Daniel Cummins
2010

Hannah More

Hannah More

The First Victorian

ANNE STOTT

OXFORD
UNIVERSITY PRESS

OXFORD
UNIVERSITY PRESS

Great Clarendon Street, Oxford OX2 6DP

Oxford University Press is a department of the University of Oxford.
It furthers the University's objective of excellence in research, scholarship,
and education by publishing worldwide in

Oxford New York

Auckland Bangkok Buenos Aires Cape Town Chennai
Dar es Salaam Delhi Hong Kong Istanbul Karachi Kolkata
Kuala Lumpur Madrid Melbourne Mexico City Mumbai
Nairobi São Paulo Shanghai Taipei Tokyo Toronto

Oxford is a registered trade mark of Oxford University Press
in the UK and in certain other countries

Published in the United States
by Oxford University Press Inc., New York

© Anne Stott 2003

British Library Cataloguing in Publication Data
Data available

Library of Congress Cataloging in Publication Data
Data available

ISBN 0-19-924532-0

1 3 5 7 9 10 8 6 4 2

Typeset by Kolam Information Services, Pvt., Ltd, Pondicherry, India
Printed in Great Britain on acid-free paper by
TJ International Ltd, Padstow, Cornwall

For Philip

PREFACE

To David Garrick she was the embodiment of all the nine Muses. Samuel Johnson thought her 'the most skilled versificatrix in the English language'. She was Horace Walpole's 'Saint Hannah'. William Wilberforce admiringly compared her to Spenser's martial heroine Britomart. On the other hand, the radical journalist William Cobbett dismissed her as 'the Old Bishop in petticoats', and a local clergyman luridly accused her of prostitution on the basis of no evidence whatsoever. The varied comments, ranging from the embarrassingly laudatory to the spitefully chauvinistic, were a tribute to Hannah More's importance. In her time she was better known than Mary Wollstonecraft, and her books outsold Jane Austen's many times over. Her now forgotten play *Percy* was the most successful tragedy of its day, only eclipsed a generation later by Samuel Taylor Coleridge's equally forgotten *Osric*. Her Cheap Repository tracts (aided admittedly by a little help from her friends) had a wider circulation than Thomas Paine's *Rights of Man*. Following her Evangelical conversion she set up Sunday schools and women's benefit clubs in Somerset that survived into the twentieth century. She campaigned against the slave trade. She wrote conduct books, political pamphlets, and a best-selling novel. Born in obscurity, she died leaving nearly £30,000, an unprecedented sum for a woman writer.

Her fame did not die with her, and for a generation or so after her death she figured in biographical series with improving titles such as 'Women of Worth' and 'Lives of Eminent and Illustrious Englishwomen'. These biographies established her as a high achiever who had done much to widen the range of activities open to women. But as 'Victorian values' came under attack, so Hannah More, the epitome of these values, became a hate object to the iconoclasts of the younger generation. The essayist and politician Augustine Birrell, who thought her 'one of the most detestable writers that ever held a pen', gleefully buried a nineteen-volume edition of her works for garden compost.[1] More, an enthusiastic gardener, might have smiled sardonically.

Who has heard of her now? Pupils and teachers at the Hannah More Primary School in Bristol and the Hannah More Infant School in nearby Nailsea, where she founded a Sunday school and set up an adult school for

[1] A. Birrell, *Collected Essays* (London, 1899), i. 255; id., *In the Name of the Bodleian and Other Essays* (London, 1905), 118.

miners and glass-workers; residents of Hannah More Close, also in Nailsea. In Baltimore, Maryland, her name lives on in the Hannah More School for emotionally disturbed adolescents, a successor to the Hannah More Academy, which was founded in her lifetime by American admirers. Alert visitors to St Mary Redcliffe, Bristol's most splendid church, might come across a tablet on the wall of St John's Chapel, bearing her verse epitaph to a Mrs Fortune Little; the politician Edmund Burke thought highly enough of the verses to learn them by heart and recite them to her when they next met. But, in the main, she is now known only to historians and literary scholars.

The road to obscurity was paved by the good intentions and bad scholarship of her first biographer, the lawyer and journalist William Roberts. He had access to her correspondence through his sister Margaret, her companion and literary executrix, and his *Memoirs of the Life and Correspondence of Mrs Hannah More* appeared in 1834, only a year after the subject's death. Though any author would have struggled to produce a four-volume biography in such a short time, there can be no excuse for Roberts's acts of vandalism: his neglect of chronology shown by his misdating of letters and his habit of running two separate letters into one without informing the reader; his distortion of his subject's character by his prim bowdlerizing of her harmless colloquialisms. The person who should have been given the task, More's beloved god-daughter Marianne Thornton, read the finished product with helpless rage.

She [More] calls Sir Tho⁵ Acland in one of her notes to me 'The recreant Knight of Devonshire', which Roberts, thinking uncivil I suppose, has altered into 'the excellent and estimable Sir T. Acland'—two words that playful woman never used in her life. Somewhere else she began to me, 'When I think of you I am gladerer and gladerer and gladerer,' which he, thinking bad English, has done into 'I am very glad'—Now if such an oaf will write a book, at least he should be honest.[2]

'That playful woman' is not the usual image of Hannah More, who, thanks partly to Roberts's omissions and 'improvements', is so often viewed as an unpleasant, authoritarian bigot: 'pushy, humourless . . . complacent, and . . . unctuously sycophantic', as one distinguished historian has described her.[3] This is exactly what Marianne feared would happen.

In a vain attempt to set the record straight, she begged Florence Nightingale's aunt not to

---

[2] Thornton Add. MS 7674/1/N, fo. 633, Marianne Thornton to Patty Smith, 11 July 1835. See also E. M. Forster, *Marianne Thornton, 1797–1887: A Domestic Biography* (London, 1956), 140. On the other hand, More's second biographer, the clergyman Henry Thompson, was extremely conscientious in his use of the more limited sources available to him. H. Thompson, *The Life of Hannah More with Notices of her Sisters* (London, 1838).

[3] L. Colley, *Britons: Forging the Nation, 1707–1837* (New Haven, 1992), 274.

judge of Hannah More by anything... that Roberts tells you she said or did. She
was a fine creature... overflowing with affection & feeling & generosity, spoilt by
adulation & hardened a little perhaps by controversy and abuse....The earliest
thing I can remember, was that she amused me more, & let me be more saucy
than anybody else.

Looking back over her childhood, Marianne remembered More's visits to her
home, Battersea Rise in Clapham. 'She used to cry when she left... & I used
to cry to go with her.' On her annual visit More would teach Marianne her
lessons, 'which would consist in her telling me fairy tales, & good woman that
she was, taught me to believe in Tom Thumb as implicitly as in Joseph and
his brethren. And for all that', she concluded angrily, 'she did not deserve... to be trodden underfoot by Roberts.'[4] Marianne saw the most attractive
side of More, but other friends also commented on her lively, cheerful, warm-
hearted character. She herself wrote unrepentantly to Marianne's mother, 'I
am afraid I do not think wit quite so wicked a thing as your good people do,'
and admitted to another friend that 'my natural gaiety of temper is not favourable to religion. Minds of a graver cast have fewer sacrifices to make!'[5] A later
generation might regret that she thought the sacrifices necessary, and can be
pleased that Evangelical seriousness never completely dampened her vitality.

The image of a solemn and sanctimonious Hannah More is now firmly
embedded in the historiography. Negative views abound, only partially offset
by a sympathetic and scholarly biography, published in 1952.[6] She has been
harshly condemned for her political conservatism, her anti-feminism, and the
allegedly repressive regime of her Sunday schools. However, at the end of the
twentieth century a more subtle picture began to emerge as, on both sides of
the Atlantic, a number of books, articles, unpublished dissertations, and web
sites reassessed her importance and made her works available for new generations of scholars.[7] The result has been mixed. There are still many scholars

---

[4] Thornton Add. MS 7674/1/N, fos. 633–4.

[5] Clark, More to Mrs H. Thornton, 'Tuesday morning' [May 1796]; A. Harford, *Annals of the Harford Family* (London, 1909), 104.

[6] M. G. Jones, *Hannah More* (Cambridge, 1952).

[7] See e.g. P. Demers, *The World of Hannah More* (Lexington: University Press of Kentucky, 1996); C. H. Ford, *Hannah More: A Critical Biography* (New York, 1996). A. Stott, 'Hannah More: Evangelicalism, Cultural Reformation, and Loyalism', Ph.D. thesis (London, 1998); ead., 'Patriotism and Providence: The Politics of Hannah More', in K. Gleadle and S. Richardson (eds.), *Women in British Politics, 1760–1860: The Power of the Petticoat* (Basingstoke: Macmillan, 2000), 39–55; ead., '"A singular injustice towards women": Hannah More, Evangelicalism and Female Education' in Sue Morgan (ed.), *Women, Religion and Feminism in Britain 1750–1900* (Basingstoke: Palgrave, 2002), 23–38. K. I. Swallow Prior, 'Hannah More and the Evangelical Contribution to the English Novel', Ph.D. thesis (Buffalo, NY, 1999); R. Hole, 'Hannah More on Literature and Propaganda', *History*, 85 (2000), 623–33; J. Nardin, 'Hannah More and the Rhetoric of Educational Reform', *Women's History Review*, 10 (2001), 211–27. For recognition of More's importance as an Anglican spiritual writer, see G. Rowell, K. Stevenson, and R. Williams (eds.), *Love's Redeeming Work: The Anglican Quest for Holiness* (Oxford, 2001), 339–42.

who show an almost personal dislike of More. The old charges have been repeated, and the dubiously Freudian accusation of 'matrophobia' added to the indictment.[8] Others, however, have re-examined her writings and detected 'bourgeois progressivism' and (what was once an oxymoron) 'counter-revolutionary feminism'.[9] They recognize that women read More in huge numbers and that by and large they interpreted her message as one of empowerment rather than submission, as, while she advocated modesty and humility, she also gave them permission to dip their toes into public life, to campaign, to organize, to develop expertise. A spokeswoman for British patriotism at a time when this patriotism was being re-examined and redefined, she claimed it for women and urged them to use their influence for the national good. This book will attempt to highlight More's complexity, and to argue that, except perhaps at the end of her long life, her conservatism was thoughtful and subtle, and that she was never a mere mouthpiece for patriarchal ideologies.

This new study of More takes account of half a century's scholarship and interpretation and a wealth of previously uncited manuscripts in Britain and the United States. For reasons of space I have been unable to develop all the issues I raise—each of which could be expanded to a sizeable monograph—as fully as I would have liked. Neither can I claim to have penetrated all the depths of More's psyche. Passionate and emotional in her youth, in later life she covered her tracks by cultivating a restrained, disciplined personality. The concealment was completed at the end of the nineteenth century when many letters that might have given more insight into her private persona were destroyed.[10] This means that whole areas of her life—most notably her broken engagement, and her relations with her parents—remain something of a mystery.

There is more than enough material, however, for a convincing narrative of More's public life. This was a woman who received no formal education, who never voted, never trained for a profession; who battled continuously with migraines, chest infections, stomach upsets, and fevers; who, like her near contemporary Thomas Chatterton, another ambitious child of a Bristol schoolmaster, went to London to seek her fortune; who mixed with literary men, bluestockings, and politicians; who, after her momentous conversion to 'vital religion', turned her life about, and travelled on horseback in all

[8] See E. Kowaleski-Wallace, *Their Fathers' Daughters: Hannah More, Maria Edgeworth and Patriarchal Complicity* (Oxford, 1991). But see C. L. Krueger, *The Reader's Repentance: Women Preachers, Women Writers and Nineteenth-Century Social Discourse* (Chicago, 1992), 95–121.

[9] M. Myers, 'Hannah More's Tracts for the Times: Social Fiction and Female Ideology', in M. A. Schofield and C. Macheski (eds.), *Fetter'd or Free? British Women Novelists, 1680–1815* (Athens, Ohio, 1986), 264–84; K. Sutherland, 'Hannah More's Counter-Revolutionary Feminism', in K. Everest (ed.), *Revolution in Writing: British Literary Responses to the French Revolution* (Milton Keynes, 1991), 27–63.

[10] C. H. Bennett, 'The Text of Horace Walpole's Correspondence with Hannah More', repr. rev. in *Walpole*, pp. xix–xxiv.

weathers through country roads that were muddy and dusty in turn in order to teach ragged children to read and to set up friendly societies for their mothers; who could turn her hand equally to an elegant poem for the London intelligentsia, a moralistic tract for polite society, an anti-slavery polemic, a chapbook story for the poor, or a work of political theory for a princess. In a period when, according to much conventional historical wisdom, women retreated into a private domestic sphere, she stood out as a public woman, sometimes commended, sometimes execrated, who proved that gender boundaries were more fluid and shifting than the rigid prescriptions of the conduct books (her own included) might suggest.

In her long life Hannah More witnessed extraordinary changes: the gathering pace of industrialization, the Evangelical revival, the American and French Revolutions, the Napoleonic wars, the struggle for parliamentary reform, and the emergence of the culture of purposeful energy and earnest moralism known by the convenient shorthand of 'Victorianism'. A key player in momentous events, she was a paradoxical figure, who worked for change while supporting existing hierarchies. She deplored attempts to extend the franchise, yet taught working men to read; though deeply hostile to overt feminism, she longed for women to realize their spiritual and intellectual potential; she was a lifelong member of the Church of England, who found many Dissenters more spiritually congenial than some of her fellow Anglicans; she was the last of the original bluestockings and the first of the Victorians. Her remarkable achievements and her multiple contradictions mean that Hannah More will always elude precise terminology, easy labels, and glib simplifications.

What could she have been in an age of greater opportunities? A woman priest, a headmistress of a good girls' school, a newspaper columnist, a scriptwriter for a famous British rural soap opera, a television presenter? Her career shows what was possible for one late Georgian woman who was neither well born nor wealthy and who did not owe her advancement to becoming the mistress of a prominent man. A narrative of female achievement, it is also one of ambiguity and complexity. With much historical writing now preoccupied with nuances and interactions and with multifaceted narratives that probe below the surface of events, this is the best of times to be revising her story and reassessing her significance.

In the nine years spent with Hannah More, first working on a Ph.D. and then writing a full biography, I have picked the brains of many fellow workers in the period. First there is Julian Hoppit, supervisor and mentor, and the other members of the Long Eighteenth Century and Modern Religious History seminars at the Institute of Historical Research, University of London. Though it is invidious to single out names, I should like to make a special

Preface

mention of Arthur Burns, Pene Corfield, Margaret Escott, Mary Clare
Martin, Mark Smith, and John Wolffe. Nigel Aston has generously shared
with me his great knowledge of the émigré clergy, and I had fruitful discussions with Peter Nockles on More's relationship with the early nineteenth-
century High Church. Nigel Aston and Elisabeth Jay read the book before
publication and I am grateful for their comments and criticisms; they have
saved me from many errors and it goes without saying that any remaining
mistakes, misinterpretations, and omissions are mine alone. I should like to
thank Sir Peter and Dame Elizabeth Anson, and Christabel Boult, for their
generous hospitality. I am grateful to my German translator, Janet Ferguson,
and to Helen Kennett for her researches into Hannah More's paternal relatives in East Anglia. I have been greatly helped by friends in the Bristol area,
notably Peter and Celia Skrine and the trustees of the Mary Webb Charities
and the Hannah More Buildings, especially Marie Taylor. The *Bristol
Evening Post* kindly sent me information about the recent sale of the Tyntesfield estate. I must thank the UCL Graduate School and the Nuffield Foundation Social Science Small Grants Scheme for making it possible for me to
visit Los Angeles and study the recently acquired Hannah More correspondence at the Clark Library. Money from the Open University's Small Grants
Fund helped pay for one of my trips to Bristol. I have received constant
support and encouragement from my editors at Oxford University Press.
Finally, I should like to thank all my family for their support, and especially
Philip. Having lived with her for so long, he has come to feel a wry affection
for 'Hannah', even to the extent of finding an appropriate passage from
Coelebs in Search of a Wife to quote in his father-of-the-bride speech. He has
borne my enthusiasms with exemplary patience, searched out pictures, and
offered a good deal of advice (not always solicited). It is only fair that the
book should be dedicated to him.

A.M.S.

ACKNOWLEDGEMENTS

I wish to thank the following for permission to quote from material in their possession: Sir Peter and Dame Elizabeth Anson; the Bodleian Library, University of Oxford; the Bristol Record Office; the British Library; the Syndics of Cambridge University Library; the Master and Fellows of the Library of St John's College, Cambridge; the Centre for Kentish Studies (Maidstone); Duke University, Durham, NC, Rare Book, Manuscript and Special Collections Library; the Folger Shakespeare Library, Washington, DC; Isaac Gewirtz, Curator of the Berg Collection of English and American Literature, New York Public Library, Astor Lennox and Tilder Foundations; the seventh earl of Harrowby (Harrowby Manuscripts Trust); the Henry E. Huntington Library, San Marino, California; the Trustees of Lambeth Palace Library; the Lilly Library, Indiana University, Bloomington, Indiana; the Osborn Collection, Beinecke Rare Book and Manuscript Library, Yale University; Somerset Record Office; the Swem Library, College of William and Mary, Williamsburg, Virginia; University College London Library; the Victoria and Albert Museum, London; the Trustees of the Mary Webb Charities and the Hannah More Building, Fishponds, Bristol; the William Andrews Clark Memorial Library, University of California at Los Angeles.

CONTENTS

LIST OF ILLUSTRATIONS

(between pp. 200–201)

LIST OF MAPS

LIST OF ABBREVIATIONS

BL	British Library
BL, Add. MS	British Library, Additional Manuscript
Bodleian	Bodleian Library, University of Oxford, MS Wilberforce
Clark	William Andrews Clark Memorial Library, University of California at Los Angeles, Hannah More MSS
CRST	Hannah More, *Cheap Repository Shorter Tracts* (London, 1798)
CRTEMR	Hannah More, *Cheap Repository Tracts, Entertaining Moral and Religious* (London, 1798)
Duke	William Wilberforce Papers, Rare Book, Manuscript and Special Collections Library, Duke University, Durham, NC
FFBJ	*Felix Farley's Bristol Journal*
Folger	Folger Shakespeare Library, Washington
Gambier	*Memorials, Personal and Historical of Admiral Lord Gambier*, ed. Georgiana, Lady Chatterton, 2 vols. (London, 1861)
Huntington	Henry E. Huntington Library, San Marino, Calif.
Life of Wilberforce	Robert Isaac and Samuel Wilberforce, *The Life of William Wilberforce*, 5 vols. (London, 1838)
MA	Martha More, *Mendip Annals; or, The Narrative of the Charitable Labours of Hannah and Martha More*, ed. Arthur Roberts (London, 1859)
PRO	Public Record Office, Kew
Roberts	William Roberts, *Memoirs of the Life and Correspondence of Mrs Hannah More*, 4 vols. (2nd edn. London, 1834)
Somerset Record Office	SRO
Thornton	Cambridge University Library, Thornton Papers
V & A	Victoria and Albert Museum
VP	Hannah More, *Village Politics Addressed to all the Mechanics, Journeymen and Day Labourers in Great Britain, by Will Chip, a Country Carpenter* (4th edn. London, 1793)

Walpole   *The Yale Edition of Horace Walpole's Corres-pondence with Hannah More et al.*, xxxi, ed. W. S. Lewis, Robert A. Smith, and Charles H. Bennett (London and New Haven, 1961)

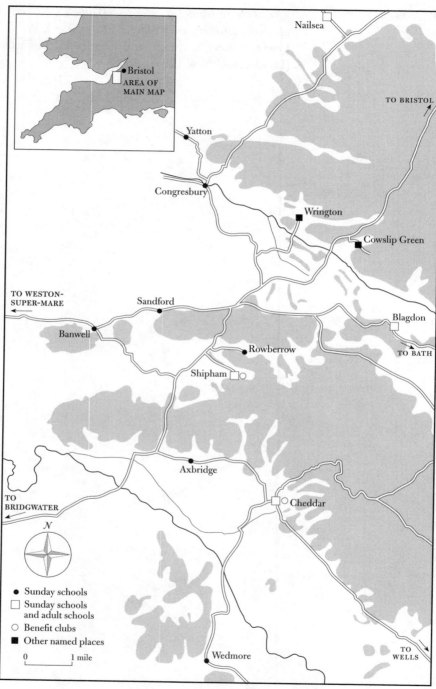

Map 1. The Mendip schools

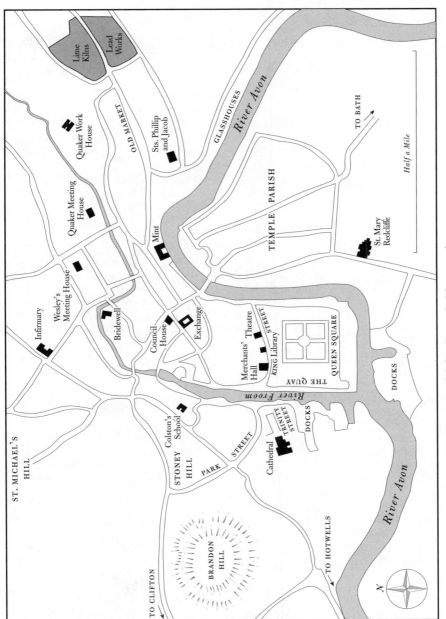

Map 2. Bristol (after Donne's Map, 1773)

Chapter 1

⟫◄⟪

Bristol Beginnings
1745–1774

IT began with failure and disappointment, missed opportunities, and loss of status. Hannah More—playwright, bluestocking, educationalist, political propagandist, and Evangelical activist—was born not into comfort and prosperity, but into a four-roomed cottage, already crammed to bursting with her parents and three elder sisters. The cottage was attached to the charity school at Fishponds in Gloucestershire, where her father, Jacob More, had recently been appointed master. On the Lady Day following his daughter's birth he received a year and three-quarters' salary, which amounted to £28; the initial sum had been £32 but the trustees, realizing their mistake, deducted the extra £4.[1] This cheese-paring must have been a bitter humiliation for a man who had hoped to be a landed gentleman. The sour taste of disappointment communicated itself to his daughters, who, through hard work, useful contacts, and shrewd investments, climbed back up the social ladder. Hannah More, who was to earn more than any other woman writer of her day, often pleaded poverty, but the truth was that she reached a degree of affluence and consequence unthinkable to her unassuming parents.

If Hannah More brooded on her father's circumstances, her reflections have not survived. When she talked about her family history in her old age, she was vague about names, dates, and her own feelings, and her reticence left her early biographers groping for facts.[2] The absence of the relevant

---

[1] Trustees of the Mary Webb Charities and the Hannah More Building, Fishponds, Bristol, 'Memorandum and Accounts relating to Mrs Webb's Charity', fo. 19b.

[2] See Roberts, i. 6–10; H. Thompson, *The Life of Hannah More with Notices of her Sisters* (London, 1838), 5–6.

parish registers means that little is known of her paternal relations. Jacob More was born about 1694 at Thorpe Hall near Harleston on the Norfolk–Suffolk border.[3] Though he became a Tory High Churchman, his family background was Roundhead and Presbyterian. Two of his uncles fought in Cromwell's New Model Army. In the persecuting days of Charles II his father 'lodged a Nonconformist Minister in his house for a year or two & comported that the charge of the keeping of this Minister & his horse amounted to ten pounds annually'.[4] The story that he had to guard his premises with a drawn sword may be a picturesque embellishment. His strong-minded wife, Jacob's mother, who was born at the time of the Great Fire of London in 1666 and lived to the age of 90, was equally staunch in her Presbyterian beliefs. She was a woman of remarkable determination. 'One of the family anecdotes which were treasured of her is that being subject to frequent & sudden attacks of pleurisy & being distant three miles from medical aid, she learnt to bleed, in order to perform this operation upon herself.'[5] Her two surviving children were Jacob and a daughter, Hannah, who married a Mr Hayle of Needham, a neighbouring village.

There was some family connection between the Mores and the Cottons, a sprawling family of better-off farmers, lesser gentry, and professional men. In 1777, when she was becoming well known, Hannah More paid a summer visit to these relations. She did the rounds of various Cottons, and on one of her visits to 'a romantic farm-house buried in the obscurity of a deep wood', she found a great number assembled 'of all ages, sexes, and characters. The old lady of the house . . . took a great deal of pains to explain to me genealogies, alliances, and intermarriages, not one word of which can I remember.'[6] A niece of one of the Cotton relatives, the daughter of a Yarmouth barrister, had married the ninth Earl of Home, though when Hannah More saw her in church one Sunday, she found her depressed and 'no countess at her heart'.[7] She had no further contact with her one aristocratic relative. It is clear that she took little interest in her paternal connections. A Bristolian through and through, she identified with her mother's relatives, the West Country Graces, rather than the East Anglian Mores and Cottons.[8]

---

[3] The date is based on More's assertion that he died at the age of 88. Clark, Hannah More MSS box 46, 'Reminiscences', fo. 17. However, it is also possible that he was born *c*.1700. See Roberts, i. 206.

[4] Clark, box 46, 'Reminiscences', fo. 22.   [5] Ibid., fos. 17, 23.   [6] Roberts, i. 99.

[7] Ibid. 104. Alexander Home, ninth earl and fourteenth baron, married, thirdly, Abigail Browne Ramey, daughter and co-heiress of John Ramey, at Yarmouth on 10 Feb. 1768. She died in Feb. 1814.

[8] More's will records a legacy of £400 to Martha Grace. There is no mention of any East Anglian relatives. PRO, PROB 11/1822, fo. 366.

Jacob More had been educated at Norwich Grammar School, and was intended for the Church. Here, however, bad luck or bad judgement intervened. Jacob believed that he was the rightful heir to a manor house at Wenhaston in Suffolk, but the inheritance was contested by a cousin. The two went to law, Jacob lost his suit and with it his fortune, estimated at more than £8,000 per annum, though this very substantial figure may have been a wild exaggeration.[9] The result was dramatic. Abandoning plans of a clerical career, he left his home and relatives, and made his way to Bristol. It seems typical of his bad luck that his books, which were sent by a separate conveyance, were lost on the way and that he could not afford to replace them. He was forced after this to rely on his remarkable memory, which his daughter was to inherit.

The hilly city of Bristol must have been something of a shock to a young man brought up in the comparatively flat landscape of East Anglia. There, some time between his twenty-fourth and thirtieth birthdays, after a period of pupillage and a written and a practical examination, he became a supervisor of the excise. This meant that he would have needed a certificate of his age from the minister of the parish where he was born, and a recommendation signed by some neighbouring gentry; he had also to produce a certificate stating that he had recently received communion according to the rites of the Church of England, and to take an oath abjuring the Catholic doctrine of transubstantiation.[10] The post involved overseeing the junior excisemen and keeping a sharp eye out for fraud and mismanagement. It was an occupation requiring shrewdness, diligence, and mathematical competence rather than a scholarly interest in Greek and Latin. It was also extremely arduous: 'a Seat of constant work', the former exciseman Thomas Paine wrote with feeling.[11] Carrying his books, measuring instruments, pen, and inkpot, Jacob would have ridden or walked many miles in a day in order to check on his juniors, and then record his findings in a diary, which had to be sent up to London every six weeks. For this he would have been paid £90 per annum: not a bad income for a bachelor, though far below that of a landed gentleman.

At some stage while he was in the West Country, Jacob came into contact with a local aristocrat, Norborne Berkeley, Tory MP for Gloucestershire (until in 1764 he was summoned to the House of Lords under the resumed title of Lord Botetourt), and owner of Stoke Park at the village of Stoke

---

[9] In its review of Roberts's *Life of More*, the *Quarterly Review* questioned this figure on the grounds that a family possessing this sum—a large one in the early 18th century—must have been very well known and therefore easy to discover. *Quarterly Review*, 52 (1834), 417–18.

[10] C. Leadbetter, *The Royal Gauger; or, Gauging Made Easy* (London, 1739), part 2, pp. 1–9. For excisemen, see J. Brewer, *The Sinews of Power: War, Money and the English State, 1688–1783* (London, 1989), 104–14.

[11] Quoted in Brewer, *Sinews of Power*, 108.

Gifford, a few miles north of Bristol. Through his connection with Berkeley, Jacob met Mary Grace, daughter of a small farmer at Stoke, a girl twenty years younger than himself.[12] Around 1737, when Mary was about 17, the two married, and their first child, Mary, was born in 1738, to be followed by Elizabeth (Betty) in 1740, and Sarah (Sally) in 1743. Very little is known of Mary Grace. The parish records for Stoke show a brother, William, his wife, Susanna, and a large family of children, contemporaries of Hannah More and her sisters. The little information we have about Mary suggests a woman of strong character who, perhaps because of her own very modest education, was ambitious not only for her daughters but for literary women in general. In 1774, when the Bristol writer Mary Deverell published her *Sermons*, a 'Mrs More of Bristol' was listed among the subscribers.[13]

Jacob had married late, and he started his family at a time when he would be running out of the physical energy required in an excise supervisor. On 6 October 1743, in a career change which involved a sharp drop in salary, he was appointed master of the free school at Fishponds, part of the parish of Stapleton, four miles north-east of Bristol. The school had been founded under a trust set up by the will of Mary Webb in 1729 'for teaching Twenty poor Boys and Ten poor Girls of the parish of Stapleton' and for housing 'three poor old Women . . . at Twelve pence p[r] Week'.[14] Lying off the road to Bristol, the school was an attractive, high-ceilinged building lit by two large windows on either side of the door. There were two wings, one for the master and his family and the other for the old women. (The building survives today, next to the nineteenth-century Fishponds church.) The master's cottage comprised four tiny rooms, and it is hard to imagine how it could eventually have held two adults and five children; the initial salary was a meagre £15 per annum, out of which he had to fund repairs. The first master, William Scutts, lasted only four years. He was dismissed in May 1734 after the trustees found him 'guilty of very obscene practices towards some of his female Schollars and . . . suspected of attempting a Rape upon one of them'.[15] His replacement died in 1743 and Jacob More became the third master, presumably through the influence of Norborne Berkeley, who was appointed trustee at the same time. As the modest curriculum of the charity schools encompassed little more than basic literacy, with writing and some arithmetic added for the boys, it was a demeaning as well as badly paid

---

[12] As Hannah More reported that Mary Grace More was 65 when she died in May 1786, she must have been born in 1720 or 1721. Anson MSS, letters and diaries of Mary Hamilton, property of Sir Peter and Dame Elizabeth Anson, doc. folder 8, More to Mary Hamilton, 3 June 1786. Quoted by kind permission of Sir Peter and Dame Elizabeth Anson.

[13] M. Deverell, *Sermons on the Following Subjects* (Bristol [1774]).

[14] Trustees of the Mary Webb Charities and the Hannah More Building, 'Memorandum and Accounts', fo. 1.

[15] Ibid., fo. 7.

occupation for a classically educated man, though it is possible that he might have given private lessons to boys requiring a more gentlemanly education. Presumably Mrs More taught needlework and housewifely skills to the girls, though her contribution is not recorded. There must have been a garden attached to the school as Jacob was able to send a present of potatoes to some friends in Norfolk, clearly a novelty in that part of the country, as his eldest daughter remembered him 'receiving with their thanks an enquiry of how they were to be prepared for the Table'.[16]

Jacob was to hold the post nominally until his death in 1783, though by then he had moved to Bristol and must have abandoned teaching years earlier. His last mention in the trustees' accounts, dated 1786, three years after his death, notes that the balances of the various accounts relating to the school 'have by the neglect of…Jacob Moore [*sic*] been hitherto omitted to be brought to account'.[17] This casual attitude to money was probably a reflection of his later years; had it been typical of his younger days, he would not have survived long as an excise officer.

The Mores' fourth daughter, Hannah, was born in the cottage on 2 February 1745; two weeks later she was baptized at Stapleton church. She was followed at the end of 1747 by a brother, Jacob, who died in May 1749 and was taken back to his mother's village, Stoke Gifford, for burial. (Presumably, if he had lived, he would have been the petted darling of the family.) Shortly after this Mary More became pregnant again, and her daughter Martha, nicknamed Patty, was born in April 1750.[18] The family was now complete. By this time Jacob's income had risen to £20 per annum, and they could afford a nurse for the younger children. This nurse had looked after the son of the poet John Dryden in his last illness, a fact that aroused little Hannah's curiosity, though in later life she did not have a particularly high opinion of Dryden's poetry.

As the children grew up, they formed themselves into the groupings natural to sisters in a large family. The eldest, Mary and Betty, were a self-contained unit, serious and responsible; as they grew into adulthood, Mary became the head of the family while Betty, kind-hearted, domesticated, and with no intellectual pretensions, became the 'wife'. The two youngest slept together, and from an early age Patty, blue-eyed and pretty, became Hannah's adoring follower and uncritical admirer. Suffering the common fate of middle siblings, Sally was free-ranging, attaching herself at various times in her life to either her elder or her younger sisters. Vivacious, quick-witted,

---

[16] Clark, Hannah More MSS box 46, 'Reminiscences', fo. 7.

[17] Trustees of the Mary Webb Charities and the Hannah More Building, 'Memorandum and Accounts', fo. 49b.

[18] This information is derived from the Stapleton and Stoke parish registers in the Bristol Record Office.

and unconventional, with a keen sense of the ludicrous, she was the family's licensed jester. William Wilberforce was later to compare her to the politician George Canning: like him, 'you saw the coming joke in her dark expressive eyes'.[19]

In the evenings the children would have had the free run of the schoolroom, and, as children do, they rearranged the furniture in order to create their own imaginative worlds. Mrs More observed the proceedings, and, according to family tradition, remembered that Hannah turned her chair into a carriage and 'called her sisters to ride with her to London to see bishops and booksellers'.[20] Hannah was also an avid collector of bits of paper, on which she would scribble little essays or poems and then hide them in the broom cupboard. In the evenings she would sit on her father's knee and hear him recite from memory stories from Plutarch's *Lives*. Such was her enthusiasm that, when she was about 8 years old, Jacob began tentatively to teach her Latin and mathematics. The child responded so readily to this masculine education that the father took fright, dreading that he was creating that much mocked eighteenth-century creature the female pedant. The mathematics stopped first, then the Latin. Here Mrs More intervened, and begged for the lessons to continue. Reluctantly Jacob agreed, but the teaching now proceeded half-heartedly. Later Hannah was to pick up her Latin studies under the guidance of the Bristol Baptist minister James Newton, who found that 'for the limited period of his instruction, she surpassed all the others he had known'.[21] But she never progressed in mathematics. 'I, a girl, was educated at random,' she later commented.[22] She claimed this was a blessing, but, in view of her attacks on the superficial nature of women's education, it is unlikely that she truly believed this. She had been short-changed, and in her heart perhaps she knew it.

It may be significant that several of Hannah More's early writings should focus on conflicts between fathers and daughters. Her first play was a close copy of *Regolo Attilio*, the most celebrated work of Pietro Metastasio, librettist at the Austrian court.[23] *The Inflexible Captive* deviates significantly from the original by exploring Regulus' relationship with his daughter Attilia. In trying to dissuade her father from handing himself over to his Chartarginian enemies and thus to a gruesome death (being rolled downhill in a barrel pierced with nails), she is given the tentative lines 'Because I *am* a daughter,

[19] Bodleian, MS d. 20, Barbara Wilberforce, 'Recollections of Mrs Hannah More and her Sisters', fo. 33. See also M. A. Hopkins, *Hannah More and her Circle* (New York, 1947), 28–31.

[20] Roberts, i. 14.

[21] J. Cottle, *Reminiscences of Samuel Taylor Coleridge and Robert Southey* (London, 1847; repr. 1970), 53 n.

[22] Clark, More to Sir William Weller Pepys, 11 Nov. 1783.

[23] P. Metastasio, *Biblioteca Teatrale Italiana*, iii (Lucca, 1762).

I presum'd,' only to be rebuffed for a 'coward mind' that 'wants fortitude and honour'.[24] Later Regulus excuses her weakness:

> We must not hope to find in *her* soft soul
> The strong exertion of a manly courage.[25]

Attilia's conflicts over the downgrading of her character and her sex provide the few moments of real passion in the play:

> I only recollect I am a *daughter*,
> A poor defenceless, helpless, wretched daughter . . .[26]

Towards the end she overcomes her female weakness. The spirit of Regulus, she decides,

> . . . shall subdue the *woman* in my soul;
> A Roman virgin should be something *more*—
> Shou'd dare above her sex's narrow limits.[27]

She took up the father–daughter conflict again in her most successful play, *Percy*. The heroine, Elwina, forced into a loveless marriage, indicts her 'barbarous father', who

> . . . dragg'd me trembling, dying, to the altar,
> I sighed, I struggl'd, fainted, and—complied.[28]

When her lover, Percy, reproaches her for this obedience, she defends herself:

> I cou'd withstand his fury; but his tears,
> Ah they undid me! Percy dost thou know
> The cruel tyranny of tenderness?
> Hast thou e'er felt a father's warm embrace?
> Hast thou e'er seen a father's flowing tears,
> And known that thou couldst wipe those tears away?[29]

These plays were not, of course, autobiographical. Jacob More, gentle and ineffectual, was not a father in either the Roman or feudal mode, and, following the success of Samuel Richardson's *Clarissa Harlowe*, the question of how much obedience a daughter owed her father was a popular topic for debate. Nevertheless, it is difficult to escape the conclusion that the young Hannah used her early writings to work through her problems with her father. Later, in *Coelebs in Search of a Wife*, she was to create an idealized father in the person of Mr Stanley, who teaches Latin to his elder daughter and mathematics to her younger sister.

---

[24] *The Inflexible Captive: A Tragedy* (Bristol, 1774), 36.   [25] Ibid. 42.   [26] Ibid. 44.
[27] Ibid. 74.   [28] *Percy: A Tragedy* (London, 1778), 12.   [29] Ibid. 45.

Whatever the truth about her relationship with her father, Hannah More must have realized early on that he could do little to help her advance in the world. She grew up in a patron–client society and soon learned how to play by the rules. One of the first to take an early interest in the clever girl and her sisters was a Mr Silas Blandford of Stoke, who, with his wife, befriended her from the age of 10. Their children, like their Grace cousins, were similar ages to the More sisters, and it is tempting to believe that they all played together as they grew up. Hannah More later recollected that he was a man 'of the most unfeigned simplicity of manners and purity of life imaginable'.[30] She paid her debt by helping to nurse him when he was dying, and she possibly wrote the newspaper obituary which claimed that 'he was always the warm friend of virtuous industry in others, and honest and laborious poverty were the objects of his protection'.[31] A year later she attended his widow in her last illness, describing her as 'the oldest friend I have in the world'.[32] The Blandfords were possibly the first of her substitute parents and patrons. Others were to follow, most famously David Garrick and his wife.

The More sisters did not have the option of sitting at home in a genteel fashion, waiting for promising young men to propose marriage. They were destined for teaching, an expanding occupation for educated women, and the training had to begin early.[33] From about the age of 14 Mary was sent to a school at Bristol to learn French, and on returning home at the end of the week she passed on what she had learned to her younger sisters. This economical educational plan opened up new horizons for the girls, bringing them into contact with the thriving cultural life of the second city in England.

Jacob More had chosen well in deciding to seek a new life in the Bristol area.[34] At the time of his arrival it was still a walled and gated city, built round two quays, and crammed with overhanging medieval buildings, but by

[30] Clark, More to Ann Kennicott, 17 Aug. 1782.

[31] *FFBJ*, 3 Aug. 1782; *Sarah Farley's Bristol Journal*, 10 Aug. 1782.

[32] Anson MSS, doc. folder 8, More to Mary Hamilton, 13 Aug. [1783].

[33] See S. Skedd, 'Women Teachers and the Expansion of Girls' Schooling in England, *c*.1760–1820', in H. Barker and E. Chalus (eds.), *Gender in Eighteenth-Century England: Roles, Representations and Responsibilities* (London, 1997), 101–25.

[34] This discussion of Bristol is based on J. Mathews, *The Bristol Guide*, 5th edn. (Bristol, n.d.); J. F. Nicholls and J. Taylor, *Bristol Past and Present*, 3 vols. (Bristol, 1881–2); J. Latimer, *The Annals of Bristol in the Eighteenth Century* ([Bristol], 1893); P. McGrath (ed.), *Bristol in the Eighteenth Century* (Newton Abbott, 1972); P. J. Corfield, *The Impact of English Towns, 1700–1800* (Oxford, 1982); P. Borsay, *The English Urban Renaissance: Culture and Society in the Provincial Town, 1660–1770* (Oxford, 1989); J. Barry, 'The Cultural Life of Bristol, 1640–1775', D.Phil. thesis (Oxford, 1985); id., 'The Press and the Politics of Culture in Bristol, 1660–1775', in J. Black and J. Gregory (eds.), *Culture, Politics and Society in Britain, 1660–1800* (Manchester, 1991), 49–81; M. E. Fissell, *Patients, Power, and the Poor in Eighteenth-Century Bristol* (Cambridge, 1991); K. Morgan, *Bristol and the Atlantic Trade in the Eighteenth Century* (Cambridge, 1993); C. B. Estabrook, *Urbane and Rustic England: Cultural Ties and Social Spheres in the Provinces 1660–1789* (Manchester, 1998).

1750 the population had grown to 50,000, and the wealthy were already moving up Clifton Hill; later speculative development was to turn the modest village of Clifton into one of the most beautiful suburbs in the country. The city's commercial life was carried on in the coffee houses at the Exchange or at the Merchants' Hall in King Street, where the Society of Merchant Venturers was based. Its philanthropy was displayed in the Bristol Infirmary, built and maintained by public subscription, its cultural life in the City Library, and its genteel sociability in the balls and public breakfasts in the Long Room at the Hotwells, a spa whose cleverly marketed medicinal waters made it second only to Bath in popularity. Its prosperity was founded on the production of copper and brass and on the expanding Atlantic trade. The dark side of this affluence could be seen by anyone who scanned through the newspapers. An entry in the *Bristol Journal* for November 1762, for example, announced the arrival in Virginia of the Bristol ship the *Hector*, carrying in its hold 512 slaves from Angola.[35] A few years later the same newspaper announced the sale of 'a healthy Negro Slave named Prince, 17 Years of Age. Measuring Five Feet and Ten Inches and extremely well grown'.[36] But Bristol was rapidly losing its dubious status as the premier slave-trading port in Britain to the energetic merchants of Liverpool. Instead it imported vast quantities of sugar (of course, a slave-worked product), and by 1750 the city had twenty refineries in operation, their scalding vats a terrible hazard for tired and inattentive workers.

The surplus wealth of the thriving urban societies of the eighteenth century was channelled into a range of leisure and cultural activities, creating a 'polite' culture of good breeding and elegant manners. This in turn brought about a new social mobility as talented men and women from relatively humble origins mixed freely with those of higher rank and greater wealth. The More sisters were part of this trend. Mary's education in Bristol brought the sisters into contact with influential members of the city's elite. One was Josiah Tucker, dean of Gloucester (half of the city of Bristol was in the diocese of Gloucester), and political controversialist; he had been burned in effigy at least twice, once in 1751 for apologizing to the Pope for his previous use of violently anti-papal language, and again in 1753 for speaking in favour of a bill to naturalize the Jews. Another was the Cornish heiress Mrs Ann Lovell Gwatkin, the cultivated wife of a Bristol merchant. She in particular offered the sisters encouragement for the ambitious venture that would make their fortune.

On 11 and 18 March and 8 and 15 April 1758 an announcement appeared in the *Bristol Journal*: 'At No. 6 in Trinity Street, near the College Green. On Monday after Easter will be opened a School for Young Ladies by Mary

---

[35] *FFBJ*, 20 Nov. 1762.   [36] Ibid., 30 Jan. 1768.

More and Sisters, where will be carefully taught French, Reading, Writing, Arithmetic, and Needlework. Young Ladies boarded on reasonable terms.' In the later advertisement an additional line was added: 'A Dancing Master will properly attend'. This was an upmarket school, offering a fashionable curriculum for the daughters of the affluent. It could not have been set up cheaply, for, in addition to finding the rent for the building and buying the furniture, fabrics, and books, the sisters were hiring some relatively expensive teachers. Given their own lack of resources, the money must have come from Mrs Gwatkin and possibly other patrons, in the form of either loans or outright gifts. The school opened behind the cathedral on Monday 10 April, presided over by its 20-year-old headmistress. It filled up immediately, the numbers continued to expand, and about four years later the sisters moved to more spacious premises in the newly built 43 Park Street, halfway up the hill to Clifton. By this time the school housed about sixty pupils, small boys as well as girls, two of whom, Martha and Frances Lintorn, remained lifelong friends.[37] The school prospered and became famous, with the sisters universally respected for their 'genius, *benevolence*, and excellent principles'.[38] Bristol gossip also credited them with shrewd financial acumen,[39] and certainly they later made enough money to remove their parents from Fishponds on their retirement and install them in comfort at Stoney Hill, near the school.

It was by any reckoning a remarkable story: the Mores had succeeded in a risky market where two other celebrated sets of sisters—the Wollstonecrafts and the Brontës—were to fail.[40] In 1776 Sally related to Dr Johnson in her inimitable fashion (burlesquing the West Country accent the sisters had, presumably, long discarded),

how we were born with more desires than guineas; and how, as years increased our appetites, the cupboard at home began to grow too small to gratify them; and how with a bottle of water, a bed, and a blanket, we set out to seek our fortunes . . . till, looking into our knowledge-boxes, we happened to find a little *larning* . . . and so at last, by giving a little of this little *larning* to those who had less, we got a good store of gold in return. 'I love you both', cried the inamorato—'I love

---

[37] Hopkins, *Hannah More*, 20–1; R. Jenkins, *Memoirs of the Bristol Stage* (Bristol, 1826), 37 n. Frances Lintorn married Captain Thomas Simmons of Bath. Their son John Lintorn Simmons was the solicitor who became one of the trustees of the Shipham Club in 1814 and handled the sale of Barley Wood in 1828. Somerset Record Office, DD/X/MMT/1; BL, Add. MS 42511, fo. 46. More left him £500 in her will. PRO, PROB 11/1822, fo. 366.

[38] Anson MSS, diary of Mary Hamilton, book 7 (23 Apr.–7 June 1784), 14 May 1784.

[39] [W. Shaw] *The Life of Hannah More with a Critical Review of her Writings by the Rev. Sir Archibald MacSarcasm, Bart* (London, 1802), 50. Sir Archibald MacSarcasm was a character in Charles Macklin's *Love à la Mode*.

[40] The school Mary Wollstonecraft and her sisters later set up in 1783 lasted two and a half years. It was unable to offer French. J. Todd, *Mary Wollstonecraft: A Revolutionary Life* (London, 2000), 55–78, 463–4 n. 1.

you all five—I never was at Bristol,—I will come on purpose to see you—what! five women live happily together! . . . God bless you; you live lives to shame duchesses.'[41]

It was not common for female teachers to see their career in terms of ambition and high adventure rather than drudgery and loss of gentility. In one of her letters to Ann Gwatkin, Patty More noted, tongue in cheek, that 'tho' I appear so genteely in the world, and have that air of fashion about me; yet it is all supported by downright vulgar industry'.[42] The classic putdown was to be delivered by Jane Austen's snobbish Emma Woodhouse: 'One should be sorry to see greater pride or refinement in the teacher of a school.'[43] No wonder Johnson, who had been a teacher himself (and an unsuccessful one), was captivated. He kept his promise and called on the Park Street school when he and Boswell visited Bristol a little later.[44]

The 13-year-old Hannah More started off as a pupil at the school before becoming a teacher herself. Denied the classical and mathematical education she had craved, she turned to the more feminine study of modern languages. She learned Italian and Spanish from visiting masters, read the fashionable works of Metastasio, and translated a Spanish poem called *Las lagrimas de San Pedro*. She made more solid progress with French. During the Seven Years' War, French officers were held on parole in the prison at Stapleton, and the More parents entertained them at home (presumably in the schoolroom), giving Hannah the opportunity to act as translator. She learned to read French fluently and with pleasure (though she did not always write it grammatically), and even in her Francophobic old age she kept her love of much French literature, with the moralistic Racine a special favourite.

The information about Hannah More in her teens is somewhat scanty. No one commented much on her personal appearance, and it is difficult to build up a consistent picture from her portraits. Friends later thought that she resembled the countess of Albany, widow of the Young Pretender, who came to London in 1791, and she herself claimed to detect a likeness.[45] This might mean that she had a pale complexion, a slightly turned-up nose, and a tendency to put on weight. There was nothing especially

[41] Roberts, i. 66–7.

[42] Indiana University, Lilly Library, Gwatkin MS, Patty More to Ann Gwatkin, 9 Aug. 1774. Quoted courtesy Lilly Library, Indiana University, Bloomington, Indiana.

[43] *Emma*, ch. 7. Compare the character in *The Watsons* who declares, 'I would rather do anything than be a teacher at a school.' J. Austen, *Lady Susan, The Watsons, Sanditon*, ed. M. Drabble (Harmondsworth, 1974), 110. For Austen's possible views on girls' schools, see C. Tomalin, *Jane Austen: A Life* (Harmondsworth, 1998), 34–42.

[44] Though Boswell made no mention of it either in his journal or in his subsequent *Life of Johnson*, he informed Hannah More of the visit when he returned to London. J. Boswell, *Life of Johnson*, ed. G. Birkbeck Hill (Oxford, 1934), iii. 50–1; Roberts, i. 80.

[45] Roberts, ii. 343.

remarkable about her features apart from her expressive eyes, noted by friend and enemy alike, and which shine out even in the portraits painted in old age. The eyes reflected her character: strong emotions, unquenchable intellectual curiosity, a great desire to shine in company, and a flirtatiousness that was later disciplined, though not entirely suppressed, by her Evangelical conversion. In her early youth she was introduced to the works of Shakespeare, and was so overwhelmed by the experience that she 'durst not read him after supper, as he shook my nerves so, as by his power of excitement to prevent my sleeping'; she was especially moved by the character of Constance in *King John* and her poignant line 'Young Arthur is my son and he is slain.'[46] Her 'nerves' continued to plague her throughout her life in the form of headaches and bilious attacks; 'I have but a foolish bundle of nerves,' she was to tell a friend, 'and spirits extremely liable to agitation.'[47] Looking back in old age, she reflected that her life had been 'a successive scene of visitation and restoration. I think I could enumerate 20 mortal diseases from which I have been raised up without any continued diminution of strength.'[48] Her frequent illnesses—which also included fevers and bronchial infections—gave her a horror of idleness and procrastination, causing her to cherish the days when she was well and to fill them with purposeful activity.

In 1763 she went to hear the renowned Scottish astronomer, mechanic, and portrait painter James Ferguson, who had come to Bristol to deliver a course of lectures on 'experimental philosophy'.[49] A brilliant speaker, and an evangelist for Newtonian science, he travelled the country addressing packed audiences; a few years earlier he had come to know the youthful Tom Paine, who was one of his great admirers.[50] Like her future enemy, Hannah More, too, was enthralled. She quickly secured an introduction, and, according to one of her biographers, he then submitted some of his compositions to her so that she could check his style.[51] It may seem unlikely that a celebrated middle-aged scholar should seek the advice of a girl of 18, but in the following decades men of even greater distinction were only too eager to flatter Hannah More. Perhaps it was the eyes.

In the summer of that year the citizens of Bristol entertained another itinerant lecturer, the Irish actor Thomas Sheridan, father of the playwright, who came to deliver a set of lectures on oratory.[52] By now a practised and persistent attention-seeker, Hannah More addressed him in (allegedly) extempore verses, which were presented to him by a common friend.

---

[46] *A Later Pepys: The Correspondence of Sir William Weller Pepys*, ed. A. C. C. Gaussen (London, 1904), ii. 390–1; Roberts, i. 252.

[47] Anson MSS, doc. folder 8, More to Mary Hamilton, 1 Sept. 1783.

[48] Duke, More to Wilberforce [Autumn 1818].   [49] *FFBJ*, 12 Feb. 1763.

[50] J. Keane, *Tom Paine: A Political Life* (London, 1996), 42–3; *FFBJ*, 12 Feb. 1763. For the popularization of science through lectures, see R. Porter, *Enlightenment: Britain and the Creation of the Modern World* (London, 2001), 142–4.   [51] Roberts, i. 16.   [52] *FFBJ*, 6 Aug. 1763.

What nobler charms in eloquence are found,
Where wit with musick, sense unites with sound!
Oh could my unfledg'd muse, the theme define,
The well-earned praise, O Sheridan, were thine![53]

And so on.

In fact, Hannah More's 'unfledged muse' was ready to hatch in the form of a pastoral verse drama *The Search after Happiness*, written for the girls at the school to perform. The theme could hardly be more conventional. Four young ladies visit a shady grove which conceals the home of the ancient shepherdess Urania and her daughters. All are dissatisfied and in search of the happiness which is only to be found in solitude and simplicity. Cleora is as ambitious as the young Hannah More.

I sigh'd for *fame*, I languished for renown,
I would be prais'd, caress'd, admir'd, and known.
On daring wing my mounting spirit soar'd,
And science thro' her boundless laws explor'd:
I scorn'd the salique laws of pedant schools,
Which chain our genius down by tasteless rules:
I long'd to burst those female bonds, which held
My sex in awe (by thirst of fame impell'd):
To boast each various faculty of mind.[54]

Later in the drama, however, she is rebuked by Urania in terms that Jacob More could well have used.

Would she the privilege of *Man* invade?
Science for *female* minds was never made;
Taste, elegance, and talents may be ours,
But *learning* suits not our less vigorous powers...
For *Woman* shines but in her *proper* sphere...
By yielding she obtains the noblest sway,
And reigns securely when she seems t'obey.[55]

At the age of 18 Hannah More had set out the contradictions found in all her subsequent writings about women. She never fully reconciled her longing for fame with the narrow code of female modesty. Her painful realization of the way the traditional prescriptions cramped women's talents was offset by her own firm reinforcement of these conventions. *The Search after Happiness* was the first of her works to present women and girls with a tortuous message impossible to disentangle into clear advice. If an admiring anecdote related by her clerical biographer Henry Thompson is to be believed, her

---

[53] Thompson, *Life of More*, 14–15.
[54] *The Search after Happiness: A Pastoral Drama* (London, 1774), 16.
[55] Ibid. 34, 38.

practice as a teacher could be even more discouraging. The sister of one of the pupils frequently stayed at the school as a visitor. She was a talented artist and her drawings were admired by everyone at the school apart from Hannah More.

One morning this young lady made her appearance rather late at the breakfast-table. Her apology was this, that she had been occupied in *putting a new binding on her petticoat*. Mrs Hannah More, fixing her brilliant eyes upon her with an expression of entire approbation, said, 'Now my dear, I find you can employ yourself *usefully*, I will no longer forbear to express my admiration of your drawings'.[56]

The priggish schoolteacher with her deflating comments and the creative artist determined to express her talents lodged uneasily within the same individual.

Bristol was proud of its cultural life, especially its theatre.[57] The Jacob's Well Theatre, situated at the foot of Brandon Hill, had been built by the comic actor John Hippisley, who had been the original Peachum in the *Beggars' Opera*. When the London theatres closed for the summer, he brought the actors down to Bristol, where they played to packed and appreciative audiences. By the summer of 1764 the city was in the grip of a 'theatrical mania' with the arrival of the famous London actor William Powell, then aged about 29.[58] A charming womanizer, a man of undisciplined energy, impetuous, quarrelsome, and undisciplined, he was a controversial and charismatic figure. When he played King Lear for his benefit on 13 August, many thought his performance outdid Garrick's; he performed the storm scene in a way that perfectly suited his unstable personality. With her keen nose for celebrity, Hannah More soon came to know Powell, and turned her facility in writing verses to her advantage. When he returned to Bristol for the 1765 season, she wrote the prologue for his benefit performance of *Hamlet*, in which she domesticated the Prince of Denmark and imbued him with contemporary notions of sensibility.

---

[56] Thompson, *Life of More*, 167 n.

[57] This discussion is based on Jenkins, *Memoirs of the Bristol Stage*; Nicholls and Taylor, *Bristol Past and Present*, iii. 200–1; K. Barker, 'William Powell: A Forgotten Star', in K. Richards and P. Thompson (eds.), *The Eighteenth-Century English Stage* (London, 1972), 73–83; ead., 'The Theatre Royal, Bristol: The First Seventy Years', in P. McGrath (ed.), *Bristol in the Eighteenth Century* (Newton Abbot, 1972), 63–88; ead., *The Theatre Royal, Bristol, 1766–1966: Two Centuries of Stage History* (London, 1974), 3–25; *The Biographical Dictionary of Actors, Actresses, &c*, ed. A. P. H. Highfill *et al.* (Carbondale, Ill., 1975).

[58] Jenkins, *Bristol Stage*, 49.

No thundering hero angry J O V E defies,
Nor impious lover storms against the skies;
To draw the gen'rous, sympathetic tear,
The *filial virtues* shall tonight appear.[59]

By the mid-1760s the Jacob's Well Theatre had outgrown its site. Perhaps because of the cramped conditions and the squash of bodies on hot summer evenings, audiences were sometimes disorderly, and on one occasion Powell himself forcibly dislodged a group of rioters. It was also inconveniently situated, being outside the city boundary and an uncomfortable distance from the gentry residences at Queen Square and St James, Barton. After the performances the audience had to walk home along a dirty, potholed road, needing linkboys to guide their steps. For these reasons, the managers decided to build a new theatre at King Street in the centre of the city. £5,000 was raised by subscribers and shareholders, and, in spite of a legal challenge from the Quakers and a protesting pamphlet describing the new building as 'the very loadstone of vice in the centre of the city',[60] the foundation stone was laid on 30 November 1764. In April 1766 David Garrick came to view the completed project and declared himself 'much pleased'.[61] On 30 May the Theatre Royal opened under Powell's management. Audiences must have gasped with delight when they entered the elaborately decorated semicircular auditorium, the first of its shape in England, and saw it glitter and sparkle under the chandeliers. With its nine dress-boxes and eight upper side-boxes, all inscribed with the names of dramatists and other literary men, it was a proudly self-conscious assertion of the cultural importance of a provincial city.

The most memorable event of a brilliant season in the new theatre was Powell's performance of *Lear*, in which his wife, Elizabeth, played Cordelia for the first time. The Park Street school, which included Powell's two daughters among the pupils, was in a state of stage-struck excitement. The school was remarkable for the number of pupils connected with the theatre. As well as the Powell girls, it included the granddaughter of the great tragedienne Hannah Pritchard, and the future actress Priscilla Hopkins, later to become the wife of the actor John Kemble and the sister-in-law of Sarah Siddons.[62] All the pupils were taken to see the play. One of them was a pretty 8-year-old girl named Mary Darby, on her first visit to the theatre. Thirteen years later, as the actress Mary Robinson, she was to create a sensation when she played Perdita in *The Winter's Tale*, and a sensation of a different kind when she became the mistress, first of the Prince of Wales

[59] *The Search after Happiness*, 44.   [60] *FFBJ*, 31 Aug. 1765.
[61] *FFBJ*, 12 Apr. 1766.
[62] *Perdita: The Memoirs of Mary Robinson* (1758–1800), ed. M. J. Levy (London, 1994), 22–3.

and then of his friend Charles James Fox. 'Of all Biographical Anecdotes', Hester Piozzi was to write, 'none ever struck me more forcibly that the one saying how Hannah More *la Devote* was the Person who educated fair *Perdita la Pecheresse*.'[63] The future 'pecheresse' and her schoolmates heard the great actor and compulsive philanderer recite an uxorious prologue written by Hannah More, which was sickly even by the standards of the day.

> ... I presume to plead a *woman's* cause;
> Tonight, the *second* aera of my life,
> I venture here my *pupil*, more—my wife! ...
> Then smile, propitious smile, and make for life
> One grateful *Husband*, and one happy *Wife*.[64]

According to Mary Robinson, however, Mrs Powell did not play 'with sufficient *éclat* to render the profession an object for her future exertions',[65] and she soon retreated into private life.

By now Powell was at the height of his fame. Cooler critics thought his performances uneven, but most Bristol theatregoers, grateful for his patronage of their city, could see no wrong in him. The young poet and forger Thomas Chatterton wrote, 'No single part is thine, thou'rt all in all': words that could easily have been echoed by Hannah More.[66] At the end of May 1769 Powell performed in Otway's *Venice Preserved*, but the following day he was struck down with a feverish chill, caught after playing cricket, which turned to pneumonia. While the fever raged, King Street was covered with straw and the magistrates directed chains to be placed across each end of it to keep out carriages.[67] He died on the evening of Monday 3 July just as the curtain was going up on *Richard III*. Somehow the actors got through their parts; when the performance was ended, the audience was told of the tragedy, the rest of the evening's entertainment was cancelled, and the theatre was shut down until after the funeral. According to one account, Hannah More, who was temporarily taking Mrs Powell's place at his bedside, was with him when he died.[68] Bristol paid its adopted son the full tribute of elaborate mourning. On 6 July his remains were taken from the College Green to the cathedral church for a service conducted by the dean. He was buried in the north aisle and a marble monument was raised over his tomb with an epitaph by the London actor–manager George Colman the elder.

---

[63] *The Piozzi Letters: Correspondence of Hester Lynch Piozzi (formerly Mrs Thrale)*, ed. E. A. Bloom and L. D. Bloom, iii: 1799–1804 (Newark, Del., 1993), 82.

[64] *The Search after Happiness*, 48–9. [65] *Perdita*, 22.

[66] Quoted in Jenkins, *Bristol Stage*, 86. [67] Ibid. 93.

[68] G. Tracey Watts, *Theatrical Bristol* (Bristol, 1915), 55; Hopkins, *Hannah More*, 44.

Here rest his praise, here found his noblest fame—
All else a bubble, or an empty name!

If Hannah More reflected that this was also the option facing her, then her choice was complicated by another factor that might have severely curtailed her hopes of literary celebrity. She was now 24, and for the last two years she had been engaged, like her mother before her, to a man twenty years her senior.

The details of the engagement have been obscured by both the reticence of Hannah More's friends and the ribaldry of her enemies. She never referred to it in later life, and her biographers had to research the story at second hand.[69] Her fiancé was a local landowner, William Turner, who lived at a house with the Shakespearean name of Belmont, on a hill six miles from Bristol. His two young cousins were pupils at the Park Street school. They spent their holidays at Belmont, and as they were about the same ages as Hannah and Patty More, it was natural that they should invite the two young teachers to stay with them. The situation

Where beauteous *Belmont* rears its modest brow
To view *Sabrina's* [the River Severn's] silver waves below,[70]

more than gratified Hannah More's intense love of scenic beauty. Turner, who was busy laying out his grounds, consulted her on his plans, and perhaps inspired what was to be her lifelong passion for landscape gardening. She was shown one of the features of the estate, a rock partially made up of red sandstone. On rainy days blood-coloured water poured from it, and, long after the relationship with Turner was over, she commemorated the phenomenon in her early poem *The Bleeding Rock*. In it the neighbouring hamlet of Failand became Fairyland, and the rock the metamorphosed nymph Lindamira, mortally wounded by her dying lover.

The life-blood issuing from the wounded stone,
Blends with the crimson current of his own.
And tho' revolving ages since have past,
The meeting torrents undiminish'd last;
Still gushes out the sanguine stream again,
The standing wonder of the stranger Twain.[71]

---

[69] For the fullest account, see Thompson, *Life of More*, 15–20; see also Roberts, i. 31–3.

[70] *Sir Eldred of the Bower and The Bleeding Rock: Two Legendary Tales* (Dublin, 1776), 27. Belmont House and the adjoining farmland and woodland now form part of the Tyntesfield estate. In June 2002, following the death of the owner, Lord Wraxall, in 2001, Tyntesfield was bought by the National Trust. Until about 1990 Belmont was used as a nursing home. The estate also includes a detached stone house known as Hannah More, and there is a memorial tablet to More in the grounds.

[71] *The Bleeding Rock*, 31.

Entranced with the clever, bright-eyed girl, Turner proposed marriage, probably some time in 1767, and she accepted. Everyone would have thought her mad to refuse. He seemed the ideal husband, as benevolent as he was wealthy; he later contributed £1,000 to the foundation stone of the new wing of the Bristol Infirmary, and the rest of his family seemed equally disposed to good works.[72] Marriage to such a man, affluent, cultivated, philanthropic, would be a Cinderella-like transformation for the daughter of a charity school master. With a glittering prospect ahead of her, More burned her boats, renounced her share in the school, and spent a good deal of money buying the clothes necessary for her new status as the wife of a wealthy man. The date was fixed for the marriage, the preparations were made, but then Turner postponed it. It was clearly at very short notice, though there is no supporting evidence for Thomas De Quincey's malicious assertion that she was jilted at the church door on the very day of the wedding.[73] A new date was arranged and the marriage was again put off; it was then postponed for the third time. There was no particular reason, save that Turner seems to have been a depressive by temperament, incapable of making a long-term commitment, but incapable too of taking the decisive step of breaking off a relationship. He dithered for about six years, at the end of which period Hannah More was 28 and past her first youth, short of money, and the butt of gossip and mockery. Such a situation called for firm action from her parents, but none was forthcoming. By now in his seventies, and out of his depth, Jacob More opted out of the duty a self-respecting eighteenth-century father owed his daughter. As he failed to confront the vacillating suitor, the elder sisters stepped into the vacuum. Determined to persuade her to renounce Turner, they sought the help of a man who was to have great importance in her life, the clergyman, doctor, and future baronet James Stonhouse. Since 1764 he had been rector of a Wiltshire living, but he spent most of the year in Bristol in order to take the waters at the Hotwells. A keen theatregoer and friend of David Garrick, he had been one of the chief mourners at Powell's funeral, and it may have been this common interest that brought him to the More sisters' attention. He became Hannah More's latest and most helpful patron, determined either to secure the marriage or to extricate her from her engagement.

With her future unresolved, and with Bristol society fluttering with gossip and unkind speculation, More succumbed to what her doctor described as

---

[72] *FFBJ*, 28 June 1788. He was also intensely moralistic and patriotic. In 1803 he donated £25 to the newly formed Society for the Suppression of Vice and 5 guineas to the Bristol Sea-Fencibles (*FFBJ*, 26 Feb., 17 Dec. 1803). See also his obituary notice, *FFBJ*, 7 Apr. 1804. The whole family seems to have been wealthy and benevolent. On 25 Oct. 1788 *FFBJ* reported the death of his unmarried sister, 'who, we have good authority to say, has left a very handsome legacy to our Infirmary'.

[73] T. De Quincey, *Collected Writings*, ed. D. Masson (Edinburgh, 1890), xiv. 107–8.

an ague, though it was probably her body's reaction to feelings of emptiness and depression. On her recovery she went on holiday to Weston-super-Mare in the late summer and early autumn of 1773, where she met the poet and clergyman John Langhorne, rector of Blagdon (a parish that was to loom large in her life), and found that a mild flirtation could do wonders for her self-esteem. Like William Powell, Langhorne was a married man and therefore 'safe', as well as being a charming and disreputable character, who enjoyed the company of clever women. They arranged to ride together along the sands, Hannah More on pillion behind a servant. When they did not manage to meet, they left letters and poems for each other in the cleft of a post near the water. On one occasion Langhorne wrote her a little poem in the sand. With her riding whip she added her own verse.

> Some firmer basis, polish'd Langhorne, choose,
> To write the dictates of thy charming muse;
> Thy strains in solid characters rehearse,
> And be thy tablet lasting as thy verse.[74]

Langhorne was the chief poetry reviewer for the *Monthly Review*, and he later used this position to give favourable reviews of More's published work.[75] Their friendly correspondence continued until his death, probably from alcoholic poisoning, in 1779. One of his letters, written in 1776, was a scatalogical conceit, using topical military language inspired by the American Revolution, to describe a recent bilious attack: 'A truce was proclaimed for twenty-four hours; when it appeared that a large body of the Biliaries had secreted themselves in the lower parts of the country I despatched the Second battalion, consisting of ... the provinces of Senna, Tamarind, and Crim Tartary, under the command of ... general Cathartic.'[76] This went on for a couple more paragraphs elaborating on metaphors of expulsion. Nearly sixty years later the *Quarterly Review* was shocked at the indelicacy of this letter, at William Roberts for printing it, and (by implication) at Hannah More for receiving and keeping it.[77] But the woman who did so much to create the conditions which made Victorianism possible had her roots in an earlier period that was less inhibited about bodily functions. Besides, after six years coping with Hamlet, it might have been a pleasure to share a dubious joke with Falstaff.

In October 1773 she was back in Bristol, with the problem of Turner still unresolved. On Stonhouse's advice she wrote to him to break off the

---

[74] Thompson, *Life of More*, 22.
[75] For his reviews of *Sir Eldred of the Bower* and *The Bleeding Rock*, see *Monthly Review*, 54 (1776), 89–99.
[76] Roberts, i. 26.   [77] *Quarterly Review*, 52 (1834), 421.

engagement.[78] He replied, in characteristic fashion, begging her to reconsider, though still not offering a wedding date. The couple then had what must have been a very difficult meeting in which he repeated his proposal, and she, hurt and angry, refused him for the last time. In recompense he offered to settle an annuity on her; in her injured pride she chose to consider this an insult and angrily turned it down. What followed next was set out in a letter from Patty to Ann Gwatkin in the first extant document emanating from a member of the More family.[79] Towards the end of 1773 Stonhouse sought another interview with Turner, who renewed the offer of the annuity, but also stated that he was ready to marry More at any time the doctor suggested 'provided she could be persuaded to consent'. Dealing with such a man must have been like wrestling with a jellyfish. Faced with this final proof that he was incapable of making up his mind, Stonhouse accepted on Hannah's behalf an annuity of £200, to be paid quarterly, together with the verbal promise that 'he would do great things in his Will'. However, the arrangement was made without her consent, and when she learned that the two men had gone over her head to sort out her life, she apparently became angrier than ever. With brutal realism Stonhouse then told her that 'the malicious world, who had so cruelly slandered her, would not provide for her', and, faced with this undeniable truth, she succumbed. Patty was delighted: '£200 P Ann is not to be sported with, tis a noble provision,' and now 'this *Poet* of ours is taken care of and may sit down on her large *behind* and *read*, no *devour*, as many books as she pleases.' But for all her robustly expressed satisfaction, Patty could not rid herself of some niggling 'doubts about the propriety of the thing'. Her fears were understandable. Having taken the money as a reasonable recompense for her six wasted years, Hannah More had to endure whispered accusations, which dogged her for the rest of her life, that she had acted out of calculation. Turner had put her in a most invidious position, and she would hardly have been human if she had not felt betrayed and humiliated.

Six years later the hurt seemed as keen as ever. In her play *The Fatal Falsehood* Guildford (another inadequate father) tells his daughter Emmelina that Orlando has rejected her.

> I will not shame thy blood; and yet, my father,
> Methinks thy daughter shou'd not be refused?
> Refus'd? It has a harsh, ungrateful sound;
> Thou shouldst have found a softer term; refus'd?

---

[78] Though the chronology here is patchy, I have assumed that More broke off her engagement shortly after her return from Weston-super-Mare.

[79] Gwatkin MS, Patty More to Ann Gwatkin, 9 Dec. 1773. It is remarkable that the letter makes no mention of the More parents, who do not seem to have had any involvement in the transaction.

And have I then been held so cheap? Refus'd?
Been treated like the light ones of my sex,
Held up to sale? been offer'd, and refus'd?[80]

Later in the play Orlando, acting remarkably like Turner, offers once more
to marry Emmelina. She refuses.

I cannot stoop to live on charity,
And what but charity is love compell'd? . . .
She who aspir'd to gain Orlando's heart,
Shall never owe Orlando's hand to pity.[81]

Perhaps *The Fatal Falsehood* helped to get Turner out of her system. At
any rate, she made no further references to jilting. Twenty years later the
couple accidentally met again outside her Somerset home, Cowslip Green.
They talked in a friendly fashion, and after this he dined with her from time
to time. According to her biographer, she 'made a point of presenting him a
copy of every work she published'.[82] What point?, one wonders. When he
died in 1804 (a bachelor), it was seen that he had kept his promise to
remember her in his will; in what seems like the expiation of a profound
sense of guilt, he left her a legacy of £1,000 and instructed his executors that
the annuity should continue to be paid her for the rest of her natural life.[83]
(No one could have predicted that she would live to be 88.)

Following the ending of her tortuous relationship with Turner, Hannah
More set herself against marriage and resolved on a literary career. Already
this was making headway. She had been under pressure for some time to
publish *The Search after Happiness*, which had for some years circulated in
manuscript around Bristol literary circles,[84] and the Quaker publisher and
newspaper proprietor Sarah Farley had offered to print the poem for the
standard price of 2s. 6d. On 8 May 1773 *Sarah Farley's Bristol Journal* had
announced the forthcoming publication of 'A PASTORAL POEM, In [*sic*]
SEARCH after HAPPINESS . . . By a YOUNG LADY'. The published poem
was dedicated to Mrs Gwatkin in tribute to 'the friendship with which you
have honor'd me from my very childhood', and it included the prologues she
had written for Powell's *Hamlet* and *Lear*.[85] The following week the rival
paper *Felix Farley's Bristol Journal* published a poem 'To the celebrated
Author of the Pastoral Poem In Search of Happiness' from 'Amicus' (Dean
Tucker or James Stonhouse?), praising More as the embodiment of both

---

[80] *The Fatal Falsehood: A Tragedy* (London, 1779), 49.   [81] Ibid. 62–3.
[82] Thompson, *Life of More*, 19.   [83] PRO, PROB 11/ 1408, fo. 291.
[84] As early as 1766 the *Bristol Journal* had published a poem 'To a certain Young Lady who
has composed an elegant Pastoral, and many other fine Pieces, which she does not care to publish.'
FFBJ, 31 May 1766.
[85] *The Search after Happiness*, pp. vii, 43–9.

masculine and feminine virtues: '*Bold* in thy song—but *gentle* in thy Heart'.[86] By the end of the month the poem was being sold in London by the Bristolian printer and bookseller Thomas Cadell.[87] This inspired a poetic tribute 'On Miss MOORE [*sic*] of Bristol. From STREPHON'.

> Sweet Daughter of the Grove! . . . the tuneful Throng
> Charm'd with thy Notes, shall listen to thy Song . . . [88]

In September, while More was at Weston, the poem went into a second edition at the lower price of 1*s*. 6*d*; in May 1774 the newspapers were advertising the fourth edition.[89] Eighteenth-century print editions were small, usually under 1,000 copies, and the copyright legislation of that year only mildly tilted the balance from publishers to authors.[90] A novice to the literary world, More was not set immediately to earn large sums of money (and even at the end of her life she believed that her publishers had cheated her of some of her earnings). Nevertheless, she had made the encouraging discovery that she could earn money from writing, and would not have to rely on her annuity alone. With characteristic generosity she marked the transition to financial independence by subscribing to the Bristol Society for the Relief and Discharge of Persons Confined for Small Debts.[91]

The decision to publish *The Search after Happiness* proved commercially shrewd. By 1800, by which time the publisher Thomas Cadell had gained the copyright, more than 10,000 copies had been printed, it had gone into twelve editions, and was performed regularly in girls' schools.[92] More was to be astonished at the popularity of a work, which she claimed she lacked the patience to reread, but pleased at her early decision to make over the profits to Patty.[93]

Stonhouse was now to perform his greatest service for More. Around the end of 1773 he sent his friend David Garrick a manuscript copy of her Roman play *The Inflexible Captive*, in the hopes that he would stage a production at the Drury Lane Theatre. Garrick declined, but neither Stonhouse nor More abandoned hope. If he turned down one play, he might be persuaded to accept another, and More had now completed a new tragedy

---

[86] *FFBJ*, 15 May 1773.
[87] Ibid., 22 May 1773. See also the poem in *Sarah Farley's Bristol Journal*, 29 May 1773.
[88] *Sarah Farley's Bristol Journal*, 10 July 1773.
[89] *FFBJ*, 11 Sept. 1773; *Sarah Farley's Bristol Journal*, 28 May 1774.
[90] For the book trade, see I. Rivers (ed.), *Books and their Readers in Eighteenth-Century England* (Leicester, 1982); J. Raven, *Judging New Wealth: Popular Publishing and Responses to Commerce in England, 1750–1800* (Oxford, 1992).
[91] *Sarah Farley's Bristol Journal*, 30 Apr. 1774.
[92] See e.g. M. Russell Mitford, *Our Village: Sketches of Rural Character and Scenery* (London, 1824), ii. 146–65.
[93] Roberts, ii. 51–2.

based on Metastasio's *Olimpiade*. In one of the great turning points of her life, she decided to seize the moment, and at the beginning of 1774 she made her first journey to London in the hope of meeting the great actor–manager. It was a brave move, but the visit was hastily arranged and proved an expensive failure. She was in town about two months (probably with Sally and Patty) but for a good deal of that period was ill with the fever which had attacked her the previous year, perhaps brought on by nervous tension. To sweat and toss in a strange bed in a dark lodging house during a smoky London winter must have been a peculiarly bleak experience; but even if she had been well, the visit would have been unsuccessful, as Garrick himself was ill and performing rarely. Frustrated, she returned to Bristol.[94]

A second visit was planned with much more care, and this time the circumstances were in More's favour. In March Cadell published *The Inflexible Captive*, which quickly went into a second edition, giving her reason to hope that it might yet be performed in Bristol or Bath, if not in London. Cadell also had her new play in manuscript, and on her request he sent it to Garrick. Mrs Gwatkin played her part in preparing the ground by writing a letter of introduction to her friend Frances Reynolds, sister of Sir Joshua and a talented painter in her own right. (Her son was later to marry the Reynolds' niece Theophilia Palmer.) With everything planned, Hannah, Sally, and Patty boarded the London coach in early May 1774, having handed over the sum of £1 7s 0d. each; jolting eastward with few stops on the way, except to change horses, they covered the eighty-mile journey in two dusty, exhausting days.[95] Their lodgings, at a Mr Howson's in Southampton Street, were just across the Strand from David Garrick's London residence, the Adelphi. This time nothing had been left to chance. She was going to meet the great man.

[94] See Stonhouse's letter to Garrick of 21 May 1774, *The Letters of David Garrick*, ed. D. M. Little and G. M. Kahrl (Cambridge, 1963), iii. 1355.

[95] For information about journey times and prices, see e.g. *FFBJ*, 18 Oct. 1766.

Chapter 2

---=>◦<=---

The Garrick Years
1774–1779

SOUTHAMPTON STREET, where the More sisters arrived with their luggage and their high expectations, linked the bustling, untidy piazza of Covent Garden to the elegant shops and wide thoroughfare of the Strand. The street was respectable—the Garricks had lived at number 27 for the first two decades of their marriage—but when the market closed for the night, the piazza and many of the surrounding streets were given over to the brothels and bagnios presided over by the 'Covent Garden abbesses' as well as to the more numerous freelance prostitutes supplementing the meagre earnings of their day jobs. Harris's annual *List of Covent Garden Ladies* was later to provide potential customers with a helpful guide to these attractions.

For the three provincial schoolteachers the sheer size of London must have been daunting. With a population of three-quarters of a million, more than ten times the size of Bristol, it was the largest city in western Europe. One in ten of the population of England lived there and the number was growing all the time. Contemporary metaphors focused on its gargantuan appetite and restless movement. Some of its public spaces—the clubs and coffee houses—were for men only, but many others were open to women. At some time the More sisters visited the British Museum, which they loved, and the Pantheon in Oxford Street, a vast auditorium that mounted masquerades, balls, and concerts, which they disliked. But they would not have allowed any of these pleasures to divert them from their great purpose of seeing Garrick perform. The capital had two licensed theatres, Covent Garden and Drury Lane, as well as the King's Theatre at the Haymarket, which functioned during the summer. Since coming from Lichfield with his former tutor Samuel Johnson, Garrick had transformed the theatrical scene, and by the power of his acting and the psychological depth of his interpretation of character had raised the prestige of his profession to new heights.[1] In 1747 he had taken over Drury Lane, and over the years he turned it into the most flourishing of the London theatres. The sisters arrived in time to see him in two of his most popular roles, Lusignan in Aaron Hill's tragedy *Zara*, performed on 13 May, and King Lear four days later. Having been disappointed on their first visit, they were keyed up for the event. Hannah More had waited months—possibly years—for this sublime experience. She expected to be electrified and was not disappointed.

Garrick's 'Newtonian' revolution in the theatre had liberated acting from the mannered and declamatory style of the early eighteenth century and replaced it with a powerful emotionalism perfectly attuned to an age of sensibility. He compensated for his lack of height and his undistinguished features by a commanding stage presence that relied heavily on his expressive eyes, his gestures, and the sheer physicality of his performances: throwing away his crutch as Lear cursing Goneril, or clenching his fists and tensing his body for a fight as the comic tobacconist Abel Drugger in Ben Jonson's *The Alchemist*. He played lovingly upon the sentiments of his audiences in a fashion equalled only by the revivalist preachers Wesley and Whitefield, and contemporaries often used the language of religious experience to describe their heightened reactions.

Her two visits to Drury Lane were certainly an overwhelming experience for Hannah More. In a breathless letter to Stonhouse she described Tuesday 17 May, when she saw *Lear*, as the 'Day of Days' (even though this was Nahum Tate's version, which pandered to the sensibilities of the age by leaving out the Fool and providing a happy ending in which Edgar and Cordelia marry). 'Surely He is above Mortality.... His Talents are capacious beyond human credibility. I felt myself annihilated before Him, & every Faculty of my Soul was swallowed up in Attention.... I thought I should have been suffocated with Grief.'[2] This was the rapture of the mystics as much as Aristotle's catharsis—ecstasy in its literal sense—and it was language which she was never, even at the height of her Evangelical fervour, to apply to her relationship with God.

As no doubt More had intended, Stonhouse passed her letter on to Garrick with a covering letter dated 21 May, introducing her as 'a young

---

[1] For Garrick, see C. Oman, *David Garrick* (London, 1958); K. A. Burnim, *David Garrick, Director* (Pittsburgh, 1961); G. W. Stone and G. M. Kahrl, *David Garrick: A Critical Biography* (Carbondale, ill., 1979); L. Woods, *Garrick Claims the Stage: Acting as Social Emblem in Eighteenth-Century England* (Westport, Conn., 1984); I. McIntyre, *Garrick* (London, 1999); J. Benedetti, *David Garrick and the Birth of the Modern Theatre* (London, 2001).

[2] *The Letters of David Garrick*, ed. D. M. Little and G. M. Kahrl (Cambridge, 1963), iii. 1357–8.

Woman of an amazing Genius, & remarkable Humility'. He reminded him that he had already shown him *The Inflexible Captive*, and that Cadell had sent him her new tragedy, and concluded optimistically that she 'has wrote some little Farces—which I have not seen—but I am told she has a good comic Genius'.[3]

David Garrick received many unsolicited plays, a fair number from ambitious young women, and he relished his role of manager–mentor in getting their work performed.[4] He could be ruthless in his criticisms, but generous where he recognized talent, and the tremulous flattery of Hannah More's letter soothed his vanity. For all his great gifts, he was an oddly insecure man, always ready to lap up praise, more especially now that he was well advanced into middle age and his health was failing. Daringly, he had played Lear when only 25; now he knew that, at 57, he was really too old for Hamlet. His marriage to the Austrian dancer Eva Maria Veigel was famously happy but it was childless, and the emergence of a potential literary daughter at a time when his career was winding down was powerfully attractive. He was prepared to like and support Hannah More.

On Monday 23 May he sent her a note telling her he would call the next day. The sisters treasured this brief message and one of them (not Hannah) wrote on the back "'twas the *first*!"[5] However, circumstances prevented this initial visit, and two days later he sent another note telling them that his coach would be ready the following Friday to take them to his home at 5 Adelphi Terrace on the other side of the Strand.[6] (It would have been far quicker to walk, but the conventions required a more genteel mode of transport.) The Adelphi was a luxurious new development, designed by the Adam brothers (hence its name), built on a series of vaulted arches overlooking the Thames. The Garricks had moved there in 1772 and furnished it expensively. The sisters entered it through the pillared hall, the first of the twenty-four rooms, and would then have been escorted into the first-floor drawing room, with its marble chimney-piece and ornately decorated ceiling crowned by a central panel of Venus adorned by the graces. But if the three young women (even the loquacious Sally) were initially tongue-tied, Garrick soon put them at their ease with his vivacious good humour. He would have been ably partnered by his wife, who was, as Fanny Burney noted, 'the most attentively polite & perfectly well bred Woman in the World—her speech is all softness, her manners all elegance, her smile all sweetness'.[7] Seeing him

[3] Ibid. 1355–6.

[4] E. Donkin, *Getting into the Act: Women Playwrights in London, 1776–1826* (London, 1995), 25–31.

[5] Clark, uncatalogued.   [6] Folger, Garrick MS Y.c. 2600 (183).

[7] *The Early Journals and Letters of Fanny Burney*, i: *1768–1773*, ed. L. E. Troide (Oxford, 1988), 148–9.

close up, Hannah More might have been struck once more by the emotion she had felt on hearing him speak the epilogue at the end of *Lear* when her heart had 'ach'd for the Depredations Time is beginning to make in his Face'.[8] Alongside the hero-worship was a maternal protectiveness and a poignant sadness at the inevitable decay of even the greatest genius.

As Garrick reported to Stonhouse, he found the sisters 'most agreeable' and did not think that Hannah More's talents had been exaggerated. However, he spoke his mind about the new play and had some useful advice for her future work.

I have seen her last imitation of Metastasio which I dont think has the merit of Regulus—the foundation and conduct of the fable is too romantic as I fairly told her for among many other good qualities I soon found that I might speak my mind sincerely without offence: her Sisters told me that she *writes* quick which is lucky; but then I woud advise her to *correct* slowly—I perceived several marks of haste—were I worthy to direct her she should first chuse a happy subject and well adapted to her genius—then she should take some time carefully to distribute her fable into Acts—*Character* & *circumstances*, alias *Situations*; shoud be well attended to . . . a Play without them is mere Dialogue. . . . I coud wish to see her *outlines*, before she writes one verse, and when the road is made a true Dramatic Turn Pike, I woud have her seat herself upon Pegasus and gallop away as fast as she pleases—if she writes without Plan I will not insure her success.[9]

There was nothing condescending about Garrick's advice. He was taking More seriously as an apprentice writer and his criticisms showed more respect for her potential than the undiscerning adulation she was used to hearing. From being so cruelly jilted, she was now having her work honestly and constructively scrutinized by the greatest actor of the age. Although he had turned down her play, her ambition was set on fire—and her emotions too. Under the benignly watchful eye of Eva Garrick the relationship would always be safe, and she could give full rein to the intensity of her feelings, knowing them to be virtuous. Garrick was more than a substitute for the flawed Powell and the indecisive Turner; he was the supportive, encouraging father she had never had. Far from confining her to a limited female sphere, he had urged her to take wings and seek her own destiny, soaring as high as her talents would allow. It was an exquisite prospect, and she loved him for it.

Her entrée to literary London was now assured. Soon after, the sisters met the opposition Whig Edmund Burke, author of the influential treatise on aesthetics *A Philosophical Inquiry into the Origins of our Ideas of the Sublime and the Beautiful*, and, like Garrick and Sir Joshua Reynolds, a member of

[8] *Letters of Garrick*, iii. 1358.
[9] Yale University, Beinecke Rare Book and Manuscript Library, Osborn Collection, MS vault file, David Garrick to Sir James Stonhouse, 31 May 1774.

Samuel Johnson's Club. Shortly after this they were introduced to Johnson at Reynolds's house. As they mounted the stairs, Reynolds warned them of the great lexicographer's uncertain moods, but when they entered the room More found him 'with good humour in his countenance, and a macaw of Sir Joshua's in his hand'. He was well prepared for the meeting, and recited for her a verse from a morning hymn she had written for Stonhouse.[10] A little later an excited Sally reported back to the family that they had been to see him in 'his *very own house*' at Johnson's Court off Fleet Street. When they entered his little parlour and found it empty, Hannah audaciously 'seated herself in his great chair, hoping to catch a little ray of his genius'. Johnson was greatly amused when he learned this, and told her he never sat on that particular chair. Sally continued:

Miss Reynolds told the doctor of all our rapturous exclamations on the road. He shook his scientific head at Hannah, and said, 'She was a *silly thing*.' When our visit was ended, he called for his hat . . . to attend us down a very long entry into our coach, and not Rasselas could have acquitted himself more *en cavalier*.[11]

Though Johnson could be famously difficult, he was here acting in character. He enjoyed the company of young women, and encouraged their literary ambitions. He later stated that Hannah More was 'the most powerful versificatrix in the English language'.[12] This, perhaps, is not saying very much, as, for all his affectionate praise, he did not believe that women could scale the high peaks of true genius.[13] Nevertheless, he had a high opinion of her work, and by the time she composed *The Bas Bleu* he was prepared to judge her by masculine standards.

After a dazzling six weeks the sisters returned to Bristol. In the autumn the city was in the throes of a particularly exciting election. Its two parliamentary seats were contested by Matthew Brickdale, the government candidate, the radical Henry Cruger, and his ally Edmund Burke, who made a dramatic entry in the middle of October.[14] The election was very raw politics, with the crisis in America emerging as the most important issue. Burke took up his headquarters in Park Street, next to the More sisters' school, so that, as Sally reported to Mrs Gwatkin, 'we are very lively at night with the Huzzas of the Mob'. Surprisingly in view of the fierce loyalism of her later politics,

---

[10] Roberts, i. 48.   [11] Ibid. 49.

[12] J. Boswell, *Life of Johnson*, ed. G. Birkbeck Hill (Oxford, 1934), iii. 293–4 n. 5.

[13] I. Grundy, 'Samuel Johnson as Patron of Women', in P. J. Korshin (ed.), *The Age of Johnson: A Scholarly Annual*, 1 (New York, 1987), 59–77.

[14] For Burke's campaign, see P. T. Underdown, 'Bristol and Burke', in McGrath (ed.), *Bristol in the Eighteenth Century*, 41–62; J. E. Bradley, *Religion, Revolution, and English Radicalism: Nonconformity in Eighteenth-Century Politics and Society* (Cambridge, 1990), 112–25.

the pro-American Cruger supporters identified Hannah More as an ally. One
night the teachers and girls at the school were drawn to the window by the
noise of the crowd, and by 'a genteel Voice among them [which] commanded them to Halt under the Window . . . and order'd them to give three
Cheers to Sappho, and the very heavens rung with More, Sappho, and
Cruger for ever', much to the bewilderment of those spectators who lacked a
classical education.[15] In between canvassing, Burke spent several evenings
with the sisters. When his victory was assured, they sent him a congratu-
latory cockade, entwined with myrtle, ivy, laurel, and bay, decorated with
silver tassels, and inscribed with the word BURKE, followed by a verse
tribute. He wore it at his triumphal chairing and the following day he called
at Park Street to thank them.[16]

In January 1775, a few weeks before her thirtieth birthday, Hannah More was
back in London with Sally and Patty, this time lodging in Henrietta Street in
Covent Garden.[17] By the middle of the month she was staying in grace and
favour lodgings at Hampton Court, possibly with Frances Reynolds.[18] From
there she made a pilgrimage to Alexander Pope's villa at Twickenham,
where she committed an act of cultural vandalism—stealing two pieces of
stone from the grotto, a sprig of laurel from the garden, and a pen from one
of the bedrooms. She showed the same eager quest for sacred relics and sites
when she visited the Garricks' Thames-side villa at Hampton. The owners
were absent, but she was able to peep into the octagonal Temple of Shakespeare; inside was Roubiliac's statue of the Bard, commissioned by Garrick,
'in an attitude strikingly pensive . . . his whole form seeming the bigger from
some immense idea with which you suppose his great imagination pregnant'.[19]

Theatrically, this London visit was a disappointment. Garrick was unwell,
and performed relatively infrequently. At Covent Garden, however, the
sisters saw Richard Brinsley Sheridan's *The Rivals*, which, after an uncertain
start, played to packed houses from late January. There were other compen-
sations, too. According to the scarcely impartial Sally, she was now established as one of Dr Johnson's particular favourites. At an evening at Sir
Joshua Reynolds's the pair of them sparkled together. 'It was certainly her
lucky night! . . . The old genius was extremely jocular, the young one very
pleasant. You would have imagined we had been at some comedy had you

[15] Indiana University, Lilly Library, Gwatkin MS, Sally More to Ann Gwatkin, 11 Oct. 1774.
[16] H. Thompson, *The Life of Hannah More with Notices of her Sisters*, (London, 1938), 25-7.
[17] Roberts, i. 38.
[18] Ibid. 41-7. More's letter to Ann Gwatkin seems from internal evidence to have been written
*c.*18 Jan. 1775.
[19] Ibid. 46-7.

heard our peals of laughter.'[20] She also secured the useful patronage of the Shakespearean critic Elizabeth Montagu: 'she is not only the finest genius, but the finest lady I ever saw...her form (for she has no *body*) is delicate even to fragility; her countenance the most animated in the world'.[21] Through her she was drawn into her circle of literary women, the celebrated bluestockings.[22] They included Montagu's sister Sarah Scott, the author of *Millenium Hall*, the poet and educationalist Anna Barbauld, and the essayist Hester Mulso Chapone. A woman with fewer literary pretensions but a great gift for friendship and for letter-writing was Frances Boscawen, the widow of the famous admiral who had captured Lagos during the Seven Years' War; she already had a slight connection with More as her daughter had married Lord Botetourt's nephew the fifth duke of Beaufort.[23] The most distinguished of all was the former journalist and renowned classical scholar Elizabeth Carter, who was to become one of More's closest friends.

The greatest service Garrick performed for her in that year was to make some minor changes to *The Inflexible Captive*, to write an epilogue (the prologue was written by Langhorne), and to oversee its production at the Theatre Royal in Bath on 18 April. A further performance followed on 6 May for the benefit of the Bath actress Mrs Keasberry. Hannah More's sisters came over from Bristol to see it, while she herself observed the performance from behind the scenes.[24] It was a sweet boost to her confidence and there was more to come.

Already *The Search after Happiness* had gone into six editions, and had brought in £100. In the summer she approached Cadell, who had offices in Bristol and London, and offered him two more poems. He volunteered to pay whatever Goldsmith had received for *The Deserted Village*. Having no idea of the price, More suggested 40 guineas. The deal was struck and the ballad tale *Sir Eldred of the Bower* went into print in December along with her earlier *The Bleeding Rock*, which she had written after her ill-starred visits to Belmont.[25] It was the beginning of a long association with the man who made many good judgements as a publisher and one spectacular misjudgement; in the following year he published the first volume of Gibbon's *Decline and Fall of the Roman Empire*, but in 1797 he was to return

---

[20] Ibid. 54.   [21] Ibid. 53.   [22] Ibid. 56–7, 62–3.

[23] For Frances Boscawen, see C. Aspinall-Oglander, *Admiral's Wife: Being the Life and Letters of the Hon. Mrs Edward Boscawen from 1719 to 1761* (London, 1940); id., *Admiral's Widow: Being the Life and Letters of the Hon. Mrs Edward Boscawen from 1761 to 1805* (London, 1942). More might have met Frances Boscawen on her first abortive visit to London, or else at Stoke, the home of the dowager duchess of Beaufort. In March 1774 she dedicated *The Inflexible Captive* to Mrs Boscawen, which would have been a considerable liberty unless there had been some prior acquaintance.

[24] Thompson, *Life of More*, 24–5; *Bath Chronicle*, 20 Apr., 4 May 1775.

[25] Roberts, i. 58–9; Thompson, *Life of More*, 15–17, 27–9.

Jane Austen's *First Impressions* (an early version of *Pride and Prejudice*) unread.

Sir Eldred was dedicated (of course) to Garrick, who returned the compliment in full. In the spring of 1776 Lord Chesterfield's letters to his son were published to much disapproving comment. Garrick fixed on his lordship's contemptuous opinion that women had no genius, and in early April he inserted an anonymous riposte in the press in the form of a six-stanza poem in praise of *Sir Eldred*.

> Thy Wit a Female Champion braves
> And blasts thy Critic's power;
> She comes!—and in her hand she waves
> *Sir Eldred of the Bower.*

The manuscript version of this poem in the Clark Library in Los Angeles is inscribed 'To *my* wild Arab. D. G.', a punning reference to a line in *The Inflexible Captive*: 'To the wild Arab and the faithless Moor'. Hannah More's letters suggest that the Arab was not herself but the vivacious Sally.[26]

Though *Sir Eldred* was little more than a piece of eighteenth-century faux medievalism, it secured More's reputation as a new literary star. In the freezing January of 1776 she returned to London with Patty and Sally to a round of gratifying praise. Garrick began to call her 'Nine' in honour of the Muses, an absurd compliment to a woman who was deaf to music and knew little about painting. Johnson had learned *Sir Eldred* by heart. One evening he called at the Garricks', read the poem over with her, and rewrote a stanza. It appeared in its improved form in subsequent editions.[27]

It was a momentous time in the history of the theatre. On 18 January Garrick sold his portion of the Drury Lane patent to Sheridan and three others in return for £35,000. This was to be his last London season. '*Sic transit gloria mundi!*', Hannah More wrote. 'Who shall supply his loss to the stage? Who shall hold the master-key of the human heart? . . . and who in short shall direct and nurse my dramatic muse?'[28] But far from deserting her, the Garricks were adopting her into their family. On 19 February he celebrated his birthday at a dinner at the Adelphi with some of his other friends. More, 'never saw Johnson in such perfect good humour'. Late in the evening Johnson and Garrick performed their party piece, 'telling old stories "e'en from their boyish days" at Lichfield. We stood around them above an hour, laughing in defiance of every rule of decorum and Chesterfield.'[29] Any lover

---

[26] V & A, Forster, F.48, F.5, vol. 1, fo. 5, More to Garrick, 28 July 1777; fo. 6, More to Garrick., 7 Aug. 1777. See also *Letters of Garrick*, iii. 1254–5.
[27] Roberts, i. 64.   [28] Ibid. 63–4.   [29] Ibid. 69–70.

of the eighteenth-century literary scene might envy Hannah More this golden occasion. It concluded with Garrick reading *Sir Eldred* in a pathetic manner that reduced More and Mrs Garrick to tears, though, by the time he reached the tragic catastrophe, both were laughing at themselves for their excess of sensibility.

At about this time the Garricks confirmed More's new status by taking her to Hampton, not as a sightseer this time, but as a favoured guest. For her future visits they promised her a little table for her writing and her studies.[30] On her return to London she vacated her cramped lodgings and moved into the spacious Adelphi, where she was allocated a bedchamber and a dressing room and given free run of the whole house and its large collection of books.[31] 'I am so much at my ease,' she wrote happily; 'have a great many hours at my own disposal, to read my own books, and see my own friends, and whenever I please, may join the most polished and delightful society in the world!'[32] She was also, of course, saving a considerable amount of money.

In April Garrick gave her his ticket for one of the sensations of the year—the trial before her peers at Westminster Hall of Elizabeth Chudleigh, duchess of Kingston, for bigamy. More's account of the trial is worth quoting in part, both for its entertainment value and for the light it throws on her already censorious attitude to aristocratic vice in the person of 'this unprincipled, artful, licentious woman'.[33] Dressed in deep mourning ('there was nothing white but her face, and had it not been for that, she would have looked like a bale of bombazeen'), the duchess hammed her part with panache. 'She... affected to write very often, though I plainly perceived she only wrote as they do their love epistles on the stage, without forming a letter.' Later she 'was taken ill, but performed it badly'.[34] A week later she was found guilty on overwhelming evidence. A professional to the end, she 'made a Curtsey to the Lords and to all the Spectators, and then with great Composure retired'.[35]

In a space of three weeks in April and May Hannah More saw Garrick's final performances of the roles that had made him famous, and she is one of our best sources for this extraordinary moment in the history of the theatre. The performances included Abel Drugger, Kitely in *Every Man in his Humour*,

[30] Ibid. 68.   [31] Ibid. 73-4.   [32] Ibid. 78.   [33] Ibid. 84.   [34] Ibid. 81-3.
[35] *Public Advertiser*, 23 Apr. 1776. Because of her rank, the duchess, now demoted to a mere countess, was not burned in the hand like a common criminal, and she was able to take a boat to Calais before proceedings could be started against her. She went to Russia, where she set up a brandy distillery near St Petersburg; when this failed, she returned to France and died in Paris in 1788. One feels she would have taken the Revolution in her stride.

Archer in *The Stratagem*, and the Shakespearean roles Benedick, Lear, and Hamlet. He went out, she wrote, 'like one of those summer suns which shine brightest at their setting', and she pitied those who would never see him act: 'Posterity will never be able to form the slightest idea of his perfections.'[36] Such was his fame that Jacques Necker, the Swiss banker who in the following year was to be appointed Louis XVI's reformist director-general of finances, came over from Paris with his wife, Suzanne Curchod, and their precocious 10-year-old daughter, Germaine, the future Madame de Staël. More met the family at the Garricks' in company with the historian Edward Gibbon.[37] Garrick had presumably primed her that Gibbon had once been in love with Suzanne, but that his father had forbidden the marriage. More's tart verdict, more than forty years later, was that Madame Necker was 'too studiously ingenious to be agreeable, and too *recherchée* ever to seem easy; in short she seemed to have been formed to be the admiration of Mr Gibbon'.[38]

London was in a feverish state. For Garrick's Lear on 13 May the crowd flocked round the Drury Lane Theatre from two o'clock, three hours before the doors opened: a disgruntled visitor from the provinces compared the melée to the Black Hole of Calcutta.[39] His Hamlet, however, had always been more controversial; many thought that his rewriting of the play leaving out the fencing scene and the low comedy of the gravediggers was a mutilation too far, and after he left the stage they were restored by popular demand. For Hannah More, however, Garrick could do no wrong. She noted of his performance on 27 April 'that, whether in the simulation of madness, in the sinkings of despair, in the familiarity of friendship, in the whirlwind of passion, or in the meltings of tenderness, he never once forgot he was a prince'. She marvelled that such a supreme master of tragedy could also draw forth roars of laughter from the audience in the role of Abel Drugger: it was as if Milton had written *Hudibras* and Butler *Paradise Lost*.[40] But she could not bear to watch his final performances, and at the beginning of June she departed for Bristol.

On 4 June, the day before his command performance as Richard III, when the house was so crowded that the start of the play was delayed for two hours, he scrawled an exhausted letter telling her that this 'will absolutely kill me—What a trial of breast, lungs, ribs, & what not'. He added, 'we have wanted You at some of our private hours—Where's ye Nine? We want ye Nine!—Silent was every Muse.'[41] She replied instantly. 'I have

[36] Roberts, i. 89, 88.   [37] Ibid. 84.   [38] Ibid. iv. 141.
[39] *Public Advertiser*, 18 May 1776.   [40] Roberts, i. 86–7.
[41] Folger, Garrick MS Y.c 2600 (215).

devoured the newspapers for the last week with the appetite of a famished Politician, to learn if my General had yet laid down arms.' She ended revealingly, 'And has the Nine really been called for? what a comfort was that piece of flattery!'[42]

Garrick's reply was written two days after his final Prospero-like farewell on 10 June, when he played Don Felix in Susannah Centlivre's *The Wonder!* His own account gives something of the flavour of the event. 'Such clapping, Sighing, crying, roaring, &c &c &c—it is not to be describ'd!—in short—it was as we could Wish, et finis coronat Opus.' He passed on a message from his wife, a response to her request for a memento of those last days: 'I have save'd his Buckles for you, which he wore in that last moment, and which was the only thing that They could not take from him.'[43] When they reached More, Anna Barbauld, who was staying with her, composed a little verse:

> Thy *Buckles*, O Garrick, thy friend may now use,
> But no Mortal hereafter shall *stand in thy Shoes*.[44]

More and Garrick were not to meet for another twelve months, and the separation played havoc with her emotions. She consoled herself by writing a little poem, entitled with mock grandiosity *Ode to Dragon*, in honour of their house dog, the 'tyrant of the yard' who terrorized all who came near the house. The summer of 1776 was a busy time for all of them. The Garricks were winding up the sale of the Drury Lane patent, and More was preoccupied with writing her new play, *Percy*, based on Buirette de Belloy's French tragedy *Gabrielle de Vergy*. On Garrick's advice she patriotically relocated her story in England, and centred it round the Douglas, Percy, and Raby families, names already familiar to readers of *Chevy Chase* and Percy's *Reliques*. Vaguely set around the time of the Crusades, the play deals with the moral dilemma faced by the virtuous heroine, Elwina, who was married against her will to Douglas but continues to love the heroic Percy. In July she sent him the first two acts. 'Do not spare the rod, dear Sir,' she begged anxiously.[45] He assured her, 'they will do, & do well with a few omissions . . . —keep up yᵉ fire, & We shall do Wonders!'[46]

[42] V & A, Forster, F.48, F.5, vol. 1, More to Garrick, 10 June 1776.

[43] *Letters of Garrick*, iii. 1108–9. The original is in the Bristol Reference Library.

[44] New York Public Library, Berg Collection of English and American Literature, Astor Lennox and Tilder Foundations, 221722B, More to G. I. Beltz, 23 Apr. 1823. These 'Don Felix' buckles remained with More for the rest of her life; in her will she bequeathed them to Sir Robert Inglis, the Tory MP who unseated Sir Robert Peel in the Oxford by-election of 1829. PRO, PROB 11/1822, fo. 367.

[45] V & A, Forster, F.48, F.5, vol. 1, fo. 3, More to Garrick, 1 July 1776.

[46] *Letters of Garrick*, iii. 1115.

After this encouragement, things went less well. First there was the bitter disappointment that the Garricks were unable to visit Bath and Bristol in August, as they had half-promised. Then there was his cool reaction to parts of the play. 'I don't think You were in y^r most Acute & best feeling when You wrote ye 3^d Act—I am not satisfied with it, it is the weakest of the four.'[47] At the end of the year he was even more discouraging. Now it was the fourth act which 'will not stand Muster—that must be chang'd greatly but how, I cannot yet say'.[48] More replied dispiritedly: 'You will be so good . . . as to put me into a way to recover the right road . . . I have blundered from the path, and cannot get back to it.'[49] It was some encouragement when in April 1777 Cadell printed a revised version of the *Ode to Dragon*.[50] The facility with which she wrote 'this charming bagatelle',[51] as Frances Boscawen called it, stood in marked contrast with her struggles over *Percy* and should have told her where her true literary gifts lay. The cleverness of her light verse exposed the laboured, derivative nature of her tragedies. Garrick should have told her this, but his affection (and possibly his vanity) blurred his usually clear judgement. He was determined to make her a playwright.

The year 1777 was to be Hannah More's *annus mirabilis*, but it opened badly with a series of arson attacks on the docks and warehouses of Bristol, which reduced the city to panic.[52] The Park Street school was dangerously near the harbour, and both teachers and pupils must have been in a state of infectious terror. The citizens set up patrols, troops were brought in from Gloucester, and substantial rewards were offered for the capture of the incendiarist. The fires were soon linked with similar incidents at the Portsmouth dockyard, where the chief suspect was a painter called John. The arsonist was arrested at the end of January. He was a Scotsman named James Aitken, a former soldier now passing on sensitive information to American agents. He was tried in Portsmouth, where he pleaded guilty, and in early March he was hanged at the dockyard on a gibbet $64\frac{1}{2}$ feet high. He was an isolated malcontent, but it took some time for the Bristolians to recover from their fears. Hannah More delayed her visit to London, 'having not put my eyes together for a minute for thirty nights'.[53] Twenty years later she was still

---

[47] Ibid. 1120. The original is in the Bristol Reference Library.
[48] Folger, Garrick MS Y.c 2600 (222), Garrick to More, 17 Dec. [17]76.
[49] V & A, Forster, F.48, F.5, vol. 1, fo. 8, More to Garrick, 21 Dec. 1776.
[50] *Public Advertiser*, 3 Apr. 1777; *Ode to Dragon, Mr Garrick's House Dog at Hampton* (London, 1777).
[51] Roberts, i. 97.
[52] See *FFBJ*, 18 Jan.–22 Mar. 1777; *The Life of James Aitken, Commonly Called John the Painter*, 2nd edn. (London, 1777).
[53] V & A, Forster, F.48, F.5, vol. 1, fo. 4, More to Garrick, 17 Apr. 1777.

dwelling on her ordeal: 'I do not know that my nerves ever have recovered ... to this hour.'[54]

Even at this trying time, however, she continued with her writing. As well as working on *Percy*, she had prepared, she told Garrick in April, 'some Essays ... for the edification of young Damsels'.[55] *Essays on Various Subjects Principally Designed for Young Ladies* came out in May, published by Cadell and dedicated to Elizabeth Montagu. In setting herself up as a moral commentator, she was creating a new role for herself, one that would long outlast her career as a playwright.

The conduct book was a fashionable genre, exemplified in writings such as James Fordyce's *Sermons to Young Women* (1765), the book which Mr Collins unsuccessfully attempted to read to the Bennet sisters in *Pride and Prejudice*. Fordyce and other male writers instructed their women readers to be modest and retiring, to recognize their intellectual limitations, and to shine in the private sphere rather than compete with men in the public. Historians variously interpret this increased insistence on the ideology of separate spheres—a doctrine at least as old as Aristotle—either as marking an important shift to a new conservatism, or as reflecting anxieties that women were trespassing into areas previously denied them. A woman writer who echoed the Fordyce prescriptions risked the charge of inconsistency. How could she recommend privacy and self-abnegation to others when, by the very act of writing books, negotiating with publishers, and engaging in debate, she was herself entering the public sphere? This contradiction runs through Hannah More's *Essays*.

The ambivalence began with the quotation on the title page: the Athenian general Pericles' advice to women to 'follow your natural modesty, and think it your greatest commendation not to be talked of one way or the other', and continued in the assertion in the main text that 'the successful flights of the Tragic Muse seem reserved for the bold adventurers of the other sex'[56]—this at a time when More was preparing the tragedy that she hoped would establish her as a playwright. A moment's reflection might have shown her the incongruity of laying down for other women a seclusion and retirement she did not intend to practise herself. There was a contradiction, too, in urging women to 'walk honourably in the road which nature, custom, and education seem to have marked out',[57] while praising Elizabeth Montagu, who in a very public fashion had ventured into the world of Shakespearean criticism, taking on Voltaire and the whole school of French classicism. Was

---

[54] Duke, More to Wilberforce, 30 Nov. 1797.
[55] V & A, Forster, F.48, F.5, vol. 1, fo. 4, More to Garrick, 17 Apr. 1777.
[56] *Essays on Various Subjects Principally Designed for Young Ladies* (London, 1777), 7.
[57] Ibid. 14.

it an adequate answer to potential critics merely to claim that Mrs Montagu was the exception that proved the rule?[58] It is possible that the Pericles quotation was an afterthought inspired by the behaviour of the historian Catharine Macaulay, whose republican politics she deeply deplored. On 2 April Mrs Macaulay had celebrated her forty-sixth birthday by holding a party at her house in Bath, where she heard a recital of six odes composed in her honour. This unwise piece of self-aggrandizement provided a golden opportunity for her many critics. 'I am actually ashamed of her,' More gleefully told Garrick.[59] It may well be that in a spasm of irritation she instructed her publisher to insert the quotation without considering how poorly it would play among her bluestocking friends, who did not relish being advised to emulate the confined lives of Athenian women. As Frances Boscawen gently pointed out, 'you *do* give up our cause too much; and where shall we find a champion, if you (armed at all points) desert us?'[60] It was particularly galling for More's women friends because only four years earlier the bluestocking Hester Mulso Chapone's *Letters on the Improvement of the Mind* had set new goals for women, encouraging them to expand their mental horizons.[61] Now More seemed to want to put them back in their cages. Eventually she herself came to regard *Essays* as 'a very juvenile production',[62] and though the work went into a fifth edition in 1791, all subsequent editions were pirates.

Garrick, meanwhile, was encouraging her to finish *Percy*: 'Let your fifth act be worthy of you, and tear the heart to pieces, or woe betide you.'[63] She received his letter just as she was about to leave Bristol, first for a short trip to London and then for the visit to her father's family in East Anglia which has already been mentioned, where she met a bewildering array of relatives and saw a couple of performances at the Theatre Royal in Norwich. Back at the Adelphi she found a coach waiting to take her to Hampton, where she was given her old room and made to feel thoroughly at home. From there she made a short visit with the Garricks to their friends the Wilmots, at Farnborough Place in Hampshire, before returning to Bristol.[64] Garrick was not in the best of spirits; he was fretting over an attack in a novel, *The Excursion*, written by the playwright Frances Brooke, whose work he had rejected. His faithful disciple

---

[58] Ibid. 12 n.

[59] B. Hill, *The Republican Virago: The Life and Times of Catharine Macaulay, Historian* (Oxford, 1992), 94 ff.; V & A, Forster, F.48, F.5, vol. 1, fo. 4, More to Garrick, 17 Apr. 1777.

[60] Roberts, i. 190–1.

[61] For Chapone, see G. Kelly (ed.), *Bluestocking Feminism: Writings of the Bluestocking Circle, 1738–1785* (London, 1999), iii, ed. R. Zuk, 257–366.

[62] *The Works of Hannah More in Eight Volumes: including several pieces never before published* (London, 1801), vol. i, p. x.

[63] Roberts, i. 116.   [64] Ibid. 111–14.

shared his indignation and, probably at Garrick's instigation, she savaged the book in the July edition of the *Monthly Review*. The wounding sarcasms were produced with such disturbing facility that she later resolved that she would never again write anything of that nature.[65]

Preparations were afoot to stage *Percy*. The Drury Lane Theatre was now controlled by Sheridan, whose own play *The School for Scandal* was first performed there in May, and More would have to wait another season for him to consider it. Garrick therefore planned to submit it to Thomas Harris, the manager of Covent Garden, a grasping businessman who, nevertheless, was prepared to take the risk of putting on new plays.[66] Before this the Garricks intended to come to Bath and Bristol, where Mrs Garrick would subject the play to a stringent, Germanic critique.[67] 'Io triumphe!' More exulted. 'I am almost out of my wits for joy!' She had not seen him for nearly fourteen months. She hoped Mrs Garrick would 'reduce me to the precise point of dramatic slenderness. She is heartily welcome to set about the same reformation in reducing my personal overmuchness.'[68] When she learned that, after all, they could not come, she covered her disappointment with jocular hyperbole: 'It was not simply lamentation and mourning—it was roaring and howling and gnashing of teeth.'[69] A week later she sent him her revised third and fourth acts, explaining that she was trying to differ from Belloy's story as much as possible. The fifth act was posing a problem. She had to kill off Percy and Douglas, make Elwina go mad with grief, and then kill her as well; she was out of her depth in melodrama, and she knew it: 'As to madness, it is a rock on which even good poets split. What then will become of me?'[70] Nevertheless, by 1 September the play was ready after 'great alterations', and she sent it to Garrick for him to pass it on to Harris. She hoped that the part of Elwina would be taken by Anne Barry, the leading tragic actress of the day.[71]

About ten days later she heard that Harris had accepted *Percy*, and on 2 November she sent the final draft to Garrick.[72] Then, just as she was planning to journey to London, she and her sisters fell ill; she was confined to her room and in considerable pain from her frequent bloodlettings. Plaintively she asked Garrick, 'Will you favour me with a line? for indeed I want

[65] *Monthly Review*, 57 (1777), 141–5. For More's authorship, see *The Private Correspondence of David Garrick with the Most Celebrated Persons of his Time*, ed. J. Boaden (London, 1821), ii. 278, and Roberts, i. 201 n. For Brooke, see Donkin, *Getting into the Act*, 41–56.

[66] C. Price, 'Thomas Harris and the Covent Garden Theatre', in K. Richards and P. Thompson (eds.), *Essays on the Eighteenth-Century English Stage* (London, 1972), 105–22.

[67] Roberts, i. 114.

[68] V & A, Forster, F.48, F.5, vol. 1, fo. 5, More to Garrick, Bristol, 28 July 1777.

[69] Ibid., fo. 6, More to Garrick, 7 Aug. 1777.

[70] *Private Correspondence of Garrick*, ii. 225.

[71] Ibid. 267.   [72] Ibid. 278.

comfort.'[73] He was publicizing the play very well without her help. He had rewritten it in parts, provided both the prologue and the epilogue, and in accordance with his usual practice, he was sending anonymous 'puffs' to the newspapers, setting his protégée against the more established playwright, the vain and hypersensitive Richard Cumberland, whose *Battle of Hastings* was also due to be performed. One of these, a letter from 'Theatricus' to the *Public Advertiser*, set up the competing playwrights as gender warriors, concluded with a double meaning.

Being told just now by a Friend, that two Candidates for the Bays, one of the *masculine* and the other of the *feminine* gender, are soon to start from the *Dramatic* Post, I am afraid the former will come off no better than Harold at the Battle of Hastings; for I never yet knew a Man measure weapons with a Woman, who was able to stand in the conflict.[74]

This invited several ripostes on similar lines.

> Miss MORE *to the* Author *of* CERTAIN EPIGRAMS.
> SAID *Hannah*, who is not in Town,
> '*Ungen'rous* is your weak Attack,
> For none, but an unmanly Clown,
> Would stab a Maid behind her BACK'.

> The Author's Answer to MISS MORE.
> 'GOOD Hannah, I am not afraid,
> To launch my Dart *before*,
> For, whether you are *Wife* or *Maid*,
> I dare do *that* and—MORE.'[75]

Possibly oblivious to this indecorous bandying of her name, More arrived in London with a filthy cold. Mrs Garrick promised to keep her at Hampton with a good fire and 'with all the lozenges and wheys in the world' and Garrick calmed her jittery nerves with sanguine predictions about the play's success.[76] *Percy* finally appeared on the night of Wednesday 10 December, and More watched it from Thomas Harris's box in a quiet corner of the theatre, from where she heard the actress Mrs Bulkely speak Garrick's provocatively feminist prologue.

> A *woman* here I come—to take a woman's part.
> No little jealousies my mind perplex,
> I come, the *friend* and *champion* of my sex;
> I'll prove, ye fair, that let us have our sing
> We can, as well as men, do any thing...

---

[73] Ibid. 278–9. [74] *Public Advertiser*, 5 Nov. 1777. [75] Ibid. 25 Nov. 1777.
[76] Roberts, i. 121–2.

That night she wrote home from Garrick's study at the Adelphi: 'He himself puts the pen into my hand, and bids me say that all is just as it should be.'[77] The following night Garrick wrote exultantly to his friend Countess Spencer, 'cordial applause; not a dry Eye in the house'.[78] The *Public Advertiser* thought Mrs Barry 'incomparably excellent' as Elwina, and noted that the applause of the audience was 'as general and continued as the most sanguine Friends of the Author could wish'.[79] The sixth performance on 17 December was for the author's benefit, and played to a full house. On the same day the text of the play was published and sold out within a fortnight. The ninth performance inspired another poetic innuendo in the *Public Advertiser*:

> NINE Times had Percy rear'd his Head
> Nine Times had sunk on H*'s Bed,
> Yet still the Wreath he bore:
> Th' enchanting and enchanted Maid,
> Fainting with Bliss ecstatic said,
> Come—nine Times—Percy—More![80]

More, who devoured the press for mentions of *Percy*, must have read this, but her reaction is not recorded. By the time the season ended in the spring of 1778, *Percy* had achieved a very respectable run of nineteen performances, each netting more than £200, an almost unprecedented achievement for a verse tragedy by an unknown author. It was, however, as More admitted, eclipsed by the huge success of *The School for Scandal* at Drury Lane.[81]

Her feelings about her celebrity were confused and contradictory. Perhaps she felt a touch of inevitable anticlimax, made worse by a prolonged attack of neuralgia;[82] perhaps she was only too keenly aware of how much the play's success had depended on Garrick. At times she professed indifference. On the night of 18 December she airily told one of her sisters, 'I never think of going.'[83] Yet she also resented their unwillingness to come to London to see the play for themselves. (Were they a little jealous?) In the New Year she was ill again; she refused an invitation to go to the Adelphi, but that evening Garrick called in his coach and brought her a meal of 'a minced chicken in the stew-pan, hot' and a canister of his wife's tea. 'Were there ever such people!' she exclaimed.[84] Friendship like this was beyond price. Fame, on the other hand, was more of a mixed blessing—as she learned when the backbiting began.

[77] Ibid. 123.   [78] Stone and Kahrl, *David Garrick*, 435.
[79] *Public Advertiser*, 11 Dec. 1777.   [80] Ibid. 16 Jan. 1778.   [81] Roberts, i. 141.
[82] Ibid. 139.   [83] Ibid. 126.   [84] Ibid. 132–3.

First, there were the criticisms of *Percy*. In spite of More's disclaimer in the printed text of the play, the *Monthly Review* concluded that Belloy's tragedy had 'manifestly engendered' the whole play.[85] Then there was the widely expressed opinion that she would have been nothing without Garrick. In March 1778 the veteran actress Kitty Clive told Garrick that *Percy* was his child not More's: 'you dandled it, and fondled it, and then carried it in your arms to *town* to nurse'.[86] The main sniping came from the circle around Samuel Johnson's friend Hester Thrale, the vivacious brewer's wife who ran an informal salon at Streatham in unofficial competition with Elizabeth Montagu's. Because Hannah More was Mrs Montagu's protégée, she was set on disliking her. She had taken under her wing the young Fanny Burney, and, when her *Evelina* was published in February 1778, she wanted her to follow up her success with a play. 'Hannah More', she told her, 'got near 400 pounds for her foolish play,—& if you did not write a better than *hers*, *I* dare say you deserve to be *whipped*.'[87] (In fact, More made £600, which Garrick had invested for her, as well as £150 from the printed text of the play.[88]) In the spring of 1778 Hester Thrale recorded an incident at a dinner at the Reynoldses' at which More and the Thrales were present. Mrs Thrale left for another engagement while her husband remained. Not knowing of the relationship, More called across to Frances Reynolds, 'Why did you never tell me, Madam, that Mrs Thrale was such a pretty Woman?' Faced with an embarrassed silence, she turned for confirmation to Henry Thrale, who said imperturbably, 'I am very glad you like her, Madam.'[89] The anecdote highlights More's provincial insecurities; she had not yet learned how to behave in metropolitan society and among those of higher rank than herself. When Hester Thrale drew up a table of the characteristics of her acquaintances, she gave More full marks (twenty out of twenty) for 'worth of heart' and useful and ornamental knowledge but only half marks for good humour, seven out of twenty for 'Conversation Powers', and zero for 'Person, Mien & Manner'.[90] This social awkwardness was picked up by Johnson when he commented, 'Hannah More has very good intellects ... but she has by no means the elegance of Miss Burney.'[91]

The context of this comment was a story circulating among the Streatham set that has done much to damn More in the eyes of posterity. In August Hester Thrale told Fanny Burney

[85] *Monthly Review*, 58 (1778), 23.
[86] *Private Correspondence of Garrick*, ii. 295.
[87] *The Early Journals and Letters of Fanny Burney*, iii: *The Streatham Years*, pt. 1: *1778–1779*, ed. L. E. Troide and S. J. Cooke (Oxford, 1994), 133.
[88] Roberts, i. 140.
[89] H. L. Piozzi, *Thraliana: The Diary of Mrs Hester Lynch Thrale (Later Mrs Piozzi) 1776–1809*, ed. K. C. Balderston (Oxford, 1942), i. 356.
[90] Ibid. 331.   [91] Burney, *Streatham Years*, 154.

a story of Hannah More, which I think exceeds, in its severity, *all* the severe things I have yet heard Dr Johnson saying. When she was introduced to him,— not long a go,—she began singing his praises in the warmest manner; & talking of the pleasure & the instruction she had received from his writings, with the highest encomiums. For some Time he heard her with...quietness...she then redoubled her charges &...*peppered* her flattery still more highly; till at length, he turned suddenly to her with a stern & angry Countenance & said 'Madam, before you flatter a man so grossly to his Face, you should consider whether or not your flattery is worth his having!' Good God, how the poor Creature must have been confounded! Yet she deserved *some* rebuke for laying it on so thick & clumsily.[92]

The story might have been forgotten had it not become part of the epic battle fought between Hester Thrale and James Boswell over Johnson's mighty corpse. Mrs Piozzi, as she became, retold the story in her *Anecdotes of Johnson* in 1786, though she added that Johnson was later 'very sorry for the disgusting speech he made her'.[93] When Boswell published his *Life of Johnson* in 1791, he too included the story, though he claimed that Mrs Piozzi had exaggerated Johnson's brusqueness.[94] But he also had a story of his own to show that More had indeed become notorious for flattery. He recorded the following conversation of Johnson for 15 April 1778:

Talking of Miss [More], a literary lady, he said, 'I was obliged to speak to Miss Reynolds, to let her know that I desired she would not flatter me so much.' Somebody now observed, 'She flatters Garrick.' JOHNSON: 'She is in the right for two reasons; first, because she has the world with her, who have been praising Garrick these thirty years; and secondly, because she is rewarded for it by Garrick. Why should she flatter *me*? I can do nothing for her. Let her carry her praise to a better market.'[95]

Johnson had his own baggage where Garrick was concerned. He could never forget his early years of poverty and obscurity in London, and unfairly, if understandably, he retained a residual jealousy of his former pupil's rapid rise to fame, which contrasted so poignantly with his own grim struggles. When Mrs Piozzi's book came out, and More found in it many harsh comments about Garrick, she was deeply indignant. She then remembered having once asked him 'why Johnson was so often harsh and unkind in his speeches, both of and to him; Why, *Nine*, he replied, it is very natural; is it not to be expected he should be angry, that I, who have so much less merit than he, should have had so much greater success?'[96] Johnson could not quite forgive More, perhaps, for attaching herself so firmly to Garrick.

---

[92] Ibid. 119–20.

[93] H. L. Piozzi, *Anecdotes of the Late Samuel Johnson, LLD, during the Last Twenty Years of his Life* (Dublin, 1786), 183.

[94] Boswell, *Life of Johnson*, iv. 341–2.   [95] Ibid. iii. 293.   [96] Roberts, ii. 15–16.

London society being as leaky as it was, More was well aware that she had acquired a reputation as Johnson's flatterer. She deflected the seriousness of the accusation by stressing that she was prepared to stand up to the great man. In a letter written in 1780 she described how he 'scolded me heartily, as usual, when I differed from him in opinion, and, as usual, laughed when I flattered him'. She added that there was only one occasion when Johnson was angry with her, when an allusion to some witty passages in *Tom Jones* drew from him a magisterial rebuke: 'I am sorry to hear that you have read it: a confession which no modest lady should ever make. I scarcely know a more corrupt work.'[97] This incident rings true, as Johnson's dislike of Fielding's racy novel was notorious, and More's later career shows that she would never have laughed off an accusation of immodesty, a much more serious offence in her eyes than a bit of flattery.

Finally, if More flattered Johnson, this was nothing to his flattery of her. There was, for example, the occasion she recorded in 1782. 'One of the company happened to say a word about poetry, "Hush, hush," said he, "it is dangerous to say a work of poetry before her; it is talking of the art of war before Hannibal." He continued the jokes and lamented that I had not married Chatterton, that posterity might have seen a propagation of poets.'[98] This from the greatest literary critic of the day! London was at this time, as More acknowledged later, a society of hyperbole and flattery in which 'the most indifferent authors' were assured that they were great geniuses.[99] In such a culture, it is hardly surprising that she allowed her enthusiasm to run away with her.

In April More returned to Bristol, from where she sent Garrick a hamper of local produce; he ended his letter of thanks with 'Ever Yours Most Affectionately Hannah of all Hannahs'.[100] She set to work on a new play, and was gratified to see *Percy* in performance at Bristol to a very crowded house, with the temperamental Anne Barry, now Mrs Crawford, playing Elwina for her benefit. More's uncharitable response was to pity her new husband.[101] But she was not easy in her mind. She was pessimistic about her latest play, recognizing its lack of drama and suspense.[102] The strain of writing in a genre unsuited to her talents was telling on her nerves, and she was plagued with 'bilious torments' for which the only remedy was to 'go to Bath and drink like

---

[97] Roberts, i. 168–9.   [98] Ibid. 251–2.   [99] *Works* (1801) i, pp. v–vi.

[100] *Letters of Garrick*, iii. 1225.

[101] V & A, Forster, F.48, F.5, vol. 1, fo. 9, More to Garrick, Bristol, 22 Sept. 1778; *Sarah Farley's Bristol Journal*, 5 and 12 Sept. 1778.

[102] V & A, Forster, F.48, F.5, vol. 1, fo. 10, More to Garrick, Bristol, 10 Oct. 1778; for Garrick's reply, see *Letters of Garrick*, iii. 1254–5.

a fish'.[103] Above all, she was increasingly aware that not all was well with Garrick. In July he wrote a distressed letter to 'My dearest of Hannahs' contradicting a groundless and spiteful rumour that he and Mrs Garrick had separated.[104] By September she was hearing 'very alarming accounts' of his health, and the truth of these accounts was confirmed by a letter from him telling her 'I have been half-dead, and thought I should never see you more.' It was no comfort that he had 'shown my love to you by a trifling legacy'.[105] (In the end More received no money from his will, as he was later persuaded by his executor, Albany Wallis, to revoke his bequest.[106]) In November he was complaining of 'a Cold & Cough wch tear my head & breast to pieces'.[107]

Garrick was suffering from something far worse than a winter cold—an irreversible kidney failure. In the new year he was taken ill at Althorp, on a visit to Earl and Countess Spencer. He returned home and was subjected to the usual well-meaning tortures of emetics, blistering, and bleeding, but he declined rapidly and died on 20 January. A distraught Hannah More heard the news three days later. At first she did not dare intrude on Mrs Garrick's grief, and wrote instead to Albany Wallis (unaware of the bad turn he had done her): 'Oh Sir! what a friend have I lost! My heart is almost broken! I have neither eat [*sic*] nor slept since, my tears blind me as I write. . . . Ask her, dear Sir, if she will allow me to come to her—I can not dry her tears, but I will weep with her.'[108] Reassured that she was needed, she dashed to London, where Eva Garrick 'ran into my arms', and gazed at the coffin until her mind 'burst with thinking. . . . He will never be disturbed till the eternal morning, and never till then will a sweeter voice than his own be heard.'[109] She had already written presciently in her *Ode to Dragon*

> For he shall shine while Taste survives
> And he shall shine while Genius lives,
> A never-setting sun.[110]

Garrick lay in state for the weekend before his funeral, which was held at Westminster Abbey on 1 February. It was one of the most magnificent of the century, comparable to Sir Isaac Newton's in 1727. There were thirty-three

---

[103] *Private Correspondence of Garrick*, ii. 320. [104] *Letters of Garrick*, iii. 1232–5.

[105] V & A, Forster, F.48, F.5, vol. 1, fo. 9, More to Garrick, 22 Sept. 1778; Roberts, i. 115.

[106] In a letter to Eva Garrick's executor More claimed that Wallis ('a man of a shallow intellect, illiterate, but affable, flattering and full of schemes') persuaded Garrick to make another will, making his bequest to his widow conditional on her staying in England and omitting any provision for More herself. Berg Collection, 221722B, More to G. I. Beltz, 23 Apr. 1823.

[107] *Letters of Garrick*, iii. 1254.

[108] Folger, uncatalogued, More to Albany Wallis, 23 Jan. 1779. [109] Roberts, i. 147–50.

[110] *Ode to Dragon*, stanza xviii.

mourning coaches, five allocated to members of Johnson's Club. The body was borne by ten pall-bearers, including the duke of Devonshire and Earl Spencer, with Sheridan the chief mourner. Johnson, Burke, and the actors in the congregation were in tears. Possession of an admission ticket did not secure Hannah More any special treatment. She and Frances Cadogan, the daughter of Garrick's physician, found themselves by some oversight locked for half an hour in one of the Abbey towers, where they gave way to some ghoulish Gothic fantasies of dying of starvation. They beat the door and cried out, and were eventually released and finally found themselves 'in a little gallery directly over the grave' where they observed the solemn stillness of the congregation. 'And this is all of Garrick!' More mused. 'So passes away the fashion of this world. And the very night he was buried, the playhouses were all full, and the Pantheon was as crowded, as if no such thing had happened.'[111] Shortly after, she and Mrs Garrick retreated to Hampton. When Dragon ran up to meet his absent master, Mrs Garrick, overcome once more, shut herself up in her room. The future she faced without the man who had been 'her *lover* as well as a most tender Husband'[112] was bleak indeed.

Hannah More was bruised, too. After the funeral she fell ill again, from grief and exhaustion.[113] It was a professional as well as a personal loss, as, deprived of Garrick's mentoring, her career as a playwright foundered. While recuperating at Bath, she worked up her play 'The Bridal Day', soon to be renamed *The Fatal Falsehood*. In the early spring she took it to London, where Thomas Harris pounced on it, and, as a dismayed Sally told Ann Gwatkin, 'carried off the piece with him, and what to be sure never happend to an Author before, he sent it to the prompter to copy, distributed the parts to the performers, put the Scene Painters & Taylors to Work, with an intention to bring it out within three weeks of his having it in possession'.[114] Having parted with her manuscript, More then panicked and 'wrote to recall it, and told him it was a very bad play and woud not succeed'. Harris tried to talk her out of her fears, but her anxiety would not go away, and a few hours after Patty joined her in London, she became ill again. Dr Cadogan diagnosed this as an ague and gave her an emetic. Unsurprisingly, her condition then worsened dramatically, and she was confined to bed for three weeks, unable to move 'hand or foot' with what the doctor had now decided was 'Rheumatic Gout'. On his recommendation, Mrs Garrick sent 2 guineas' worth of out-of-season strawberries to aid her recovery.[115]

---

[111] Roberts, i. 156–8.
[112] Ibid. 159; Anson MSS, diary of Mary Hamilton, book 7 (23 Apr.– 7 June 1784), 14 May 1784.
[113] Clark, Ann Kennicott to More, 9 Feb. 1779.
[114] Gwatkin MS, Sally More to Ann Gwatkin, 'Thursday afternoon' [1779].
[115] Ibid.

'If the piece escapes Damnation in my opinion tis a miracle,' was Sally's gloomy prediction.[116] She had good reason to be apprehensive. *The Fatal Falsehood* was performed at Covent Garden on 6 May. This was late in the season, the main parts were miscast, and the success of the work was not helped by Sheridan's sour epilogue mocking lady scribblers, something he would never have written if Garrick had been alive. It lasted only three nights, just long enough for a single benefit, and was never revived. On the second night the playwright Hannah Cowley, another of Garrick's proté-gées, allegedly stood up in the theatre and shouted 'That's mine! That's mine!' On 7 May the *Morning Chronicle* asserted that *The Fatal Falsehood* was 'astonishingly similar' to an unpublished manuscript by Mrs Cowley. When her *Albina, Countess Raimond* opened at the Haymarket on 31 July, the critics pounced and accused More of plagiarism, a charge that had already been levelled at her over *Percy*. She felt she had to reply. From Bristol she wrote a letter, dated 10 August, versions of which appeared in various papers.

It is with the deepest regret that I find myself compelled to take a step repugnant to my own Feelings, and to the delicacy of my Sex; a Step as *new* to me as it is *disagreeable*...My moral character thus grossly attacked, I am under the necessity of solemnly declaring that I never saw, heard, or read, a single line of Mrs Cowley's tragedy, nor did I ever hear she had written a tragedy, till after the Fatal Falsehood came out at Covent-garden, when I was accused of the above fraud.[117]

More then learned the hard way that a woman could not win in this game. If she stayed silent, she must be guilty, if she defended herself she was indulging in unfeminine conduct. Hannah Cowley led the attack: 'I wish Miss More had been still more sensible of the indelicacy of a newspaper altercation between women, and the ideas of ridicule which the world are apt to attach to such unsexual hardiness.'[118] She went on to repeat the charge of plagiarism in the preface to the printed text of *Albina*. This time More remained silent.

It is true that the two plays have some similarities of plot. In both an Iago-like character plots to destroy a romance, a gullible character is deceived, and a character is killed at the end, mistaken for another. However, in *Albina* there is no equivalent to Emmeline's jilting, which provided the best-received moment of *The Fatal Falsehood*.[119] Circumstantial evidence also argues strongly against plagiarism. More had no opportunity to see *Albina* as it was in Garrick's possession during the fourteen-month period when they did not meet. Moreover, after her embarrassment over *Percy* she specifically

---

[116] Ibid.   [117] *Morning Post*, 13 Aug.   [118] *Morning Chronicle*, 14–17 Aug.
[119] T. Davies, *Memoirs of the Life of David Garrick, Esq.* (London, 1780), ii. 330–1.

asked him to 'recollect any other tragedy that it is like, as I shall be most careful of that'.[120] Hannah Cowley, therefore, was almost certainly wrong in her accusation. Behind it, however, lay a genuine grievance. She was thrashing about for a reason for her failure to have a play accepted by the London winter management, and blaming Hannah More for the deeper malaise facing female playwrights following Garrick's death.[121] Their vulnerability was highlighted by an attack in the *St James's Chronicle* of 8 May.

We are tired of indulging Authours [*sic*] because they are Females.... The Success of these Amazonian leaders brought forward a Mrs Griffith, a Mrs Cowley, and a Miss More. Some well-timed Flattery to a late Manager and Actor brought on the Tragedy of Percy, the most interesting parts of which were borrowed from a French Play, without the common good Manners of acknowledging it.

In spite of the chilling of the climate, Mrs Cowley recovered and went on to write successful plays. Hannah More never wrote again for the stage. Her sisters had already noted that she seemed 'mighty indifferent' over the failure of *The Fatal Falsehood*.[122] She had written it to please Garrick and with his death she lost interest in the theatre. She had always been dubious about actors, disapproving of their affectations and deploring their private lives. Now, apart from her affection for Mrs Garrick, there was nothing to connect her to that world. It is difficult to see this as a great loss. Though *Percy*, with its fine dramatic moments and its heroine's touching moral predicament, was a better than average tragedy, it had been as much Garrick's as hers and failed to do justice to her real talents. There are occasional flashes in her later works, notably some passages in the early part of *Coelebs in Search of a Wife*, which suggest that she could have produced an entertaining comedy of manners for the stage, perhaps almost up to the standard of Fanny Burney's *A Busy Day*. But this was never going to happen. With Garrick's death she had reached a standstill in her career and her personal life, and she could have had little inkling of the new avenues that would open up for her.

There is one intriguing coda to her short career as a playwright. In 1779 *Percy* was translated into German and performed in Vienna, where it was very well received, and a copy was found among Mozart's possessions when he died in 1791.[123] As a result of Garrick's embellishments the plot was certainly dramatic enough for tragic opera (it bears a striking resemblance to *Lucia di Lammermoor*), and, given the right librettist, who knows what he might have done with it if he had not died prematurely?

[120] V & A, Forster, F.48, F.5, vol. 1, fo. 10.

[121] See Donkin, *Getting into the Act,* 57–76; also P. Demers, *The World of Hannah More* (Lexington, Ky: 1996), 39–40.

[122] Roberts, i. 163.   [123] I am indebted to Professor Peter Skrine for this information.

Chapter 3

Living Muse
1780-1785

IT took ten erratic but inexorable years for Hannah More to change her career by transforming herself from intermittently successful playwright to Evangelical campaigner. She began the decade bruised and despondent following Garrick's death, and ended it full of energy and purpose with the writing of her first major conduct book in 1788 and the founding of the Cheddar Sunday school the following year. In the intervening period, deprived of an obvious purpose in life, her main preoccupation was to develop one of her greatest gifts, her talent for friendship. Until the end of the decade most of her writings were personal compositions, inspired by her relationships with her friends and initially intended for them alone; and it was through these friends that, in spite of her relatively low productivity, she was able to find a significant niche in London literary society.

The friend who had most call on her time and attention was Mrs Garrick, who in the aftermath of her bereavement was touchingly dependent on her for support and comfort. Though More spent the second half of each year with her family in Bristol, between January and June she functioned as Mrs Garrick's companion. The press saw this as part of a contemporary pattern of female patronage and semi-dependency: 'Miss Burney ... is now domesticated with Mrs Thrale in the same manner that Miss More is with Mrs Garrick, & Mrs Carter with Mrs Montagu.'[1] She was at Hampton in January

---

[1] Quoted in B. Rizzo, *Companions without Vows: Relationships among Eighteenth-Century British Women* (Athens, Ga., 1994), 93.

1780 for the first anniversary of Garrick's death, and as the fatal 20th approached, she described their joint solitude: 'We never see a human face but each other's.... We dress like a couple of Scaramouches, dispute like a couple of Jesuits, eat like a couple of aldermen, walk like a couple of porters, and read as much as any two doctors of either university.'[2] A year later she wrote that Mrs Garrick 'keeps herself in secret as a piece of smuggled goods, and neither stirs out herself or lets any body in'.[3] That summer she took her to Bristol for a change of scene, where she met the More family, and took a particular fancy to Jacob.[4] The visit was so enjoyable that, when the time came to part, Mrs Garrick became distressed and More travelled back with her as far as Marlborough, a journey of about forty-five miles.[5] As well as her sympathetic companion, she was also her social secretary, as Mrs Garrick, a notoriously bad correspondent, left it to her to arrange meetings with friends such as Fanny Burney.[6] Her least conventional role, according to James Boswell, was to act as Mrs Garrick's domestic chaplain; meaning presumably that she read prayers to the servants in place of their Catholic mistress.[7]

Even in her reclusive widowhood, Mrs Garrick maintained her interest in clothes; years later More reminisced that she was famous for her taste, and gave ladies advice on what to wear when being presented at court.[8] In an attempt to make More dress more fashionably, she gave her an elegant cap to wear at a reception in the early spring of 1780. This, however, turned out to be a disaster, for when More arrived she found 'every human creature in deep mourning, and I, poor I, all gorgeous in scarlet. I never recollected that the mourning for some foreign Wilhelmina Jacquilina was not over.... Even Jacobite Johnson was in deep mourning.'[9] As she struggled through the embarrassing evening, she longed for the tranquillity of Hampton. She was much happier at a gathering at Frances Boscawen's, where she renewed her friendship with Elizabeth Carter, the translator of the Stoic philosopher Epictetus. Happily abandoning the card players, they 'fastened on each other, and agreed not to part for the evening'.[10]

Elizabeth Carter was a generation older than More, and her matronly appearance and unpretentious manners concealed the formidable intellect and unremitting self-discipline that had made her the most learned woman

[2] Roberts, i. 167.   [3] Ibid. 197.   [4] Ibid. 215, 271.
[5] Ibid. 215; E. Montagu, *Mrs Montagu, 'Queen of the Blues': Her Life and Friendships*, ed. R. Blunt (London, 1904), ii. 111.
[6] New York Public Library, Astor Lennox and Tilder Foundations, Berg Collection MS 198090B, More to Fanny Burney [1786?].
[7] J. Boswell, *Life of Johnson*, ed. G. Birkbeck Hill (Oxford, 1934) iv. 96.
[8] Clark, box 46, 'Reminiscences', fos. 2–3.   [9] Roberts, i. 170–1.   [10] Ibid. 173.

of her day.[11] In marked contrast to Jacob More, her father, the curate of Deal in Kent, had taught her Greek, Latin, and Hebrew; in 1738 she had taken the adventurous step of going to London to write for the *Gentleman's Magazine*. Since then she had lived more quietly, writing for Johnson's *Rambler*, working on her translation, learning Portuguese and Arabic, and looking after her nephews and nieces. Johnson famously described her as one who 'could make a pudding as well as translate Epictetus', though a friend in a better position to know insisted that she had 'never raised a pye'. Hannah More was to carry on the domestic theme when she posthumously praised 'acquirements which would have been distinguished in a University, meekly softened, and beautifully shaded by the gentle exercise of every domestic virtue'.[12] This focus on Elizabeth Carter's housewifely skills was a way of coping with her extraordinary achievements. A learned lady who combined in herself the apparent opposites of 'inelegant domesticity and philosophical genius'[13] posed no very obvious threat to conservative values.

More's own fame was kept alive by occasional revivals of *Percy*; in January 1781, for example, Sarah Siddons was an epically tragic Elwina in Bristol.[14] In 1780 Frances Reynolds painted her as a learned lady, with a sheaf of papers before her, a pen in one hand, her head lightly resting on the other hand in the classic pose of contemplation. Three years later she was made a member of the Academy of Arts at Rouen, though, characteristically, she tried to keep this hidden on the grounds that there was something 'ridiculous in the idea of an *ignorant*, and above all, of a *female* Academician'.[15] It was a sign of her high reputation that when the painter Richard Samuel paid tribute to some of the more prominent women of the day he included her in their number.

Samuel's compliment initially took the form of an engraving entitled *The Nine Living Muses of Great Britain*, distributed in *Johnson's Ladies New and Pocket Memorandum for 1778*. Another version was exhibited as a finished painting in the Royal Academy exhibition of 1779. In both the painting and the engraving the 'Muses', attired in vaguely classical garb,

[11] See S. Harcstack Myers, *The Bluestocking Circle: Women, Friendship and the Life of the Mind* (Oxford, 1990); D. Williams, 'Poetry, Pudding, and Epictetus: The Consistency of Elizabeth Carter', in A. Ribeiro and J. G. Basker (eds.), *Tradition and Transition: Women Writers, Marginal Texts and the Eighteenth-Century Canon* (Oxford, 1996), 3–24; H. Guest, *Small Change: Women, Learning, Patriotism, 1750–1810* (Chicago, 2000).

[12] J. Boswell, *Life of Johnson*, ed. G. Birkbeck Hill (Oxford, 1934), i. 123 n.; *Coelebs in Search of a Wife: Comprehending Observations on Domestic Habits . . . Religion, and Morals* (9th edn. London, 1809), ii. 249.

[13] Guest, *Small Change*, 108.   [14] *Sarah Farley's Bristol Journal*, 13 Jan. 1781.

[15] Anson MSS, Property of Sir Peter and Dame Elizabeth Anson, doc. folder 8, More to Mary Hamilton, 24 June 1783. It is not clear why the Academicians of Rouen should have known about More.

form two unequal groups gathered before the temple of Apollo. The stand-ing, centrally placed figure playing a harp is the singer Elizabeth Linley, wife of Richard Brinsley Sheridan. The portraitist Angelica Kauffmann is shown seated at her easel. The others, who are harder to identify individually, represent some celebrated literary women: Elizabeth Montagu and Elizabeth Carter; Catharine Macaulay, the historian; the educationalist Anna Barbauld; the actress and playwright Elizabeth Griffith; the novelist Charlotte Lennox; and Hannah More. Though More cannot be identified in the engraving, she appears in the painting holding a cup, the symbol of Melpomene, the Muse of tragedy, a sign of her increased recognition following the success of *Percy*. The swoony figure bears no resemblance to the sturdy, plump-cheeked young woman painted by Frances Reynolds; but then *The Nine Living Muses* was not really a portrait. The fact that the women were given this degree of prominence is a tribute to their achievements, but the undifferen-tiated way in which they were depicted, so different from the rugged indi-viduality of the portraits of Johnson, Burke, and Goldsmith, shows how far they had to go to achieve equality of esteem.

The choice of figures to make up the nine Muses was arbitrary, and the image of a united group was misleading. More was friends with only three of them, Anna Barbauld, Elizabeth Montagu, and Elizabeth Carter. It was through the latter pair that she had gained access to the circle described by Hester Thrale as 'the female Wits—a formidable Body, & called by those who ridicule them, the *Blue Stocking Club*'.[16]

The mockery of learned ladies was part of a literary tradition going back to Molière's portrayals of the *précieuses* of seventeenth-century France, and brought up to date by Fanny Burney's unsisterly lampooning of Elizabeth Montagu in her unperformed play *The Witlings*. The term 'bluestocking' is said to have arisen around 1756 out of an apology made by the botanist Benjamin Stillingfleet, who declined an invitation to a literary meeting at Elizabeth Vesey's house in Bath because he was not properly dressed for an evening assembly. To which she replied, 'Don't mind dress! Come in your blue stockings!': meaning informal worsted stockings rather than fashionable silk stockings.[17] In the following decade the term 'the blue stocking Philoso-phy' appeared in Elizabeth Montagu's correspondence, by which she meant the type of polite learning, good manners, and elegant conversation found to

[16] H. L. Piozzi, *Thraliana: The Diary of Mrs Hester Lynch Thrale (Later Mrs Piozzi) 1776–1809*, ed. K. C. Balderston (Oxford, 1942) ii. 381 n. 3. For the bluestockings, see J. Hemlow, *The History of Fanny Burney* (Oxford, 1958); M. Doody, *Frances Burney: The Life in the Works* (New Brunswick, NJ, 1988); Myers, *Bluestocking Circle*; K. Chisholm, *Fanny Burney: Her Life, 1752–1840* (London, 1998); G. Kelly (ed.), *Bluestocking Feminism: Writings of the Bluestocking Circle, 1738–1785* (London, 1999); C. Harman, *Fanny Burney: A Biography* (London, 2000); N. Clark, *Dr Johnson's Women* (London, 2000).

[17] *Memoirs of Dr Burney*, ed. Madame d'Arblay (London, 1832), ii. 113.

dazzling effect in the French salons. Learned and semi-learned ladies who relished the chance to shine in the bluestocking assemblies included Frances Boscawen, Margaret, dowager duchess of Portland (mother of the Whig prime minister), and her widowed friend Mary Delany, whose botanical drawings were to win her much posthumous fame. In contrast to Johnson's all-male Club, bluestocking gatherings were open to both sexes, and included the musicologist Dr Charles Burney and the amiable classical scholar Sir William Weller Pepys, brother to the king's physician and future master-in-chancery. However, it was the women who presided and who set the tone.

The undisputed Queen of the Blues was the Shakespearean critic Elizabeth Montagu, a thin, fragile, but vivacious woman, acknowledged to be one of the great conversationalists of the age. The death of her husband in 1775 left her wealthy and independent, and at the end of 1781 she moved into a new neo-classical house in Portman Square, where she held court in great magnificence. According to Fanny Burney, she would arrange her guests in a semicircle, 'with a precision that made it seem described by a Brobdingnagian compass'.[18] She positioned herself centrally, from where she could view and dominate the company, though her dignity and severity often stifled the very conversation she wished to stimulate.

It was very different at the chaotic home of the eccentric Elizabeth Vesey—known as the Sylph because of her wispy appearance—whose husband, the Irish MP Agmondersham Vesey, was a member of Johnson's Club. In contrast to the regimentation of Elizabeth Montagu's assemblies, chairs and sofas were arranged haphazardly, with the seats often back to back, to the neck-wrenching discomfort of guests who attempted to talk to their neighbours. As More was to put it in *The Bas Bleu*,

> See V ESEY's plastic genius make
> A Circle every figure take;
> Nay, shapes and forms which would defy
> All science of Geometry . . .[19]

Elizabeth Vesey's conversation was as jumbled as her furniture, and was further hampered by her deafness. Fanny Burney recollected that 'she had commonly two or three more ear trumpets hanging to her wrists, or slung about her neck; or tost upon the chimney-piece or table; with the intention to try them severally and alternately upon different speakers as the occasion might arise'.[20] With such a restless hostess, it was often impossible to sustain

---

[18] Ibid. ii. 270.

[19] *Florio: A Tale for Fine Gentlemen and Fine Ladies; and, The Bas Bleu; or, Conversation* (London, 1786), lines 140–5.

[20] *Memoirs of Dr Burney*, ii. 266.

a conversation, and Hannah More and Elizabeth Carter found their delightful discussions about books constantly interrupted by Mrs Vesey 'frequently clapping, in her hurry, the broad part of the brazen ear to her temple'. Having killed all talk, she would then lament that 'as soon as I come near any body, nobody speaks'.[21] But her salons were well attended. On a good evening guests could see the young duchess of Devonshire, the leader of the *bon ton*, hear Sir William Hamilton, British ambassador in Naples (whose wife, Emma, was to make him the most celebrated cuckold of the age), learnedly describing the ruins of Pompeii, or else listen to Burke reading aloud from a book or pamphlet that had caught his eye. At one evening at Mrs Vesey's, More met the great orientalist Sir William Jones; on another she was introduced to the Corsican nationalist leader General Paoli, with whom, on a later occasion, she tried unsuccessfully to practise her extremely basic Italian.[22] Though she was still missing Garrick, London had much to offer, and she had not yet begun to weary of it.

Garrick's former teacher was still very much part of her life. In April 1781 she and Mrs Garrick met Johnson at a party at the home of Jonathan Shipley, bishop of St Asaph. James Boswell was also present. He recorded the meeting as having taken place at the home of Beilby Porteus, bishop of Chester, but his memory of the evening was clouded by alcohol. Hannah More, who remained sober, remembered it better. She had met Boswell five or six years before, and like most women she was initially charmed with his lively manners; on this occasion, however, she saw the other side of his character. After dinner he came upstairs to join the ladies 'much disordered with wine, and addressed me in a manner which drew from me a sharp rebuke, for which I fancy he will not easily forgive me'. Faced with her icy response, he retreated.[23]

On 20 April Mrs Garrick courageously confirmed her re-entry into the world by hosting a little party at the Adelphi. Both More and Boswell, now reconciled, remembered the evening with great pleasure; the company was agreeable, the conversation brilliant.[24] Johnson was in particularly good form. When More accused him of not doing justice to Milton's pastoral poetry, he retorted that 'he was a Phidias that could cut a Colossus out of a rock, but could not cut heads out of cherry stones'. Boswell reminded More that she had once been made 'umpire in a trial of skill between Garrick and Boswell, which could most nearly imitate Dr Johnson's manner'. She remembered that she diplomatically 'gave it for Boswell in familiar

[21] Ibid. 267–8.   [22] Roberts, i. 212, 214, 242.
[23] For More's account of the evening, see Roberts, i. 210–11; for the confusion of dates, see Boswell, *Life of Johnson*, iv. 88 n. 1.
[24] Compare Roberts, i. 212–13; Boswell, *Life of Johnson*, iv. 96–9.

conversation and for Garrick in reciting poetry'. At some point in the evening Boswell leaned over to Frances Boscawen, who, in More's words, 'shone with her usual mild lustre', and whispered, 'I believe this is as much as can be made of life.' In this mellow atmosphere Johnson turned ponderous. Referring to a woman of their acquaintance, he declared that she 'had a bottom of good sense'. While the company struggled for composure, Boswell noticed that 'Miss Hannah More slyly hid her face behind a lady's back who sat on the same settee with her.'

This stay in London gave More the opportunity to develop one her most enduring friendships. Ann Kennicott was the wife of the biblical scholar and canon of Christ Church, Oxford, Dr Benjamin Kennicott. With no children to distract her, she had learned Hebrew in order to help her husband in his studies, and proved a tireless and efficient research assistant. In 1780 More visited the couple at Oxford and met George Horne, president of Magdalen College and future dean of Canterbury and bishop of Norwich.[25] The two Oxford clerics vied with each other in writing punning poetic tributes to More. Horne's contribution was

> Muses nine there were of yore,
> But Kennicott has shown us MORE.

Kennicott wrote his eulogy shortly after More left Christ Church:

> With avarice, a virtuous passion! Fir'd,
> Moore I receiv'd, yet Moore I still desir'd.[25]

An old-fashioned High-Churchman, Horne might not seem an obvious soulmate for Hannah More, whose spiritual pilgrimage was moving her in a more Evangelical direction. However, his best-selling book on the Psalms crossed the bounds of churchmanship and greatly appealed to Methodists and Evangelicals. More respected his religious fervour and relished his wit. She showed her own brand of wit to advantage when she wrote 'An Heroick Epistle' for his 3-year-old daughter Sally on the blank leaves of the child's copy of *Mother Bunch's Tales*.[26] Sally later became a pupil at the Mores' school.

On her return to Park Street in the summer of 1781, accompanied by Mrs Garrick, More heard a story of a young woman who for the past four years had taken up residence in a haystack in the parish of Bourton near Bristol, in

---

[25] Yale University, Beinecke Rare Books and Manuscripts Library, Osborne Collection, files 17452, 17453. I am grateful to Dr Nigel Aston for bringing these poems to my attention. For Horne, see N. Aston, 'Horne and Heterodoxy: The Defence of Anglican Beliefs in the Late Enlightenment', *English Historical Review*, 108 (1993), 895–919.

[26] *Works* (1801), iv. 133.

spite of the pleas of the local ladies that she come indoors. 'The Lady of the Haystack' had become a local celebrity. All who saw her were struck with her disarming sweetness of manner, which contrasted so poignantly with the wildness of her appearance and incoherence of her speech. The mystery of her identity kept everyone guessing. Some detected a German accent. The speculation intensified and her story spread. Hannah More and Eva Garrick took advantage of a fine day to visit the stranger, soon to be named Louisa. They found her 'handsome, young, interesting, enough Mistress of her reason carefully to shut up from our observation every avenue that might lead to her secret'. When they begged her to leave her haystack, she refused, telling them that 'trouble and misery dwelt in houses'. Her determination left them 'much troubled what to do with this unfortunate and inexplicable creature'.[27]

It was not in her nature to leave well alone. The *St James's Chronicle* of 10–13 November contained a piece by her headed A TALE OF REAL WOE by 'Philalethes', in which the story of the beautiful bag-lady was affectingly told in a high-flown style, full of the language of sensibility.[28] The article had been written in the hope that a reader might recognize Louisa and restore 'an amiable and wretched young Creature into the Arms of (perhaps) a broken-hearted parent'. It certainly brought the story to national attention. Queen Charlotte, in particular, was intrigued by her true identity. All More could report was that Louisa told her 'that her Father was a German, her Mother an Italian; that she has one brother and one Sister; that her father had a very fine garden full of olive and orange Trees'.[29]

Early in 1782 Louisa was confined in the madhouse at Hanham, near Bristol, which was presided over by the humane Methodist schoolmaster Richard Henderson. There she was visited on several occasions by John Wesley, who described her as 'pale and wan, worne [*sic*] with sorrow, beaten with wind and rain . . . partly insane, partly silly and childish'. Two years later he found she had deteriorated and become 'quite furious'.[30] By this stage rumours abounded that she was the illegitimate daughter of Francis I, late emperor of Austria and thus the half-sister of Marie Antoinette, driven out of her own country in order to avoid scandal. Wesley was sceptical, but the story was irresistibly romantic and as late as 1801 Hannah More's friend the Revd George Henry Glasse was still peddling it, possibly with More's connivance.[31]

[27] Clark, More to Ann Kennicott, Bristol, 15 June [1781].   [28] Roberts, i. 222–3.

[29] Anson MSS, doc. folder 8, More to Mary Hamilton, 29 June 1782.

[30] *The Journal of John Wesley*, ed. N. Curnock (London, 1915), vi. 343–4, 482–3.

[31] [G. H. Glasse], *Inconnue: Louisa. A Narrative of Facts supposed to throw light on the Mysterious History of 'The Lady of the Haystack*, (3rd edn. London, 1801). See also *The Affecting History of Louisa, the Wandering Maniac; or, 'Lady of the Haystack' . . . supposed to be a Natural Daughter of Frances I, Emperor of Germany* (London, 1803).

Hannah More continued to visit Louisa. In the autumn of 1783 she gave a full account of her condition to her young friend Mary Hamilton, niece of Sir William and an attendant to the king's daughters (where she was for a brief, uncomfortable period the unwilling recipient of the attentions of the prince of Wales) until November 1782.[32] She and Hannah More had become very intimate, and their affectionate, lively correspondence provides one of the best insights into More's emotions and opinions in the 1780s. She wrote to reassure her and their common friend Horace Walpole, who had also taken up Louisa's cause,[33] that she was being treated well.

She is not put into a Cell, my dear ... but in a chamber, where she is constantly in bed.... At first I paid fifty Pounds a year for her, but now I have prevailed on them to keep her for thirty. My friends have been very good and my resources are not yet exhausted. When they are, I intend to apply to a few particular friends for a very small annual Contribution as I cannot conveniently afford to be at the whole expence, and it wou'd grieve my heart to send her to Bedlam, as my friends wish me to do.

She was now, she continued, 'much altered: and has almost lost all that beauty and elegance which I am afraid had too great a share in *seducing my affections*. I dare not ask myself whether it was her calamity or her attractions which engaged my heart to serve her.' Her condition continued to be pitiable.

Mad as she now is, you wou'd have been touched to the very soul had you seen with what incomparable grace she lately took the white ribbons out of my Cap, to make herself Bracelets, the only ornament she seems to delight in; but as soon as I had tied them on her arms, she tore them off again and threw them at me; then begged I wou'd bind them round her fine dark hair, and then looked at herself in a little glass I had carried her, but was shocked at her own figure, tore off the ribbons and wrapped herself up in her bed cloths full of grief and disgust remembering, I fear, with what a different Spectacle that glass used to present her.

She concluded sadly, 'May her mother, if she has one, never know the misery of seeing that emaciated form and ruined intellect.'[34]

In her old age she remembered one particularly harrowing visit made late in 1788 at the time of George III's first outbreak of what was thought to be insanity.

Whilst waiting alone in a parlour, a tall wan looking man came into the room & shutting the door after him seated himself by her on the Sofa to her very great dismay; he then pulled a small book out of his pocket & printed in the black letters nearly 200 years before & showed her, in which it was foretold that about the time

---

[32] For Mary Hamilton, see E. and F. Anson (eds.), *Mary Hamilton, afterwards Mrs John Dickenson at Court and at Home. From Letters and Diaries 1756 to 1816* (London, 1925).

[33] *Walpole*, 208.   [34] Anson MSS, doc. folder 8, More to Mary Hamilton, 21 Oct. 1783.

in which they were 'the Kingly Power should be lost but not the King's life'.... She could not help (notwithstanding her dread at being so near an insane person & alone) being extremely surprized at seeing with her own eyes a prediction in a book of so early a date which this melancholy case appeared so exactly to fulfil.[35]

When Louisa was later transferred to St Luke's Hospital for the Insane in London, More 'was persuaded to go over the house, & was so extremely affected by it that she was obliged to put off an engagement she had for the next day, & for two or three days she could not recover her spirits but was continually in tears'.[36]

Louisa was eventually moved to Guy's Hospital, and More subscribed £10 per annum until she died in 1801. The obituary in the *Gentleman's Magazine* concluded with a verse tribute suggesting that she had been wronged by interested parties in very high places.[37] Modern commentators might conclude instead that the great wrong had been to remove her from her haystack, where she had known happiness of a sort, presumably with the consent of the farmer. Her story seems a striking vindication of the argument of the French philosopher/historian Michel Foucault that the late eighteenth century saw a growing urge to confine and control the insane.[38] But the conditions of Louisa's various confinements were far removed from the brutalized madhouses often thought to be typical of the age, and Hannah More's letters show deep compassion as much as a desire to control. She could easily have walked away; instead she devoted time, money, and emotional energy in trying to alleviate her condition. If she acted wrongly, it was from the best of intentions. No one had a better solution.

During her stay in London in the first half of 1782 More continued to socialize with a succession of agreeable people, including the aristocratic Shute Barrington, bishop of Llandaff, later to be in turn bishop of Salisbury and Durham, who was to become one of her closest episcopal friends. She saw a good deal of Johnson in this period and enjoyed several arguments with him. One day a distinguished visitor, the elderly widower James Burnett, Lord Monboddo, a luminary of the Scottish Enlightenment, called for breakfast at the Adelphi. More's verdict was that 'among much just thinking and some taste...he entertained some opinions so absurd that they would be hardly credible, if he did not deliver them himself, both in writing and conversation, with a gravity which shows that he is in earnest'.[39] She and

[35] Clark, box 46, 'Reminiscences', fos. 14–15.   [36] Ibid.
[37] *Gentleman's Magazine*, 71/1 (1801), 280–1.
[38] M. Foucault, *Madness and Civilization*, trans. A. Sheridan-Smith (London, 1967). But see R. Porter, *Mind-Forg'd Manacles: A History of Madness in England from the Restoration to the Regency* (London, 1987).
[39] Roberts, i. 252–3.

Mrs Garrick had been interrogating him on his widely mocked and notorious view that the orang-utan was a species of human, lacking only the gift of speech. 'Monkey' Monboddo had a strong personal motive in making his call. In August Horace Walpole's well-tuned ears picked up some gossip that he had proposed to Mrs Garrick, and at the end of the year he reported that he had proposed again.[40] The first proposal was confirmed by More when she related it late in life to her friends Margaret and Mary Roberts, the sisters of her biographer:

In one of his Visits to Hampton, after walking with him round the Grounds, she asked him if he did not think them very complete, to which he replied that it was a perfect Paradise, & that it only wanted an Adam; this Speech amused her much because the Speaker was ignorant that her Italian name was Eve; & what gave more point to this Anecdote is, that L^d M——made a Matrimonial proposal to Mrs G——[41]

Many years later More's friend John Scandrett Harford picked up a variation of this story: that she herself had received a proposal from Monboddo while walking with him in the garden at Hampton. When he was refused, he 'returned to the drawing-room, when he amused Mrs Garrick not a little by telling her what had just occurred, adding, "I am very sorry for this refusal: I should have so much liked to teach that nice girl Greek" '.[42] But Harford, who was born two years after the events he described, had got the wrong end of the stick. The fact seems to be that Monboddo proposed to Mrs Garrick for a third time in 1783, this time by means of a poetical letter. On 28 June she read the letter out to an amused gathering that included Walpole and Mary Hamilton, but not Hannah More, who was back in Bristol.[43] Miss Hamilton then wrote to More and received the following reply:

You condole with me very kindly on the loss I have sustained, thro' Mrs Garrick's rejection of her antiquated lover. I am glad you were so well amused with the *Scotch Edition of Ovid's Epistles*. Don't you think I shou'd have had an admirable Tutor? I dare say he would have taught me

> —to speak Greek
> As naturally as Pigs squeak—

In truth 'he is a very foolish fond old man'.[44]

---

[40] H. Walpole, *Correspondence with William Mason*, ed. W. S. Lewis, G. Cronin Jr., and C. H. Bennett, xxix (London, Conn., 1955), 271; id., *Correspondence with the Countess of Upper Ossory*, ed. W. S. Lewis and A. Dayle Wallace (London, 1965), xxxiii. 363.

[41] Clark, Hannah More MSS box 46, 'Reminiscences', fos. 3–4.

[42] J. S. Harford, *Recollections of William Wilberforce, Esq.* (London, 1864), 274.

[43] Anson, *Mary Hamilton*, 137.

[44] Anson MSS, doc. folder 8, More to Mary Hamilton, 20 July 1783. For the chronology of the relationship between Mrs Garrick, Hannah More, and Lord Monboddo, see E. L. Cloyd, *James Burnett, Lord Monboddo* (Oxford, 1972), 95–7.

Monboddo did indeed wish to teach her Greek, but only as a by-product of his marriage to Mrs Garrick; she was to be a surrogate daughter, not a wife.

In June 1782 she called at Oxford on her way home to Bristol, a guest of Dr William Adams, the master of Pembroke. There she again met Johnson, who was staying at his old college. After dinner he showed her round, pointing out the rooms of all the poets who had been there. 'We were a nest of singing birds,' he told her. In the common room the pair were delighted to find a large framed print of Johnson, which had been put up by the resourceful master that very morning. Under the print was a motto from More's *Sensibility*, which had been published earlier in the year: 'And is not Johnson ours, himself a host?'[45]

Back at Bristol, More settled into her familiar routine. She read Fanny Burney's new best-seller *Cecilia* ('this fascinating, provoking, ingenious, absurd, lively, tiresome, interesting, disgusting performance'), and though she felt let down by the rather sombre ending, she continued to be amazed at the talents of the 'extraordinary girl'.[46] She entertained Anna Barbauld and her husband, and at the end of November the Kennicotts stayed for a couple of days.[47] But she refused to acknowledge that her father was now declining. Seeing what she wanted to see, she told Mrs Garrick that he was 'weak but not worse; nothing but a great change in him will keep me longer than the time mentioned as I truly long to see you'.[48] Having persuaded herself that Mrs Garrick needed her more, she left for London at the end of the year and returned just as *Percy* was being revived at Covent Garden.[49] On 5 January Jacob More died at Stoney Hill and was buried at Stoke three days later.[50] Hannah More was in town when the black-edged letter arrived, and she found it waiting for her when she returned to Hampton. The news shocked her into inertia. For three weeks she stayed indoors, not even venturing into the garden.[51] He had been 'the dearest and best of Fathers', she told Mary Hamilton.[52] In her reply to her sisters she tried to take comfort from the fact 'that he was removed when life began to grow a burden to himself—that he did not survive his faculties . . . that his life was so exemplary, and his death so easy'. Yet there was a strong residue of guilt. 'I wish I had seen him. Yet that is a vain regret. I hope he did not inquire after me or miss me.'[53] Her thoughts later turned to the plight of her 'solitary mother'.[54] But she did not return home. Was it the difficulty and expense of

[45] Roberts, i. 261–2.

[46] Clark, More to Ann Kennicott, Bristol, 10 Oct. 1782; see also Anson MSS, doc. folder 8, More to Mary Hamilton, Sept. [1782], typescript copy.

[47] Folger, W.b. 487, fo. 79, More to Eva Garrick, 23 Nov. 1782.

[48] Clark, Ann Kennicott to More, Oxford, 20 Jan. [1783]; Folger, W.b. 487, fo. 79, More to Eva Garrick, 23 Nov. 1782.

[49] *Public Advertiser*, 19 Dec. 1782.   [50] *FFBJ*, 11 Jan. 1783.   [51] Roberts, i. 271.

[52] Anson MSS, doc. folder 8, More to Mary Hamilton, 12 Jan. 1783.

[53] Roberts, i. 270–1.   [54] Ibid. 280.

transport that kept her at Hampton, or was it her semi-official post as Mrs Garrick's companion?

The evidence that could give a fuller insight into Hannah More's relations with her parents has not survived. Several commentators have seen her as very much her father's daughter, yet the evidence is uncertain. In his biography William Roberts quoted extensively from her letters to her sisters but made no mention of any to her parents. In 1781 she had written to her sisters commending her father's verses in a rather patronizing fashion ('I do not think I shall write such verses at eighty-one') but apparently did not communicate with him directly.[55] Perhaps he was now too much in awe of her to presume to write himself. She and her mother do not seem to have corresponded either, though the fact that in later life she took care not to neglect her Grace relatives indicates that the relationship might have been closer than the surviving evidence suggests. But whatever fondness she retained for her parents, they had been relegated to the back row. In her letter of condolence Ann Kennicott noted, 'It has made you *serious* but not *sad*. Your loss, though certainly affecting, cannot be called afflictive.'[56] This was true; but, observant though she was, Mrs Kennicott might have missed the complexity of her friend's reaction to her bereavement.

The months after Jacob More's death saw the development of one of the most curious of his daughter's friendships. Her relationship with Horace Walpole, son of the great prime minister, wit, author, connoisseur, and incorrigible gossip, was an apparent mismatch of opposites that was to cause much embarrassment to her first biographer, writing at a time when Walpole's reputation had been savaged by Macaulay's notorious essay in the *Edinburgh Review*.[57] But there was nothing surprising about the association; they were both celebrities and celebrity hunters. A passionate lover of the theatre, he had gone to see *Percy* in December 1777, and though he thought it too religious and the last act 'very ill-conducted and unnatural and obscure',[58] he liked the play well enough to buy it and to mark the passages he especially approved. Within the pattern of overlapping circles which was London society, he and More had many associates in common and were bound to come together at some stage.

[55] Ibid. 206.   [56] Clark, Ann Kennicott to More, Oxford, 20 Jan. [1783].

[57] The following is based on H. Walpole, *A Description of the Villa of Mr Horace Walpole* (Twickenham, 1784); R. Wyndham Ketton-Cremer, *Horace Walpole* (London, 1940); P. Sabor (ed.), *Horace Walpole: The Critical Heritage* (London, 1987); T. Mowl, *Horace Walpole: The Great Outsider* (London, 1996); M. R. Brownell, *The Prime Minister of Taste: A Portrait of Horace Walpole* (New Haven, 2001); also on *The Yale Edition of Horace Walpole's Correspondence*, ed. W. S. Lewis *et al.* (London and New Haven, 1937–83), esp. vol. xxxi.

[58] Walpole, *Correspondence with the Countess of Upper Ossory*, xxxii. 404–5.

Walpole's many interests and hobbies included the collecting of correspondents, a policy, inspired by the example of his heroine Madame de
Sévigné, whose letters to her daughter from the court of Louis XIV set
standards of elegance for English polite society. His own letters, which fill
more than forty fat volumes in the Yale collection, were carefully crafted
works of art modelled on her style: the touch was light and pleasant, the
tone easy and conversational, the discourse wide-ranging, encompassing art,
literature, history, politics, and anecdote. The whole letter was a finished
piece carefully adapted to the tastes of the reader, who, as often as not, in
this feminized genre, would be a woman. Hannah More was simply the latest
in the long line of recipients of these elegant, essentially impersonal compositions.

In 1780, when they first became friends, Walpole was 63 years old and
afflicted by gout, though his love of gossip and the bursts of malice and
kindness that went to make up his complex character were undiminished.
He was small, he walked in a mincing fashion that one observer likened to a
peewit, and in moments of animation he could emit little screams. In modern
parlance, he would be described as camp. He was the comical antithesis of
Sir Robert Walpole, the bluff, sometimes crude Norfolk squire, and after his
death the rumour circulated that his true father was his mother's friend Carr,
Lord Hervey, elder brother of Pope's effeminate 'Sporus'. In his lifetime he
had to face the veiled charge of homosexuality. The accusation remains
unproven, but certainly no one, then or later, ever saw him as a red-blooded
male awash with testosterone. Until his meeting with the Berry sisters near
the end of his life the only woman he loved deeply was his mother. Hetero-
sexual sex seems to have frightened him, and when the blind *salonnière*
Madame du Deffand declared her love, their friendship went into painful
decline. His wariness of emotional involvement was also reflected in his
attitude to religion. He had learned deism at Cambridge and he viewed
Methodist ardours with cool contempt. However, he detested the atheism of
the French *philosophes*, and, for a while at least, More's Christianity was no
barrier to their friendship. He called her 'Saint Hannah' or 'Holy Hannah',
and it might have been his private joke that 'a Hannah' was his term for a
kept woman.

In becoming friends with Walpole, More had to overcome her Bristolian
prejudices. Walpole was hated in her native city as his well-merited scepticism about the authenticity of Thomas Chatterton's 'Rowley' poems was
believed to have caused the young poet's suicide.[59] For a time More, a
strong believer in the authenticity of the poems, was inclined to go along

[59] E. H. W. Meyerstein, *A Life of Thomas Chatterton* (London, 1930), 254–77; P. Baines, *The House of Forgery in Eighteenth-Century Britain* (Aldershot, 1999), ch. 7.

with this harsh and unjust verdict. She was friendly with Chatterton's mother, Sarah, who like her was a native of the parish of Stapleton, and two years later she was recorded as having collected subscriptions of £30 'from Sundry Persons' in aid of the mother and sister.[60] But her views were softening and, for all her sympathy with the family, she now conceded that Walpole had a good case though she was 'not *quite* a convert'.[61] The conversion eventually followed.

Shortly after this More went with Mrs Garrick to Strawberry Hill, his 'bauble villa' by the Thames at Twickenham, a Gothic extravaganza reflecting in stone and glass, portraiture and porcelain, the catholic range of his tastes and interests. She was awed, as all visitors were, by this phantasmagoric creation, monastery, castle, and gentleman's villa, remarkable for its battlements, turrets, and cloister, its narrow arched windows and stained glass, and its magpie horde of classical, medieval, and Renaissance artefacts, all reflecting its owner's formidably eclectic taste. For all its magnificent incoherence, Strawberry Hill was more than the whim of a rich dilettante. Walpole produced two editions of a meticulous guide in which every room and every object within the room was described in loving detail. Visitors paid to view one of the wonders of the age and went away inspired or overwhelmed. The lucky ones like Hannah More were admitted free. Those who were especially privileged had their works printed on the private Strawberry Hill press, which had been set up in a garden close to the house.

The visit was a bewildering experience. There was so much to see and take in, and Walpole devoted himself most assiduously to showing her his collection. The day was as delightful 'as elegant literature, high breeding and lively wit can afford' but More was left feeling that 'I have so little of virtû [*sic*] and antiquarianism about me that I really felt myself quite unworthy of all the trouble he took for me.'[62] She might have turned instead with some relief to make a fuss of Tonton, the bad-tempered little dog bequeathed by Madame du Deffand.

It is one of the contradictions of More's life that, though she contrived to be absent at the deaths of both her parents, she was an assiduous attender at the deathbeds of others. In August 1783 Benjamin Kennicott died in Oxford in More's presence, and she had to break the news to his widow. 'These great scenes are almost too much for me,' she told Mary Hamilton.[63] She also attended his funeral, drew up a sketch of his character, and helped Mrs Kennicott come to terms with the consequences of her bereavement, both emotional and financial.[64] Either then or in the following year Ann Kennicott

---

[60] Meyerstein, *Life of Chatterton*, 487–8.   [61] Roberts, i. 187.   [62] Ibid. i. 287.
[63] Anson MSS, doc. folder 8, More to Mary Hamilton, 1 Sept. 1783.
[64] Roberts, i. 288–95; Clark, More to Sir William Weller Pepys, Bristol, 18 Sept. 1783.

came to Bristol to stay with the Mores and enjoyed there some 'excellent gipseying days'. Her graceful letter of thanks gives a rare insight into the lives and characters of the More sisters at this stage.

Tell Governess [Mary], I have sent my Stays to the Mantua-makers' and I expect to be quite in Shape when my gown is made to fit them, Miss Betty More I have thought of every bit of Furniture I have been deliberating upon. The sight of a Mutton chop not only makes my mouth water, but my eye too; at the remembrance of Sally, and as to my new Friend P[atty] I cannot begin to speak of her at the Bottom of a Page.[65]

Mrs Kennicott and Patty claimed to be 'sentimental friends', a literary conceit popularized in many contemporary novels, possibly reflecting the widow's loneliness and the intensely emotional nature of the youngest More sister.

In the month before Dr Kennicott's death More wrote from Bristol to Sir William Weller Pepys, telling him that she had been 'scribbling a parcel of idle verses' to divert Elizabeth Vesey, whose husband had taken her off, an unwilling captive, to Ireland. This was the *The Bas Bleu*, her celebration of the bluestockings. Having a 'terror of newspapers' following her experiences over the Hannah Cowley business, she wished for anonymity, but at the same time she wanted the poem circulated and corrected.[66] She sent half the verses to Pepys (celebrated in the poem as 'Laelius'[67]) and the other half to Mary Hamilton, 'so if you shou'd be prudish and not chuse to send for the Gentleman to come to you, you are not likely to know what they are about'.[68] The two parts were to be put together and sent off to Mrs Vesey, and More was eager to 'know the whole history of the little bustle which I hope my Frisk will put you into'.[69] When the poem began to be circulated, she tried to offset the rather endearing vanity of this elaborate secrecy with some equally characteristic self-deprecation. Writing to Pepys a couple of months later, she assured him that 'all the little *affected* display of knowledge in the Bas bleu may be picked up in Newberry's sixpenny histories, or the mottoes to the Spectator'. As for '*learning*—what a big word! I think I never used it before with reference to myself.'[70]

None of this feminine shrinking could conceal the cleverness and ingenuity of the poem in which the whole bluestocking project was wittily set out: the equal participation of men and women in the cultivation of true learning and elegant taste; the banishing of acrimony and party conflict from polite society; the reverence for rational conversation, described by Enlightenment

[65] Clark, Ann Kennicott to More, n.d.   [66] Roberts, i. 296-7.   [67] Ibid. iv. 273.
[68] Anson MSS, doc. folder 8, More to Mary Hamilton, Bristol, 24 July 1783.
[69] Ibid.   [70] Clark, More to Pepys, Bristol, 18 Sept. 1783.

thinkers as one of the defining marks of civilized society. Friends were named and praised. 'BOSCAWEN sage' and 'bright MONTAGU' had 'rescued the ravag'd realms of Taste' (lines 45–7). In contrast to the pretensions of pedants and *précieuses*, Walpole combined erudition with gaiety and Elizabeth Carter 'taught the female train / The deeply wise are never vain' (lines 50–5). At bluestocking assemblies

> Here sober Duchesses are seen,
> Chaste Wits and Critics void of spleen;
> Physicians, fraught with real science,
> And Whigs, and Tories in alliance;
> Poets, fulfilling Christian duties,
> Just Lawyers, reasonable Beauties;
> Bishops who preach, and Peers who pay,
> And Countesses who seldom play;
> Learn'd Antiquaries, who, from college,
> Reject the rust, and bring the knowledge... (lines 168–77)

Though Hannah More herself is the great absence from the poem, the particular tone—a combination of the witty, the arch, and the priggish—was all her own. She was celebrating her friends, but also the fact that she was part of this delightful circle. She had come a long way since Hester Thrale had rated her social skills so poorly. Through her talents, her adaptability, her delicate flattery, and above all perhaps, the warmth of her affections, she had become valued and accepted by literary London. It was small wonder that the poem was an instant success, though, somewhat surprisingly, Elizabeth Montagu wanted to know 'what connection has stockings with conversation'.[71] Elizabeth Carter thought it 'delightful'; Fanny Burney longed for a copy of her own—no doubt because Pepys had told her that the silent figure of 'Attention' in the poem was a portrait of herself; this was confirmed when More told Mary Hamilton that 'that sweet girl really sat for the Picture to my imagination'.[72] Johnson described it to Hester Thrale as 'a very great performance'.[73] In his first extant letter to More, written in March 1784, Walpole praised the 'quantity of learning [that] has all the air of negligence instead of that of pedantry'.[74] The king liked it so much that he wanted a copy of his own, and More sat up one night to write it out for him.[75] The poem was finally printed in 1786 along with another poem, *Florio: A Tale for Fine Gentlemen and Fine Ladies*, a celebration of the virtues of the country

---

[71] *Mrs Montagu*, ii. 3.

[72] *Letters from Mrs Elizabeth Carter to Mrs Montagu*, ed. M. Pennington (London, 1817), iii. 202–3; F. Burney, *Diary and Letters of Madame d'Arblay* (London, 1842), ii. 284–5; Harman, *Fanny Burney*, 181; Anson MSS, doc. folder 8, More to Mary Hamilton, 29 Dec. 1783.

[73] *The Letters of Samuel Johnson*, ed. Bruce Redford, iv: *1782–1784*, (Princeton, 1994), 317.

[74] *Walpole*, 212.   [75] Roberts, i. 319.

over the town, which was dedicated to Horace Walpole. (By that time Elizabeth Vesey was widowed and sinking into decrepitude, and Johnson, the grand old man of letters, was dead. In the printed version More added a tribute to 'rigid CATO, awful Sage / Bold Censor of a thoughtless age', who now 'with ROSCIUS [Garrick] sleeps' (lines 198, 203.)

On her return to London in January 1784 More paid a call on Johnson; she found him ill, but in reasonable spirits. She did not stay long 'for it was at his own house...[and] he let in so many men that I began to feel awkward and so sneaked off'.[76] On 23 January she dined at Mrs Vesey's, where she met Elizabeth Carter again, as well as Fanny Burney and her father, Sir Joshua Reynolds, and Horace Walpole. In spite of this agreeable company, the relentless round of sociability was beginning to pall, and she 'did not much enjoy the Day'.[77] On another occasion she complained to Ann Kennicott, 'This evening I go to the Bishop of St Asaph's, tomorrow to Mrs Walsingham's, next day to Mrs Vesey's and so on sans fin and sans cesse.'[78] This note of weariness would resound through her correspondence with increasing insistence. Outwardly, however, she was cheerful, and most of her friends had little idea that there were troubled currents below the calm surface.

She was a close observer of one of the most exciting election campaigns of the century, Charles James Fox's successful attempt to retain his Westminster seat during a general election which saw his Whig party trounced and William Pitt returned triumphantly. Mrs Garrick, a passionate adherent of the Pittite candidate, sent a servant out at the close of every day to find the state of the poll. More herself was playing a delicate balancing act. She too was a Pittite, and was to remain the young prime minister's devoted supporter until his death, but when she visited the Whig dowager Countess Spencer at St Albans, she had to keep her politics to herself.[79] All eyes were on Lady Spencer's daughter, the duchess of Devonshire, whose spirited campaign for Fox was winning her praise in the opposition press and many inventive innuendoes elsewhere. Mary Hamilton, who encountered the duchess on her campaigns, exclaimed in horror, '*What a Pity* that any of our Sex should ever forget what is due to female delicacy.'[80] Hannah More

---

[76] Clark, More to Ann Kennicott, Hampton, 26 Jan. [1784].

[77] Ibid. Compare the account of the day given by Mary Hamilton: Anson MSS, diary, book 4 (17 Jan.–17 Feb.), 23 Jan. 1784.

[78] Clark, More to Ann Kennicott, London, 22 Apr. [1784].   [79] Roberts, i. 311–13.

[80] Diary of Mary Hamilton, book 7 (23 Apr.–20 June), 27 Apr. 1784. See also A. Stott, ' "Female Patriotism": Georgiana, Duchess of Devonshire and the Westminster Election of 1784', *Eighteenth-Century Life*, 17 NS (Nov. 1993), 60–84; P. Deutsch, 'Moral Trespass in Georgian London: Gambling, Gender, and Electoral Politics in the Reign of George III', *Historical Journal*, 39 (1996), 637–56; A. Foreman, *Georgiana, Duchess of Devonshire* (London, 1999), ch. 9.

was more blunt, telling Mrs Kennicott, 'I wish her husband wou'd lock her up or take away her Shoes, or put her in the Corner or bestow on her any other punishment fit for naughty children. All the windows are filled with Prints of her, some only ludicrous, others I am told seriously offensive.'[81] She had an exciting little adventure of her own to relate. One evening she was about to be carried in a chair through Covent Garden, a perilous journey, as armed men were on the lookout for Fox's supporters. Though the chairmen were persuaded to turn back, 'a vast number of people followed me, crying out, "It is Mrs Fox; none but Mr Fox's wife would dare to come into Covent Garden in a chair; she is going to canvass in the dark." Though not a little frightened, I laughed heartily at this, but shall stir no more in a chair for some time.'[82]

She and Walpole joked together about the election. He proposed 'that everybody should forfeit half a crown who said anything tending to introduce the idea either of *ministers* or *opposition*'. More 'added that whoever even mentioned *pit coal* or a *fox-skin muff*, should be considered as guilty'.[83] It was a relief when Fox was finally declared the victor after a campaign that lasted six weeks and exhausted participants and spectators alike.

During and after the election More's life continued its relentless round. At various Bas Bleu parties she resumed old friendships, made new ones, and her letters name-dropped as much as ever. In April she discovered a new admirer in General James Oglethorpe, the founder of Georgia, with whom she flirted 'prodigiously'. It was a window into a bygone age; now aged 90, he had been foster-brother to the Pretender and was 'one of the three persons still living who were mentioned by Pope'. She found him 'quite a preux chevalier, heroic, romantic and full of the old gallantry'.[84] In the following month she and Frances Boscawen attended a birthday party for another venerable survivor, Mary Delany, where she mended some fences with Burke. Irritated with his fiery pro-American speeches during the War of Independence, she had criticized him in *The Bas Bleu* as 'Hortensius', whose obsession with politics had made him 'Apostate now from social Wit' (line 204); but now she found him 'the agreeable Mr Burke I once knew and admired'.[85] On 14 May Mrs Garrick assembled a party at the Adelphi: Mary Hamilton, Elizabeth Carter, the Burneys, and Johnson. Mary Hamilton found the old man 'in good spirits' and full of anecdotes. He told the company how Goldsmith had been caught out in a lie when he claimed that his brother was dean of Durham, at which More exclaimed, 'Surely the *Red Book* [the clerical directory] would have inform'd him better.' Johnson replied that 'he was so ignorant of common things that he did not know

---

[81] Clark, More to Ann Kennicott, London, 22 Apr. [1784].
[82] Roberts, i. 315–16.   [83] Ibid. 311.   [84] Ibid. 317.   [85] Ibid. 359.

there was such a book'.[86] On the following day he dined at the Essex-Head Club, where Boswell recorded his qualified praise of More and her friends:

He told us, 'I dined yesterday at Mrs Garrick's, with Mrs Carter, Miss Hannah More, and Miss Fanny Burney. Three such women are not to be found: I know not where I could find a fourth except Mrs [Charlotte] Lennox, who is superior to them all.' BOSWELL. 'What! had you them all to yourself, Sir?' JOHNSON. 'I had them as much as they were to be had; but it might have been better had there been more company there.'[87]

In the summer she planned to 'flirt' with him again at Oxford, but he was not well enough to stay. She was grieved to learn that 'his mind is still a prey to melancholy, and that the fear of death operates on him to the destruction of his peace'; this seemed inexplicable in such a devout Christian.[88] Johnson was soon to find another reason for depression, when in June Hester Thrale wrote to inform him of her approaching marriage to the Italian musician Gabriele Piozzi. The terrible letter he sent in reply, a wounded beast's howl of pain, put an end to all hopes of a true reconciliation.

Hester Thrale's marriage cut her off from the bluestockings, whose viciously uncharitable reactions have shocked many later commentators.[89] But in their eyes she had offended very deeply. At the supposedly decorous age of 42, in a scenario Fielding or Sterne would have enjoyed, she had apparently gone out of her way to pursue the man who had given music lessons to her daughters, who was, moreover, a foreigner and a Roman Catholic; she was now preparing for a tour of Europe with her new husband, leaving her daughters to fend for themselves. In ignoring so many social taboos, she had reinforced all the old sneers about female frailty, and this at a time when some women were fighting to be taken seriously as rational beings able to rise above their sexual natures. The unforgiving Fanny Burney decided that she had been 'duped by ungovernable passions'.[90] Elizabeth Montagu solemnly pronounced a verdict of lunacy. It was too painful to believe otherwise.

In her resentment at her ostracism, Hester Piozzi singled out Elizabeth Montagu and Hannah More as her chief detractors, claiming that they 'have written long letters about this cruel business, which are read about the town'.[91] She wrote this in August 1784, when More was staying at Sandleford Priory, Elizabeth Montagu's Gothic mansion in Berkshire, and it is certainly hard to believe that, while they were together, they would have

---

[86] Anson MSS, diary of Mary Hamilton, book 7 (23 Apr.–7 June 1784), 14 May 1784.

[87] Boswell, *Life of Johnson*, iv. 275.   [88] Roberts, i. 330.

[89] See J. L. Clifford, *Hester Lynch Piozzi (Mrs Thrale)* (Oxford, 1941), 222–31.

[90] Ibid. 223.

[91] *The Piozzi Letters: Correspondence of Hester Lynch Piozzi (formerly Mrs Thrale)*, ed. E. A. Bloom and L. D. Bloom, i: *1784–1791* (London, 1989), 91 n. 7.

refrained from discussing the scandalous marriage.[92] But if More did for a while add her own note to the chorus of censoriousness, she soon desisted, and in subsequent years, when the More sisters and the Piozzis became neighbours in Bath, the relationship was far more cordial than it had ever been in Hester Thrale's Streatham days.

Perhaps More was able to distance herself from some of the turmoil surrounding the Piozzi marriage because she spent much of June 1784 in Kent. Teston (pronounced Teeson), a village on the road between Maidstone and Tonbridge lying amid hills and hop fields and overlooking the River Medway, was the beautiful home of Elizabeth Bouverie, a wealthy and philanthropic spinster, niece of Lord Radnor and cousin to the future Tractarian leader Edward Bouverie Pusey. Living with Mrs Bouverie (single women of mature age were given this courtesy title) in a curious threesome were a remarkable couple. Sir Charles Middleton, the son of a Scots collector of customs and cousin of the politician Henry Dundas had become comptroller of the Navy and head of the Navy Board during the American war; in the recent election he had been returned for the nearby naval constituency of Rochester. His wife, Margaret, a friend of Mrs Bouverie's from her youth, was a woman of keen intelligence and deep idealism and also a talented painter, who, like More, mixed with London society and knew Mrs Garrick.[93] All three were devout Christians, inclining to the unfashionable Evangelical religion. With them More could be herself without the need to pretend to be happier than she was or conceal the progress of her religious quest. She wrote in raptures to Mrs Kennicott: 'such an enchanting Country, such Books! such Nightingales! such Roses! Then within Doors such goodness, such Charity, such Piety!...I hope it is catching.'[94] To complete the harmony of the group, another of her friends, Porteus of Chester, had his residence at Hunton, only a few miles away, 'where he lives in all the simplicity of a little Country Clergyman'.[95] As these friendships deepened, More herself changed, as slowly, with many doubts and hesitations, she began to shed her old life.

Towards the end of August More left Elizabeth Montagu and returned to Bristol, where she began her momentous association with the poetic milkwoman Ann Yearsley, which will be discussed below. In September she explored the beautiful Mendip Hills in Somerset, and her effusions of sensibility were worthy of Marianne Dashwood. She told Elizabeth Carter, 'Every morning I rode though the most delightful vallies [*sic*] or crept

[92] Roberts, i. 354–6.   [93] See J. Pollock, *Wilberforce* (London, 1977), 49–52.
[94] Clark, More to Ann Kennicott, 7 June 1784.
[95] Anson MSS, doc. folder 8, More to Mary Hamilton, 8 June 1784.

along the sides of the most beautiful hanging woods, where the blue smoke, ascending from the cleanest white cottages in the world, had the prettiest effect imaginable.' She spent a day in Cheddar Gorge, 'a narrow and deep valley under a vast ledge of rocks, so lofty and stupendous as to impress the mind with ideas the most solemn and romantic'.[96] Her imagination was carried back to the days of chivalry, and, as she told Pepys, 'the delight was of so serious a nature that I could scarcely refrain from crying'.[97] The heightened language of sentiment was a sign of the subterranean change taking place in her consciousness. There was an unexpressed purpose to her lonely rides, and as she approached the milestone of her fortieth birthday, the urge to refashion her life could no longer be denied.

She was back in London in December 1784. Johnson had died on the 13th, leaving an irreplaceable gap in her circle of friends. Her readiness to believe that he had experienced an Evangelical conversion on his deathbed shows the direction of her own religious pilgrimage. He had, she reflected, 'a zeal for religion which one cannot but admire, however characteristically rough'.[98] The bluestockings continued to flourish. She told a sister that 'We have had a pleasant *Vesey* or two lately. Mrs Carter, Mr Walpole and I make our own parties and ask or exclude just whom we like. Our last was a little too large, and had too many great ladies; and we have agreed to keep the next a secret.'[99] It was in these circumstances of pleasurable intimacy that she wrote her first extant letter to Walpole, an anonymous futuristic parody of 'the *bon ton* gabble of the present age', which took the form of a letter from a fashionable lady to her friend, written from 'A-la-mode Castle' in 1840 during the reign of 'George V'.[100] This offering, revealing More's keen sense of satire and sharp ear for dialogue, was a fitting addition to Walpole's collection. He recognized the author and wrote back immediately.

I did wish you to write another *Percy*—but I beg now that you will produce a specimen of *all* the various manners in which you can shine; for since you are as modest as if your issue were illegitimate, I don't know but, like some females really in fault, you would stifle some of your pretty infants, rather than be detected in a blush.[101]

She was now admitted to the ranks of his correspondents and, having sought the privilege, she could not lay it down. When she proved dilatory in replying, she was punished with a reproachful letter that made her feel guilty and caused her to work again at the type of elegant, witty, and chatty missive

---

[96] Roberts, i. 355. [97] Ibid. 348. [98] Ibid. 394. [99] Ibid. 399.
[100] *Walpole*, 223–5. [101] Ibid. 226–7.

which he loved to receive. Paradoxically, the correspondence was established just at the time she was beginning to loosen her ties with the world he represented.

This change was shown most strikingly on Lady Day (25 March) 1785, when she signed and settled the purchase of Cowslip Green, a plot of land two miles outside the small Somerset market town of Wrington. She found it 'the most perfect little hermitage that can be conceived', and immediately commissioned the builders, who proceeded 'at a ruinous rate'.[102] It was to be her own home, unlike Hampton and the Adelphi, where she was Mrs Garrick's guest, or the Park Street school, which was primarily her sisters' territory. Although just off the Bridgwater road, it was ten miles from Bristol, too remote for a postal delivery and out of the range of newspapers. The isolation was deliberate. Like the hero of her poem, *Florio*, she wished to turn from 'well-bred crowds, and mobs polite' and learn from 'Nature's all-instructive book'.[103] Cowslip Green was to be everything London was not, a place for solitude, contemplation, and prayer. It was also to be a pastoral idyll, according to the taste of the age: a one-storey thatched cottage, surrounded by a bowery garden, fragrant with roses and honeysuckles. The situation of the house was quite low-lying but it had a variety of views, all admired by visitors. To the south lay the Mendip Hills, then open and unenclosed, with a view of the tower of Blagdon church, which was to play such a significant part in her life. Her friends helped her fill the little house. Walpole was asked for a copy of his *Castle of Otranto* and Elizabeth Montagu later sent a pretty pair of painted chairs. Soon they were to be asked to send money for struggling local families.[104] London was not forgotten, but it was beginning to occupy a subordinate place in her concerns.

Just before Johnson's death at the end of 1784 he had been visited by Fanny Burney. To divert the sick man she gave him 'a history of the Bristol milk-woman, and told him the tales I had heard of her writing so wonderfully, though she had read nothing but Young and Milton. He then animated, and talked upon this milk-woman ... with as much fire, spirit, wit and truth of criticism and judgment, as ever yet I have heard of him.'[105] The milkwoman was Ann Yearsley. She had been 'discovered' in the summer by Hannah More, and her poems were soon to be published. It was an association that began with generous hopes and ended in tears: a patron–client relationship,

[102] Roberts, ii. 87; Clark, More to Ann Kennicott, Apr., Friday [1785].
[103] *Florio*, lines 341–2, 884.
[104] *Walpole*, 231, 349–51; Huntington, MO 3996, More to Elizabeth Montagu, 20 July 1788, MO 4001, More to Elizabeth Montagu, 20 Dec. 1790.
[105] Burney, *Diary and Letters of Madame d'Arblay*, ii. 328–9.

fraught with dangers, in which the two women began as warm friends and ended as bitter enemies.[106]

Early in 1784, at the end of an unforgiving winter, Ann Yearsley, her husband, a failed small farmer, her mother, and her surviving children had been found destitute in a stable in Clifton, where they were rescued by a benevolent gentleman. After the birth of her sixth child, she took up the trade of milkwoman, selling milk from door to door in Bristol. She was then aged 31, a woman of courage and energy, a natural survivor. She rose quickly to modest prosperity and was determined to better herself still further. In the summer she began to call on the Mores' school in Park Street, and reached an unofficial arrangement with their cook by which she collected the kitchen slops to feed her pigs: part of an unofficial servants' economy that was later to become a matter of controversy. During her conversations with the cook, she handed her a copy of some verses she had written. These were passed on to Hannah More, who read them, and then met the milkwoman, possibly shortly before her August visit to Elizabeth Montagu at Sandleford. The pattern established in her dealings with 'Louisa' and with Mrs Chatterton and her daughter repeated itself, and in her impulsive, well-meaning, managing fashion, she rushed in to help: together with Mrs Montagu, champion of Shakespeare and patroness of learning, she would introduce this new poetic talent to the literary world.

On returning from Sandleford, she wrote to thank Elizabeth Montagu for her gift of money for Ann Yearsley, and to tell the milkwoman's story as she heard it from her own lips. Putting her own gloss on it, she depicted her marriage (almost certainly misleadingly) as a ludicrous caricature of the aristocratic marriage of convenience: Yearsley 'was sacrificed for *money* at 17 to a silly Man whom she did not like; the Husband had an Estate of near Six *pounds* a year, and the marriage was thought too advantageous

---

[106] This narrative is based on Hannah More's account in her 'Prefatory Letter to Mrs Montagu', in *Poems on Several Occasions, by Ann Yearsley, a Milkwoman of Bristol* (London, 1785), pp. iii–xii, and on Ann Yearsley's version in *Poems on Various Subjects, by Ann Yearsley, a Milkwoman of Clifton, near Bristol* (London, 1787), pp. xv–xxx; also J. M. S. Tomkins, *The Polite Marriage, also the Didactic Lyre, the Bristol Milkwoman, the Scotch Parents, Clio in Motley and Mary Hays, Philosophess* (Cambridge, 1938); L. Zionkowski, 'Strategies of Containment: Stephen Duck, Ann Yearsley, and the Problem of Polite Culture', *Eighteenth-Century Life*, NS 3 (13/1989), 91–108; D. Landry, *The Muses of Resistance: Laboring-Class Women's Poetry in Britain, 1739–1796* (Cambridge, 1990); M. Waldron, 'Ann Yearsley and the Clifton Records', *The Age of Johnson: A Scholarly Annual*, 3 (New York, 1990), 301–25; ead., *Lactilla, Milkwoman of Clifton: The Life and Writings of Ann Yearsley, 1753–1806* (Athens, Ga., 1996); P. Demers, ' "For mine's a stubborn and a savage will": "Lactilla" (Ann Yearsley) and "Stella" (Hannah More) Reconsidered', *Huntington Library Quarterly*, 56 (1993), 135–50; ead., *The World of Hannah More*, 63–75; M. Kahn, 'Hannah More and Ann Yearsley: A Collaboration across the Class Divide', *Studies in Eighteenth-Century Culture*, 25 (Baltimore, 1996), 203–23.

to be refused'.[107] She had already made up her mind that John Yearsley was a wastrel and his wife would need to be protected from him. She continued,

I asked her who were her favourite Authors? 'Among the Heathen, said She, I have met with no such Compositions as Virgil's Georgics'. How I stared! besides the choice was so *professional*. Of English poets her favourites are Milton and Dr Young, the latter she said had an ardour and boldness in his Imagination that was very delightful to her.[108]

Yearsley had gained her literary knowledge from the books given to her mother by her employers and from looking at the prints displayed in the Bristol bookshops. Her spontaneous love of Virgil's great pastoral poem (in translation) harmonized with Hannah More's own preference for natural, untaught feelings and probably helped to validate her growing determination to break free of London society. She approved, too, of the milkwoman's enthusiasm for Milton and for Edward Young's *Night Thoughts*, a long, lugubrious piece of nature poetry, which was particularly admired by Anglican clergymen. Even more striking was Yearsley's enviable calm, which contrasted with More's own unsettled emotions.[109]

The existence of the 'primitive', plebeian genius, the 'mute, inglorious Milton', who understood by instinct what the educated had to strive to acquire, was welcomed by many in polite society as it seemed to indicate that taste was acquired by nature rather than nurture. It was a message More, who reverenced the 'unlettered' genius of Shakespeare and Chatterton, and who was increasingly disillusioned with the artificiality of fashionable society, wanted to hear. Her 'discovery' of Ann Yearsley—'a Milker of Cows, and a feeder of Hogs, who has never even seen a Dictionary'[110]—followed a tradition begun by Queen Caroline, the wife of George II, who had patronized the agricultural labourer Stephen Duck. His poems went into ten editions and such was his (temporary) prestige that he was at one time considered a likely poet laureate. Though she went out of her way to stress that she wanted 'bread' rather than 'fame' for Yearsley,[111] More felt an understandable triumph at the thought that she had a protégée of her own to bring forward: the Bristol milkwoman as a worthy successor to the Wiltshire thresher. But with the Duck precedent in mind, she struck a cautionary note in her next letter to Mrs Montagu. 'I am *utterly* against taking her out of her station. *Stephen* was an excellent Bard as a *Thresher*, but as the Court Poet and Rival of Pope, detestable.'[112]

---

[107] Huntington, MO 3986, More to Elizabeth Montagu, 27 Aug. 1784.
[108] Ibid.   [109] Ibid.
[110] Huntington, MO 3998, More to Elizabeth Montagu, 22 Oct. 1784.
[111] *Poems on Several Occasions*, pp. xi–xii.
[112] Huntington, MO 3987, More to Elizabeth Montagu, 27 Sept. 1784.

Under More's patronage Yearsley came to the notice of polite society, and was graciously inspected by the dowager duchess of Beaufort (sister and heiress of her father's patron, Lord Botetourt), Lady Spencer, and Elizabeth Montagu. 'I hope all these honours will not turn her head, and indispose her for her humble occupations,' More wrote to Frances Boscawen.[113] Utterly convinced that she knew what was right for Ann Yearsley, and that her protégée would meekly acquiesce in the future being mapped out for her, she doled out her beneficence in carefully measured portions, supplying her with 'a *little* Maid to help her feed her pigs, and nurse the little ones, while she herself sells her Milk'. In hiring the cheapest possible servant she was following the policy advocated by Elizabeth Montagu that 'she shou'd not be corrupted by being made *idle* or *useless*'.[114] But, for all her professed caution, she was rushing ahead with her plans and did not pay enough attention to Walpole's condescending but shrewd warning.

Were I not persuaded . . . that this good thing has real talents, I should not advise her encouraging her propensity lest it should divert her from the care of her family, and after the novelty is over, leave her worse than she was. . . . She must remember that she is a Lactilla, not a Pastora, and is to tend real cows, not Arcadian sheep.[115]

Meanwhile, More and Elizabeth Montagu were preparing a subscription volume of the milkwoman's poems.[116] By April the manuscript was nearly ready for the press, by which time some of More's friends were speculating that she had added her own improvements to Ann Yearsley's verses. In a letter to Ann Kennicott she denied that she had altered one particular poem (though this did not necessarily preclude alterations to other poems) and gave an account of her progress in raising subscriptions.

By the by, I am quite angry at you for leaving half a guinea with Lady B[athurst?] did I not charge you to give only a Crown? That is as much as many *Peeresses* have given. I continue to get subscriptions every day, quite unsolicited; you will be glad to hear that I have near eight hundred names. Mrs Montagu has given twenty Guineas, Lord Stormont 5, Duke of Northumberland 5 . . . That most munificent woman the Duchess Dow^r of Portland yesterday gave me another ten pound Bill, but I refused to take it, as I know those *giving* Spirits have always demands on their bounty, beyond the ability of their Purse to satisfy.[117]

In the same letter she told her friend about the expense involved in building Cowslip Green, and added archly, 'I wish I may not be tempted to convert some of Lactilla's Guineas into Shrubs, and to embellish my little Lawn with

---

[113] Roberts, i. 332.
[114] Huntington, MO 3988, More to Elizabeth Montagu, 22 Oct. 1784.
[115] *Walpole*, 220–1.   [116] See *Bath Chronicle*, 24 Feb. 1785.
[117] Clark, More to Ann Kennicott, Apr., Friday [1785].

her Bank Bills. Dont you think the temptation perilous when one poor Bard is bound to another?' But the issues of literary property and finance, treated so light-heartedly here, were to come back to haunt her.

Poems on Several Occasions finally came out in June. It contained Yearsley's poems, an account of her story as described by More in a prefatory letter to Elizabeth Montagu, and a list of subscribers which was an impressive trawl through More's friends. Much of the collection was autobiographical, detailing the relationship of 'Lactilla' and her muse, 'Stella' (More), who represents civilization and society. In 'To the Same; on her accusing the author of flattery . . .', 'Lactilla' defends the warmth of her friendship and the depth of her gratitude, but with an energy and truculence that might have given her patron pause for thought.

> For mine's a stubborn and a savage will;
> No customs, manners or lost arts I boast,
> On my rough soul your nicest rules are lost;
> Yet shall unpolish'd gratitude be mine,
> While STELLA deigns to nurse the spark divine.   (lines 8–12)

More ominous still was the poem 'Address to Friendship', in which Yearsley considers the inequality of her relationships with patrons who also call themselves her friends, and describes true friendship as

> That name which never yet cou'd dare exist
> But in equality.   (lines 78–86)

Yet equality was the one gift More did not offer.

With the poems published, More's next concern was to establish Yearsley's finances in a way that would make her independent of her unsatisfactory husband. From Teston she wrote to her publisher, Cadell, on 12 June asking him to purchase '*immediately* as agreed in the 5 Pr Cents', breaking her increasingly strict sabbatarian principles in order to catch the post.[118] From the Adelphi she wrote a letter full of triumph and innocent rectitude to Elizabeth Montagu.

Were you not surprised, dear Madam, to see so magnificent a book . . . We printed 1250 and are obliged to sell the supernumerary copies at 6s to indemnify us a little; I paid near fourscore pounds *all* expences; have lodged £350 in the Five Pr Cents which will produce about £18 a year; and shall take her down about £20 to cloathe her family and furnish her House. . . . I have laid out the money in *your* name, Madam and mine, having first had an instrument drawn by the Lawyer signed by Yearsley and his wife allowing us to controul the money, and putting it out of the Husband's power to touch it.[119]

[118] Huntington, HM 1837, More to Cadell, 12 June 1785.
[119] Huntington, MO 3990, More to Elizabeth Montagu [June 1785].

Although preoccupied with Ann Yearsley's finances, she was also full of a shocking piece of London gossip: Agmondersham Vesey had died of apoplexy, and the sham of his marriage was revealed to the world. To More's great indignation he had 'left that dear woman *nothing* but that hole of a house; and the old Coach! The plate to Ld Lucan after the death of the heir . . . and £1000 go to his W——'.[120] Having relieved her feelings with an indelicate expression, she busied herself with 'the horrors of packing' in preparation for her meeting with Ann Yearsley at Bristol.

The deed of trust signed by the Yearsleys set up Hannah More and Elizabeth Montagu as joint trustees and empowered More to invest the proceeds from the poems in government stock, and to dispose of principal and interest in ways she considered benefited Ann Yearsley and her children (not her husband). This left Yearsley full of misgivings, feeling that she was not being trusted to look after her children's interests. Yet More believed she had some reason for her lack of confidence, as on her return to Bristol she was disturbed to hear from Yearsley that she owed £10. She agreed to pay her debt, and over dinner a few nights later she handed over the money. According to Ann Yearsley, she then said, 'I can do no more, if any thing should happen; the money lodged in the funds is three hundred and fifty pounds, which nobody but myself or Mrs Montagu can ever call out. You have complained much of being in debt—we hear it from every quarter.' As More felt herself the aggrieved party, she was outraged when Yearsley then belligerently demanded a copy of the deed of trust. 'Are you *mad*, Mrs Yearsley?', she exclaimed, 'or have you drank [*sic*] a glass too much?' Yearsley retorted it was quite reasonable for her to have a copy of a deed as 'a little memorandum' for her children. At this stage the normally silent Betty More intervened: 'I don't think you unreasonable, Mrs Yearsley, but there is a manner of speaking.' She might have put her finger on the problem, but her remark only aggravated Ann Yearsley's prickly awareness of her lack of social graces. After more angry exchanges, she left the house. It was several weeks before she and More met again and in the intervening time they were engaged in a petty dispute over the ongoing pigswill transaction between Yearsley and the Mores' cook.[121]

Ann Yearsley's account of the quarrel shows the two women behaving in character, each convinced of her own righteousness. The apparently innocuous request for a declaration of the deed of trust fanned out into a series of grievances that left both feeling betrayed. At a further meeting, this time in front of witnesses called in to examine the accounts, Yearsley, according to More, 'behaved more like a Demon than a human Creature. I gave her eleven Guineas which I had by me for her present use; she dash'd it at me,

[120] Ibid.   [121] Yearsley, *Poems on Various Subjects*, p. xxvii.

and said she never wou'd take that or any thing else from me for that "I had added insult to the weight of imaginary obligations".'[122] (In Ann Yearsley's account of this meeting she did not touch the money, which remained on the table; she 'spoke but little', concealing her emotions while More called her 'a savage' and 'a bad woman'.[123]) More confided her bewilderment in a difficult letter to Elizabeth Montagu.

I have spent above 8 months entirely in this business, I have written a thousand pages on her subject and with your generous concurrence have got near five hundred pounds; I believe it will be more, for I am preparing a second Edition, and am trying to get the husband a place, I do not see her of which she is very glad, as she says I am such a Tyrant; I hear she wears very fine Gauze Bonnets, long lappets, gold Pins etc. Is such a Woman to be trusted with the poor Children's Money?[124]

In a further disagreeable letter in September she copied out part of a stinging letter from Yearsley:

You tax me with ingratitude, for why? . . . You have led me to sign a Settlement which defrauds me of my right, and makes it ever received your peculiar gift. Your bankruptcy or death may lose it for ever, and let me ask you Miss More what security You have ever given my children whereby they may prove their claim?[125]

Outraged by what she saw as Yearsley's betrayal, More did not stop to consider that, for all its belligerent phrasing, the question was perfectly reasonable.

Worst of all, from More's perspective, was her embarrassment at having implicated Elizabeth Montagu in the transaction, and she longed to free them both from the whole business. In October she was able to report that she had prevailed upon one of Yearsley's friends to take charge of the trust, but her troubles were not over. Mrs Yearsley now had a new patron in Frederick Hervey, the worldly bishop of Derry and fourth earl of Bristol ('how suitable the Patron to the Protégée'), and she let it be known in Bristol that she was 'going to bring out her Poems as she originally wrote them, before they were spoilt by me'. She ended her letter grimly: 'What a holiday to me when I have done with her and her business which has occupied near a whole year of my Life!'[126] In December she thankfully relinquished the trust in what she hoped was 'an honourable and conscientious manner'.[127]

[122] Berg Collection, 222809B, More to Eva Garrick, 12 Aug. [1785].
[123] *Poems on Various Subjects*, p. xx.
[124] Huntington, MO 3991, More to Elizabeth Montagu, 21 July 1785.
[125] Huntington, MO 3992, More to Elizabeth Montagu, 16 Sept. 1785.
[126] Huntington, MO 3993, More to Elizabeth Montagu, 20 Oct. 1785.
[127] Folger, W.b. 487, fo. 80, More to Eva Garrick, 30 Nov. 1785.

When Ann Yearsley came to lay her case before the public in the preface to her *Poems on Various Subjects* (1787), she accused More of high-handedness, of exaggerating her poverty, and of altering her poems without her permission. As More had to admit that she had destroyed the manuscripts of Yearsley's poems after their publication, she was unable to refute the latter charge convincingly. She had behaved in the manner of an old-fashioned patron, and had ignored Yearsley's rights to her literary property. It was some comfort that her friends readily accepted her version of the story and accused Yearsley of shocking ingratitude bordering on insanity.[128] Many modern commentators, however, have reversed this verdict, and painted Yearsley in the best possible light and More in the worst. Unwilling to give More credit for her undoubted desire to do her best for Yearsley, they have found her guilty of arrogance and condescension and a failure to spot the inevitable class antagonisms involved in the patron–client relationship. But perhaps the key lay in More's inexperience rather than her arrogance. In her dealings with Yearsley she had for the first time become a patron rather than a client. She herself had shown nothing but gratitude and deference to Mrs Gwatkin, David Garrick, Elizabeth Montagu, and all the others who had helped her, and she must have been completely taken aback by Ann Yearsely's aggressive insistence on her autonomy. Having allowed Garrick to handle the profits from *Percy*, she had taken it for granted that her own protégée would show a similar trusting compliance. For her part Yearsley refused to credit her former patroness with any good motives, seeing malice and deceit where there was only well-intentioned clumsiness. Trapped in their mutual antagonism, each constructed a caricatured picture of the other, devoid of nuance, ambiguity, or shades of grey.

Far from being the standard-bearer for proletarian resistance that some of her admirers have assumed, Ann Yearsley was to prove determinedly upwardly mobile. Like More, she published a poem on the slave trade, and wrote her own Gothic tragedy, *Earl Godwin*, which was performed at Bath. In about 1793 she set up a circulating library at the Hotwells, from where she dispensed medicine for flatulence as well as books and pamphlets.[129] She continued quarrelsome, engaging in disputes with a former mayor of Bristol and with those who planned to open a new library next to her own. Defending herself against unfair competition, she inserted a newspaper advertisement claiming that 'she came an orphan into the Republic of Letters, was received with indulgence and kindly adopted'.[130] This was not a peace-offering to Hannah More, though she might have reflected that she

---

[128] W. W. Pepys, *A Later Pepys: The Correspondence of Sir William Weller Pepys, Bart., Master in Chancery 1758–1825*, ed. A. C. C. Gaussen, 2 vols. (London, 1904), ii. 258; *Letters from Elizabeth Carter*, iii. 246–7; *Walpole*, 254.

[129] *FFBJ*, 26 Apr. 1794.   [130] Ibid. 9 Aug. 1793.

had only entered this republic through More's efforts. In the end the market for her works dried up, and she published nothing after 1796. She died at Melksham in Wiltshire in 1806 and was buried at Clifton near the spot where her family had been rescued twenty-two years earlier.

Impulsively, Hannah More had rushed into action without taking sufficient thought for the implications: a pattern that was to repeat itself during the even more traumatic experience of the Blagdon controversy, when her enemies gleefully raked over the coals of the Yearsley affair.[131] Her troubles with Ann Yearsley came at a critical time, when she was building Cowslip Green and loosening her roots in fashionable society. The experience humbled her and deepened her disillusion. She was later to claim that she was indebted to Yearsley 'for the most effectual blow to her love of reputation'.[132] This suggests that she came to realize that there might have been something conceited and self-serving about her wish to take on the patron's role and bring the milkwoman to public notice. The whole distressing business was a further inducement to turn away from the applause of fashionable society and to seek peace within her own soul.

[131] E. Spencer, *Truths respecting Mrs Hannah More's Meeting-Houses and the Conduct of her Followers* (Bath, 1802), 75; [W. Shaw] *The Life of Hannah More, with a Critical Review of her Writings, by the Rev. Sir Archibald MacSareasm, Bart* (London, 1802), 48.

[132] Thornton, Add. MS 7674/1/L1, fo. 35, Henry Thornton to Patty More, 14 Apr. 1794.

Chapter 4

Zion's City
1780–1789

EVEN at the height of her worldly success Hannah More was a convinced Christian, and her ostensibly secular plays and poems were infused with Christian values. Her father practised his religion from conviction as well as expediency, and in her old age his daughter remembered the wry term 'house Protestants' (a variation on the Elizabethan 'church papists') he applied to his non-churchgoing neighbours.[1] But for all his Dissenting ancestry, Jacob More was a High Churchman, and therefore unlikely to have been one of the 'many serious souls' Charles Wesley found when he preached at Fishponds in 1748.[2] More later claimed that she owed the first glimmerings of her spiritual awakening to the clergyman–doctor James Stonhouse, who, for all his association with the theatre, was an Evangelical of sorts, and a famously eloquent preacher.[3] His story follows the standard conversion narrative: a youth spent in whoring, blasphemy, and religious scepticism, and a change of heart under the influence of the great Dissenting minister Philip Doddridge, whose (now unreadable) *Rise and Progress of the Soul* was an Evangelical classic. Shortly afterwards he was ordained by a somewhat reluctant bishop of Hereford.

During Hannah More's early years in London he performed the role of a critical friend, eagle-eyed in faulting any tendency to slip into the ways of the world. Some time in 1775 he rebuked her for going to Elizabeth Montagu's on a Sunday; she was duly chastened, though she did not immediately mend

---

[1] Clark, More to Ann Kennicott, 22 July [1815?].
[2] *The Journal of Charles Wesley*, ed. T. Jackson (London, 1849), ii. 15.
[3] Roberts, iv. 186.

her ways.[4] Her practice became stricter over the next couple of years. One Sunday evening in the late summer of 1777 Garrick excused her from participating in music: 'Nine, you are a *Sunday woman*; retire to your room—I will recall you when the music is over.'[5] His kindness rescued her from an embarrassing predicament, but it only served to emphasize her sense of displacement and her haunting reflection that 'no earthly pleasure can fill up the wants of the immortal principle within'.[6] Sooner or later something would have to give. She could permit herself to enjoy the pleasures of the fashionable world even if they took place on a Sunday; or she could go out on a limb and risk drawing down on her head the unwelcome appellation of 'Methodist'.

With her psychological need for strong meat, Hannah More was never going to adopt an undemanding, latitudinarian Christianity. Perhaps if she had been born a generation or so earlier she would have been drawn to the High Church piety of Samuel Johnson and Elizabeth Carter, and nourished herself spiritually on a work like William Law's *Serious Call to a Devout and Holy Life*. But the decade before her birth witnessed one of the most remarkable spiritual awakenings in the history of Christianity, and it is hardly surprising that, growing up as she did during the first phase of the Evangelical revival, she should come to adopt its precepts, theology, and forms of devotion.

   The Evangelical awakening took many forms: revivalism in Scotland and Massachusetts, pietism in Germany, the preaching of the Wesley brothers and George Whitefield in England.[7] At its core lay a return to the Reforma-

---

   [4] Ibid., i. 56.   [5] Ibid. 113.   [6] Ibid. 57.
   [7] F. K. Brown, *Fathers of the Victorians: The Age of Wilberforce* (Cambridge, 1961); J. Walsh, 'Origins of the Evangelical Revival', in J. D. Walsh and G. V. Bennett (eds.), *Essays in Modern English Church History* (London, 1966), 132–62; id., 'The Anglican Evangelicals in the Eighteenth Century', *Aspects de l'Anglicanisme* (Paris, 1974), 87–102; id., 'The Church and Anglicanism in the "Long" Eighteenth Century', in J. Walsh, C. Haydon, and S. Taylor (eds.), *The Church of England, c.1689–c.1833: From Toleration to Tractarianism* (Cambridge, 1993), 1–64; I. Bradley, *The Call to Seriousness: The Evangelical Impact on the Victorians* (London, 1976); E. Jay, *The Religion of the Heart: Anglican Evangelicalism and the Nineteenth-Century Novel* (Oxford, 1979); D. W. Bebbington, *Evangelicalism in Modern Britain: A History from the 1730s to the 1980s* (London, 1989); B. Hilton, *The Age of Atonement: The Influence of Evangelicalism on Social and Economic Thought, 1785–1865* (Oxford, 1991); W. R. Ward, 'The Evangelical Revival in Eighteenth-Century Britain', in S. Gilley and W. J. Sheils (eds.), *A History of Religion in Britain: Practice and Belief from Pre-Roman Times to the Present* (Oxford, 1994), 252–72; id., *The Protestant Evangelical Awakening* (Cambridge, 1994); J. Wolffe, *Evangelicals, Women and Community in Nineteenth-Century Britain* (Milton Keynes, 1994); id. (ed.), *Evangelical Faith and Public Zeal: Evangelicals and Society in Britain, 1780–1980* (London, 1995); M. A. Noll, D. W. Bebbington, and G. A. Rawlyk (eds.), *Evangelicalism: Comparative Studies of Popular Protestantism in North America, the British Isles, and Beyond, 1700–1900* (Oxford, 1994); C. Podmore, *The Moravian Church in England, 1728–1760* (Oxford, 1998). For More and Evangelicalism, see A. Stott, 'Hannah More: Evangelicalism, Cultural Reformation, and Loyalism', Ph.D. thesis (London, 1998), ch. 1.

tion doctrine of justification by faith: the belief that, because human beings were fallen creatures incapable of rescuing themselves, salvation was gained not through intellectual assent to Christian doctrine, nor even through a life of strict morality, but through faith alone—through repentance from sin and trust in the atoning death of Christ for salvation. To be saved was to be converted, to be born again, to move from death to life, to be transformed by a new spiritual identity. This could be a highly charged, deeply emotional experience. 'I felt my heart strangely warmed,' wrote John Wesley, looking back to the meeting in the chapel in Aldersgate that turned the failed missionary into one of the most powerful evangelists of his generation. Orthodox Churchmen were dismayed at the behaviour of the crowds that attended the Methodists' open-air meetings and the disturbing manifestations of 'enthusiasm' among social outcasts such as the miners of Cornwall and Kingswood.[8] Powerful springs of spiritual energy had been released, and the results were unpredictable, difficult to confine within the channels of an ecclesiastical establishment.

Evangelicalism overlapped the denominations. The Moravians, who brought from Germany the *Herzensreligion* of their founder, Count Zinzendorf, were recognized by Parliament as 'an Antient Protestant Episcopal Church of England'.[9] Philip Doddridge, Stonhouse's mentor, remained a Dissenter, though widely read by Anglicans. The Wesleys and Whitefield remained within the Church of their baptism and it was only after their deaths that separate Methodist denominations developed. Other Anglican clergy were energized by the revival but continued their parochial work; Elizabeth Gaskell's biography of Charlotte Brontë gives a vivid picture of one of them, the eccentric William Grimshaw, curate of Haworth.[10] The Evangelicals were also divided theologically. Whitefield and his followers were old-school Calvinists, but Wesley, an Arminian, rejected the doctrine of predestination, and insisted that the offer of salvation was open to all. Disputes around this notoriously contentious issue—which Milton's fallen angels had debated so unprofitably—came to a head in Bristol in August 1771, when the followers of the Calvinist Selina, countess of Huntingdon prepared to disrupt Wesley's annual conference in the city.[11] Though Hannah More might have been too stage-struck at this time to take much notice of the controversy, she would have known of the activities of the countess, who had built a Gothic-style chapel for her new 'Connexion' in

[8] See e.g. J. Rule, 'Explaining Revivalism: The Case of Cornish Methodism', *Southern History*, 20–1 (1998–9), 168–88.

[9] Podmore, *Moravian Church in England*, 1.

[10] E. Gaskell, *The Life of Charlotte Brontë* (Harmondsworth, 1975), 69–71.

[11] B. S. Schlenther, *Queen of the Methodists: The Countess of Huntingdon and the Eighteenth-Century Crisis of Faith and Society* (Durham, 1997), 108.

Bath, and whose work in proselytizing the upper classes who frequented the spa towns prefigured her own attempts to reform polite society.

Hannah More, William Wilberforce, and their friends in the Clapham sect were to be the leading figures in the second wave of the revival. The link between the two generations was provided by a set of remarkable Anglican clergyman, two of whom, Thomas Scott and John Newton, were to influence More profoundly. Newton's career was extraordinary.[12] If all men were sinners in need of a Saviour, then few had sinned as spectacularly as this former first mate of a slave ship, 'the old African blasphemer' as he later described himself. A storm at sea had awakened his sense of religion, though it was only after a severe fever when he returned to land that his conversion was complete. He then resolved on a career in the Church but found that bishops were reluctant to ordain a self-taught man who associated with irregulars like George Whitefield. However, his ordination was secured through the offices of the Evangelical peer Lord Dartmouth, and he became curate of Olney in Buckinghamshire, where he was joined by the poet William Cowper. At the end of 1779 the Evangelical merchant John Thornton (whose son was to become one of Hannah More's closest friends) offered him the living of the smart City church, St Mary Woolnoth, where his evening lectures attracted a large body of attenders.

Newton was a Calvinist: only sovereign, irresistible grace could have transformed the life of one who, in his own words, had been so 'big with mischief'.[13] He was later to tell Hannah More that 'no scheme of religion can afford me relief, but that which is accommodated to the state of the unworthy, helpless sinner . . . having nothing of his own, but evil and misery'.[14] As he put it in the great Evangelical dualisms of his best-known hymn,

> Amazing grace! (how sweet the sound)
> That sav'd a wretch like me!
> I once was lost, but now am found,
> Was blind but now I see.[15]

But he did not share the dogmatic vehemence of the countess of Huntingdon, and it is unfair to blame him for poor Cowper's descent into melancholia. He was a spiritual director rather than a polemicist, emphasizing the disposition of the heart rather than the minutiae of Calvinist doctrine. He had

[12] D. Bruce Hindmarsh, *John Newton and the English Evangelical Tradition between the Conversions of Wesley and Wilberforce* (Oxford, 1996); id. 'The Olney Autobiographers: English Conversion Narratives in the Mid-Eighteenth Century', *Journal of Ecclesiastical History*, 49 (1998), 61–84.

[13] [J. Newton] *An Authentic Narrative of Some Remarkable and Interesting Particulars*, 6th edn. (London, 1786), 53.

[14] Roberts, ii. 184.

[15] [J. Newton and W. Cowper] *Olney Hymns in Three Books*, 5th edn. (London, 1788), 1. 41, st. 1.

developed an expertise in counselling souls in distress. In his way, he was as eager a letter-writer as Walpole, though the purpose of his long, unwittingly egotistical letters could not have been more different. In 1781 he published anonymously his two-volume epistolary *Cardiphonia; or, The Utterance of the Heart*.[16] One of the first purchasers was Frances Boscawen, who made a present of the book to Hannah More at a time when she was still mourning Garrick. Here perhaps, in these letters by an unknown author, so full of 'vital, experimental religion' and 'rational and consistent piety',[17] was the key to a more fulfilling existence. *Cardiphonia* did not secure More's immediate conversion, but it helped set her feet on a new path.

The result was seen early in the following year, when she made her first literary attempt to reconcile the two halves of her life by publishing in the same volume *Sacred Dramas* and *Sensibility*: the one an attempt to make the Bible familiar to young readers, the other an advocacy of the religion of the heart.[18] Garrick would have deplored the absence of dramatic tension in *Sacred Dramas* and agreed with her publisher, Cadell, that she was now 'too good a Christian for an author'.[19] Under the influence of Racine's severe classicism, David kills Goliath off stage, and Daniel's lions are talked about rather than seen (or heard). But for all their theatrical short comings, the *Dramas* became an Evangelical classic, the staple reading, for example, of the pious ladies of George Eliot's *Scenes of Clerical Life*.[20]

Included in the same volume was *Sensibility: A Poetical Epistle*, in which she engaged with a highly topical theme. The term sensibility carried a range of meanings, encompassing sensitivity, compassion, and imagination. More's own definition—'the Sympathy divine Which makes, O man, the woes of others thine'[21]—is close to the modern concept of empathy. The piece was dedicated to Frances Boscawen, who, as a naval widow, the mother of a son who had died young and another who was fighting in America, had known more than her share of sorrow. More believed that the intensity of her grief sprang from superior powers of feeling.

---

[16] *Cardiphonia; or, The Utterance of the Heart; in the Course of a Real Correspondence* (London, 1781).

[17] Roberts, i. 188.

[18] *Sacred Dramas: Chiefly Intended for Young Persons: The Subjects Taken from the Bible. To which is added, Sensibility, a Poem* (London, 1782). See P. Demers, *The World of Hannah More* (Lexington, Ky., 1996), 40–7.

[19] Roberts, i. 172.   [20] *Scenes of Clerical Life*, ed. T. A. Noble (Oxford, 1988), 183.

[21] *Sacred Dramas and Sensibility*, 281. For sensibility, see J. Todd, *Sensibility: An Introduction* (London, 1986); G. J. Barker-Benfield, *The Culture of Sensibility: Sex and Society in Eighteenth-Century Britain* (Chicago, 1992).

> That grief a thousand entrances can find,
> Where parts superior dignify the mind;
> Would you renounce the pangs those feelings give,
> Secure in joyless apathy to live?[22]

Unconsciously, perhaps, More was also writing about herself, and never more so than when she mourned Garrick:

> N'er shall my heart his lov'd remembrance lose;
> Guide, critic, guardian, glory of my muse! . . .
> Tho' Time his silent hand across has stole,
> Soft'ning the tints of sorrow on the soul,
> The deep impression long my heart shall fill,
> And ev'ry mellow'd trace be perfect still.[23]

However, the downside of sensibility was a facile emotionalism that placed feelings above duty. In itself neutral, it made the good better and the bad worse, and was therefore a fatal gift for those who lacked a firm grounding in moral principles. But, for all its ambivalence, it had the potential to rescue religion from arid formalism.

> Cold and inert the mental pow'rs would lie
> Without this quick'ning spark of Deity.[24]

Sensibility, the 'ethereal flame which lights and warms', could provide the soil and climate in which the religion of the heart could be nurtured and flourish. On the whole, therefore, More (for the time being) approved of sensibility.

One of the friends celebrated in *Sensibility* was Beilby Porteus, bishop of Chester, author of a much admired (later inevitably derided) prizewinning poem, *Death*, a friend since More's visit to London in 1776.[25] He was one of the few bishops who shared her own militant moral rigour. A gentle, sometimes timid man, he disliked acrimony, but did not shrink from attacking what he saw as the vices of the rich. In particular, he set his face against the rapidly growing London debating societies, which encouraged participants—women as well as men—in free, often sceptical discussion of religious topics, often on a Sunday evening. In 1780 he introduced a bill to ban them. The result was the Act of 1781, which declared that any house or room used for public entertainment or debates on the sabbath 'shall be deemed a disorderly house or place': a measure which, more than 200 years later, was still in force to prevent young people from clubbing on a

---

[22] *Sacred Dramas and Sensibility*, 276.   [23] Ibid. 273, 276.   [24] Ibid. 288.
[25] Roberts, i. 146. For Porteus, see R. Hodgson, *The Life of the Right Reverend Beilby Porteus, DD*, 2nd edn. (London, 1811).

Sunday.[26] He was never an Evangelical in John Newton's sense, but his spirituality, his moralism, and his conscientious care of his diocese won Hannah More's respect, while his cultivation and urbanity made him one of her most agreeable companions. On Sunday 24 March 1783 she had breakfast with him and went to the Chapel Royal to hear him preach before the royal family, in his role as king's chaplain. It was not her natural territory. The chapel was 'but a disagreeable place to go to' with 'more music, and more bustle, and more staring than I like'. She did her own share of royal watching, however, and observed that the king and queen 'both looked very pale'. As for the sermon, she noted ambiguously that, though 'I should have blamed it in a village', it 'was very well suited to a court'.[27] Newton would probably not have approved. Yet a year later, she was reading Porteus's sermons with interest, and once more taking breakfast with him and his wife, Margaret.[28] A friendship had begun which was to remain warm and unbroken for twenty-five years.

More had already come a long way since Stonhouse had rebuked her for breaking the sabbath, and she now took pride in her growing reputation as 'a rigid Methodist'.[29] As her practice became more strict, she turned (much to Johnson's annoyance) to the writings of the French Jansenists, whose stern moralism more than atoned, in her eyes, for their Catholicism.[30] Perhaps there were some aspects of Catholicism that held a dangerous attraction for her. The Austrian Catholic Mrs Garrick was a punctilious attender at Mass. More never went with her, but when at the beginning of Lent her friend went to London 'to have her forehead *Ashwednesday'd*', she remarked, 'I think that wou'd not have been a bad part of Popery to have retained; we have kept some things which I dislike more.'[31] (Was she thinking about the wording of the baptismal service, with its references to the un-Evangelical doctrine of baptismal regeneration?) Ultimately, however, she was too robustly Protestant to succumb to the allure of Rome; but where, in the Church of England, could she find what she was seeking? Porteus was the most devout Christian she had met among the higher clergy, but even he did not quite fit the bill. She was looking at this stage for someone harsher and more abrasive, ready to expound with uncompromising passion the doctrine of human corruptibility and the new birth; and if this drew on him the mockery of polite society, so much the better.

[26] W. B. Whitaker, *The Eighteenth-Century English Sunday: A Study of Sunday Observance from 1677 to 1837* (London, 1940), 155–8; Hodgson, *Life of Porteus*, 71–83; D. T. Andrew, 'Popular Culture and Public Debate: London 1780', *Historical Journal*, 39 (1996), 405–23.

[27] Roberts, i. 241–2; *Public Advertiser*, 25 Mar. 1782.

[28] Clark, More to Ann Kennicott, 20 May 1783.   [29] Roberts, i. 283.

[30] Ibid. 211, 278.   [31] Clark, More to Ann Kennicott, 'Hampton, 25th'.

Help came in the form of Thomas Scott, a self-educated grazier turned clergyman and biblical scholar. In 1781 he had succeeded Newton to the curacy of Olney, and at Christmas 1785, when More was preparing to move into Cowslip Green, he was appointed lecturer at St Mildred, Bread Street, in the City of London and chaplain to the Lock Hospital for venereal diseases, situated at Hyde Park Corner. Such apparently marginal appointments were all that most Evangelicals could hope for at a time when mainstream livings were denied them; they proved an effective means of infiltration. For all its unpleasant associations, the Lock had become one of the most prominent Evangelical pulpits in London, ministering to a congregation that included Lord Dartmouth. Hannah More was one of many residents in the fashionable West End who, ignoring the parochial structure, came to hear Scott; sometimes, too, she walked the six miles to Bread Street to hear him preach (she would not have used a carriage on a Sunday). She recollected, 'With the worst voice, the most northern accent, and very plain manners, sound sense and sound piety were yet so predominant that like Aaron's serpent, they swallowed up the rest.'[32] The influence of his written words spread even wider; Cardinal Newman was to see him as 'the writer who made a deeper impression on my mind than any other, and to whom (humanly speaking) I almost owe my soul'.[33]

While More was attending Scott's sermons, another troubled soul was embarking on his own spiritual pilgrimage. This was William Wilberforce, the brilliant young member for Yorkshire, a close friend of Pitt the prime minister, and a member of Brookes's gaming club, the haunt of Charles James Fox and the Whig grandees. In the summer of 1785 he toured the continent with his friend Isaac Milner, then a tutor at Queens' College, Cambridge, later to be its president, and one of the leading Evangelical clergyman of his generation. After an intense spiritual experience in Spa, he returned to England, and at the end of the year made contact with John Newton.[34] In the subsequent months he turned his life round. On Newton's advice he determined not to retire from public affairs, but in some, as yet unresolved, way to use his parliamentary career in the service of God. On Easter Day 1786 he walked into the countryside, his heart bursting with 'praise and thanksgiving', his conversion apparently complete.[35] At about the same time More was still licking her wounds over the Yearsley affair, groping towards the serenity he had now found, living in two worlds and at rest in neither.

---

[32] Roberts, iv. 191–2, 201.
[33] J. H. Newman, *Apologia pro Vita Sua*, ed. I. Kerr (Harmondsworth, 1994), 26.
[34] *Life of Wilberforce*, i. 96–9.   [35] J. Pollock, *Wilberforce* (London, 1977), 39.

On Sunday 8 May 1786 her mother died at the home her daughters had provided for her on Stoney Hill.[36] By this time, following her usual practice, More was at the Adelphi with Mrs Garrick. She had not seen her mother since December, having spent Christmas not at Bristol but at the home of the bluestocking Charlotte Walsingham, at Thames Ditton. Replying to Mary Hamilton's letter of condolence, she noted, 'The age indeed of my poor Mother was not great, she was only 65, but her sufferings were extreme.' She hoped she had now become resigned to her bereavement, though, she added, 'I suffered very sensibly for a time, and the uneasiness produces its usual consequence, a disorder in my stomach.'[37] At the end of the month she went with Mrs Garrick to Teston, where she poured out her heart to her substitute mother, Lady Middleton. 'She is made up of feeling and compassion,' she reported gratefully. 'Her kindness, which you would think must needs be exhausted on the negroes, extends to the suffering of every animal.'[38] The reference to Africans is a pointer to the fact that this visit to Teston was a turning point in More's life.

She remained there until about 10 June. Shortly afterwards the young Cambridge graduate Thomas Clarkson, author of a prizewinning essay on slavery, came to Teston.[39] He spent a month with the vicar, James Ramsay, former rector of St Kitt's, who at the request of Lady Middleton, the first woman known to have associated herself with the abolitionist movement, had written two anti-slavery pamphlets.[40] One evening over dinner with the Middletons Clarkson blurted out to his delighted hosts his readiness to devote himself to the cause. On leaving Teston, he visited the port of London, and for the first time boarded a slave ship. While in London he met John Newton, whose first-hand experience of the trade made him an especially valuable witness. He then called upon William Wilberforce, who told him 'that the subject had often employed his thoughts, and that it was near his heart'.[41]

At the beginning of the eighteenth century hardly anyone questioned the morality of slavery and the slave trade. At the end of the century, however, the moral high ground had been surrendered to the abolitionists, and those who argued for its retention usually did so on the grounds of expediency and utility. Various factors—religious, cultural, possibly economic—combined

---

[36] *FFBJ*, 14 May 1786.

[37] Anson MSS, doc. folder 8, More to Mary Hamilton, 3 June 1786.   [38] Roberts, ii. 24.

[39] This paragraph is based on T. Clarkson, *History of the Rise, Progress, and Accomplishment of the Abolition of the African Slave Trade by the British Parliament* (London, 1839), 145–55. For Clarkson, see E. Gibson Wilson, *Thomas Clarkson: A Biography* (Basingstoke, 1989).

[40] J. Ramsay, *An Essay on the Treatment and Conversion of African Slaves in the British Sugar Colonies* (London, 1784); id., *An Enquiry into the Effects of Putting a Stop to the African Slave Trade* (London, 1784). For Ramsay, see F. Shyllon, *James Ramsay: The Unknown Abolitionist* (Edinburgh, 1977).

[41] Clarkson, *Abolition*, 154.

to bring about one of the most remarkable changes in sensibility in human history.[42] For a start, the complacent belief that Britain was uniquely the home of liberty was hard to reconcile with the enslavement of fellow human beings. It was on these grounds that Lord Chief Justice Mansfield, in his landmark judgment of 1772, reluctantly decided that a slave whose master had brought him to England could be freed; the last public sale of a black slave in England took place in Liverpool in 1779. At the same time moral philosophy extolled the virtue of benevolence, and the cult of sensibility privileged compassion, while the popular themes of primitivism and the noble savage found dramatic form in Thomas Southerne's play *Oroonoko*, based on Aphra Behn's novel. It was performed throughout the eighteenth century, and, in setting up the negro as a hero and the Europeans as villains, it disturbingly inverted traditional racial hierarchies. Devout Christians, too, were increasingly outraged by the sheer cruelty of what John Wesley called 'this infernal traffic'.[43] Samuel Johnson startled an Oxford gathering when he drank to 'the next insurrection of the negroes in the West Indies', and during the American Revolution enquired with memorable sarcasm, 'how is that we hear the loudest *yelps* for liberty among the drivers of negroes?'[44]

But though most right-thinking people deplored the slave trade (and some went further and opposed the very institution of slavery), it was hard to fight the powerful vested interests that supported it, not least in Hannah More's city of Bristol.[45] As Thomas Clarkson was to discover, 'everybody [in Bristol] seemed to execrate it, though no one thought of its abolition'.[46] But the whole nation was compromised. The sugar that women put in their tea and cake mixtures, the tobacco the men stuffed into their pipes, the rum beloved of the Royal Navy, were products of the slave plantations. Textiles and hardware manufactured in Britain were transported to Africa to be traded for slaves. The high-minded More sisters ran a school that included the daughters of planters among its pupils. To overturn the nation's participation, voluntary and involuntary, in a trade that affected so many aspects of its life would be a Herculean effort involving reserves of courage, energy, and perseverance that few could aspire to.

The movement for abolition began with the Quakers. In 1783 the London Yearly Meeting presented a petition to the Commons arguing, in a synthesis

---

[42] See e.g. R. Anstey, *The Atlantic Slave Trade and British Abolition* (London, 1975); C. Bolt and S. Drescher (eds.), *Anti-Slavery, Religion and Reform: Essays in Memory of Roger Anstey* (Folkestone, 1980); H. Thomas, *The Slave Trade: The History of the Atlantic Slave Trade, 1440–1870* (Basingstoke, 1998), 447–556.

[43] Quoted in Anstey, *Atlantic Slave Trade*, 240.

[44] Quoted in J. Boswell, *Life of Johnson*, ed. G. Birkbeck Hill (Oxford, 1934), iii. 201.

[45] Morgan, *Bristol and the Atlantic Trade*, 123–51; D. Richardson, *The Bristol Slave Traders: A Collective Portrait* (Bristol, 1996).

[46] Clarkson, *Abolition*, 182.

of Christian and Enlightenment thinking, that the trade was inconsistent not only with Christianity but also with humanity, justice, and the natural rights of mankind. In the same year Beilby Porteus, himself the son of a Virginia tobacco planter, denounced it in a powerful sermon before the Society for the Propagation of the Gospel,[47] and the abolitionist Granville Sharp brought a prosecution against the owners of the Liverpool slave ship the *Zong*, whose captain had thrown slaves overboard during a storm at sea in order to save the insurance money, an incident that was later to be portrayed in one of Turner's most disturbing paintings. The failure of the prosecution, on the grounds that slaves were disposable livestock, exposed as nothing else could the horrifying implications of the trade. Ramsay's pamphlets appeared in the following year, to be followed by the publication of Clarkson's essay in 1786.

This was the situation when Hannah More discussed the slave trade with Lady Middleton in the early summer of 1786. She had already practised her arguments against the trade on Lord Monboddo,[48] and with all her closest friends so firmly abolitionist, it is hardly surprising that she too should have become caught up in the cause. In the spring and summer of 1787 the movement took off and became the first of the great middle-class pressure groups that have so influenced British politics and society.[49] In March Wilberforce was invited by a gathering that included Clarkson and Sir Charles Middleton to assume the parliamentary leadership of the embryonic movement.[50] Clarkson was to assign great significance to this meeting; however, Wilberforce's sons, in their eagerness to snub a man they saw as their father's rival, made much more of a meeting with Pitt and the prime minister's cousin George Grenville at Keston in Kent on 12 May, when the prime minister is alleged to have asked him to 'give notice of a motion on the Subject of the Slave Trade'.[51] The unseemly bickering was a diversion; by various means and through an assortment of individuals and groups, the abolitionist movement was coming into being as a national movement. On 22 May 1787 the Committee for the Abolition of the Slave Trade (the London Committee) was set up, composed mainly of Quakers, but with Granville Sharp as chairman. This Committee formally requested Clarkson to investigate the slave trade. He duly set out for Bristol, and on a hazy June evening he had his first glimpse of Hannah More's 'savage town' and 'began now to tremble . . . at the arduous task I had undertaken of attempting to subvert one

---

[47] B. Porteus, *A Sermon Preached before the Incorporated Society for the Propagation of the Gospel in Foreign Parts* (London, 1783), 16–17.

[48] Roberts, i. 254.

[49] J. R. Oldfield, *Popular Politics and British Anti-Slavery: The Mobilisation of Public Opinion against the Slave Trade, 1787–1807* (Manchester, 1995).

[50] Clarkson, *Abolition*, 160.   [51] Pollock, *Wilberforce*, 58.

of the branches of the commerce of the great place which was then before me'.[52]

Clarkson's account of his visit is a brilliant piece of investigative journalism.[53] He quickly learned that the seamen on the slave ships were impressed when they were drunk, and, once caught up in the trade, suffered almost as much as the slaves themselves from the brutality of the captains. The business tainted all who touched it and Bristol became a nightmare place to Clarkson, containing 'nothing but misery'.[54] But in the city he met many convinced abolitionists, in particular the Quakers and Hannah More's friend Dean Tucker. He also had some contact with More herself, who arrived there a few days before him. Like him she sought out the Quakers and found them, as she told Middleton at the end of July, 'all charmed with the Negro Project'.[55] By September, however, she was more critical, complaining to Lady Middleton that 'nothing could be more lukewarm, cautious, and worldly wise than they are'. But she was able to report that 'Clarkson desires us to canvass for him from the Member of Parliament down to the common seaman'.[56] (The fact that his subsequent narrative made no mention of her is probably an indication of the cooling of his relationships with the Clapham sect in the wake of later political and personal differences.) The Clarkson visit energized More. Not only was she ready to canvass opinion, but she was even prepared to forget her growing scruples about the theatre. Could they not, she suggested to Lady Middleton, persuade Richard Brinsley Sheridan, the manager of the Drury Lane Theatre, to stage *Oroonoko* once more—'this on condition that they leave out the comic part, which is indecent and disgusting'? Could they not as well 'get some good poet to write an affecting prologue, descriptive of the miseries of those wretched negroes'? She wanted Sheridan to undertake this, 'but in case a *good* poet will not take the pains, I know a *bad* one who would attempt it, though she should be sorry not to see the campaign in better hands'.[57] She herself, of course, was the 'bad poet'.

Some time in the summer of 1787, before she came to Bristol, More had at last met William Wilberforce, and described him enthusiastically to Elizabeth Carter as a young man with 'the zeal of an apostle'.[58] His small frame, mobile features, quick-wittedness, irresistible charm and humour, his love of company, and his passionate commitment to his chosen calling might have reminded her of Garrick and drawn from her a similar emotional response.

---

[52] *Gambier*, i. 178; Clarkson, *Abolition*, 180.

[53] Clarkson, *Abolition*, 180–217; Peter Marshall, *The Anti-Slave Trade Movement in Bristol* (Bristol, 1996).

[54] Clarkson, *Abolition*, 217.   [55] *Gambier*, i. 167.   [56] Ibid. 169.   [57] Ibid. 170.

[58] Roberts, ii. 70–1.

She was not in love with him in a conventional sense, but, next to Patty, he came to mean more to her than any other individual. She was now advancing on her spiritual journey. Earlier in the year she had at last made contact with Newton, heard him preach, 'and afterwards went and sat an hour with him, and came home with two pockets full of sermons'.[59] They began to correspond, and in a letter from Cowslip Green on 1 November 1787 she poured out her heart.

I am certainly happier than in the agitation of the world, but I do not find that I am one bit better. . . . I can contrive to make so harmless an employment as the cultivation of flowers stand in the room of vice, by the great portion of time I give up to it, and by the entire dominion it has over my mind. You will tell me that if the affections be estranged from their proper object, it signifies not much whether a bunch of roses or a pack of cards effects it. I pass my life in intending to get the better of this, but life is passing away, and the reform never begins.[60]

Newton replied with understanding, telling her that she was on the first stage on the road to conversion, a process which was not necessarily sudden or dramatic;[61] and indeed Hannah More was never to experience an instantaneous transformation on the lines of John Wesley. There was no Damascus road, no sudden entering into the blessings of joy and peace, and she was later to condemn those who made such an experience the litmus test of true religion. But though she was unable to recount a single defining event, it was becoming clear that her life had taken a new direction.

At the end of the year she was back at the Adelphi with Mrs Garrick, gratified at the news that Porteus had been appointed bishop of London. Meanwhile, the bluestocking circle was changing irrevocably, as, following her husband's death, Mrs Vesey had lapsed first into depression and now into mental confusion. In the spring Hester Piozzi published Johnson's letters to her, which raised all the usual problems of raking over the lives and opinions of the recently dead. More's verdict was that 'they are such letters as ought to have been *written*, but ought never to have been *printed*'. When she and Burke discussed the burgeoning Johnson industry, he famously commented, 'How many maggots have crawled out of that great body!'[62] (Meanwhile, Boswell was assiduously gathering the materials for the *Life* that would surpass all the others.) She herself was once more in the news. Early in the year Sarah Siddons played Elwina at Drury Lane. The *Morning Post*, which did not love More, claimed that Mrs Siddons gave 'animation' to the play's 'dramatic insipidities' and attracted 'a tolerably numerous and elegant audience'.[63] Louis XVI's former finance minister Charles-Alexandre de Calonne had been whiling away his temporary exile by translating the play into French. But if

[59] Ibid. 54.   [60] Ibid. 88.   [61] Ibid. 89–93.   [62] Ibid. 100–1.
[63] *Morning Post*, 4 Jan. 1788.

More's vanity was tickled, she was careful to conceal it, and was unmoved when Walpole 'quite raved' at her for not going to see Mrs Siddons.[64] *Percy* was part of her past. Her priorities had shifted. She had two other literary projects in hand, and she was concerned to rush them both out early in the year in order to ensure maximum publicity.

Slavery: A Poem came out on 8 February, handsomely bound, priced at half a crown. At the same time John Newton's *Thoughts upon the African Slave Trade* was published.[65] In March John Wesley delivered a fierce anti-slavery sermon at the New Rooms in Bristol, and More achieved one of her wishes when *Oroonoko* was performed at Covent Garden. The purpose of this rush of activity was to soften up public opinion for the Commons debate in May on the bill put forward by Sir William Dolben, a leading Anglican layman and the MP for Oxford University, to regulate the number of slaves to be carried on each ship; in response, over a hundred petitions were presented to Parliament from all over the country. In many respects it was an unsatisfactory bill, and was open to the objection that, by making the crossing of the marginal passage slightly less horrific, it legitimized the trade. But it was a start and showed that the abolitionists meant business. The two members for Liverpool opposed the bill bitterly, as did Matthew Brickdale, one of the Bristol MPs. On the other hand, with strong support from Pitt, the bill was passed by the Commons, and after some complicated amendments by the Lords became law. It was round one to the abolitionists, but the supporters of the slave trade were now beginning to organize and it was to be nineteen years before the trade was finally abolished.

Hannah More was dismissive about *Slavery*, thinking the poem 'too short and too much hurried'.[66] The modern reader would probably consider it long enough for its purpose and would happily dispense with the strained rhetoric and the pseudo-classical sentimentality. However, the description of the effects of a slave raid, 'the burning village, and the blazing town', 'the shrieking babe, the agonizing wife' (lines 98, 100), is uncomfortably vivid, as is the passionate indictment of the forcible separation of parents and children.

> By felon hands, by one relentless stroke,
> See the fond links of feeling Nature broke!
> The fibres twisting round a parent's heart,
> Torn from their grasp, and bleeding as they part.   (lines 107–10)

The effectiveness of a passage like this depends on the ability of the white reader to identify with the sufferings of Africans, and it was part of More's purpose to refute theories of racial inferiority and climatic determinism by

---

[64] Roberts, ii. 99.
[65] J. Newton, *Thoughts upon the African Slave Trade* (London, 1788).   [66] Roberts, ii. 99.

showing that they had the same needs and emotions as Europeans and were equally made in the image of God.

> In every nature every clime the same,
> In all, these feelings equal sway maintain.   (lines 118–19)

She was engaging in an Enlightenment debate about the nature of human-kind. The botanist Carl Linnaeus had classed Africans as *Homo monstrosus*. David Hume had argued that they were 'naturally inferior' to whites, deficient in 'action and speculation. No ingenious manufactures amongst them, no arts, no sciences.' Even some abolitionists had a low view of their potential.[67] Many Christians accepted the legend that the blacks were the children of Ham, for ever accursed, their sole destiny (conveniently) being to serve the needs of the white man. However, neither Rational Dissenters such as Priestley nor Evangelicals like More could accept such a view, which had no foundation in the text of the Bible.

> What! does th' immortal principle within
> Change with the casual colour of a skin?   (lines 63–4)

In a possibly contradictory fashion, More linked this belief in the essential unity of the human race with the romantic concept of the noble savage. She had been deeply moved by Ramsay's tale of the negro Quashi, who cut his throat rather than face the indignity of the whip: a gesture of pagan nobility reminiscent of her earlier hero Regulus.

> A sense of worth, a conscience of desert,
> A high, unbroken haughtiness of heart;
> That self-same stuff which erst proud empires sway'd,
> Of which the conquerors of the world were made.
> Capricious fate of men! that very pride
> In Afric' scourg'd, in Rome was deified.   (lines 77–82)

The poem contains themes that were to resurface in her later political writings: a whiggish concern for rights and liberties, and a patriotic providentialism that took it for granted that Britain was a chosen nation with a special destiny. *Slavery* came out in the centenary year of the Glorious Revolution and thus coincided with a rethinking of the foundation principles of the eighteenth-century British state. Though a growing number of radicals were agitating for the reform of Parliament and the electoral system, Hannah More, with her 'conservative Whig' or Pittite politics, firmly believed that the Revolution had created a polity that was as near perfection as was possible in a fallen world. Its great achievement had been to guarantee the right to

---

[67] P. J. Marshall and G. Williams, *The Great Map of Mankind: British Perceptions of the World in the Age of Enlightenment* (London, 1982), 244–8.

liberty and property; but this threw into sharp relief the terrible contradiction that Britain, the freest state on earth, was also the leading slave-trading nation.

> Shall Britain, where the soul of Freedom reigns
> Forge chains for others she herself disdains?
> Forbid it, Heaven! O let the nations know
> The liberty she loves she will bestow;
> Not to herself the glorious gift confin'd,
> She spreads the blessing wide as humankind.   (lines 251–6)

Such sentiments can be read in two ways: as a critique of British hypocrisy or as typical British complacency. It can certainly be argued that patriotic language such as More's made the anti-slavery discourse fundamentally 'safe', with the slaves conveniently distanced from the British poor, whose miseries could be safely ignored. Abolition legitimized Britain's claim to be the arbiter of the civilized and uncivilized world, and gave the governing elite a painless way of claiming moral superiority.[68] In *Slavery*, Britons are encouraged to feel good about themselves, to contrast 'gentle Cook' and 'peaceful Penn' with the murderous Cortez, and Columbus, the 'detested Lord' of 'plunder'd realms' (lines 220–50). The poem ends with a vision of a world freed from the slave trade: 'FAITH and FREEDOM spring from Mercy's hands.' In later editions of the poem this was changed to 'Britain's hands'. Patriotism and humanity were to go hand in hand, providing a convenient justification for the subsequent expansion of the British empire.

However, to press this argument too far is to underplay the hard fight the abolitionists faced in persuading the nation to take a very real economic and political risk.[69] It is to make light, as well, of the personal toll: the constant supping with horrors as they studied the details of the trade, the nervous strain of coping with vitriolic press attacks, the sheer marathon reserves of energy and endurance needed to sustain them over the wearisome twenty-year fight. During the long years of struggle it was not always possible to allow the nation to bask in a glow of superiority. In November 1795 More was to publish the Cheap Repository ballad *The Sorrows of Yamba; or, The Negro Woman's Lamentation*. At a time when abolitionists were tempted to tone down their arguments in the face of the threat of radicalism, she risked taking the anti-slavery arguments to a wider audience. The baptized slave Yamba uses the patriotic language of a nation at war, echoing *Rule Britannia* and *Heart of Oak*, but in order to condemn British policy.

---

[68] L. Colley, *Britons: Forging the Nation, 1707–1837* (New Haven, 1992), 359–60.

[69] See S. Drescher, *Econocide: British Slavery in the Era of Abolition* (Pittsburgh, 1977); id., *Capitalism and Antislavery: British Mobilization in Comparative Perspective* (New York, 1987); id., 'Whose Abolition? Popular Pressure and the Ending of the British Slave Trade', *Past and Present*, 43 (1994), 136–43.

British laws shall ne'er befriend me,
They protect not slaves like me.

Britons must therefore abandon their cruel hypocrisy.

Ye that boast 'ye rule the waves'
Bid no slave-ship sail the sea;
Ye that *'never will be slaves'*
Bid poor Afric's land be free.

Involving as it did a doctrine of spiritual equality, a critique of government complicity, and an attack on vested interests, abolition was always potentially subversive: even when its protagonist was a political conservative like Hannah More.

More's second publication of 1788 was superficially very different, though in reality it was simply another facet of the increasingly ambitious Evangelical agenda for the transformation of society. At the end of 1787 Wilberforce had recorded in his diary, 'God Almighty has set before me two great objects, the suppression of the Slave Trade and the Reformation of Manners.'[70] Many, then and later, have praised his long and dogged campaign for abolition, but have looked askance at the moral harshness that lay behind his concern to regulate the conduct of others; but he saw no contradiction. Abolition and the reformation of manners were two aspects of the same urgent need for the nation to clear its moral debts before it faced the inevitable judgement of a righteous God. Furthermore, anxieties about the state of the nation ranged well beyond the Evangelical community. Moralists had been vocal throughout the eighteenth century, but became increasingly active in the 1780s. The decade had opened unpropitiously with the Gordon riots, defeat in America, and a growing concern with crime and poverty. Faced with these problems, many believed religious reform was the key to national revival.[71] The following years saw a revival of the charity school movement, the founding of Sunday schools, and an increase in the number of sermons and tracts advocating the stricter enforcement of the sabbath and the laws against vice. Porteus's successful bill banning debating societies was one aspect of this trend.

---

[70] *Life of Wilberforce*, i. 149.
[71] For the reformation of manners, see M. Quinlan, *Victorian Prelude: A History of English Manners, 1700–1830* (New York, 1941); J. Innes, 'Politics and Morals: The Reformation of Manners Movement in Later Eighteenth-Century England', in E. Hellmuth (ed.), *The Transformation of Political Culture: England and Germany in the Late Eighteenth Century* (Oxford and London, 1990), 57–118 ; D. T. Andrew, *Philanthropy and Police: London Charity in the Eighteenth Century* (Princeton, 1989); ead., ' "Adultery à-la-Mode": Privilege, the Law, and Attitudes to Adultery, 1770–1809', *History*, 82 (1997), 5–23.

On 1 June 1787, in a sign of the new moral climate, George III acted on a request from the archbishop of Canterbury, who had himself been primed by Porteus and Wilberforce, and issued a proclamation for the discouragement of vice. Many magistrates responded with enthusiasm, resolving to be more vigilant in issuing alehouse licences and to control disorderly entertainments. Meanwhile, in his diary of 5 August 1787 Porteus recorded that he was 'approached by friends about the formation of a society... *for the Reformation of Manners* ... to enforce the Execution of the Laws against Drunkenness, Lewdness, indecent Prints & indecent Publications, disorderly Public Houses & all the various Profanations of the Lord's Day'.[72] In November the Society for Carrying into Effect His Majesty's Proclamation against Vice and Immorality held its first formal meeting, though it did not officially come into being until early in the following year.

Though it clearly anticipated many of the characteristics of 'Victorianism', the Proclamation Society was modelled on an earlier reformation of manners movement, when William III, Mary II, and Queen Anne had issued proclamations against vice and immorality, and local interest groups and voluntary societies had put pressure on the magistrates to enforce the laws against blasphemy, prostitution, and Sunday trading.[73] Its members were predominantly laymen, mainly from the gentry, mercantile, and parliamentary classes, with strong support at the local level, from the county magistrates. The Society's critics saw its activities as thoroughly class-biased, aimed solely at suppressing the pleasures of the poor. This, however, was not the intention of the founders, who continually stressed that the vices they wished to eradicate took place in the elegant streets and squares of St James's as well as in village alehouses. As some Westminster magistrates pointed out, 'it is not only vain, but highly *partial* and *cruel* to execute the laws on the lower ranks of people only'.[74] But in practice it was impossible for the Proclamation Society and the Vice Society which succeeded it (and with which it is often confused) to be even-handed. When the king prohibited 'all our loving subjects of what degree or quality soever, from playing on the Lord's Day at dice, cards, or any other game whatsoever, either in public or in private houses', the raffish set that congregated round the duchess of Devonshire and Charles James Fox responded with derision, and the law was powerless against them.[75] While the poor could be coerced, the rich had to be persuaded: a more demanding task, everyone agreed.

---

[72] Lambeth Palace, Porteus Correspondence and Papers, 2099, fo. 160.

[73] G. V. Portus, *Caritas Anglicana; or, An Historical Inquiry into those Religious and Philanthropical Societies that Flourished in England between the Years 1678 and 1740* (London, 1912).

[74] *Morning Herald*, 20 Mar. 1788.

[75] Quoted in Quinlan, *Victorian Prelude*, 54; A. Foreman, *Georgiana, Duchess of Devonshire* (London, 1999), 195.

One such attempt at persuasion was Hannah More's *Thoughts on the Import-ance of the Manners of the Great to General Society*, which was written immediately after the proclamation, and published anonymously in early March 1788. It sold out quickly, and within three months had gone through seven editions. Porteus, who had received a draft of part of the book, wrote to congratulate her on her 'delicious morsel', assuring her that it would be 'an excellent precursor to our society, and do half its business beforehand', and indeed the book had been written with this purpose in mind.[76] Yet its slant was subtly different, as More's fundamental target was neither the disorderly poor, nor the incorrigible gamblers at Devonshire House, but the religious complacency of the respectable, those who 'may be termed *good kind of people* . . . persons of rank and fortune who live within the restraints of moral obligation and acknowledge the truth of the Christian religion'.[77] Like the rich young ruler in the Gospel, such outwardly admirable individ-uals were basking dangerously in 'a treacherous security' and 'a fatal indo-lence', with hearts hardened by luxury and prosperity.[78] Their unthinking sabbath-breaking—attending Sunday concerts, walking in public gardens on Sunday—was merely the outward sign of their religious laxity.[79] Yet Sunday was 'a kind of Christian Palladium', the last citadel of the city of God against the forces of secularization.[80] Secure in their comfortable lives, the rich failed to recognize their obligations to those below them, such as the hairdressers they kept from church by employing them on the sabbath.[81] They wrongly assumed that the poor would not notice the unfairness of legislation that punished them alone. Yet, 'will not the common people think it a little inequitable that they are abridged of the diversions of the public-house and the gaming-yard on Sunday evening, when they shall hear that many houses of the first nobility are on that evening crowded with company?'[82] For this reason, 'Reformation must begin with the GREAT, or it will never be effec-tual. . . . To expect to reform the poor while the opulent are corrupt, is to throw odours into the stream while the springs are poisoned.'[83]

Uncomfortably aware that she did not 'live up to my song', and that 'my own life is not as strict as the life I recommend', More was anxious to preserve her anonymity.[84] Knowledge of the book's authorship soon seeped out, how-ever. Queen Charlotte was one of the earliest readers, as Mary Hamilton (Mrs Dickenson) told More when they met after a long absence in 1825:

When she came to the passage which censured the practice of ladies in sending on Sundays for a hair-dresser, she exclaimed, 'This I am sure is Hannah More; she is

---

[76] Roberts, ii. 83; *Thoughts on the Importance of the Manners of the Great to General Society* (4th edn. London, 1788), 30.
[77] *Manners of the Great*, 3. [78] Ibid. 5–10, 13–14. [79] Ibid. 40–1, 48–9.
[80] Ibid. 55–7. [81] Ibid. 37. [82] Ibid. 119–21. [83] Ibid. 117.
[84] *Gambier*, i. 166.

in the right, and I will never send for one again.' She did not mean she would not have her hair dressed on a Sunday, but she would not compel a poor tradesmen to violate the Sabbath, but rather employ her own household.[85]

The queen lent the book to Fanny Burney, then her deputy mistress of the robes, who confided to her journal, 'The design is very laudable, and speaks a mind earnest to promote religion and its duties; but it sometimes points out imperfections almost unavoidable, with amendments almost impracticable.'[86] There was unequivocal praise, however, from More's episcopal friend Shute Barrington of Salisbury (he became bishop of Durham in 1791). When she introduced him to another female reformer, Sarah Trimmer, Sunday school founder and editor of the *Family Magazine*, she told a sister, 'The Bishop diverted us by saying he was between two very singular women, one who undertook to reform all the *poor*, and the other all the *great*; but he congratulated *her* on having the most hopeful subjects.'[87] This commendation highlighted the role women were beginning to take in the reformation of manners movement. Female participation was to increase greatly during the subsequent decades, and make the all-male Proclamation Society look somewhat old-fashioned. When the Vice Society was founded in 1802, women made up 39 per cent of its initial membership, and the Society went out of its way to solicit the 'Patronage and Support of Ladies'.[88] A new type of female activism was coming into existence with important consequences for the future.

One regrettable consequence of the book was the straining of More's friendship with Walpole, though his condemnation of her 'Puritanism' left her unmoved.

He defended (and that was the joke)—religion against me...that the Fourth Commandment was the most amiable and merciful law that ever was promulgated, as it entirely considers the ease and comfort of the hard-working poor, and beasts of burden; but that it was never intended for people of fashion, as they never do any thing on the other days....He really pretended to be in earnest, and we parted mutually unconverted.[89]

Following this altercation, the two of them worked hard at re-establishing common ground. Returning to her beloved 'casa mia' in November, she sent him one of her most spontaneous letters. She had a piece of news that she knew would tickle his fancy: the great John Locke had been born in 'a little

---

[85] Roberts, iv. 264.   [86] *Diary and Letters of Madame d'Arblay* (London, 1842), iii. 108–9.

[87] Roberts, ii. 101.

[88] Stott, 'Hannah More', 137–8. For the Vice Society, see M. J. D. Roberts, 'The Society for the Suppression of Vice and its Early Critics, 1802–1812', *Historical Journal*, 26 (1983), 159–76.

[89] Roberts, ii. 111.

white house' in Wrington. 'He did not intend to have been born here, but his mother was on a visit when she produced this bright *idea*, and so bequeathed me something to boast of.'[90] The author of *Slavery* could indeed take pride in the link. It was Locke who was the founding father of the doctrines of rights and liberties that had been such an indispensable part of her argument, and his views on education were to influence her own practice when she set up her Sunday schools. There is no evidence that she read his political writings in any systematic fashion, and she ignored the radicalism behind his assertion that the people had the right to overthrow an unjust sovereign. For her he stood, in a vague but satisfying fashion, for enlightenment in general. His achievement, as she told Walpole, in a thoroughly eighteenth-century contempt for medieval philosophy, was that he 'broke the ranks of Aristotle and swept away the metaphysical cobwebs which the subtle spiders of casuistry had been weaving with fruitless industry for many an age'.[91] In 1791 Elizabeth Montagu, who shared her admiration, presented her with an urn inscribed

> To John Locke
> (born in this village)
> This memorial is executed
> by Mrs Montagu
> and presented to Hannah More.[92]

She took it with her when she moved to Barley Wood, where it delighted a couple of Persian visitors who called on her some time in 1818, and was a feature of the grounds long after her death.[93] (There are now busts of More and Locke on either side of the door of Wrington church.)

Cowslip Green was relaxing in a way London could never be. She could dress casually and had only herself to please. She told Mary Hamilton (Mrs Dickenson) that she had 'not dressed my hair, or written a Card or told a Lye (not in writing I mean) these seven weeks'. She spent her days riding round the countryside, gathering watercress and digging up wild flowers for her garden. In the afternoons she drank tea in a little root-house she had built—a garden-house formed from roots, stumps, and gnarled branches, and now covered with periwinkles and honeysuckle.[94] Her only frustrations were that the birds were attacking her cherry trees, causing her, she told Charlotte Walsingham, to lose her sentimental attachment to 'the harmonious thieves ...I talk of imprisonment and murder with as much sang froid as an African Slave merchant. I, who cou'd once be pathetic over a pigeon pye,

---

[90] Ibid. 122.   [91] Ibid.
[92] Huntington, MO 4002, More to Elizabeth Montagu, 14 Aug. 1791.
[93] Clark, More to [Zachary Macaulay], Tuesday morning [1818].
[94] Anson, *Mary Hamilton*, 291–2.

can now talk with spiteful delight of Sparrow dumplings, water wagtail Tarts, yellow-hammer fricasees, and—I had almost said—Robin redbreast pudding.'[95]

Yet in another mood she could see this very delight in the countryside as spiritually dangerous. As she told Newton, 'When I am in the great world, I consider myself as in an enemy's country... and this puts me upon my guard.' At Cowslip Green, however, surrounded by 'the lovely wonders' of nature, she would forget God, 'were it not for frequent nervous headaches and low fevers, which I find to be wonderfully wholesome for my moral health'.[96] She reflected bleakly that her retreat to the country seemed to have achieved the exact opposite of its purpose.

With the tensions between the two sides of her nature still unresolved, she returned to London at the end of the year to find the political world in turmoil. The king had apparently gone mad and the prime minister and the Foxite Whigs were locked into the tragi-comedy of the Regency Crisis. If the prince of Wales were confirmed as regent with full powers, then Pitt would be out of office. The crisis confirmed More's high opinion of Pitt and her distaste for the opposition. She was already disgusted with their conduct over the prosecution of Warren Hastings in the previous June, and she had returned her ticket rather than witness Sheridan's final peroration, thus missing the moment of high drama when he collapsed fainting into the arms of Burke.[97] But she followed closely the progress of the king's illness and was delighted at his recovery. In March she dined with his 'mad doctor' Dr Willis, and found him 'quite a good, plain, old-fashioned country parson'.[98] (The poor king saw him in a different light.) In April she had a ticket for the thanksgiving ceremony at St Paul's, where Porteus preached the sermon. She was 'very much affected at the sight of the king' but characteristically concerned that the 6,000 charity children, there at the queen's request, seemed to have nothing to eat or drink.[99] If she heard the crowd hiss the prince of Wales, or observed his very improper behaviour during the service, her comments have not been preserved.

Her life had fallen into a new pattern. Her stays with Mrs Garrick were shorter, and she spent weeks at a time either with the Middletons or at Fulham Palace, Porteus's residence as bishop of London. In the spring the abolitionist movement mounted its second great challenge, with the parliamentary campaign now spearheaded by Wilberforce. He spent some time with the Middletons working on his speech, and More hoped that Teston would be 'the Runnymede of the negroes, and that the great charter of

---

[95] Clark, More to Charlotte Walsingham, 23 July 1788. [96] Roberts, ii. 116–17.
[97] Ibid. 108–9; *Morning Herald*, 20 June 1788; *Morning Post*, 14 June 1788.
[98] Roberts, ii. 144. [99] Ibid. 153.

African liberty will be there completed'.[100] On 12 May he delivered his speech—a virtuoso piece of oratory lasting three and a half hours—and was supported by Fox and Burke. But the opponents of abolition, including (again) the members for Bristol and Liverpool, closed ranks and the bill was lost. His journal of 23 June contained the dispiriting entry: 'Slave business put off till next year.'[101]

The spring of 1789 gave More a further opportunity to renew her friendship with Walpole. With Porteus now installed at the bishop of London's residence at Fulham, only a short distance from Strawberry Hill, the two men began to visit each other, with Hannah More providing a further link between them. One day Walpole was dining at Fulham with More, Ann Kennicott, and Mrs Garrick. Mrs Kennicott later reminisced about how the ladies were alarmed at seeing their host's face 'assume a most cadaverous appearance... and how they were lamenting in the Drawing room till I assured them it was occasioned by his blowing his nose with a new blue handkerchief'.[102] At about this time Porteus cut a narrow walk through the thicket of his grounds, opening it up to the light, and named it 'Monk's-Walk'. When More visited him in June, this Gothic conceit inspired her to write a poem, *Bishop Bonner's Ghost*. Edmund Bonner, Porteus's notorious predecessor as bishop of London, was the chief persecutor of Mary Tudor's reign, the villain of Foxe's *Acts and Monuments*, and an easy target in the decade that had begun with the anti-Catholic Gordon Riots. In the poem his disconsolate shade rebukes his successor for his symbolic gesture in opening up a dark glade. The ghost describes Porteus with horror as 'a prelate with a wife', who joins his 'pious labours' with 'domestic bliss', and supports the great causes of abolition and religious toleration.

> Nor clime nor colour stays his hand;
> With charity depraved,
> He wou'd from Thames to Gambia's Strand
> Have all be free and sav'd.
>
> And who shall turn his wayward heart,
> His wilful spirit turn?
> For those his labours can't convert,
> His weakness will not burn.[103]

Enchanted with the poem, Walpole had 200 copies printed. A breakdown of the rolling press caused a short delay, but the poem was out on 18 July, the last of the Strawberry Hill publications.[104]

---

[100] Ibid. 156.   [101] *Life of Wilberforce*, ii. 224.
[102] Clark, Ann Kennicott to More, 23 Sept. [1808?].
[103] *Bishop Bonner's Ghost* (Twickenham, 1789); also in *Works* (1801), i. 35–41.
[104] Roberts, ii. 158–60; *Walpole*, 300–2, 306, 309, and n.

Zion's City

With the publication of *Bishop Bonner's Ghost*, Hannah More's reputation as (to quote a grudging Hester Thrale Piozzi) 'the cleverest of all us Female Wits'[105] was further enhanced. But she was to write no more works of this kind. By the end of the year she was preoccupied with the Sunday school she had founded at Cheddar and had neither the time nor the inclination to amuse her friends with her poetry. As the long gestation of her conversion came to fruition, she reached the turning point of her life, the second phase of her remarkable career. Walpole noted with regret the growth of her 'enthusiasm'; more bluntly, Mrs Garrick was to tell her that religion had spoiled her 'fine disposition'.[106] But if some friendships cooled, she made others of a younger generation—Wilberforce, Henry Thornton, Zachary Macaulay. Her new life seems on the whole to have made her happier, though it brought with it stresses greater than any she had previously experienced, and the nervous illnesses that had beset her all her life continued to prostrate her for days on end. Her surviving diaries show that she continually reproached herself for lack of the required religious fervour. At her best moments, however, with the pleasing assurance that she was now living the life God had intended for her, she achieved a sort of serenity. Though she never had the Calvinist's comfortable certainty of persevering to the end, she was able to echo the words of one of Newton's *Olney Hymns*.

> Saviour, if of Zion's city
> I thro' grace a member am;
> Let the world deride or pity,
> I will glory in thy name:
> Fading is the worldling's pleasure,
> All his boasted pomp and show;
> Solid joys and lasting treasure,
> None but Zion's children know.[107]

---

[105] H. L. Piozzi, *Thraliana: The Diary of Mrs Hester Lynch Thrale (Later Mrs Piozzi) 1776–1809*, ed. K. C. Balderston (Oxford, 1942), ii. 699.

[106] Clark, More to Mrs H. Thornton, 1798.   [107] *Olney Hymns*, 1. 60, st. 5.

Chapter 5

The Mendip Schools
1789–1795

HANNAH MORE entered her fifth decade believing it might be her last. The move to Cowslip Green was to be the final opportunity to find the peace she had been seeking. Away from the distractions of London she could attend to her soul; her idyllic cottage would be the tranquil antechamber of death. It was not to be. In spite of her frequent illnesses, the genes she had inherited from her father and grandmother had destined her for a long life, while her own busy nature gave her no rest. She was still driven, and always would be, by the powerful ambitions that had brought her to London fifteen years before. The fact that they were now directed to a different end, the glory of God rather than the advancement of Hannah More (though her critics might argue that the distinction was not clear-cut), meant that, if anything, her life was more strenuous and demanding than ever. In the next ten years she and her sister Patty (who was now the most significant person in her life) were to set up a series of schools in the Mendip area (at Cheddar, Shipham, Rowberrow, Sandford, Banwell, Congresbury, Yatton, Nailsea, Axbridge, Blagdon, and Wedmore), which, at the height of their prosperity, were attended by about 1,000 children; as late as 1824, when the elderly sisters had long delegated the work, there were 620 children in the remaining schools.[1] Though clerical hostility or sheer lack of viability forced the closure of most of the schools, those at Cheddar, Shipham, and Nailsea survived into the

---

[1] Bodleian, c. 48, fos. 36–7, More to Wilberforce, 31 July 1824.

twentieth century. The More sisters did more than any other individuals to establish elementary education in Somerset.[2]

The schools had their inimitable chronicler in Patty, whose journal, covering the years 1789 to 1799, was published as *Mendip Annals* in 1859 by Arthur Roberts, the son of Hannah More's biographer.[3] As the original journal seems to have been lost or destroyed, there is no means of knowing how intensively it was edited; however, the formlessness of the narrative, the repetitions, and the robust comments on the shortcomings of the local clergy suggest that the printed text is a reasonably faithful transcription of a journal that was written down at the time, rather than one composed with the benefit of hindsight.[4] In spite of a jarringly condescending tone, Patty showed considerable sympathy for the plight of the Mendip poor, and much indignation at the farmers who 'oppressed' them and the clergymen who 'neglected' them. The Mendip people emerge vividly from her narrative. She named names, gave details of their lives, and set down their views and attitudes, sometimes in tones of amused incredulity at their 'ignorance' and 'superstition'. Hannah, too, filled in the details in her Cheap Repository tracts, in particular, *The Sunday School* and *Hester Wilmot*, stories rooted in her own experiences.

The initiative for the schools is said to have come from William Wilberforce, now established after his great Commons speech of 12 May 1789 as the champion of the abolition of the slave trade. When Parliament was prorogued, he travelled to Bath with his sister Sarah. On Thursday 21 August the pair arrived at Cowslip Green for the first of many visits. The following morning Wilberforce was persuaded to visit Cheddar Gorge, though the women stayed at home. He set off, his carriage stocked with cold chicken and wine, but the spectacular landscape made little impression compared with the shock of his encounter with the destitute people scratching an existence in the caves, 'wretchedly poor and deficient in spiritual help' and 'grateful beyond measure' for the money he was able to give them.[5] On his return, when the meal was served and the servant sent away, he unburdened himself: 'Miss Hannah More, something must be done for Cheddar... If *you* will be at the trouble, *I* will be at the expense.'[6]

---

[2] P. Belham, 'The Origins of Elementary Education in Somerset, with Particular Reference to the Work of Hannah More in the Mendips', MA thesis, Bristol University, 1953; A. Stott, 'Hannah More: Evangelicalism, Cultural Reformation, and Loyalism', Ph.D. thesis (London, 1998), ch. 5.

[3] *MA*.

[4] A letter to Wilberforce reveals that in 1800 Patty was keeping a journal and had done so for some time. Duke, More to Wilberforce, *c.*28 Oct. 1800.

[5] H. Thompson, *The Life of Hannah More with Notices of her Sisters* (London, 1938), 85–6; *Life of Wilberforce*, i. 238–9.

[6] *MA* 13.

The story thus related both by Patty More and by the Wilberforce sons in their biography of their father has about it a mythic, dramatized quality that must contain an element of distortion. Hannah More's long friendship with Wilberforce had only just begun, and a venture as ambitious, expensive, and time-consuming as the Mendip schools could hardly have owed its existence to a single incident. If any individual was the driving force behind the schools, it was Patty, whose efforts, herculean but self-effacing, surpassed her sister's. But it was More's practice to rationalize her grand projects and fend off accusations of presumption by asserting that she had been pressed into action by some prestigious male. In this case, Wilberforce's offer to fund any project she chose to undertake harmonized with her own unformed wishes. She had retreated to the countryside for some urgently felt but nebulous purpose; now she had found it.

By 'something' Wilberforce meant a Sunday school. Sunday schools were the most fashionable form of philanthropy, and the work of Robert Raikes at Painswick in Gloucestershire was being copied in many parts of the country, including the Bristol area.[7] Wilberforce's plea was made a mere four years after the foundation of the interdenominational Sunday School Society, of which he was a patron. By July 1789 the Society's schools contained over 41,000 scholars, and the numbers were rising all the time.[8] The schools were a response to the ever-present fears (shown in the formation of the Proclamation Society) of the lawless, uneducated poor. Unlike the charity schools, they did not take children away from their weekday work; their modest agenda concentrated on literacy, enabling the pupils to read the Bible, and on the inculcation of the socially desirable virtues of punctuality, cleanliness, and honesty. Influential supporters included two of More's friends, George Horne, then dean of Canterbury, and Beilby Porteus.[9] Women were prominent in the whole venture. Sarah Trimmer's school at Brentford had received wide publicity through her *Oeconomy of Charity*, and had gained the accolade of Queen Charlotte's patronage. More had visited it in 1788 and found it 'a scene ... of instruction and delight'.[10] At about the same time that the Mendip schools

---

[7] For examples of favourable reports of local Sunday schools, see *Bonner and Middleton's Bristol Journal*, 16 Oct. 1784; 9, 30 June, 14 July, 1787. When More began her work, there were also fifty-five charity schools in Somerset, the majority founded by endowment. Wrington, More's own village, had a Sunday school and a free school. Belham, 'Origins of Elementary Education', 11–16, 315, 150. For charity schools, see M. G. Jones, *The Charity School Movement: A Study of Eighteenth-Century Puritanism in Action* (Cambridge, 1938).

[8] *Woodfall's Register*, 14 July 1789.

[9] J. Gregory, 'The Eighteenth-Century Reformation: The Pastoral Task of the Anglican Clergy after 1689', in J. Walsh, C. Haydon, and S. Taylor (eds.), *The Church of England: From Toleration to Tractarianism c.1689–c.1833* (Cambridge, 1993), 77–9; B. Porteus, *A Letter to the Clergy of the Diocese of Chester concerning Sunday Schools* (London, 1786).

[10] S. Trimmer, *The Oeconomy of Charity; or, An Address to the Ladies concerning Sunday Schools* (London, 1787); Roberts, ii. 115.

were founded, Dorothy Wordsworth set up a little school in Norfolk, encouraged by Wilberforce, who promised her 10 guineas a year for the project.[11]

In spite of this respectable support, Sunday schools were still controversial, and those who advocated them were often forced onto the defensive. Critics believed that they gave the poor ideas above their station, unfitted them for their lowly occupations, and enabled them to read seditious literature. They have been condemned since by left-leaning historians for an agenda of regimentation which instilled into the poor the work disciplines appropriate for an industrializing society. E. P. Thompson famously portrayed the schools as counter-revolutionary institutions imposing an alien value system through 'psychological atrocities'. However, they have also been viewed more sympathetically as essentially the product of working-class communities, staffed by working-class teachers, and organized around local and neighbourhood needs.[12] More recently an interpretation influenced by the writings of Foucault sees the type of middle-class charity that the More sisters engaged in as an attempt to master and control the explosive and disruptive tendencies of the lower-class body.[13] However, the problem with hegemonic models, whether Marxist or Foucauldian, is that they deprive the poor of agency and identity, seeing them as essentially passive recipients of programmes that were opposed to their own best interests. The reality, as Hannah More was to discover, was that the Mendip people had ideas of their own, and, because they did not fear her, because she was not a clergyman, a magistrate, or a landlord, they were quick to give her their opinions and, if necessary, to obstruct her plans. Far from lording it over tame and submissive people, she constantly negotiated and compromised, winning some battles but retreating in others.

As if charging her batteries for her future endeavours, More went on a series of short holidays. On 24 August she and Patty accompanied William and Sarah Wilberforce first to Bristol and then over the Bristol Channel to the Wye Valley, a destination recently made popular by the publication of the second edition of William Gilpin's description of his tour.[14] With his book

---

[11] *The Letters of William and Dorothy Wordsworth*, i: *The Early Years, 1787–1805*, ed. E. de Selincourt, 2nd edn., rev. C. L. Shaver (Oxford, 1967), 26–7.

[12] E. P. Thompson, *The Making of the English Working Class* (Harmondsworth, 1968), 414; T. W. Laqueur, *Religion and Respectability: Sunday Schools and Working Class Culture, 1780–1850* (New Haven, 1976). See also K. Thompson, 'Religion, Class, and Control', in R. Bocock and K. Thompson (eds.), *Religion and Ideology* (Manchester, 1985), 126–53; D. Hempton, *Methodism and Politics in British Society, 1750–1850* (London, 1984), 87–90; K. D. M. Snell, 'The Sunday-School Movement in England and Wales: Child Labour, Denominational Control, and Working-Class Culture', *Past and Present*, 164 (Aug. 1999), 122–68.

[13] E. Kowaleski-Wallace, *Their Fathers' Daughters: Hannah More, Maria Edgeworth and Patriarchal Complicity* (New York, 1991), 68–72.

[14] *Life of Wilberforce*, i. 243; W. Gilpin, *Observations on the River Wye and Several Parts of South Wales* (2nd edn. London, 1789).

in hand, they journeyed by water from Chepstow to Tintern Abbey, and saw (as More told Pepys) the requisite number of 'ruined Abbeys, and dismantled Castles'. They 'admired the depredations of time, and deplored the devastations of Cromwell and Henry the eighth, those great Masters, as Mr Gilpin calls them, of picturesque Beauty'.[15] One wonders whether the party agreed with Gilpin's decidedly un-Wordsworthian criticisms of the 'vulgarity' of the shape of the gables of Tintern Abbey, or his view that 'a mallet judiciously used (but who durst use it?) might be of service in fracturing some of them'.[16] More seems to have read him slightly tongue in cheek. On the way home she paid a courtesy visit to the dowager duchess of Beaufort at Stoke, where the 'lovely scenery and delightful order tried to reconcile me as well as they cou'd to the total want of decay and absence of desolation'.[17] She finally returned to Cowslip Green with Mrs Garrick.[18] It was not until the third week in September that she and Patty visited Cheddar, in order to assess the state of the village.[19]

Cheddar, famous for its dramatic gorge and its cheeses, was a substantial, though impoverished, village of about 200 houses and over 1,000 inhabitants. The great majority worked in agriculture, though many of the women were employed in knitting and spinning or worked at the paper mill.[20] The spiritual needs of the village were served by the absentee vicar, the Revd John Rawbone, who passed most of his time in Oxford, and a curate who lived eight miles away in the pleasant cathedral city of Wells. The pair of them made little impact on the villagers, who, as Wilberforce put it, 'never saw the sun but one day in the year, and even the moon appeared but once a week for an hour or two'.[21] There was no kindly squire to offset the neglect of the parsons, though a Mrs Stagg, the proprietor of a white-lead works in Bristol, was described as the lady of the manor. But the Mendips were inhospitable territory for paternalism, and, with gentry thin on the ground, it was the farmers who mattered. They employed the poor as labourers, carried out inoculation programmes, and, through their control of the vestry, ruled the parishes. During her stay at Cheddar Hannah More quickly realized that these were the people, hard, unsentimental men, with a ruthlessly functional view of their labourers, she had to conciliate.

She soon learned that she could not take their support for granted. As she told Wilberforce,

---

[15] Clark, More to Pepys, 14 Sept. 1789.   [16] Gilpin, *Observations*, 47.
[17] *Walpole*, 320.
[18] Huntington, MO 3998, More to Elizabeth Montagu, 2 Sept. [1789].   [19] *MA* 13.
[20] J. Collinson, *The History and Antiquities of the County of Somerset* (Bath, 1791), iii. 572–7.
[21] *Life of Wilberforce*, i. 247.

I was told we shou'd meet with great opposition if I did not try to propitiate the chief Despot of the village, who is very rich and brutal; so I ventured into the Den of this monster, in a country as savage as himself, near Bridgewater. He begg'd I wou'd not think of bringing any religion into the Country; it was the worst thing in the world for the poor, for it made them lazy and useless.[22]

She likened her initial tour to an election canvass.

I found friends must be secured at all events, for if these rich savages set their face against us, and influenc'd the poor people, I thought nothing but hostilities wou'd ensue; so I made Eleven of these agreeable visits; but I was by this time improved in the arts of canvassing, and had better success. Miss Wilberforce wou'd have been shocked had she seen the petty Tyrants whose insolence I stroked and tamed, the ugly children I praised, the Pointers and spaniels I caressed, the cider I commended, the wine I drank and the brandy I might have drunk.

She found the farmers remarkably ignorant, 'drunk every day, and plunged in such vices as make me begin to think London a virtuous place'. Her plea to them was carefully worded: 'I ... said that I had a little plan which I hoped would secure their orchards from being robbed, their rabbits from being shot, their game from being stolen, and *might* lower the Poor Rates.' This argument, so shamelessly geared to the farmers' self-interest, worked. One family told the sisters that they had read about Sunday schools in the Bristol papers, and believed that 'their apples would be safer if the children were confined'.[23] Having been won over, the farmers found them a large unused ox-house, 'which, when a partition is taken down, and a window added, will receive a great number of children'.[24] Beside it was 'an excellent Garden of almost an acre of ground'. Drawing a deep breath, More agreed to take it for seven years at $6\frac{1}{2}$ guineas a year. 'There's courage for you!' she told Wilberforce triumphantly.[25] The long, single-storey, white-washed building, known locally as the Hannah More cottage, is now one of the landmarks of Cheddar.

Another decision made at this time was courageous to the point of being foolhardy. In the same letter she told Wilberforce that she had hired a teacher, a 'Mrs Easterbrook of whose judgment (Demons out of the question) I have a good opinion. I hope Miss W[ilberforce] won't be frightened, but I am afraid she must be a Methodist.'[26] Sarah Wilberforce might well have been apprehensive, as the name Easterbrook was at that time notorious not only in Bristol, but also in London. Mrs Easterbrook was probably the recently widowed mother of the Revd Joseph Easterbrook, vicar of the Temple church in Bristol and one of the most prominent clergyman in the city. In June 1788 he had been controversially involved in an incident in

---

[22] Bodleian, MS d. 17, fo. 6, More to Wilberforce, 24 Sept. 1789.   [23] *MA* 15.
[24] Bodleian, MS d. 17, fo. 6.   [25] Ibid.   [26] Ibid.

which a tailor named George Lukins, from the Mendip village of Yatton, had claimed to be possessed by demons. He and six 'Wesleyan' ministers performed an exorcism in front of a great crowd in the Temple church, after which Lukins was described as calm, happy, and thankful for his deliverance. Later, however, witnesses came forward to describe Lukins as a clever ventriloquist and confidence trickster.[27] More took the side of the sceptics. When Horace Walpole wrote her an indignant letter about 'the abominable mummery', she replied, like a fully paid-up Enlightenment rationalist, deploring 'the operation of fraud upon folly'.[28] But, as with so many of her letters to Walpole, this was a selective expression of her true opinions. Though she did not believe in the alleged miracle, she was prepared to overlook Mrs Easterbrook's credulity in the interests of finding a suitably evangelical teacher; 'enthusiasm' was always better than cold formalism. Wilberforce agreed with her action, yet sympathized with her dilemma. 'I fear with you', he wrote, 'nothing can be done in a regular way.' His advice was to 'send for a comet', and he recommended that More approach John Wesley.[29]

This letter later embarrassed Wilberforce's High Church sons, who pointed out (correctly) that the Methodist schism had not yet occurred and that the Wesley brothers were Anglican clergy. They added that Wilberforce met Charles Wesley at Hannah More's house in 1786.[30] Though no confirmatory evidence has been found, it was not an impossible scenario. Charles Wesley spent much of his time in Bristol; whatever her later reservations, More was on reasonably friendly terms with Methodists, and, as will be shown, she believed that they made the best Sunday school teachers. She later told friends that she regarded them as a form of alternative medicine: '*spiritual quacks* when the regular clergy fail to awaken & alarm, these will often produce the desired effect'.[31] Though for some reason Mrs Easterbrook was not appointed, this did not reflect a change of mind on More's part, as the new teacher, a widow from Yatton named Sarah Baber, was appointed on Mr Easterbrook's recommendation. It was Mrs Baber who had first alerted Easterbrook to Lukins's 'possession', and she was to show herself as zealous in her new vocation as any of the itinerant Methodists who were causing such anxiety in more sober religious circles.

The building had been found and the teacher hired. Wilberforce repeated his promise to fund the venture, and informed More about another source of

---

[27] *A Narrative of the Extraordinary Case of George Lukins of Yatton* (Bristol, 1788); J. Easterbrook, *An Appeal to the Public Respecting George Lukins, Called the Yatton Demoniac* (Bristol, 1788); S. Norman, *Authentic Anecdotes of George Lukins, the Yatton Demoniac* (Bristol, n.d.).

[28] *Walpole*, 276, 279–80.   [29] *Life of Wilberforce*, i. 247.   [30] Ibid. 248.

[31] M. J. Crossley-Evans (ed.), 'The Curtain Parted; or, Four Conversations with Hannah More, 1817–1818', *Transactions of the Bristol and Gloucestershire Archaeological Society*, 110 (1992), 202.

funding, his friend and second cousin Henry Thornton, banker and MP for Southwark, son of the wealthy philanthropist who had placed Newton in St Mary Woolnoth.[32] More wrote back approvingly. She had heard of Thornton's work in assisting the Sunday School Society's work of supplying books, and hoped he would be able to provide her own school with Bibles and prayer books.[33] This was the beginning of the warm and creative triangular relationship of More, Wilberforce, and Thornton. It was further cemented in 1792 when the two men set up a 'chummery' together in Thornton's house, Battersea Rise, situated to the west of Clapham Common, a marshy area undergoing rapid development. By the time Wilberforce moved into his house, Thornton had become very wealthy, having inherited £40,000 from his father; until his marriage he devoted six-sevenths of his income to charities, among which the Mendip schools were a high priority. A reserved, aloof man, Thornton was temperamentally very different from More. She was sometimes amused at his seriousness and at other times puzzled and hurt by the coldness of his manners, while he could misjudge her spectacularly in a way Wilberforce never did. Yet they cared deeply for each other. He fretted over her frequent illnesses, and lived in constant and gloomy expectation of her death. He died of tuberculosis in the harsh winter of 1815, predeceasing her by eighteen years.

By the beginning of October the More sisters were totally preoccupied with 'forming our little Colony'. Like most missionaries, they were dismayed at the attitudes of the natives. Their house visits unearthed only one Bible, and this was used as a stand for a geranium pot.[34] 'I find the People so ignorant so poor and so vicious,' Hannah More told Elizabeth Montagu, who along with Elizabeth Carter, was an early subscriber, 'that I consider it as a sort of Botany Bay Expedition.'[35] She was to recycle this newly topical analogy a good deal as she extended her work. On a pouring wet day, one of the worst of a dismal autumn, Sarah Baber, her daughter, who was to be the under-teacher, and a spinning mistress arrived at Cheddar in a cart. The sisters assembled the drenched women in the kitchen of the public house and they all tucked into a shoulder of mutton brought from the neighbouring market town of Axbridge. The school finally opened on 25 October, with 140 children. The More sisters, the teachers, and the children all processed to a church crowded with villagers eager to take a good look at 'the ladies'. The normally elusive clergyman, Patty wrote, 'was so very judicious as to give us a twelve minutes' discourse upon good Tory principles, upon the laws of the

---

[32] *Life of Wilberforce*, i. 247. For Thornton, see S. Meacham, *Henry Thornton of Clapham, 1760–1815* (Cambridge, Mass., 1964).

[33] Duke, More to Wilberforce [1789].   [34] *Gambier*, i. 176.

[35] Huntington, MO 3999, More to Elizabeth Montagu, 10 Oct. [1789].

land and the Divine right of kings; but the Divine right of the King of kings seemed to be a law above his comprehension'.[36]

The following day the sisters set up the spinning school, a weekly school for thirty girls, and then retreated, 'leaving poor Mrs Baber to encounter these savages, in a place where she was a total stranger'.[37] In spite of the sisters' efforts, the school of industry failed as such schools usually did, being unable to compete with established businesses. The Sunday school itself, however, proved such a success that some months later an evening class was set up for the parents. The programme was modest—the sisters read a chapter of the Bible and a sermon, sang a psalm, and closed with a prayer—but it persuaded John Rawbone, the absentee vicar, to put in an appearance at the adult class and to examine the children on their religious knowledge, after which, Patty noted dryly, 'he received his tithes and marched off'.[38]

A year later the sisters opened a school in the combined parishes of Shipham and Rowberrow, two poor and isolated villages high up in the Mendips, where the inhabitants mined *lapis calaminaris*, an ingredient used to convert copper into brass. When washed, baked, and sifted, the substance was sent in bags to the Bristol brass works. In Shipham many of the mines, from six to twelve fathoms deep, were found in the street, the yards, and even in the houses. In contrast to the agricultural areas, wages were high, sometimes a guinea a day, but employment was precarious, at the mercy of market fluctuations.[39] If Patty More is to be believed, it was a lawless area, where the constable did not venture, and such was their isolation that the villagers suspected that the sisters were about to sell their children into slavery.[40] The 94-year-old rector (unsurprisingly another absentee) allowed them to fit up his deserted parsonage house as a schoolroom, though, as More noted caustically, he insisted on charging rent.[41]

The search for a female teacher proved equally fruitful.

We heard in a tea-circle that a young woman, a poor farmer's daughter, who was employed in the laborious work of a dairy had, from the love of doing good, and a great desire of instructing the ignorant, raised a little Sunday-school of her own poor neighbours, and had actually collected thirty poor children, and from her little pittance bought books and provided rewards of gingerbread for those who improved most.[42]

The name of this paragon was Patience Seward. The sisters mounted their horses in pursuit of her, and found her milking her cow. 'All we had heard

---

[36] *MA* 22.   [37] Ibid. 22–3.   [38] Ibid. 25.

[39] Collinson, *History of Somerset*, iii. 599–600.

[40] However, she was probably exaggerating, as John Wesley had preached there in 1782 and had met with an encouraging response. *The Journal of John Wesley*, vi, ed. N. Curnock (London, 1915), 336.

[41] *MA* 30; *Gambier*, i. 179.   [42] *MA* 28.

we were now convinced was true, and even fell short of this girl's usefulness. She possessed a good understanding... could read and write very prettily, was deeply serious, and seemed pretty well acquainted with the Scriptures.'[43] It is worth examining Patty's vocabulary. The terms 'usefulness' and 'deeply serious' were part of the Evangelical code and show that the More sisters regarded Patience Seward as a true Christian who, young and untried as she was, could be entrusted with the spiritual welfare of the children of Shipham in preference to a teacher from a higher social stratum who lacked the 'vital religion' the Evangelicals believed was the essence of true Christianity. She was hired as mistress, and her half-sister Flower Waite, another farm servant, became the teacher at Rowberrow, along with two male teachers. In the next year, evening readings for adults were instituted at Shipham on the same pattern as those of Cheddar. These were held on a Thursday, under the control of the teacher, but on their visits the More sisters took over.

By this time the pattern was set for the foundation of further schools, at Sandford, Banwell, Congresbury (pronounced Coomesbury), Yatton, and Axbridge. It followed a formula: the cultivation of the parish elites, the finding or construction of a suitable building, the meeting with the parents, the hiring of the teachers (one male, one female, with under-teachers where necessary). Of the new schools the one at the ancient corporation town of Axbridge proved the most problematic. The eccentric incumbent, Thomas Gould, was described in lurid terms by Patty: 'the black shades of his character are too melancholy even to be sketched here'. The town itself was 'all anarchy and malice' while the 'ignorance and impertinence' of the people were indescribable. Yet rector and corporation declared that they had no objection to the school, which duly opened in September 1791 with 'upwards of a hundred poor, little dirty, wretched-looking creatures'. The master and mistress could not match Sarah Baber or Patience Seward in Evangelical fervour, being 'merely decent people', but, as Patty noted, 'nothing else presented'.[44] All in all, the sisters were rather gloomy about Axbridge.

During the summer of 1791 they explored the prospect of founding a school at Nailsea, another mining village. Situated eight miles of tortuous road from Wrington, it was an important centre of Mendip industry. Coal had been mined there for centuries, and in 1788 John Lucas, a glass-bottle manufacturer from Bristol, had set up a factory which manufactured green glass, dark for bottles, light for windows. One of the coal works was under contract to serve the glass-houses.[45] It was an area of relatively high wages but appalling working conditions, which bred tough, independent-minded workers, who, like the Kingswood colliers on the other side of Bristol, were

---

[43] *MA* 29.   [44] *MA* 41–2.
[45] *Victoria County History: A History of Somerset* (London, 1911; repr. 1986), ii. 385 and 431.

ready to take direct action when it suited them.[46] On 1 October the foundation stone of the school was laid, and in February 1792, in a move that was to have wide repercussions, the sisters hired a couple from Bath, 'well recommended for religious zeal and industry', as teachers.[47] This was their first encounter with Henry Young; ten years later the name of this obscure teacher with his Methodist sympathies and abrasive, tactless personality was to become notorious. The new school was attended by the children of poor farmers and colliers, and within a few months evening meetings were set up for the village teenagers, 'the great collier boys and some great girls'.[48]

One group remained untouched: the glass-house workers and their families, 200 people squeezed into wretched houses, an existence which for squalor and ignorance surpassed all the sisters had previously seen. But even this paled before the Dantesque horror of the furnaces where they worked. 'The high buildings of the glass-houses ranged before the doors of these cottages—the great furnaces roaring—the swearing, eating, and drinking of these half-dressed, black-looking beings, gave it a most infernal and horrid appearance.'[49] The men politely welcomed the sisters to 'Little Hell' and listened attentively as they talked about the school. Nothing was said about religion, which, as Patty realistically admitted, 'would have been a very indiscreet, and, I fear, unsuccessful beginning'. Instead, the sisters talked about their children 'making good servants, getting top places, going out into the world': in other words, escaping the hell of the glassworks.[50] However, when they returned the next year, they were 'civilly and kindly received' by the parents, but were given 'many lame apologies' for not sending their children more regularly.[51]

The Nailsea picture was mixed, but the rewards, when they came, were very great. The colliers' and farmers' children proved, 'to our great surprise, sharp and quick to learn', and many of them were able to read the Bible fluently after twenty-two weeks.[52] In the late summer of 1792 the whole of this mining area was disrupted by a series of strikes, spreading from Somerset to Kingswood, which resulted in across-the-board increases of pay: the hauliers', wages rose to 17*d.* a day, and those of the miners from 16*d.* to 18*d.*[53] The 'great boys' of the Nailsea school had joined the strike, and the sisters proved surprisingly understanding of their action. By September, however, they were back at the school. 'It would create a smile in a fine gentleman or lady to behold our mutual pleasure on meeting,' wrote Patty; 'it was something quite transporting.'[54] At the end of the year the sisters took

---

[46] R. Malcolmson, ' "A Set of Ungovernable People": The Kingswood Colliers in the Eighteenth Century', in J. Brewer and J. Styles (eds.), *An Ungovernable People: The English and their Law in the Seventeenth and Eighteenth Centuries* (London, 1980), 85–127.

[47] *MA* 55.   [48] *MA* 63.   [49] *MA* 62.   [50] *MA* 62.   [51] *MA* 90.

[52] *MA* 61.   [53] *FFBJ*, 23 Aug. 1792.   [54] *MA* 70.

their leave of this infant colony, and because the roads were almost impass-able they had to be brought out by men on horseback. The following Sunday (2 December) they took their leave of Cheddar. The children followed their chaise into the lane and they all parted 'with equal reluctance, mutually blessing and praying for each other'.[55] After this unsophisticated affection, the elegant artificiality of Bath must have come as an unwelcome culture shock.

By the time the Nailsea school was opened, the More sisters had expanded their activities in their other schools. At Cheddar they were greatly cheered by the fact that they had secured an Evangelical curate in the person of John Boak.[56] With his co-operation they organized the first of the school feasts. It was held on Callow Hill on 4 August 1791, and 500 children were fed. As Cheddar recorded a total population of 1,150 in the 1801 census, this must have included the great majority of the village children, and possibly some from outside the parish.[57] Decorated wagons left Cowslip Green early in the morning, carrying servants, pieces of beef, plum puddings, cakes, loaves, and a great cask of cider. The children lay hidden in a valley until the meal was ready, then at the sound of a horn the procession began, led by a boy carrying a flag, followed by Mrs Baber and the More sisters, and watched by 4,000 people. The children sang psalms as they processed, the girls carrying nosegays and the boys white rods; then they sat down to their food, which was served by visiting ladies, in a decorously Saturnalian inversion of the social order.[58] This colourful spectacle, which must have taken weeks to prepare, provided ritual, drama, and *tableaux vivants* to match the more elaborate ceremonies of Catholic countries. It was modelled on the feasts given by Robert Raikes at Painswick, and approximated on some degree to the existing parish wakes, which were also attended by visiting gentry.[59] Such manifestations of popular Anglicanism were attempts to help people identify with their parish churches, and to promote solidarity between classes and neighbourhoods, a particularly important consideration in the ideologically charged 1790s.

At other times the children were provided with lesser treats to keep them from the enticing counter-attractions of summer, listed by More as 'Birds' nesting, gathering nuts—robbing orchards—going miles to get wild straw-berries &c'. As she admitted to Wilberforce, 'These attractions wou'd quite thin the schools did we not watch for the seasons and counteract their

---

[55] *MA* 73.   [56] *MA* 42.
[57] *Victoria County History, Somerset*, ii. 352.   [58] *MA* 36; *FFBJ*, 13 Aug. 1791.
[59] R. W. Malcolmson, *Popular Recreations in English Society, 1780–1850* (Cambridge, 1973), 16–19; D. Hempton, *Religion and Political Culture in Britain and Ireland from the Glorious Revolution to the Decline of Empire* (Cambridge, 1996), 15–18.

temptations by pleasures of the same kind—such as giving out one Sunday that on the next fruit, Gingerbread or tarts will be provided.' In winter, she added realistically, 'bribes are less necessary'.[60] This strategy of bribery shows that, far from being harsh and oppressive, the Mendip schools had to work hard at being popular. If the pupils disliked them, they could simply stay away.

After two hectic years the sisters turned their attention to the women of the parishes. Preoccupied with the endless task of feeding their families on pitifully low incomes, many of them had proved very resistant to sending their children to Sunday schools. Some time later More put her experiences with such women into her Cheap Repository story *Hester Wilmot*. The energetic Mrs Jones (a thinly disguised Hannah More) calls on Rebecca Wilmot to ask her to send her 14-year-old daughter to the school. At first, Rebecca says she will only do this if Mrs Jones pays. Learning that this is out of the question, she changes tack and declares:

Religion is of no use that I know of but to make people hate their flesh and blood; and I see no good in learning, but to make folks proud and lazy and dirty . . . Hester has other fish to fry, but you may have some little ones if you will. No, said Mrs Jones, I will not. I have not set up a nursery but a school. I am not at this expence to take crying babes out of the mother's way, but to instruct reasonable beings in the way to eternal life; and it ought to be a rule in all schools not to take the troublesome young children unless the mother will try to spare the elder ones who are capable of learning.[61]

Rebecca is given the last word. 'The moment [Mrs Jones] went out of the house, Rebecca called out loud enough for her to hear, and ordered Hester to get the stone and a bit of sand to scrub out the prints of that dirty woman's shoes.'[62] Such rudeness might have been untypical, but Rebecca's readiness to use the school as a free nursery and her reluctance to dispense with her daughter's services were representative of the reactions of many of the Mendip mothers who, unconvinced of the value of religion or literacy, wanted domestic help and a free crèche. Even when they agreed to send their children, they could create difficulties; when she accompanied the More sisters to the Axbridge school in 1797, Barbara Wilberforce saw them confronted by an indignant mother angered at her son's 'petty punishment' for some trivial misdemeanour.[63]

Showing some sensitivity to the drudgery and insecurity of the women's lives, the sisters proposed to set up female benefit clubs, 'the men in this, as

---

[60] Duke, More to Wilberforce [1792 or 1793].   [61] *CRTEMR* 346–7.   [62] Ibid. 348.
[63] Bodleian, MS d. 20, Barbara Wilberforce, 'Recollections of Mrs Hannah More and her Sisters', fo. 38.

in most other things, having the advantage of such comforts'.[64] Female clubs had existed since the 1730s, and, thanks in part to the initiatives of upper- or middle-class women, they were on the increase at the end of the eighteenth century.[65] The More sisters wished to follow the traditional practice of such clubs, providing the women with sickness pay and a caudle drink after childbirth in return for a subscription of $1\frac{1}{2}d$. a week. This was a difficult project in the light of the women's poverty, and in some cases it could only give the illusion of self-reliance; in practice, the soft-hearted Hannah More often found herself privately subsidizing the scheme.[66] However, the plan, though sensible and compassionate, was drawn up without consultation, and when the sisters called a general meeting for the women of Rowberrow and Shipham to discuss its implementation, they faced an unexpectedly stormy reaction.

These wretches, half-naked, and . . . some of them almost half-starved, had a long contention with as much fury as they dared exhibit before us, declaring they would rather relinquish the comforts and blessings of assistance at their lying-ins, to enrich the stock and procure a handsome funeral; and I myself heard a Rowberrow woman declare—'What did a poor woman work hard for, but in hopes she should be put out of the world in a tidy way?' This was a pitch of absurdity almost beyond bearing.[67]

Faced with this clash of values (a few weeks later the women of Cheddar reacted in precisely the same way), the sisters negotiated a compromise: the women would be given the traditional caudle after childbirth *and* their families would receive 6*d*. when they died. At the same meeting a second proposition was put. This was that on her marriage a bride 'of good character' should receive 'a pair of white worsted stockings of our own knitting, five shillings and a Bible'. On hearing this, 'a universal smile graced their ferocious countenances'. Encouraged, the sisters put forward their third proposition, 'To prevent . . . the indecency of women appearing in a public house [we] promised to give tea and cakes on the annual day of the meeting; and for this we were indulged with another smile.'

This was the origin of the club feasts, mentions of which occur so frequently in Hannah More's correspondence. They were accompanied by a sermon and the reading of the 'Charge' (which rapidly taught the Mendip women that there was no such thing as a free lunch). The first was held at Shipham in September 1792 and was quickly followed by the Cheddar feast, and, as with the Sunday school celebrations, it showed the More sisters

---

[64] *MA* 63–4.

[65] P. Clark, *British Clubs and Societies, 1580–1800: The Origins of an Associational World* (Oxford, 2000), ch. 10. For the Mendip clubs, see E. J. Yeo, *The Contest for Social Science: Relations and Representations of Gender and Class* (London, 1996), 11–14.

[66] *MA* 64; Roberts, ii. 304.   [67] *MA* 64–6.

skilfully adapting existing traditions. Over a hundred women, all wearing the club's blue breast-knot, processed to the church, preceded by the Sunday school children and watched by a party of 'ladies'. 'The bells were set a-ringing, the singers assembled, and a band of musicians very gallantly stepped forward and played "God save the King" before us.' Throughout, as Patty recorded with some surprise, 'they all behaved incomparably'.[68] Complacently, the sisters chose to interpret this as evidence of their beneficial influence. Not everyone approved of what they were doing, however, and some critics accused them of 'spoiling' the women. This forced Hannah More on to the defensive, and made her refuse to use donated money to finance the feasts. She defended her practice in a letter to Wilberforce, whose sister was one of those who doubted the wisdom of her methods.

I do not think the generality are tender enough in their charity—judging of human nature partly by myself, I believe a kindness is often valued more than a benefit. Including the Women's Club-feasts and the children's dinner, I contrive in the course of this month to treat about 1700 in what *they* think a *grand way* for a little more than thirty Pounds—And why shou'd not these poor depressed creatures have one day of harmless pleasure in a year to look forward to?[69]

In 1793 she sent Ann Kennicott an account of the Shipham Feast of that year, held on a blazing July day. The sermon was preached by James Jones, but the star performers were the More sisters, who featured 'in the august Character of Presidents'. ('Painful pre-eminence', Hannah More added hastily, always sensitive to conduct that transgressed female propriety.) They placed themselves 'at the head of our grand procession, the music of half a Dozen Villages parading before us with *God save the King*, and then making Tea for these hungry hundreds; who, we diverted ourselves with calculating, drank twelve hundred dishes'. The women wore 'smart linen Gowns and good black hats' which they had bought out of their meagre wages. Two brides received their awards, and Hannah More 'presented these marriage prizes with as much ceremony, and they received them with as much joy as if they had been Marriage Settlements on twenty Sheets of Parchment'.[70] The presence of clergy and 'ladies' contributed, if More is to be believed, to a warm atmosphere of class harmony, and the careful intertwining of ritual, food, patriotism, and moralizing was typical of the club feasts as a whole.

The 'Charges' that followed the feasts were used to scold the women into 'good' behaviour, and at a distance of two centuries their exhortations can seem outrageously smug and moralistic. But what is equally striking is the fact that, having no external authority over the women, the sisters were

[68] *MA* 67.   [69] Bodleian, MS c. 48, fo. 53, More to Wilberforce, 8 Aug. [1793].
[70] Clark, More to Ann Kennicott, 18 July, 1793.

forced on to the defensive. Behind the bossy harangues of the Shipham Charge of 1795 lurked a good deal of anxiety. In the harsh conditions of that year the villagers were restive, and needed to be reminded of their lowly place in the divinely ordained hierarchy.

We are as much better judges than you can be who ought to preside over this school as the bishops are who ought to be minister of your parish . . . remember that rebellion against rulers first brought on the troubles in France. Grieved as we are to say, that in the distress of last winter there were people who *petitioned* against the hand that brought them assistance. Let the conscience of those ungrateful people ask them if they had the *smallest* relief from any *other* quarter.[71]

In the Cheddar Charge of the same year the women were reproached for spreading 'an evil tale' about the club and 'inventing complaints about the method of payment'.[72] They evidently grumbled about the sisters, both behind their backs and to their faces, feeling freer to complain to other women than to male authority figures. At the Shipham Club feast of 1795, not having grasped the principles behind an insurance policy, they came 'ripe for revolt . . . determined to complain of their good health always having prevented their taking out any of their own subscription'. They had to be won over by the presence of the 'genteel people', the generosity of the gifts, and the fact that the articles of the club were about to be printed (an indication of their respect for the written culture).[73] The very complaining was a tribute to the club enterprise; had it been of no account, they could simply have ignored it. When the scheme became fully established, a woman received 3s. a week sickness benefit and 7s. 6d. for a lying-in, a respectable sum in an economy where the average male agricultural wage was a shilling a day. The clearest sign of their success lies in their survival. In 1823 More told Henry Thornton's daughter,

I have appointed two Trustees to manage my clubs after my death . . . Tho my clubs receive but sixpence a month, you will see how rich we are. Dear P. and I put in a little sum at setting out, and we had *then* honorary members but we have had no help for many years, tho I entertain all the ladies in the country at a grand tea feast, on the Anniversary of each Club which costs me about ten pounds. It will add to my happiness in death that I will leave in these Clubs 14 or 15 hundred pounds; they are in parishes which never gave the smallest assistance. In a Club so rich I think no new Members should be admitted without five Shillings entrance.[74]

Colloquially known as the Hannah More clubs, they continued to exist until the twentieth century, when the creation of the welfare state seemed to make

---

[71] *MA* 46–52.   [72] *MA* 164.   [73] *MA* 146.
[74] Huntington, HM 25785, More to Marianne Thornton [1823].

them superfluous.[75] The Cheddar Club went out in style. The final meeting was held on 30 April 1951, when about £800 was distributed among the remaining ninety-five members, though they were informed that the original £1,117 which Hannah More left on trust could not be touched. The evening closed with a singing of 'Auld Lang Syne', and the official links were finally severed with 'the Great Lady', as the vicar called her. At about the same time the final payments were made from the Shipham Club.[76]

On any calculation the setting up of the schools and clubs was a remarkable venture for two middle-aged women, neither of them in good health. Male commentators were awed by a courage and determination that hardly fitted contemporary stereotypes of the frailer sex. Wilberforce thought the whole enterprise 'truly magnificent' and 'really sublime', and he compared the More sisters to Edmund Spenser's 'lady knights'.[77] The editor of the *Mendip Annals* resorted to classical history and compared Hannah and Patty to Xenophon's Ten Thousand.[78] As a good Calvinist, John Newton saw the fact that 'such an athletic service should be appointed for such delicate instruments' as a manifestation of the inscrutable power of God.[79] The whole project arose naturally from the sisters' deep religious commitment—relatively new in Hannah's case, perhaps more long-standing in Patty's—and in particular from the imperatives of Evangelical religion that laid such stress on the life of active goodness. It would be simplistic and reductionist to see this as no more than the religious masochism of a couple of pious spinsters. Of course there were sacrifices in abundance of time and money, but it is also likely that these two childless women, both of them gifted teachers, enjoyed their contacts with the children, their parents, and grandparents. Nevertheless, at times of sickness, discouragement, and sometimes crisis, exceptional qualities of perseverance were called for, and these qualities sprang out of a deep inner conviction which alone could sustain the momentum. They were working themselves almost to death (or so it seemed at times) for the immortal welfare of the Mendip people. This was an agenda that went far beyond the reinforcement of the social order.

To make this point is not to underplay the conservative and utilitarian aspects of More's programme or to deny that she was attempting to alter the

---

[75] Because of new legislation on friendly societies, the articles of the Cheddar Club were rewritten in 1908 and the club was reconstituted in 1909. A copy of the new articles is in the Wrington church rooms. The club's foundation date is given as 25 Sept. 1792. For 20th-century correspondence on the Cheddar Club, see SRO, D/P/ched. For the Shipham Club indentures from 1814 to 1892 and the winding up of the club by the Charity Commission, see SRO, DD/X/HMT/1.

[76] SRO, D/P/ched/17/6/5, club minute book, 1914–51 [unpaginated].

[77] *Life of Wilberforce*, i. 238, 249. See P. Demers, *The World of Hannah More* (Lexington, Ky., 1996), 15.

[78] *MA* 5.   [79] Roberts, ii. 286.

culture of the poor: to make them hard-working, God-fearing, law-abiding, and self-supporting, and thus to lessen the workload of the magistrates and the parish officers and to ease the financial burdens of the middle classes, the people who paid the poor rate. This was the argument she had used with some success to the Cheddar farmers. Her own practice in the Mendips showed that she took this seriously. She insisted, as far as possible, on a respectable outward appearance. In her Cheap Repository story *The Sunday School,* 'many a willing mother lent her tall daughter her hat, best cap and white handkerchief, and many a grateful father spared his linen waistcoat and bettermost hat, to induce his grown-up son to attend'.[80] Where, as was often the case, the poor could not afford to clothe themselves, she sometimes shamed the farmers into making donations towards their clothing.[81] In 1793 she commended the Shipham women 'on the ground of the children being kept cleaner and more civil'.[82] The Cheddar women were warned against the profanation of the sabbath 'by scenes exhibited in the cliffs too shocking and indelicate to be named here' and reproached for gossiping and complaining at the baker's shop and the paper mill ('that sink of sin and wickedness').[83] Other Charges delivered routine condemnations of fairs and dances, leaving the impression that the More sisters were highly suspicious of any pleasures that were not under the supervision of trustworthy members of the elite. Above all, the bribing of virginal brides with money and stockings was an unashamed piece of social engineering.

Indignation about such bossiness, however, can lead to a caricatured picture of More's programme as an instrument of class oppression. The sentiments of one particular letter have been quoted again and again, though with scant reference to the context: 'My plan for instructing the poor is very limited and strict. They learn of weekdays such coarse works as may fit them for servants. I allow of no writing. My object has not been to teach dogmas and opinions but to form the lower class to habits of industry and virtue.'[84] The letter was written to the extreme conservative Dr John Bowdler (brother of the 'bowdlerizer' of Shakespeare), who needed to be reassured that the schools were not subversive. In seeking the support of those who were more reactionary than herself, More felt obliged to stress the utilitarian aspects of her programme at the expense of more controversial aims. She was forced to guard against critics like Dr Edward Tatham, the fiery High Church, high-Tory rector of Lincoln College, Oxford, 'a blind and furious stickler for Aristocracy'. 'I had hoped to be a favourite with him', she told Wilberforce, 'but now he says I am labouring to ruin this Country by enlightening the Common people, the *source of all national ruin.*'[85] A few years later, writing

---

[80] *CRTEMR* 330.   [81] *MA* 68.   [82] *MA* 82.   [83] *MA* 158, 164.
[84] *MA* 6.   [85] Duke, More to Wilberforce, 3 Aug. 1796.

to George Pretyman, bishop of Lincoln, she still felt the need to deride the view that 'gross ignorance will infallibly secure obedience. Did France, did Ireland, find this to be the case?'[86] Her public statements about the limited nature of her schools have to be read in the light of her need to guard her right flank.

Her private correspondence, on the other hand, shows her contempt for the ultra-conservatives. For example, in a letter to Wilberforce at the height of the club feasts season she wrote sarcastically about the local landowner Hiley Addington, brother of the future prime minister and a man she regarded as 'extremely hostile to the education of the poor'.[87]

You will be pleased to hear that the Addingtons are so affected by one of those meetings, Sermon &c which they attended that *he* declared that he would not have missed it for £50 and she wept the whole time, but then alas, the only inference they drew was a political one, viz: that if *every body* did the things we do, there would not be a *Democrat* in the kingdom.[88]

More was no more a political democrat than the Addingtons, but her programme for the poor was far more ambitious than theirs. Essential though it was to teach obedience, industry, contentment, and chastity, she believed that moral reformation, unaccompanied by a fundamental change of heart, would merely create plebeian versions of the 'good sort of people' that she targeted in her conduct literature. Such were the types she found at Congresbury, where the people were 'though not in the same state of *barbarity* with our other villages, yet quite as far from *Christianity*'.[89] It was a considerable achievement to turn naughty boys and wayward girls into solid citizens, but the distinction between outward respectability and true inward religion could never be forgotten. It was the belief that they were dealing with the eternal destiny of the Mendip people that ultimately inspired the sisters to undertake the work.

It also exposed them to considerable risks. One evening in Cheddar in 1792 Patty taxed Mrs Baber about the 'state of the poor people's minds' and received a solemn assurance that 'upwards of twenty were under the deepest convictions, and as many more in a hopeful way'.[90] This was Methodist language, and the old woman in the Shipham workhouse who declared that the prayers conducted there were '*Wesleying*' was not alone in her suspicions.[91] Patty's description of an event at Nailsea in 1793 could have come from John Wesley's journal: 'Three young men, (one profligate to excess) and three old ones appeared, bowed down as it were by the weight of their

---

[86] Centre for Kentish Studies, Stanhope U1590/S5/3/6, More to the bishop of Lincoln, 24 Sept. 1800.
[87] Duke, More to Wilberforce, 18 Mar. 1801.   [88] Duke, More to Wilberforce [1799].
[89] *MA* 34.   [90] *MA* 60.   [91] *MA* 54-5.

sins, groaning under the heavy burden, and crying aloud to the Physician of souls.'[92] Religious emotions thus awakened were difficult to control, and were not always compatible with the hierarchical society the More sisters said they wished to reinforce. An impoverished labourer converted to vital religion became the spiritual equal of any other Christian and, even more to the point, the spiritual superior of those bishops and aristocrats whose religion was merely formal. As the conservative reaction deepened at a time of national danger, the inevitable contradictions in their programme were to rise up and threaten to engulf the schools.

There were those who increasingly argued that Hannah More had taken too much upon herself and was usurping the functions of the clergy. But she thought she had no choice. It was intolerable to leave Cheddar to the ministrations of its 'galloping curate' or Shipham to its ancient rector, who 'had claimed the tithes for fifty years, but had never catechised a child or preached a sermon for forty'.[93] The eighteenth-century church, once reviled by historians for its sleepy complacency, has now been partially rehabilitated.[94] The More sisters, too, were deeply partisan, and it is possible that they exaggerated the neglect and indifference they perceived around them. How literally, for example, should we take this comment to Sir Charles Middleton, probably written at the end of 1789? 'I have been in a district where three Welsh curates, without morals, without learning, and almost without bread, serve ten or eleven churches. These poor men dig potatoes and make cider for their maintenance, and dance and play at cards with the servants of the gentry for their amusement afterwards. They drink hard when it is given them.'[95] However, even if such lurid comments are discounted, it is still clear that the Mendips, presided over by a frail, octogenarian bishop, were an area of inadequate diocesan structures and impoverished and often neglectful clergy. To counter these obstacles to her programme, More's solution was to use such influence as she had in order to place 'her' clergy in key positions. In July 1791 the aged rector of Shipham finally died, and the dean and chapter of Wells replaced him with her friend James Jones. This promotion of this poor but zealous curate was, claimed Patty, due to 'the interference and perseverance of Hannah'.[96] John Newton, who had preached at Shipham during the interregnum, wrote to congratulate her: 'The Lord has made you the instrument of relieving a poor but deserving servant of his.'[97] At about the same time she secured the curacy of Cheddar for Boak, and when he was moved on, he was replaced with the equally Evangelical Thomas Drewitt. Patty ascribed it all to a 'kind providence' and

---

[92] *MA* 96.   [93] *MA* 29.
[94] W. M. Jacob, *Lay People and Religion in the Early Eighteenth Century* (Cambridge, 1996).
[95] *Gambier*, i. 175–6.   [96] *MA* 44.   [97] Roberts, ii. 281.

joyfully noted that the rector and bishop had both agreed that 'no clergyman should come to Cheddar but with our entire approbation, and no-one who would not assist and countenance all our schemes!'[98] In the flush of her innocent triumphalism, she did not take stock to consider how the neighbouring clergy might view this unofficial lay patronage.

Good teachers were equally essential, if only because for most of the time the sisters were not around. Hannah More's retreat from the world was still far from total. Every spring she still made her annual journey to London; this involved visits to Fulham to visit the Porteuses, a journey to Kent to stay with the Middletons, and (with decreasing frequency) a stay at Hampton or the Adelphi with Mrs Garrick. When winter set in, the sisters retreated to Bath. Even when she and Patty were both in Cowslip Green, they could only visit half their schools on a given Sunday (Nailsea, Yatton, and Congresbury one week, Cheddar, Shipham, and Axbridge the other). Virtually everything, therefore, hinged on the teachers. Supreme among them was Sarah Baber at Cheddar. She proved so outstanding in her gifts, able to teach adults and children with equal success, that the sisters exhausted their vocabulary of praise when describing her. As often as not they inverted the gender conventions and spoke of her as 'Bishop Baber'. 'Not the finest writer perhaps of the four and twenty', as More told Wilberforce, 'but certainly not the worst Divine.'[99] Unlike the absentee clergy, she lived in the village, and proved a compassionate friend to the sick and needy. She addressed the people with a 'righteous boldness' that drew from them 'an undeviating respect and attention'.[100] Wilberforce was deeply moved by one of her addresses to the children.[101] Another appreciative male observer was John Boak, who stayed one Sunday to watch her conduct her class. Patty saw this as 'an important and striking revolution', and indeed it was a remarkable achievement for a charity school mistress, a lower-middle-class imperfectly educated woman, to be held up to a clergyman as such a shining example.[102] The only problem lay in a ne'er-do-well son, and More wrote a couple of anxious letters to Wilberforce begging him to find a place at sea for him. 'We don't so much want to serve him as to get rid of him,' she wrote brutally, 'for fear he should lessen his mother's great usefulness.'[103]

Few teachers, however, were as gifted or zealous. At the other end of the spectrum were the Congresbury teachers, so spiritually inert that Patty described them as 'the two stones'. As a price for hiring the highly satisfactory Nancy Keene at Sandford, the sisters 'were obliged to be saddled with her dull husband for a master'. However, Mrs Keene, who had a realistic

[98] *MA* 184.   [99] *MA* 93; Duke, More to Wilberforce [1792?].   [100] *MA* 116.
[101] *Life of Wilberforce*, i. 304–5.   [102] *MA* 95.
[103] Duke, More to Wilberforce, 'Saturday night' [1790 or 1791].

appreciation of her husband's shortcomings, 'worked for both', enabling the More sisters to open a school in their cottage for about sixty pupils.[104] With the labour market offering men a greater range of occupations, it was often difficult to find suitable male teachers.[105]

The sisters tried to rectify deficiencies where they existed and impose some uniformity of teaching by drawing up a plan of instruction which More variously called her 'method' or her 'system'. She set out the details in a letter to Wilberforce.[106] She divided the children into older and younger. (Though she did not specify the age at which the division was made, the children started the schools at the age of 6.) The older children were made to read a chapter or two of the Bible, after which the teacher questioned them to discover how much they had remembered and understood. They started with the parables, as being 'easy and entertaining', but soon went on to the meat of Evangelical theology: the passages in Genesis, Isaiah, and St John concerning the fall and redemption of man. The children were encouraged to learn whole chapters by rote, and many of them, like Stendhal's Julien Sorel, accomplished prodigious feats of memory. As well as the Bible, they learned the church catechism, the Lord's Prayer, and the Creed. Meanwhile, the younger children were instructed in the 'Mendip School Questions', drawn up by the sisters, as well as the catechism, the collects, and Watts's hymns. More insisted that the teachers should always 'try to make it pleasant by cheerful manners, by striking out a hymn when labour has been long continued, and by avoiding corporal punishment—whatever makes them hate Sunday is wrong'.[107] 'I have never tried the system of terror', she wrote in 1801, 'because I have found that kindness produces a better end by better means.'[108]

The grading of the learning in order of difficulty, the attempts to vary the routine, the avoidance of physical punishment, the use of rewards, were all typical of the methods used in Sunday schools throughout the country. More was realistic enough to know that, if the children were to be trained into 'pious' and 'useful' members of the community, they needed to enjoy their lessons, and she had some very modern-sounding views about the best methods of instruction. After nearly a decade of experience she criticized over-reliance on rote learning and urged teachers to encourage children to take part in 'lively discussion'. She also wanted their language to be appropriate to the children's circumstances. 'Teach them rather, as their Blessed Saviour taught, by interesting parables, which, while they corrected the heart, left some exercise for the ingenuity in the solution, and for the feelings in their application. Teach, as HE taught, by seizing on surrounding objects, passing events, local circumstances, peculiar characters, apt allusions, just analogy, appropriate

---

[104] *MA* 33.   [105] *MA* 40.   [106] Bodleian, MS c.3, fos. 246–7.
[107] Duke, More to Wilberforce [1792 or 1793].
[108] Duke, More to Wilberforce [21 July 1801].

illustration.'[109] She practised what she preached. Henry Thornton's daughter Marianne retained vivid memories of 'Mrs Hannah's or Mrs Patty's eloquent exhortations to the whole School made in the most homely language, full of anecdotes of the people round them, as well as of the good people who lived in old times, and full of practical piety—brought down into such minute detail one never hears now'.[110]

Of the two sisters, Patty, with her commanding presence, her voice of bell-like clarity, her unflagging stamina, and her fierce devotion to the Mendip people, was the better teacher.[111] 'She never thinks of a holiday six months together,' More told Sir Charles Middleton.[112] On one evening of 'tremendous weather', while she was at home nursing an illness, she wrote anxiously to Wilberforce that Patty had been forced to go to Nailsea without her. 'I wish she were home, this road being the only perilous one we have.'[113] She could never free herself of her guilty awareness that the chief burden of the schools rested on the shoulders of this most loyal of lieutenants, the person she loved most in the world. She knew that Patty was prepared to do more than half the work, yet to allow her beloved Hannah to claim most of the credit; that was the way their relationship worked.

[109] *Strictures on the Modern System of Female Education, with a View of the Principles and Conduct Prevalent among Women of Rank and Fortune* (London, 1799), i. 253–4.

[110] Thornton, Add. MS 7674/1/L10, fo. 39.

[111] Bodleian, MS d. 20, fo. 41, 'Recollections of Mrs Hannah More'; Clark, Hannah More's diary, 1794 [uncatalogued and unfoliated], Sunday 10 Aug.

[112] *Gambier*, i. 234.   [113] Duke, More to Wilberforce, 14 July 1798.

Chapter 6

Revolution and Counter-Revolution
1789–1793

THE foundation and expansion of the Mendip schools coincided with cataclysmic events in Europe which by the end of the 1790s were to impact on Hannah More herself, calling her political loyalism into question and threatening the very existence of her schools. In response to these events she refashioned herself yet again, this time as a political controversialist, and discovered a talent for popular writing that was to make her one of the more interesting proponents of conservatism in the war of ideas that characterized that troubled decade.

In the late summer of 1789 the British newspapers were giving extensive coverage to what was already being called the French Revolution.[1] Perhaps

---

[1] For the French Revolution, see e.g. W. Doyle, *Oxford History of the French Revolution* (Oxford, 1989); S. Schama, *Citizens: A Chronicle of the French Revolution* (London, 1989); *The Longman Companion to the French Revolution*, ed. C. Jones (Harlow, 1990). For the British reaction, see A. Cobban, *The Debate on the French Revolution, 1789–1800* (2nd edn. London, 1950); E. P. Thompson, *The Making of the English Working Class* (Harmondsworth, 1968); R. Dozier, *For King, Constitution and Country: The English Loyalists and the French Revolution* (Lexington, Ky., 1983); C. Jones (ed.), *Britain and Revolutionary France: Conflict, Subversion, and Propaganda* (Exeter, 1983); H. T. Dickinson, *Liberty and Property: Political Ideology in Eighteenth-Century Britain* (London, 1977), chs. 7 and 8; id., 'Popular Loyalism in Britain in the 1790s', in E. Hellmuth, *The Transformation of Political Culture: England and Germany in the Late Eighteenth Century* (Oxford, 1990), 503–33; id., *The Politics of the People in Eighteenth-Century Britain* (Basingstoke, 1995), chs. 7 and 8; id. (ed.), *Britain and the French Revolution, 1789–1815* (London, 1989); D. Bindman, *The Shadow of the Guillotine: Britain and the French Revolution* (London, 1989); R. Hole, *Pulpits, Politics, and Public Order in England, 1760–1832* (Cambridge, 1989), part II; G. Claeys, *Thomas Paine: Social and Political Thought* (Boston, 1989), id., 'The French Revolution Debate and British Political Thought', *History of Political Thought*, 9 (1990),

this term was so quickly adopted because events in France followed closely on the centenary celebrations of the Glorious Revolution of 1688, and opposition politicians, Protestant Dissenters, and abolitionists were already making use of the rhetoric of British rights and liberties in order to advance their causes. Unsurprisingly, the French Revolution was initially interpreted in the light of British concerns. The papers welcomed the symbolism of the fall of the Bastille, but also reported the accompanying theatre of violence, when the heads of the governor and the chief magistrate of Paris were stuck on pikes and paraded through the streets. As readers tried to get behind the gory details and uncover the deeper meaning of the events, it was natural for whiggish commentators to assume that the French Revolution was a rerun of the Revolution of 1688. Triumphantly, if incautiously, Charles James Fox declared that the fall of the Bastille was 'much the greatest event that has ever happened in the world, and . . . much the best'.[2] Similar sentiments were expressed in poems and letters to the newspapers. As Hannah More was to put it retrospectively,

What English heart did not exult at the demolition of the Bastile [*sic*]? What lover of his species did not triumph in the warm hope that one of the finest countries in the world would soon be one of the most free? . . . Who . . . that had a head to reason and a heart to feel did not glow with the hope that . . . a beautiful and finely framed edifice would in time have been constructed?[3]

She had a personal reason for following events closely. The immediate cause of the storming of the Bastille had been Louis XVI's dismissal of his finance minister and the associated fears of a royalist counter-coup; and, as has been shown, she had met Jacques Necker and his family when they came to England in 1776 for Garrick's final performances. More recently, Germaine Necker, now Madame de Staël, had sent her 'a very eloquent and ingenious Eloge on Rousseau' in remembrance of old times.[4] But the events of 14 July came when she was caught up in a domestic crisis. One of her neighbours, the owner of Mendip Lodge a few miles from Wrington, was the clergyman magistrate Thomas Sedgwick Whalley, a minor literary figure

59–80; J. Dinwiddy, 'Conceptions of Revolution in the English Radicalism of the 1790s', in Hellmuth (ed.), *Transformation of Political Culture*, 535–60; M. Philp (ed.), *The French Revolution and British Popular Politics* (Cambridge, 1991); id., 'Vulgar Conservatism, 1792–3', *English Historical Review*, 110 (1995), 42–69; J. Mori, *William Pitt and the French Revolution, 1785–1795* (Edinburgh, 1997); E. Vincent Macleod, *A War of Ideas: British Attitudes to the Wars against Revolutionary France, 1792–1802* (Aldershot, 1998); E. Royle, *Revolutionary Britannia? Reflections on the Threat of Revolution in Britain, 1789–1848* (Manchester, 2000).

[2] Quoted in L. G. Mitchell, *Charles James Fox* (Harmondsworth, 1997), 110.
[3] *Remarks on the Speech of M. Dupont, made in the National Convention of France on the Subjects of Religion and Public Education* (London, 1793), 7–8.
[4] Roberts, ii. 154–5. The work was *Lettres sur les écrits et le charactère de J.-J.Rousseau* (1788), translated into English in 1789.

much given to genteel friendships with learned ladies. Early in July, when he and his wife were on their way to visit More, their phaeton overturned in a stream, leaving Mrs Whalley gravely injured. Too ill to be moved, she had to be treated at Cowslip Green. The distraught husband and anxious family, together with their servants, crowded into 'this nutshell of a house' which was full already as her sisters were down from Bristol waiting for their new home in Bath to become habitable. What with nursing, catering for visitors, and snatching sleep at odd moments, More was left to contemplate the ruin of her summer; to cap it all, it rained all the time.[5] (Later, however, her sacrifice would pay dividends, when she was able to call in her debt to Whalley during the Blagdon controversy.) When Mrs Whalley was finally sent home, she was then presented with Wilberforce's challenge to do something about Cheddar. A few days later she was touring the Wye Valley with her thoughts full of picturesque scenery and her Sunday school plans rather than politics.

In France events moved at bewildering speed. In August, while the countryside erupted into chaos, the National Assembly at Versailles promulgated the Declaration of the Rights of Man, based on the ideology of inalienable natural rights. Later Hannah More came to detest the whole novel concept, but at this stage, like many people of moderately conservative opinions, she was in two minds about the direction of the Revolution. As she told Elizabeth Montagu,

As to French politics, whatever may be the *end*, they do not much rejoyce one's heart by the *means*. I comfort myself however that if despotism dies by the hand of the Execution, Popery must of course die a natural death; and yet after all if anarchy and atheism are to succeed to Popery and Despotism, it will not be a very gainful bargain.[6]

Her letter was written a few days after two of the most dramatic of the revolutionary *journées*. On 5 October the Parisian market women advanced on Versailles, and early the next morning more Parisians poured into the palace. In the ensuing confusion two guardsmen were killed, the queen allegedly fled in fear of her life, and the royal family were forced to leave Versailles, which they never saw again. This event confirmed More's nagging apprehension that France might be descending into godless anarchy, and she speculated to Walpole about what the feelings of her *bête noire* Louis XIV, would be if he could only know that his once mighty throne had been 'overturned by fishwomen!'[7]

---

[5] Folger, W.b. 487, fo. 64, More to Eva Garrick, 23 July 1789; Huntington, MO 3997, More to Elizabeth Montagu, 7 July [1789]; Roberts, ii. 173.

[6] Huntington, MO 3999, More to Elizabeth Montagu, 10 Oct. 1789.

[7] *Walpole*, 329.

Already the nation was beginning to divide. While her friend George Horne, now dean of Canterbury, fulminated against the sinfulness of rebellion, the Unitarian minister Dr Richard Price, a very representative specimen of the progressive clergyman, preached a sermon which appeared to rejoice—even gloat—at the fact that the king was now forced to live in his own capital among his own people. This was later published under the title *A Discourse on the Love of our Country*—much to the disgust of Hannah More, now moving rapidly into the counter-revolutionary camp.[8]

By this stage, with winter closing in and the Mendips unseasonably covered with snow,[9] she was preparing to retreat to Bath, where the new house in Great Pulteney Street was being prepared. The eldest More sisters had now retired from teaching, and had handed over the school to Selina Mills and her sisters Mary and Fanny, Anglican daughters of the Quaker Thomas Mills, a Bristol bookseller who specialized in publishing works of mystical devotion.[10] All the sisters, but especially Patty, were charmed with Selina, 23 years old, pretty, sweet-tempered, apparently docile, and they treated her as an honorary sister. With the transaction completed, Mary, Betty, and Sally could look forward to a life of well-earned leisure in pleasant and sociable surroundings. For Hannah More, however, it was frustrating to put up with the frivolity of spa society when there were souls to be saved in Cheddar, and she chafed at the fact that the poor insulation of Cowslip Green forced her to retreat from the field of action.

Meanwhile, one of her friends had been brooding over the French Revolution in general and Dr Price's sermon in particular. The storm loured for months then burst forth in a thunder clap when, on 1 November 1790, Edmund Burke dissociated himself from his fellow Whigs and published his *Reflections on Revolution in France*, which is now seen as one of the seminal texts of conservative philosophy. His fierce onslaught set the tone for all future loyalist comment, including the writings of Hannah More. At one level it was an attack on Price. Far from hailing the women's march as the triumphant dawn of a new era, he saw in the fury of the *poissades* 'all the unutterable abominations of the furies of hell, in the abused shape of the vilest of women'.[11] Their actions were an affront to the king as father

---

[8] Roberts, ii. 201.   [9] *St James's Chronicle*, 10–12 Nov. 1789.

[10] *FFBJ*, 1 Jan. 1790. The *Bristol Directory* of 1793–4 records Fanny Mills as head of the 'Ladies' Boarding School, Park Street'. In her will in 1819 Patty left 19 guineas to 'Frances Mills of Park Street' and 'Madame Amelin'. PRO, PROB 11/1621, fo. 271. Subsequent editions of the *Directory*, up to and including 1831, record Fanny Mills and Madame Amelin as proprietors of the school and give the school address as 10 Park Street. In 1824 both women visited More at Barley Wood. Huntington, MY 709, More to Selina Macaulay, 19 Jan. 1824. Hannah More left Madame Amelin £40 in her will. PRO, PROB 11/1822, fo. 366.

[11] *Reflections on the Revolution in France*, ed. C. C. O'Brien (Harmondsworth, 1982; repr. 1986), 165.

of his family and to the queen as a woman and a mother. 'The age of chivalry', he lamented in the book's most quoted passage, 'is gone. That of sophisters, calculators and economists is upon us.'[12] His embarrassing idealization of Marie Antoinette was a gift to the caricaturists, who depicted him as a lean and bespectacled Don Dismallo riding to the defence of despotism and Catholic bigotry; Thomas Paine memorably accused him of pitying the plumage but forgetting the dying bird.[13]

Never a man to spoil a case by understatement, Burke had certainly laid himself open to criticism, yet behind the sentimental excesses lay serious arguments. Earlier than most commentators he discerned in the secular radicalism of the French Revolution the seeds of a fundamental assault on Christian civilization.[14] Its ideology was a 'mechanic philosophy', its doctrine of the rights of man a mere abstraction.[15] In contrast, Englishmen enjoyed specific, concrete liberties such as access to justice and ownership of property, granted by Magna Carta and the common law.[16] These rights, rooted in history and custom, formed 'a partnership not only between those who are living, but between those who are dead and those who are to be born . . . the great primaeval contract of eternal society'.[17] But did this emphasis on precedent and tradition mean that nothing could ever be changed? Faced with the uncomfortable fact that the British themselves had had a revolution 100 years previously, Burke claimed that, far from setting a precedent, the Glorious Revolution was a once and for all event, 'a small and a temporary deviation from the strict order of a regular hereditary succession'.[18] He did not allow it to deflect him from the thrust of his argument, which pitted a passionate upholding of ancient authorities in Church and State against what, in an unfortunate phrase, he called the tyranny of 'a swinish multitude'.[19]

The book was a strong brew, and opinions were quickly polarized. While Horace Walpole and the bluestockings were enthusiastic in their praise, Whigs and radicals rushed into print to denounce it. Their outrage, together with the amused condescension of the caricaturists, reflected a common perception that, not for the first time, Burke's passionate enthusiasm had got the better of his reason. In 1790 the violence in France seemed to have passed and the country was in the throes of institutional reform. British citizens of reforming views made a point of crossing the Channel to observe

[12] Ibid. 170.
[13] Bindman, *Shadow of the Guillotine*, 17, 107; T. Paine, *Rights of Man*, ed. E. Foner (Harmondsworth, 1969; repr. 1987), 51.
[14] See N. Aston, 'A "lay divine": Burke, Christianity, and the Preservation of the British State, 1790–1797', in id. (ed.), *Religious Change in Europe, 1650–1914* (Oxford, 1997), 192–4; *Reflections*, 186–7, 171.
[15] *Reflections*, 172. [16] Ibid. 149–50. [17] Ibid. 194–5. [18] Ibid. 101.
[19] Ibid. 173. For More's implied criticism, see her story 'The Delegate', in *The Works of Hannah More: A New Edition* (London, 1818), vi. 406.

events for themselves and to send sympathetic reports back home. William Wordsworth twice toured the country, in 1790 and 1791. He visited the site of the Bastille and pocketed a stone from the ruins, just as a later generation of tourists would collect parts of the Berlin Wall. As he travelled through France, he saw around him 'a People risen up | Fresh as the morning Star' on the verge of a new era of liberty and social justice.[20] Few could have predicted the ugly turn of events that would vindicate Burke and force the defenders of the Revolution onto the back foot.

In the years before the Revolution Hannah More had come to disagree with much of Burke's politics, in particular to deplore the violence of his language, whether he was attacking the government's American policy or prosecuting Warren Hastings. She was now in no position to make an immediate response to the *Reflections*. After a busy summer spent in opening the Shipham and Rowberrow schools she was in agony from a toothache which made her delirious. It was cured by extraction—'and a terrible operation it was for such a detestable coward as I am', she complained to Elizabeth Bouverie.[21] The Bath house was finally ready, but again she tried to put off the evil day when she had to leave Cowslip Green. A new concern was preoccupying her: that, as she told Mrs Garrick, of 'obtaining redress for the poor in the important article of bread'. This involved putting pressure on the magistrates of Wrington to step up their inspections of the weight and quality of the bread that was being sold in the markets.[22]

In February 1791 Cadell published her second major conduct book, with the self-explanatory title of *An Estimate of the Religion of the Fashionable World*. This took up and expanded the themes of the *Manners of the Great*, being an assault on luxury, a critique of polite society, and a call to self-denying Christianity. In its attacks on absentee landlords, unrestrained consumerism, and the impersonal nature of institutionalized charity, it was nostalgic and backward-looking. But it also envisaged a new society in which 'politeness' would lose its elegant veneer and shed its elitism. Remoralized, it would comprise the useful virtues of punctuality, hard work, time management, and truthfulness, the attributes of the hard-working middling sort rather than the leisured classes. For Hannah More, profligacy, luxury, and dissimulation were symptoms of a social and spiritual malaise, a '*practical irreligion*' more dangerous than outright scepticism, which filtered down through society, infected 'servants and inferiors', and contributed to rising crime.[23] In contrast, true Christianity was not an opinion or a performance but 'a disposition, a

---

[20] *The Prelude*, IX. 63–80, 389–92.　　[21] *Gambier*, i. 186.

[22] Folger, W.b. 487, fo. 69, More to Eva Garrick, 11 Dec. 1790; *FFBJ*, 20 Nov. 1790.

[23] *An Estimate of the Religion of the Fashionable World by One of the Laity* (3rd edn. London, 1791), 18, 20, 140–1.

habit, a temper . . . a turning of the whole mind to God; a concentration of all the powers and affections of the soul into one steady point, an uniform desire to please *Him*'.[24] With this avowal of her deepest beliefs, she had bared her soul and thrown down her challenge to the spirit of the age.

Although the book was published anonymously, the secret of the authorship emerged when John Newton blurted it out in company, causing her great, though temporary, embarrassment. The reason, she told him, with typical self-deprecation, was that 'neither my sex, my abilities, nor my conduct are such as fully to justify me in my own eyes for the things which I attempt, merely because others better qualified will not do it'.[25] The work sold out rapidly, though, even with five editions printed by 1793, it was never the most successful of her conduct books. Horace Walpole confided his mixed feelings to Mary Berry: 'It is prettily written, but her enthusiasm increases, and when she comes to town, I shall tell her that if she preaches to people of fashion, she will be a Bishop *in partibus infidelium*.'[26] Possibly More would not have been displeased at this description, which confirmed what Newton had already told her: 'You have a great advantage, madam;—there is a circle by which what you write, will be read; and which will hardly read any thing of a religious kind that is not written by you.'[27] The whiggish *Monthly Review* seemed to concede this point. It believed that the book would have little influence, but admitted that it had become the fashion to read Hannah More.[28]

In the following month a book was published that was to have a far greater impact, the first part of Thomas Paine's *Rights of Man*. In a ferocious attack on Burke's traditionalist arguments, Paine declared that the venerated British constitution, founded on the injustice and irrationality of inherited privilege, was flawed in its very essence: 'The idea of hereditary legislation is as inconsistent as that of hereditary judges, or hereditary juries; and as absurd as an hereditary mathematician, or an hereditary wise man; and as ridiculous as an hereditary poet laureate.'[29] Porteus read the book with horror and foreboding. He recognized that Paine wrote in 'a plain, familiar, forcible style, very well calculated to captivate common Readers', and feared that his book would be widely distributed by the various reforming societies already in existence, poisoning and perverting the minds of the people.[30] Yet, fearful of turning him into a martyr, the authorities refused to prosecute. They trusted

[24] Ibid. 58.   [25] Roberts, ii. 257.

[26] *Horace Walpole's Correspondence with Mary and Agnes Berry*, ed. W. S. Lewis and A. Dayle Wallace, xi (New Haven, 1944), 214.

[27] Roberts, ii. 265.   [28] *Monthly Review*, NS 6 (1791), 306–7.   [29] *Rights of Man*, 83.

[30] Lambeth Palace, Porteus MS 2100, fos. 25–8. For Paine's style, see O. Smith, *The Politics of Language, 1791–1819* (Oxford, 1984), 35–57.

that the prohibitive price of 3s. would be a sufficient disincentive, but their hopes collapsed as the book sold 50,000 copies in 1791 alone, breaking every publishing record and putting Burke's sale of 30,000 copies of his *Reflections* in the shade. The result of this popularity, Porteus gloomily surmised, might be the introduction of a democracy, a fickle, unstable form of government condemned by the great majority of classical and modern political theorists.[31]

There can be no doubt that these were Hannah More's views as well. She had always been a supporter of Pitt's government, and did not look kindly on attacks on the settlement of 1688. However, she was not in a position to shake her head over Paine's book with her friends, as in the early spring of 1791 she was in Bristol, tied up in a crisis that was to become a national cause célèbre. On 21 March she wrote an agitated letter to Mrs Garrick.

We are in a great affliction at a most distressing Event which carried my Sister to Bristol in the middle of last night. A young Lady who was left under our care, a Scotch child, and placed by my Sister at Miss Mills' School at Bristol, is now run away with a Fortune hunting Ruffian, we know not whom . . . and this innocent young creature only fourteen years old, with the purity of an angel, is now God knows where, in France or Scotland perhaps . . . We are half distracted, we know not what steps to take.[32]

The 'young Lady' was Clementina Clerke, pupil at the Park Street school, and niece and sole heiress of a Scots merchant, George Ogilvie, who, having made his fortune in Jamaica, had recently died leaving her £6,000 a year. As soon as the news was out, Richard Vining Perry, surgeon and apothecary at Bristol, made covert advances to her through one of the servants at the school. On 19 March an over-trusting Selina Mills allowed Clementina to leave the school, ostensibly to visit her aunt. A few hours later she and Perry were in a fast post-chaise on their way to Gretna Green, where they could be married according to the relaxed Scots law. On the journey the chaise overturned and the couple arrived at Gretna pale and shaken with their heads bandaged. The official, who had presumably seen stranger sights, performed the marriage without asking any questions.

Meanwhile, Selina's sister Mary, her 17-year-old brother, and a local landlord had set off in pursuit. They failed to overtake the couple but met them in Cumberland on their way back. The road was narrow and both coaches stopped. When asked if he would allow Mary Mills to speak to his new wife, Perry replied in the manner of a true eighteenth-century villain, a Lovelace or a Valmont, 'No, not a word by God—drive on.' Unable to turn their coach round, the pursuing party were obliged to continue their journey

---

[31] Lambeth Palace, Porteus MS 2100, fos. 26–8. [32] Folger, W.b. 487, fo. 70.

northwards. A day or so later a dejected Miss Mills was back in Bristol, minus her former pupil.[33]

Shortly after this she went to London with Hannah and Patty More to seek out possible legal remedies and to try to find the couple, now believed to be hiding there. They took temporary lodgings near Bow Street, only to have Patty fall ill the day after they arrived. Hannah's time was passed 'with thief takers, officers of justice and such pretty kind of people' including the Bow Street magistrate Sir Sampson Wright. A reward of £1,000 was offered for the return of Mrs Perry. She made flying visits to Barrington and Porteus 'in my dishabille' but had not had any opportunity to see any other friends apart from Henry Thornton, whose knowledge of the law and lawyers was invaluable. As she told Ann Kennicott, it was a furtive, underworld existence.

When we had information brought us of any house where our unhappy child and her atrocious companion were supposed to be, Miss M[ills] and I were obliged to go under pretence of wanting lodgings. One lawyer went with us into the house to look at the rooms, another stood at the door: a hackney coach full of Sir Sampson Wright's men at a little distance: to these we were directed to make signals, in case we had discovered the object of our pursuit... You know, I believe, my silly terror of fire-arms—it is inexpressible. What therefore made these visits so particularly distressing to me was the assurance that P[erry] never sat without a pistol on the table, which he seized at every noise.[34]

Horace Walpole relished the melodrama. 'Good Hannah More is killing herself by a new fit of benevolence,' he wrote to Mary Berry. However, he continued, 'Mrs Garrick... suspects as I do, that Miss Europa is not very angry with Mr Jupiter.'[35] Perry was certainly a villain, but had he broken the law? There being no legal age of consent, he could not be accused of sexual relations with an under-age girl. The charges if any had to be rape or forcible abduction, both of them hanging offences, but as Miss Clerke had shown herself only too willing to elope, these would be hard to prove. The cartoonists were thoroughly enjoying themselves. One caricature entitled 'A Perry-lous Situation: or the Doctor and his Friends keeping the Bum-brusher and her Myrmidons Away' portrayed Mary or Selina Mills as 'Mistress Sharp', the madam of a flagellant brothel; she is holding up a birch-rod in a threatening fashion, while Clementina appeals to Perry: 'Dear Doctor, save me from my governess.'[36]

Feeling London too dangerous for them nevertheless, the Perrys took a ship to Ostend. An increasingly desperate Mary Mills followed them to

[33] This account is taken from *The Trial of Richard Vining Perry* (Bristol, 1794).
[34] Roberts, ii. 335–6.   [35] Walpole, *Correspondence with Mary Berry*, xi. 253–4.
[36] *British Museum Catalogue of Political and Personal Satires*, vi, ed. M. D. George (London, 1978), 7991.

Flanders, though she was unable to find them there. The couple remained in Europe until the fuss died down.

With the Perrys out of reach, More concentrated on her schools for the rest of the summer. At the end of 1791 she was at her sisters' Bath house, and as usual she was unwell. This time her complaint was gallstones ('the most excruciating pain to be conceived') accompanied with a bout of jaundice that turned her skin 'not overwhite naturally...yellow as Gold'. But the house was habitable, and in spite of the building works around them, Great Pulteney Street was at last 'accessible without danger of breaking our neck'. When the pain subsided, More found herself racked with a cough. However, she was able to go to the Pump Room in a chair, and she found that the sulphurous waters did her good.[37] The sedan chair also took her to Argyll Chapel, situated almost opposite the More sisters' house, where the brilliant young Independent (Congregationalist) preacher William Jay, the son of a stonemason, was beginning to attract large congregations comprising Anglicans as well as Dissenters.

For Hannah More, Bath reeked of sickness and death that January. Two young cousins of William Wilberforce, Harriet and Mary Bird, had come to settle in the town, and at the turn of the year Harriet was taken ill. After eighteen days of intense suffering she was dead. During this distressing time one or other of the More sisters was always with her, and Hannah was with her the night she died. 'It was such a death as I wou'd not but have seen for the world,' she told Mrs Garrick, 'all peace and joy, indeed she was an angel before she went to Heaven.'[38] In an age of anaesthetics and antibiotics it is easy to accuse More, and those who shared her fascination with exemplary deaths, of ghoulish morbidity. But deaths such as Harriet Bird's provided a triumphant validation of the truths of Christianity. As her obituary notice insisted, 'during this Affliction her hope and consolation in the Author of her being were, as the evident reward of her piety, remarkably conspicuous'.[39] The restrained language concealed some very intense feelings, and for a while More could think of little else.

Harriet's eyes had scarcely been closed when, a hundred yards away in Queen Square, George Horne, who had lately become bishop of Norwich, died, and the widow turned to Hannah More, just as Mrs Garrick had done in another dark January thirteen years before. She and her lively daughter Sally came to stay in their house along with Mary Bird, though the bereaved women were careful to keep away from each other.[40] The bishop's death had

---

[37] Folger, W.b. 487, fo. 74, More to Eva Garrick, Bath, 19 Dec. 1791; fo. 75, More to Eva Garrick, Bath, 27 Jan. 1792.
[38] Folger, W.b. 487, fo. 75.   [39] *Bath Chronicle*, 26 Jan. 1792.
[40] Folger, W.b. 487, fo. 75.

been as edifying as Harriet Bird's, the culmination of a lifetime's devotion to the Church. 'How wise and how witty, how pleasant and how good he was, we shall often remember,' More wrote to Ann Kennicott.[41]

In the following month she turned her attention to the outside world. She and Patty took a trip out to Nailsea to superintend the opening of the school and to see the new teachers, the Youngs, begin their work. After a short return to Bath she travelled to London, where she met her old friends again, with the exception of Horace Walpole, who was ill. Perhaps she was relieved not to see him, as in the previous month he had written her a letter which gently scolded her for sabbatarianism.[42] In April 1792 Wilberforce put forward his second motion for the abolition of the slave trade in a marathon three-hour speech. The motion was defeated. More and her friends were becoming sadly used to such discouragements. This time, however, she took comfort from Pitt's passionate speech in support of abolition; quoting one of Patty's favourite expressions, she declared she could hug him for it.[43] In the following month she was at Fulham with the Porteuses. By July she was back at Cowslip Green, setting up the women's benefit clubs.

It seemed then as if little had changed in the rhythm of her life; in reality, nothing would be the same. The political establishment was shaken to its foundations as in the wake of the French Revolution and the publication of *Rights of Man* working men—artisans, journeymen, small mechanics, shopkeepers—began to form themselves into reforming societies aimed at securing manhood suffrage. In many respects these earnest, thoughtful men were similar in character to those Nailsea miners whose attempts at self-improvement were to make them one of the great success stories of the Mendip schools. But whereas Hannah More could approve wholeheartedly of the aspirations of upwardly mobile Sunday school teachers, the political demands of working men filled her with horror. Though most of these reformers dissociated themselves from revolutionary violence, she was quite correct in her belief that, were their programme to be implemented, it would be the end of the political world she knew.

Conservative anxieties were greatly intensified by the publication of part 2 of *Rights of Man* in February, originally published at 3s., but within a few months republished at the greatly reduced priced of 6d. Those who had been horrified by part 1 were even more outraged by its sequel; the language was more provocative, the proposals for social reform more far-reaching. In place of a class-ridden society Paine advocated an egalitarian republic in

---

[41] Roberts, ii. 325.   [42] *Walpole*, 365–6.
[43] *The Parliamentary History of England* (London, 1817), xxix. 1134; Roberts, ii. 315.

which the poor were freed from destitution by family allowances and old age pensions: proposals which, however admirable in intention, might seem at variance with his belief that republican government was cheap government. What alarmed many of Paine's readers, even those who considered themselves political reformers, was the tone of his book, its class antagonism and mockery of ancient institutions. Sales have been estimated at about 200,000, but the number of readers was probably far greater. It was read, not merely in the form of a lengthy pamphlet, but in cheap, popular, easily digestible selections. The government responded with something like panic. Within a week of its publication part 2 was officially condemned as a seditious libel. In December Paine was tried in his absence and found guilty. By this time he was in France, elected a member of the Convention, and was being burned in effigy in various parts of England.[44] To the dismay of the More sisters one of their more 'hopeful' Mendip people, 'overtaken with liquor', joined in a Paine-burning at Axbridge.[45] These rituals may well have been orchestrated by members of the elite, but they could not have taken place without the consent of sizeable numbers of the labouring population. For all the phenomenal sales of *Rights of Man*, it is not clear how far Paine's iconoclasm was shared by the mass of the people, for whom John Bull may have been a more potent symbol than the cap of liberty.

In the spring of 1792 the French Revolution took off in uncharted directions. France was now at war with Austria and Prussia, and a new humanitarian method of execution, the guillotine, claimed its first victim (a highwayman). As the more zealous revolutionaries hunted out the traitors in their midst, British newspapers chilled their readers by printing (with a translation) the latest revolutionary song, the 'Ça Ira' ('That will be all right'), its harsh, jagged rhythms summing up all the bloodthirsty energy of the Revolution and its hatred of priests and aristocrats.

> Ah ça ira, ça ira, ça ira,
> Les aristocrats, à la lanterne!
> Ah ça ira, ça ira, ça ira,
> Les aristocrats, on les pendra!

In September this gruesome threat was fulfilled, when 1,000 prisoners, including many priests, were massacred in the Paris prisons. A few weeks later the monarchy was abolished. The French were now seen as a monstrous people, outside the normal bounds of humanity. In a genocidal rage Horace Walpole told Hannah More that the whole nation should be exterminated.[46] James Gillray drew a nightmarish caricature of a family of working-class

---

[44] See e.g. *FFBJ*, 22 Dec. 1792. For Paine-burning, see N. Rogers, *Crowds, Culture, and Politics in Georgian Britain* (Oxford, 1998), 202–7.
[45] *MA* 94.   [46] *Walpole*, 372.

revolutionaries, the *sans-culottes*, basting a baby, dismembering a corpse, and dining off human eyes, hearts, and entrails.[47] News from the battlefield was even more alarming. In the autumn the French entered Brussels, from where they issued a decree of fraternity and help to all subject people. The Revolution was now for export and Europe was confronted with a full-scale ideological war.

In Britain the loyalist response was now in full flow. In November the barrister John Reeves founded his Association for Preserving of Liberty and Property Against Levellers and Republicans at the Crown and Anchor tavern in London, and placed advertisements in the newspapers calling for the formation of loyalist bodies throughout the country. The mobilization of the traditional elite had begun as loyalist societies mushroomed all over the country. Once the Association for Preserving Liberty and Property (APLP) was founded, Reeves received many letters full of suggestions about the best way of combating radicalism. Some argued the need to counter Paineite literature by circulating loyalist tracts.[48] An anonymous woman plucked up the courage to enter the public sphere of politics and to propose setting the poor right 'through the medium of *vulgar ballads* ... Every serving man and maid, every Country Girl and her Sweetheart ... will buy a halfpenny ballad to a popular tune.'[49] Other correspondents sent in samples of popular literature, either written by themselves or by others. One of the tracts was *One Penny Worth of Truth from Thomas Bull to his Brother John*, written by the prominent High Church clergyman William Jones of Nayland, a friend of the late Bishop Horne. This tract and the other Thomas and John Bull pamphlets that followed it were among the most successful (that is to say, most widely distributed) of the loyalist pamphlets.[50]

The John Bull tracts took the form of dialogues between John and Thomas Bull and were a mixture of conservative political theory, British patriotism, black humour, knockabout abuse of the French, and scurrilous half-truths about Thomas Paine. Common arguments run through these and similar writings: the British political system is organic and slow-growing, the French constitution a botched, hastily manufactured affair; the French Revolution has led to violence and disorder; human beings are naturally unequal, yet in England all are equally protected by the law; complete economic equality (which Paine had never advocated) would end the division of labour and impoverish everyone.

[47] *British Museum Catalogue of Political and Personal Satires*, 8122.
[48] BL, Add. MS 16919, Reeves MS, fo. 148.   [49] BL, Add. MS 16920, Reeves MS, fo. 99.
[50] They can be found in [W. Jones] *Liberty and Property Preserved against Republicans and Levellers: A Collection of Tracts*, i:. Nos. 1 and 11 (London [1792]).

It is almost certain that Hannah More read some of these tracts. If not, many of her friends did, including William Weller Pepys, one of the many people of mildly reformist inclinations who had turned conservative. He wrote to her on 5 December 1792, 'Both Mrs Montagu and I most *earnestly* request you to exact your admirable Talents at this Juncture for the Good of your Country (Which is in great Peril)...We think you wou'd do it most successfully in the way of a Dialogue between two persons of the lowest order.'[51] As so often in More's life, a plea from a valued friend gave her the necessary justification to do what was probably already in her mind. Who knew the common people—the pattern of their lives, their hopes and fears, their colloquialisms, the rhythms of their speech—better than she? Who was better qualified to address them? Spurred into action, she sat down one day in Bath at the end of 1792 and penned at white-heat a 5,000-word survey of the main loyalist arguments, which she entitled *Village Politics Addressed to all the Mechanics, Journeymen and Day Labourers in Great Britain, by Will Chip, a Country Carpenter*. While she was writing, 'Louis Capet' was on trial for his life before the revolutionary Convention.

Like the other popular loyalist tracts, *Village Politics* takes the form of a dialogue in which the novelty and violence of the French Revolution is contrasted with the tried and trusted virtues of the British political system. In one respect it is more democratic than the others, as the loyalist case is put into the mouth of a blacksmith called Jack Anvil. His opponent, Tom Hod, a mason, has picked up *Rights of Man* and finds from it 'that I'm very unhappy and very miserable, which I should never have known if I had not had the good luck to meet with this book'.[52] Jack's function is to put him right using arguments which represent Hannah More's conservative, Pittite Whiggism rather than unreconstructed Toryism. Most of the arguments of the allegedly 'reactionary' *Village Politics* turn out to be the same as those of the more 'progressive' *Slavery*, and were to emerge again in a more extended and intellectual fashion in the *Hints towards Forming the Character of a Young Princess*, which More wrote for the young Princess Charlotte in 1805. Jack's politics are those of the balanced constitution allegedly set up by the Glorious Revolution to prevent the abuse of power. Unlike the French, subjected first to the whims of an absolute monarch and then to the fury of the mob, Englishmen enjoy the protection of the law, security of property, and freedom of worship. If they fall on hard times, they are aided by charity-parish, private, or institutional. Like the other loyalist writers, More insisted

---

[51] *A Later Pepys: The Correspondence of Sir William Weller Pepys, Bart.*, ed. A. C. C. Gaussen (London, 1904), ii. 283-4.
[52] *VP* 4.

that the British state benefited the poor as well as the rich and that it was an act of rational self-interest to support it.

The physical context of the debate is skilfully sketched in. The village is both allegorical and rooted in an idealized contemporary reality somewhere in Somerset. There is a resident squire, Sir John, a benevolent Sir Roger de Coverley figure, with a French manservant and the kind of restless, extravagant wife who was the butt of so much contemporary moralizing. The quasi-feudal castle in which he lives is a symbol of his paternal care for the villagers. He supports the Sunday school and the school of industry that teaches Jack's daughters to sew and knit. Other villagers include the tailor (Snip), the butcher (Hackabout), a farmer called Furrow, and an exciseman called Standish, who is the local radical. The meeting-place for the men of the village is the Rose and Crown, which, in spite of its traditional name, is a scene of vehement political arguments.

Running through *Village Politics* is a semantic debate, reflecting the loyalist attempt to wrest control of the political language from the revolutionaries and restore the older, less ideologically charged usages. At the beginning of the pamphlet Jack is deliberately obtuse. When Tom says, 'I want a new constitution', he responds with, 'Why, I thought thou hadst been a desperate healthy fellow. Send for the doctor directly.' Tom then declares that he wants 'Liberty, Equality and the Rights of Man', thus enabling Jack to respond with the language of John Reeves's Association: 'Thou art a leveller and a republican, I warrant!' When Tom uses the word 'reform', Jack gives it a moral rather than a political meaning: 'The shortest way is to mend thyself.'[53] At the end of the dialogue Tom shows his conversion to the loyalist case by echoing Jack's inversion of the revolutionary vocabulary: liberty is the right to murder; a democrat is 'one who likes to be governed by a thousand tyrants, yet can't bear a king'; equality is 'for every man to pull down every one that is above him'; the new Rights of Man are (in the language of the Prayer Book) 'battle, murder and sudden death'.[54]

Though the tone of *Village Politics* is less xenophobic than that of the John Bull tracts, More is happy to abuse the French when it suits her argument. Like the other loyalist writers, she makes much of the violence of the Revolution: 'If they don't like a man's looks, they make free to hang him without judge or jury, and the next lamp-post does for the gallows.'[55] Even before the Revolution 'they could clap an innocent man into prison, and keep him there too, as long as they would, and never say with your leave, or by your leave, Gentleman of the Jury'.[56] In contrast, Englishmen live under the rule of law, and as for liberty, 'Why, we've got it, man!...we're there

---

[53] Ibid.   [54] *VP* 19.   [55] *VP* 5.   [56] *VP* 5–6.

already! Our constitution is no more like what the French one was than a mug of our Taunton beer is like a platter of their soup-maigre.'[57]

Though More takes it for granted that all are equal in the sight of God, she advances two different sets of arguments to support a hierarchical, unequal society. One is religious, the traditional great chain of being schema familiar from Tudor times: Providence has ordained that 'the woman is below her husband, and the children are below their mother, and the servant is below his master'.[58] This is reinforced by free quotations from two of the staple texts of Anglican political theory: 'Render unto Caesar the things that are Caesar's' (Matthew 22: 21) and the much-used opening verses of Romans 13: 'Let every soul be subject to the higher powers; for the powers that be are ordained of God.'[59] The other argument was secular, utilitarian, and primitivist. In a familiar distortion of the radical case, Jack assumes that an egalitarian society would mean a general division of land that would do away with the division of labour. But if everyone were to be given an acre of ground apiece, he would be unable to mend a broken spade, 'Neighbour Snip would have no time to make us a suit of cloaths, nor the clothier to weave the cloth; for all the world would be gone a digging.'[60] This would be no idyllic Rousseauean paradise but Hobbes's state of nature. 'If such a sturdy fellow as I am, was to come and break down thy hedge . . . I'm not so sure that these new-fangled laws would have thee righted.'[61] Equality 'wou'd not last while one cou'd say Jack Robinson'.[62]

One of the most effective passages in *Village Politics* takes the form of a sustained metaphor encapsulating Burke's arguments. (Like many of the writings on either side of the political argument, it was also tinged with misogyny.)

When Sir John married, my Lady, who is a little fantastical, and likes to do everything like the French, begged him to pull down yonder fine old castle, and build it up in her frippery way. No, says Sir John; what shall I pull down this noble building, raised by the wisdom of my brave ancestors; which outstood the civil wars, and only underwent a little needful repair at the Revolution; and which all my neighbours come to take a pattern by—shall I pull it all down, I say, only because there may be a dark closet, or an inconvenient room or two in it? My lady mumpt and grumbled; but the castle is let stand, and a glorious building it is; though there may be a trifling fault or two, and though a few decays want stopping; so now and then they mend a little thing . . . But no pull-me-down works.[63]

---

[57] *VP* 13.   [58] *VP* 11.

[59] *VP* 12. More later expanded Jack's argument by stressing that St Paul obeyed the Emperor Nero even though he was 'a monster' who set fire to Rome and persecuted the Christians. *Works* (1801), i. 334.

[60] *VP* 7.   [61] *VP* 8.   [62] *VP* 7.   [63] *VP* 8–9.

It is because of passages such as this that *Village Politics* has been wittily described as 'Burke for Beginners'.[64] However, other parts of the tract are pure Hannah More. Jack's daughter attends a charity school and, like the more promising children in the Mendip schools, she has been allowed to bring home a book. Her father has picked it up and read a story from Roman history showing how the patricians and plebeians ('the Belly and the Limbs') all need each other. More's ideal society was hierarchical, but it was also mutually interdependent, with the poor as necessary as the rich to the smooth running of the state.[65] And as she went out of her way to point out that both Jack and his daughter could read, it was clear that she did not advocate that they should be kept in ignorance.

An equally characteristic passage was in part a rerun of the arguments of her *Estimate of the Religion of the Fashionable World,* and her victim was Sir John's idle, hypochondriac of a wife. Yet though the satire was sharper than ever, More's attack on luxury was ambiguous. She was forced to admit that it had its uses.

Tho' my Lady is too rantipolish, and flies about all summer to hot water and cold water, and fresh water and salt water, when she ought to stay at home with Sir John; yet when she does come down, she brings such a deal of gentry, that I have more horses than I can shoe, and my wife more linen than she can wash. Then all our grown children are servants in the family, and rare wages they have got. Our little boys get something every day by weeding their gardens; and the girls learn to sew and knit at Sir John's expence, who sends them all to school of a Sunday.[66]

In the absence of paternalistic care, institutional charity is on hand to help the poor, such as the Bristol Infirmary, where Tom had been treated.[67] There was, as Jack points out with more rhetoric than accuracy, nothing comparable in France: 'no 'firmaries, no hospitals, no charity schools, no sunday-schools ... For who is to pay for them? *equality* can't afford it'.[68]

Another characteristic Hannah More touch came in the treatment of religion. Unlike the High Church pamphleteers, she advocated tolerance and inclusion.

There's many true dissenters, and there's hollow churchmen; and a good man is a good man, whether his church has got a steeple to it or not ... Now, tho' some folks pretend that a man's hating a Papist or a Presbyterian, proves him to be a good *Churchman*, it don't prove him to be a good *Christian*, Tom. As much as I hate republican works, I'd scorn to *live* in a country where there was not liberty of conscience; and where every man might not worship God his own way.[69]

---

[64] M. G. Jones, *Hannah More* (Cambridge, 1952), 134.   [65] *VP* 9–10.   [66] *VP* 15–16.
[67] *VP* 16.   [68] *VP* 16–17.   [69] *VP* 18.

It was an important part of More's argument that the French had moved from religious repression to an equally intolerant irreligion. They had murdered their priests, abolished the sabbath, and chosen a new god, 'a wicked old fellow' whose 'rotten bones' were dug up so that he could be worshipped.[70] This was a scornful dismissal of the elaborate ceremony of 11 July 1791 in which Voltaire's corpse was taken to the Panthéon, a ceremony which anticipated Robespierre's deistic, quasi-Masonic cult of the Supreme Being.

Finally, Jack appeals to the multifaceted concept of patriotism: 'While Old England is safe, I'll glory in her, and pray for her; and when she is in danger, I'll fight for her, and die for her.'[71] In a generalized sense patriotism was bound up with Protestantism and anti-French sentiment and had been grow-ing throughout the century. More specifically, however, it had been claimed by the opposition politicians, most recently during the American war. (This was why Johnson had famously condemned patriotism as the last refuge of a scoundrel.) Now More and her fellow conservatives were reclaiming it for loyalism.[72] However, when Tom declares his intention to burn both his book and an effigy of Tom Paine, Jack quickly discourages him. 'If thou wouldst show they love to thy King and country, let's have no drinking, no riot, no bonfires.' Instead, as the parson instructed them, they are to 'Study to be quiet, work with your own hands and mind your own business.'[73] With this dismissal of the more raucous manifestations of John Bullism, More ended her pamphlet on a characteristic note.

On the surface *Village Politics* seems a very simplistic work, misrepresenting the radical case and setting out a bucolic, harmonious version of Old Eng-land as she never was. In fact, its conservatism is ambiguous and paradox-ical. The poor are invited to enter a political debate at the same time as they are told that they have no expertise in politics. Yet Jack's grasp of politics reveals him to be a more eloquent and thoughtful commentator than many a booby squire, and if the right to vote is to rest on an understanding of political issues, it becomes difficult to justify his exclusion. More even holds out the hope that some of her readers may eventually win the franchise, not through direct action, which will only raise prices, but by quietly and stead-ily improving their economic prospects.[74] This was an unrealistic argument in 1792 and was to become more so in the grim years that followed.

---

[70] *VP* 14, 20.   [71] *VP* 23.
[72] See D. Eastwood, 'Patriotism and the English State in the 1790s', in Philp (ed.), *French Revolution and British Popular Politics*, 146–68; id., 'Robert Southey and the Meanings of Patriot-ism', *Journal of British Studies*, 31 (1992), 265–87; L. Colley, 'The Apotheosis of George III: Loyalty, Royalty and the British Nation', *Past and Present*, 102 (1984), 94–129; ead., *Britons: Forging the Nation, 1707–1837* (New Haven, 1992), chs. 5–7 and *passim*.
[73] *VP* 23–4.   [74] *VP* 11.

Nevertheless, she suggests that no man need consider himself irrevocably excluded from the franchise.

A second paradox concerns her concept of hierarchy. For all his defence of an unequal society, Jack is critical of magistrates: 'We have the best laws in the world, if they were more strictly enforced.'[75] The 'if' is significant, as is his critique of the upper classes.

And as to our great folks, that you levellers have such a spite against; I don't pretend to say they are a bit better than they should be; but that's no affair of mine; let them look to that; they'll answer for that in another place. To be sure, I wish they'd set us a better example about going to church and those things . . . and . . . if I was a parson I'd go to work with 'em.[76]

Behind the tugged forelock lies a sharp and critical mind. The sentiments, of course, are Hannah More's. In literature apparently aimed exclusively at the plebeian population she could not refrain from castigating the vices of the rich and encouraging her readers to share her condemnation.

There was a contradiction lying at the heart of all the popular loyalist propaganda. Writing for the educated elite, Burke excluded the lower orders, but the Reeves correspondents knew that they had to persuade the poor with reasoned argument. Of all the 'vulgar' authors Hannah More went furthest in this direction. The suggestible Tom is able to make some sort of case for the radicals, while in the process of his conversion he has been given a set of criteria by which to judge a government: equal justice, property rights, press freedom, social benefits.[77] How else can he be convinced that the British state is better than the French? More's tactic was risky but unavoidable. As the only major loyalist pamphleteer who had actually taught literacy to the poor, she above all knew that it was no longer possible to pretend that the mass of the population could be excluded from political debates. In competing with radical propaganda, the conservative pamphleteers had to court, entertain, and persuade their readers, to canvass for their loyalty if not their votes. Unavoidably, in the long term, they played into the hands of their opponents.

Village Politics was published anonymously at the end of December 1792. To cover her tracks More chose Rivington rather than Cadell, and did not send copies out to her friends.[78] The only exception to the self-imposed secrecy was Mrs Garrick, and More's defensive tone in her letter suggests an anxious attempt to repair a friendship that was cooling: 'I tell you fairly you wont like

---

[75] *VP* 23. [76] *VP* 14–15.

[77] See Philp, 'Vulgar Conservatism', 62–3; D. Herzog, *Poisoning the Minds of the Lower Orders* (Princeton, 1998), 130–3.

[78] Roberts, ii. 345.

it, and I shall not be affronted if you tell me so, for it is not written for the polished but the ignorant.'[79] Mrs Garrick apparently did not enthuse, but Porteus, who was in the secret from the beginning, and promised not to divulge the authorship, circulated it assiduously, as did the APLP.[80] It was an instant success. The royal family liked it very much (they would have been ungrateful if they had not).[81] Not knowing it was by one of her acquaintances, Fanny Burney quoted it with approval a few days after its publication. 'Let every one mend one, as Will Chip says, & then States, as well as families may be safely reformed—I hope you like "Village Politics". It makes much noise in London, & is suspected to be by some capital Author.'[82] Frances Boscawen sent a packet to her daughter, the duchess of Beaufort; she found the work superior to Archdeacon William Paley's deeply complacent *Reasons for Contentment* because the author 'understood the language much better'.[83] (More had also prudently refrained from Paley's bizarre suggestion that the rich should envy the poor rather than the other way round.)

When the secret emerged at the beginning of February, many wrongly believed *Village Politics* had been commissioned by Pitt. This, as Henry Thornton pointed out, was untrue.[84] However, the prime minister's 3-guinea contribution to the Cheap Repository in 1795 (he was the only member of the government to subscribe) was a measure of his appreciation. Another admirer was Horace Walpole. Though increasingly uneasy at the rigorous tone of More's writings for fashionable society, he believed that here she had triumphantly succeeded, producing a work that was 'infinitely superior to anything on the subject, clearer, better stated, and comprehending the whole mass of matter in the shortest compass'.[85]

Anecdotal evidence suggests that the tract was a success and that More had resoundingly trumped most of her male fellow pamphleteers. There is no evidence that she was criticized for her bid to bring the poor into the political debate. A year later *Village Politics* received the compliment of imitation in the form of *The Country Carpenter*, a scurrilous tract full of unpleasant gloating over Tom Paine's imprisonment in Luxembourg, claiming to come from the author of *Village Politics*.[86] More's reaction was ambivalent. In her diary for 9 November 1794 she wrote, 'My dear friends

---

[79] Folger, W.b. 487, fo. 81, More to Eva Garrick, 8 Jan. 1793.

[80] Roberts, ii. 347–8; A. Stott, 'Hannah More: Evangelicalism, Cultural Reformation, and Loyalism', Ph.D. thesis (London, 1998), 216–17.

[81] Roberts, ii. 348.

[82] *Journal and Letters of Fanny Burney (Madame d'Arblay)*, ii: *Courtship and Marriage, 1793*, ed. J. Hemlow (Oxford, 1972), 14.

[83] Roberts, ii. 351.

[84] Thornton, Add. MS 7674/1/L7, fo. 73, Thornton to Zachary Macaulay, 20 Feb. 1796.

[85] *Walpole*, 380.

[86] *A Country Carpenter's Confession of Faith* (London, 1794). Both the British Library and the Cambridge University Library catalogues incorrectly attribute the tract to More.

were not deceived...I pray however that this book which is good in the main may do good.'[87] But *The Country Carpenter* simply coasted along in the wake of the success of *Village Politics*, in which More had shown that, more than other loyalist propagandists, she could write a short, simple, popular tract that could convey quite complicated political ideas in colloquial language, vivid dialogue, and clear, effective metaphors. She had mapped out a new career as a writer of popular literature.

On 21 January 1793 Louis XVI was executed; two days later the news reached a shocked Britain. Court and Parliament went into mourning and the theatres closed. At Bath the Catholic chapel was hung in black and a requiem mass was heard by a tearful congregation.[88] In the following days the papers filled up with stories of the king's dignified demeanour at his trial and execution and the sufferings of his family. Their readers could not get enough of a story so full of human interest. The More sisters were typical. 'We have done little else but weep for him, talk of him, and read of him,' Hannah told Mrs Garrick.[89] The execution was 'the murder of the most innocent and perhaps the only really Christian king which ever sat upon their throne'.[90] 'From liberty, equality, and the rights of man, good Lord deliver *us*!' she exclaimed to Walpole.[91] He wrote back immediately to 'dear holy Hannah'. 'I have no words that can reach the criminality of such *inferno-human* beings.' The present age could well be styled 'the diabolic age'—there had never been another like it in human history and no one could tell where it would all end.[92] By this time Britain and France were at war. The fundamental cause lay in French expansionism rather than the king's execution, but horror at Louis's death intensified a widespread feeling that the war was just and necessary. No one anticipated that it would last for twenty-two years.

As usual Hannah More was ill, but still immersing herself in pamphlet literature. She told Walpole, 'I wonder if I shall ever live to read a book again that shall cost a shilling. I have lived so long on halfpenny papers, penny cautions, twopenny warnings and threepenny sermons, that I shall never be able to stretch my capacity even to a duodecimo!' These studies, she added, were 'harassing to the nerves, and although like dram-drinking, they invigorate for a moment, yet like that too, they add to the depression afterwards'.[93] But she was engaged in a new project, and the exhilaration of

---

[87] Clark [uncatalogued] More's diary for 1794. For her denials of authorship, see Duke, More to Wilberforce, 29 Nov. 1794; *Gambier*, i. 268.
[88] *St James's Chronicle*, 24–6 Jan. 1793; *FFBJ*, 26 Jan., 2 Feb. 1793.
[89] Folger, W.b. 489, fo. 82, More to Eva Garrick, 2 Feb. 1793.
[90] Clark, More to Ann Kennicott, Bath, 4 Feb. 1793.   [91] *Walpole*, 375.
[92] Ibid. 377–80.   [93] Ibid. 375–6.

the task kept her going. She was writing a pamphlet, designed this time for an educated readership, and her purpose was to aid a particularly deserving group of unfortunates—the French émigré clergy driven out of their own country for the sake of conscience, traumatized, poverty-stricken, and in need of urgent relief.

The plight of these clergy dated from the summer and autumn of 1790, when the Constituent Assembly promulgated the Civil Constitution of the Clergy, and the deputies decided to dismiss all clerics who did not accept the new order, and to impose a loyalty oath to test their acceptance. Unintentionally perhaps, the Assembly had created the conditions by which monopolistic religious privilege was to be replaced by secular intolerance.[94] About half the clergy refused to subscribe, and, with so many of the priests recalcitrant, opposition to the Revolution grew among many laity in the large provincial cities and in the deeply Catholic rural areas in western France. By the middle of 1791 most bishops had left the country; the priests were to follow in the winter of 1791–2. Many of those who remained were to perish in the carnage of the September massacres.

By 1793 more than 2,000 priests were in Jersey or the English mainland, the numbers rising all the time.[95] In a curious reversion of history, Britain, which, a hundred years before, had welcomed Huguenots fleeing from the tyranny of Louis XIV, was now offering shelter to the representatives of the religion that had persecuted them. Dissenters, radicals, and many local parishioners were predictably hostile, but, led by the archbishop of Canterbury, the higher clergy of the Church of England extended them the hand of friendship. The warmth of their reception is not as surprising as it might seem. Many Anglican clergy, particularly High Church Tories, saw the national-based Gallican Church in France as a sister Church, trinitarian, anti-deistic, uniting throne and altar, and forming a bulwark against fashionable infidelity.[96] It was a time for established Churches to band together. In September 1792 John Eardley Wilmot, MP for Coventry and son of Garrick's old friends, set up a National Relief Committee for the émigrés. At Burke's request, Wilberforce joined the committee, partly to extricate himself from the embarrassment at having been declared an honorary French citizen along with Paine and Priestley.[97] Subscriptions began to pour in, and one of

---

[94] J. McManners, *Church and Society in Eighteenth-Century France*, i: *The Clerical Establishment and its Social Ramifications* (Oxford, 1998), 4.

[95] For the émigré clergy, see D. Bellinger, 'The Émigré Clergy and the English Church, 1789–1815', *Journal of Ecclesiastical History*, 34 (1983), 392–410; K. Carpenter, *Refugees of the French Revolution: Émigrés in London, 1789–1802* (Basingstoke and New York, 1999); ead. and P. Mansell (eds.), *The French Émigrés in Europe and the Struggle against Revolution, 1789–1814* (Basingstoke and New York, 1999).

[96] Aston, 'A "lay divine"', 200–6.   [97] *Life of Wilberforce*, ii. 369–70.

the bankers taking the money was Henry Thornton's bank, Down, Thornton, and Free. However, by March 1793 the fund for the clergy was drying up, and a renewed effort was required if more money was to be raised.

In the same month Walpole wrote to More, mischievously thanking her for the news of her 'pregnancy' (a word she later crossed out and demurely changed to 'publication').[98] The 'pregnancy' was her latest publication, *Remarks on the Speech of M. Dupont*. Jacques Dupont was a member of the Convention, deputy for Indre-et-Loire, who in December 1792 had made a violently anticlerical speech, which was being circulated in translation in an English pamphlet. Both tone and subject matter confirmed More's Burkean belief that at the dark heart of the French Revolution lay an assault on religion that went far deeper than any attack on kings. When she received a copy of the speech, she knew she had found her subject. *Dupont* was published by Cadell on 1 April with More's name on the title page; Porteus had overruled her stated intention to remain anonymous, and as usual she submitted to male authority when it harmonized with her unconscious wishes.[99] It was priced at 2s. 6d., and readers were informed that the profits were to go to the French clergy. A couple of weeks later it had gone into a second edition.[100] It was quickly translated into French, though many of the émigré clergy found the tactless anti-Catholicism of parts of the pamphlet hard to stomach.[101] The subscribers' committee eventually received £240 from the sales.[102]

Unlike *Village Politics*, the pamphlet was aimed at an affluent readership and geared specifically to women, a fact made clear by its 'Prefatory Address to the Ladies . . . of Great Britain', which contained a defence of the right of a private individual, even a woman, to intervene in a public issue: there were occasions 'so extraordinary that all the lesser motives of delicacy ought to vanish before them'.[103] In the main text she launched into Dupont's 'monstrous impiety'. The aim of the French Revolution 'is not to dethrone kings, but HIM by whom kings reign'.[104] The French Revolution was fundamentally a moral evil: the danger came not from 'French bayonets' but 'the contamination of French principles', and the 'real and pressing evils' in England arose less from external threats than from 'our own corruption'.[105] The true remedy was for the Church to reform itself: 'No degree of orthodoxy can atone for a too close assimilation with the manners of the world.'[106] But the nation could also protect itself by banning 'corrupt and inflaming publications . . . the crooked progeny of treason and blasphemy' such as the writings of Voltaire and d'Alembert.[107] Readers might also

[98] *Walpole*, 384.   [99] Ibid. 382.   [100] *St James's Chronicle*, 11–13 Apr. 1793.
[101] Roberts, ii. 388; Clark, More to Ann Kennicott, 18 Nov. 1793.   [102] Roberts, ii. 359.
[103] *Remarks on the Speech of M. Dupont*, p. iii.   [104] Ibid. 2–3, 26.   [105] Ibid. 44, 15.
[106] Ibid. 19–20.   [107] Ibid. 21–2.

ponder the possibility that the French had been sent by God 'as a scourge for the iniquities of the human race'. If so, let everyone consider how his offences might have contributed to 'that awful aggregate of public guilt'.[108] Or, as Jack Anvil had put it more pithily, let each one mend himself.

Basking in the success of *Dupont*, More paid her usual May visit to Teston, now sadly depleted after the sudden death of Lady Middleton the previous October, and eagerly followed the progress of Wilberforce's bill to limit the importation of slaves into the British sugar colonies. By June she was back supervising her schools. In the following month Wilberforce and John Venn, the rector of Clapham, visited her and, ignoring the resentment building up among some of the local clergy, she secured the Axbridge and Cheddar pulpits for Venn.

By this time she had made the acquaintance of a prominent émigré priest, who was spending a week at her sisters' house in Bath. She was impressed with his broad-mindedness, thinking it 'rather extraordinary that he joined in the Family Prayer, and looked over the book as Patty read it'.[109] Nearly two years later she was to become friends with one of the most distinguished of the émigré clergy, Urbain de Hercé, bishop of Dol in Brittany.[110] A man of apostolic simplicity, he had given out large amounts of his personal income to relieve distress in his poor and remote diocese; the annual feast he used to hold before the beginning of Lent bore some resemblance to the Mendip feasts.[111] His unbending Catholicism apart, he was exactly More's type of clergyman, 'the most virtuous and pious bishop...in France'.[112] In June 1795 he set off with 12,000 émigrés and some fellow clergy on the disastrous Quiberon expedition, only to be captured, tried by a military commission, and executed by firing squad, along with his brother on 28 July. 'I consider them as sort of martyrs,' More wrote to Wilberforce, 'for they expected the destruction they have met, but they thought it their duty to return.'[113]

This was in the bleak future. In the meantime *Dupont* continued to make waves; Burke recommended it to Anne Crewe, the political hostess.[114] Many Whigs and Dissenters, however, disliked its tone and message and the fact that More had condemned the whole French nation on the basis of a single

---

[108] Ibid. 42–3.   [109] Clark, More to Ann Kennicott, 18 July 1793.

[110] As he and More were both in London in March and April 1795, it was likely that they met then. For Urbain de Hercé, see C. Robert, *Urbain de Hercé, Dernier Évêque et Comte de Dol* (Paris, 1900).

[111] McManners, *Church and Society in France*, i. 290.

[112] *Gambier*, i. 286, More to Elizabeth Bouverie, 14 Aug. 1795.

[113] Duke, More to Wilberforce, 27 Aug. [1795].

[114] *Correspondence of Edmund Burke*, vii, ed. P. J. Marshall and J. A. Woods (Cambridge and Chicago, 1968), 426.

speech.[115] An extraordinarily offensive assault was mounted in an anonymous publication entitled *Gideon's Cake of Barley-Meal*: More had lied when she praised the good character of the French clergy; she was therefore 'most evidently the daughter of the "Father of Lies"'; she 'must have drank freely "of the wine of fornication of that mother of harlots"', and she was probably descended from 'that bitter persecutor Sir Thomas More' and saw 'such wonderful glory and honour in Popery, there is no doubt she would have made an excellent maid of honour to that bloody queen'.[116] More professed herself greatly amused—the author of *Bishop Bonner's Ghost* described as Mary Tudor's waiting woman!—and urged Elizabeth Bouverie to read it in order to enjoy its unique flavour.[117] She believed that it had been written by the Dissenting preacher and former coal-heaver the high Calvinist William Huntington, who used the letters S.S. ('Sinner Saved') after his name, and knew an attack from such a quarter could be laughed off.[118] She was more concerned to learn that a defence of her character had been published, thus keeping her in the public eye, when she wanted the whole furore to die down of its own accord.[119]

More was not the only woman to respond to the needs of the clergy. In November Fanny Burney, who had recently married the émigré Alexandre d'Arblay, published her own pamphlet.[120] By this time Mrs Crewe and the Irish Catholic heiress the marchioness of Buckingham had formed their own Ladies' Society, with Dr Burney as treasurer, designed to raise subscriptions and heighten public awareness of the plight of the émigré clergy.[121] A delegation of these ladies approached More, and, as she told Ann Kennicott, 'wished to make me their *Chair-woman or female Mr Wilmot*'. She pleaded ill health, but the real reason lay in 'the ostensibleness and publicity attached to such an office'.[122] As so often, she had helped open up a new opportunity for women's participation in the public sphere, only to shrink from the consequences of her action.

One of the most noteworthy public events in the late summer of 1793 was the outrageously biased trials in Edinburgh of the radicals Thomas Muir and Thomas Palmer and their subsequent transportation. But like other conservatives More was more preoccupied with the fate of Marie Antoinette, guillo-

[115] *Analytical Review*, 17 (1793), 94–5; *Monthly Review*, NS 11 (1793), 118–19.

[116] *Gideon's Cake of Barley-Meal: A Letter to the Rev. William Romaine . . . with some Strictures on Mrs Hannah More's Remarks published for their benefit* (London, 1793), 51, 61–3.

[117] *Gambier*, i. 221–2, 230.

[118] *Gideon's Cake* was probably written by the Calvinist polemicist Michael Nash.

[119] This was *A Charitable Morsel of Unleavened Bread for the Author of a Letter to the Rev William Romaine, entitled Gideon's Cake of Barley Meal, being a reply to that pamphlet* (London, 1793).

[120] F. Burney, *Journal and Letters*, ed. Hemlow, ii. 14 n. 4.

[121] Ibid. 5–6; *Memoirs of Dr Burney* (London, 1832), ii. 185–7.

[122] Clark, More to Ann Kennicott, 18 Nov. 1793.

tined on 16 October. Mere plumage she might be, in Paine's famous phrase, but it was hard for newspaper-reading women to dissociate themselves from her sufferings. The details were graphically reported: what Hannah More called her 'narrow and squalid prison', the plight of the little dauphin who had been taken from his mother, the trial with its bizarre charges of child abuse, the courage with which she faced death.[123] The next royal victim, More speculated correctly to Mrs Garrick, would be the king's sister, 'that spotless saint, Princess Elizabeth', who had turned down the opportunity to escape in order to remain with her brother. In the same letter More gave her friend an intriguing piece of news. Some time back two young French sisters had been teachers, one after the other, at the Park Street school. 'The letters they used to receive from their mother and brothers show'd they were fierce, ambitious, romantic, irreligious, but very philosophising and meddling in politics.' It turned out that one of the brothers was none other than Dupont and that one of the sisters had married Jacques-Pierre Brissot, the recently guillotined Girondin leader.[124]

In the following April the school was in the news again. Richard Vining Perry was in Bristol prison ready to be tried for his life for abduction. His wife had joined him in prison along with their young child; she was pregnant once more.

---

[123] See e.g. *St James's Chronicle*, 3–5, 22–4 Oct. 1793; *Analytical Review*, 17 (1793), 418–26.

[124] Folger, W.b. 487, fo. 87, More to Eva Garrick, 21 Nov. 1793. In 1782 Brissot married Félicité Dupont. According to Helen-Maria Williams, she 'partageait l'enthousiasme de son mari pour les principes qui firent la règle de sa conduite'. L.D. Woodward, *Une Anglaise Amie de la Révolution française* (Paris, 1930), 61. She died in 1818. She had three sisters, Marie-Thérèse, Julie Henriette, and Marie Anne. E. Ellery, *Brissot de Warville: A Study in the History of the French Revolution* (Boston, 1915).

Chapter 7

The Greeks and the Barbarians
1794–1798

HANNAH MORE is known to have kept a spiritual diary for at least four years of her life. Those for the years 1798, 1803, and 1804 apparently survive only in the pages of her biographer William Roberts and have clearly been heavily censored. However, the actual diary for 1794 is now in the Clark Library, Los Angeles, and though some pages have been cut out and other sections have been very thoroughly scored through, it provides a unique record of the hidden More that lay behind the façade of self-confident busyness. It was written at a significant period in her life, as she entered her fiftieth year; it was round about this time that, in the middle-aged spinster's rite of passage, she assumed the courtesy title 'Mrs More' and began to cover her greying hair with powder. The diary is part of a Puritan and Evangelical genre, a highly self-critical daily or weekly self-analysis in which the writer continually lacerates him- or herself for such faults as weak faith, lack of fervour in prayer, or general inattention to religious duties. These diaries fulfilled the function of the confessional in a Catholic culture. For all their apparent individualism, they were highly stereotyped, and because they inevitably concentrated on failures they do not necessarily give a better guide to the author's personalities than their more public personae. Who would guess from reading Wilberforce's lugubrious diaries at the ebullient quicksilver of his character? The same mismatch is found with Hannah More, where the amusing companion and the compulsive self-flagellator existed side by side. For example, in late July and early August, when she was staying with Henry Thornton at Battersea Rise, she wrote to Patty describing a visit to Betch-worth, where she met a friend of the prince of Wales. 'He says the Prince breakfasted with him the day before & told him that all was over between him and Mrs Fitzherbert. I asked him if he thought they were ever married— he thinks not but is not sure.'[1] In private she duly punished herself for this piece of enjoyable royal gossip, while a subsequent hand, possibly that of William Roberts, scored through the self-condemnation: 'dined next day with Wilb. & H Thornton went to Betchworth ... ~~my mind not in a good frame—worldly, engaged on trifles~~'.[2]

The diary gives a record of a crowded year in More's life. In the summer she noted the death of her 'poor afflicted aunt' Susanna Grace.[3] She went to London in the early spring, dined with Elizabeth Montagu, and reproached herself with a familiar text: 'What does thou here Elijah? felt too much pleasure at that express'd by so many accomplished friends at the sight of me.'[4] Even at Fulham Palace, the home of the Porteuses, she was restless: 'much kindness, literary & elegant society, but the habits of polished life, even of virtuous and pious people are too relaxing'.[5] On a visit to Richmond with Frances Boscawen later in the year she lamented that 'this dear friend has excellent qualities and much piety— ~~but does not see some great matters in a Gospel light~~'. It was becoming increasingly hard for even her more devout friends to match her exacting standards. Back home she faced a different set of trials. On Sunday 28 September she recorded 'a painful trying day' on her visits to Nailsea, Cheddar, and Yatton, where she found much enmity against religious Schemes, opposition, labour, & bodily fatigue. She was also distressed by the 'many scenes of woe' in the workhouses. At the same time she was beset by some personality clashes, possibly with her sisters, as, for all the outward harmony, their ménage sometimes came under strain. Part of the page has been cut away, but the remaining part reads, 'I am much tried as to others tempers. Lord subdue my own evil tempers.'[6]

The pattern of the year as a whole was one of unrelenting activity in which Sunday schools and club feasts jostled with visits to the comfortable homes of her wealthy friends. Increasingly she was coming to see her life as one of variety and contrast, and defining her mission, in terms borrowed from St Paul, as one to the Greeks and the barbarians, the fashionable world and the rural poor. Whereas other moral and religious reformers had tended to concentrate on one or other end of the social spectrum, she worked with both groups and had to adapt her tactics accordingly.

Before further analysing this joint mission, it should be noted that the most dramatic event of the year never found its way into the diary: it was too

---

[1] Thornton, Add. MS 7674/1/L1, fo. 31.   [2] Clark, diary for 1794, *post* Wednesday 23 July.
[3] Ibid., Sun. 31 Aug. She was buried on 19 Aug. Bristol Record Office, parish records for Stoke Gifford.
[4] Ibid., London, 1 Mar.   [5] Ibid., Sunday 4 May.   [6] Ibid.

painful to be set down. More was not in Bristol for the predictable humiliation of Richard Perry's trial but had prudently decamped to London. This did not make its impact any easier to bear. The trial, conducted by the recorder of Bristol, Sir Vicary Gibbs, was a painful farce, ending with his triumphant acquittal and leaving his wife considerably worse off as the costs came from her estate.[7] The defence was led by the brilliant Whig barrister Thomas Erskine who had earlier defended Thomas Paine (unsuccessfully), and later in the year was to defend the members of the London Corresponding Society (with conspicuous success). Like all the great advocates he could be a brutal interrogator. Selina Mills in particular was roughly handled, and her friends feared for her reputation after he belligerently insisted on interpreting her nervous smile as irresponsible levity. No mention was made of the fact that she had been hoodwinked into allowing Clementina to leave the school by a forged letter, purporting to come from the girl's aunt. On the judge's insistence, the defence were permitted to cross-examine Mrs Perry, and when she told the court that she had gone voluntarily with Perry, he instructed the jury to return a Not Guilty verdict. The court erupted with triumphant shouts and the couple embraced ecstatically; in a later age they would have sold their story to the newspapers.

For all Mrs Perry's apparent rejoicing, it was a bleak verdict for women. In a letter to a newly married friend Hester Piozzi put her finger on the girl's dilemma.

Miss Mills is a Maiden Lady, but dear Mrs Pennington knows better now sure than to dream of a Woman's bastardizing her own Babies, and hanging the Father, who could scarcely have been so had there not been some consent on her Side...what must the Girl do? ruin her own children and write herself up a [whore] for the patriotic Desire of saving future Heiresses! I have no notion that such a Girl can be found.[8]

Henry Thornton was equally unsurprised but less sympathetic. He wrote philosophically to Patty,

The poor girl is an object of compassion. I am not surprised at the metamorphosis in her manners and character...She has the advantage in point of reputation in being married, but the effrontery of the poor girl's conduct—the evident metamorphosis of her character & the boldness of the forgery, place her far below the rank of many an unmarried woman in my view & make her ruin much deeper in the eyes of those who look to God & not the world when they are estimating the degrees of vice.[9]

---

[7] Folger, W.b. 487, fo. 88, More to Eva Garrick, 10 Feb. [1794]; *The Trial of Richard Vining Perry* (Bristol, 1794).

[8] H. L. Piozzi, *The Piozzi Letters: Correspondence of Hester Lynch Piozzi*, ii: *1792–1798* (London, 1991), 117.

[9] Thornton, Add. MS 7674/L1, fo. 35.

In the eyes of one man at least she was worse than a prostitute. Even those who appreciated the predicament of a girl who had made an irrevocable decision at the age of 14 were limited in their sympathy. There was no outcry for the law to be changed to protect the young and emotionally immature or to free wives from the power of unscrupulous husbands. By the time Mary Mills had tried to confront her on the road from Gretna, Clementina Perry was beyond the reach of those who would have saved her from herself.

In the same month Hannah More made a significant new friendship when she came to know Horace Walpole's great-niece Laura, Lady Waldegrave; in the following year she met her mother, the duchess of Gloucester, the king's sister-in-law. The duchess, a woman of great beauty and operatic temperament, was one of the most controversial women of the age. Born Maria Walpole, she was the illegitimate daughter of Edward Walpole, Horace's brother.[10] In 1759 at the age of 22 she married James, second Earl Waldegrave, who, though he was twice her age, was considered a very good match indeed for the daughter of a milliner's apprentice. She set up house with her husband at Navestock in Essex, conveniently situated on the road to the Newmarket racecourse, and quickly bore him three famously beautiful daughters, Elizabeth Laura, Charlotte Maria, and Anne Horatia. The marriage was happy, but it was brutally cut short when Lord Waldegrave died suddenly of smallpox in 1763. Three years later, out of ambition or loneliness, the widowed countess took a step which barred her for ever from court society when she secretly married the king's brother William Henry, duke of Gloucester, who was seven years her junior. The rumour of the marriage was one of the causes of the passing of the Royal Marriage Act in 1772, which forbade members of the royal family to marry without the monarch's permission. With the truth out, the new duchess was ostracized by the court. Two children were born, Sophia Matilda in 1773 and William Frederick in 1776, but, as Horace Walpole had feared, the marriage proved a disaster; perhaps it is no coincidence that Sir Joshua Reynolds painted her in the pose of Dürer's *Melancholia*. Tiring of his temperamental wife, the duke began a liaison with her former lady-in-waiting Lady Almeria Carpenter, who give birth to his daughter in 1782. Five years later, hoping for his

---

[10] This discussion is based on V. Biddulph, *The Three Ladies Waldegrave* (London, 1938), J. C. D. Clark (ed.), *Memoirs of James, Second Earl Waldegrave* (Cambridge, 1988), and *The Correspondence of Horace Walpole*, chiefly vol. xxiv (*Correspondence with Sir Horace Mann*, ed. W. S. Lewis, W. H. Smith, and G. L. Lam (London and New Haven, 1967), vol. xxxi (*Walpole*), and vol. xxxvi (*Correspondence with the Walpole Family*, ed. W. S. Lewis and J. W. Reed Jr. (London and New Haven, 1973). In 1750, when Maria was 14, Edward Walpole was indicted on a charge (almost certainly false) of attempted homosexual rape. For the failure of the prosecution and Walpole's ruthless revenge, see N. Murray Goldsmith, *The Worst of Crimes: Homosexuality and the Law in Eighteenth-Century London* (Aldershot, 1998), 109–96.

reinstatement in the king's favour, he wrote penitently to his brother about the duchess's 'very unfortunate turn of mind and temper', which he saw as a punishment for his 'juvenile indiscretion'.[11] After this a disgusted Walpole took care to avoid the duke. His embittered wife passed much of her time abroad, away from the family that had slighted her but also from her daughters by her first marriage and from the uncle who loved her.

Meanwhile the daughters made brilliant careers in London society and were painted by Reynolds as 'the three Ladies Waldegrave'. (This painting is now in the National Gallery of Scotland.) In 1782 Laura married her cousin George, Viscount Chewton, who on the death of his father became the fourth Earl Waldegrave. The children followed rapidly: a daughter, Maria, and then four sons. The couple were happily in love, but the growing family was expensive and the earl's estates were cumbered with debt. In 1786 his mother-in-law swallowed her pride and sent William Wilberforce the kind of letter eighteenth-century women were accustomed to write on behalf of their male relatives. 'I hope through your mediation that Mr Pitt will be so good as to remind His Majesty how very acceptable a Regiment of Dragoons will be to Lord Waldegrave.'[12] But the earl died suddenly in October 1789 leaving his pregnant widow numb with grief.[13] As the years passed and she continued to live the life of a recluse, her great-uncle's concern deepened and he was eager to introduce her to a sympathetic woman who could give her the religious consolation he certainly could not provide. Who better than Hannah More?

Either at Walpole's instigation or on her own initiative More, who had already corresponded with the family, expressed a wish to meet Lady Waldegrave. The meeting took place at Walpole's Berkeley Square house at the end of April 1794; mischievously, he described his own role as 'pimping between two female saints'.[14] In her diary More recorded, 'Saw Lady W, struck with her pious dispositions, & considering she had no human means of gaining them I cannot but infer it to the influence of the divine teacher.'[15] In June she visited her at Navestock, met her sister Maria, now Lady Euston, and 'conceived lively hopes from the pious dispositions of both'. She evidently evangelized them with some vigour as she went on to write, 'Wish I may not have done harm by my over zeal but thought such golden opportunities not to be neglected.'[16]

Soon after this she was given a further opportunity to dispense comfort and the Evangelical message to the unhappy countess. On 29 June, just after his tenth birthday, her eldest son, the fifth earl, was drowned while bathing

---

[11] *Horace Walpole's Correspondence with the Walpole Family*, xxxvi, nn. 244–5.
[12] Bodleian, MS c. 3, fo. 2, duchess of Gloucester to Wilberforce, 4 Feb. 1786.
[13] *Horace Walpole's Correspondence with the Walpole Family*, xxxvi. 269–70.
[14] Ibid. 394. [15] Clark, diary for 1794, 'Sund. April 27'. [16] Ibid., 'Sund. June 1st'.

at Eton. To make matters even worse, the king picked up the rumour that the child had been bullied and had rushed into the water to escape from his tormentors, though everyone was careful to keep this from his distraught mother.[17] Wilberforce, who was staying at Windsor, heard the news the following day and immediately wrote to Hannah More. With the insouciance of a childless man, he made little of the mother's grief compared with the opportunity for evangelism presented by the tragedy.

Considering the State of her Mind when she last wrote to you, the age of the Boy &c &c I own I could never regret the Accident—& it was impossible not to recognize the Rod of him who guides us in ways which now we see not, but of which we shall hereafter discover... & acknowledge the providential kindness— What if you were to sally forth & drive to Lady W. or *to ask her to invite herself for a* few days to your Cottage by way of a Change of Scene &c &c.[18]

More too recognized the opportunity, but felt more compassion for the bereaved mother. 'Her eldest son!' she exclaimed to another aristocratic friend. 'She the fondest of mothers! a lovely young broken hearted widow!'[19] She wrote immediately to Lady Waldegrave, and the reply, moving and heartfelt, came not from the mother but the grandmother. 'O my dear Madam, you do not know what a loss we *all* sustain in that dear, that uncommon child.' She ended the letter, 'your very great admirer—and for all your excellent works very much obliged'.[20] More was taken aback at this praise from such a proud and illustrious woman, and was apprehensive at the roles of bereavement counsellor and spiritual director that were being thrust on her. She told Wilberforce,

By return of post, I received a long letter not from Lady Waldegrave but from the Duchess of Gloucester, so humble and respectful that you would have thought I had been the Princess and she the Cowslip-Green woman. She... desires this sad occasion to begin an acquaintance which she has long desired—She thankfully accepts my offer of coming to her broken-hearted daughter... She forms great hopes of the comfort Ly W. will receive from *me*—and I feel so little equal to the work![21]

The journey to Navestock could not be made immediately, however; Patty was overwhelmed with work, and could not be left to man the field on her own. More did not set out therefore until the end of July. The company was joined by Lord Cornwallis, former governor-general of India, and More questioned him eagerly about the news of the fall and execution of

---

[17] *Horace Walpole's Correspondence with the Walpole Family*, xxxvi. 329.
[18] Bodleian, MS d. 15, fos. 190–1.
[19] BL, Add. MS 46362, fo. 62, More to dowager countess of Haddington.
[20] Biddulph, *Three Ladies Waldegrave*, 333–4.
[21] Duke, More to Wilberforce, 10 July 1794.

Robespierre in the Thermidor coup which had just taken place. But the main business was Lady Waldegrave's soul. More confided to her diary that she found her 'piously disposed but a little afraid of going too far' and ignorant of 'the great doctrines'.[22] But, as she wrote with rather more humility to Elizabeth Bouverie, 'I may be very glad to learn of her that great and important point, submission to the Divine Will. In this point of duty she is quite exemplary, and I feel her decided superiority to myself.'[23]

In the following April, when she was staying with Mrs Garrick, she met Lady Waldegrave's mother. The duchess had given her a green gown, which she wore to Gloucester House, where she was introduced to her children by her first marriage, Prince William and Princess Sophia. She had heard much of Maria Gloucester's vanity and ambition, she told Elizabeth Bouverie, but she found her 'religiously disposed' though she 'took the liberty to contradict some of her *notions* which I thought not sound'. But then 'the doctrine of human corruption is not likely to be very palatable to great beauty or exalted rank'.[24] 'Where in *their* station, shall they look for comfort and assistance when they told me that tho' acquainted with several Bishops, they never cou'd get a word of profit from any of them?' she wrote to Wilberforce. 'I caught myself talking of *the New Birth* when it might have been safer to have rested in lower views and doctrines less novel and terrifying.'[25] Of course the Waldegrave women could not have failed to notice that she was angling for their souls, but they chose to be impressed rather than offended. Lady Euston, the duchess's second daughter, was a lost cause when she converted to the Unitarianism of her father-in-law, the third duke of Grafton, 'the faith *never* delivered to the saints', More wrote sniffily to Wilberforce.[26] But Maria Gloucester herself moved steadily nearer to the Evangelical camp. She contributed 5 guineas to the Cheap Repository tracts and gave an enthusiastic welcome to Wilberforce's *Practical View*, the manifesto of the Clapham sect. She retained her independence of mind, however, and in 1798 she wrote a spirited little memorandum giving vent to her exasperation with Evangelical sabbatarianism. She supposed that Wilberforce would consider her a mere nominal Christian, but for her part she did not see any harm in taking a Sunday evening drive in summer and thought it wrong of 'pious people' to make the lives of the poor a misery.[27] But though the duchess never accepted Evangelicalism in its full strictness, her religious commitment deepened over the years. She died in 1807. After her stormy passage she was fully prepared for death, and her Clapham friends did not doubt her salvation.[28]

[22] Clark, diary for 1794, 10 Aug.   [23] *Gambier*, i. 258   [24] Ibid. 282–3.
[25] Bodleian, c. 3. fo. 242, More to Wilberforce, 18 June [?1795].
[26] Duke, More to Wilberforce, 17 Aug. 1801.
[27] Biddulph, *Three Ladies Waldegrave*, 287.
[28] Clark, More to Mrs H. Thornton, 12 Sept. 1807.

The friendship with Lady Waldegrave continued until her death in 1816. The poor woman had more sorrows ahead of her. In 1805 her daughter, Lady Maria Micklethwaite, died in childbirth after a year's marriage. She wrote a broken letter to her mother with the plea, 'I wish to hear from Hannah More,' and once again More had to give what comfort she could. Lady Waldegrave, she decided, had 'one of the most decided marks of God's own children—that of a frequent visitation from His own hand'.[29] In fact her troubles tested the comfortable Evangelical doctrine of providence. Lady Maria's death caused a puzzled Wilberforce to write her mother a frank but scarcely comforting letter. 'Perhaps the Sentiment in which my Surprize bottomed . . . was that you had already suffer'd so much that it was utterly unlikely that another Stroke, scarcely less severe than any of the former, should succeed.'[30] There was more to come. In 1809 her son Edward was drowned like his brother, on his way home from Sir John Moore's unsuccessful Corunna expedition. Her eldest surviving son, James, the sixth earl, was wild and extravagant, and his mother's last years were spent fretting over his conduct. Try as they might her Evangelical friends had difficulty in discerning a divine purpose behind such sufferings.

These contacts with 'the Greeks' made a piquant contrast with More's work among her 'barbarians' in the Mendips. As her experience with the Waldegraves had shown, different strategies were needed for the two groups. Whereas she could try to nag or bribe the poor into good behaviour and 'vital' Christianity, her behaviour to her social superiors had to be more subtle and accommodating, and she ran the risk of resorting to the flattery her accusers were quick to detect in her. One has only to compare the bossy language of the club feast Charges with the letter she wrote to the duchess of Gloucester when she had suggested holding a Sunday concert for charitable purposes.

I am inclined to think, that no *amusement*, however modified, can be made consistent with the Christian observance of that day, for though the act itself might, to a religious mind, be made even an act of piety; yet, as your Royal Highness observes, many difficulties respecting performers &c. would attend such a plan. I hazard this remark, in the full confidence I have, that truth and candour are more pleasing and acceptable to your royal Highness than anything of a more accommodating or flattering complaisance.[31]

It was difficult to preach the plebeian 'Methodist' doctrine of salvation to aristocratic women, who thought themselves good Christians, but liked their

[29] Biddulph, *Three Ladies Waldegrave*, 336.
[30] Bodleian, MS c. 31, fos. 65–6, Wilberforce to Lady Waldegrave, 15 Apr. 1805.
[31] Roberts, ii. 407.

religion calm, rational, and undemanding. In a previous generation the abrasive Lady Huntingdon had failed to convert the fashionable world. Hannah More, humbly born and more diffident, had to tread a careful path—to teach the truth as she saw it without alienating her social superiors. In her conduct books she was setting out the Evangelical message in an increasingly overt and controversial manner, and her private conversations were geared to probing the spiritual conditions of her fashionable acquaintances without alienating them. It was a balancing act that exposed her to much criticism. Henry Thornton wrote to Zachary Macaulay to defend her against the charge that she flattered the upper classes. After assuring him that she had not written *Village Politics* at Pitt's instigation, he went on,

He little knows her who thinks she is afraid of the upper classes or subject to them, for she has in fact lost many of her great and worldly friends through the opposition she has made to them and the distance to which her principles have thrown her, and having tried almost in vain she has turned to the poor like the Apostle Paul when he said Lo! we turn to the Gentiles![32]

However, the distinction was not so clear-cut as Thornton implied. She might have a poor opinion of the members of polite society, but at the same time, like other middle-class reformers with limited incomes, she tirelessly flattered her fashionable acquaintances into supporting her projects for the poor. 'Your *name* will be the great thing,' she told Elizabeth Montagu, when persuading her to subscribe to the Sunday School Society.[33] Her tactics paid spectacular dividends when she persuaded large numbers of titled and other elite women to contribute often substantial sums of money to the Cheap Repository tracts. Where she could save souls and raise money for her pet causes she could indeed be said to have killed two birds with one stone.

One very distinguished aristocratic acquaintance was Elizabeth, dowager duchess of Beaufort, who lived at Stoke Park. Around this formidable matriarch clustered an influential group of female relatives: her daughter-in-law Elizabeth (wife of the fifth duke and daughter of Frances Boscawen), her daughter Mary Isabella, the beautiful and fashionable widow of the fourth duke of Rutland (and the Pittite rival to the Whig duchess of Devonshire), and her granddaughters Lady Elizabeth and Lady Katherine Manners. More's relationship with the Beaufort family had uneasy patron–client overtones. They were the largest landowners in the area. As has been shown, Elizabeth Beaufort's late brother Norborne Berkeley, Lord Botetourt, had been one of the trustees of the Mary Webb Charity which had set up the Fishponds charity school, and her late husband, the fourth duke, had been

---

[32] Thornton, Add. MS 7674/1/L7, fo. 73, Thornton to Macaulay, 20 Feb. 1796.
[33] Huntington, MO 4003, More to Elizabeth Montagu, 12 Sept. 1791.

the treasurer, responsible for paying Jacob More's meagre salary. It was difficult for More to speak out boldly to a great lady who had known her when she was no more than the daughter of a penniless schoolteacher. In 1794 she lamented her lack of progress in converting the dowager to Evangelical religion. The chief problem, as she described it in the censorious privacy of her diary, was that her manners were 'of perfect decency, regularity and sober-mindedness leaving little room for blame as to life and conduct', making her unable to 'bear vital Xtianity' or to 'understand that *heart* depravity can consist with so much outward order'.[34] A year later she told Wilberforce that, though she had been invited to stay with the dowager and her family at Stoke, 'I can do them no good...I think I have done with the aristocracy—I am no longer a debtor to the Greeks, but I am so to my poor Barbarians.'[35] After a visit in 1798 she vented her feelings in language of biblical coarseness: 'I do not flatter myself that any thing was done except making some of the party uncomfortable—but the dog will return to his vomit.'[36] She told Mrs Thornton that she found the dowager duchess

most exact in her mint anise and Common observances, and paying herself for her external correctness by invections against the general impiety and vices of the great. She laments the deadness and extravagance of the times, but I observe rather abridges her charities than her state, tho her great income wou'd suffice amply for both. Vital Xtianity seems as new to her as the introduction of a sixth sense would be.[37]

If the Beaufort women had known More's low opinion of their spiritual state, they might have been less willing to contribute to the Cheap Repository. They might also have detected some duplicity in More's fulsome dedication of her *Sacred Dramas* to the dowager duchess, in which she praised 'the many amiable and distinguished qualities which adorn her mind and add lustre to her rank'. However, though she singled out the duchess's 'excellence in the maternal character', More did not pay any tribute to her piety; there were limits she was not prepared to cross. But it was a delicate game to play, and with her dual strategy of angling for the souls of aristocratic women while at the same time exploiting their money and prestige to further the reformation of manners, it is not surprising that she had to pray to be 'no mean respecter of persons'.[38] No wonder she found the 'barbarians' less of a problem.

---

[34] Clark, diary for 1794, 6 Dec. 1794.
[35] Duke, More to Wilberforce, 'Cowslip Green, Saturday' [1795].
[36] Bodleian, MS c. 3, fo. 46, More to Wilberforce, 18 Dec. [1798].
[37] Clark, More to Mrs H. Thornton, 1798.
[38] Roberts, iii. 58.

As the More sisters emerged from their winter quarters in the spring of 1794, the Youngs sent them a piece of bad news from Nailsea—the village was infected with smallpox and, though the farmers were inoculating as fast as possible, it would be a while before it was free of infection.[39] Otherwise the news seemed good. When Hannah More returned to the Mendips after her London and Navestock visits, she found her visit to Cheddar and Shipham (Sunday 8 June) 'a day of great comfort—All flourishing & improving, 93 boys & 76 Girls at Cheddar—150 old folks in Eveg. There have been 200 in Winter of the children's Parents to our School.'[40] At the feasts Patty noted that the children were nearly the same in number, the dinner was eaten with the usual appetite, 'the same pleasure appeared to dance upon the countenances of all who possessed a kind heart. The farmers' wives attended as before, riding in the waggons with their children.' Two things, however, marred the enjoyment of the day. One was that a group of people described vaguely by Patty as 'our neighbours' poured abuse on them, an ominous reminder that there were many who still viewed Sunday schools with hostility.[41] The second event was that the Cheddar children attended without Sarah Baber, who was in bed with a fever. Within a fortnight this most beloved of teachers was dead.

It is impossible to exaggerate the effect of Sarah Baber's death on the More sisters. Hannah was at Navestock with Lady Waldegrave when she heard the news. Patty's account of the funeral, written in a lachrymose style anticipating that of Queen Victoria, was described by E. M. Forster as 'one of the great masterpieces of macabre literature'.[42] Hundreds attended, all with some tokens of mourning about them, the children, thoroughly wound up by the occasion, mopping their eyes with their ragged handkerchiefs. Unusually for a woman of her class, Sarah Baber was buried inside the church. John Boak, the curate of Cheddar, took the service, and Patty and Mrs Baber's sister were chief mourners. Mastering his own tears, Boak dared to declare in front of the vicar, 'This eminent Christian first taught *salvation* in Cheddar.' A prayer was then offered for her daughter Betsy, that, like Elisha succeeding Elijah, she might be given a double portion of her mother's spirit. 'She will now suddenly be called into great power,' Patty observed in an irregular feminized inversion of the High Church doctrine of the apostolic succession.[43] (In fact, Betsy Baber was no Elisha. In 1796 she insisted on marrying a man the More sisters disapproved of and had to be dismissed.[44]) She went on to relate that during the interment she herself felt power descend on her, and experienced the need, more associated with

---

[39] *MA* 102–3.   [40] Clark, diary for 1794.   [41] *MA* 120.
[42] E. M. Forster, *Abinger Harvest* (Harmondsworth, 1967), 265.
[43] Roberts, ii. 442.   [44] *MA* 185–6.

Quakers than Anglicans, to speak a message. She restrained herself when she recollected that 'I had heard somewhere a woman must not speak in the church. Oh! had she been interred in the church yard, a messenger from Mr Pitt should not have restrained me.'[45] Conquering the urge to speak, and leaving the mortal remains of this 'mother in Israel', she took the children back to the schoolroom and tried to comfort them.

Hannah More's reaction was hardly less effusive. In a letter to Wilberforce she noted how the achievements of a woman like Mrs Baber broke down the barriers of class.

Last night I was earnest in talking with [Lord Cornwallis] on the politics of France and Flanders, but today Cheddar has driven Robespierre out of my head . . . If Lord C. knew that it was only the death of the poor Mistress of a Charity School which prevents my going down to take leave of him, how cheap wou'd he hold me! But how little in my estimation are the most brilliant Heroes to this dear woman, who has turn'd *many*—I had almost said *hundreds*—to righteousness![46]

'Such talents as those I am regretting', she told Elizabeth Bouverie, 'make all states honourable.'[47] In September the sisters paid their final tribute in the local press, praising her 'humble benevolence and active piety' and using 'the unspeakable felicity she evidenced at the approach of the last enemy' as an example to believers and a warning to the irreligious.[48]

In marked contrast to the language used about Ann Yearsley, Sarah Baber was consistently described throughout her short but momentous association with the Mores in terms that undermined existing hierarchies of class, gender, and clerical status, and make nonsense of assertions that Hannah More was a blinkered and dogmatic supporter of patriarchy. It has already been noted that the sisters referred to her as Bishop Baber, that on her death John Boak saw her as Cheddar's first true pastor, and that Hannah More compared her favourably to the eminent soldier–politician Lord Cornwallis. Significantly, Patty called her a 'mother in Israel', a term commoner in sectarian than Anglican circles. Initially applied to the Old Testament prophetess Deborah, it was bestowed on women of exceptional courage and devotion; it gave women preachers in the Dissenting sects a public role and provided a justification for circumventing St Paul's prohibition of women preachers.[49] For a strong, charismatic woman like Sarah Baber, ostensibly a member of the established Church and therefore barred from preaching, it neatly deflected the charge of acting in an improper fashion.

---

[45] Roberts, ii. 443. [46] Duke, More to Wilberforce [Aug. 1794].
[47] *Gambier*, i. 260. [48] *FFBJ*, 13 Sept.; *Bath Chronicle*, 11 Sept. 1794.
[49] D. Valenze, *Prophetic Sons and Daughters: Female Preaching and Popular Religion in Industrial England* (Princeton, 1985), 35–7. For the application of the term to the autocratic Lady Huntingdon, see B. S. Schlenther, *Queen of the Methodists: The Countess of Huntingdon and the Eighteenth-Century Crisis of Faith and Society* (Durham, 1997), 39, 102.

In the lean and turbulent summer of 1795, when the price of bread almost doubled and desperate rioters were attacking flour mills, Hannah More received a visit from Henry Thornton, 'the sage and Ancient Harry' as she described him, tongue-in-cheek, to Wilberforce.[50] He went round the schools with them, and inspected the dreadful Yatton workhouse.[51] While he was with them, the sisters received a visit from the overseer and churchwarden of Blagdon, a village to the south of Cowslip Green, begging them to open a school. A woman had been condemned to death for attempting to begin a riot and for purloining some butter that was being sold by a tradesman at a price she and her companions thought unreasonable. The records do not show that a Blagdon woman was hanged for these particular crimes, but the fear of execution threw the parish into a panic. The male elites felt helpless and were afraid to set foot in one particularly lawless area. Instead, commented Patty, they 'wished to send two nervous women'.[52] The sisters hesitated for all sorts of common-sense reasons. More told Wilberforce, 'Henry stimulates me and says we *must* engage in it—but my health is bad, my time and Patty's does not more than suffice to our present schemes, and our expences are already very heavy.'[53] The hesitation was predictably short-lived. They accepted the request and selected as teacher the Nailsea master, Henry Young, whose quarrel with the farmers was disrupting the progress of the school.[54] Removing him from Nailsea must have seemed an ingenious way to solve two problems in one stroke, yet further consideration might have made them hesitate. Young was a prickly, self-important character, and Patty had shrewdly picked out his faults as 'pride and a consciousness of really tolerable abilities'.[55] Ignoring the possibility of further conflict in this new mission field, the sisters brought Young and his wife to Blagdon, and in October the school was opened.

It was an affecting sight. Several of the grown up youths had been tried at the last assizes; 3 were the children of a person lately condemned to be hang'd;—many thieves! all ignorant, prophane and vicious beyond belief. Of this Banditti we have enlisted 170. And when the Clergyman, a hard man, who is also the magistrate, saw these Creatures kneeling round us, whom he had seldom seen but to *commit* or to punish in some way, he burst into tears.[56]

The 'hard man' was Thomas Bere, curate of Blagdon, and also rector of the neighbouring parish of Butcombe; like an increasing number of his fellow clergy, he was also a magistrate, a responsibility that might have undermined his pastoral effectiveness. It was perhaps because they feared their curate that the people of Blagdon turned so readily to the More sisters, who offered

---

[50] Duke, More to Wilberforce, 27 Aug. [1795].   [51] *MA* 166.   [52] *MA* 167.
[53] Duke, More to Wilberforce, 27 Aug. [1795].   [54] *MA* 166-9.   [55] *MA* 128.
[56] Duke, More to Wilberforce, 14 Oct. 1795.

them maternal care (and maternal bossiness) rather than the terrors of the penal code.

The success of the school took More by surprise. At the end of the year she told Wilberforce that of the 185 pupils, 'near one half are grown up, the greater part of whom had scarcely been in a Church since they were christen'd, nor cou'd they literally tell who had made them'. In addition thirty attended the weekly day school and another thirty the night school.[57] More was moved at their eagerness to learn. As she wrote to Sir Charles Middleton in the middle of harvest-time in the following year, 'A good many young labourers are so desirous of improvement that it would affect you to see them come in at nine o'clock after a hard day's mowing, just to hear a chapter or two before they rest their weary limbs.'[58] The Youngs were unable to cope with the workload and had to be reinforced every Sunday by '3 stout Missionaries' from Cheddar '(10 or 12 miles there and back)'.[59] It seemed as well as if the parish elites were on her side. The adult pupils included some farmers and their wives 'as blind and ignorant as Africans' who, ashamed to admit their illiteracy, came to the school in secret.[60] The curate, Bere, was apparently another of More's growing band of clerical allies. In December 1796 he gave a glowing report of the school and its 'clever and useful' master, who 'has done more essential good by informing and therefore quietening the people than their Squireships and Worships will effect in the whole process of this turbulent business'.[61] A notorious parish had become quiet and orderly. The only fly in the ointment was More's increasing dislike of the curate.

At the end of 1795 Sir James Stonhouse died: 'the oldest friend I think I ever had in the world', More told Mrs Garrick. She was late coming to Bath this year and only deserted Cowslip Green when she found 'every thing about me was so wet and dirty that I could not stir out'. She found the city 'remarkably full, the high people take much to our low quarter of the Town as they find it more convenient'. (With their usual instinct for a good investment, the sisters had chosen to build their house in an expanding and fashionable area.) The new Pump Room, 'a most noble, spacious room', had opened in December, the day before More's arrival.[62] But nothing could redeem Bath in her eyes, and as usual she regarded her enforced stay there as a time of exile and inactivity. The mild winter helped her coughs, however, and by March she was planning to visit Teston again.[63]

[57] Duke, More to Wilberforce [1795].   [58] *Gambier*, i. 305.
[59] Duke, More to Wilberforce [1795].   [60] Duke, More to Wilberforce, 25 Jan. [1796].
[61] Duke, Thomas Bere to More, 3 Dec. 1796.
[62] Folger, W.b. 488, fo. 4, More to Eva Garrick, 29 Dec. 1795.
[63] Ibid., fo. 6, More to Eva Garrick, 17 Feb. 1796.

While the Blagdon school was expanding and prospering, the More sisters were also preoccupied with events at the mining and glass-house village of Nailsea, where in 1793 they saw 'several grim colliers shed contrite and penitential tears'. 'Alas!' Hannah More added, 'my faith is much weaker than theirs.'[64] On Whitsunday 1795 they had taken communion along with eight young colliers, and appointed one of them, John Haskins, as under-master to Henry Young.[65] Later in the year, when Young was moved to Blagdon, the Mores appointed Haskins in his place. 'This young collier has a very quick apprehension, and a lively understanding. It is a situation of great honour and power for so young a man . . . who had no sort of knowledge a very little time ago—who, in short, in every respect, was very ignorant.' The marvel was, Patty continued, that 'this stupid race of farmers . . . should suffer us to place him over their children'.[66]

At the end of 1795, however, Haskins was horribly injured in a mining accident ('Jaw broke in 3 places, a fractur'd skull, his Eyes pushed out of their orbits'). In the following May he had to be taken to the Bristol infirmary; as a subscriber, More was able to nominate a patient to be treated there.[67] To the surprise, gratification, and even alarm of the More sisters, his two young under-masters, both of them miners, Tommy Jones and Johnny Hart, carried on his teaching in his absence. By the summer of 1796 Haskins was recovering and, in spite of the loss of an eye, seemed well enough to resume his Sunday school teaching. But the mining was a different matter. His nerves as well as his physique had been shattered by his accident, and More feared that he was 'threatened with insanity by the damps of the pit'. In order to save him from this horror, she accepted a proposal put forward by the farmers to make him the master of a weekday school for their sons. To enable him to qualify, she 'put him to a good school to improve in writing and arithmetic of both which he knows something', and the farmers agreed that they would each subscribe sixpence a week to support him while he was receiving his education. During his apprenticeship he walked twelve miles every Saturday night in order to teach at his Sunday school, and returned to his lessons on the Monday morning.[68] He progressed so rapidly that within a few months the sisters were able to set him up in a small house in the parish, and were delighted at the thought that 'a creature of such parts and piety would be put into a situation for the exercise of his talents'.[69] By the end of the year Patty was able to observe with some astonishment that 'our poor collier' was 'at the head, not only of

[64] *Gambier*, i. 234, More to Sir Charles Middleton, 5 Dec. 1793.
[65] *MA* 144.   [66] *MA* 169–70.
[67] Duke, More to Wilberforce [1795]; *MA* 174–5.
[68] *Gambier*, i. 308–9, More to Elizabeth Bouverie, 17 Aug. 1796; *MA* 177–8, 180.
[69] *Gambier*, i. 316, More to Elizabeth Bouverie, 24 Dec. [1796].

the school, but also of the parish'.[70] Haskins's promotion, though, was to be short-lived, as in the winter he was seized with convulsions and died within a few days.[71] 'He was so loved', More told Elizabeth Bouverie, 'that several parishes attended him to the grave, and the Clergyman gave for him a funeral Sermon.'[72]

This promising young man seemed irreplaceable. However, when the sisters visited Nailsea in the spring of 1797 they found that his two former under-teachers, Jones and Hart, had carried on with the Sunday school on their own initiative. Patty was awed at their achievement.

A Higher Power not only presided over, but greatly blessed these two poor youths, who are concealed from all human sight in the bowels of the earth six days out of seven, and on the seventh day they emerge like two young apostles ... we can with truth assert that we have no teachers of any age that excel them.[73]

The farmers, moreover, went out of their way to support the school, binding themselves with forfeits if they did not attend. In June 1798 Hannah More found 140 children 'taught the Scriptures by two young colliers, whom I taught their letters!'[74] Like any good teacher she was delighted in the progress of her pupils, and, as with Sarah Baber, the success of the colliers caused her to reflect on the social hierarchy. In the same diary entry she prayed to be cured of 'delicacy' (snobbery) and to 'delight in the company of a Christian collier more than in that of a witty and great man if he were not pious'.[75] An earlier letter to Elizabeth Bouverie suggests that she was not thinking about spiritual equality alone.

You will think I am become a perfect democrat, when I tell you that this brilliant company was no other than a society of young colliers, who have really more in them than half my acquaintance. When I contemplate the natural good sense, the degree of religious knowledge, the civilized manners, the handsome Sunday clothes of these poor young men, some of them married (and staying all day at school with their children) I could not help thinking there was less disproportion in human conditions, certainly less in human happiness, than we are apt to believe. But then (more democratic still you will say) I could not forbear regretting that more pains were not taken in scouring off the crust from these rough diamonds, and that so many bright ones are left to perish in the mine without being brought to light and usefulness.[76]

The colliers proved long stayers, and Patty More's will, dated 1819, a few months before her death, left £40 to Hart and 19 guineas to Jones.[77] The motives of these teachers can only be guessed at. Perhaps the unpleasant and

---

[70] *MA* 194.   [71] *MA* 195–6.   [72] *Gambier*, i. 316.   [73] *MA* 199.
[74] *MA* 205.   [75] Ibid.
[76] *Gambier*, i. 332, More to Elizabeth Bouverie, 6 Sept. 1797.
[77] PRO, PCC 11/1621, fo. 271.

dangerous nature of their work made them especially receptive to Evangelical religion; John Wesley had preached with great success to the colliers of Kingswood and Cornwall. But in the Mendip context these young men were exceptional, but not unique. Another teacher from the early days of the schools, Flower Waite (now Trip and removed from Rowberrow to Ship-ham), received £10 from Patty's will. Take too the Banwell mistress Nelly Spenser, a former nursemaid at an apothecary's family, full of intellectual curiosity and thwarted ambition. 'An old mother had taught her to read, and here ended her education; but her love of books was so great, she would procure them from her master's study, and, rather than not read, she would amuse herself with medical books.'[78] The Cheap Repository heroine Hester Wilmot likewise shows 'a quick capacity'; she soon learns to spell and read and her teacher lends her a little book to take home; by rising an hour earlier than the rest of her family, she reads St John's Gospel; eventually she becomes an under-teacher at the school, with the prospect of one day be-coming headmistress. Such case-studies, whether real or fictional, cast fresh light on Hannah More's repeated claims that her sole aim was to teach the pupils to be servants. Though this was true in the majority of cases, there were significant exceptions. In spite of her assertions that she allowed no writing, it is clear that the collier teachers were taught this skill. It is highly possible, too, that Nelly Spenser learned it as well: how else would she have managed to keep a register? In both rural and industrial parishes, among both the young men and women, teachers arose from within the ranks of the labouring classes, and proved at least as competent as those with more obvious qualifications. Without making light of the religious commitment which inspired them to sacrifice their hard-earned leisure, it is clear that they were eager for knowledge and found teaching more congenial than their normal occupations. Whatever her protestations to the contrary, Hannah More, the robust anti-democrat, the friend of duchesses and countesses, was proving a surprising agent of social mobility.

[78] *MA* 33.

Chapter 8

The Cheap Repository Tracts
1795–1798

IN March 1795 a Bristol newspaper reported a gathering outside Hazard's library in Bath which had taken place a few days earlier. 'A number of hawkers attended, decently dressed, with characteristic ribbands in their hats, and an assortment of instructive and entertaining works in poetry and prose were presented to each by a subscription of ladies and gentlemen there present.' The newspaper offered its good wishes for the success of 'this most benevolent plan...which originated with, and has been thus far carried into execution by the indefatigable zeal and abilities of that most excellent woman—Miss HANNAH MORE'.[1] This was the start of More's Cheap Repository tracts, her 'Plan to promote good morals among the Poor...a great scheme, which opens upon me daily, and hardly leaves me time to eat'.[2] It was to be one of the most ambitious projects of the decade and was to have a host of imitators, as other middle-class people—some conservative, some radical—made use of her methods in order to disseminate their various messages among the labouring poor.[3]

The success of *Village Politics* had already proved her expertise in the area of popular publications, and now, in the eyes of the conservatively minded, the need was greater than ever. Early in 1794 the war of ideas widened out

---

[1] *FFBJ*, 7 Mar. 1795.   [2] Duke, More to Wilberforce [1795].

[3] For the Cheap Repository, see G. H. Spinney, 'Cheap Repository Tracts: Hazard and Marshall Edition', *The Library*, 4th ser., 203 (Dec. 1939), 295–340; S. Pedersen, 'Hannah More Meets Simple Simon: Tracts, Chapbooks, and Popular Culture in Late Eighteenth-Century England', *Journal of British Studies*, 25 (1986), 84–113.

from the purely political with the publication of Paine's deistic *Age of Reason*, an irreverent attack on orthodox Christianity. An alarmed Bishop Porteus begged More to write a riposte 'brought down to the level of Will Chip and Jack Anvil'. She declined, feeling inadequate to the task, but the thought lingered in her mind.[4] If she did not undertake it, who would? In September she suggested to a visiting clergyman what she described in her diary as 'a Plan for abolishing ballad singing, & trying to substitute religious Papers—Hymns, ~~Communions~~—happy deaths'.[5] In the following month she told Sir Charles Middleton, 'I am getting acquaintance with all the hawkers, pedlars, and matchwomen in town and country, and to secure a stall at country fairs, I propose to make a friendship in Bath and Bristol, with all such gentry as stick out penny literature in little shops in lanes and alleys.'[6] By the end of the year, once more reluctantly holed up in Bath, her attention wandered during the Christmas sermon to 'my new Institution which I intend to call the Cheap Repository [which] engages my whole heart'.[7] Shortly after this she held a breakfast party, which was attended by the Dissenting minister William Jay, whose chapel she now attended outside the hours of Anglican worship. Jay was one of her great admirers. They shared a common Evangelical spirituality, and on a social level he liked the 'ease and elegance' with which she spoke and the way she did not dominate the conversation or spread gossip. At her clearly stage-managed gathering More produced a story called *The Shepherd of Salisbury Plain* and called upon Jay to read it. He complied, and his voice broke with tears as he read this tale of honest poverty submissively born.[8] With this encouragement she went ahead, and in February 1795 she registered the first batch of tracts with the Stationers' Company for publication in March. The Cheap Repository was born.

The Cheap Repository tracts were the newest comers in a well-established field, part of a tradition going back to the Protestant Reformation, and represented in the eighteenth century by Isaac Watts's hymns, abridged versions of *Pilgrim's Progress*, and an assortment of cheap literature published by various religious organizations.[9] In 1787 Sarah Trimmer published *The*

---

[4] Roberts, ii. 366–7; Clark, diary for 1794.   [5] Clark, diary for 1794, Sept.
[6] *Gambier*, i. 268.   [7] Diary for 1794, 21 Dec.
[8] *The Autobiography and Reminiscences of the Rev. William Jay*, ed. G. Redford and J. A. James (London, 1855), 329, 339–40.
[9] W. O. B. Allen and E. MacClure, *Two Hundred Years: The History of the Society for Promoting Christian Knowledge, 1698–1898* (London, 1898), 166–99; S. G. Green, *The Story of the Religious Tract Society for One Hundred Years* (London, 1899); R. D. Altick, *The English Common Reader: A Social History of the Mass Reading Public, 1800–1900* (Chicago, 1957); V. E. Neuburg, *Popular Education in Eighteenth-Century England* (London, 1971), 128–38; J. Feather, *The Provincial Book Trade in Eighteenth-Century England* (Cambridge, 1986).

*Servants' Friend: An Exemplary Tale Designed to Enforce the Religious In-
structions Given at Sunday and Other Charity Schools*, though at 113 pages,
and with such an unseductive title, this must have been bought, if at all, by
employers rather than the servants themselves. The same was true of her
short-lived *Family Magazine*, though it is likely that the 'Village Dialogues',
which appeared in some of the 1789 editions, inspired the title for *Village
Politics*. The magazine's influence can also be seen in two Cheap Repository
tracts, *The Cottage Cook* and *The Sunday School*, where More's hyperactive
Mrs Jones is lifted straight from Sarah Trimmer's Mrs Andrews.

The *Family Magazine* folded at the end of 1789, leaving nothing in its
place until the spate of popular loyalist pamphlets in 1792 and 1793, by
which time the agenda for reforming the poor had become inextricably
bound up with politics. In his *Politics for the People* the radical journalist
Daniel Eaton mixed ballads, songs, fables, and dreams and ingeniously
reworked the national anthem.

> God save great Thomas Paine,
> The Rights of Man explain
> To every soul.[10]

The spread of such literature was viewed with great alarm by More's friend
Urbain de Hercé, the émigré bishop of Dol, who told her that he had
'laboured with Louis to oppose the pestilential writings which overturned
France'. But, as More sadly told Elizabeth Bouverie, 'he was not listened to
by that wretched king'.[11]

The political agenda was unmistakable, but the tracts also had the wider
programme of undermining the influence of the more traditional literature of
the poor. This was spread through chapbooks, so called because they were
sold by travelling pedlars (chapmen), and broadside ballads, which were
sung in the streets by salesmen and women. Chapbooks were miniature soft-
cover storybooks of between four and twenty-four pages, usually measuring
$3\frac{1}{2}$ inches by 6, selling for between 1*d.* and 3*d.*, and illustrated by somewhat
crude woodcuts. Broadsides, single sheets with a poem, song, or story, often
illustrated by a woodcut, and selling for 1*d.* or $\frac{1}{2}$*d.*, were an even earlier
form of popular literature. The seller would sing the ballad to a popular
tune, people in the streets would gather round, and those who could not
afford to buy it or who could not read the words could learn it by heart.
Broadsides were often bought simply for the illustration, and could be used
to decorate private houses or alehouses. With their combination of oral,

---

[10] Quoted in M. Wood, *Radical Satire and Print Culture 1790–1832* (Oxford, 1994), 91.
[11] Duke, More to Wilberforce, 27 Aug. [1795]; *Gambier*, i. 287.

verbal, and visual elements, they helped bridge the gulf between the literate and the illiterate.[12]

Most chapbook literature was produced in London by the firm of Richard Marshall & Cluer Dicey at Aldermary Churchyard, but there were also thriving publishers in the provinces. The trade was big business. More told Hester Piozzi that '30,000 Hawkers are maintain'd by this dissolute Traffic, and Boat loads of it are sent away from the Trading Towns to infect the villages.'[13] The earthy humour of many of the ballads deeply offended her sensibilities. Her Cheap Repository story, *The Sunday School* describes how 'an old blind fiddler and a woman who led him . . . I am sorry to say she was not his wife' sell the farm serving-maids ballads of 'such ribaldry as [the clergyman] was ashamed even to cast his eyes on'.[14] Farmer Hoskins, their employer, is no better, as he has his kitchen 'hung around with songs and ballads' of an indecent nature.[15] Her protagonist, Mrs Jones, declares that she can hardly cross a hayfield without hearing 'young girls singing such indecent ribaldry as has driven me out of the field though I knew they could not read a line of what they were singing, but had caught it from others'.[16] Her complaints were almost as old as the popular printed literature, and lasted until the time when, according to the veteran radical Francis Place, 'the songs have all dissappeared [*sic*] and are altogether unknown to young girls'.[17]

---

[12] For chapbooks, see M. Spufford, *Small Books and Pleasant Histories: Popular Fiction and its Readership in Seventeenth-Century England* (London, 1981); P. Anderson, *The Printed Image and the Transformation of Popular Culture, 1790–1860* (Oxford, 1991). A selection of chapbooks have been reproduced in J. Ashton (ed.), *Chapbooks of the Eighteenth Century* (London, 1882; repr. n.d.). For ballads, see R. Palmer (ed.), *A Ballad History of England from 1588 to the Present Day* (London, 1979). See also the bibliography in I. Dyck, *William Cobbett and Rural Popular Culture* (Cambridge, 1992), 276–7. For early modern 'godly' ballads, see T. Watt, *Cheap Print and Popular Piety, 1550–1640* (Cambridge, 1994).

[13] Yale University, Beinecke Rare Book and Manuscript Library, Osborn Collection, More to Hester Piozzi, Bath, Feb. [1795].

[14] *CRTEMR* 336.   [15] Ibid. 333.   [16] Ibid. 338.

[17] *Autobiography of Francis Place*, ed. M. Thale (Cambridge, 1972), 57. The songs that scandalized Mrs Jones were probably similar to those recollected by Place and his friends. A verse of one of these went,

> One night as I came from the play
> I met a fair maid by the way;
> She had rosy lips and a dimpled chin
> And a hole to put poor Robin in.

Another was

> First he niggled her, then he tiggled her
> Then with his two balls he began for to batter her
> At every thrust, I thought she'd have burst
> With the terrible size of his Morgan Rattler.

Ibid. n. 58–9. See also his evidence to the Select Committee on Education, 30 June 1835, *House of Commons Sessional Papers: Select Committee on Education*, vol. 7, p. 70.

Most of the ballads and chapbook stories were superstitious rather than obscene. The Suffolk poet John Clare remembered how his father enjoyed 'Old Nixon's Prophesies, Mother Bunch's Fairy Tales, and Mother Shipton's Legacy etc, etc'.[18] Middle-class people were not entirely free from the contagion of these superstitions, as Hannah More learned to her dismay when, in response to her request for material, volunteers sent in stories of 'Ghosts, Dreams, Visions, Witches, Devils and all the wild machinery of folly and Enthusiasm'.[19] But, for all her censoriousness, More did not condemn popular literature out of hand. She probably agreed with Farmer Bragwell, another of her fictional farmers, when he says that he would 'rather read Tom Hickathrift or Jack the Giant Killer a thousand times' than the frivolous novels his daughters bring home from the circulating library.[20] Because they could not be confused with real life, fantasy and extravagance posed less of a threat to religious and moral values than so-called 'realistic' fiction.

It is an oversimplification to see popular literature as the antithesis of the polite literature read by the middle classes.[21] A good story crosses barriers of class and education and can bridge the generation gap. *Robinson Crusoe* and *Jane Shore* (a variation on the eternally interesting theme of the royal mistress who comes to a bad end) were printed in both chapbook form and the more expensive hard-cover versions. As has been noted, Hannah More herself entertained the Thornton children at Clapham with the chapbook story of Tom Thumb. James Boswell's childhood was enlivened by the popular romances 'which in my dawning years amused me as much as Rasselas does now'.[22] In the manner of films and soap operas today, these tales, comic, romantic, and tragic, conservative, and subversive in turn, were cultural unifiers, accessible to a wide range of readers and listeners, and indicating some sharing of moral and imaginative worlds across class divisions. Hannah More undoubtedly set herself a difficult task in attempting to reach out to a plebeian readership, but, as she shrewdly pointed out to Elizabeth Bouverie, 'We are very apt to forget [that the poor] have the same tastes, appetites, and feelings with ourselves; ay, and the same good sense too, though not refined

---

[18] Spufford, *Small Books*, 3.

[19] Centre for Kentish Studies (Maidstone), Stanhope U1590/S503/S6, More to the bishop of Lincoln, 21 Jan. [1795].

[20] *CRTEMR* 145. See also Sarah Trimmer's *Family Magazine* (Apr. 1789), 259, and *The Two Farmers: An Exemplary Tale* (London, 1787), 7.

[21] See R. Chartier, 'Culture as Appropriation: Popular Cultural Uses in Early Modern France', in S. L. Kaplan (ed.), *Understanding Popular Culture: Europe from the Middle Ages to the Nineteenth Century* (Berlin, 1984), 229–53; T. Harris, 'Problematising Popular Culture', in id. (ed.) *Popular Culture in England, c.1500–1850* (London, 1995), 1–27; J. Mullan and C. Reid (eds.), *Eighteenth-Century Popular Culture: A Selection* (Oxford, 2000), 1–28.

[22] *Boswell's London Journal, 1762–1763* (Yale edn.), ed. F. A. Pottle (London, 1950), 299.

by education.'[23] If she enjoyed her stories, there was a chance that the poor would as well.

On 9 February 1795 Bishop Richard Hurd of Worcester wrote to a clergyman in his diocese,

I have this morning your favour of the 7th inclosing *two* copies of the Plan . . . These good Ladies [Hannah and Patty More] & good Bishops would needs have the poor people be taught to read: with a good design no doubt: but who shall hinder them from reading *bad* books as well as good; nay, from giving a preference to the former? Teach them to read, & they will chuze for themselves or suffer bad people to chuze for them. I doubt therefore the success of this project for a Repository.[24]

The 'Plan' was the official proposal for the Cheap Repository drawn up by Henry Thornton (who became treasurer), and Hurd was one of many recipients. More spent the last part of January engaged in sending out to potential supporters a summary of the reasons for the formation of the Repository, as well as specimens of the first batch of tracts. 'The object of this institution', readers were informed, was 'the circulation of Religious and Useful Knowledge as an antidote to the poison continually flowing thro' the channel of vulgar and licentious publications'.[25] Wilberforce received several copies and was admonished to disseminate them; another recipient was George Prettyman, bishop of Lincoln.[26] Beilby Porteus and Shute Barrington responded with predictable enthusiasm; so did Horace Walpole, who subscribed 5 guineas.[27] Even Hurd, once he had overcome his distrust of any scheme for educating the poor, was prepared to subscribe. His clerical correspondent was more sanguine, and dared to hope that 'this fair and zealous moralist' would 'accomplish the Herculean Task she has undertaken'.[28] More would have agreed with this description of her work; she found 'the arranging and bringing to bear my plan has been a labour beyond all conception'.[29]

Though at first she seems to have contemplated a primarily local scheme, by February 1795 she was envisaging a nationwide network of distribution, 'establishing Correspondences in various parts of the kingdom', as she told Hester Piozzi.[30] By May she was sending tracts to Newcastle, where the

---

[23] *Gambier*, i. 276.   [24] BL, Egerton MS 1958, fo. 140.

[25] [H. Thornton] *A Plan for Establishing by Subscription a Repository of Cheap Publications, on Religious & Moral Subjects* (1795).

[26] Duke, More to Wilberforce, 1795; Centre for Kentish Studies, Stanhope U1590/S503/S6, More to the bishop of Lincoln, 21 Jan. [1795].

[27] Roberts, ii. 455; *Walpole*, 396-7.   [28] BL, Egerton MS 1958, fo. 140.

[29] *Gambier*, i. 274, More to Elizabeth Bouverie, 24 Jan. 1795.

[30] Osborn Collection, More to Hester Piozzi, Feb. [1795]. For more on the distribution of the Cheap Repository, see A. Stott, 'Hannah More: Evangelicalism, Cultural Reformation, and Loyalism', Ph.D. thesis (London, 1998), 154-6.

mayor was a subscriber, using Ralph Beilby, the metal engraver, and former master and partner of Thomas Bewick, as a distributor.[31] Her booksellers were two well-known publishers, John Marshall in London and Samuel Hazard in Bath. Both were new to her; Cadell was her usual publisher, and *Village Politics* had been produced by Rivington, the SPCK publishers. Marshall, who had published Sarah Trimmer's *Family Magazine*, was familiar with chapbook literature, and able to pass off the Cheap Repository as a plausible imitation. Both the ballads and the chapbooks looked exactly like the popular literature that was sold in the streets of London and the larger towns, or was carried by chapmen around the country. Like their secular competitors, they carried illustrations in the form of wood engravings. *The Shepherd of Salisbury Plain* shows a shepherd identified by his crook and his dog. In the background is a labourer's hovel, and on the right a well-dressed man on a horse, representing the benevolent Mr Johnson. In contrast to many of the normal chapbook illustrations, the Cheap Repository picture bore some resemblance to the text, ensuring that, visually at least, the buyers were getting superior products for their pennies and halfpennies. John Lee, who engraved some of the later tracts, was proud enough of his handiwork to sign them, though the names of the earlier engravers are not known.

The usual chapmen were paid to distribute the Cheap Repository, and in imitation of the existing publications, the tracts and ballads were sold at 1*d.* and ½*d.* respectively. There were discounts for bulk orders. As More told Hester Piozzi, '*One* Shop in any great Town who wou'd supply the Hawkers will be served with penny Books for 3/3 per Hund—all other Shops at 3/6— half penny books in proportion.'[32] There were discounts, too, for 'the Gentry' to give away at twenty-five for 1*s.* 6*d.* The opening day was at Hazard's Library in Bath on Tuesday 3 March. In their packs the hawkers carried runs of eleven broadsides and twenty-two tracts, which included the ballads *The Gin Shop; or, A Peep into a Prison* and *The Market Woman, a True Tale; or, Honesty is the Best Policy*, together with the first part of *The Shepherd of Salisbury Plain* and a new edition of Watts's *Divine Songs*. (This large list did not set a precedent. In the subsequent months—from May 1795 onwards—three tracts or ballads only were published.) Many of the buyers were More's friends. When she visited Porteus in the spring, she found his table 'full of our penny literature. Above a thousand, I suppose; some of which he gives to every hawker that passes.'[33] The duchess of Gloucester sent her lady of the bedchamber to try to persuade an orange-seller to sell the tracts. The woman refused, telling them that she only sold

---

[31] Osborn Collection, More to Mr Bielby [*sic*], 1 May 1795.
[32] Osborn Collection, More to Hester Piozzi, Feb. [1795].   [33] Roberts, ii. 431.

oranges, and the two aristocratic ladies, freed from the necessity of earning their own livings, were amused at her firm sense of demarcation.[34]

The plan was soon pronounced a success and the printers could not prepare the tracts fast enough for the demand. On 16 April the *Bath Chronicle* reported that 300,000 had been sold since the end of March. At the end of the month Marshall told More that 'on Account of the extraordinary demand for the Tracts, he had not yet been able to fulfil any of the Orders in the distant Counties'.[35] By July the numbers mounted to 700,000, and 2 million tracts were distributed by the end of the year. (Paine's *Rights of Man* had sold about 100,000 by 1793.) None of this, however, proves that labourers and maidservants were queuing up to read moralistic little tracts; what it shows is that, like *Village Politics*, the Cheap Repository was a huge hit among the middle classes, who, as Henry Thornton informed readers and subscribers, had set up 'very respectable Societies' throughout the country in order to distribute them.[36]

However, the sums did not add up. The generous discounts, combined with the need for the publishers to make a profit, meant that the tracts could not pay their way. Early into the scheme Cadell told More gloomily that 'he would not stand my shoes at the end of the year, for five hundred pounds over and above the subscription; nay, according to another calculation, a *thousand* pounds would not do it at any rate'.[37] 'I found', More told Mrs Pretyman, the bishop of Lincoln's wife, in June, 'I was got on too expensive a plan.'[38] This led to some crisis management, the details of which remain unclear. But there were two consequences. The first was that one copy of each tract was to be sent out to More's (mainly clerical) supporters throughout the country, so that they could judge which best suited local needs. The second, much more important change was that John Marshall was officially designated Printer to the Cheap Repository, and Henry Thornton's diary suggests that Hazard's nose was put out of joint by the downgrading of his own role (though the unsympathetic More believed the business had been 'very gainful' to him).[39] Early in 1796 the scheme was reorganized again, in response to gentry and middle-class demand for more durable editions. In addition to the cheap versions for the poor, the tracts were now published in annual collected volumes, priced 3*s.* 6*d*; ballads were printed in eight-page octavo booklets as well as in broadside form so that they could be bound in

---

[34] Ibid. 435.   [35] Osborn Collection, More to Mr Bielby, 1 May 1795.

[36] This statement, together with a list of subscribers, is found at the back of *Cheap Repository Tracts Published during the Year 1795* (London, 1797). Another copy is in the Clark Library.

[37] Roberts, ii. 431.

[38] Centre for Kentish Studies, Stanhope U1590/S503/S36, More to Mrs Pretyman, 11 June 1795.

[39] Spinney, 'Cheap Repository Tracts', 305; Thornton, Add. MS 7674/1/R, fo. 121;Thornton, Add. MS 7674/1/E/1, More to Thornton, 12 Sept. [1798].

with the rest.[40] This, More hoped, would put the Cheap Repository on a sound footing and reduce the need to raise further large sums of money; she did not, at this time, however, envisage a time when she could do without subscriptions altogether.[41]

The Cheap Repository was too large a venture to be carried on by one person, and More relied on friends, acquaintances, and other well-disposed individuals to supply money and stories. According to a list of subscribers, dated, by internal evidence, April 1796, over 760 individuals subscribed, of which 420 are known to be men and 327 women.[42] The majority subscribed one guinea or half a guinea (10s. 6d.). The subscribers included ten peers, several of them Pittite creations, though none of Cabinet rank, and all, with the very conspicuous exception of Horace Walpole, associated with the reformation of manners movement. John Moore, the archbishop of Canterbury, subscribed, as did eleven bishops, including More's diocesan, Charles Moss, bishop of Bath and Wells, and a High Church friend, William Cleaver, bishop of Chester. Fourteen MPs subscribed, but only one, the prime minister, William Pitt, who subscribed 3 guineas, was of Cabinet rank. The others were Wilberforce and his friends and relations, all associated in some way with abolition and the reformation of manners. Fifteen naval and military men, contributed, a tribute to wartime patriotism and the zealous networking of Sir Charles Middleton and his friends; one, Lady Waldegrave's cousin Admiral Waldegrave, the future Lord Radstock, was to be very prominent in the Vice Society. Other moral reformers who subscribed were the Evangelical peer the second earl of Dartmouth, Thomas Bernard, the founder of the Society for Bettering the Condition of the Poor, and the ultra-conservative High Churchman John Bowdler. The Proclamation Society subscribed 10 guineas to the scheme, the most substantial single donation. By far the largest category of male subscribers were lower clergy. Two less predictable subscribers were the Revd William Gilpin, the enthusiast for the picturesque, and the great naturalist Sir Joseph Banks, formerly botanical collector on James Cook's Pacific voyage. But the Whig politicians and many higher clergy were conspicuous by their absence. The reasons for their failure to subscribe might have included distrust of Evangelicalism, and dislike of any project associated, even at one remove, with Wilberforce.

[40] These were sold as vol. i, *Cheap Repository Tracts Published during the Year 1795* and vol. ii, *Cheap Repository Tracts Published during the Year 1796* (London and Bath [1797]). In both volumes Marshall was listed as 'Printer to the Cheap Repository', though Hazard and the Edinburgh publisher J. Elder were named on the title page as subsidiary printers and booksellers.

[41] *Gambier*, i. 284–5, More to Elizabeth Bouverie, 14 Aug. [1795].

[42] See n. 36 above. For the subscribers, see Stott, 'Hannah More', 137–8, 156–8, 279–83.

The most remarkable fact about the Cheap Repository subscribers is that women made up more than two-fifths of the total. Mrs Garrick apart, the great majority of More's female friends, including Elizabeth Montagu, Elizabeth Carter, and the dowager duchess of Beaufort, subscribed, but they were greatly outnumbered by a host of unknown women, whose imaginations had been captured by the scheme. The Cheap Repository was another sign of the feminization of the reformation of manners agenda, which had already been noticed by Bishop Barrington.

Though the tracts were written anonymously, the authorship of many of them can be established. Those marked 'Z' were written by Hannah More and those marked 'S' by Sally. Outside the More household the most enthusiastic author was Henry Thornton. Much of his diary for 1795 was taken up with the Cheap Repository, and the entries show a revealing combination of pleasure in authorship and furtive self-doubt over the propriety of his literary activities.[43] He wrote a Sunday reading, *On the Religious Advantages of the Present Inhabitants of Great Britain*, and a story, *The Beggarly Boy*.[44] He took out of More's hands one story he especially liked, *The Lancashire Collier Girl*, which was apparently taken from real life, and reworked it before its publication in May.[45] But the effort of writing this one tract exhausted him. He was never able to match More for speed; like many an aspiring author he was defeated by dialogue, and he never again expended so much effort on one story.[46]

Other authors can be identified. The Sunday reading *The Touchstone* was written by the abolitionist Zachary Macaulay.[47] William Mason, one of those eighteenth-century poets who were well regarded in their day and then forgotten, sent in some ballads, out of which More selected *The Ploughboy's Dream* for inclusion.[48] John Venn, rector of Clapham, contributed Sunday readings.[49] Many others volunteered their services, but, as has been noted, in some cases their efforts were too similar to the chapbook stories to be acceptable. The result, as More told Elizabeth Bouverie, was that 'I have been obliged to turn *sans-culotte* author myself.'[50] Overwhelmingly, the Cheap Repository was her creation and her work.

It is difficult to better More's own irony-free summary of the Cheap Repository literature: 'striking Conversions, Holy Lives, Happy Deaths, Providen-

---

[43] See e.g. Thornton, Add. MS 7674/1/R, fos. 36–7.

[44] Thornton, Add. MS 7674/1/R, fos. 93, 117, 118.

[45] For the tract's convoluted history, see P. Langford, *Public Life and the Propertied Englishman, 1689–1798* (Oxford, 1994), 389; *Gentleman's Magazine* (1795), 197–9, 336, 486; Thornton, Add. MS 7674/1/R, fo. 96.

[46] Thornton, Add. MS 7674/1/R, fo. 108.   [47] Clark, More to Macaulay, 14 Jan. 1796.

[48] Roberts, ii. 432.

[49] M. Hennell, *John Venn and the Clapham Sect* (London, 1958), 196–8.

[50] *Gambier*, i. 274.

tial Deliverances, Judgments on the Breakers of Commandments, Stories of Good and Wicked Apprentices, Hardened Sinners, Pious Servants &c'.[51] The tracts were attacked even in their own day. William Shaw, rector of Chelvey and ally of More's enemy Thomas Bere, found them full of 'blood-loving, hypocritical cant'.[52] Horace Walpole, who came to regret his sub-scription, criticized their 'ill-natured strictness'.[53] Today, whether seen as political propaganda or conduct literature, the tracts are widely disliked for preaching the doctrine that the poor must passively await their salvation at the hands of the upper classes.[54] They are also highly predictable. More's devout upwardly mobile heroes and heroines rise through their own efforts and the benevolence of kind-hearted ladies, zealous magistrates, and godly clergymen—far-fetched scenarios in the traumatic 1790s. Her good characters are rewarded, and her villains die unhappily—in prison, in Botany Bay, or at the end of a rope. As Oscar Wilde's Miss Prism says, 'The good ended happily and the bad unhappily. That is what Fiction means.'

It is easy therefore to poke fun at the Cheap Repository, yet even its sternest critics have at times found themselves disarmed by the sheer skill of the storytelling. The tracts abound in colloquial metaphors, lively dialogue, and precise and vivid descriptions of street life and the work patterns of rural communities.[55] If More's work is set alongside that of others in the field, the comparison is all to her advantage. Not only was she a born narrator, but her own circumstances worked in her favour. She had grown up in a cramped cottage, surrounded by the chatter of her father's pupils. She knew about the lives of the farmers from her contacts with her mother's family. At Cowslip Green, though she had become famous and reasonably affluent, she still mixed with farmers, and in her relatively small house she could not have avoided snatches of her servants' conversation that would have given her some insight into their mental world. Her work in the Mendips led her to plead, bargain, and negotiate with the villagers. Whereas most women of her class derived their knowledge of the poor from the occasional philanthropic visit, she had trudged round cottages seeking out children, collected pennies and halfpennies for benefit clubs, taught reading in draughty unfinished buildings, and organized mass distributions of cakes and cups of tea. Much of this rubbed off onto her stories.

---

[51] Ibid. 268.

[52] [W. Shaw] *The Life of Hannah More, with a Critical Review of her Writings* (London, 1802), 123.

[53] Roberts, ii. 435.

[54] See e.g. O. Smith, *The Politics of Language, 1791–1819* (Oxford, 1984), 90–6.

[55] See M. Myers, 'Hannah More's Tracts for the Times: Social Fiction and Female Ideology', in M. A. Schofield and C. Macheski (eds.), *Fett'rd or Free? British Women Novelists 1670–1815* (Athens, Ohio, 1986), 267–9.

Some of More's least convincing writing is found in *The Shepherd of Salisbury Plain*, which was probably the first of the tracts to be written, and remained in print for nearly a hundred years. It was published in two parts. Part 1 went out with the first batch in March 1795. It ended with a promise of more to come, and the sequel was published in June. It was based on the exemplary life of a poor shepherd, who was a model of piety, hard work, and contentment. The story is told from the perspective of a Mr Johnson, 'a very worthy, charitable gentleman'.[56] On first meeting the shepherd he notices that he is wretchedly poor, but of respectable appearance. His stockings are covered with darns of different colours, 'but had not a hole in them', and 'his shirt, though nearly as coarse as the sails of a ship, was as white as the drifted snow'.[57] All this is a tribute to 'the neatness, industry and good management of his wife', Mary. Yet this remarkable woman has eight children to look after; she suffers from rheumatism brought on by lack of firewood and sleeping under a leaky thatch; her husband cannot afford an apothecary's bill; and like the rest of her family she exists on a diet of gruel, bread, and potatoes.[58] Cold, sick, and malnourished, she nevertheless keeps her husband's shirts and stockings in immaculate condition. The family insist on being deeply grateful for what they see against all the evidence as their extreme good fortune. When they sit down to a dish of potatoes for their Sunday dinner, the little girl Molly says, 'Father, I wish I was big enough to say grace, for I am sure I should say it very heartily today, for I was thinking what must *poor* people do who have no salt to their potatoes.'[59] It was sentiments such as this that led William Cobbett, after he had renounced his enthusiasm for the Cheap Repository, to condemn 'the religious mouse, who lived upon dropped crumbs, and never, though ever so hungry, touched the cheese or bacon on the racks of shelves'.[60] It is far easier for the modern reader to sympathize with Cobbett's reaction, or with Ford K. Brown's wittily ironical demolition, than with Wilberforce's assertion that he would sooner have written *The Shepherd of Salisbury Plain* than the works of Scott or Byron.[61]

The story ultimately fails not merely because of its complacency, but because it is an unconvincing marriage of the realistic and the pastoral. Descriptions of a family's desperate expedients to ward off cold and hunger are interspersed with lyrical, even moving, praise of the life of the shepherd and its opportunities for contemplation.[62] The daughter Molly is 'a fine plump cherry-cheek little girl', but a couple of paragraphs on we are told that the children go without shoes and stockings and 'the pinching cold . . . cramps

---

[56] *CRTEMR* 1. [57] Ibid. 2–3. [58] Ibid. 7–9, 18–19, 34. [59] Ibid. 19.

[60] Quoted in, G. Spater, *William Cobbett: The Poor Man's Friend* (Cambridge, 1982), i. 203.

[61] F. K. Brown, *Fathers of the Victorians: The Age of Wilberforce* (Cambridge, 1961), 144–50; Bodleian, MS c. 48, fo. 39, Wilberforce to More, 12 Aug. 1824.

[62] *CRTEMR* 4–7.

their poor little limbs'.[63] The shepherd insists on calling his house a cottage; to his benefactor, Mr Johnson, however, it is 'that hovel with only one room above and below, with scarcely any chimney'.[64] In the downstairs room, which has to house ten people during the day, the family can fit 'four brown wooden chairs, which with constant rubbing [by a woman with rheumatic hands!] were become as bright as a looking glass' and 'an old carved elbow chair and a chest of the same date which stood at the corner'. However, More had the honesty to note that the 'poor old grate . . . scarcely held a handful of coal' and the spit 'was kept for ornament rather than use'.[65] At the end of the story the shepherd and his family are lifted out of their poverty. The parish clerk dies and the shepherd takes his place and moves into a better cottage. He is also made the master of a new Sunday school, and 'honest Mary' becomes the mistress of a school of industry (even though More's experience at Cheddar had taught her the problems of such schools). Their lives will be frugal, but they will be warm and they will have enough to eat. Predictably, the couple burst into tears of gratitude, even though they had previously assured Mr Johnson that they were fully content with their existing lot. This leaves it hard to understand how readers were meant to interpret the story. Did it preach submission or aspiration? Were the poor meant to be content or to hope for the arrival of a *deus ex machina*? At the end More compounded the contradictions that run through the story by obscuring her moral message.

In the later editions of the story readers were told that the shepherd had hung the Cheap Repository ballad *Patient Joe, the Newcastle Collier* on the walls of his cottage. This came out in July 1795, and like all ballads was intended to be heard, viewed, and read. Like its secular competitors, it was to be sung to a popular tune. The elaborate pattern in the margin, combined with the picture of two men at a pithead, a pit pony turning a machine, and a dog gnawing at a bone, gave it visual interest. It is possible that it was specifically intended for the Newcastle market, which, as has been noted, contained reliable distributors as well as a friendly diocesan. Each tract and ballad had its own particular slant, and this was designed to win the poor away from their belief in chance and to recognize instead the workings of Providence. Convinced of St Paul's doctrine that everything works together for good, the miner Joseph insists on praising God in spite of the unpromising outward circumstances: war, high taxes, a sickly wife, a dead child. The necessary counterfoil is

> Idle Tim Jenkins, who drank and who gam'd,
> Who mock'd at his Bible, and was not asham'd.[66]

---

[63] Ibid. 10.   [64] Ibid. 8, 34.   [65] Ibid. 20–1.

[66] The quotations here are taken from the original broadsheet. The ballad was also published, with a different illustration, in *CRST* 386–8.

When a dog seizes Joe's bacon joint, Tim naturally mocks, 'Is the loss of thy dinner too, Joe, for the best?' But Joe refuses to accept a passive role; like his creator, he believes the workings of Providence do not absolve human beings from the need to act. He therefore goes off in search of the dog and his bacon. When he returns, the colliers greet him with 'horror and fear'.

> What a narrow escape hast thou had, they all said,
> The pit is fall'n in, and Tim Jenkins is dead.

Of course.

The message that everything works for good was reworked in the ballad *Turn the Carpet; or, The Two Weavers*, which was especially admired by Porteus: 'Here you have Bishop Butler's Analogy, all for a halfpenny.'[67] Another ballad, *The Gin Shop*, subtitled *A Peep into a Prison*, argued that the 'deadliest pest' in Britain was not war but drink. *The Market Woman* and *The Roguish Miller* warned against dishonest trading, a much discussed misdemeanour at a time of poor harvests and high prices. *The Riot; or, Half a Loaf is Better than no Bread*, published in August 1795, was especially topical. Jack Anvil and Tom Hod of *Village Politics* were resurrected. The always suggestible Tom is about to riot, until the loyal Jack dissuades him by a series of common-sense arguments.

It is quite a shock to turn from the world of the tracts—where everything always turns out for the best provided one goes to church and keeps the sabbath—to Hannah More's letters to her closest friends, where, freed from the need to censor herself, she showed a more subtle recognition of the grim realities of rural life in the 1790s. *The Riot* was written to counter the spate of attacks on mills and bakers' shops that broke out in the spring and summer of 1795. Some took place at Kingswood, a few miles from More's birthplace.[68] Far from being spasms of mindless hooliganism, they are now seen as traditional and considered responses to shortages of food, reflecting an older 'moral economy' of just prices and fair trading.[69] Millers and bakers came under attack because they stood between the poor and their grain and were believed to be hoarding food in order to raise the price still further. In this turbulent summer the nation was deep in a food crisis, with its twin threats of hunger and social disturbance.[70] The harvest of 1794 was poor,

---

[67] Roberts, ii. 433. For the admiration of moderate Evangelicals for Joseph Butler's *Analogy of Religion* (1736), see B. Hilton, *Age of Atonement: The Influence of Evangelicalism on Social and Economic Thought, 1785–1865* (Oxford, 1991), 173–83.

[68] *FFBJ*, 9 and 16 May 1795.

[69] E. P. Thompson, *Customs in Common* (Harmondsworth, 1991); A. Randall and A. Charlesworth (eds.), *Moral Economy and Popular Protest* (Basingstoke, 2000).

[70] This discussion is based on J. Stevenson, *Popular Disturbances in England 1700–1832* (2nd edn. London, 1992), 114–43; J. R. Poynter, *Society and Pauperism: English Ideas on Poor Relief,*

and by the spring of the following year the price of the high-density quartern loaf, the basic diet of the poor, had risen from $7\frac{1}{2}d$. to $12\frac{1}{2}d$. This was the final intolerable load on a population already suffering from the strains of war, unprecedented population growth, a reduction of income from domestic industry, and an erosion of property rights. The smallholder was being turned into a wage labourer at a time when he was least able to cope with a decline in his status and income. The so-called Speenhamland system, the device adopted by some Berkshire magistrates whereby the agricultural wage was supplemented by parish relief, was an emergency response to an intolerable situation and was soon adopted in many parts of the country. Critics argued that it created a dependency culture among labourers and absolved the farmers from paying decent wages. This may have been true, but what was the alternative? In this time of hardship two of More's friends, Wilberforce and Barrington, joined with the philanthropist Sir Thomas Bernard in 1796 to set up the Society for Bettering the Condition and Increasing the Comforts of the Poor. The Society distributed pamphlets containing plans for soup kitchens, subsidized village shops, and cheap, nutritious recipes for the poor. Its ideology of self-help and self-improvement fitted in well with the moral mission of the Cheap Repository, and no doubt its recommendations, when implemented, improved the condition of the poor at the margins; but the magnitude of the crisis showed the limitations of philanthropic bodies.

Faced with heart-rending local manifestations of this crisis of poverty, Hannah More's moralistic agenda became entangled with her practical attempts to improve the lot of the poor. She was concerned to acquaint her influential friends, especially members of Parliament, with the local situation in order to stir them into action. When Thornton visited her in the summer of 1795, she took him round the Yatton workhouse, and showed him scenes of 'want, misery, vice, cruelty and oppression'. 'I could now', she wrote to Sir Charles Middleton, another political contact, 'convict some overseers of murder, if those who could redress the grievance would listen to me.'[71] She fretted over public indifference. 'I have written on the subject to some of our young Reformers, but those who do good have already so much to do, and the rest of the world cares so little whether it is done or not, that I grow hopeless on all points of domestic reformation and redress.'[72]

She also tried to encourage government action. During her visit to London in the spring of 1796 she spent five hours with Pitt's adviser and

1795–1834 (London and Toronto, 1969); R. Wells, *Wretched Faces: Famine in Wartime England, 1763–1803* (Gloucester, 1988); D. Eastwood, 'Patriotism and the English State in the 1790s', in Mark Philp (ed.), *The French Revolution and British Popular Politics* (Cambridge, 1991), 161–8.

[71] *Gambier*, i. 291, More to Sir Charles Middleton, 13 Oct. 1795.
[72] Ibid. 262–3, More to Elizabeth Bouverie, 20 Oct. [1794].

former secretary the bishop of Lincoln, with a copy of the prime minister's proposed Poor Law Bill in front of her, making 'pretty free use of our pencils in the margin'.[73] Her predictable contribution was to suggest amendments in the areas of 'female economy and religious instruction', an agenda that harmonized well with the wider public debate. The failure of the bill, complicated and incoherent as it turned out to be, must have been a bitter disappointment, and there were no other major legislative attempts to meet the problems of poverty in her lifetime.

Deprived of guidance from the government, the magistrates were forced to improvise, and the results, from More's point of view, were unsatisfactory. In the tracts she exhorted the poor to trust the authorities; in real life she believed such trust was vain. The summer of 1795 was cold and wet, though the harvest was less disastrous than that of the preceding year, but, as More complained to her Teston friends in the following summer, 'we give a shilling a pound for butter', while 'the white loaves which our poor buy at the bakers are very little larger than they were this time twelvemonth—the period of greatest scarcity'.[74] By this stage, she believed, the problem lay less with the vagaries of the weather than with the attitudes of the authorities. 'We alas! have no magistrates who care for the poor and needy, nor who seek to right the oppressed . . . They are full fed themselves, and will not believe the misery which I see with my eyes.'[75] The rich farmers and the 'tyrannical overseers' were even worse, all 'as insolent aristocrats as any of the ci-devant nobles of France'.[76]

It was comforting to resurrect time-honoured criticisms of the poor and to argue that most of their miseries were primarily due to their own bad management and their tastes for such luxuries as tea. More subscribed to this orthodoxy, but only in part. Her tract *The Way to Plenty*, written at speed in the crisis summer of 1795, was one of many well-meaning attempts to suggest to the poor some cheap, nutritious, but fuel-intensive recipes such as baked potatoes and rice pudding, which she had acquired from the Teston steward; as she rather disarmingly confessed, she had little idea herself about 'receipts for leek-porridge and rice milk'.[77] There is little evidence that the poor paid much attention to such advice. During a later food crisis Ann Kennicott handed out some of More's recipes to the poor at Windsor, and encountered some consumer resistance to rice: 'the people there do not care for anything but bread "'tis so handy like"'. In addition, as Mrs Kennicott was forced to admit, 'the high price of firing favours their indolence'.[78]

---

[73] Ibid. 310, More to Elizabeth Bouverie, Friday, 1796.   [74] Ibid. 306–7.

[75] Ibid. 304, 308, More to Elizabeth Bouverie, 2 July, 17 Aug. 1796.

[76] Ibid. 227, More to Elizabeth Bouverie, 17 Oct. 1793. This letter shows that More's hostility to the parish elites pre-dated the food crises of 1795–6.

[77] *CRST* 279–303; *Gambier*, i. 285–6, More to Elizabeth Bouverie, 14 Aug. 1795.

[78] Clark, Ann Kennicott to More, 8 Feb [1800 or 1801?].

Aware that it was difficult for the poor to use her recipes, More gave out strong hints to her middling-sort and gentry readers; the kind farmer's wife Mrs White buys up a large quantity of rice, sells it to the poor at a low price, and makes sure that the farm workmen are able to get skimmed milk.[79] In *The Cottage Cook*, published at the beginning of 1797, Mrs Jones the Sunday school founder deplores 'the new bad management' which has caused many cottages to be built without ovens. She nags the gentry into building a parish oven, following which, 'at a certain hour, three times a week, the elder children carried their loaves which their mothers had made at home, and paid a halfpenny, or a penny according to their size, for the baking'.[80] In such cases, the poor are dependent on the good will of the better off; there was little alternative. For all its fake pastoralism, *The Shepherd of Salisbury Plain* had shown that the agricultural wage of a shilling a day was insufficient to support a family, however pious, prudent, and enterprising. In the end, therefore, More, like the politicians, was defeated by the gravity of the crisis. If her response was inadequate, she was no different from most of her contemporaries, with only Paine and the even more radical Thomas Spence prepared to advocate a fundamental (and politically unrealistic) redistribution of wealth.[81] Failing this, the paternalist strategies suggested in the tracts could have rescued at least some of the poor from utter destitution.

The Cheap Repository is wartime propaganda, full of all the special pleading associated with this type of literature, and More saw self-censorship as a patriotic duty at a time of national emergency. *The Riot* tackled the uncomfortably topical subject of food riots in a way that was acceptable to the government, putting the scarcity of food down to bad weather, and (conveniently) to the mysterious workings of Providence. But More's real feelings about rioting were more complicated. Following the publication of the ballad, she wrote to Elizabeth Bouverie, 'I told the Bishop of London I would screen the collateral and subordinate causes of the scarcity, as much as my *conscience would allow me*, for the sake of keeping peace at home ... I hope it is not Jesuitical to tell the truth without telling the *whole* truth.'[82] The 'collateral and subordinate causes', as she saw them, were primarily 'the wickedness of monopolizers ... forestallers [and] contractors, [and] the negligence of the rich'.[83] The evidence was all around her. Though Somerset was not one of the counties most affected by the enclosure movement, part of the waste and commons of Blagdon had recently been sold at auction.[84]

---

[79] *CRTEMR* 294, 297.   [80] Ibid. 315–16.

[81] For poverty and poor relief, see J. Innes, 'The "Mixed Economy of Welfare" in Early Modern England: Assessments of the Options from Hale to Malthus (*c*.1683–1803)', in M. Daunton (ed.), *Charity, Self-Interest, and Welfare in the English Past* (London, 1996), 139–80.

[82] *Gambier*, i. 287–8.   [83] Ibid. 307.

[84] *Bonner and Middleton's Bristol Journal*, 27 Aug. 1785.

The result of the expansion of capitalist farming was that 'hardly any poor man can now get a bit of ground for a cow, as all the land in a parish is swallowed up by a few great farms'. Profiteers were making the situation worse: 'Jobbers go round and buy up the butter, which they again sell to little shops, so that there are three profits before the poor get it.' Following her visits to the poor, she came home 'to my own good dinner...sad and discontented'—and guilty too at her own inability to help.[85] But while she poured out her heart to her friends at Teston, only the barest hints of her anger and frustration found its way into the tracts. Under the tense circumstances of 1795 it is easy to understand why she kept her criticisms for the eyes of her friends; but it is a pity for her posthumous reputation that she seemed so much more complacent in public than she was in private.[86]

More wanted to preach patience and subordination to the poor, but she was not so naive as to assume that they would accept this message in an undiluted form. 'I am resolved', she told Elizabeth Bouverie, 'in trying to *reform* the poor, to *please* them, too, a point I think we do not sufficiently attend to.'[87] Not all her creations were as static as the shepherd of Salisbury Plain. In some of the later stories she managed to depict likeable characters with whom her readers could identify, and to allow them to rise in the world partly through their own efforts. One example is Tom White, the upwardly mobile postilion, who becomes a (benevolent) farmer. Another is Betty Brown, the St Giles's orange girl (the name taken from Johnson's *Rambler*), who falls into the clutches of a loan shark; her story follows very closely a section in the magistrate Patrick Colquhoun's influential *Treatise on the Police of the Metropolis*.[88] Like Hester Wilmot, the promising Sunday school pupil, this intelligent, hard-working girl is presented with dilemmas that test her character and her moral code.

More was proud of *Betty Brown*, 'a composition on which I am afraid I rather value myself, as it shows my intimate acquaintance with the night-cellars and other places of polite resort in the metropolis'.[89] Betty 'was born nobody knows where and bred nobody knows how...The longest thing that [she] can remember, is, that she use to crawl up out of a night cellar,

[85] *Gambier*, i. 296, More to Elizabeth Bouverie, 7 Dec. 1796.

[86] This discussion of More's views on poverty differs in emphasis from Boyd Hilton's discussion on the attitudes of the 'moderate' Evangelicals to political economy (*Age of Atonement*, *passim*, but especially pp. 15–16). In keeping with her distrust of theory, More disclaimed all knowledge of works of 'political economy': 'I neither know them nor their Character.' Duke, More to Wilberforce, *c*.18 Jan. 1805. The pragmatism found in her practice and her writings makes it difficult to place her decisively in either the 'extreme' or 'moderate' Evangelical camp on economic issues.

[87] *Gambier*, i. 275–6.

[88] P. Colquhoun, *A Treatise on the Police of the Metropolis* (London, 1796), 177–9.

[89] *Gambier*, i. 309.

stroll about the streets, and pick cinders from the scavengers' carts.' However, the girl has the courage and resilience to seize the pleasures she can. 'Among the ashes she sometimes found some ragged gauze and dirty ribbons; with these she used to dizen herself out, and join the merry bands on the first of May.'[90] (Had More seen such sights on her Mayday visits to Elizabeth Montagu, who entertained the sweeps on that day at her grand house in Portman Square?) Betty's great ambition is to have her own barrow and sell fruit. But in order to raise the money, she borrows 5*s*. from the aptly named Mrs Sponge, who lives in the notorious Seven Dials, and is then trapped in crippling interest payments. Tempted as she is, she does not beg or steal, and the unwritten subtext is that she refuses to turn to prostitution. The predictable *dea ex machina* arrives in the form of a kind lady, whose husband 'was one of the Justices of the new Police' (created by the Middlesex Justices Act of 1792) and who explains her dire situation. 'My poor girl ... do you know that you have already paid for that single five shillings the enormous sum of 7*l* 10*s*?'[91] In order to make her self-reliant, the lady chooses not to give Betty the money she owes, but she gives her good advice, and, by applying it, Betty works her way out of her debts. The lady gives her a gown and a hat 'on the easy condition that she should go to church'.[92] Betty is converted to 'vital' Christianity, and eventually she is able to leave her orange-selling, 'a dangerous trade' though not necessarily 'a bad one'.[93] She progresses 'by industry and piety' until she becomes the keeper of 'a handsome Sausage-shop near the Seven Dials, married to an honest Hackney Coachman'.[94]

The name Hester Wilmot was almost certainly suggested to More by her work for the émigré clergy, as John Eardly Wilmot and John Hester were respectively chairman and secretary of the association set up on their behalf. Unlike Betty Brown, Hester lives in the country; both her parents are alive and are moderately prosperous. The first part of *The History of Hester Wilmot* was published in June 1797, and reflects More's eight years of experience in the running of Sunday schools.[95] It is chiefly notable for its portrayal of the ferociously houseproud Rebecca Wilmot.

It was no fault in Rebecca but a merit, that her oak table was so bright you could almost see to put your cap on it; but it was no merit but a fault that when John, her husband, laid down his cup of beer upon it so as to leave a mark, she could fly out into so terrible a passion that all the children were forced to run into corners; now poor John, having no corner to run into, ran to the ale-house ... She would keep poor Hester from church to stone the space under the chairs in fine patterns and whim-whams. I don't pretend there was any harm in this little

---

[90] *CRST* 112–13. [91] Ibid. 121. [92] Ibid. 124. [93] Ibid. 126.
[94] Ibid. 128. [95] *CRTEMR* 341–55.

decoration, it looks pretty enough…But still these are not things to set one's heart upon, and besides Rebecca only did it as a trap for praise.[96]

When Rebecca grudgingly allows her daughter to attend the school, Hester soon learns to spell and read (writing is not mentioned) and is allowed to take a book home. She rises early to study and like Betty Brown she is soon converted. When she becomes too old for the Sunday school, she joins the evening class run by Mrs Jones. At the end of the story More promises her readers a second instalment the following month. This duly came out in July, entitled *The History of Hester Wilmot; or, The New Gown*. For a year Hester has been saving up the money she earns from her spinning so that she can have a new gown for Mrs Jones's May Day feast. However, her feckless father has as usual been keeping 'Saint Monday', the pre-industrial worker's unofficial holiday, in the alehouse. He runs up a gambling debt, and, as a dutiful daughter, Hester lends him the money she has saved for her gown. She resolves to go to the feast nevertheless, though she knows she must endure the gleeful reaction of the other girls. Sure enough, 'there was a great hue and cry made at seeing Hester Wilmot, the neatest girl, the most industrious girl in the school, come to the May-day feast in an old stuff gown when every other girl was so creditably drest'.[97] She survives her humiliation, and, shortly after, both parents are converted. Hester herself is later rewarded. 'Last Christmas-day she was appointed an under teacher in the school, and many people think that some years hence…Hester may be promoted to be head mistress.'[98] Having undergone the teenage girl's ultimate horror experience, she is well placed to move up the social ladder.

As well as setting up these likeable girls as role models, More also created a colourful villain in her two-part tract *Black Giles the Poacher*, published in November and December 1796, a story which reveals a rather disconcerting knowledge of rural criminality. Giles lives at 'that Mud Cottage with the broken windows stuffed with dirty rags, just beyond the gate…You may know the house from a good distance by the ragged tiles on the roof, and the loose stones which are ready to drop out from the chimney.'[99] When a chaise approaches the nearby gate, his children ('ragged brats, with dirty faces, matted locks and naked feet and legs') rush to open the gate and terrify the horses. (Today, they would be cleaning car windscreens.) More adds feelingly, 'I know two ladies who were one day very near being killed by these abominable tricks.'[100] Abusing the right of the poor to use the common, Giles has appropriated the land for his own use, keeping two or three half-starved asses and beating them cruelly.[101] He is thus depriving his

---

[96] Ibid. 342–3.   [97] Ibid. 364.   [98] Ibid. 373.   [99] Ibid. 60.
[100] Ibid. 61.   [101] Ibid. 63.

fellow villagers of one of their customary rights, and as her intended readers would have known very well, he is also behaving like the engrossing land-lords More disliked so much. She took the added risk of raising the vexed question of the notoriously class-biased game laws. Giles is a poacher; so too is a much more sympathetic character, an 'honest fellow', named Jack Wes-ton. Giles informs against him, and he is brought before Mr Wilson (one of the pious clergyman and upright magistrates who people the Cheap Reposi-tory but were rarely found in the real world of the Mendip villages), charged with 'having knocked down a hare'. The manner in which Jack pleads guilty shows that More was well aware of plebeian attitudes to poaching. 'He did not deny the fact, but said he did not consider it as a crime, for he did not think game was a private property.' This is countered by Mr Wilson's 'It is not your business nor mine, John, to settle whether the game laws are good or bad. Till they are repealed, we must obey them.'[102] The sentiment is trite. What is noteworthy is More's refusal to mount a defence of the class-biased game laws beyond a general assertion of the sacredness of property. She did not want to be the uncritical mouthpiece of the landed classes, and she knew perfectly well that, if she assumed this role, she would lose her intended readers. She had to convince the poor that she was on their side.

Jack, a small-time opportunist, is let off with a fine, the payment staggered over the year. Black Giles, on the other hand, is a professional, and his poaching is part of a wider criminality. At all costs, he must not engage the sympathies of the reader. To prevent this, More is careful to stress that his crimes are against his own kind. He has already been exposed as an informer. In the second part of the story he and his sons rob a poor widow first of the onions that she uses to flavour her broth and then of her Red-streak cider apples, which are the envy of the whole village. Once more, local detail adds credibility and interest. Giles tries to shift the blame onto a neighbour, but he is eventually discovered and dies in despair. Having made him a traitor to his fellow workers, More could briskly dispose of him, hoping that she had kept her readers on board.

Bishop Porteus declared himself 'charmed with the amiable character of Black Giles'.[103] More, too, seems to have liked her creation and been reluc-tant to let him go. Giles is dead, but his wife, Tawney Rachel, the subject of a tract published in April 1797, matches him in villainy.[104] She travels the country and 'pretends to get her bread by selling laces, cabbage nets, ballads and history books, and used to buy old rags and rabbit skins'.[105] This, More adds, is a perfectly honest trade, but Rachel's motive is to get into farmers' kitchens in order to tell fortunes. Like her late husband, her crimes are against her own class. Her victims are mainly credulous young girls, perhaps

---

[102] Ibid. 70–5.　　[103] Roberts, iii. 5.　　[104] *CRST* 95–111.　　[105] Ibid. 95.

the type who would have worked as servants at Cowslip Green. One of the girls, Sally Evans,

delighted in dream books, and had consulted all the cunning women in the country to tell her whether two moles on her cheek denoted that she was to have two husbands or only two children ... She never made a black-pudding without borrowing one of the Parson's old wigs to hang in the chimney, firmly believing there were no other means to preserve them from bursting.[106]

Deceived by Rachel's trickery, Sally cannot concentrate on her work. 'She put her rennet into the butter-pan instead of the cheese-tub. She gave the curd to the hogs, and put the whey into the vats.'[107] She is lured into a disastrous marriage and then an early death. Rachel is sent to Botany Bay, 'and a happy day it was for the county of Somerset, when such a nuisance was sent out of it'.[108]

Inevitably, the dramatic interest of even the best Cheap Repository stories is undermined by the predictability of the endings. In the interest of her moral and religious message, More deliberately stifled her undoubted potential for writing innovating social novels. However, using her own experiences of the rural poor, whose hardships she now knew so well, she depicted sympathetic characters and placed them in realistic situations. She thus gave them a dignity denied them by Burke, making them individuals rather than undifferentiated parts of a swinish multitude. Far from being mere propaganda for the ruling classes, the tracts are mementoes of the accomplished minor novelist she might have been.

[106] Ibid. 99–100.   [107] Ibid. 105.   [108] Ibid. 109.

Chapter 9

The Emergence of Clapham
1795–1799

NEITHER the Sunday schools nor the Cheap Repository would have been possible without the active support, moral and financial, of an influential group of Hannah More's Evangelical friends, who, conveniently for tidy-minded historians, lived in close proximity around Clapham Common, four miles south-west of London. The group's centre of activity was Henry Thornton's home, Battersea Rise, which he had shared with Wilberforce from 1792. It began as a dignified Queen Anne house, but Thornton added two wings and a fine oval library designed by Pitt, which opened onto a lawn bounded by elms and tulip trees.[1] On the edge of the common he built two smaller houses, one, Broomfield, rented by Edward Eliot, Pitt's brother-in-law, and the other bought by Charles Grant, who had been a member of the Board of Trade at Calcutta. The little colony was later joined by John Shore (Lord Teignmouth), Warren Hastings's successor as governor-general of India, the lawyer James Stephen, and the abolitionist Zachary Macaulay.

[1] For Clapham, the 'Clapham sect', and its wider influence, see J. Stephen, 'The Clapham Sect', *Edinburgh Review*, 80 (1844), 295–307; id., *Essays in Ecclesiastical Biography* (London, 1875), 523–84; D. Pym, *Battersea Rise* (London, 1934); E. M. Howse, *Saints in Politics: The 'Clapham Sect' and the Growth of Freedom* (London, 1952); E. M. Forster, *Marianne Thornton* (London, 1956), chs. 1 and 2; N. G. Annan, 'The Intellectual Aristocracy', in J. H. Plumb (ed.), *Studies in Social History* (London, 1955), 243–87; M. Hennell, *John Venn and the Clapham Sect* (London, 1958); I. Bradley, 'The Politics of Godliness: Evangelicals in Parliament, 1784–1832', D.Phil. thesis (Oxford, 1974); id. *The Call to Seriousness: The Evangelical Impact on the Victorians* (London, 1976); J. Pollock, *Wilberforce* (London, 1977); C. Tolley, *Domestic Biography: The Legacy of Evangelicalism in Four Nineteenth-Century Families* (Oxford, 1997); F. K. Brown, *Fathers of the Victorians: The Age of Wilberforce* (Cambridge, 1961). For an incisive critique of Brown, see D. Newsome, 'Father and Sons', *Historical Journal*, 6 (1963), 295–310.

This dense conglomeration of Evangelicals, comprising bankers, members of Parliament, and colonial administrators, all devoted to the abolition of the slave trade and the dissemination of 'vital religion', became known as the Saints; by the middle of the nineteenth century they had acquired the retrospective title of the Clapham sect. Their group solidarity was remarkable; some thought it sinister. They went on holiday together, intermarried, and stood godparents to each other's children. In the Revd John Venn they had (almost) their own domestic chaplain; he had (of course) been presented to the living of Clapham by Henry Thornton. For all its many virtues and great reforming energies, the sect had many of the characteristics of a cosy coterie which are so comforting to those within the magic circle and so infuriating to those on the outside. It is no accident that some prominent members of the Bloomsbury group were descended from the Claphamites: E. M. Forster was the great-grandson of Henry Thornton; Virginia Woolf and Vanessa Bell were the great-granddaughters of James Stephen by his first wife. (His second wife was the widowed Sarah Clark, Wilberforce's sister.)

Hannah More was the honorary man of Clapham, the only woman to be attached in her own right rather than through kinship or marriage. As her ties to Mrs Garrick loosened, she was an ever more frequent guest at Clapham, where she was greeted rapturously by the eager children, who relished her kindly interest in their doings and her gift for making Bible stories exciting. When she returned home, their parents took time out of their hectic lives to write to her, pouring out their thoughts, seeking her advice, asking anxiously about her health. A decade older than most of them, and apparently comfortable with her single status, she was the safest kind of female friend. But the relationships were not always problem-free. In the second half of the 1790s, as three of the Clapham men fell in love and married, the emotional eddies spread out to trouble her own life and it took time for her to regain her balance and composure.

Early in 1796 Henry Thornton married the Yorkshire banker's daughter Marianne Sykes. Hannah More thoroughly approved of the match, describing the bride as 'a lady . . . of great sense and goodness, and of a disposition to make him happy, as she is fond of retirement and not at all disposed for the gaieties of life'.[2] But the marriage soon made her deeply unhappy, not because of any dissatisfaction with the new Mrs Thornton, but because of the strange attitude of her husband. The reasons lie in Thornton's complex psyche, much of which was unknown to her. His diary for 1795 reveals that in the last year of his bachelorhood he was coping with a sexual crisis involving a habit of masturbation he found hard to break and some very

---

[2] Folger, W.b. 288, More to Eva Garrick, 17 Feb. 1796.

complicated feelings (part hostile, part adulatory) about More herself. While recognizing that he gained credit from her friendship, he also went out of his way to be brusque and hypercritical.[3] It got worse after his marriage, perhaps because he associated her with a time of frustration and moral failure, and punished her accordingly. With her enormous need for friendship and affection, his rebuffs were more than she could bear. Hurt and bewildered, she confided in Wilberforce in August 1796.

I am greatly pleased with that Lady's good sense and piety, and with her kind and friendly behaviour to me, but I must say that while *she* marries me into the affection of an old friend, Mr Thornton freezes me into the distance and reserve of a new Acquaintance—and it is no hard matter, for tho' an old woman, I am repulsed as easily as a Child. You may tell him the above when you have an opportunity.[4]

Wilberforce clearly did speak to him, and Thornton responded by sending More a very warm letter telling her that Marianne 'would be much more sorry to drop your friendship than that of any other woman to whom I have introduced her'.[5] In September Mrs Thornton wrote to confirm her husband's sentiments. 'Do you not . . . know that removed as I am from all my own natural friends, I must look to you next to my Husband as the friend from whom I may hope to receive tenderness & sympathy & the best advice?'[6] This was not mere words. Marianne Sykes Thornton was a nervous, sensitive woman, prone to anxiety. Like Lady Waldegrave, she found More a good friend in trouble. When a child died ten hours after its birth, she confided, 'I now know that the loss of a child can create a pang unlike any other—it seems so contrary to nature, that it could only be inflicted in anger on sinful parents & it is wounding to every gentle feeling of one's heart.'[7] It is a tribute to More's gifts of sympathy, that in spite of her childlessness, she was expected to enter into the feelings of a bereaved mother.

On the whole, though, Mrs Thornton's letters conveyed happier news. On 10 March, just over a year after her marriage, she gave birth to the first of her nine surviving children, a daughter named after her mother. This lively, intelligent girl, later her father's confidante and amanuensis, became one of Hannah More's closest friends and the most entertaining of her correspondents. Posterity owes her an ambivalent debt. On her parents' deaths she destroyed most of their correspondence, but not before transcribing their

[3] Thornton, Add. MS 7674/1/R, fo. 75, 'Saty m[ornin]g. [6 Mar.]'; fo. 79, 'M[onda]y. m[ornin]g'. For indications of masturbation, see fos. 105, 114, and 124.

[4] Duke, More to Wilberforce, 3 Aug. [1796] [catalogued *c.* 1799].

[5] Thornton, Add. MS 7674/1/L1, fo. 96, Thornton to More, 26 Aug. 1796; also 7674/1/N, fo. 66.

[6] Thornton, Add. MS 7674/1/L1, fo. 96b, Mrs H. Thornton to More, 2 Sept. 1796; also 7674/1/N, fo. 67.

[7] Thornton, Add. MS 7674/1/N, fos. 79–80, Mrs H. Thornton to More, 17 Aug. 1798.

letters, no doubt with many omissions, into a series of notebooks which she bequeathed to her great-nephew E. M. Forster, who used them to compile his domestic biography *Marianne Thornton*. Along with her parents' letters she set down her views on various members of the Clapham sect, their wives, and their children. She had strong likes and dislikes. She despised Barbara Wilberforce, thought the Wilberforce sons a pale shadow of their great father, saw Tom Macaulay as too clever by half, and described Hannah More in terms of deep, though not uncritical, affection.

The temporary estrangement between More and Henry Thornton in the summer of 1796 was caused in the main by his unfortunate manner and uptight personality. But More herself was more vulnerable than usual at that time, perhaps prone to see slights where none were intended. She was passing through one of the most distressing emotional experiences of her life.

It began in the summer of 1795, when she received a new visitor to Cowslip Green, a young Gaelic-speaking Highlander of awkward manners and heroic ambition. He was Zachary Macaulay, son of John Macaulay, a Presbyterian minister in Argyll, who had met and argued with Samuel Johnson on his Highland tour in 1773. Through the marriage of his sister Jean to the Evangelical abolitionist Thomas Babington, a college friend of Wilberforce and the owner of the imposing Leicestershire manor house Rothley Temple, he had been drawn into the Clapham sect. On the recommendations of Wilberforce and Thornton he had been appointed governor of the freed slave colony Sierra Leone. He was now in England on leave and, on Thornton's urging, he set out that summer on a visit to Hannah More and her Sunday schools, by now a place of Evangelical pilgrimage. More was delighted to meet a man who had sacrificed so much for the freed Africans. The visit was a success, and Macaulay became an enthusiast for the Cheap Repository, which had been launched earlier that year; Henry Thornton asked him to check Hannah and Sally More's anti-slavery ballad *The Sorrows of Yamba* for inaccuracies.[8] At some stage on this visit he must have met Selina Mills, then aged 29 and still teaching at the Park Street school. He reached an understanding with her, and confided his feelings to his Babington relations, who were as encouraging as a man in love could wish.[9]

At the turn of the year he spent three days with the Mores in Bath, where Selina was also passing the Christmas vacation. It seems that Hannah More, correctly interpreting some unguarded expressions on his first visit, had guessed at his feelings. She was reluctant to discuss the matter, but when

---

[8] Thornton, Add. MS 7674/1/L1, fos. 47–8, Thornton to Zachary Macaulay, 6 Oct. 1795.

[9] The following narrative is based largely on M. Knutsford, *Life and Letters of Zachary Macaulay* (London, 1900), 98–115, and the correspondence of Zachary Macaulay and Selina Mills in the Huntington Library.

Macaulay insisted on bringing it into the open, she gave him to understand that Selina was indifferent to him. This was duplicitous; the truth was that she feared for Patty's happiness should she lose her young friend to a man they hardly knew. Dinner that afternoon was a difficult meal. Macaulay hardly dared look at Selina, while she had great difficulty in concealing her distress; a considerable amount of food must have been sent back to the kitchen. Macaulay was due to leave that evening, and he bade a polite, formal farewell to the More sisters in the drawing room. On the way down-stairs to the carriage, however, he accidentally saw Selina in a room on her own, weeping bitterly. He went to her, began to console her, and within a few minutes both had declared their love. He then stepped into the coach, leaving the house in turmoil.

Some days later, and as if nothing had happened, Hannah More sent him a letter about the Sunday reading he had contributed to the Cheap Repository. 'Miss Mills has been busy at work transcribing your *Communicant*...We much approve of what you have done but have ventured to abridge in a few instances. Pray don't forget to bring her previous performance, as I dare say she would be miserable to have it lost, and I must return the manuscript.'[10] But about ten days later she wrote to Thomas Babington, telling him that Selina was 'resolved not to entangle herself'; she was also determined not to go to Africa herself, and would think less of Macaulay if he abandoned his great schemes for love of her. This sounded rather cold-blooded, but Selina was (More assured Babington) 'naturally...of a very calm composed mind, has no violent passions, but is of an orderly regular spirit and tho not *deficient* in sensibility has not those acute sort of feelings which torment the possessor'. She added that she hoped the letter 'will tend to allay the disquiet of Mr Macaulay's mind, and give him that sort of reasonable consolation which is all that, sorry as I am to say it, the state of the case admits'.[11]

More was right about Selina's determination not to go to Africa, but in all other respects she had misjudged her. Macaulay was back before the end of the month; he and Selina were now prepared to meet the sisters and tell them the truth about their relationship. The resulting confrontation was stormy and distressing. As the More sisters retained a strict *omertà* on the whole business, the details survive only in hints in Macaulay's correspond-ence and in the family tradition recorded by his granddaughter. From this it emerges that Macaulay had at least one discussion with Patty on her own, after which, he told his sister Jean Babington, he was astonished at 'the extraordinary turn' her mind had taken. 'She received my questions with such a repulsive coldness as quite surprised me, and made me soon quit the

---

[10] Clark, More to Zachary Macaulay, 14 Jan. [1796].
[11] BL, Add. MS 63084, fos. 4–5, More to Thomas Babington, c.25 Jan. 1796.

subject.'[12] However, the main drawback was not Patty's attitude but Selina's refusal to accompany him to Africa. With the matter still unresolved, Macaulay left for London on 1 February; six days later he wrote Selina a puzzled, rambling letter in which he twice accused the Mores of 'violence' in their opposition.

You will not readily suspect me of wishing to lessen the great obligations you are under to the Miss Mores, especially H. and P. or to detract from the singular excellence of their characters. God who knows my heart, knows that I should be glad to follow them as they follow Christ . . . But I w^d not conceal it from you that I cannot help thinking them outrageously violent on several points. . . . One of the points I allude to is the effect of Marriage in narrowing the heart, and hardening it against the impressions of former friendships, whence they draw conclusions hostile to marriage itself. . . . that in some cases, there appears in these dear Ladies a degree of violence, a little unwarrantable.[13]

On 18 February he was complaining that 'Miss Patty's dislike to marriage appears whimsical. She ought to suspect that the effect she complains of arises from herself.'[14] Jean Babington was more forthright. 'I believe them to be very good Women,' she wrote to her brother, 'but they certainly see things much too strongly. I cannot think that they have acted with perfect candour in this affair.'[15]

The extreme reaction of the Mores to a marriage proposal from a man who was liked and trusted by such Evangelical luminaries as Wilberforce and Thornton was at odds with their carefully cultivated image of good sense and calm restraint. It appears that during the painful conversations they inveighed against marriage in general as the destroyer of friendship. They were thrashing about for rationalizations of disturbing emotions which they were unprepared to acknowledge and for which they might not even have had a vocabulary. A crude but obvious conjecture is that Patty, who was the most violent in her opposition, was an unacknowledged lesbian, in love with the pretty teacher. However, apart from her opposition to Selina's marriage, the only other evidence of homoerotic feelings is her 'sentimental' friendship with Ann Kennicott, which probably reflected literary convention rather than sexually charged emotions.[16] Later Barbara Wilberforce picked up a quite different rumour about her:

She had endured a very painful trial, having relinquished an attachment very strong on her part, & which was mutual, in order to gratify her Sisters, who for some cause which I could never learn, could not endure her becoming the Wife of

---

[12] Quoted in Knutsford, *Macaulay*, 103.
[13] Huntington, MY 441, Zachary Macaulay to Selina Mills, 7 Feb. 1796.
[14] Huntington, MY 451, Zachary Macaulay to Selina Mills, 18 Feb. 1796.
[15] Knutsford, *Macaulay*, 107. [16] Clark, Ann Kennicott to More, 19 July [?].

the individual for whom she felt this decided predilection, her wishes were sacrificed to gratify her family, but the struggle was long and severe.

In an innocent anticipation of Freud, Barbara Wilberforce speculated that 'perhaps the foundation of her deep & animated piety might be laid amidst the pangs & contending feelings of this early trial'.[17] If Selina Mills was indeed the Mores' surrogate sister, and had replaced Patty as the baby of the family, then the common factor in the two narratives is the possessive closing of ranks against marriage, seen as the mortal enemy of their special relationship. It was a breaking of the fellowship, a rift in the warm solidarity they had built up against a world all too ready to mock and despise single women. To desert the sisterhood for the sexual and emotional demands of a man and the constrained lifestyle of a married woman was the ultimate betrayal. If Patty had nearly succumbed and then drawn back at the cost of considerable personal distress, this may help to explain the intensity of her hostility when she saw Selina apparently re-enacting her own painful story.

In mid-February she attempted to repair the relationship and made a short visit to Park Street to see Selina. The visit did more harm than good as Patty talked at rather than to her and gave the impression that she thought it impossible 'to retain kind affections for ones relations and friends after marriage'.[18] Macaulay himself had not helped his case by blurting out one of those thoughtless remarks which cannot be unsaid but are never forgotten. He told his sister that in his interview with Patty he had let out 'an involuntary expression of surprise that those women who possessed the greatest share of intrinsic worth did not seem to possess that degree of estimation in the eyes of men which they merited. I could have bit my tongue with vexation, but the words were irrevocable.'[19] In his abrupt, honest fashion, he had probably inflicted a greater wound than he knew.

On 23 February Macaulay set sail from Portsmouth. He did not return for three years, and in that period he often did not hear from Selina for months on end. In September 1797 Hannah More sent him a chatty letter full of information about the Cheap Repository, telling him that she had not seen Selina lately but that her sister, Mary Thatcher, had paid them a visit.[20] In 1799 he resigned his position as governor of Sierra Leone. On returning to England he was appointed secretary of the Company with a salary of £500. At Battersea Rise he met More again and found her full of 'friendly attentions'. He had sent over some African children to be educated in England, and when they arrived in Clapham Hannah More, always the pedagogue,

[17] Bodleian, MS d. 20, Barbara Wilberforce, 'Recollections of Mrs Hannah More and her Sisters', fo. 35.

[18] Huntington, MY 379, Selina Mills to Zachary Macaulay, 17 Feb. 1796.

[19] Quoted in Knutsford, *Macaulay*, 103.

[20] Clark, More to Zachary Macaulay, 8 Sept. 1797.

'began to catechise one of them a little and was much pleased with his ready answers'.[21] (Some of the children died shortly after, and those who survived the English climate were later put to school in Clapham.) The long-awaited marriage finally took place in Bristol on 26 August 1799. Selina had sent Patty an invitation to the wedding, and received an emotional refusal full of dark hints that they would never meet again in this world.[22] After the wedding party left Bristol, the More sisters collapsed into collective grief, sobbing themselves into an exhausted acquiescence. A short while later, Selina Macaulay sensibly choosing to ignore Patty's forebodings, visited Cowslip Green, and friendly relations were resumed. After this, everyone agreed to 'forget' the whole business.

Zachary Macaulay continued to labour for the abolitionist cause, and he became editor of the *Christian Observer*, the influential Evangelical house journal. In her old age Hannah More relied on him to sort out her complicated finances, which he did with great patience and good humour in spite of the pressing concerns of his own affairs. Selina Macaulay kept up her links with the West Country, and as her family grew she brought her children on summer visits to Wrington. A daughter, born in 1810, was named Hannah More Macaulay after her godmother, though More laughingly protested: 'I think it very hard upon the poor babe to be obliged to carry about such an ugly name with her all her life.'[23] (She later married the civil servant Sir Charles Trevelyan and became the mother of George Otto Trevelyan and the grandmother of the historian George Macaulay Trevelyan.)

By far the most celebrated of the Macaulay children was their first-born, Thomas Babington Macaulay, born at Rothley Temple on 25 October 1800. Anecdotes of this extraordinary child soon began to abound, showing the cocksure historian firmly embedded in the precocious toddler: how he sat perched on a table and read to the housemaid out of a book as big as himself; how he regaled his nurse and mother with interminable stories constructed with a vocabulary and a phraseology far in advance of his years. One anecdote relates to Hannah More. She called at the Macaulays in Clapham and 'was met by a fair, pretty, slight child . . . about four years of age, who came to the front door to receive her, and tell her that his parents were out, but that if she would be good enough to come in he would bring her a glass of old spirits'.[24] When his amused visitor asked him what he knew about old spirits, he replied that Robinson Crusoe had often had some. Another, very famous story shows how More's friendship with the Waldegrave family had tied them firmly into the Clapham sect. Zachary Macaulay took his son to see Laura Waldegrave at Strawberry Hill. After she had

[21] Knutsford, *Macaulay*, 220–2.   [22] Ibid. 235.
[23] Clark, More to Zachary Macaulay, 5 Apr. 1810.
[24] G. O. Trevelyan, *The Life and Letters of Lord Macaulay* (London, 1876), i. 27–8.

shown him round Horace Walpole's collection, he was taken to the great gallery, where a servant spilled some hot coffee over his legs. A concerned Lady Waldegrave fussed over the distressed child, and after a few minutes asked him how he felt. He looked up at her and replied, 'Thank you, madam, the agony is abated.'[25]

The year 1797 was one of notable deaths. Mary Wollstonecraft's death in childbirth seems to have passed Hannah More by, but she could not ignore the passings of Edmund Burke and Horace Walpole (who had inherited his uncle's title, Lord Orford). She last saw Burke in February. Broken in spirit since the death of his only son, he was vainly seeking a cure in Bath, and, as More told Mrs Garrick, he looked 'so altered that people hardly knew it to be the same man'.[26] He was to die in June. More's feelings about him were mixed. Much as she welcomed the brilliance of his assault on the French Revolution, she continued to believe that he spoiled a good case by lack of judgement. The hardships of war and the advent of a new, less ideologically driven government in France in the summer of 1794 had drawn her and many of her fellow Bristolians—'moderate and reasonable persons', she assured Wilberforce—into the peace camp.[27] This meant that she was harshly critical of Burke's *Letters on a Regicide Peace*, two very hawkish pamphlets published at the end of 1796: 'a wild malignant rhapsody', she told Elizabeth Bouverie, that 'kept me in a violent ill humour the whole time it was reading. We want emollients now, and not inflamers.'[28] Eventually she was to decide that, for all the abusive violence of his political diatribes, he had been vindicated by the events of the French Revolution, where 'happily for his fame, all the successive actors in the revolutionary drama took care to sin up to any intemperance of language which even Mr Burke could supply'.[29]

Walpole had died in March, uncharacteristically fretful and complaining in his final days. Though More's conversion had driven a wedge between them, his last letter drafted in an infirm hand in the preceding August was deeply affectionate, and she was saddened by his death.[30] 'Poor Lord Orford,' she wrote to Patty. 'Twenty years' unclouded kindness and pleasant correspondence cannot be given up without emotion. I am not sorry now that I never flinched from any of his ridicule or attacks, or suffered them to pass without rebuke.'[31] His last gift to her had been Bishop Wilson's superbly bound three-volume edition of the Bible, inscribed 'To his excellent friend MISS HANNAH MORE ... as a mark of his esteem and gratitude'.[32]

---

[25] Ibid. i.28.   [26] Folger, W.b. 488, fo. 5, More to Eva Garrick, 7 Feb. [1797].
[27] Duke, More to Wilberforce, 29 Nov. 1794.   [28] *Gambier*, i. 315.
[29] *Hints towards Forming the Character of a Young Princess* (2nd edn. London, 1805), ii. 205.
[30] New York Public Library, Berg Collection, Walpole to More, 29 Aug. 1796.
[31] Roberts, iii. 13.   [32] *Walpole*, 399.

He left his Berkeley Square house and Strawberry Hill to his friend Anne Damer, with the reversion to Lady Waldegrave. In the following year Mary Berry, who had inherited his literary estate, published their correspondence, though not before More had excised some of his earthier expressions; for example, where Walpole had written 'dugs enough to suckle' she scratched out the offending words and substituted 'sucklings'.[33] The prudery is understandable if indefensible. She was well aware that her friendship with Walpole raised eyebrows among some Evangelicals, and she had to defend her carefully guarded reputation against any hint of indelicacy.

The volume of correspondence contained as a frontispiece an engraving of John Opie's portrait of More, which had been painted in 1787. Walpole, an avid collector of portraits, had seen it in Elizabeth Montagu's drawing room and liked it so much that he had ordered a copy of his own.[34] More discovered the engraving of 'my hideous picture' when thumbing through the book at the duchess of Gloucester's house. 'I almost screamed,' she told Patty.[35] In her lugubrious diary she wrote that she 'laboured to hinder' its publication and prayed to be kept 'humble . . . under a deep sense of the emptiness of earthly honours'.[36] It seems that she knew very well that, far from being 'hideous', it was the most flattering of her portraits, and she was vain enough to be pleased.

A month after Walpole's death Wilberforce became engaged. Henry Thornton's marriage had ended the bachelor chumminess of their shared household at Battersea Rise, and at the age of 37, perhaps in a panic that he would end his days rootless and alone, he proposed to a pretty, dark-haired girl in her twenties whom he had only known for eight days. She was Barbara Spooner, the daughter of a family of Birmingham merchants, bankers, and ironmasters. On her mother's side she was rather better connected, being the niece of the Evangelical peer the first Lord Calthorpe. Unsurprisingly, the pair had met at Bath: as Jane Austen's Mrs Elton was to point out to Emma Woodhouse, the advantages of Bath to the young were very well understood. A cynical friend believed that she had mugged up the slave trade in order to get an introduction.[37] The news of this very sudden engagement came as a shock to Wilberforce's friends. Hannah More's anxieties were apparent beneath the surface of the letters she wrote at this time, the first to Wilberforce, the others to Elizabeth Bouverie. She was evidently anxious that her friend's love life, already an open secret in Bath, should distract him from following up the progress of his recently published *Practical View of the Prevailing Religious System*, a work she had been gently nagging him to produce.[38]

---

[33] Ibid., p. xi.   [34] Roberts, ii. 68, 98.   [35] Roberts, iii. 30.
[36] Ibid. 59.   [37] Pollock, *Wilberforce*, 156.
[38] W. Wilberforce, *A Practical View of the Prevailing Religious System of Professed Christians in the Higher and Middle Classes . . . contrasted with Real Christianity* (London, 1797).

1. Hannah More, 1780, by Frances Reynolds: in the aftermath of *Percy* More is portrayed as a literary celebrity. Reproduced with kind permission from the Bridgeman Art Library.

Heath Sculp!

2. Hannah More, 1787, by James Heath, after John Opie: Hannah More called this 'my hideous picture' but Walpole liked it so much that he had an engraving made for Strawberry Hill. Picture courtesy of The Lewis Walpole Library Print Collection, Yale University.

(Positively The Last Night but Two.)

For the BENEFIT, of

Mrs. BUTLER.

At the *THEATRE*, in the Market-place, *ABINGDON*.

On FRIDAY, Evening, the 27th, of *March*, 1789.

Will be performed a TRAGEDY, *(Never Acted Here,)* call'd

PERCY.

Or the FATAL CHEVIOT CHACE.

The French Drama, founded on the famous old Story of Raoul de Coucy, suggested to the Author, some circumstances in the former part of this Beautiful Tragedy, and the famous old Song of Cheviot Chace furnishes other Hints. If to hold out an Example of Purity, Fortitude and honour in the midst of severest Difficulties and misfortunes and animate by sympathy a female Breast, and make them emulous of comparing and vieing with a Roman Horatia; let them (as they may without a Blush) view an Example of Resplendent Merit in Elwina, and view a Scene,

Where Love, Revenge, Jealousy's wild Rage,
Rouse all the Genious of ... sioned Stage.

(Written by Miss HANNAH MORE.)

Percy, *(Earl of Northumberland,)* Mr. LEE.
Earl of Raby, Mr HAYDEN.
Sir Hubert, Mr. COOPER.
Edric, Mr. BUTLER.
Harcourt, Mr. CROSS.
Knights, Messrs. CRAVEN. and HITCHCOCK.
And Douglas Mr. SHATFORD.

Birtha, Mrs. CRAVEN.
And Elwina, Mrs. SHATFORD.

SINGING, by Mr. BUTLER,

To which will be added (By particular Desire,) a COMEDY, call'd

The Midnight Hour.

(Written by Mrs. INCHBALD.)

The Marquis, Mr. CROSS.
Sebastian, Mr. LEE.
Nicholas, Mr. SHATFORD.
Ambrose, Mr. HAYDEN.
Mathias Mr. BUTLER.
And the General, Mr. CRAVEN.

Cicely, Mrs. CRAVEN. Flora, Mrs. SHATFORD.
And Julia, Mrs. BUTLER.

BOXES 3s. TPT. 2s. GALLERY 1s.----To begin half past Six o'Clock.
TICKETS, to be had at the Principal Inns, of Mrs. Butler, at Mr. Gregorys

3. Playbill, 1789, for *Percy*: showing that *Percy* continued to be performed in the provinces after it had ceased playing on the London stage.

4. 'A Perry-lous Situation', 1791: mocking Clementina Clerke's elopement and showing the respectable Park Street school in the worst possible light. Picture by permission of the British Museum.

5. Mr and Mrs Garrick by the Shakespeare Temple at Hampton by Johann Zoffany: More was for many years a privileged guest at Hampton. Picture courtesy of the Yale Center for British Art, Paul Mellon Collection.

6. The Nine Living Muses, 1779, by Richard Samuel: More is Melpomene, the Muse of Tragedy, the figure holding the cup.
Picture courtesy of the National Portrait Gallery, London.

7. Elizabeth Carter, by Thomas Lawrence: the translator of Epictetus and the most learned woman of her day. Picture courtesy of the National Portrait Gallery, London.

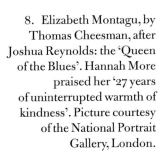

8. Elizabeth Montagu, by Thomas Cheesman, after Joshua Reynolds: the 'Queen of the Blues'. Hannah More praised her '27 years of uninterrupted warmth of kindness'. Picture courtesy of the National Portrait Gallery, London.

9. William Wilberforce,
by Thomas Lawrence:
the great abolitionist
was More's closest
friend and most
enthusiastic admirer.
Picture courtesy of the
National Portrait
Gallery, London.

10. Horace Walpole, by
William Danielle: in 1784
Walpole recruited More
into the ranks of his cor-
respondents.
In 1789 he published
Bishop Bonner's Ghost
on the Strawberry Hill
Press. Picture courtesy
of The Lewis Walpole
Library Print Collection,
Yale University.

11. Cowslip Green: 'this nutshell of a house', More's home from 1785 to 1801. The picture shows later enlargements. Reproduced by permission of the British Library, ADD. 42511 f.22.

12. Barley Wood: More's home from 1801 to 1828. She frequently compared it to Paradise. Reproduced by permission of the British Library, ADD. 42511 f.31.

13. Hannah More, 1809: More in her sixties, a celebrated author, but suffering from failing health.

14. Hannah More, 1824 after Frederick Richard Pickersgill: described by a friend as 'an excellent likeness of her in her old age'.

15. *The Shepherd of Salisbury Plain*: the most celebrated of the Cheap Repository Tracts, first published in March 1795.

16. The Closure of the Cheddar Club (1951): after more than 150 years the 'Hannah More Club' was wound up. By permission of Somerset RO.

Now that it was out, however, she almost feared to write about it for fear that 'if I were now to fill up my paper with any other Subject but this fair *Barbara* you would think me a dull, prosing, pedantic, unfeeling old maid, who was prating of the *book* when she should be talking of the *Wife*'.[39] More candidly told Mrs Bouverie that 'the wife follows so fast upon the book that he hardly gives one time to breathe between the two'.[40] At first she favoured secrecy, but then changed her mind because she feared the damage a hasty marriage might do to Wilberforce's reputation.[41] Inevitably she hoped he had chosen the right woman. 'I feel anxious on this head, as I consider the credit of Mr Wilberforce in some degree connected with the credit of religion itself.'[42] She was eager to call in at Bath on her way back to Cowslip Green, to see the prospective bride, 'and purpose to make a beginning of a friendship which I hope will never have an end'.[43] She seems to have half-known Barbara Spooner already, as she was 'one of a little set of young ladies with whom . . . I was beginning to be acquainted at Bath'.[44] From what she knew of her she believed that she would readily fall in with his habits, 'many of which would not be pleasant to a gay young woman of the world'.[45]

Beneath Hannah More's careful language lay the unspoken assumption that she never thought Barbara Spooner worthy of the high honour of being the wife of such a man. Her description of her to Zachary Macaulay as 'a pretty, pleasing, pious young woman' seems rather cool.[46] In contrast to the volume of her correspondence with Marianne Thornton and Selina Macaulay, she wrote few letters to Mrs Wilberforce. Intellectually Barbara could not compete with these other Clapham wives. Temperamentally, too, she and More had little in common. Barbara was a fussy hypochondriac, and after the couple moved into Broomfield, Edward Eliot's old house on Clapham Common, she ran her household with a parsimonious inefficiency that made visits something of a trial to her guests. She was prolific in the type of embarrassing evangelical effusions that More disliked because she believed they gave the cause a bad name. It is difficult to believe that such a woman could have provided her husband with much mental stimulation. This, however, might have been the last thing Wilberforce wanted from a wife. There were plenty of people—his male friends, his parliamentary colleagues, Hannah More—with whom he could discuss religion, politics, tactical moves in the abolition debates, the formation of parliamentary alliances, the latest

---

[39] Duke, More to Wilberforce, 25 Apr. 1797.
[40] *Gambier*, i. 320, More to Elizabeth Bouverie, 2 May [1797].
[41] Duke, More to Wilberforce, Apr. 1797.
[42] *Gambier*, i. 325, More to Elizabeth Bouverie, 15 June 1797.
[43] Duke, More to Wilberforce [Apr. 1797].   [44] *Gambier*, i. 320.
[45] Ibid. 322–3; More to Elizabeth Bouverie, 28 May [1797].
[46] Clark, More to Zachary Macaulay, 8 Sept. 1797.

issue of the *Christian Observer*. What he found at home was deep devotion, unstinting admiration, and (presumably) sexual satisfaction after years of abstinence. As a man who lived in cheerfully creative chaos, he did not notice her bad housekeeping or her inability to manage servants. He loved her dearly and was patient with her irritating characteristics, on which count alone, in the acerbic Marianne Thornton's opinion, he qualified as an angel.[47] She was unwilling to consider what might have been the truth—that he needed his wife deeply and would have been crushed if she had died first.

The couple were married in Bath on Tuesday 30 May. Like most weddings at that time it was low-key, with few friends attending, and at a time of war there was no prospect of a honeymoon trip abroad. Instead there was to be a tour of the Mendip schools, an itinerary which on its own would have mapped out for Barbara the shape of her future life. There is something rather chilling in the fact that, according to Hannah More, it had been Wilberforce's long-standing resolution 'to make his wife (if he ever did marry) set out with an act of humility by bringing her to pass the first Sunday &c at my cottage and with our poor'.[48] On the day before the wedding More sent Wilberforce a letter setting out their programme, which is worth noting in some detail for what it reveals of her personality and the extent of the Sunday school work at this stage.[49]

The couple were to arrive on Saturday 3 June. Because the cottage was small, the sisters could lodge 'an humble footman' but not 'a fine Valet de Chambre'. One of the parlours would serve as a dressing room. 'As to the Lady', More wrote, with one of her odd bursts of flirtatiousness, 'I will be handmaid myself to her. "I'll weave her Garlands and I'll pleat her hair."' The reference, as Wilberforce must have known, was to Matthew Prior's song *Emma and Henry*, in which the rejected Emma agrees to wait on her successful rival in love. He and Barbara were both delighted at the quotation and read no deeper meaning into it. The Sunday was to be a gruelling day. At half past eight two chaises, one carrying the Wilberforces, the other the More sisters, were to set out first for Shipham, then to Axbridge and Cheddar; after this eleven-mile journey they would endure the relative hardship of a cold lunch at the inn (the servants were not to be made to cook on the sabbath). At Cheddar, More told Wilberforce, 'the Church, School, and evening devotions will keep us there till about seven; then we call in on another little Society at Axbridge and get home after nine'. The one problem was that Cheddar was under inoculation so the attendances there would be poor. If Wilberforce was unable to fit in with this plan, then the following Sunday they would do a tour of the schools that lay in the other direction

[47] Thornton, Add. MS 7674/1/L/10, fo. 19; 76741/N, fo. 503.
[48] *Gambier*, i. 324, More to Elizabeth Bouverie, 15 June [1797].
[49] Bodleian, MS c. 3, fos. 31–2, More to Wilberforce, 29 May 1797.

(Nailsea, Yatton, and Blagdon). It says much either for Barbara Wilberforce's marital submissiveness or for her Evangelical commitment (or both) that she was willing to fit in with such an arduous programme.

For all her shortcomings, Barbara could be a perceptive observer, as is shown in the account of this day that she wrote years later for her son Samuel, the future 'soapy Sam', bishop of Oxford.[50] After the predicted early start the couple found a reception awaiting them at Shipham church in the form of 'a row of... parishioners up the little Gravel walk all strewed with flowers in honour of the Bride'. At Axbridge, a town with a 'narrow and miserable main street', they called in on John Boak's 'dismal little parlour', where his wife was dying of cancer.[51] On entering the schoolroom they were confronted by a 'furious dirty woman' who was noisily withdrawing her son because of 'some petty punishment'. But what took their attention in particular was the sight of an animated little girl wearing a cap, whose 'fixed attention & intelligent answers caught our attention'. The newly-weds were much taken with this lively child and distressed to learn from Patty that she was suffering from 'a Cancer in her head which the little Cap had concealed'. After a cold lunch at the Cheddar inn they attended a service in the church, which was 'full to overflowing—the Pews well peopled & the middle Aisle down which rows of benches were ranged were filled with quiet orderly attentive Children'. The Wilberforces were told that, before the foundation of the school, there had only been twelve or fourteen in the congregation. The rest of the afternoon was spent in the schoolrooms hearing the children answer questions on the Bible (with Wilberforce asking his own somewhat unrealistic questions) and repeat passages from memory. When their attention flagged, the sisters, true to their normal practice, got them to stand up and sing. After a break for tea the parents, villagers, and older children assembled for the evening reading of prayers, conducted by Patty, who, so Barbara believed, 'excelled her Sister in that service'. They then returned to Cowslip Green, presumably exhausted. If the following day was typical of Hannah More's Mondays, she would have spent it in bed, enduring the agonies of one of the migraine attacks that plagued her, sometimes for days, following her punishing Sundays.[52]

If Mrs Wilberforce's narrative is to be believed, the schools were by this stage a triumphant success. She was, of course, a partial observer, and she wrote from hindsight. Her glowing tributes to More's pet clergy, Jones of Shipham, Drewitt of Cheddar, Boak of Axbridge, reflected her own Evangelical zeal. On her own admission she was at this stage ignorant of Sunday schools and unable to bring a critical perspective to bear on the More sisters'

---

[50] Bodleian, MS d. 20, fos. 34–43. [51] She died in Feb. 1799; Bodleian, MS c. 3, fo. 265.
[52] Clark, More to Zachary Macaulay, 8 Sept. 1797.

aims and methods. She only visited half the schools (though she visited others on subsequent visits) and might not have been aware of the fact that the sisters had recently had to close the Congresbury school.[53] She was vague about numbers; for example, she described the Shipham congregation as large, but gave no indication of the percentage of its nearly 500 inhabitants who were at church or Sunday school on that particular day. Above all, perhaps, she viewed everything from the perspective of a woman in love, determined to make her husband's life's work her own. But when all the qualifications are made, the success of the schools seems beyond doubt. Cheddar had new pews, and the school now had two rooms, as a barn had been added to the original schoolroom that had been rented so recklessly nearly eight years earlier. In July 500 women attended the benefit club feasts.[54] In spite of setbacks, Hannah More was able to report to Elizabeth Bouverie at the end of the year, 'everything flourishing and increasing'.[55] A year later, however, the picture would darken.

The publication of Wilberforce's *Practical View* in April 1797 turned out to be one of the most significant events in the history of the Clapham sect, and the book was soon established as the classic text of Evangelical Anglican theology. More might also have influenced the subject matter. Writing in the early spring of 1797, when it must have been going to the press, she urged him 'to insert a short tolerating clause in a small degree to lower its unmitigated *High Church-ness* as I know many good Dissenters will read it, and I trust, profit by it'.[56] When it finally came out, it was praised by John Moore, archbishop of Canterbury, as well as by the usual episcopal suspects (Porteus and Barrington), and it was said to have comforted Burke in the last weeks of his life.

Though, according to the duchess of Gloucester, More was in raptures over the finished product,[57] not everyone shared her enthusiasm. On the book's publication Wilberforce received a letter from Charles Daubeny, then vicar of North Bradley in Wiltshire and prebendary of Salisbury, a High Churchman, who was about to open a free church in Bath in order to counteract the schismatical tendencies he saw in that town of pick and mix religion. A forceful, zealous, and combative man, Daubeny was ready to go into battle on behalf of 'the friends of the Church' against the 'false friends', among whom he was inclined to number Wilberforce and other Evangelicals. Though courteously, even emolliently, worded, the letter was highly critical of Wilberforce's interpretation of the Evangelical doctrine of justification by faith, arguing that he had implied (unwittingly) that Christians were released

[53] *MA* 197.   [54] *Gambier*, i. 326, More to Sir Charles Middleton, 28 July 1797.
[55] Ibid. 333.   [56] Duke, More to Wilberforce 'Teston, Saturday' [1797] [catalogued 1798?].
[57] Bodleian, MS c. 3, fo. 20, duchess of Gloucester to Wilberforce, 14 Apr. 1797.

from the obligation to perform good works.[58] Wilberforce filed the letter, but does not seem to have replied. Early in the following year Daubeny published his influential *Guide to the Church*, the manifesto of pre-Tractarian High-Churchmanship before the High Church existed as a recognizable party.[59] The book asserted the apostolic succession and the necessity for episcopal ordination, attacked Dissenters and Calvinists, and, again, criticized Wilberforce for his alleged theological error. This drew the Evangelical baronet and member of Parliament Sir Richard Hill into the controversy, and a pamphlet war between him and Daubeny rumbled on for several years, conducted with the type of acrimony once common among religious people.[60] All this was to impact on More's life.

By the time of the Wilberforces' visit to the Mendip schools, the Cheap Repository project was winding down. It was too much work for one woman, and was fast destroying Hannah More's fragile health. After the first rush of enthusiastic volunteers the authors dropped off one by one, so that, as she told Zachary Macaulay, she had 'often been driven to the necessity of furnishing three monthly pieces myself'.[61] In August 1797 the previously reliable Henry Thornton wrote sheepishly, 'I am grieved to tell you that I have been guilty of neglecting to send to Marshall the ballad for the next month's Repository.'[62] The September list, therefore, had two titles only, a Sunday reading, *The Pilgrims*, by Hannah More, and Sally's *History of Diligent Dick*. Worn out by the effort, she wrote her last tract in November. One hundred and fourteen had been printed, of which she wrote (or contributed to) nearly 50 per cent. Having done all that was humanly possible, she ended the project without regrets. A year later it was formally wound up. In her diary for 22 September 1798 she wrote, 'Cheap Repository is closed.—"Bless the Lord, O my soul!" that I have been spared to accomplish that work.'[63]

However, the closure was not the smooth operation she would have wished. After the initial problems the Cheap Repository had turned into a profitable concern, with the hardback editions selling well among the middle classes. What had begun as a charitable venture was now vulnerable to the vagaries of the market and the whims of the publisher. The choice of Marshall had been Henry Thornton's, and More had deferred to him as a friend, a man, and a banker. But in January 1797 she complained of his 'neglect and other faults'.[64] Tough talking did little to improve the situation, and later in

[58] Bodleian, MS d. 13, fo. 112, Daubeny to Wilberforce, 22 Apr. 1797.
[59] C. Daubeny, *A Guide to the Church in Several Discourses...Addressed to William Wilberforce, Esq., MP* (London, 1798).
[60] Brown, *Fathers of the Victorians*, 172–9.
[61] Clark, More to Zachary Macaulay, 8 Sept. 1797.
[62] Thornton, Add. MS 7674/1/L1, fos. 124, 125a, Thornton to More, 28 Aug. 1797.
[63] Roberts, iii. 61.   [64] Clark, More to Zachary Macaulay, 30 Jan. [1797].

the year she was describing Marshall as 'selfish, tricking, and disobliging from first to last'.[65] In November 1797, with the writing of her last tract, she severed her connections with him, and appointed Evans and Hatchard as the new publishers to the Cheap Repository. They concentrated mainly on reprints. A three-volume, hard cover, uniform edition of the tracts was published by the SPCK publisher Rivington, in partnership with Evans, Hatchard, and Hazard, in May 1798, designed for a middle- and upper-class market.[66] The contract, negotiated by Thornton, generously gave Rivington the ownership of the copyright, and also the right to half the profits.[67]

Meanwhile, her difficulties with Marshall continued. Angered at the severance of the contract, he thought of prosecuting her on the grounds that he had not been given copyright.[68] In December 1797 he began to bring out his own tracts under the imprint of the Cheap Repository, and because these looked exactly like the genuine tracts, with similar titles and with wood engravings by Lee, there was much confusion among prospective purchasers. More was still partially dependent on Marshall's reprints simply because they were in his possession. He retained as well most of the original woodblocks, and thus continued to exercise some control over the Cheap Repository even when the connection was officially broken.

The spurious tracts were causing great confusion, and More had to warn prospective purchasers against them. She told one correspondent,

I have enclosed some papers containing the list of all *my* Tracts . . . These papers also announce a new and correct Edition of all the Tracts bound in three volumes and arranged in a regular manner, so that the Stories form a complete series . . . You must be careful to distinguish this by the name of *Rivington's* Uniform Edition of Cheap Repository Tracts.

But she also had to inform him that 'all that are already printed will continue to be sold as usual, and either Evans or Marshall will reprint such as are out of print and are most called for'.[69]

Another potential purchaser who had to be reassured and given correct information was William Cobbett; he later became a celebrated radical and critic of the Cheap Repository, but at this stage was a staunch supporter. In the summer of 1797, when in Philadelphia, he came across some of her tracts and wrote to More requesting her to send out a batch. As she told Macaulay,

[65] Ibid., 8 Sept. 1797.
[66] These were sold as *Cheap Repository Tracts, Entertaining, Moral and Religious; Cheap Repository Shorter Tracts; Cheap Repository Tracts for Sunday Reading*. All were published by Rivington in 1798. (BL catalogue 854.d. 22–4.)
[67] Huntington, MY 671, More to Zachary Macaulay, 23 Sept. 1815.
[68] Clark, More to Ann Kennicott, Bath, Christmas Day [1797]; Thornton, Add. MS 7674/1/L1, fo. 156, Thornton to Zachary Macaulay [1798].
[69] BL, Add. MS 42511, fo. 5, More to William Bankes, 20 Sept. [1798].

he 'says that, among all the clubs, societies, and institutions, which have abounded in America, not one has been attempted for the instruction of the common people. He is resolved to make this trial if he can get support.'[70] In June 1798 Mrs Thornton told More, 'I have written a note to Marshall indicating that Cobbett wished only for *your* Cheap Repository & that he had better send none of his own, lest they should be returned on their hands.'[71] A few months later Thornton bought the remaining tracts from Marshall at a cost of between £20 and £30 and the whole messy business was finally completed.[72]

With the Cheap Repository wound up, the Evangelicals were able to pronounce it a success. However, it was success of a specialized kind. Marshall's decision to issue his own imitations is a clear indication of its commercial importance, but this owed less to the general popularity of the 2 million tracts and ballads printed and distributed than to the enthusiasm of the subscribers. Once their money dried up, he ceased printing his spurious tracts. This inevitably raises the question of how far the poor themselves were prepared to buy and read More's popular literature. Even to pose the question presents difficulties. Which poor? Were the putative readers mainly men or women, skilled or unskilled, young or old? What about possible regional variations? Did the illustrations make a greater impression than the words? Finally—to use a useful concept familiar to historians of culture—did they 'appropriate' the tracts by internalizing them and reinterpreting their meaning.[73]

There are only a few indications of their response. In 1796 Selina Mills and her sister Mary Thatcher sallied forth to Pills, a disreputable area that was part of the port of Bristol. They found that the prostitutes and sailors' wives wanted sailors' songs and tragedies, which they were unable to supply; for want of anything better, they gave them 'The History of the Plague in London'.[74] In 1835 Francis Place was asked by the House of Commons Select Committee on Education if he thought the Cheap Repository had been useful. While expressing general approval, he replied that the tracts circulated mainly in rural areas; he does not seem to have come across any in London, and overall he was inclined to discount their influence.[75] A Baptist labourer and former militiaman found the Cheap Repository and

---

[70] Clark, More to Zachary Macaulay, 8 Sept. 1797.
[71] Thornton, Add. MS 7674/1/L1, fos. 133–4, Mrs H. Thornton to More [16 June] 1798.
[72] Ibid., fo. 159, Thornton to More, 20 Sept. 1798.
[73] R. Chartier, 'Culture as Appropriation: Popular Cultural Uses in Early Modern France', in Steven L. Kaplan (ed.), *Understanding Popular Culture: Europe from the Middle Ages to the Nineteenth Century* (Berlin, 1984) 229–53.
[74] Huntington, MY 383, Selina Mills to Zachary Macaulay, 2 May 1796.
[75] *House of Commons Sessional Papers: Select Committee on Education, 1835*, vol. 7, p. 85.

other tracts circulating among the Dissenting communities in the south of England in the difficult post-war period. He was not a receptive reader, seeing *The Shepherd of Salisbury Plain* and other similar stories as designed 'to perswade [*sic*] poor people to be satisfied in their situation and not to murmur at the dispensations of providence'. The tracts 'drove me almost to despair for I could see their design'.[76]

There was no such hostility in the responses of middle-class Evangelicals. In 1815, following the death of Henry Thornton, More learned from Macaulay, who had taken over dealings with Rivington, how profitable the hardcover editions had been for the publisher. Looking back on the whole transaction, she concluded ruefully that 'our dear friend Henry was not a good hand at a bargain'. Rivington's monopoly had 'obliged me to refuse permission to various printers in the North, who formally applied to me for that purpose'.[77] In the six- or seven-year period after the crisis years of 1816 and 1817 Rivington sold a further 7,100 bound volumes, which 'would have been a little fortune', More told Macaulay later, 'if I had not given half the profits to him'.[78]

The middle-class market was a profitable by-product. The experience of the Cheap Repository encouraged many earnest moralists to believe that they had found the correct formula for reaching the labouring classes. The dissemination of the tracts was not confined to Britain; some were translated into Italian and circulated in Rome and Bologna.[79] Porteus sent shiploads to the West Indies.[80] William Pitt heard with satisfaction that 40,000 tracts had been sent to America, where More's earlier works were already in circulation.[81] Some of these found their way to Philadelphia, where, as has been seen, they were read and admired by William Cobbett. In 1800 they were printed more systematically and sold weekly by B. & J. Johnson of Philadelphia. With the official ending of the Cheap Repository, expanded tracts of thirty-six pages generally comprising a story, a ballad, a hymn, and a prayer were sold for 4 cents. Individual tracts continued to be sold in the United States. In 1826 the American Sunday School Union published a revised addition of *The Shepherd of Salisbury Plain*. As late as 1851 the American Tract Society published eight volumes of Cheap Repository Tracts with fifty-two illustrations.[82] The rural England of Black Giles, Taw-

---

[76] *The Autobiography of Joseph Mayett of Quainton (1753–1839)*, ed. A. Kussmaul, Buckinghamshire Record Office, no. 23 (1986), 70.

[77] Huntington, MY 671, More to Zachary Macaulay, 23 Sept. 1815.

[78] Huntington, MY 680, More to Zachary Macaulay, 12 Nov. 1822.

[79] Clark, More to Ann Kennicott, Bath, Christmas Day [1797].

[80] Roberts, iii. 5.

[81] Roberts, ii. 470. For the publishing history of Hannah More's earlier works in the United States, see H. B. Weiss, *Hannah More's Cheap Repository Tracts in America* (New York, 1946), 5.

[82] Weiss, *Cheap Repository Tracts*, 5–6, 10, 21.

ney Rachel, and Hester Wilmot, and the slums of Betty Brown's St Giles's, had successfully crossed the Atlantic.

In Britain it was quickly recognized that the winding up of the Cheap Repository had left a gap in the market, and in 1799 the Religious Tract Society, an Evangelical movement encompassing most Protestant denominations, was set up. Its founders believed that Hannah More had sugared her pill too thoroughly, and though they published *The Shepherd of Salisbury Plain* until as late as 1884, they made sure that their own stories were 'of a more decidedly religious character than hers'.[83] Legh Richmond's *The Dairyman's Daughter* was the most celebrated of the new range of tracts, though it is difficult to imagine barely literate readers struggling through the elaborate descriptions of scenery and the long religious effusions. But whatever the limitations of this type of literature, the mass distribution of reading matter and the formation of auxiliaries paralleled the work of the missionary societies, the Bible Society, and the SPCK, and played a part in creating the Victorian Evangelical culture. This was part of an even more important change; the upper levels of the working classes were becoming better informed. Zachary Macaulay, one of the earliest supporters of the Cheap Repository, also became a member of the Society for the Diffusion of Useful Knowledge, whose weekly *Penny Magazine*, with its woodcut illustrations, was their most popular publication. Political radicals, too, copied the tactics of the religious propagandists. In November 1816, in a back-handed compliment to his enemies, Cobbett reissued his *Political Register* as a broadsheet, and reduced the price to 2*d*. with discounts for bulk orders.[84] Hannah More's mission to spread improving literature among the poor was arguably more successful than she could have dreamed. But if readers chose to move on from her prayers, ballads, and stories to Cobbett's *Twopenny Trash* or William Hone's irreverent parody of the Creed and the catechism, that was something beyond control of the Evangelicals.

The Religious Tract Society was a movement encompassing all Evangelicals, Dissenters as well as Anglicans. But on 12 April 1799 a public meeting held under the aegis of the Claphamites agreed to establish the Society for Missions to Africa and the East, which, though equally Evangelical, would be firmly Anglican.[85] The Church Missionary Society, as it was known from

---

[83] W. Jones, *The Jubilee Memorial of the Religious Tract Society* (1850), 12. For the long publishing history of *The Shepherd of Salisbury Plain*, see E. Green, *Bibliotheca Somersetensis* (Taunton, 1902), iii. 84–5.

[84] G. Spater, *William Cobbett: The Poor Man's Friend* (Cambridge, 1982), ii. 347–8.

[85] E. Stock, *The History of the Church Missionary Society* (London, 1899), i. 60–72 and *passim*; E. Elbourne, 'The Foundation of the Church Missionary Society: The Anglican Missionary Impulse', in J. Walsh, C. Haydon, and S. Taylor, *The Church of England, c.1689–c.1833: From Toleration to Tractarianism*, (Cambridge, 1993) 247–64.

1812, was a new type of creature, marking the decisive arrival of the Evangelical Anglicans—the Clapham sect and beyond—on the religious scene. John Moore, archbishop of Canterbury, was equivocal. Fearing the setting up of a church within a church, he informed a delegation comprising Wilberforce, Grant, and Venn that 'he could not with propriety express his full concurrence and approbation'.[86] Something new was happening in the Church of England and old-fashioned High Churchmen were getting worried. Over the next few years their anxieties were to intensify.

[86] Stock, *Church Missionary Society*, i. 72.

Chapter 10

Praise and Opposition
1798–1799

IN retrospect, the Wilberforces' honeymoon visit can be seen as the high-water mark of the Mendip schools. In the following year the clouds gathered, and Hannah More found herself headed for choppy waters. June 1798 found her in her usual state of exhaustion. The heat and fatigue of the Shipham Club feast, which was attended by about 400 people (the women, their families, and the usual interested observers), 'knocked me *up* or rather *down*, for I cou'd not get out of bed yesterday'. In fact, the energetic Patty had been far more active. 'To her great dismay' she had been obliged to deliver the club Charge before an audience, which included about a dozen clergy. She was not exactly preaching, but her action was a potentially indecorous intrusion into male territory. Of course, as More assured Sarah (Wilberforce) Clarke, 'we don't much like it, but we are brought to consider that duty is paramount to mere delicacy'.[1] (But one feels that the sisters might have rather enjoyed breaking gender conventions in a good cause. Two years previously More had reported gleefully to Mrs Thornton that one Sunday in May 'we visited about 500 of our poor children, and at night in one of our usual disorderly inversions Patty *preached* and had two parsons among her *Auditory*'.[2]) The sermon proper was delivered by Thomas Fry, an Axbridge inhabitant, 23 years old, who had been ordained for only a year, and who, in in spite of his youth, 'preached with the boldness of an old Confessor'.[3] A couple of weeks later the Cheddar Club feast was held and the preacher

---

[1] Duke, More to Sarah Wilberforce Clarke, 30 June 1798.
[2] Clark, More to Mrs H. Thornton, 'Tuesday morning' [May 1796].
[3] Duke, More to Sarah Wilberforce Clarke, 30 June 1798.

was another young Oxford graduate, James Vaughan, who 'preached most evangelically to a grand audience'.[4]

Perhaps most women in their fifties would have felt they had achieved enough. At Cheddar and Shipham the schools and clubs were well established. The devoted work of the Nailsea colliers was paying dividends in their tough area. Blagdon was now an orderly village. In deeply unpromising territory, neglected for many years, the More sisters had built up what Wilberforce called a 'little Christian communion of saints'.[5] Yet the successes had been bought at a heavy price of time, money, and sheer exhaustion, and the arguments for slowing down might have seemed overwhelming. It says much for Hannah More's intensely driven nature that she refused to ease up. In part she was energized by Fry and Vaughan, whose youthful optimism was a welcome tonic when she was tempted to flag. With her consent Fry set out on a voyage of discovery and found a new harvest field in the large village of Wedmore, fifteen miles from Wrington, which made it their most ambitious project to date.

Flesh says 'spare thyself', for alas! *there and back* will be about four and thirty miles... and to sleep out will break in much on our time, besides the expence of two days' chaises: Add to this, if we do it at all, we purpose to do it on a large scale like Cheddar and Blagdon, so that it will be a very expensive establishment.[6]

In their enthusiasm Fry and Vaughan volunteered to contribute, and the impecunious curates Boak and Drewitt each offered £5 out of their £100 a year salaries. More brushed these offers aside and instead asked Wilberforce to talk over the finances with Henry Thornton. It was clear that she had already made her decision.

Shortly after this the sisters visited Wedmore and were surprised at its size; with a scattered population of 2,000 recorded in the 1801 census it was almost twice as big as Cheddar. As before, they 'canvassed' the farmers and were dismayed to unearth some alarmingly unreconstructed attitudes. John Barrow, churchwarden and wealthy farmer, declared that 'we should not come there to make his ploughmen wiser than himself; he did not want saints but workmen'. His wife believed that the lower classes were destined to be poor and ignorant; the sisters wrote her off as a fatalist.[7] But the mass of the village seemed enthusiastic about the school, and the sisters arranged a meeting in the church the following Sunday.

This meeting went reasonably well, helped by a sermon from John Boak, now curate of the neighbouring parish of Brockley. The opposition was momentarily silenced, and the sisters began thinking about finding a schoolhouse. In early August, however, a tense scene took place in Wedmore

---

[4] Duke, More to Wilberforce, 14 July 1798. [5] *Life of Wilberforce*, ii. 299.
[6] Duke, More to Wilberforce, 14 July 1798. [7] *MA* 210.

church, which More described in a vivid letter to Wilberforce. At the end of the service, which was conducted by her friend Thomas Drewitt, the Cheddar curate, the clerk gave notice, on behalf of John Barrow the hostile farmer and churchwarden, that the parish were to meet on the following Friday 'to consult on the best means for opposing the Ladies who are coming to set up a School'. Drewitt promptly responded by announcing from the pulpit, 'And on Sunday next the Parish are desired to meet the Ladies who intend opening the School at nine o clock.' The congregation must have been on the edge of their seats. 'It will be a hard contest', More commented wryly, 'whether John Barrow or Hannah More will be the successful Candidate.'[8] In spite of this hostility, which was reinforced by an ominous lack of support from both vicar and curate, the plans for Wedmore went ahead and More found a 'damp, half finish'd house' which would serve at a pinch for a schoolroom. But the following days saw her crippled with an excruciating nervous headache. At the height of her distress she fell over in a faint, cut her face, and lay unconscious on the floor until her sisters found her. For a while she thought she was dying, and she lay in bed tormenting herself with her recurrent guilt that she had 'not done enough for God, and what wou'd poor Patty do by herself?'[9] By September, though, she had forced herself back into harness, ready once more to do battle for her new school.

Her presence was certainly needed. On the Sunday of her return, a day of continuous rain, she found the children shivering in a room without a floor, a door, or a window, and with none of the farmers offering them more suitable accommodation. The reason soon emerged. The children had been learning one of Isaac Watts's hymns, and this convinced a farmer that the sisters were '*Methodys*'. He told them that his hostility to the Methodists dated from the time when an itinerant Methodist had preached in his orchard under his mother's best apple tree. Immediately after, the leaves had withered and the tree died, after which the farmers had beaten all the Methodists out of the parish. 'This is the enlightened nineteenth century!' More exclaimed, somewhat prematurely, to Henry Thornton.[10]

At the same time the Wedmore schoolmaster was posing problems and was to create more before he was eventually dismissed. He was John Harvard, a failed trader, and nephew of Hazard, the Bath printer of the Cheap Repository, and, in order to hire him, More was forced to pay £25 to cover his debts. She believed the money, together with his £35 a year salary and a decent house, was well spent as he and his wife were able and zealous teachers, but it had left her with debts of her own, which had led to her refusing medical assistance after her accident.[11] But money was not her main

[8] Duke, More to Wilberforce, 15 Aug. [1798] [catalogued *c*.1799].   [9] Ibid.
[10] Thornton, Add. MS7674/1/E/1, More to Thornton, 12 Sept. [1798].   [11] Ibid.

worry. A year later she admitted to Sir Charles Middleton that Harvard had been 'a preacher in Mr Wesley's connexion', a damning fact in a parish 'where they would prefer a Mahometan to a Methodist'.[12] But she had known about the attitudes of the parish when she had appointed him, and a little foresight would have spared her much future embarrassment.

Problems were piling up. In September 1798 Elizabeth Bouverie, the patron of the schools, and a friend of twenty-six years' standing, died. She left More a legacy of £300 and an annuity of £100 per annum, but, generous though it was, this could not compensate for the loss of a previously assured income of £300 per annum for the schools.[13] By the end of the year Wilberforce and Thornton had agreed to make good the shortfall and to supply the sisters with a much-needed post-chaise.[14] The money came as a relief to More, who knew that she would feel the pinch when Pitt's novel income tax came into being. It was all very well for her sisters, she told Wilberforce crossly, for once not at all pleased with her idol. Because their Bath house was already highly rated by the assessed (property) taxes, they would not notice the change, 'but to me whose Little Cowslip, was so little taxed, it will make the difference from about £5 a year to nearly 50'.[15]

For all her complaining, in the following summer she was able to afford a holiday at the elegant seaside resort of Christchurch, staying with the Thorntons at the Priory. It was a large house, she told Mrs Garrick, with two conservatories and grape houses, though it had the disadvantage of being two miles from the sea. She thought of bathing, but was deterred by a bowel complaint.[16] The illness rapidly became more serious. She was soon in agony, and for a while the Thorntons believed she was dying. But she recovered enough to enjoy the company of little Marianne, now a lively 2-year-old.[17] However, in spite of walks by the seaside and in shrubberies and visits to the bishop of Lincoln and his wife, who were staying nearby, Wedmore was never far from her thoughts. In her absence a vestry meeting was called to consider the future of the school.[18] At about the same time the farmers presented her at the archdeacon's visitation for teaching the poor without a licence. She told Wilberforce that they had employed 'a pettifogging Attorney of bad character' to prosecute her, not under the Conventicle Act, but 'on some old, and I believe obsolete Statute, which requires every *School Master* to take out a licence'.[19] Her troubles were exacerbated by the

---

[12] *Gambier*, i. 370–1.   [13] Duke, More to Wilberforce, 'Saturday night' [c.29 Sept. 1798].
[14] *Life of Wilberforce*, ii. 301–2.
[15] Bodleian, MS c. 3, fo. 45. More to Wilberforce, 18 Dec. [1798].
[16] Folger, W.b. 488, fos. 13–14, More to Eva Garrick, 11 July [1799], 31 Aug. 1799.
[17] Thornton, Add. MS7674/1/L2, fos. 34–5, Mrs H. Thornton to Mrs R. Thornton, 17 Aug. 1799.
[18] E. Spencer, *Truths respecting Mrs. Hannah More's Meeting Houses and the Conduct of her Followers* (Bath, 1802), 21.
[19] Duke, More to Wilberforce [Aug. 1799?].

fact that Wedmore was a peculiar under the authority of the dean of Wells, and out of the control of the diocesan bishop. In another parish, meanwhile, the farmers went to a fortune-teller to learn if the schools were Methodist, but following classical precedent 'the Oracle returned an ambiguous answer'.[20]

To cap it all, she had to cope with severe personal problems. Two of her sisters (presumably Mary and Betty) were very ill, and one of them had 'a kind of paralytic attack with a grievous dejection'. It is sad to think of their hard-won retirement being ruined by depression. The presence of a nurse and physician made Cowslip Green overcrowded and dismal. More had to delay her return, and when she did get back, a whole set of engagements, including a visit from Lady Waldegrave and her daughter, had to be put off.[21] With troubles piling up for her schools, it was the worst possible time to be experiencing severe social isolation, and, under this trying combination of circumstances, Hannah and Patty decided on a tactical retreat. Towards the end of the year they dismissed Harvard as soon as his wife had recovered from childbirth, and transferred Mrs Carroll, their reliable Axbridge teacher, to Wedmore, though this meant that the embattled Axbridge school had to close.[22] They had secured a breathing space, no more.

By this time, for all the mounting troubles at Wedmore, More was enjoying a renewal of celebrity following the publication early in 1799 of her most important conduct book, *Strictures on the Modern System of Female Education*. The book was an instant talking point, both for its comparatively ambitious agenda for women's education and also because it contained the most explicit avowal to date of her Evangelical theology. It was addressed to women in fashionable society, 'the ladies of *ton*',[23] though its sales and popularity show that its readership extended well into the middle classes. Writing at the end of a decade in which women had entered public life, writing or disseminating political literature, collecting subscriptions, presenting colours to regiments, More had no doubts about the potential political importance of genteel women. At a time of 'the most tremendous confederacies against religion, and order, and governments which the world ever saw; what an accession would it bring to the public strength could we prevail on beauty, and rank, and talents, and virtue . . . to come forward with a patriotism at once firm and feminine for the general good!'[24] In *Village Politics* she

---

[20] Duke, More to Wilberforce, 11 Sept. 1799. This incident inspired Charlotte M. Yonge to write a charming story, *The Cunning Woman's Grandson: A Tale of Cheddar a Hundred Years Ago*, for the National Society.

[21] *Gambier*, i. 369–70; Folger, W.b. 488, fo. 13, More to Eva Garrick, 11 July [1799].

[22] *MA* 226.

[23] *Strictures on the Modern System of Female Education* (5th edn. London, 1799), i. 15.

[24] Ibid. 5–6.

had sought to reclaim the language of patriotism from the radicals. Now she was appropriating it for upper-class women, a group which included both titled aristocrats and the wealthy genteel: in other words, her 'Greeks'.

She had begun the book on her visit to London in the spring of 1798, and among the friends she sounded out was Sir William Weller Pepys. On 25 May he sent her a letter urging her to 'impress upon the Minds of our Fair Countrywomen, that their Sphere of doing good is far more extensive than they imagine'. For example, no man would fight a duel if he knew that women would afterwards treat him with contempt.[25] The letter could not have been more topical. On the day it was written a ferocious Commons clash occurred between the prime minister, Pitt, and the radical MP George Tierney, after which Pitt challenged Tierney to a duel: this at a time when Britain was at war, Ireland was about to erupt, and invasion was threatened. The two men met on Putney Heath, both fired into the air and honour was satisfied. Three days later Wilberforce strained his friendship with Pitt to the limits by giving notice of a censure motion against the practice of duelling, though he abandoned it a week later. More was driven to distraction by the duel. 'What a dreadful thing, that a life of such importance should be risked (or indeed any life at all) on the miserable notion of false honour! To complete the horror, too, they chose a Sunday!'[26] Though it is easy to mock the apparent bathos of the last sentence, her position had an inner consistency. The aristocratic practice of duelling was part of a code that valued personal honour above the Christian imperatives of meekness and forgiveness; to fight on a Sunday was a further demonstration that the reputation of an individual was of more importance than the honour of God.[27]

Pepys's remarks about the importance of women were well taken, but More believed that they could only influence the conduct of men if their own behaviour was reformed and they turned away from the obsessive pursuit of 'accomplishments'. On her return to Cowslip Green, she wrote to Elizabeth Bouverie, who did not live to see the completion of *Strictures,*

I saw so much of the shocking way of going on in the short time I was in town, that I *must* acquit myself to my conscience on this momentous subject before I die, if it please God. Dancing and music fill up the whole of life, and every *Miss* of fashion has *three* dancing, and a still greater number of music masters.[28]

With her usual lack of confidence she sent copies of her manuscript while it was in progress to Wilberforce and the Thorntons. It was as well she did, as

[25] *A Later Pepys: The Correspondence of Sir William Weller Pepys, Bart.*, ed. A. C. C. Gaussen, 2 vols. (London, 1904), ii. 285–7.

[26] Roberts, iii. 31.

[27] See D. Andrew, 'The Code of Honour and its Critics: The Opposition to Duelling in England, 1780–1850', *Social History*, 5 (1980), 426–74.

[28] *Gambier*, i. 338–9.

they prevented her from dedicating the book to the princess of Wales, who at that time had unofficially separated from her husband. But for her friends' advice, her message could have been drowned in a tide of knowing ridicule.[29]

The *Strictures* was More's first two-volume work, a loose, baggy monster containing a range of seemingly contradictory statements that, pulled out of context, can be used to depict her as a protofeminist or an antifeminist. Inevitably it has to be judged alongside Mary Wollstonecraft's *Vindication of the Rights of Woman*, which had been published early in 1792 at the height of the Burke–Paine controversy. From the start More had been extremely hostile to Wollstonecraft's book, and had refused on principle to read it. A political conservative, deeply hostile to what she saw as the speculative philosophy of the French Revolution, she went out of her way to distance herself from the whole language of women's rights. In *Strictures* she correctly noted that human rights are indivisible, but she used this insight to condemn the whole doctrine.

The *rights of man* have been discussed till we are somewhat wearied with the discussion. To these have been opposed with more presumption than prudence *the rights of woman*. It follows . . . that the next stage of that irradiation which our enlighteners are pouring in upon us will produce grave descants on the *rights of children*.[30]

Earlier, writing to Horace Walpole in the summer of 1793, she had railed against the language of rights as 'metaphysical jargon . . . fantastic and absurd'. In the same letter she added an intriguingly vague piece of autobiography in which she chose to ignore the very real disabilities of married women (as opposed to spinsters with an independent income like herself), and to make an implied criticism of her indulgent parents: 'I am sure I have as much liberty as I can make a good use of, now that I am an old maid, and when I was a young one, I had, I dare say, more than was good for me.' She went on to state that

so many women are fond of government, I suppose, because they are not fit for it. To be unstable and capricious, I really think, is but too characteristic of our sex; and there is perhaps no animal so much indebted to subordination for its good behaviour as woman. I have soberly and uniformly maintained this doctrine, ever since I have been capable of observation, and I used horribly to provoke some of my female friends, *maîtresses femmes*, by it, especially such heroic spirits as poor Mrs Walsingham. I believe they used to suspect me of art in it, as if I wanted to court the approbation of the other sex, who, it must be confessed, politically encourage this submissive temper in us.[31]

[29] Thornton, Add. MS7674/1/L2, fo. 24, Mrs H. Thornton to More, 2 Feb. 1799.
[30] *Strictures*, i. 147.   [31] *Walpole*, 370.

It suited More to allow herself to be seen as the polar opposite of Mary Wollstonecraft, the woman Walpole insisted on abusing as a 'hyena in petticoats'. The dichotomy, so flattering to her image among conservatives, was taken up in Richard Polwhele's poem of 1798 *The Unsex'd Females.* The poem condemned Wollstonecraft, 'the intrepid champion of her sex', as well as More's old pupil 'Perdita' Robinson, her aggrieved enemy Ann Yearsley, and her friend Anna Barbauld. In a footnote he described Hannah More as 'diametrically opposite to Miss Wollstonecraft; excepting indeed her genius and her literary attainments'. The conclusion of the poem praised the blue-stockings for their mildness, and at the end invoked More.

> She ceas'd; and round their MORE the sisters sigh'd!
> Soft on each tongue repentant murmurs died;
> And sweetly scatter'd (as they glanced away)
> Their conscious blushes spoke a brighter day.[32]

So much for the texts. In reality the sighs and blushes were a male fantasy and neither More nor her bluestocking friends were much given to them. Neither did her life and experience fit the *la donna è mobile* trope that she had so gratuitously invoked in her letter to Walpole. At the time of this letter she was busily expanding her Sunday schools and using as her indispensable helpers two tough, dogged, determined women, Patty More and Sarah Baber. 'I prefer Women,' she was to tell Richard Beadon (who became her diocesan bishop in 1802), 'and find it does better.'[33] The sentiments in the letter to Walpole were not echoed in her other letters, and they reveal more about her ambivalent relationship with the most worldly and sceptical of her friends than her true view of woman's nature and capabilities. For reasons of her own, she chose to set herself up as an antifeminist in opposition not merely to Mary Wollstonecraft, which was understandable, but to the much milder feminisms of bluestocking friends such as Frances Boscawen and Charlotte Walsingham. As a result she was praised by the antifeminists of her day and has been denounced ever since.

Yet for all her apparent denigration of her own sex, several contemporary women saw her as a role model. One of these was the duchess of Gloucester. In 1802 Ann Kennicott told More that, when Lord Harcourt had ventured some mild criticisms of her, the duchess 'flew into one of her passions, & said it was the pride of Man who never could hear the superiority of woman, and when they could not deny them parts, denied them judgment'.[34] In July 1798 a new journal, the *Ladies' Monthly Museum*, began publication. Its

---

[32] Quoted in V. Jones (ed.), *Women in the Eighteenth Century: Constructions of Femininity* (London, 1990), 188–9.

[33] Cambridge University, St John's College Library, MS k. 34, fo. 21.

[34] Clark, Ann Kennicott to More, 15 July [1802].

frontispiece contained an engraving of More (the glamorous dark-haired, turbaned figure bears no resemblance to any of her portraits) and its first article was given over to an account of her life. The following editions celebrated other literary women, such as Anna Barbauld, Sarah Trimmer, and Anna Seward. Though the type of feminism these women represented was ambiguous at best, their lives and writings did much to bolster women's self-esteem. Compared with the radical feminists, they were safe and respectable, and could be held up as exemplars of what women could achieve rather than awful warnings of the fate of those who stepped outside their allotted sphere. For all their caution, perhaps because of it, they did much to advance the cause of women.

Strictures has to be set in the context of a debate about women's education, which rumbled through much of the eighteenth century and exploded in the revolutionary 1790s, when a surprising consensus emerged among otherwise divergent women. Mary Wollstonecraft was the most notable participant, but she was joined by 'Perdita' Robinson and the historian Catharine Macaulay in a condemnation of 'the absurd notion that the education of females should be of an opposite kind to that of males'.[35] Though conservatives like More were more circumspect in their language, their analysis of the problem was similar: women were being fobbed off with a trivial and superficial education that left them intellectually crippled, morally defective, and ill equipped to be companionable wives or effective mothers. It was a compelling critique, the result of a set of material, intellectual, and political factors that came together at the end of the eighteenth century. These included the growth of a middle-class reading public, the influence of Enlightenment thought, and the moral crisis that arose in the wake of the French Revolution.

Literary women such as Hannah More were beneficiaries of a rise in the numbers of the middle classes, improvements in education and the expansion of girls' schooling, the growth of printed literature, and a whole culture of polite learning which provided a public for an aspiring author.[36] Women were going into print as never before, and for every writer there had to be many hundreds of readers. The female reading public extended far beyond the intellectuals of the bluestocking circle to include many other women,

---

[35] C. Macaulay [Graham], *Letters on Education with Observations on Religious and Metaphysical Subjects* (London, 1790), 471; [M. Robinson] *A Letter to the Women of England on the Injustice of Mental Subordination* (London, 1799).

[36] See O. Hufton, *The Prospect before Her: A History of Women in Western Europe*, i: *1500–1800* (London, 1997), 419–57; A. Vickery, *The Gentleman's Daughter: Women's Lives in Georgian England* (New Haven, 1998), 258–9 and *passim*; John Brewer, *The Pleasures of the Imagination: English Culture in the Eighteenth Century* (London, 1997), 56–9, 79, 84, 120, 194–7; S. Skedd, 'Women Teachers and the Expansion of Girls' Schooling in England, *c.*1760–1820', in H. Barker and E. Chalus (eds.), *Gender in Eighteenth-Century England* (London, 1997) 101–25.

whose names will never be known. Though they remained disadvantaged compared with men, they gained status and mental stimulation from the expansion of the print culture.

Other developments of the period, however, were more problematic; in particular the cult of sensibility risked setting up women as lesser beings. In her poem to Frances Boscawen, More had praised sensibility, at the same time as warning of its downside. But by the 1790s the moral climate had changed, and sensibility was now seen as full of dangers—especially for women.[37]

Though sensibility had existed since Chaucer's prioress wept at the sight of a mouse caught in a trap, it was not until the eighteenth century that science and psychology could provide intellectual reinforcement for earlier stereotypes. Women were now constructed as possessing delicate nerves, faculties that were imaginative rather than analytical, and reasoning that was lively rather than solid, making them creatures of feeling rather than thought. Sensibility was represented in its most powerful form in Jean-Jacques Rousseau's sensationally popular novel *La Nouvelle Héloïse* (1761), where the heroine's conflict between her violent love for her former tutor and her duty to her family leads to her inevitable death. The book met with an extraordinary reaction, shattering the emotions of normally sober readers, transporting them out of their prosaic lives into orgasmic sensations of pain and pleasure, passion and tears.[38] However, with the great shift of cultural attitudes that came with the French Revolution, the book was re-evaluated and condemned as part of an insidious 'new morality' bent on undermining the ethical foundations of society; and, just as women readers had been particularly stirred by Rousseau's novels, so in the conservative counter-attack it was they who were perceived to be most at risk from the perversions of 'Jacobinism', a shorthand for the whole ideology of the French Revolution.

The polarity of thinking man and feeling woman was thus part of the Enlightenment's ambiguous legacy to gender politics. But other tributaries which fed into that broad river allowed for a more positive view of women's intellectual potential.[39] Followers of Descartes—both French and English—argued that women, possessing minds and souls like men, should be taken seriously as rational and spiritual beings. The pioneer sociologists of the

[37] C. Jones, *Radical Sensibility: Literature and Ideas in the 1790s* (London, 1993).

[38] R. Darnton, 'Readers Respond to Rousseau: The Fabrication of Romantic Sensibility', in id., *The Great Cat Massacre and Other Episodes in French Cultural History* (New York, 1984), 215–56; R. Wittmann, 'Was there a Reading Revolution at the End of the Eighteenth Century?', in G. Cavallo and R. Chartier (eds.), *A History of Reading in the West*, trans. L. G. Cochrane (Cambridge, 1999), 284–312.

[39] The following discussion is based on R. Perry, *The Celebrated Mary Astell: An Early English Feminist* (Chicago, 1986), 70, 171–3, 332; J. Rendall, *The Origins of Modern Feminism: Women in Britain, France and the United States, 1780–1800* (Basingstoke, 1985), 7–32; S. Tomaselli, 'The Enlightenment Debate on Women', *History Workshop Journal*, 20 (1985), 101–24; S. O'Donnell,

Scottish Enlightenment showed that societies differed from each other and evolved over time; thus, far from being fixed by nature, the position of women was contingent upon social developments and therefore capable of improvement. Most famously, John Locke's theory of the *tabula rasa*, the belief that the mind of the newborn infant is like a blank tablet, ready for whatever impressions are made on it, inevitably highlighted the importance of women; everyone agreed that the child's first impressions were supplied by his mother or his nurse. This point was taken up by a man who was to become a close friend of Hannah More, the Evangelical clergyman Thomas Gisborne, who observed in a well-respected book that came out two years before *Strictures*, 'The mind is originally an unsown field, prepared for the reception of any crop; and if those to whom the culture of it belongs, neglect to fill it with good grain, it will speedily be covered with weeds.'[40] If this Lockean point was conceded, then the argument for giving women a sound education seemed irrefutable; both sexes would benefit.

More set out her stall in her opening sentence, one of the most feminist she ever wrote: 'It is a singular injustice which is often exercised towards women, first to give them a most defective Education, and then to expect from them the most undeviating purity of conduct.'[41] This was a faithful, though unwitting, echo of the complaints of Mary Astell, writing 100 years earlier,[42] and was a standard feminist trope throughout the eighteenth century. However, her message, as it developed, was mixed to say the least. A few hundred pages on she was making the usual separation between the female domestic and the male public sphere, and confining women to the domestic realm. 'A woman sees the world, as it were, from a little elevation in her own garden, whence she makes an exact survey of home scenes, but takes not in that wider range of distant projects which he who stands on a loftier eminence commands.'[43] Like previous conduct book writers, she recommended a modest and retiring manner as appropriate for this female private sphere. In language which would never have been used by Catharine Macaulay or Mary Wollstonecraft, she condemned 'the bold and independent beauty, the intrepid female, the hoyden, the huntress, and the archer; the swinging arms, the confident address'.[44] Such a woman lacked propriety;

'Mr Locke and the Ladies: The Indelible Words on the Tabula Rasa', *Studies in Eighteenth-Century Culture*, 8 (London, 1979), 151–64; T. Lovell, 'Subjective Powers? Consumption, the Reading Public and Domestic Woman in Early Eighteenth-Century England', in A. Bermingham and J. Brewer (eds.), *The Consumption of Culture, 1600–1800: Image, Object, Text* (London, 1995), 23–41; B. Caine, *English Feminism, 1780–1980* (Oxford, 1997), ch. 1.

[40] T. Gisborne, *An Enquiry into the Duties of the Female Sex* (London, 1797), 45.
[41] *Strictures*, vol. i, p. ix.
[42] M. Astell, *A Serious Proposal to the Ladies* (3rd edn. London, 1696).
[43] *Strictures*, ii. 27.   [44] Ibid. i. 75.

and to More, who is cited in the *Oxford English Dictionary* as one of the earliest users of the term, 'Propriety is to a woman what the great Roman critic says action is to an orator; it is the first, the second, the third requisite. A woman may be knowing, active, witty, and amusing; but without propriety she cannot be amiable.'[45]

With this in mind, she urged women not to become 'female warriors' or 'female politicians: I hardly know which of the two is the most disgusting or unnatural character'.[46] 'A female Polemic', she added, conveniently forgetting her own writings, 'wanders nearly as far from the limits prescribed to her sex, as a female Machiavel or warlike Thalestris.'[47] The intellectually ambitious woman too received a sharp, self-punishing slap on the wrist. 'Let her who is disposed to be elated with her literary acquisitions check her vanity by calling to mind the just remark of Swift "that after all her boasted acquirements, a woman will, generally speaking, be found to possess less of what is called learning than a common schoolboy".'[48] Some painful experiences lay behind much of her argument here.

There is one *human* consideration which would perhaps more effectually tend to damp in an aspiring woman the ardour of literary vanity...than any which she will derive from motives of humility or propriety or religion; which is that in the judgment passed on her performances, she will have to encounter the mortifying circumstance of having her sex always taken into account, and her highest exertions will probably be received with the qualified approbation, *that it is really extraordinary for a woman.* Men of learning...are apt to consider even the happier performances of the other sex as the spontaneous productions of a fruitful but shallow soil.[49]

With Elizabeth Carter and Elizabeth Montagu in mind, she was careful to make an exception for 'real genius'. It was a bitter little moral, nevertheless, as if she had now come to despise the once delicious flattery of Garrick, Johnson, and Horace Walpole.

But *Strictures* was a work of many moods, and for most of the book the tone was not resentful or pessimistic but bracing, as More continually urged women to improve their minds and to wean themselves from vanity in order to accomplish their true purpose. Bringing the full weight of Lockean psychology and Evangelical theology to bear, she declared education to be a school for life, and life a school for eternity.[50] This message was especially important for mothers, who, in the education of their children, exercised '*power*, a power wide in its extent, indefinite in its effects and inestimable in its importance'.[51] Yet instead of being educated for this supremely important role, girls were caught up in what she sardonically termed the 'phrenzy of

---

[45] Ibid. 6.   [46] Ibid.   [47] Ibid. 7.   [48] Ibid. 187–8.   [49] Ibid. ii. 13–14.
[50] Ibid. i. 63–4.   [51] Ibid. 59.

accomplishments', especially an overemphasis on music, which meant that 'a young lady now requires, not a master, but an orchestra'.[52] 'The wise mother', she asserted, 'knows that the superstructure of the accomplishments can be alone safely erected on the broad and solid basis of Christian humility.'[53]

Taking it for granted that mothers should supervise their daughters' reading, she mounted a ferocious, 'anti-Jacobin' attack on the literature of sensibility. By alluring the warm-hearted and impressionable and by giving vice 'so natural an air of virtue', Rousseau had constructed 'a net of... exquisite art and inextricable workmanship, spread to entangle innocence and ensnare experience'.[54] But in the Francophobe culture of the 1790s she saw Rousseau as less of a threat than 'the modern apostles of infidelity and immorality'[55] the German Romantics Goethe and Schiller, and the playwright Kotzebue, whose play *The Stranger* was in performance at Drury Lane at the time of her visit in the spring of 1798. Later in the year, while *Strictures* was being finalized and published, his *Das Kind der Liebe*, translated by Elizabeth Inchbald as *Lovers' Vows*, was performed at Covent Garden. Such was the play's subsequent scandalous reputation that Jane Austen could assume that the readers of *Mansfield Park* were thoroughly familiar with its values and plot and could appreciate the wonderfully ironical layering as the amateur actors in her novel are subsumed into their roles.[56] The notoriety of the German drama of sensibility gave More an opportunity for a dig at Mary Wollstonecraft, 'the Female Werter [sic]' whose unfinished feminist novel *Maria; or, The Wrongs of Woman* seemed to condone adultery provided the participants were in love.[57]

The new German literature coincided with another of More's pet hates, the proliferation of romantic novels supplied by John Lane's Minerva Press, which multiplied 'with unparalleled fecundity... overstocking the world with their quick-succeeding progeny... till every fresh production, like the progeny of Banquo is followed by "Another, and another, and another!"'[58] To More, both plays and novels elevated a flabby sentimentality devoid of moral principles, which flourished in shallow soils, nurtured on 'the streams of *Abridgements, Beauties*, and *Compendiums*, which form too considerable a part of a young lady's library... an infallible receipt for making a superficial mind.'[59] Her remedy was 'dry, tough reading', 'serious study' which 'lifts the reader from sensation to intellect... concentrates her attention, assists her in

[52] Ibid. 69, 79.   [53] Ibid. 94.   [54] Ibid. 34.   [55] Ibid. 41.

[56] M. Butler, *Jane Austen and the War of Ideas* (Oxford, 1987), 229–36.

[57] *Strictures*, i. 48. For Wollstonecraft's unfinished feminist novel *Maria; or, The Wrongs of Woman*, see V. Sapiro, *A Vindication of Political Virtue: The Political Theory of Mary Wollstonecraft* (Chicago, 1992), 264–8.

[58] *Strictures*, i. 188–9; D. Blakey, *The Minerva Press, 1790–1820* (London, 1939).

[59] *Strictures*, i. 178.

the habit of excluding trivial thoughts, and thus even helps to qualify her for religious pursuits'.[60] This is very much the voice of the former teacher, addressing her readers as if they were adolescent girls in the schoolroom; in effect, she was telling them to grow up—morally, intellectually, and emotionally.

The implications of her plea for rational education were far-reaching, and she was not always prepared to follow through her argument. In a thoroughly conventional passage she claimed that women lacked the masculine 'faculty of comparing, combining, analysing and separating'. However, she also asserted that

there is so much truth in the remark, that till women shall be more reasonably educated, and until the native growth of their mind shall cease to be stinted and cramped, we shall have no juster ground for pronouncing that their understanding has already reached its highest attainable perfection, than the Chinese would have for affirming that their women have attained to the greatest possible perfection in walking, while their first care is, during their infancy, to cripple their feet.[61]

Until women received an education more approximating to men's, the question 'will always remain as undecided as to the *degree* of difference between the masculine and feminine understanding, as the question between the understandings of blacks and whites'. Given their existing disadvantages, it was premature to assume the intellectual inferiority of either women or Africans.

The overall message, discernible in spite of the twists and turns, the contradictions and inconsistencies, has much in common with Wollstonecraft's. For all their political differences these two writers, so often seen as at opposite poles, agreed that women had been short-changed, stunted in their development by a faulty system of education. Sharing what some commentators have seen as a common misogyny, both believed that the cult of sensibility had trivialized and corrupted them, making them slaves to the demands of their bodies and to their over-heated emotions. Wollstonecraft's call for 'a revolution in female manners' so that women would 'labour by reforming themselves to reform the world' was echoed by More's plea that elite women 'will not content themselves with polishing when they are able to reform, with entertaining when they may awaken; and with captivating for a day, when they may bring into action powers of which the effects may be commensurate with eternity'.[62] Mary Berry, who read *Strictures* side by side with the *Vindication*, noted wryly, 'it is amazing, or rather it is not amazing but impossible, they should do otherwise than agree on all the great points

---

[60] Ibid. 184–5.   [61] Ibid. ii. 30.
[62] M. Wollstonecraft, *Political Writings*, ed. J. Todd (Oxford, 1994), 113; *Strictures*, i. 4.

of female education. H. More will, I dare say, be very angry with me when she hears this, though I would lay a wager that she never read the book.'[63]

Whatever More might have intended, *Strictures* inevitably raised fundamental questions about gender relations. Her 'counter-revolutionary feminism' coexisted uneasily with her very traditional assumptions about the separation of the male and female spheres.[64] By placing women on the front line in the battle against 'Jacobinism', she, wittingly or not, undermined her metaphor of the 'little garden', with its limited views and narrow prospects. The implication of her call for feminine patriotism was that politics in its broadest sense could not be the preserve of men alone. Home and nation were not discrete entities, and, as keepers of the domestic hearth, women were also the moral guardians of the country. They could not be conveniently tucked away in a private world isolated from the great public issues.[65]

On the whole *Strictures* was well received. By October 1799, seven months after its publication, it had gone into a sixth edition and it continued to be widely discussed and praised. In a typical comment the *Ladies' Monthly Museum* thought that 'the tendency of the whole is so exalted that we really think her labours above all praise'.[66] As far as the education of genteel women was concerned, More was operating from within a growing consensus. Less friendly readers, however, selected one passage for mockery: a robust, schoolmistressy attack on the new fashion of 'baby-balls', the provision of grown-up dances for little girls, which she saw as 'a sort of triple conspiracy against the innocence, the health, and the happiness of children'.

[63] *Extracts from the Journals and Correspondence of Miss Berry from the Year 1783 to 1852*, ed. T. Lewis (London, 1865), ii. 91–2. For illuminating comparisons between More and Wollstonecraft, see M. Myers, 'Reform or Ruin: "A Revolution in Female Manners"', *Studies in Eighteenth-Century Culture*, 11 (1982), 199–216, and H. Guest, *Small Change: Women, Learning, Patriotism, 1750–1810* (Chicago, 2000), 271–89. It could be argued, however, that More's attitude to sensibility was more consistent that Wollstonecraft's—perhaps because, whatever her earlier feelings for William Turner, she never experienced anything like Wollstonecraft's hopeless passion for Gilbert Imlay.

[64] K. Sutherland, 'Hannah More's Counter-Revolutionary Feminism', in K. Everest (ed.), *Revolution in Writing* (Milton Keynes, 1991), 27–63.

[65] For the public sphere, see J. Habermas, *The Structural Transformation of the Public Sphere: An Inquiry into a Category of Bourgeois Society*, trans. T. Burger (Oxford, 1989). For the ideology of separate spheres, see C. Hall, 'The Early Formation of the Victorian Domestic Ideology', in S. Burman (ed.), *Fit Work for Women* (London, 1979), 15–32; L. Davidoff and C. Hall, *Family Fortunes: Men and Women of the English Middle Class* (London, 1987); E. Janes Yeo, 'Introduction. Some Paradoxes of Empowerment', in ead. (ed.), *Radical Femininity: Women's Self-Representation in the Public Sphere* (Manchester, 1998), 1–24. For critiques of the separate spheres model, see A. Vickery, 'Golden Age to Separate Spheres? A Review of the Categories and Chronology of English Women's History', *Historical Journal*, 36 (1993), 383–414; ead., *Gentleman's Daughter*; H. Barker and E. Chalus (eds.), *Gender in Eighteenth-Century England: Roles, Representations, and Responsibilities* (London, 1997), 1–28. For an overview, see R. B. Shoemaker, *Gender in English Society, 1650–1850: The Emergence of Separate Spheres?* (London, 1998).

[66] *Ladies' Monthly Museum*, 2 (1799), 485.

Against the depressing scene of 'lilliputian coquettes, projecting dresses, studying colours, assorting ribbands and feathers, their little hearts beating with hopes about partners and fears about rivals' she painted a lyrical, almost Wordsworthian, picture of the 'native simplicity' of childhood in which 'every object teems with delight, to eyes and hearts new to the enjoyment of life'.[67] To many in fashionable society the passage confirmed More's reputation for prudery. Some time later she wrote to Henry Thornton telling him that 'a Lady gave a very great children's Ball, at the upper end of the Room on an elevated place was dressed out a figure to represent *me* with a large rod in my hand prepared to punish them all for such naughty doings!'[68] Hester Piozzi, meanwhile, heard that the boys of Westminster School had burned More in effigy 'for writing against the Dissipation of Youth'.[69] The book had its unintended entertainment value as far as the unregenerate were concerned.

Today *Strictures* is discussed almost entirely in terms of its protofeminism or antifeminism, but at the time the book was mainly controversial for the explicit espousal of Evangelical theology in its final chapters. More began by attacking what she called a 'worldly spirit' rather in the manner of the early eighteenth-century High Church moralist William Law. In a sardonic passage she contrasted the moderate demands of Christianity with the rigour of fashion.

How really burdensome would Christianity be if she enjoined such sedulous labours, such a succession of fatigues! If religion commanded such hardships and self-denial, such days of hurry... such nights of broken rest, such perpetual sacrifices of quiet, such exile from family delights as Fashion imposes, then indeed the service of Christianity would no longer merit its present appellation of being a '*reasonable* service'.[70]

She moved into more explicitly Evangelical territory when she dealt with what she called the doctrine of human corruption.[71] This rigorous reworking of the Christian doctrine of original sin was the starting block of Evangelical theology as it provided the essential condition for their doctrine of the atonement. As in her earlier works, she attacked the tolerant easygoing religion of many of her friends, condemning a 'cheap and indolent Christianity', and stressing the need for conversion (though she made very sparing use of the term itself).[72] This caused Richard Watson, latitudinarian bishop of Llandaff, to scoff at her 'elegant Methodism'.[73] The *Monthly Review* also

[67] *Strictures*, i. 95–100.   [68] Duke, More to Thornton, 'Bath, Tuesday' [1800].
[69] H. L. Piozzi, *Thraliana: The Diary of Mrs Hester Lynch Thrale*, ed. K. C. Balderston (Oxford, 1942), ii. 3 n.
[70] *Strictures*, ii. 220–1.   [71] Ibid. 264–87.   [72] Ibid. 292, 294–6.
[73] Duke, More to Wilberforce [1810].

detected 'Methodism' and believed that 'her religion is of too rigid a cast for enlightened society'.[74] Mary Berry thought, 'There are many excellent details in it, much good sense and an infinity of wit, for which I think all H. M.'s prose is quite remarkable; but there is in her writings, as in Mr Wilberforce's, a principle radically false, which ... vitiates every system built upon it and saps the very foundation of morality.'[75] As More was to learn to her cost, Miss Berry was not alone in such criticisms, and the anti-Jacobins who had praised her as one of themselves were swiftly becoming more ambivalent.

Richard Watson apart, most of the bishops liked it. George Pretyman of Lincoln wrote rather pompously to tell her that 'no age ever owed more to a female pen than to yours'.[76] But nothing could match the praise lavished on her by Porteus. In the published version of his Charge to the clergy of his diocese, he praised More as the most accomplished moralist and stylist of her generation: 'such brilliancy of wit, such richness of imagery, such variety and felicity of allusion, such neatness and elegance of diction, as are not, I conceive easily to be found so combined and blended together in any other work in the English language'.[77] This was too much for one satirist, the ex-clergyman, ex-doctor John Wolcot, who wrote under the pseudonym of Peter Pindar. Bishops and bluestockings were among his prime targets, and this was too good an opportunity to miss. In a mischievous poem, *Nil Admirari; or, A Smile at a Bishop*, he mocked Porteus's eulogy and More's literary pretensions.

> I own Miss Hannah's life is *very good*.
> But then her verse and prose are *very bad*.[78]

He went on to concoct a scurrilous fantasy about how Hannah More, middle-aged and overweight, was helped to win a race against younger and lighter competitors by the firm hand of the gallant bishop. The implication, of course, was that the *Strictures* had been largely the work of Porteus.

> Did no *kind* SWAIN his hand to Hannah yield
> No BISHOP'S hand to help a HEAVY REAR,
> And bear the NYMPH triumphant o'er the field?[79]

More immediately found a spirited defender in the Tory polemicist John Gifford, editor of the newly launched *Anti-Jacobin Review and Magazine*, who attacked 'Peter Pindar' as a 'contemptible rhymster' and praised the

---

[74] *Monthly Review*, enlarged series, 30 (1799), 411.

[75] Berry, *Journals and Correspondence*, ii. 91–2.   [76] Roberts, iii. 94.

[77] B. Porteus, *A Charge Delivered to the Clergy of the Diocese of London in the Years 1798 and 1799* (London, 1799), 35–6 n.

[78] [J. Wolcot] *Nil Admirari; or, A Smile at a Bishop ... by Peter Pindar Esq.* (London, 1799), 9.

[79] Ibid. 26.

Strictures as 'excellent'.[80] This, however, was to be the last piece of praise she received from that particular quarter for a long time. The magazine had already published some moderate criticisms of *Strictures* in a largely friendly review by the Anglo-American High Church loyalist clergyman Jonathan Boucher, but it was soon to become much more hostile.[81] In writing the book she had exposed a vulnerable flank, and for the next few years she was to be the target of relentless criticism, less from radicals than from the elements within the Tory High Church, disappointed perhaps that she was not after all the staunch churchwoman they had thought her to be.

Both Mary Berry and the *Monthly Review* had linked More's doctrine of human depravity with the message of Wilberforce's *Practical View*, a work which, as has been seen, owed much to More's encouragement. It has already been noted that, on that book's publication, Wilberforce had received a critical letter from the Revd Charles Daubeny, which eventually sparked off a full-blown theological controversy. The publication of *Strictures*, two years after the *Practical View*, provided Daubeny with fresh ammunition. This time he did not confine his criticisms to a private letter that might not receive an answer, but published them in a pamphlet entitled *A Letter to Mrs Hannah More*,[82] in which he fastened on More's description of Christian duties as 'the natural and necessary' productions of the 'living root' of Christian faith.[83] His keen nose sniffed heresy: 'Madam, this is not the language either of Scripture or of the Church of England,' but, he implied, of Calvinist determinism.[84] More was convinced she had been misunderstood,[85] but, following her usual practice after the Hannah Cowley experience, she allowed others to defend her. An anonymous pamphlet by 'a minister of the Church of England' praised her extravagantly and abused Daubeny for deliberate misrepresentation.[86] Daubeny was unabashed. 'I have spoken blasphemy', he wrote to his friend Jonathan Boucher, 'against the great Diana of the Ephesians.'[87] Battle lines were being drawn up within

---

[80] *Anti-Jacobin*, 4 (1799), 331–7. The master copy of the first six volumes of the *Anti-Jacobin* (P.P. 3596 in the BL catalogue) has the names of the contributors inked in.

[81] *Anti-Jacobin*, 4 (1799), 190–9.

[82] C. Daubeny, *A Letter to Mrs Hannah More on Some Part of her Late Publication Entitled 'Strictures on Female Education'* (Bath and London, 1799).

[83] *Strictures*, ii. 307.   [84] *Letter to Mrs Hannah More*, 39.

[85] When the first complete edition of her works came out in 1801 she refused to change the offending passage, arguing that she had been misinterpreted. *Works* (London, 1801), vol. i, p. xiv n.

[86] *A Letter to the Rev. Charles Daubeny on Some Passages Contained in his Guide to the Church and his Letter to Mrs Hannah More, by a Minister of the Church of England* (Bath and London, 1799).

[87] College of William and Mary, Swem Library, Jonathan Boucher Papers, B/5/11, Daubeny to Boucher, 23 Oct. 1799.

the Church, and he was eager to enlist the *Anti-Jacobin* in the person of its reviewer Boucher to his side. He thought his friend was too kind to More, and was anxious to put him right.

I read her well-meaning, but neither well informed nor well judging. Inflated with adulation and encircled with not the wisest men. What I have written, I have written *tenderly* because the ground was tender. But if weighed in the balance of the Sanctuary, however right she may be in some things...she w^d doubtless quoad the gen^l Doctrine be found wanting.—Her faith like that of Mr Wilberforce is Calvinism in disguise; her practice, like his, is schismatical: her Attachment to the Church of England, like his, of a very doubtful kind.[88]

Not for the first or last time, an author helpfully supplied a friendly reviewer with his best lines. In the following issue of the *Anti-Jacobin* Boucher reviewed the *Letter to Hannah More* and quoted his friend word for word. Daubeny's letter must have been in front of him as he wrote, 'If Mrs More be really of Mr Wilberforce's school, her faith is, like his, Calvinism in disguise; and her attachment to the Church of England of a very question-able kind.'[89] He ascribed More's error to her 'lively imagination', the usual put-down of a woman writer.

The *Anti-Jacobin Review and Magazine*, launched in July 1798, was the ultra-loyalist successor of a short-lived weekly newspaper of the same name founded by the ambitious young politician George Canning. Its editor, John Gifford, received a government pension of £300 a year and a police magis-tracy of £400.[90] The contributors included, in addition to Boucher, the conservative polemicist John Reeves (the founder of the loyalist Association for the Preservation of Liberty and Property), the High Church clergymen William Jones of Nayland and Richard Polwhele, and William Cobbett, who only a year before had been an enthusiastic supporter of the Cheap Reposi-tory. More Pittite than Pitt, it was extremely hawkish in foreign policy, following the agenda of the war minister, William Windham, who, now that Burke was dead, carried the torch for uncompromising hostility to peace negotiations with France. The ecclesiastic whom they most admired was Samuel Horsley, the inflexible High Church bishop of Rochester, a firm opponent of a negotiated peace.

The journal was the product of the loyalist panic of the late 1790s and at the comfortable distance of 200 years it is easy to be disdainful of the paranoia that infected many otherwise balanced people. It was a difficult

---

[88] Boucher Papers, B/5/10, Daubeny to Boucher, 24 Sept. 1799.

[89] *Anti-Jacobin*, 4 (1799), 255.

[90] E. L. de Montluzin, *The Antijacobins, 1798–1800: The Early Contributors to the 'Anti-Jacobin Review'* (Basingstoke, 1989), 1–40; S. Andrews, 'Pitt and Anti-Jacobin Hysteria', *History Today*, 48 (Sept. 1998), 49–54; J. Sack, *From Jacobite to Conservative: Reaction and Orthodoxy in Britain, c.1760–1832* (Cambridge, 1993), 24 n. 78.

period for Britain, a time of 'crisis upon crisis'.[91] One by one her allies, Prussia, Spain, and Austria, dropped out of the war, leaving Pitt's patient coalition-building policy in ruins. While, as in 1940, the country stood alone, Bonaparte's Army of England camped at Boulogne as part of an elaborate invasion bluff. Early in 1797 the French landed at Fishguard in south Wales, a comic-opera fiasco which nevertheless exposed the vulnerability of Britain's long coastline. In the spring sailors, inspired in part by radical propaganda, mutinied at the Nore and Spithead. A year later the uprising of the United Irishmen heralded one of the bloodiest periods of Irish history.

In these dark days many conservatives were eagerly reading an extraordinary book, published in 1794, the émigré Jesuit Augustin Barruel's *Mémoire pour servir à l'histoire du Jacobinisme*. A conspiracy theorist of a high order, Barruel depicted the French Revolution as the culmination of a grand international plot led by freemasons, Encyclopedists, and the Bavarian Illuminati. Were it unauthenticated, Hester Piozzi commented, it 'would be by all rational Creatures deem'd a Sick Man's Delirium'.[92] A book with a similar theme, by John Robison, professor of natural philosophy at Edinburgh, *Proofs of a Conspiracy against all the Religions and Governments of Europe*, was dedicated to Windham and readily accepted by many bishops including Porteus and the normally sane and sceptical Pretyman.[93] In this feverish atmosphere the vague but emotive term 'Jacobinism' worked in the way 'Bolshevism' did in the early twentieth century, becoming a shorthand for a comprehensive revolutionary ideology set on undermining the constitution, the Church, and public and private morality. Like communism in McCarthyite America, Jacobinism was not merely an external threat but the enemy within, a plague spreading from the radical societies, to the 'Puritan fanatics' in the Dissenting conventicles and to Ireland. The enemies of the state were insidiously present in every part of the kingdom and at every level of society. 'Our worst enemies', declaimed Boucher in his Carlisle Assize sermon, 'may be those of our own household.'[94]

How were these subversives to be described? Looking back to the Civil War, the *Anti-Jacobin* became obsessed with Puritanism and Calvinism, the creed that had destroyed Charles I. A more recent and home-grown manifestation was 'Methodism', a term which had been the focus of conspiracy theories for fifty years. Wesley's enemies had described his followers as Jesuits in disguise; alter this to Jacobins and the association was suitably

[91] This is the title of C. Emsley's chapter in his *British Society and the French Wars, 1793–1815* (London, 1979).

[92] Piozzi, *Thraliana*, ii. 973.

[93] J. M. Roberts, *The Mythology of the Secret Societies* (London, 1972), 118–45, 188–202; R. A. Soloway, *Prelates and People: Ecclesiastical Social Thought in England, 1783–1852* (London and Toronto, 1969), 36–43.

[94] J. Boucher, *A Sermon Preached at the Assizes held at the City of Carlisle* (Carlisle, 1798), 13.

updated. How did they spread their message? The answer was easy; it was through itinerant preaching and the setting up of Sunday schools. The *Anti-Jacobin* noted that 'a vast number' of former Sunday school pupils 'were wandering from their proper callings, had become fanatical teachers, had deemed themselves qualified to hold disputations upon religious topics, were turned sceptics, and infidels and anarchists, and were spreading a malignant influence through the mass of the community'. The largest Sunday school in London, it added triumphantly, was 'under the exclusive direction of *Methodists*'.[95] This then was the conspiratorial context in which Daubeny accused Hannah More of 'Calvinism in disguise'. It was a serious charge and was intended to discredit her. Because it was made when the Wedmore school was facing the charge of Methodism and her master at Blagdon was under attack, the timing could not have been worse.

[95] *Anti-Jacobin*, 7 (1800), 216–17.

Chapter 11

The Blagdon Controversy
1799–1803

In January 1799, while *Strictures* was being prepared for the press, Hannah More, then in her winter quarters in Bath and confined to bed with violent headaches,[1] received a letter from Sarah Bere, wife of the curate of Blagdon. Even before breaking the seal she must have guessed that the letter spelled trouble. She had never liked Thomas Bere and recently the relationship between them had sharply deteriorated. In the previous summer she had vented her views to Henry Thornton. He was, she said,

such a hypocrite that he affected to shed tears when I was ill and said in a canting tone 'what would become of the Country' yet he is doing all he can to knock up the school, thro' a genuine hatred to Xtianity and a personal hatred of one of our serious young Ministers who has awakened a dying woman and several others. This Blagdon Parson has been reading Socinian books and now boldly preaches against the Trinity, St Paul etc, and tells the people that they need pay no attention to any part of Scripture but the Sermon on the Mount...I am extremely distressed what to do having no Bishop nor Rector who cares for any of those things.[2]

Most of the elements of the future Blagdon controversy were in that letter: the personal animosity, the accusations of heresy (Bere's alleged denial of the divinity of Christ), the lack of episcopal authority, More's belief that she

---

An earlier version of this chapter is found in A. Stott, 'Hannah More and the Blagdon Contro-versy, 1799–1802', *Journal of Ecclesiastical History*, 51 (2000), 319–46, published by Cambridge University Press.

[1] Folger, W.b. 488, fo. 10, More to Eva Garrick, 9 Jan. [1799].
[2] Thornton, Add. MS7674/1/E/1, More to Thornton, 12 Sept. [1798].

carried on her shoulders the spiritual responsibility for the Mendip region. The comments about Bere were made at a fraught time when she was trying to set up the Wedmore school, and she was not disposed to be charitable to those who stood in her way. For his part, Bere was quick to take advantage of More's problems at Wedmore by preaching indirectly against the school in his own parish, so that, according to Patty, 'from a full school and considerably above two hundred at the evening reading, it all at once fell off to thirty-five'. The More sisters confronted Bere, reminded him of his previous letters approving of the school, and forced him to acknowledge 'before witnesses' the benefits the school had brought to the parish.[3] A milder man would have found such a humiliation hard to forgive.

Bere's opportunity to exact revenge came in the form of another proud, quarrelsome man, the schoolmaster Henry Young. By the end of 1798, while the Axbridge and Wedmore schools were trying to fight off accusations of enthusiasm, he was holding Monday evening meetings distinct from those the More sisters had established, which in their structure and spiritual intensity closely resembled the class discipline of the Methodists. At the end of the year Bere's wife and a woman friend attended one of the meetings and saw Young question those present. What Sarah Bere observed disturbed her so much that in January 1799 she wrote to More, and lit the slow-burning fuse which eventually exploded into the Blagdon controversy.

When the people were dismissed, I observed to Mr Young that these were a very happy set of people indeed, if they did not deceive themselves, which I hoped they did not ... I feared, if the like questions had been put to me, I could not have given such satisfactory answers. Mr Young said, 'perhaps, madam, you have not sought the Lord in the same way they have'.[4]

Sarah Bere went on to say that on that evening there had been no extempore prayers, but that she had been informed that such prayers were customary at that time. As neither Young nor More ever questioned this account of the evening, it seemed clear that the schoolmaster had acted in an irregular fashion. A layman, he was usurping the spiritual authority of the ordained clergyman and behaving like the itinerant preachers, both Methodist and Dissenting, who were beginning to cause such concern to the established Church.[5] The incident demonstrated one of More's key problems, her inability to control from a distance the actions of her teachers. It also highlighted what was to become one of the issues in the Blagdon controversy, the authority of the parish clergyman over the Sunday schools. In this case

[3] *MA* 215–16.

[4] T. Bere, *The Controversy between Mrs Hannah More and the Curate of Blagdon, relative to the Conduct of her Teacher of the Sunday School in that Parish* (London, 1801), 10.

[5] D. W. Lovegrove, *Established Church, Sectarian People: Itinerancy and the Transformation of English Dissent, 1780–1830* (Cambridge, 1988).

Bere could have used his powers as a magistrate and ordered Young to cease his meetings. The fact that he chose not to take this course probably shows that he wished to embarrass More. Whatever the curate's motives, it was essential to her reputation that she dealt with the situation promptly. Young was ordered to stop his irregularities, after which the abuses apparently came to an end. However, pleading sickness, More did not relay this information to Sarah Bere until 4 April, and this enabled the Beres to claim that they had been slighted. In the subsequent months the Axbridge school was forced to close, and Mrs Carroll, the new teacher at Wedmore, found herself accused of Methodism.

For a year nothing much happened in Blagdon, though relations between the curate and the schoolmaster continued to be poor. The storm finally broke in April 1800, when Bere's servant vouched on affidavit that Young had spoken slightingly of the curate. On the following day Bere wrote to More, describing the master as 'a turbulent, troublesome person', and declaring that if he continued in the school 'I must infer . . . that it is avowedly with intent to render my ministration in the church as little effectual as possible'.[6] More was then in London, about to set off for Teston. Unwilling to conduct the business by correspondence she suggested that they use a mediator, and recommended Sir Abraham Elton, the owner of the medieval Clevedon Court, a clergyman and magistrate, and the head of a distinguished family of Bristol merchants.[7] (He was also the future grandfather of Tennyson's friend Arthur Hallam.) He turned out to be an unfortunate choice, pompous, ill-judging, and sometimes ridiculous. Unwilling to accept him as a mediator, Bere wrote to his rector, Dr George Crossman, complaining of Young's meetings, though its chief members were only 'the smith's wife and a poor brain-shook old woman'.[8]

Crossman was in no position to act decisively. Incapacitated by asthma, he divided his time between his rectory at West Monkton and Bath, and, fitting neatly into the stereotype of the eighteenth-century clergyman, he rarely visited Blagdon, though he was also the patron of the living.[9] Throughout the controversy he relied on hearsay and like a cushion bore the imprint of the latest posterior to have sat on him. Alarmed by Bere's letter, he wrote back that if Young continued in this fashion the curate ought to prosecute him as an unlicensed preacher. More seems to have counter-attacked swiftly but covertly, and by the late summer Crossman began

[6] Bere, *Controversy*, 17–18.
[7] M. Elton, *Annals of the Elton Family, Bristol Merchants and Somerset Landowners* (Far Thrupp, Stroud, 1994).
[8] Bere, *Controversy*, 20–1.
[9] J. Collinson, *The History of the Antiquities of the County of Somerset* (Bath, 1791), iii. 570.

receiving reports from unspecified sources of his curate's unorthodoxy. The substance of the accusations was sent to the bishop of Bath and Wells, the octogenarian Dr Charles Moss, who for some time had left the running of the diocese to his son, another Dr Charles Moss, the diocesan chancellor. The bishop's incapacity highlights the structural and administrative problems facing many eighteenth-century bishops, and their frequent inability to control their dioceses: they were often appointed late in life, they had little administrative experience, they were required to spend much of their time in London, and, regardless of incapacitating infirmities, they held their offices until removed by death. This might not have mattered if Moss the younger had been able to control the situation; but, like Crossman, he found himself unable to act decisively, buffeted to and fro by the gales of the Blagdon controversy. And for the time being events were moving Bere's way. In early September More wrote to Wilberforce:

The Blagdon Bark will be soon ingulfed. The list of follies and crimes transmitted by the Curate and believed by the Rector will oblige me to give up the School ... It is said the Rector has let his Tythes to Bere, which being an illegal transaction he cannot easily part with him. So instead of coming up, as Dr Moss desired, as examining things on the spot, where false allegations cou'd have been refuted, he sent for Bere down to him; where, as Lord North once said, 'all the reciprocity being on one side, we are tried, found guilty, and condemned'. We have no chance with people who make nothing of oaths, but on the slightest subjects swear thro thick and thin.[10]

In the meantime Elizabeth Montagu had died just before her eightieth birthday. Always diminutive, she had become very frail and nearly blind. She had been a true friend, an understanding ally during the Ann Yearsley business, and a generous contributor to More's charities. More wrote to Wilberforce, '27 years unintermitted warmth of kindness cannot easily be forgotten. She had a large and manly as well as a gay and brilliant mind, much veracity, kindness and great fidelity in friendship. But the world ran away with her!' She had a faith of a kind, 'but it was not of the vital influential sort'.[11] She had been an extraordinary person, she told another correspondent, 'one of the richest and without exception the wittiest woman in this Country'.[12] Another link with her bluestocking past was severed. A friend had gone from the scene at a time when she needed all the support she could get.

Meanwhile, with Crossman's permission Bere was gathering a series of affidavits against Young, while the dubious legality of his collecting statements in his own cause was overlooked. (Perhaps More was right about the

---

[10] Duke, More to Wilberforce, 2 Sept. 1800.   [11] Ibid.
[12] Clark, More to [?], 1 Sept. 1800.

tithes.) 'People start up out of ditches, or from under hedges, to listen to the talk of poor pious labourers as they are at work, and then go and make oath,' she wrote to Wilberforce in late September. The affidavits alleged that Young was a Methodist and a Calvinist, that he ran secret meetings, that he called the clergy dumb dogs, that he and members of his little group prayed extempore, and that he prayed for the French. As for More herself, she was (amazingly) treated as if she were a seditious radical like the English Jacobins Thomas Hardy or John Thelwall. Worse still, Dr Moss, the chancellor, had written ordering her to dismiss Young. The school was lost to her, apparently, and, as she walked in her garden and looked up at the steeple of Blagdon church, she was close to despair.[13]

It was a relief to pour out her heart to Wilberforce, but he was unable to give her his full attention. In August the Wilberforces and Thorntons were on holiday at Bognor when the pregnant Barbara Wilberforce contracted typhoid. She recovered in October and gave birth to a daughter, Elizabeth (for whom More was godmother), but in the meantime Wilberforce was naturally distracted from what was happening at Blagdon. The affidavits, meanwhile, were mounting up. They were '*such* trash', More wrote to him at the end of October, when his family crisis had passed, 'so absurd on the very face of them you never saw. How a man of Moss's sense and knowledge of the world can lend himself to such a business is inconceivable, but ... the high Church spirit *must* protect its own!' She was refusing to dismiss Young, 'being determined to die hard'.[14] She had in the meantime found a new champion in her neighbour Thomas Sedgwick Whalley, whose wife she had nursed in the summer of 1789.[15] The fact that he was not an Evangelical made him a particularly valuable ally, his 'warmth and friendship' contrasting with 'the oyster of Wrington', as Patty contemptuously described their own rector, William Leeves, who was prudently keeping his head down.[16]

By the beginning of November 1800 Bere, armed with his evidence, such as it was, called a group of sympathetic local magistrates and clergy to a meeting at the George Inn at Blagdon for 12 November. 'We shall have but an unfair Jury, in people who think one extempore prayer a greater evil than breaking the ten commandments,' Patty wrote to Wilberforce.[17] Her fears were reasonable. One of Bere's letters summoning a magistrate has survived; it shows that he regarded the matter as a foregone conclusion as the letter

---

[13] Duke, More to Wilberforce, 29 Sept. 1800.

[14] Duke, More to Wilberforce, 28 Oct. 1800.

[15] For the full More–Whalley correspondence on the Blagdon controversy, see *Journals and Correspondence of Thomas Sedgwick Whalley, D.D.*, ed. H. Wickham (London, 1863), ii. 144–227.

[16] Ibid. 150. [17] Duke, Patty More to Wilberforce, n.d.

ends with a postscript: 'I hope to have the pleasure of your company to dinner—the business, I apprehend, will not require one hour's attention.'[18] The gathering heard the depositions and unanimously decided that Young should be dismissed. That evening the church bells were rung in Blagdon, and Mrs Bere paid the ringers a guinea. On 16 November, rather than dismiss Young, More closed the school, in line with her policy of refusing to run a school without the support of the parish clergyman, leaving the parish also bereft of its clothing club and school of industry.[19]

As usual she poured out her heart to Wilberforce. 'In Blagdon is still "a voice heard lamentation and mourning" and at Cowslip, "Rachel is still weeping for her Children and refuses to be comforted because they are not"—instructed. This heavy blow has almost bowed me to the ground.' To make matters worse she had received 'a most ambiguous and alarming note' from a nervous Porteus apparently to the effect that 'this *mock* trial has been fabricated by Bere's Emissaries into an *official* one and that I am found guilty of sedition and perhaps taken up and sent to Prison'. She was not comforted by an emollient letter from Moss *fils*, when she believed that at heart he was Bere's ally. 'There is a sort of Esprit de Corps that makes [clergy] support each other in public even when (as in the present case) their private language is different.'[20] Faced with this clerical solidarity what could one woman do?

At the beginning of 1801 William Pitt resigned as prime minister, having clashed with the king over the question of Catholic emancipation. In March the king asked Henry Addington, the speaker of the House of Commons and brother of More's neighbour Hiley Addington, to form a ministry. The bemused and contemptuous reaction of much of the nation was summed up in George Canning's little rhyme: 'Pitt is to Addington | As London is to Paddington.' The More sisters were desolate at the change of government. 'We have almost broken our hearts at the abdication of Mr Pitt,' More wrote to Wilberforce, 'and are very ill reconciled to his feeble and inefficient successor.'[21] By then, however, the Blagdon controversy had moved on, and she was unable to give much attention to national affairs.

Her resolve to die hard had not left her. Whalley was proving a tireless networker and advocate, causing some of the magistrates who had been present at the meeting at the George to think again, and lobbying the bishops. Porteus, for one, was relieved to hear that the 'alehouse conclave' had been a travesty of justice.[22] From the end of December More was in Bath, where she was twice visited by Dr Crossman. She regaled him with tales of Bere's unorthodoxy, and unwisely the suggestible rector chose to act

[18] Clark, Hannah More MSS box 12, Bere to G. P. Seymour, 3 Nov. 1800.
[19] *Journals of Whalley*, ii. 152–3.   [20] Duke, More to Wilberforce, 2 Dec. 1800.
[21] Duke, More to Wilberforce, 18 Mar. 1801.   [22] *Journals of Whalley*, ii. 169.

on More's allegations without checking them. In a series of letters to Bere he informed his curate that he was not satisfied of his Trinitarian orthodoxy, and finally in a letter of 23 January he told him that the bishop had ordered his dismissal.[23] Two days later, with a haste that More herself recognized was indecent, the school was reopened and Young was reinstated, with the full approval of the rector and chancellor.[24] Patty presided over the ceremony. With her usual feel for drama, she collected the children, took them to the church, read some prayers, and delivered a little sermon which left her audience 'much affected'.[25] On 2 February Bere received formal notification that he was no longer curate.[26] 'As a fallen man, I pity him,' More wrote in Pecksniffian fashion to Whalley.[27]

Naturally Bere was devastated, though as he was also rector of the neighbouring parish of Butcombe he was not left destitute. He complained with some justification of his 'invisible enemies' who had levied charges which he had never seen in full, giving him no opportunity to answer them. He therefore refused to resign, and the rector proved reluctant to use his authority as patron of the living to deprive him of his curacy. In his darkest hour he regained the initiative. In early spring More told Wilberforce, 'He is gone to London . . . either to publish a book against us, or to institute a process at law or both,' in company with William Shaw, rector of Chelvey, who was to prove the most scurrilous of all her enemies.[28] In March Bere published a pamphlet, *The Controversy between Mrs. Hannah More and the Curate of Blagdon*, in which he skilfully presented himself as the victim 'of a designing, artful and remorseless PARTY'.[29] The effect was what he had wished. 'The whole neighbourhood is still up in arms,' More told Wilberforce. Even more worryingly, Hiley Addington was on Bere's side, and she feared that his brother, 'now, alas, Premier, has the same prejudices'. She added that she would 'not answer the book tho it accuses me of all the crimes committed since the murder of Abel'.[30] The book led the *Anti-Jacobin* (now, thanks to Charles Daubeny, thoroughly hostile to More) to give over part of its June issue to an attack from the Bath layman Edward Spencer.[31]

Though More refused to respond to the book herself, she commissioned Elton to publish a reply. With many misgivings he complied, though, as he wrote to Whalley 'there is no getting rid of the grand objection with the public—that of Bere's loss of his curacy'.[32] His pamphlet, *A Letter to*

---

[23] Bere, *Controversy*, 91–105.   [24] *Journals of Whalley*, ii. 180.
[25] *Gambier*, i. 386, Patty More to Sir Charles Middleton, 9 Feb. 1801.
[26] Bere, *Controversy*, 106.   [27] *Journals of Whalley*, ii. 178.
[28] Duke, More to Wilberforce [1801] [catalogued *c*.1800].   [29] Bere, *Controversy*, 128.
[30] Duke, More to Wilberforce, 18 Mar. 1801.   [31] *Anti-Jacobin*, 9 (1801), 201–3.
[32] *Journals of Whalley*, ii. 197.

the Rev Thomas Bere, defended More in unconvincingly hyperbolic terms.[33] Bere published a sneering riposte in July, accusing him of being the Mores' familiar—'Paddock never appears at the call of the Weird sisters but in the last extremity.'[34] All this gave the *Anti-Jacobin* a further excuse to wade into the controversy.[35] Meanwhile, Bere was still refusing to vacate his curacy, and on 1 August he was informed by Moss the chancellor that he was still curate of Blagdon.[36] He had been restored, More told Wilberforce, 'to quiet a clamour'.[37] Her own position was now impossible. In a sad little ceremony in September 1801 attended by Patty, the Blagdon school was closed again, and never reopened, though Bere set up a school of his own to which More sent secret subscriptions. Henry Young ended up in Ireland, where the Evangelical La Touche family found him a post.

But by this time, however, with the controversy now public property, the chief issue was no longer the Blagdon school but More's reputation and the future of her remaining schools. This was all-out war, and a contest she had to win. A further series of pamphlets was published, full of confusing assertions and counter-assertions. The Mendip clergy lined up, some on Bere's side, but most on More's. The High Church *British Critic* supported her, but the *Anti-Jacobin* attacks mounted in ferocity. In two particularly offensive pamphlets her private life came under attack.[38] She was depicted as the representative of a faction within the Church whose covert programme was to undermine the establishment. The accusations that had dogged her ever since she set up the Cheddar school were now aired openly. The dispute had moved beyond Henry Young, who was too obscure to matter a great deal, to encompass More herself and the whole Evangelical movement represented by the Clapham sect. It thus became a significant moment in the history of the Church of England.

The Blagdon controversy is the most problematic episode in More's career. It has been variously seen as part of the debate on the education of the poor, as a symbol of the Evangelical programme of bringing about a revolution in Church and State, and as a clerical reaction to More's assertive

---

[33] A. Elton, *A Letter to the Rev. Thomas Bere...Occasioned by his Late Unwarrantable Attack on Mrs Hannah More (London and Bath, 1801).*

[34] T. Bere, *An Appeal to the Public on the Controversy between Hannah More, the Curate of Blagdon, and the Rev. Sir A. Elton* (London, 1801), 7.

[35] *Anti-Jacobin*, 9 (1801), 277–96.

[36] T. Bere, *An Address to Mrs Hannah More on the Conclusion of the Blagdon Controversy* (Bath and London, 1801), 30.

[37] Duke, More to Wilberforce, 17 Aug. 1801.

[38] E. Spencer, *Truths respecting Mrs Hannah More's Meeting Houses and the Conduct of her Followers* (Bath, 1802); [W. Shaw] *The Life of Hannah More, with a Critical Review of her Writings* (London, 1802).

female activism.[39] Relatively trivial in itself, it gained wider significance because it erupted at a moment of national crisis, a crisis with religious, cultural, political, and military dimensions. While Bonaparte was threatening invasion, the MP Michael Angelo Taylor was promoting a bill to regulate Dissenting meeting-houses and Dissenting preachers. In the months when More's opponents were at their most hysterical, peace negotiations with France were proceeding, much to the distress of the more extreme anti-Jacobins. While the attacks reached their peak, an Evangelically inspired bill to abolish bull-baiting was being thrown out by the Commons on the grounds that the 'Puritanism' of the bill's proponents represented a 'Jacobin' assault on the English character and the English way of life. The issue ceased to be an obscure Sunday school teacher in a Somerset village few people had heard of. Instead it was part of a battle waged on behalf of an established Church by those who had come to see More and Wilberforce as its mortal enemies. In the smoke and confusion any perceived ambivalence on Hannah More's part towards the Church of England was seized on, highlighted, and misrepresented, and by a supreme paradox the woman who had regarded herself as an impeccable political conservative found herself identified with all the forces of subversion within the state.

It is fruitless to discuss all the polemical literature in detail, and impossible to assess the accuracy or otherwise of every allegation: whether, for example, Henry Young showed dumb insolence in his demeanour to Bere, whether Bere's key witness was a disreputable woman, whether the Blagdon villagers were hostile to Young or terrorized by Bere. The Blagdon literature set out two contradictory narratives: one of a blameless Christian woman set upon by malignant enemies, the other of a victimized curate and a beleaguered Church assailed by Puritan fanatics and let down by its pusillanimous bishops. Inevitably, there are many significant gaps in the surviving evidence. Private conversations, arm-twistings, discreet or brutal, and the varied pressures brought to bear on the protagonists have been lost to posterity. One fact, however, emerges clearly: More ultimately survived her ordeal because her enemies failed to enlist the main body of High Churchmen to their side. The reason for their failure is to be found in her assiduous networking of potentially sympathetic clergy and friends in polite society undertaken in the years before Blagdon. At her moment of crisis she was able to exploit these previous contacts, and, finding themselves isolated, her enemies prudently ceased their attacks. Having charged into battle, her opponents found them-

---

[39] M. G. Jones, *Hannah More* (Cambridge, 1952), 172–83; F. K. Brown, *Fathers of the Victorians* (Cambridge, 1961), 182–3, 187–233; B. Fowkes Tobin, *Superintending the Poor: Charitable Ladies and Paternal Landlords in British Fiction, 1770–1860* (New Haven, 1993), 109–12; M. Myers, ' "A Peculiar Protection": Hannah More and the Cultural Politics of the Blagdon Controversy', in B. Fowkes Tobin (ed.), *History, Gender and Eighteenth-Century Literature* (Athens, Ga., 1994), 227–57.

selves outnumbered and therefore retreated with as much dignity as they could muster, leaving her exhausted and demoralized, but in possession of the field.

It is now time to examine in more detail the substance of the case against Henry Young. The charge of Calvinism made in the late summer of 1800 echoed the accusations of Daubeny and Boucher against More in the *Anti-Jacobin*. More complained bitterly to Wilberforce of the theological incoherence of the accusation.

It makes me almost sick to tell you that the Blagdon Inquisition have driven our poor Schoolmaster to take an oath that he is not a Calvinist! 'Murderers of fathers and murderers of mothers' are good people compared with those whom they accuse of Calvinism. It is a nickname. They do not at all know what it means. The poor man's being a Disciple of John Wesley's cou'd do it with a safe conscience, but distinguished those points in which he was and was not.[40]

She was technically correct, as the Methodist movement had split over the dispute between the Calvinism of George Whitefield and the countess of Huntingdon and the Arminianism of the Wesley brothers. But she was also missing the point. In the current conspiratorial climate the term 'Calvinism' was no longer used with any precision; it was a synonym for 'Puritanism' and 'Methodism' and it spelled subversion. This left More very vulnerable, when on her own admission she had appointed a known Methodist to Blagdon in the same way that she had placed Sarah Baber in Cheddar and John Harvard in Wedmore. When the Cheddar adult school was set up in 1790, she had almost boasted to Sir Charles Middleton of its Methodist characteristics: 'Finding at the end of nine months that neither Rector or Curate had ever been near us, or catechized a child, I thought myself justified in "proclaiming open Methodism" as I suppose it will be called.'[41] Years later this readiness to appoint Methodist teachers was confirmed by William Jay, the Bath Dissenting minister.

She more than once applied to me to recommend such as, she said, would be called Methodists; adding, 'I find none seem to do my poor children good beside'...When her parochial accuser [Bere] published these things, with his colourings and enlargements, void of the circumstances of explanation or excuse, some took great alarm, and, eager for her defence, plunged incautiously into the dispute; and, judging only by what they knew of her then, they denied things which many living could not but own had been substantially true.[42]

---

[40] Duke, More to Wilberforce, 2 Sept. 1800.   [41] *Gambier*, i. 180.
[42] *Autobiography of and Reminiscences of the Rev. William Jay*, ed. G. Redford and J. Angell James (London, 1855), 337 n., 338.

This was not as dreadful as it later appeared. At the time when More set up the Cheddar school, the Methodists had not split away from the Church of England, but in the years after the death of Wesley in 1791 the movement became a separate denomination in competition with the established Church, with Bristol and the industrial villages of the Mendips key areas of growth. Much of the initiative came from radical artisans, many of whom were also itinerant preachers, whose opposition to religious hierarchy easily spilled over into hostility to the government. In 1799 George Pretyman, bishop of Lincoln, commissioned a survey of his large diocese. The report's alarming findings, published in the following year, revealed the existence of 'a wandering tribe of fanatical teachers from the lowest and most illiterate classes of society'.[43] In the same year the bishop put his influence behind the bill for the closer regulation of Dissenting meeting-houses. His concerns were echoed by his fiercely High Church colleague Samuel Horsley of Rochester, whose well-publicized Charge of 1800 linked together Sunday schools, Methodists, and itinerant preaching in one grand indictment of Jacobin conspiracy.[44]

The Mendip schools were potential victims of these changed circumstances in which any association with Methodism or Dissent became fraught with danger. As early as 1794 More's friend John Boak was dismissed from one of his curacies for being a 'Methodist'; four years later the Yatton mistress was publicly reprimanded by the curate–magistrate 'for daring to go and hear a Methodist'.[45] At Wedmore it was alleged that John Harvard 'had called the Bishops dumb Dogs—that he had said all who went to church and did not come to hear him would go to Hell, and that he distributed books called "A Guide to Methodism" '.[46] As Methodism spread in the Mendips, More's enemies believed that, by her undermining of the clergy and her encouragement of 'enthusiasm', she had paved the way for religious subversives. She countered the charge by arguing that her schools kept the people away from the Dissenting or Methodist meeting-houses.[47] Privately she maintained a clear distinction between 'these new seceding Methodists' with their 'terrible Principles' and Wesley and Whitefield, whom she regarded as fundamentally sound.[48] They, of course, had lived and died as members of the Church of England. Herein lay the ambiguity of the charge of Methodism and the difficulty of refuting it.

---

[43] R. A. Soloway, *Prelates and People: Ecclesiastical Social Thought in England, 1783–1852* (London and Toronto, 1969), 6–9, 20–1, 50–1; D. Hempton, *Methodism and Politics in British Society, 1750–1850* (London, 1984), 77.

[44] S. Horsley, *The Charge of Samuel, Lord Bishop of Rochester, to the Clergy of his Diocese* (London, 1800).

[45] Duke, More to Wilberforce, 10 July 1794; *MA* 216.

[46] Duke, More to Wilberforce, 11 Sept. 1799.   [47] *Journals of Whalley*, ii. 210–11.

[48] Duke, More to Thornton [1800].

But it was not merely the change in circumstances that created problems. Some of the teaching materials used in the schools could be viewed as highly suspect by High Church sacramentalists. The main instruction book, after the Bible and the Church catechism, was the penny booklet *Questions and Answers for the Mendip and Sunday Schools*, presumably written by the More sisters.[49] Whereas the official Anglican catechism asks the child 'Who made you?' and proceeds rapidly to questions about baptism, the Mendip *Questions* ascribe salvation, in true 'Methodist' fashion, entirely to personal faith in a way that highlighted the differences between Evangelical and High Church teaching on salvation. Alongside the Evangelical teaching material went the risky toleration of enthusiasm which has already been noted. Similarly, the reaction to the death of Sarah Baber shows how the Evangelical bypassing of the sacraments and hierarchy of the Church in favour of personal conversion could lead to the devaluing of non-Evangelical clergy. Her funeral sermon, preached by the then curate, John Boak, included a tribute startling to anyone but an Evangelical: 'This eminent Christian first taught *salvation* in Cheddar.'[50] (There had been a church at Cheddar since at least 900.) At the height of the Blagdon controversy More told Wilberforce that her enemies were resurrecting the old High Church battle-cry 'the Church in Danger'.[51] She should not have been so surprised.

There was another danger signal she might have spotted. By 1800 she had become one of the most influential lay people in the Mendips, and she was using this influence in an almost reckless fashion, which was bound to raise the hackles of some local clergy. When she brought in Evangelical clergy to preach at her club and Sunday school anniversaries, this could easily be represented as intrusion. In 1791 the poet Anna Seward, staying at the Whalleys, claimed to have heard Newton preach 'a violently methodistical sermon'; in 1793 Wilberforce brought with him the rector of Clapham, John Venn, who preached at both Axbridge and Cheddar.[52] Four years later Thomas Fry, a mere two months after his ordination, preached before a gathering of local clergy, some of whom must have been more than twice his age; unflatteringly, More hoped that 'this admirable discourse may be of service to them, as I am convinced the greater part never heard anything comparable to it'.[53]

By this time she had also became a prominent ecclesiastical patron. She was, of course, no Lady Catherine de Bourgh, a wealthy aristocrat who had inherited a right of presentation. All she had was her influence, which was formidable. The local clergy whom she favoured gained preferment, those

---

[49] The 14th edition is listed 3504 a 84 in the BL catalogue; the 16th edition is listed 3504 de g.
[50] Roberts, ii. 440.   [51] Duke, More to Wilberforce, 29 Sept. 1800.
[52] Brown, *Fathers of the Victorians*, 204–7; *MA* 44, 83.   [53] *Gambier*, i. 328.

whom she disliked languished in obscurity. William Jay surmised, possibly correctly, that Bere's early ingratiating manners to More sprang from a wish for promotion and that his subsequent hostility was the result of her failure to secure him a better living.[54] Her letters reveal her contempt for many of the local clergy and her diligent efforts to secure livings for Evangelicals. For example, the rector who had dismissed Boak for 'Methodism' 'keeps a mistress, gets tipsy before dinner and last week treated 40 [of] the poorest wretches he cou'd find to a strolling play, because Boak had preached against plays the Sunday before. This Rector is our chief Magistrate! Don't we stand in need of a little visit from the French?'[55] (Perhaps it was the expression of similar sentiments that lay behind the charge that Henry Young had prayed for the French.) To the fury of some local clergy, she persuaded the dean and chapter of Wells to appoint John Jones to the living of Shipham, and first John Boak then Thomas Drewitt to Cheddar—presumably because they were reluctant to take a stand against a determined woman with a national reputation.[56] As it happened, both Boak and Jones were devoted clergy. Jones worked tirelessly until his eighties, and when he died More felt she had lost her right-hand man. (There is a plaque to him in Shipham church with a verse tribute by More.) He was a worthy appointment, but to More's enemies this was beside the point. Not content with planting 'her' clergy in key positions, she felt no qualms about instructing them in what she believed was the right direction. Boak, for example, was told, 'I think your definition of faith not an inaccurate one. Your track seems to be right; you only have to pursue it.'[57] Fry humbly 'received my private criticism, and the little errors which I pointed out to him in his sermon'.[58] In a layman, this might have been perceived as trespassing. Coming from a woman, it became all the more offensive to those clergy who did not share More's Evangelical theology.

Her actions were noted with outrage by Daubeny, the choleric defender of clerical status, who complained bitterly to Boucher that

Mrs H: M: keeps a sort of school for the younger Clergy in which they gain as much knowledge in a few Lectures, as old Divines have been able to draw from a whole row of bulky Folios... This hop, skip & jump Divinity, as I call it, never fails to be accompanied with much confidence, self importance, and consequent contempt of all who do not study in the same school with themselves.[59]

The troubles at Wedmore and Axbridge can be seen as the inevitable reaction to her 'intrusion' and showed that Bere was not speaking simply for

---

[54] *Autobiography of Jay*, 37.   [55] Duke, More to Wilberforce, 10 July 1794.
[56] *MA* 44, 184; Bodleian, MS d. 20, fo. 36, 'Recollections of Mrs Hannah More'.
[57] Roberts, iii. 119.   [58] *Gambier*, i. 328.
[59] College of William and Mary, Swem Library, Jonathan Boucher Papers, B/5/15, Daubeny to Boucher, 16 Apr. 1800.

himself and his thwarted hopes. In his pamphlets he listed as his clerical enemies: 'Mr Jones, the rector of Shipham, which Mrs More procured for him; Mr Boak, the rector of Brockley, which the said Mrs More procured for him; and your worthy friend Mr Drewitt, who as yet has not been remunerated, but stands first on the party list.'[60] This conspiracy theme was taken up in the August 1801 edition of the *Anti-Jacobin*.

Of the existence of an *organized confederation* for the purpose of increasing the number of methodists; of training them up to the church; of purchasing small livings for them, and by this means, of perverting the pure doctrines of the Gospel of Christ, as taught by the Established Church of England; and also of bringing that Establishment into discredit; we have long had indisputable proofs. *Clapham Common* is the seat of its power; and we shall some day take occasion to notice its chiefs, and expose its manœuvres.[61]

It was now clear that the fundamental issue behind the Blagdon controversy was not the education of the poor or the conduct of Henry Young but wider fears of Evangelical infiltration into the Church of England. The *Anti-Jacobin* had declared war on the whole Evangelical party.

With the hostilities out in the open, Bishop Porteus was becoming increasingly anxious. At the end of 1801 he was hinting that More should close the schools for the sake of her health and reputation—a proposal fiercely resisted by Wilberforce.[62] Perhaps, still smarting from 'Peter Pindar's' attack, he feared that, for all his well-known anti-Calvinism, he would be judged guilty by association. The threat contained in the February 1802 edition of the *Anti-Jacobin* to expose 'the secret manœuvres of the *false friends* to the church' seemed to be directed at the bishops.[63] The April issue, which marked the high-water mark of its campaign, attacked the bishops generally and the episcopal supporters of Hannah More in particular.[64] How long would it be before Porteus was outed as a covert supporter of 'Methodism'?

There is little doubt that the bishop felt the ground cut from under his feet by a revelation in this issue of the *Anti-Jacobin*. Two years previously Daubeny had revealed to Boucher what was common knowledge in Bath: that More had been part of Jay's congregation, though her attendance was a supplement to not a substitute for her participation in Anglican worship.[65]

---

[60] Bere, *An Appeal to the Public*, 38; see also id., *Address to Mrs Hannah More*, 45.

[61] *Anti-Jacobin*, 9 (1801), 390.

[62] *The Correspondence of William Wilberforce*, ed. R. I. and S. Wilberforce, 2 vols. (London, 1840), i. 235.

[63] *Anti-Jacobin*, 11 (1802), 194. For the hostility of Daubeny and Boucher to Porteus, see Boucher Papers, B/5/12, B/5/14.

[64] *Anti-Jacobin*, 11 (1802), 424–5.

[65] Boucher Papers, B/5/14, Daubeny to Boucher, 27 Feb. 1800.

More had never concealed this, seeing Jay as 'almost the only preacher of religion in this silly, dissipated place. The church clergy here are uncommonly lukewarm and selfish.'[66] This information had enabled Boucher to issue a veiled threat in the March 1800 issue of the *Anti-Jacobin*, where he accused More of 'listening to unauthorised preachers and frequenting other places of worship than the established church'.[67] But now, two years later, a much more damaging revelation emerged, with the *Anti-Jacobin* hyperventilating over 'the positive fact of [More's] having received THE SACRAMENT from the hands of a *Layman*!!!'[68] Attendance was one thing; taking communion from a 'schismatical' minister, a layman in High Church eyes, was a graver matter. In May William Cobbett, now firmly in the camp of More's enemies, wrote triumphantly to the anti-Jacobin politician William Windham, 'This decides the controversy...It is a fearful thing to think of, that this woman had under her tuition the children of a large portion of England.'[69]

In the circumstances of 1802, with Anglican paranoia at its most feverish, this seemed damning. Porteus ruefully commented later that 'it had been better, especially for the sake of her friends, not to do it'.[70] Yet her taking communion in a Dissenting meeting-house only acquired its sinister significance at a time of conspiracy theories. Patty More assured Whalley that 'till the French Revolution when Tom Paine &c. began to show their cloven feet', it was common even for 'High church people' to do the same.[71] More herself engaged in a fruitless dispute with Jay about whether she had taken communion once only or more frequently. 'Had I been to a *hundred* Masquerades', she wrote bitterly to Wilberforce, 'nobody would care about it.'[72] The key point, however, is that under the malice and misrepresentation lay a stratum of truth. More regarded Jay as a 'serious' minister of the gospel, and though she never attended his chapel at the hours of Anglican services, she saw nothing wrong with deriving spiritual nourishment from outside the established Church. Ultimately, the 'godliness' of a clergyman mattered more to her than his denomination, and it was this that lay behind the charge that the Evangelicals represented a church within a church.

Cobbett clearly hoped that this revelation would finally sink More. But it did not. Her Blagdon school never reopened, but within a year or so her

---

[66] *Gambier*, i. 210, More to Sir Charles Middleton, 8 Jan. 1793.

[67] *Anti-Jacobin*, 5 (1800), 330. This quotation is from the edition catalogued P.P. 3596 in BL.

[68] *Anti-Jacobin*, 11 (1802), 429. See also *Bath Chronicle*, 4 Mar. 1802.

[69] BL, Add. MS 37853, fo. 38.   [70] *Autobiography of Jay*, 332.

[71] *Journals of Whalley*, ii. 225.

[72] Duke, More to Wilberforce, 17 Aug. 1802; *Autobiography of Jay*, 332; Boston (Mass.) Public Library, Dept. of Rare Books and Manuscripts, MS Eng. (197) (2), More to Jay, 14 Aug. 1802; Clark, More to John Bowdler, 17 June 1802.

reputation had recovered, thanks in part to the efforts of her friends. Wilberforce, Thornton, Porteus, and Barrington worked hard behind the scenes on her behalf. Whalley's *Animadversions on the Curate of Blagdon's Three Publications*, published anonymously in March 1802, had some enjoyable knockabout fun at Bere's expense; Sally More overheard some of the Bath clergy discussing it favourably in Hazard's bookshop.[73] Ann Kennicott, intelligent, popular, and free from the taint of 'enthusiasm', proved a skilled and effective campaigner.[74] Support from these quarters could be taken for granted. What is more remarkable is the fact that throughout the controversy More retained powerful allies on the episcopal bench, in the High Church *British Critic*, and among most of the Mendip clergy.

Part of the reason for this lay in the nature of the High Church itself, which, in these pre-Tractarian days, represented a spectrum of views rather than a monolithic party.[75] Their reasons for supporting or opposing More were often personal: did they like or dislike, trust or distrust, her? This affected how many of them interpreted the controversy. If they saw it as concerned with Methodism and intrusion, then More was on weak ground. On the other hand, if they viewed it as a debate about what, if anything, the poor should be taught, then they were likely to support her, as even deeply conservative bishops had come to believe that the education of the lower orders would reinforce rather than undermine the establishment. It was fortunate for More that two important orthodox bishops chose to believe her assertion that her only concern in setting up her schools had been to secure the obedience of the pupils to both Church and State. In the autumn of 1800 she wrote a carefully worded letter to George Pretyman, bishop of Lincoln, a man she privately distrusted, but who had subscribed 3 guineas to the Cheap Repository.[76] She and the Pretymans had met again when she was on holiday at Christchurch in 1799 and had passed a good deal of time in each other's company.[77] His reply offered warm support, allowing More to claim that 'the Bishop of Lincoln acquits us of

[73] T. S. Whalley, *Animadversions on the Curate of Blagdon's Three Publications . . . with Some Allusions to his Cambrian Descent* (London, 1802); *Journals of Whalley*, ii. 216–17.

[74] See e.g. her letter to More: 'I find your letter gives perfect satisfaction to all who have read it.' Clark, Ann Kennicott to More, 15 July [1802]. See also 7 Feb. [1803].

[75] For the High Church, see F. C. Mather, *High Church Prophet: Bishop Samuel Horsley (1733–1806) and the Caroline Tradition in the Later Georgian Church* (Oxford, 1992); P. Nockles, 'Church Parties in the Pre-Tractarian Church of England 1750–1833: The "Orthodox"—Some Problems of Definition and Identity', in J. Walsh, C. Haydon, and S. Taylor (eds.), *The Church of England: From Toleration to Tractarianism c.1698–c.1833* (Cambridge, 1993), 334–59; id., *The Oxford Movement in Context: Anglican High Churchmanship, 1760–1857* (Cambridge, 1994). See also A. Burns, *The Diocesan Revival in the Church of England, c.1800–1870* (Oxford, 1999).

[76] Centre for Kentish Studies, Stanhope U1590/S5/03/6, More to the bishop of Lincoln, 24 Sept. 1800. Cheap Repository Subscription List (Clark Library copy). For More's distrust of Pretyman, see Duke, More to Wilberforce, 3 Aug. 1796; Duke, More to Mrs H. Thornton [c.1800].

[77] Folger, W.b. 488, fo. 14, More to Mrs Garrick, 31 Aug. 1799.

enthusiasm and irregularity'.[78] It is extremely likely that either she or one of her friends wrote a similar letter to Horsley, the other bishop who had to be brought on board.[79] However, the task of persuading this apparently unbending High Churchman was not as difficult as might appear. His Charge of 1800 showed that, far from disapproving of Sunday schools, he was eager for their establishment provided that they were 'under the management of the Parochial Clergy'.[80] This was exactly what More claimed to be doing. With the bishops of London, Durham, Lincoln, and Rochester behind her, and with no one on the episcopal bench prepared to break rank and join the *Anti-Jacobin* attack, she won a major round in the contest.

However, national support counted for little if she could not gain the backing of the local clergy, as she had to demonstrate that her schools had been conducted under their supervision. In September 1801 a pamphlet was issued, entitled *A Statement of Facts relating to Mrs. H. More's Schools, occasioned by some late Misrepresentations*, a collection of statements gathered from nine local clergymen, gathered in July. Though the pamphlet is usually ascribed to Charles Moss, the diocesan chancellor, the author was almost certainly John Boak.[81] The idea, however, did not come from any of her tame clergy but from a High Churchman and former contributor to the *Anti-Jacobin*, Francis Randolph, who preached at the Shipham Club feast in July.[82] Randolph was chaplain to the duke of York and spiritual adviser to the troubled duchess of Devonshire. More knew him in three capacities: as the proprietor of Laura Chapel, which she attended while in Bath; as a subscriber to the Cheap Repository; and as the principal resident in Banwell, where she had a school until 1797. The country knew him as the man who had lost some indiscreet private letters the princess of Wales had sent back to her family in Brunswick in the early days of her disastrous marriage. It was fortunate for More that he took more care of her reputation than he did of Caroline's.

The *Statement of Facts* proved a propaganda coup. Of the nine clergy who testified (derided by their opponents as 'Hannah More's ninepins') three, Boak, Jones, and Drewitt, were her protégés and needed no persuasion. But it must have required some pressure to wring from the Revd S. T.

[78] Stanhope U1590/S5/03/6, More to the bishop of Lincoln, 30 Dec. 1800; Duke, More to Thornton, Jan. [1801].

[79] *Journals of Whalley*, ii. 217.

[80] *The Charge of Samuel Lord Bishop of Rochester*, 25–6. See also Mather, *High Church Prophet*, 278–83.

[81] On 1 Sept. 1801 Henry Thornton wrote to More, 'Mr Boak's pamphlet appears to me likely to have its use as it goes to discredit Bere by the public statement of some facts which can be authenticated.' Thornton, Add. MS 7674/1/L2, fo. 148.

[82] Duke, More to Wilberforce, *c*.21 July 1801. See also Duke, More to Wilberforce, 5 Nov. 1800. His wife was an equally energetic ally, and successfully sold More's version of the controversy to the royal family. Clark, Ann Kennicott to More, 15 Dec. [1801?].

Wylde, anti-Methodist curate of Yatton, who had been one of the clergy present at the meeting at the George, that the school was 'constantly under his inspection' and that the teachers were 'nominated by him'.[83] In a somewhat self-condemnatory statement J. Sparrow, curate of Nailsea, declared that he had visited the Sunday school whenever time allowed and had 'never seen any thing done there contrary to my approbation'.[84] Still more remarkable was the statement from John Rawbone, absentee vicar of Cheddar, who claimed from his Oxford residence that he had observed the great good done by the schools.[85] There were some dissidents remaining, notably the vicar and curate of Wedmore, who proved implacable.[86] Nevertheless, Randolph's zeal paid off, and with most of the local clergy lining up to support her, More was acquitted on a majority verdict.

Most importantly, there remained her own diocesan. In April 1802 Bishop Moss died and was replaced in the summer by the bishop of Gloucester, Richard Beadon, who like Pretyman had been a Cheap Repository subscriber. Again, More was quick to get her case in first. Before Beadon set foot in Wells, she sent him a dignified thirty-one-page letter which must have taken days to write, substantially accurate, though at times economical with the truth, in which she dissociated herself from the 'excesses' of some of her teachers, stressed her own loyalty to the Church, and minimized the '*single irregularity*' of taking communion from Jay.[87] The new bishop, happily ignorant of her scathing private comments about many of his clergy, accepted her version of events, though, after so much hesitation and equivocation from the Mosses, More found it difficult to accept that the tide had turned. She told Wilberforce that she would wait until he came to Wells 'to see if his conduct corresponds with his profession and to let him be a volunteer if he be so disposed, in his good offices in that land of Enemies [the cathedral]'.[88] But she need not have worried; thoroughly won over, the bishop thought well enough of her letter to keep it and later bequeath it to his old college (St John's, Cambridge).

With the failure of the clerical elites to rally to them, More's opponents had to retreat. Boucher and Daubeny had played a covert role throughout the controversy, willing to wound yet afraid to strike openly. They now sensed defeat, and by 1803 Daubeny was duplicitous enough to dissociate himself from his own notorious phrase. 'The Anti-Jacobin Reviewers', he wrote, 'appear to have been more quick-sight than myself . . . by representing

---

[83] [J. Boak] *A Statement of Facts relative to Mrs H. More's Schools Occasioned by Some Late Misrepresentations* (Bath and London 1801), 6.

[84] Ibid.   [85] Ibid. 19.

[86] More admitted this in her letter to Beadon. Cambridge University, St John's College Library, MS k. 34, fo. 24.

[87] Ibid.   [88] Duke, More to Wilberforce, 10 Sept. 1802.

this position of Mrs M. to be "Calvinism in disguise".[89] He had discovered that the net of More's friendships and influence spread widely and encompassed those of a churchmanship different from her own, none of whom recognized the subversive fanatic of the *Anti-Jacobin* caricature. The most critical of her friends believed that at worst she had made an honest mistake in trusting Young.[90] She proved a difficult target for her enemies; they might wing her, but they were unable to deal a mortal wound.

The wounds were real enough, however, and kept raw and bleeding by a persistent undercurrent of misogyny. More herself was well aware of the gender implications of her predicament. 'I owe much of my suffering to my defenceless Sex,' she complained to John Bowdler Jr (nephew of the man who edited out the improper passages in Shakespeare).[91] Her strategy of refusing to reply directly but relying on two male members of the local elite infuriated her opponents, though they would have criticized her still more if she had responded in person. Twenty years before she had written a temperately worded letter to a newspaper defending herself from the charge of plagiarism and found herself accused of Billingsgate behaviour. Now she went to great lengths to conceal her part in Elton's and Whalley's pamphlets. This was duplicitous, of course, but the subterfuge was forced on her by gender conventions that damned a woman if she kept silent and damned her still more if she defended herself. Her reticence did not protect her from the slurs of her opponents. Neither did the law. At various times both Wilberforce and Thornton considered consulting Sir Vicary Gibbs, the recorder of Bristol, but the thought of legal action had to be dropped; the result was too uncertain and the airing of the various libels would only add to her distress.[92]

The hostile pamphlets gleefully used a range of negative stereotypes of women. More was one of Macbeth's witches, 'Scipio in petticoats', a 'silly woman', 'Pope Joan'. Even the conventionally feminine aspects of her work were ridiculed, as in the description of Hannah and Patty More 'placing themselves under the Gothick arch of the Church porch and as the children pass in procession, give each the pious pat on the head and exclaim, "there are my *Dears*! there is my *Goody*!"'[93] The most virulent of her critics was William Shaw, rector of Chelvey, whose *Life of Hannah More* was too strong even for the *Anti-Jacobin*. Rooting round for disreputable 'facts' in

[89] C. Daubeny, *Vindiciae Ecclesiae Anglicanae* (London and Bath, 1803), 23.
[90] Clark, Ann Kennicott to More, 12 June[?].
[91] Clark, Hannah More MSS box 12, More to Bowdler, fo. 18.
[92] Bodleian, MS d. 16, fo. 1, Wilberforce to More, 11 Dec. 1801; *Journals of Whalley*, ii. 211–14.
[93] Bere, *Appeal to the Public*, 6; id., *An Address to Mrs Hannah More*, 5; Spencer, *Truths Respecting Meeting Houses*, 64, 49.

the manner of a modern tabloid journalist, he invented a racy youth and moved on to what seems like an accusation of prostitution—the client being, presumably, her former fiancé, William Turner.

About this time Miss H. More was attending the play-houses, picking up all the knowledge she could meet with, to qualify herself for a play-wright. She had, it is said, more than one offer of matrimony. A gentleman on the stage made her proposals . . . but his troops decamping, on his departure with them, a sea-Captain next presented himself. During the sailor's visits, and while his vessel was preparing for her voyage, a man of good fortune made his appearance, and being dressed in a red coat, always ensnaring to the female heart, every attention was paid him, and love obtained an easy victory; but after a long and tedious courtship, whether owing to her violence of temper, or to what cause I have not been able to discover, it ended in a separation . . . It was at this time, too, she met with an advantageous bargain, by purchasing an annuity of 200*l* a year for her life, at *a very easy rate*.[94]

Her alleged defeat was compared to a rape: 'The Curate has . . . *laid Miss Hannah on her back*, on the couch of reason and argument.'[95] The innuendo set the tone for further comments. Possibly tongue-in-cheek, in the late summer of 1801 *The Times* reported her 'marriage' to Crossman and composed an epigram to celebrate the event.

> Spotless she liv'd till past three score;
> But now poor HANNAH is no MORE.[96]

Ten days later, after the harm had been done, it published a facetious retraction: 'The marriage of Miss HANNAH MORE appears to be no more than a consummation devoutly to be wished.'[97] 'My enemies have left off worrying me and are fallen upon Hannah More,' Hester Piozzi observed, half-sympathetic, half-relieved.[98] The fact that More was a woman moving out of her proper sphere (Daubeny's 'Diana of the Ephesians'[99]) undoubtedly roused her enemies to special venom, and might well have prolonged the controversy. It might lie behind the wildest accusation of all (though it was only made verbally) that she was implicated with Charlotte Corday in the assassination of Marat.[100] As a tactic, however, it backfired, and the crude sexism enabled Whalley to ask Bere, 'Is such persevering, such obdurate vengeance towards a *woman* worthy of a *man*?'[101]

---

[94] [Shaw] *Life of Hannah More*, 22. [95] Ibid. 104.

[96] *The Times*, 25 Aug., 2 Sept. 1801. [97] Ibid., 12 Sept. 1801.

[98] H. L. Piozzi, *The Piozzi Letters*, ed. E. A. Bloom and L. D. Bloom (Newark, Del., and London, 1989–93), iii. 327.

[99] Boucher Papers, B/5/11.

[100] H. Thompson, *The Life of Hannah More* (London, 1938), 193–4.

[101] Whalley, *Animadversions*, 45.

As the assaults became ever wilder and more spiteful, the reading public became first disgusted then bored with a controversy that, as Lewis Bagot, bishop of St Asaph, in Shakespearean vein told Mrs Piozzi was 'Sour, *Stale, flat and unprofitable*'.[102] Towards the end of 1801 it acquired a further political dimension when it became tied up with the debate on the peace negotiations with France. The *Anti-Jacobin*, Cobbett, and Windham saw a clear link between the activities of More and the search for peace at any price: both warmly supported by Wilberforce, both part of the same threat to the establishment. Their attitudes emerge from a letter from Windham to Randolph on 9 March 1802.

I have been a great admirer ... of the writings of Mrs. H. Moore [*sic*] ... But I must confess my whole opinion is changed, as to the character and tendency of her labours; nor have I ever beheld with a favourable eye the progress of the sect, to which I now find, more than I had ever before supposed, that she may be considered as belonging.

The state of public affairs is as bad as it is possible to be, so much so, that if I am to speak fairly my opinion, the country is going apace ... into the state of a province to France.[103]

The juxtaposition of the Blagdon controversy and the Treaty of Amiens (only two weeks away from finalization) in Windham's mind says much about the conspiratorial agenda of More's most implacable opponents. But most of the public now seemed ready to accept Sunday schools along with peace, and all the bishops except Horsley voted for the Treaty. The *Anti-Jacobin* found itself temporarily out on a limb, Windham lost his Norwich seat in the June general election, while, in the previous October, Cobbett's windows had been broken by the peace-loving mob. In August 1802 the *Anti-Jacobin* backtracked, and launched a fierce attack on William Shaw's 'worthless' pamphlet.[104] By this time, anyway, both More and Bere were ill with nervous exhaustion. There was no way the controversy could develop, and so it fizzled out. But the issues behind Blagdon had not gone away, and they were to resurface in 1804 in the debate on the Bible Society, when, with Anglicans and Dissenters controversially co-operating, the High Church was able to present a more united front. There was more trouble to come, but never again would Hannah More be so painfully exposed to such opprobrium.

As if More did not have enough on her plate in 1801 she was also involved in the time-consuming, stressful, and expensive process of moving house.

---

[102] *Journals of Whalley*, ii. 201; *Piozzi Letters*, iii. 336.
[103] Bodleian, MS d. 14, fo. 329. Windham's half-brother George Lukin was dean of Wells.
[104] *Anti-Jacobin*, 12 (1802), 444.

Cowslip Green, delightful as it was, was small and poorly insulated and, lying in a valley, it was prone to damp. Early in 1800 she bought some land about half a mile from Cowslip Green and called in the architects and the builders. The building began in April and the roof was ready by August, the progress helped by the fine weather.[105] Then everything began to go wrong, and, like most building projects, it cost more and took longer than had originally been expected. In the summer of 1801 the builder died, without leaving any accounts, forcing her into the expensive and time-consuming process of having the land and building materials revalued. As a result, she speculated gloomily to Mrs Garrick, 'it will be very well if you do not at last hear of my being in Prison for debt'.[106] (Prison was much on her mind at this time.) When she finally moved in late September, it was 'into a half finish'd house, about which we have had nothing but vexation, loss and disappointment'.[107] But with the move accomplished Cowslip Green, which still had four and a half years of its lease to run, was advertised in the newspapers.[108]

The teething troubles over at last, More grew to love Barley Wood, and to think of it as her earthly paradise.[109] It was built in the fashionable cottage style, two storeys high with a thatched roof and a wide veranda running round the first storey. It was sheltered by hills from the north-east winds, enabling More to grow a vine outside her bedroom window. The view from the west looked out over the Mendips to the Bristol Channel and the hills of south Wales beyond. There were nearly twenty acres of grounds, and in the spring of 1802 she found solace in spending more than she could afford in planting trees and shrubs. It was well supplied with bedrooms and rooms for servants, so for the first time she could provide accommodation for her friends without racking her brains about how they were to be put up. It remained her home, the place of pilgrimage for her many admiring visitors, until she was forced to leave it under sad circumstances in 1828.

For a while it looked as though she would be unable to benefit from the move, as for much of 1802 her friends and family thought her on the point of death. The illness was diagnosed as her recurrent ague, and the feverish symptoms were similar to those which followed the ending of her engagement to William Turner. She was shielded from news of the progress of the

---

[105] Folger, W.b. 488, fo. 16, More to Eva Garrick, 1 Aug. 1800.
[106] Ibid., fo. 21, More to Eva Garrick, 25 July 1801.
[107] Duke, More to Wilberforce, 17 Aug. 1801.
[108] See e.g. *Bath Chronicle*, 24 Sept. 1801.
[109] For Barley Wood, see P. Demers, *The World of Hannah More* (Lexington, Ky., 1996), 133; Thornton, Add. MS7674/1/N, fos. 638–9, Marianne Thornton to Laura Forster, 11 June 1857.

controversy, and her correspondence, a great torrent in 1800 and 1801, slowed to a trickle. In September 1802 Wilberforce wrote to ask her to contribute to the new Evangelical journal the *Christian Observer*, edited by Zachary Macaulay. He wanted from her 'some religious and moral novels, stories, tales, call 'em what you will'. Without her light touch, he believed, the work would sink under its own solemnity.[110] More's reply suggests a textbook case of depression.

I have been so batter'd daily and monthly for the last two years about the wicked-ness and bad tendency of my writings, that I have really lost all confidence in myself, and feel as if I never more cou'd write what any body wou'd read... I hesitate and procrastinate for days when I have even a common letter to write. I used to defy mere pain and sickness and found little difference when any thing was to be written whether I was well or ill. But the late disorders of the body have introduced new diseases into my mind, listlessness and misapplication, two words of which before I scarcely knew the meaning.[111]

Not wishing to leave her alone, her sisters let the Bath house and stayed with her for the winter.[112] There was no visit to London or Teston. Instead she spent the May of that year in Cheltenham and from that time her health began to improve.[113] Such was the essential resilience of her temperament that by the summer she was bouncing back. If she could not yet write for the *Christian Observer*, she could see where it was going wrong and give Henry Thornton hints on how to improve it.[114] One fine late afternoon in October the Thorntons and little Marianne descended on Barley Wood, their first visit to the new house. They were greeted with joy, though Mary More was somewhat put out because the guests insisted on sharing the remains of the sisters' dinner rather than wait 'till two beautiful fowls were boiled'. Mrs Thornton was delighted at what she found.

They all seemed so well & hale & stout sitting all in the evening with the street door open & a very small fire, that I looked at them till I began to suspect that all this mighty cavil about Mr Bere etc. had been a dream. Hannah More looks far better than ever & Patty about ten years younger than when we last saw them. Sally was rather hoarse but abounding in bon mots—poor Betty was silent & Madame [Mary] very attentive to us all...H. More never mentioned her past troubles, but she as well as the rest were very eager about politics. Sally whispered to me that Hannah had made a new conquest. The young Duke of Cumberland who is on military duty at Bristol is become quite enamoured & raves about her.[115]

[110] *Life of Wilberforce*, iii. 66–7.   [111] Duke, More to Wilberforce, 10 Sept. 1802.
[112] Pierpont Morgan Library, New York, Misc. Eng. MA 3751, More to Eva Garrick, 31 Jan. [1803].
[113] *Gambier*, i. 391.
[114] Thornton, Add. MS7674/1/L3, fo. 89, Thornton to More, 9 Sept. 1803.
[115] Thornton, Add. MS7674/1/L3, fos. 93–6, Mrs H. Thornton to Mrs R. Thornton, 14 Oct. 1803.

There were clouds as well. The king's son, the unsavoury duke of Cumberland (an unlikely beau for an Evangelical spinster), was in the neighbourhood because the fragile peace with France had ended, and he had been appointed general of the Severn district. The telegraphs and beacons sprouting on the high hills of Somerset and south Wales were constant reminders that the Bristol Channel lay open to invasion.[116] To rally the newly formed Somerset Volunteers, More had composed some 'merrily loyal' songs, 'The Ploughman's Ditty' and 'Will Chip's *True* Rights of Man', which argued that the poor had nothing to gain and everything to lose from 'Boni's' landing.[117] In November the sisters patriotically offered to give up Barley Wood to the officers at Bristol and were guiltily relieved to receive a friendly refusal. They continued to be anxious, however. As More told Mrs Garrick early in 1804, 'We are so near the Coast, that we are under apprehensions of the French landing within sight of our Windows. We have however, *at last* obtained from the Government a man of war which we have the comfort of being able to see from our chambers tho at the distance of 7 or 8 miles.'[118]

Meanwhile, Drewitt, the faithful curate of Cheddar, had died in October 1803, to be followed in November by the ailing Dr Crossman; a couple of sour little notices in the *Orthodox Churchman's Magazine* were reminders of their roles in the Blagdon controversy.[119] The wounds were healing, but some could not resist picking at the scabs. In the following years Hannah More brooded over her ordeal and learned to discern a divine purpose behind her sufferings. In a moving passage in *Practical Piety* published in 1811 she ventured uncharacteristically into autobiography.

By a life of activity and usefulness, you had perhaps attracted the public esteem. An animal activity had partly stimulated your exertions. The love of reputation begins to mix itself with your better motives . . . It is a delicious poison which begins to infuse itself into your purest cup . . . He who sees your heart, as well as your works, mercifully snatches you from the perils of prosperity. Malice is awakened. Your most meritorious actions are ascribed to the most corrupt motives. You are attacked where your character is least vulnerable. The enemies whom your success raised up, are raised up by God, less to punish than to save you . . . Your fame was too dear to you . . . It must be offered up . . . He makes us feel our weakness, that we may have recourse to his strength, he makes us sensible of our hitherto unperceived sins, that we may take refuge in his everlasting compassion.[120]

---

[116] *FFBJ*, 23 July 1803.

[117] Roberts, iii. 196–7; Clark, Ann Kennicott to More, 26 Dec. [1803]; *Works* (London, 1818), i. 316–24.

[118] Folger, W.b. 488, fo. 22, More to Eva Garrick, 21 Jan. 1804.

[119] *Orthodox Churchman's Magazine*, 6 (1803), 62–3; 7 (1804), 227–8.

[120] *Practical Piety; or, The Influence of the Religion of the Heart on the Conduct of the Life* (London, 1811), i. 181–4.

The Blagdon Controversy

To More's biographer the Blagdon controversy, more than any other episode in her career, highlights the ambiguities of her conservatism. How many other loyalists of the period believed themselves in danger (however remote) of being imprisoned for sedition? It also reveals two important aspects of her work in the Mendips. Given a free hand, she worked energetically to spread the Evangelical message and to promote 'gospel' preachers in a way that alarmed many in the political and religious mainstream who did not share her theological views. On the other hand, when she found herself in a tight corner, she was flexibly prepared to seek the support of High Churchmen and to underplay the more controversial aspects of her programme. The controversy also reveals something that is hard to recover at this distance of time, but was nevertheless vital: the fact that more people liked her than disliked her, and that she had a network of friends and supporters, built up over many years, ready to hand when she needed them.

She was greatly helped by the fact that the principle of lower-class instruction, which had long been supported by many influential clerics, was now firmly established even among the most conservative. In this climate the remaining Mendip schools, prudently purged of any taint of Methodism, survived and flourished. On More's death in 1833 the Cheddar school was rehoused in a new and larger building and developed into a weekday school on the lines of those established by the National Society. The Shipham school was also rehoused, though Nailsea continued on its existing site. Both became national schools, and in the twentieth century were absorbed into the state system.[121] By the simple criterion of survival, the More sisters' achievement was extraordinary.

Observers certainly believed that they were witnessing something remarkable. The accounts of the school given by More's Evangelical admirers[122] may be taken as *parti pris*, but others were equally impressed. A visitor to Cheddar in 1797 found 300 children in attendance at the church (a figure confirmed by Barbara Wilberforce's description of the Cheddar church as 'full to overflowing').[123] He noted that the children answered questions and behaved well both in school and in church, while in the evening the farm servants came in from milking the cows, 'not ashamed to . . . give answers along with the children'. This visitor was typical of the many who came out of curiosity, and his enthusiastic praise helps to explain why most Churchmen were reluctant to attack a figure as respected as Hannah More over the increasingly uncontroversial issue of Sunday schools.

[121] P. Belham, 'The Origins of Elementary Education in Somerset', MA thesis, Bristol University, 1953, 242–3, 235–44, 250.

[122] See *Of the Education of the Poor; being the first part of a Digest of the Reports of the Society for Bettering the Condition of the Poor* (London, 1809), 112–21.

[123] *Gentleman's Magazine*, 68 (1798), 292; Bodleian, MS d. 20, fo. 34.

The favourable comments about the Mendip schools were a reflection of a developing consensus. In the early nineteenth century the (Dissenting) British and Foreign Schools Society and the (Anglican) National Society founded schools on the monitorial system, which taught writing and mathematics as well as reading. Towards the end of her life More was uneasy over what she saw as the extravagant and unrealistic plans of the 'ultra-educationists' to teach 'fine arts and professional sciences'. She told Wilberforce, 'It is in my poor judgment preposterous to think of making labouring men profound Historians, Philosophers &c—if they could find the money, where would they find the time?'[124] But she had played her part in creating a climate in which such advanced views could be promulgated.

This then was her fundamental ambiguity, a point her enemies seized on and grossly distorted. Her attempt to carry out what was in effect a programme of cultural transformation at a time of war, paranoia, and religious division had been shown to be fraught with dangers. Her agenda was indisputably conservative. But though she deplored ambitious schemes for the education of the poor, she had introduced them to the written culture, stimulated their minds, and awakened their religious energies. Her aim was to create a spiritual elite in the midst of a social hierarchy, to bring about a new meritocracy while sustaining the existing political order. She wanted to change people's lives at a time when the very suggestion of change carried with it the implications of subversion. She used 'worthy' clergymen as her allies, but where she believed the parish clergy to be inadequate for the task, she paid no more than lip-service to their authority. However unjust the bulk of the accusations against her, however scurrilous the hostile propaganda, she had laid herself open to attack, and it is not surprising, therefore, that her most venomous enemies were to be found on the political right, and within her own Church.

---

[124] Bodleian, MS c. 48, fos. 29–30, More to Wilberforce [1820]. She was referring to *An Essay on the Evils of Popular Ignorance* (London, 1820), written by the radical Baptist John Foster, 'whom however, I greatly admire'. The admiration was mutual. See Jones, *Hannah More*, 216.

Chapter 12

The Princess and the Bachelor
1801–*c*.1809

WITH the winding down of the Blagdon controversy and her recovery from her long illness, More's life entered its last phase. However, this was no slow descent into old age. She was now in her late fifties, worn out, and with her reputation dented and her confidence shattered, yet within a few years she had bounced back and recovered much of her drive and determination. In the following decade she was to forge two new careers, as a writer of political theory and a novelist; and at the same time she continued with her schools and clubs, and devoted as much time as ever to maintaining her friendships. Her relationship with her sisters, especially Patty, was now all-important. Their ties with Bath were becoming more tenuous, and at the end of February 1804 they sold the Great Pulteney Street house and moved permanently into Barley Wood, where they were to remain until one by one they died and were buried in the churchyard at Wrington.[1]

It says much for Hannah More's essential resilience that even while the Blagdon storm was raging round her, she found the time and the energy not only to move house but also to supervise the publication of a handsomely bound eight-volume edition of her works that came out in 1801. The most controversial aspect of this publication was the long preface to the third volume, in which, in 'a candid declaration of my altered view', she rejected the theatre that had made her famous, and decried the pernicious influence on the young of 'the feeling, fiery hero' (her own Percy?), and the heroine

---

[1] Roberts, iii. 215–16.

'who is able to love with so much violence and so much purity at the same time' (Elwina?).[2] But she paid the theatre a backhanded compliment by declaring that it was 'by universal concurrence allowed to be no *indifferent* thing. The impressions it makes on the mind are...deeper and stronger than are made by any other amusement.'[3] However suspect as a generalization, this was a revealing piece of autobiography. For her, the theatre's powerfully addictive properties meant there could be no half measures; as Johnson had told her when she urged him to take a little wine, 'I can't drink a *little*, child, therefore I never touch it.'[4]

But the past could not be undone and old friends could not be disowned. She risked ruining her argument by inserting a footnote praising Garrick for doing so much to purify the stage, and, in an effort to keep a flagging friendship going, she continued to write about the theatre to his widow.[5] Her refusal to dissociate herself completely from her early associations might have raised eyebrows among her Evangelical friends. A few years earlier John Newton had solemnly told a gathering of his fellow Evangelical clergyman that her innocuous *Sacred Dramas* 'have done injury. They have associated an idea of innocence with the drama. I know two young men now on the stage in consequence of being taught to act in Mrs. M.'s sacred dramas.'[6] Though she believed she was steering a middle way between support for the theatre and an Evangelical tendency to reject all imaginative literature out of hand, she laid herself open to the accusation of inconsistency, and compounded the charge by allowing her plays to be published in this volume: a fact seized on by her most strident Blagdon enemy, who crowed that her name 'will continue to stink in the nostrils of all consistent, honest persons'.[7] Straddling playwriting past and Evangelical present, she was in danger of pleasing no one.

The publication of the *Collected Works* was the last burst of energy before More's long collapse into illness, a period of inactivity relieved only by occasional hospitality, the publication of her loyalist songs, and her appointment (along with Sally) as executrix of the will of Chatterton's sister Mary Newton, and the guardian of her daughter Mary Ann, then aged 20.[8] But at the beginning of 1804, though 'tormented with rheumatism in my face and head',[9] she came to life again. In February she sent Zachary Macaulay an

[2] *Works* (1801), iii. 2-3, 33, 37-8.   [3] Ibid. 51.   [4] Roberts, i. 251.

[5] *Works*, iii. 9 n.; New York Public Library, Berg Collection of English and American Literature, 222811B, More to Eva Garrick, 22 Nov. [1804]; BL, Add. MS42511, fos. 9–10, More to Eva Garrick, 1 Jan. 1806.

[6] J. H. Pratt (ed.), *Eclectic Notes; or, Notes of Discussions on Religious Topics at the Meetings of the Eclectic Society, London, during the Years 1798–1814* (London, 1856), 158.

[7] [W. Shaw] *The Life of Hannah More* (London, 1802), 39.

[8] E. H. W. Meyerstein, *A Life of Thomas Chatterton* (London, [1930]), 495.

[9] Folger, W.b. 488, fo. 22, More to Eva Garrick, 21 Jan. 1806.

article for the *Christian Observer* as a belated response to Wilberforce's plea that she help to liven up the magazine's stodgy worthiness. She told Macaulay that it was written with some difficulty: 'Writing is becoming very irksome to me, and I cannot sit at it as I used to,' and, fearful of her reputation following the Blagdon controversy, she insisted on anonymity.[10] 'Hints towards Forming a Bill for the Abolition of the White Female Slave Trade in the Cities of London and Westminster' by 'An Enemy to All Slavery' appeared in the March issue, a spirited little attack on the despotism of the 'arbitrary, universal tyrant... FASHION', which relied for its satirical force on the language of abolitionism.[11] This retread of the arguments she had already expounded in *Strictures* once again set More at odds with the world of public entertainments which had opened up to women in the Georgian period. She was part of the new puritanism steadily gaining ground in the wake of the French Revolution, which urged women to turn their backs on the allurements of the ball and the pleasure garden and find their vocations in the duties of home and the expanding world of philanthropy. As will be shown, this message was not as restrictive as it might seem; it was an invitation not for seclusion or confinement but for a different type of public activity. It is no accident, therefore, that in the same year in which she published this critique of the world of genteel pleasures, Hannah More embarked on her most innovatory excursion into the public sphere.

In the summer of 1804 many who read the newspapers or listened to the gossip emanating from Windsor were reflecting on the fate of a child whose life was so privileged in one respect and so unenviable in another. The 8-year-old Princess Charlotte, the daughter of the prince of Wales and his eccentric wife, Caroline of Brunswick, was a strong-willed little girl, whose short life had been dominated by the collapse of her parents' calamitous marriage. As reconciliation was unthinkable, and there was little prospect of a brother to displace her from the succession, it was reasonable to assume that she would one day be queen. For this reason, her grandfather George III, insisting that her education 'cannot be alone that of a female, but she being the presumptive heir of the Crown must have one of a more extended nature', proposed that the child should in future live at Windsor rather than with her father, whom he clearly thought an unsuitable parent.[12] After lengthy negotiations, conducted through mediators as the king and prince were not on speaking terms, it was agreed that Charlotte should live half the year at Windsor with her grandfather and the other half at Warwick House

---

[10] Huntington, MY 672, More to Zachary Macaulay, 16 Feb. [1804, catalogued *c*.1816?].

[11] *Christian Observer*, 3 (Mar. 1804), 151–4.

[12] *The Correspondence of George, Prince of Wales, 1770–1812*, ed. A. Aspinall (London, 1968), v. 138.

with her father. At the same time the princess's governess, the gentle Lady Elgin, was to retire and the search was on for a younger, more assertive preceptor.[13]

More learned of all this, partly through the newspapers, but mainly through Ann Kennicott, who was now spending part of every year at Windsor. The news must have carried her mind back to the morning in the spring of 1799 when she and Porteus had called on Lady Elgin at Carlton House, where they had met the little princess. She had eagerly shown them round the palace, opening drawers and uncovering curtains and furniture, and More had been delighted with her character, finding her 'wild and natural, but sensible, lively, and civil'.[14] Now, her heart went out to her, the child of a broken marriage, the focus of disputes within a dysfunctional family. Not only was her own happiness at risk, but (More believed), if, as a result of faulty education, she turned out badly, this would be a tragedy for her future subjects, who would naturally look to her for an example. How was the child to be rescued? There was only one way she knew. In early March an unspecified person—probably Dr Robert Gray, biblical scholar and prebendary of Durham—urged her to write a pamphlet on 'the education of a certain royal personage'.[15] As usual, she declared her reluctance, but by the late summer she was in full flow over the manuscript of something far more ambitious than a mere pamphlet. She was audaciously embarking on the prestigious genre of advice books to princes, a humanist project associated with Machiavelli, Erasmus, and Rabelais, and in the early eighteenth century with Bolingbroke's *Patriot King*; more recently Catharine Macaulay had included a short section entitled 'Hints towards the Education of a Prince' in her *Letters on Education* (1790).[16] But the example most in her mind was *Télémaque* (1699), written for Louis XIV's grandson the duc de Bourgogne by the distinguished French ecclesiastic François de Salignac de la Mothe Fénelon, bishop of Cambrai. Living under an absolute monarch, Fénelon, a prominent opponent of Louis XIV, had to phrase his advice and criticisms in an allegory. As a citizen of a free country, More could speak more plainly, though as a woman venturing into a male world, a woman moreover whose enemies had done their best to destroy her, she was determined to publish anonymously.

While the book was in progress in the autumn of 1804, she was entertaining a guest who was to have much influence on the finished product. This was an intense and charismatic Irish layman, Alexander Knox, who, after a

---

[13] C. Hibbert, *George IV* (Harmondsworth, 1976), 266–71; T. Holme, *Prinny's Daughter: A Biography of Princess Charlotte of Wales* (London, 1976), 52–3; F. Fraser, *The Unruly Queen: The Life of Queen Caroline* (London, 1996), 142–6.

[14] Roberts, iii. 105.   [15] Ibid. iii. 216–17; Clark, More to Ann Kennicott, 11 Jan. 1805.

[16] C. Macaulay [Graham], *Letters on Education* (London, 1790), 223–34.

brief flirtation with the United Irishmen, had been private secretary to Lord Castlereagh when he was chief secretary for Ireland. They had first met at the beginning of 1800 and had taken to each other immediately. (He thought her Blagdon persecution 'a *national disgrace*'.[17]) Theologically and temperamentally he was at the opposite pole from More. An epileptic and a depressive, he had turned his back on politics and had retired from the world. Though the child of Methodist parents, he was, on his own admission, 'a primitive Churchman' who loved 'Episcopacy, the surplice, festivals, the communion table set altar-wise, antiphonal devotions'.[18] 'He is not in all points our way,' More told Wilberforce, which was understating the case.[19] Between them they made an unlikely couple: Mary and Martha, the nervous contemplative and the bustling activist, the High Church Platonist and the practical Evangelical. But she admired, though she could not emulate, his mystical spirituality, and he thought her 'a most extraordinary person; such as I am sure is not in the world again'.[20] Knox seems to have sought out More in order to gain an entrance into the Evangelical world, partly to move it in a more High Church direction, partly to convert the parliamentary Claphamites to the cause of Catholic emancipation. But if she was useful to him, he was equally helpful to her. She intended to write about the Church of England, and with Archdeacon Daubeny, '*the High Church Dragon*',[21] an imaginary presence at her shoulder, she needed the imprimatur of someone with impeccably Orthodox credentials.

In September she sent drafts of the manuscript to Wilberforce, then on holiday at Lyme in Dorset.[22] Though plagued with stomach complaints, she was writing quickly out of a sense of urgency.

I know how desirable it is that I shou'd take more time to finish it, but when you consider the state of things, there is not a month to be lost—The poor child is going on most miserably, and the change talk'd of is likely to be from bad to worse—much worse—the D[uche]ss of Devon[shire] being actually talked of by the unworthy Father as the next Directress—God forbid it shou'd really be so. I have little expectations but that my attempt will be scanted—But it will be a duty done.[23]

[17] Roberts, iii. 162.

[18] A. Knox, *Remains* (London, 1837), iv. 207. See also *Thirty Years' Correspondence between John Jebb and Alexander Knox*, ed. C. Forster (London, 1836); J. T. A. Gunstone, 'Alexander Knox, 1757–1831', *Church Quarterly Review*, 157 (1956), 463–75; G. T. Stokes, 'Alexander Knox and the Oxford Movement', *Contemporary Review*, 3 (1887), 184–205. I am grateful to Dr Peter Nockles for allowing me to see his article on Knox for the forthcoming *New Dictionary of National Biography*.

[19] Bodleian, MS d. 15, fo. 71, More to Wilberforce, 24 Sept. 1804; for Knox's input into the *Hints towards Forming the Character of a Young Princess*, see Clark, More–Knox correspondence for 1805; Duke, More to Wilberforce 'Thursday Morn' [Nov. 1804].

[20] Knox, *Remains*, iv. 168.   [21] Clark, More to Knox, 6 Jan. 1805.

[22] Bodleian, MS d. 16, fo. 28; Wilberforce to More, 15 Sept. 1804.

[23] Bodleian, MS d. 15, fo. 70, More to Wilberforce, 24 Sept. 1804.

The chapters were delivered to Wilberforce via an unreliable carter, causing More much nervous anxiety. In the meantime she confounded some of her critics by spending a few days with Bishop Beadon at Wells, though, as she told Wilberforce, 'it was running my head into a very hornet's nest.—My sworn enemies however kept aloof, but my visit I heard caused great speculation in the Chapter and it was said that I had won over the new Bishop as I had done the old one.'[24] No wonder she felt she needed Knox.

The two-volume disquisition entitled *Hints towards Forming the Character of a Young Princess* came out in the early spring of 1805. More told Ann Kennicott, 'I have avoided the word *Education* in the title because we have been Educated to Death by so many books on the subject.'[25] By the time the book appeared, a new governess had been found (not the duchess of Devonshire) and a tutor had been appointed, Dr John Fisher, bishop of Exeter. He was not an Evangelical, but as vice-president of the Bible Society he was an ecclesiastic to More's liking, and when the second edition came out, she gained his permission to add a prefatory letter apologizing for her presumption.[26] In the main preface she excused her trespass into such novel territory: 'Had the Royal Pupil been a Prince, these Hints would never have been intruded on the world, as it would then have been naturally assumed that the established plan usually adopted in such cases would have been pursued.'[27] But having got the self-deprecation out of the way she launched into patriotic hyperbole. With Bonaparte, the newly crowned emperor, a looming presence across the Channel, 'one of the most momentous concerns which can engage the attention of an Englishman, who feels for his country like a patriot' must be the education of Princess Charlotte, a 'providentially distinguished female' who would one day be responsible for the well-being and happiness of 'millions'.[28]

If this seems an unrealistically high view of monarchy in the early nineteenth century, More was also concerned to keep the royal feet firmly on the ground. A prince should learn 'that the dignity being hereditary, he is the more manifestly raised to that elevation, not by his own merit, but by providential destination; by those laws, which he is himself to observe with the same religious fidelity as the meanest of his subjects'.[29] There is no

[24] Duke, More to Wilberforce, 10 Oct. [1804].

[25] Clark, More to Ann Kennicott, 11 Jan. 1805. For an earlier version of the following discussion, see A. Stott, 'Patriotism and Providence: The Politics of Hannah More', in K. Gleadle and S. Richardson (eds.), *Women in British Politics, 1760–1860* (Basingstoke, 2000), 39–55.

[26] *Hints towards Forming the Character of a Young Princess* (London, 1805), vol. i, pp. v–vii.

[27] Ibid., p. xii.

[28] Ibid., pp. ix–x, 9. For a discussion *Hints*, see S. C. Behrendt, *Royal Mourning and Regency Culture: Elegies and Memorials of Princess Charlotte* (Basingstoke, 1997), 47–59.

[29] Ibid. 42.

divine right of kings here. The *Hints* was a conservative Whig celebration of the limited monarchy and the balanced constitution, 'that temperament of monarchic, aristocratic, and popular rule' which More believed had come in with the Glorious Revolution.[30] Such an interpretation of the events of 1688 set her apart from Tories, with their grudging acceptance of the Revolution, and from radical Whigs such as Catharine Macaulay, who detested William III as the man who betrayed the liberties of the people.[31] But though she never came remotely near Macaulay's republicanism, she was anxious to stress the limited nature of the post-Revolution monarchy, warning Charlotte in one Lockean passage that 'a bold oppressor of the people, the people would not endure. A violent infringer of the constitution, the parliament would not tolerate.'[32] It was the same ideology she had set out in *Village Politics* when Jack Anvil had assured Tom Hod that even the king could not send them to prison. As well as stressing the limited nature of monarchical power, More was dismissive of the ceremonial trappings of the office: 'in themselves they are of little value... beneath the attachment of a rational, and of no substantial use to a mortal being'.[33] A ruler was important not because he wielded immense political powers but because he was, as Henry V told Princess Catherine, 'the maker of manners', setting the tone for the whole nation.[34]

With this in mind, More set out a guide for Charlotte's reading, and the unbookish princess was given a long list of favoured authors including Plutarch, Clarendon, and Fénelon. For lighter reading she was guided to Addison's essays, where a whiggish ideology was set out in a form devoid of overt party spirit, but warned off Hume because of his religious scepticism.[35] In order to gain a true view of the providential direction of English history, Charlotte needed to turn instead to the shining examples of two previous monarchs, Alfred and Elizabeth, from whose example she would learn to be, as the whiggish *Monthly Review* noted approvingly, 'a patriot Princess'.[36] More was continuing the attempts she had made in *Village Politics* and the later editions of *Slavery* to turn the previously oppositional language of patriotism into a celebration of a providentially chosen nation: a message that could be traced back to the Venerable Bede but which had acquired new urgency at a time of revolution and war.[37]

---

[30] Ibid. ii. 327–8.
[31] See J. G. A. Pocock, 'Catharine Macaulay: Patriot Historian', in H. L. Smith (ed.), *Women Writers and the Early Modern British Political Tradition* (Cambridge, 1998), 243–58.
[32] *Hints to a Princess*, i. 264.   [33] Ibid. 43.   [34] Ibid. ii. 51.   [35] Ibid. i. 154–61.
[36] *Monthly Review*, 47 (1805), 180. For the cult of Alfred, see G. Newman, *The Rise of English Nationalism: A Cultural History, 1740–1830* (London, 1987), 189–91; C. A. Simmons, *Reversing the Conquest: History and Myth in Nineteenth-Century British Literature* (New Brunswick, NJ, 1990).
[37] For Bede and English nationhood, see A. Hastings, *The Construction of Nationhood: Ethnicity, Religion and Nationalism* (Cambridge, 1997), 36–9.

It was that goodness which made us an island, that laid the foundation of our national happiness...Thus, then, we behold ourselves raised as a nation above all the nations of the earth, by that very circumstance which made our country be regarded, two thousand years ago, only as a receptacle for the refuse of the Roman Empire![38]

The most original part of the book lay in its celebration of the providential singling out of female sovereigns, a strategy that allowed More to feminize political discourse in a way not open to classic republicanism, where the virtuous citizen was defined as a male. She set out her message through two contrasting pairs of sisters: the wise and tolerant Elizabeth, a great queen in spite of her faults, and her sister, 'the bigot', Mary Tudor; the pious Mary II, and the 'much less impressive' Anne, whose 'good qualities' were better fitted for private life than the throne.[39] She paid tribute to Elizabeth's policy of toleration and her shrewd choice of ministers, 'the characteristic mark of a sagacious sovereign'.[40] Even more exemplary was Mary II. Following the argument of Gilbert Burnet's *History*, she declared that her marriage to William of Orange was appointed by Providence 'to protect our liberties', and that her character, 'strictly and habitually devout amid all the temptations of a court', was as important as her dynastic role.[41] Though she could discern a providence in Queen Anne's dependence on the duchess of Marlborough, she wanted Charlotte to be a more positive force for good, and Mary II, the reformer of manners and patron of the Church, suited her purposes perfectly. She was the ultimate role model for the young princess, proof that in a monarchy that allowed female succession, Providence singled out women as well as men; proof too that the private virtues of a woman ruler were a public benefit to her country. More's survey of recent history virtually ignored kings and princes. She focused instead on the electress Sophia, providentially chosen from her dispossessed and scattered family to be the mother of the first Hanoverian king, and on George II's wife, Caroline of Ansbach, the skilful politician and conscientious ecclesiastical patron, who had turned down the future emperor rather than abandon her faith.[42] These royal women, set apart for a high purpose, were part of the necessary myth of patriotic Protestantism.

Towards the end of the second volume More launched into a panegyric of the Church of England, which Charlotte was to head, in which she defended the institution of a visible Church and a religious establishment and

[38] *Hints to a Princess*, ii. 331.
[39] Ibid. i. 180; ii. 366–8. For Mary, see L. Schwoerer, 'Images of Queen Mary II, 1689–95', *Renaissance Quarterly*, 42 (1989), 82–101.
[40] *Hints to a Princess*, i. 178. [41] Ibid. ii. 366–7.
[42] Ibid. 268–74. For Caroline, see S. Taylor, 'Queen Caroline and the Church of England', in S. Taylor, R. Connors, and C. Jones (eds.), *Hanoverian Britain and Empire: Essays in Memory of Philip Lawson* (Woodbridge, 1998), 82–101.

described the Church of England as a *via media*; not, as Knox and later the Tractarians were to assert, between Rome and continental Protestantism, but between Lutheran ritual and Calvinist severity.[43] Its forms of worship united 'Christian liberty' with 'Christian sobriety'; its ethos was one of rational learning and sober piety rather than superstition and fanaticism.[44] The *Monthly Review* thought this part of the book at odds with the 'enlarged and liberal views' of the rest.[45] The *Christian Observer* hinted that More's Blagdon experiences had caused her to tone down her Evangelical sentiments; Knox, however, thought she had ignored the catholicity of the Church of England.[46] On the whole, though, More might have considered that she had now decisively mended her fences with the Church; she had gone as far as she could without compromising her Evangelicalism.

Though it never sold as well as the conduct books designed for a wider readership, the book was well received by the people who mattered most, the queen and the bishop of Exeter.[47] Poor Charlotte saw matters differently: 'The Bishop is here & reads with me for an hour or two every day from Mrs *Hanna* [*sic*] *More's* "Hints for forming the education of a Pss". This I believe is what makes me finde the hours so long. I *am not quite good enough* for that.'[48] She grew to detest her well-meaning mentor, and in one fit of teenage petulance (perhaps when he was reading More's book to her) she snatched his wig and threw it into the fire.[49] At about the same time Ann Kennicott was ruefully telling More, 'What Her Royal Highness's Education is in the material branches I know not, but her manners are not such as would be approved by the Authoress of the Hints.'[50] The sunny child was growing unmanageable, while the adults fought their battles around her. More observed this with sorrow, noted too Charlotte's steady preference for the Whig opposition (even when her father deserted them), but continued to hope for her, pray for her, and even to love her.

One good friend did not live to see the publication of the *Princess*. In February 1805 Frances Boscawen died, aged 86, and More was touched to learn that she had bequeathed her her edition of the works of the Jansenists, the dissident French Catholics she had always admired. The forty volumes of edifying reading occupied her all summer. She told Wilberforce that, 'popish fooleries' apart, they were superior in 'pithy learning and solidity to our methodistical writers... they are so *very* practical! so fathoming the human

---

[43] *Hints to a Princess*, ii. 302.   [44] Ibid. 309, 316–17.
[45] *Monthly Review*, 47 (1805), 189.
[46] *Christian Observer*, 4 (1805), 497–8; Knox, *Remains*, iv. 300–5; Forster, *Thirty Years' Correspondence*, i. 198–9.
[47] Roberts, iii. 223; Forster, *Thirty Years' Correspondence*, i. 197.
[48] A. Aspinall (ed.), *Letters of Princess Charlotte, 1811–1817* (London, 1949), 38.
[49] Hibbert, *George IV*, 318.   [50] Clark, Ann Kennicott to More, 13 July [1812].

heart'.[51] In other words, they shared the rigorous Evangelical moral code and their bleak view of unredeemed human nature. She was especially drawn to Pierre Nicole's minute attention to *'les petites morales*... —the domestic charities—conquests over temper—prejudices—petty indulgences—self-love &c'.[52] His correspondence with aristocratic ladies seemed to prefigure her own attempts to reform the fashionable world, and made him a kindred spirit.

The *Princess* was written against a particularly troubled background. The newly crowned emperor Napoleon intensified his plans for the invasion of England, and 150,000 men were assembled at Boulogne ready to cross the Channel. In the meantime, following Henry Addington's resignation in the spring of 1804, William Pitt was prime minister once more, though his second ministry was a shadow of the first. In April 1805 his government was shaken to its foundations when the Commons voted to impeach his closest political friend, his first lord of the Admiralty, the ambitious and powerful Scotsman Lord Melville, for alleged financial irregularities during his previous post as treasurer of the Navy. To Pitt's dismay, Wilberforce was one of those who voted for impeachment. The impeachment failed in the Lords in June 1807, but by then the career of 'this poor delinquent',[53] as Henry Thornton called him, was over. Once he had fallen, the Saints were free to feel compassion, but their belated sympathy did not still the voices of those who believed Wilberforce had self-righteously deserted his friend the prime minister when he most needed him.

To the delight of the Claphamites, the disgraced minister was replaced on 30 April 1805 by his 78-year-old cousin Sir Charles Middleton, long since retired from naval administration, and on 1 May he was elevated to the peerage as Lord Barham. By a fortunate chance, More was at Teston (immediately renamed Barham Court) when the news broke. She dashed off an exultant letter to Wilberforce: 'There is something so Providential in the whole History which he gave us last night. Strange! That the Plans which he has been forming for near twenty years, and had thrown aside in utter despair he shou'd now be called himself to put in Execution in the Plenitude of Power.'[54] This suggests that, like Churchill in 1940, Barham believed that his whole life had been a preparation for this moment. Pitt's gamble—if such it was—paid off, and Barham's instructions to his admirals during the tense spring and summer of 1805, when Nelson pursued Villeneuve across the Atlantic and back again, helped save the country from invasion.

---

[51] Duke, More to Wilberforce, Barley Wood, 16 Oct. [1805].
[52] *The Correspondence of William Wilberforce*, ed. R. I. and S. Wilberforce (London, 1840), ii. 129–30.
[53] Thornton, Add. MS 7674/1/L3, fo. 118, Mrs H. Thornton to More, 26 June 1805.
[54] Duke, More to Wilberforce, 'Barham Court, Alias Teston' [May 1805].

News of Nelson's victory and death at Trafalgar on 21 October reached the Admiralty in the early hours of 6 November. In January the country buried its greatest admiral with elaborate honours in St Paul's Cathedral, and his status as a popular hero was commemorated in paintings, engravings, and poems. More, who had dreaded a French invasion as much as anyone, was ungracious—even cynical—in her response to this extravagant mourning. Outraged that the credit was given to a notorious adulterer rather than to the all-wise Providence, she wrote to Wilberforce, 'They seem to me (with all my warmth on the Subject) to be exceeding the just bounds in the honours paid to Nelson—It is not a funeral but an Apotheosis.' In a flash of wicked irony, she added, 'However it will I hope encourage other great men to be shot.'[55] Wilberforce is unlikely to have shown this letter to Lord Barham.

Joy over Trafalgar was rapidly overshadowed by bleak news from Europe. In December 1805 Austria and Russia were heavily defeated at Austerlitz and the third of Pitt's anti-French coalitions was smashed. No wonder the More sisters, like so many others, were 'dismay'd about Continental affairs'.[56] Meanwhile, Pitt's fragile health collapsed, and his vital organs failed. Henry Thornton told More that he 'has grown very thin, has lost his voice & his stomach will only retain eggs & brandy twice a day'.[57] On the day he wrote these words on 23 January, Pitt died. Four days after the prime minister's death Wilberforce delivered a eulogy in the House and a month later was a banner-bearer at his funeral.

The passing of Pitt, 'the pilot that weathered the storm', ushered in a new political era, with momentous consequences for the Evangelicals in Parliament. The king reluctantly offered the premiership to Pitt's cousin (more recently his political opponent) Lord Grenville, knowing that this would mean the hated Fox's inclusion in the government as foreign secretary. The 'Ministry of all the Talents', which hardly lived up to its optimistic name, was a broadly based government, fundamentally Whig, but including the former prime minister, Addington, now Viscount Sidmouth, and More's old Blagdon adversary William Windham; Thomas Erskine, defender of Thomas Paine and Richard Vining Perry, became lord chancellor. For the Evangelicals, one great prize—the abolition of the slave trade—now seemed within their grasp, as both Grenville and Fox were abolitionists. But, with Sidmouth and Windham, not to mention the West Indian lobby, still adamantly opposed, the moves had to be planned carefully. The winning smoke and mirrors strategy was devised by Wilberforce, his brother-in-law James Stephen, and the heads of the Talents Ministry. A bill forbidding the import-

---

[55] Duke, More to Wilberforce, 1 Jan. 1806.   [56] Ibid.
[57] Thornton, Add. MS 7674/1/L3, fo. 144, Thornton to More, 23 Jan. 1806.

ation of slaves into captured enemy colonies and the fitting out of British ships to trade in slaves with foreign territories was craftily presented as a self-interested move, denying future commercial advantages to former enemy powers when the war ended. It was slipped through a thin House on 2 May and through the Lords on 16 May, with Wilberforce keeping well out of the way to disarm suspicions. When the bill became law, the slave trade was reduced by three-quarters, and much of its rationale had gone. On 10 June Fox made the abolitionist speech of his life, immediately supported by Wilberforce. But it was late in the session and Fox quickly became gravely ill. He died on 13 September, depriving the cause of its most powerful voice within the government.

In the autumn the Talents Ministry went to the country, winning the election handsomely; Wilberforce was returned for his Yorkshire constituency—the largest in the country. The victory strengthened Grenville's hand against the king, who had always supported the slave trade, and the way was now open for its abolition. The abolitionists left nothing to chance. Mrs Thornton told Patty More that they had hired a house in Downing Street and met every day armed with lists of members of Parliament to lobby.[58] In February the debate began in the Lords. The slave trade was defended by the duke of Clarence (the future William IV) but, to the delight of the Evangelicals, opposed by Maria Gloucester's son the new duke of Gloucester, who had succeeded to the title on his father's death in August 1805. The bill passed the Lords, and on 23 February the Commons approved the second reading by 283 to 16. In a stirring and emotional scene the House then gave Wilberforce a standing ovation, while he sat with head bowed, tears of joy pouring down his cheeks. On 16 March it passed its third reading unopposed.

In contrast to the high-profile role she had played twenty years earlier, Hannah More remained an observer on the sidelines. She had been confined to bed since the previous July, suffering from 'eight months of the most violent fever that almost any creature ever recovered from'. Though by March she could now 'creep about my Room with the aid of a Stick', she was still in great pain and had been 'bled and blister'd more than twenty times'.[59] But, sick though she was, and suffering from a weakness in her eye that made writing difficult, she sent an ecstatic letter to Wilberforce. 'The Lord is King—the hearts of men (Lords and all) are in *his* hand . . . God bless you!—What an honoured instrument has he made you in an event which involves the fate of millions.'[60]

---

[58] Thornton, Add. MS 7674/1/L4, fo. 1.
[59] Folger, W.b. 488, fo. 23, More to Eva Garrick, 20 Mar. 1807.
[60] Bodleian, MS d. 14, fo. 8, More to Wilberforce, n.d.

All was not over, as the slave trade was still carried on by the other European powers and slavery itself was not to be abolished within the British empire until 1833. But the first of the great humanitarian campaigns in British history had been fought and won. More rightly gave full credit to Wilberforce, but she could feel some legitimate satisfaction at having played her own role in this great event; she had done all that was possible for a woman to do.

By the time the Abolition Bill received the royal assent, the king had dismissed his ministers over their plan to grant some modest concessions to Roman Catholics. The new government was composed of ex-Pittites (increasingly prepared to call themselves Tories), headed by the duke of Portland, with the Evangelically inclined Spencer Perceval, chancellor of the exchequer. In the spring a general election was called, and both Wilberforce and Thornton had to fight hard to defend their seats.

Hannah More followed the fortunes of her two friends with see-sawing emotions. Henry Thornton's difficult campaign for Southwark was fought partly on the Catholic question, the running sore in British politics for the first quarter of the nineteenth century. His neutrality on the issue caused him to be hissed on the hustings, but his friends rallied round. Mrs Thornton, a shy woman just recovered from childbirth, forced herself to canvass the ladies, and by 11 May he was safely returned.[61] It was much harder for Wilberforce, who had to fight the most protracted and expensive campaign of his career.[62] Once Southwark was safe for Thornton, the Evangelicals rushed up to York, while Mrs Thornton held the fort at Battersea Rise.[63] At the same time Wilberforce's friends were setting up fund-raising committees throughout the country; in Bristol, where one committee was especially active, Sally and Patty More worked hard to raise contributions, and Hannah contributed £50.[64] When the result was declared on 4 June, Wilberforce topped the poll. More relapsed into her fever under the strain of it all. Writing to express 'the most thorough joy at your Catastrophe', she told Wilberforce that 'Other friends have felt for you perhaps as much with their *minds*, but I believe no one with their *bodies*. The Yorkshire Election really flushed back my Pulse again up to a hundred and my apothecary told me he shou'd send me double Doses of opium till the Contest was over.'[65] It was perhaps fortunate for her drug dependency that the election was not even more protracted.

---

[61] Thornton, Add. MS 7674/1/L4, fos. 11–18, Mrs H. Thornton to More, 11 May 1807.

[62] E. A. Smith, 'The Yorkshire Elections of 1806 and 1807: A Study in Electoral Management', *Northern History*, 2 (1967), 62–80.

[63] Thornton, Add. MS 7674/1/L4, fo. 23, Mrs H. Thornton to More, 25 May 1807.

[64] Ibid., fo. 31, Mrs H. Thornton to More [May 1807]; fo. 48, 9 July 1807.

[65] Wilberforce, Bodleian, MS c. 3, fo. 89.

In spite of her recovery, More was feeling her age. The death of Elizabeth Carter the previous year had severed another link with her past. In July 1807 the Porteuses paid a visit, but, as she told Mrs Thornton, it was 'a grief of heart to me to see the Bp. so reduced (nothing makes *me* thin)'. As for the Thorntons' suggestion that she go with them to Cheltenham, 'I should as soon think of going to Egypt—I sometimes question if I shall ever be a *loco-motive* animal again.'[66] In August the duchess of Gloucester died. 'I never had a warmer or more ardent friend,' she told Mrs Thornton, 'one that entered more zealously into my joys and sorrows. She always behaved as if I had been the Princess and she the nobody. I truly believe she was pious.' She added judiciously, with a discreet reference to the duchess's well-known marital unhappiness, 'Impetuosity was her fault—a fault to which for *certain reasons* I am apt to be tender.'[67] She was more conscious than ever that her life was closing in, admitting sadly to Sir William Pepys, 'I have never failed but this once to make my annual migration Eastward every Spring, yet my health has been so broken these last seven years that I have been forced to content myself with hovering about the vicinity of London, not having been able to pass a single night in it without a fresh attack of illness.'[68] Then at the end of December John Newton, her old spiritual mentor, died. He was 82 and the event had been long expected, but it confirmed the inexorable passage of time.

In June 1808, however, she was well enough to undertake 'a crawling tour to Weymouth', travelling at one stage a day. There she had the enormous pleasure of seeing one of her first pupils 'in full regimentals, acting as pay-master and sergeant-major!' and described by one of his officers as 'the greatest master of military tactics we have'.[69] Though she was too ill to attend the Shipham feast on her return, the numbers were as good as ever, while October saw the twentieth anniversary of the Cheddar school, now attended by the children of former pupils.[70] The school feasts and anniversaries were a constant in a world of flux. In the autumn the close network of Evangelicals round Clapham Common changed irrevocably with the depart-ure of the Wilberforces for a new house at Kensington Gore. For once More let slip her mask of discretion in order to complain of Barbara Wilberforce's 'want of decency...in not concealing her satisfaction at quitting a place so pleasant, so advantageous, so congenial to her husband'.[71]

---

[66] Clark, More to Mrs H. Thornton, 14 July [1807].
[67] Clark, More to Mrs H. Thornton, 12 Sept. 1807.
[68] Clark, More to Pepys, 14 Dec. 1807.
[69] Clark, More to Zachary Macaulay, 28 June 1808; Roberts, iii. 249.
[70] Roberts, iii. 249.
[71] Thornton, Add. MS 7674/1.E/2, More to Mrs H. Thornton, 5 Apr. [1808].

Meanwhile Britain's interminable war with France had entered a new phase with the revolt of the Spaniards against Napoleon. The More sisters perked up at the news. Wilberforce joked that Patty might go to Spain as a volunteer, while Hannah revived her girlish interest in Spanish, and made 'all my clever young friends learn the language of these noble patriots'.[72] Elizabeth Carter had left her a 'nice edition of Don Quixote', which she was enthusiastically recommending to bewildered friends, who thought she had given up novels. Ann Kennicott, who was staying with the Porteuses, assured her that 'We here are as Spanish as you can wish. The Bp, has got four sets of Travels in Spain, besides Don Quixote, and his Maps so cover the breakfast Table, that we have hardly room for our bread and butter.' She added wistfully, 'How Don Q. reminds one of the pleasant time when we read it together at Hampton!'[73]

In the cold spring of 1808, at the instigation of Pepys, now her last link to the bluestocking days, More had read a far more notorious novel, Madame de Staël's *Corinne; ou, L'Italie*, which brought back memories of the young Germaine Necker, whom she had known as a girl in a blue silk gown.[74] Since then she had married a Swedish diplomat, to whom she had been routinely unfaithful, had established a famous salon, had been banished by Napoleon, and had travelled in Italy, where she took a new lover, a Portuguese aristocrat. *Corinne* was the product of the tour and the affair. A thinly disguised and intensely idealized piece of autobiography, with a heroine who turns her back on conventional feminine duties in order to fulfil her destiny, the novel was a celebration of the individualistic morality and Rousseauian sensibility Hannah More so deplored. She told Pepys, 'There never *was* such a book! such a compound of genius and bad taste! such a fermentation of love and nonsense!' Yet it had the same powerful addictive quality as the theatre, so that 'though like Pistol I swallowed and execrated, yet I went on swallowing'.[75]

More's own views about the function of imaginative literature had changed little from the time she had complained to Mary Hamilton in 1782 about the lack of religion in Fanny Burney's novels. When, twenty years later, the *Christian Observer* made the same point about the novels of Maria Edgeworth, she thought the comments '*very* able and striking'.[76] She was deeply

---

[72] *Life of Wilberforce*, iii. 371; Roberts, iii. 261.

[73] Roberts, iii. 261; Clark, Ann Kennicott to More, 23 Sept. [1808].

[74] Clark, More to Olivia Sparrow, 18 Oct. 1815.

[75] Roberts, iii. 251–2.

[76] Anson MSS, letters and diaries of Mary Hamilton, property of Sir Peter and Dame Elizabeth Anson, doc. folder 8, More to Mary Hamilton, 30 Oct. 1782; *Christian Observer*, 11 (1812), 797 (see also *Eclectic Review*, 8 (1812), 979–1000); Huntington, HM 30592, More to Jane Hoare, 4 Feb. [1813].

critical of two writers who were far more excitingly dangerous than these very moral authors: Byron was 'one of the erring geniuses', and the sensational romantic novelist Lady Morgan was venomously dismissed as 'that witch'.[77] Her attitude to the new romantic poetry was uncertain and shifting. Though she found Sir Walter Scott's *The Lady of the Lake* 'full of beauty', most of it passed her by; in an ill-considered moment she dismissed Wordsworth as 'the silly Poet'.[78] A few years later, however, if the not always reliable Thomas De Quincey is to be believed, she was prepared to open her mind and buy *The Excursion* when it came out in a cheaper edition.[79] A trip to the Lakes made by Lady Olivia Sparrow and her daughter, in 1814, brought back memories of the enthusiasms of her girlhood: 'And so you not only saw the picturesque beauties of the Lakes, but the Poets also...I suppose Millicent was in raptures with all this Etherial [*sic*] Society. I remember when I was her age the sight of a *live* poet used to make me wild.' But she added that though she admired the talents of the Lake poets, 'the taste of their compositions does not exactly fall in with my old-fashioned notions. I was formed in another school.'[80]

Indeed her tastes and preferences had hardly changed. She continued to defend her beloved Shakespeare from Evangelical criticisms, and when her newly converted friend Lady Southampton proposed selling 'almost all her books which were not religious', she 'begged quarter' for her beloved bard.[81] Judging from the number of times she and Wilberforce quoted from both parts of *Henry IV* in their letters to each other, the plays must have been joint favourites. Unmoved by Johnson's criticisms, she still reverenced Milton and turned again and again to *Paradise Lost*, her conscious mind ignoring the erotic charge that pervades his descriptions of Adam and Eve in Paradise. When Elizabeth Bouverie lent her *The Task*, a long devotional–pastoral poem by the Evangelical poet William Cowper, she was delighted: 'I have found what I have been looking for all my life, a poet whom I can read on a Sunday.'[82] And it was in the summer of 1808, possibly after her return from Weymouth, that, meditating on Milton, Cowper, and Madame de Staël, she conceived a plan for a new type of literary work, aimed at the subscribers to the burgeoning circulating libraries: an anti-*Corinne*, which, by setting out the message of her conduct books in fictional form, would fulfil what she

---

[77] Clark, More to Olivia Sparrow, 18 Oct. 1815; Thornton, Add. MS 7674/1/E/7, More to Marianne Thornton, Nov. 1817. For Lady Morgan, see A. H. Jones, *Ideas and Innovations: Best Sellers of Jane Austen's Age* (New York, 1986), 185–223.

[78] Bristol City Council, Bristol Record Office, 28048/C68/18, More to J. S. Harford, 1810; Clark, More to Ann Kennicott, 20 Feb. [1810].

[79] *The Letters of William and Dorothy Wordsworth*, iii: *The Middle Years*, p. 11: *1812–1820*, ed. E. de Selincourt, rev. M. Moorman and A. G. Hill (Oxford, 1970), 213, 221.

[80] BL, Egerton MS 1965, fo. 16, More to Olivia Sparrow, 26 Oct. [1814?].

[81] Duke, More to Wilberforce, 7 Sept. 1813.   [82] *Gambier*, i. 154.

saw as the true function of a novel.[83] This step was as daring in its way as the *Hints to a Princess*, and for once she acted solely on her own initiative, with only Ann Kennicott in on the secret. The result was the publication in December 1808 of the anonymous two-volume *Coelebs in Search of a Wife*. The book became an immediate best-seller, and wherever it was read and discussed two questions were aired: who was the author and how was the hero's name pronounced?

The hero's real name is Charles, 'Coelebs' being simply a variation of the word 'celibate'. Charles is a sententious 23-year-old, and his opinions on the education of women are such an exact echo of Hannah More's that is remarkable that anyone could have been in doubt about the author's identity.

For my own part I call education, not that which smothers a woman with accomplishments . . . [and] which is made up of the shreds and patches of useless arts, but that which inculcates principles, polishes taste, regulates temper, cultivates reason, subdues the passions, directs the feelings, habituates to reflection, trains to self-denial, and, more especially, that which refers all actions, feelings, sentiments, tastes, and passions, to the love and fear of God.[84]

In pursuit of his quest, Charles travels to London, where he meets a variety of fashionable women including 'a Machiavelian [*sic*] mother', who 'knew by instinct if a younger son was in the room, and by a petrifying look checked his most distant approaches', and a rich and selfish dowager, who refuses to give to a deserving family and complains that property taxes make her 'quite a beggar'.[85] But 'the acknowledged queen of beauty and ton' is Lady Melbury: 'warm-hearted, feeling, liberal, on the one hand; on the other, vain, sentimental, romantic, extravagantly addicted to dissipation and expence'.[86] Alert readers would have recognized the duchess of Devonshire, who had died in agony in March 1806, aged only 49. ('Alas, poor Duchess of Devonshire!' More had exclaimed to Lady Waldegrave on hearing the news.[87]) Lady Waldegrave herself featured in *Coelebs* as the pious and melancholy Lady Aston.[88] For those in the know, the book might have had some of the characteristics of a *roman-à-clef*, and part of the delight in reading it was to identify the various characters.

---

[83] Roberts, iii. 313–14. For comparisons between *Corinne* and *Coelebs*, see C. H. Ford, *Hannah More* (New York, 1996), 234–45.

[84] *Coelebs in Search of a Wife* (London, 1809), i. 14.

[85] Ibid. 112–18.   [86] Ibid. 151–2.

[87] Clark, Patty More to Lady Waldegrave, 3 Apr. 1806. The identification was picked up by Georgiana's friend Dr Francis Randolph. Roberts, iii. 287.

[88] Compare *Coelebs*, i. 210 ff. with Henry Thornton's diary of 13 May 1795 (Thornton, Add. 7674/1/R, fo. 123) and Duke, More to Wilberforce, 1 Jan. 1806.

Failing to find a wife in London, Charles goes to the country house of his late father's friend Mr Stanley, a man who combines strict religious principles with easy and agreeable manners. His wife matches him in piety and elegance, and the couple have a family of daughters, the eldest, Lucilla, approaching her nineteenth birthday. At this stage, a third of the way through the first volume, Coeleb's quest is in effect over; the heroine is introduced, and there are no obstacles in the way of their union. Lucilla is hard-working, practical, and unselfish. She rises early, inspects the household accounts, makes her parents' breakfast, assists in teaching the younger children, visits the poor, and attends the Sunday school.[89] She is also that much mocked creature the learned lady; her father has taught her Latin and she reads a portion with him every day. At first, Mr Stanley only meant to teach her the minimum required to understand English grammar, but, 'her quickness in acquiring led me on, and I think I did right; for it is superficial knowledge that excites vanity. A learned language, which a discreet woman will never produce in company, is less likely to make her vain, than those acquirements which are always in exhibition.'[90] Here More was making an almost heroic attempt to reconcile the contradictions and inner conflicts within her own life. While delivering her posthumous riposte to the father who had refused to continue to teach her Latin, she showed how painfully she had internalized his prejudices against educated women. An anecdote Barbara Wilberforce later told her son Samuel demonstrates her pathological fear of allowing her classical learning to overstep the boundaries of female decorum.

Your father spoke of her real modesty & retirement of Character with much pleasure, saying he had known her long before he could discover whether she understood the learned Languages tho' anxious to ascertain the point he had repeatedly thrown out *baits*, which in one whose vanity had not been under strict government would infallibly have drawn forth the secret.[91]

It is only because Lucilla is so 'gentle and unassuming' that she is allowed to appropriate masculine knowledge, and to see off 'the illiberal sarcasms of men'.[92]

Lucilla is also an enthusiastic gardener, a passion she shares with Milton's Eve and also with her creator. In the throes of landscaping Barley Wood, More had admitted ruefully to Pepys that 'Planting, which was the first passion of my Youth still reigns with undiminished force ... my sin was that of Jereboam, worshipping in *Groves* and *high places*'.[93] To counter her

---

[89] *Coelebs*, i. 180 ff.   [90] Ibid. ii. 230–1.   [91] Bodleian, MS d. 20, fo. 35.

[92] *Coelebs*, ii. 232–3, 148–9. For Lucilla's education and reading, see J. Pearson, *Women's Reading in Britain, 1750–1835: A Dangerous Recreation* (Cambridge, 1999), 88–92; J. Nardin, 'Hannah More and the Rhetoric of Educational Reform', *Women's History Review*, 10 (2001), 211–27.

[93] Clark, More to Pepys, 14 Dec. 1807.

obsession, Lucilla hangs up her watch in the conservatory so that she does not forget the time.[94] (Probably More did the same.) Gardening is no mere private indulgence. She has planted a piece of waste ground with fruit trees, and when a servant or a Sunday school pupil marries, 'she presents their little empty garden with a dozen young apple trees . . . never forgetting to embellish their little court with roses and honeysuckles'.[95]

The roses and honeysuckles symbolize the powerful rural nostalgia which pervades the book and which echoes Cowper's message in *The Task*: 'God made the country, and man made the town.'[96] In the main, the town-dwellers are dissatisfied individuals, leading empty lives, careless of religion and the needs of the poor. At Stanley Grove, on the other hand, the tenants are cared for with old-fashioned hospitality. Christmas is a time of 'blazing fires' and 'abundant provisions'. 'The roasting and the boiling and the baking', a servant exclaims to Charles. 'The house is alive!'[97] The clergyman, Mr Barlow (so different from the sorry specimens More had encountered in the Mendips), models himself on George Herbert's exemplary Country Parson.[98] Even Mr Stanley's neighbour Squire Flam, literary descendant of a long line of eighteenth-century booby squires, represents something 'politically valuable', and Charles decides that he 'should not be sorry to see a new edition of these obsolete squires, somewhat corrected and better lettered'.[99] This is the old 'country' Tory ideology brought up to date for an age of commercialized agriculture and Evangelical moral earnestness.

More's Cheap Repository tract *The Sunday School* described a middle-class widow who through her energy and perseverance becomes a force for good in her neighbourhood. In *Coelebs* she reinforced this message, promoting a new, Evangelically inspired ideal of useful womanhood. In what was to become the most influential sentence in the novel, Mrs Stanley declares, '*Charity is the calling of a lady; the care of the poor is her profession.*'[100] Unlike men, who 'have little time or taste for details', the wives of the landed gentry are 'intimately acquainted with the worth and wants of all within their reach'.[101] Philanthropy, More adds, giving her familiar paternalist argument a semi-political twist, 'is rather justice than charity . . . to assist their own labouring poor is a kind of natural debt, which persons who possess great landed property owe to those from the sweat of whose brow they derive their comforts, and even their riches'.[102]

If the imperatives of social justice cannot persuade women to attend to the needs of the poor, More has another argument up her sleeve. The key scene

---

[94] *Coelebs*, ii. 113–14.   [95] Ibid. 50.   [96] *The Task*, bk. 1: 'The Sofa', line 749.
[97] *Coelebs*, ii. 115–16.   [98] Ibid., i. 196.   [99] Ibid. i. 410–11.   [100] Ibid. ii. 20.
[101] For the application of this argument to Elizabeth Montagu, see H. Guest, *Small Change: Women, Learning, Patriotism, 1750–1810* (Chicago, 2000), 96–8.
[102] *Coelebs*, ii. 22.

in the book occurs when Charles, unobserved, comes across Lucilla and her sister attending to a poor old woman.

Her voice was inexpressibly sweet and penetrating, while faith, hope, and charity seemed to beam from her fine uplifted eyes. On account of the closeness of the room, she had thrown off her hat, cloak, and gloves, and laid them on the bed; and her fine hair, which had escaped from its confinement, shaded that side of her face which was next the door and prevented her seeing me . . . It was a subject not unworthy of Raphael.[103]

Lucilla's dishevelled hair is a reminder of Milton's Eve, and Charles, clearly aroused by the spectacle, becomes something of a voyeur. Philanthropy, it seems, is an excellent way of gaining a good husband—much more productive of long-term happiness than a ball or an assembly. This far from subtle message might explain why so many middle-class young women eagerly devoured a book almost entirely devoid of incident.

And devour it they did. The book went into 'ten large Editions' in its first six months; four American editions quickly followed, and during More's lifetime thirty editions of 1,000 copies were printed in the United States.[104] Among the middle classes of Colchester *Coelebs* was 'the book of the day', and helped turn visiting the poor into a fashionable activity.[105] Some readers even fell in love with Charles, one 'young Lady' swearing that 'she will not marry till she meet with a Coelebs'.[106] Among the more unlikely enthusiasts was Nancy Cobbett, the illiterate wife of More's bitter enemy, who begged her husband for a copy of the book.[107]

At first there was considerable speculation about the author. With amazing obtuseness Henry Thornton refused to believe it could be More, but Wilberforce immediately detected her fingerprints: 'What! did I not know thy old ward, Hal?,' he wrote exuberantly.[108] An irritated More learned that at Bath the authorship had become 'the chat of the place' and that the booksellers had given up trying to keep it a secret.[109] With her cover blown, she received an angry letter from the Catholic priest Joseph Berington, complaining of a slighting reference to 'popery'.[110] A conciliatory reply failed to mollify him, and he would have been more implacable still if he had seen her letters to Ann Kennicott on the subject.[111] Lacking any empathy for

---

[103] Ibid. 279–80.   [104] Clark, More to Ann Kennicott, 21 July 1809; Roberts, iii. 273.

[105] L. Davidoff and C. Hall, *Family Fortunes: Men and Women of the English Middle Class, 1780–1850* (London, 1987), 158; F. K. Prochaska, *Women and Philanthropy in Nineteenth-Century England* (Oxford, 1980), 118.

[106] Clark, Ann Kennicott to More, 12 Jan. [1809].   [107] BL, Add. MS 22907, fo. 164.

[108] Thornton, Add. MS 7676/1/L4, fo. 88; Thornton to More, 2 Jan. 1809; *Life of Wilberforce*, iii. 399.

[109] Clark, More to Marie-Aimée Huber, 23 Feb. 1809.

[110] For the Berington correspondence, see Roberts, iii. 274–85.

[111] Clark, More to Ann Kennicott, 21 July 1809, 20 Feb. [1810].

a mentality forged over centuries of discrimination and hostile propaganda, she took it for granted that Berington—in reality a liberal, ecumenically minded man—had acted from bad motives: 'I am sure it must be Bonner's Ghost for which they owe me a spite—the offence of Coelebs was so slight.'[112] (However, his criticisms might well have struck home, for in her later *Christian Morals* she went out of her way to pay tribute to aspects of Catholic worship and to the qualities of many Catholic writers, who showed 'a genius, a sublimity, and an unction, that have rarely been surpassed'.[113])

One of the many readers who enthused over the novel was Cassandra Austen. Her sister Jane, however, was dismissive: 'You have by no means raised my curiosity about Caleb [*sic*];—My disinclination for it before was affected but now it is real; I do not like Evangelicals.—Of course I shall be delighted when I read it, like other people, but till I do, I dislike it.'[114] A week later, having learned that she had misspelt the name of the book, she was more resistant still. She had now decided that its only merit 'was in the name Caleb, which has an honest, unpretending sound; but in Coelebs, there is pedantry & affectation.—Is it written only to Classical Scholars?'[115]

Yet it is very likely that Austen conquered her prejudice and read it. The famous scene in *Emma* when Mr Elton comes across Harriet Smith visiting the poor, and Emma muses (misguidedly), 'To fall in love with each other on an errand such as this...to meet in a charitable scheme; this will bring a great increase on each side', is probably an ironical commentary on *Coelebs*.[116] Towards the end of her life she included a reference to *Coelebs* in a revision of *Catharine*, an unfinished piece of juvenilia. Rebuking her niece for 'improper' conduct, the heroine's prudish and censorious aunt declares, 'I had hoped to see you respectable and good...I bought you Blair's Sermons and Coelebs in Search of a Wife.'[117] Many commentators, too, have noticed the thematic resemblance between *Coelebs* and *Mansfield Park*, with its condemnation of the slave trade and private theatricals.[118] Edmund Bertram seems remarkably like Charles, while in her shyness, intelligence, seriousness, and effusions over nature, Fanny has much in common with

---

[112] Ibid., 20 Feb. [1810].   [113] *Christian Morals* (London, 1813), ii. 290.

[114] *Jane Austen's Letters*, ed. D. Le Faye (Oxford, 1995), 169–70.

[115] Ibid. 172.   [116] *Emma*, ch. 10.

[117] J. Austen, *Catharine and Other Writings*, ed. M. A. Doody and D. Murray (Oxford, 1993), 222.

[118] *Quarterly Review*, 24 (1821), 359; R. A. Colby, *Fiction with a Purpose: Major and Minor Nineteenth-Century Novels* (Bloomington, Ind., 1967), 79–86; C. L. Johnson, *Jane Austen: Women, Politics and the Novel* (Chicago, 1988), 18, 141–2; B. F. Tobin, *Superintending the Poor: Charitable Ladies and Paternal Landlords in British Fiction, 1770–1860* (New Haven, 1993), 74–97. See also M. Waldron, 'The Frailties of Fanny: *Mansfield Park* and the Evangelical Movement', *Eighteenth-Century Fiction*, 6 (1994), 259–81, and ead., *Jane Austen and the Fiction of her Time* (Cambridge, 1999), 84–111.

Lucilla. The spoilt and selfish Bertram girls are the products of the kind of flawed female education More repeatedly condemned in her conduct books. There is an explicit reference to Evangelicalism in Mary Crawford's derisive references to conversion and 'methodism'. But for all the seductive resemblances between the two novels, *Mansfield Park* cannot be recruited into the Evangelical ranks. For a start, no Evangelical novelist would have created characters like Dr Grant or Mary Crawford: the one a flawed clergyman, the other a seductively vivacious anti-heroine.[119] And More, who was later to condemn novelists who lavished 'fascinating qualities' on the seducer, would not have approved of the subtle characterization of the attractive anti-hero, Henry Crawford.[120] The imperatives of a great novel—even one as didactic as *Mansfield Park*—cannot be reconciled with the simplicities of a fictionalized conduct book. If More and Austen seemed at times to be speaking the same moral language, it is because in their critiques of the shallowness of female education and the slick superficiality of metropolitan values they were both part of a wider reaction to romantic individualism, a reaction that extended beyond the Evangelical movement.

One difference between *Coelebs* and *Mansfield Park* is that Austen received no reviews when her novel was published in 1814, whereas More was inundated with them.[121] Most were cool. Reviewers were dissatisfied with the characters of Charles (boring and sententious) and Lucilla (too good to be true); those who disliked Evangelicalism detected 'methodism' and 'religious cant'; nearly all of them complained of the lack of a plot. Sidney Smith's whiggish *Edinburgh Review* mocked More's assertion that men were far more charmed by a modestly dressed woman than one decked out in the fashionable near nudity: 'If there is any truth in this picture, nudity becomes a virtue; and no decent woman, for the future, can be seen in garments.'[122] More wounding by far was the review in the *Christian Observer*. The reviewer disliked Coelebs, finding him 'given to prosing . . . not very delicate . . . apt to be vulgar'. One unquoted passage was deemed to verge on the indecent. Recognizing the novelty of More's attempt, the reviewer added, 'we would caution others not to enter rashly on the same project . . . Divinity is an odd ingredient in a work of imagination.'[123]

---

[119] More later received a letter from the novelist Jane West complaining 'of my censure in Coelebs on a passage which she rightly guesses was on one of her books, where I bemoaned that the Clerical character is so lowered in works of invention—and instanced that after the Author had made a Clergyman a model of piety she concluded by carrying him to a masquerade. I did instance this but without naming her.' Huntington, HM 30592, More to Henrietta Hoare, 4 Feb. [1813].

[120] *Moral Sketches of Prevailing Opinions and Manners, Foreign and Domestic* (1820), 243–4.

[121] See Ford, *Hannah More*, 244 n. 163.

[122] *Coelebs*, i. 189; *Edinburgh Review*, 14 (Apr. 1809), 150.

[123] *Christian Observer*, 8 (Feb. 1809), 109–11, 121, 115.

Coming from the house journal of the Clapham sect, the review stung More as nothing else could. It was Brutus' dagger, Judas' kiss, and it caused her to break her rule of never replying to criticism. In a letter uncharacteristically marred by blotches and crossings out, she turned on Zachary Macaulay, the unfortunate editor: 'That sort of sneer I expect from a Scotch but not from a Christian critic.' Most wounding of all were the complaints about Coelebs's character. To call him vulgar was bad enough, 'but that he is also *"indecent"* would have inexpressibly shocked me had not Mr H. Thornton made the same discovery before!!' Worst of all, 'The Critic *well* knew the writer was a woman . . . He knew *I* wrote it.' The accusation of impropriety was so damaging because it highlighted yet again the risks run by any respectable woman who ventured into the public arena. It might have brought back memories of Johnson's angry reaction to her admission that she had read *Tom Jones*; of a more recent rebuke from Knox for ignoring the 'filthily indelicate' passages in Dryden's *Absalom and Achitophel*;[124] above all, of the sexual slanders of the Blagdon pamphleteers. She concluded wearily that perhaps the reviewer was right. 'Three years' excruciating illness which has battered my body has probably injured my mind and I shall take this review as an admonition to write no more.' She wondered whether to write to the reviewer asking him to point out the indecent passage: 'I have searched closely, but cannot even guess at it.'[125] Modern readers might search like More for the offending passage, and search in vain, and wonder as well how Knox could have found the book 'as low as it well can be'.[126] Yet the strait-laced critics had a point of sorts. It is clear throughout that Charles has the normal sexual responses to a pretty young woman, and the novel ends with a hint of his frustration at the thought of the three-month postponement of his marriage.[127] But More, whose literary tastes had been formed in a more outspoken age, dared not admit that she was less prudish than most of her religious friends. As she later wrote to Macaulay when she had calmed down and could think more objectively, 'My morality as a woman was so much more alive than my vanity as an author that the charge of immodesty filled my mind to the exclusion of all other considerations.'[128]

The review had hit her when she was at a very low ebb, following a winter of 'deplorable suffering' consisting of 'spasms in my head [and] intolerable pains in my teeth' until finally she had '*seven* teeth drawn at a sitting'.[129] In the spring she had five more teeth extracted: 'the rending of so

[124] Knox, *Remains*, iv. 300.

[125] Huntington, MY 667, More to Zachary Macaulay, 7 Mar. 1809.

[126] *Thirty Years' Correspondence between John Jebb and Alexander Knox*, i. 540–1.

[127] M. Mason, *The Making of Victorian Sexual Attitudes* (Oxford, 1994), 77.

[128] *Letters of Hannah More to Zachary Macaulay, Esq., containing Notices of Lord Macaulay's Youth*, ed. A. Roberts (London, 1860), 29–30.

[129] Clark, More to Marie-Aimée Huber, 23 Feb. 1809.

many firm rocks from the centre' causing 'tortures greater than I can describe'.[130] (Two more teeth were drawn the following year.[131]) Brought low by misunderstandings and physical suffering, she could not enjoy her new status as a best-selling novelist. It was gratifying, though, to have made £2,000 in the first year, the same sum Scott received for *The Lady of the Lake*, and far above the £350 Austen made from *Mansfield Park*; and this time, having learned the ways of publishers, she kept the copyright.[132] But though the book made her wealthy, she had no intention of repeating the experiment: a pity in the view of James Stephen, who wanted her to be 'as much more novelish as you please'.[133] This was an unusual sentiment for an Evangelical, but not so surprising perhaps in the great-grandfather of Virginia Woolf.

Within ten years *Coelebs* had become a European phenomenon. In 1817 it was translated into French as *Coelebs; ou, Le Choix d'une épouse*. (As will be shown, it was commended by no less a person than Madame de Staël.) A year earlier it had appeared in a two-volume German edition, published in Stuttgart as *Cölebs; oder, Der junge Wanderer der eine Gattin sucht* together with a subtitle 'Ein Beitrag zur genauern Kenntniß der häuslichen Gewohnheiten und Sitten Englands' ('An Article with More Precise Knowledge of English Domestic Customs and Morals'). It is at least possible that the German translation influenced the Swiss poet–priest Jeremias Gotthelf, whose three *Brautschau* ('search for a bride') stories acquired great popularity when they were published in the 1840s.[134]

More's refusal to provide her readers with more of the same left a vacuum which opportunists were not slow to fill with imitations, unauthorized sequels, and parodies.[135] In *Don Juan* (1818) Byron satirized More and other 'improving' women writers.

> In short, she was a walking calculation,
>> Miss Edgeworth's novels stepping from their covers,
> Or Mrs Trimmer's books on education
>> Or 'Coelebs' Wife' set out in quest of lovers,
> Morality's prim personification . . . [136]

[130] Duke, More to Wilberforce, 4 May [1809]; Clark, More to Mrs H. Thornton, 9 May [1809].
[131] Roberts, iii. 319.
[132] Ibid. 318–19; C. Tomalin, *Jane Austen: A Life* (Harmondsworth, 1998), 328 n. 5.
[133] Roberts, iii. 310.
[134] P. Skrine, 'Die Brautschauerzählung bei Jeremias Gotthelf und Hannah More', *Erzählkunst und Volkserziehung. Das literarische Werk des Jeremias Gotthelf* (Tübingen, 1999), 289–303.
[135] R. A. Colby, *Fiction with a Purpose: Major and Minor Nineteenth-Century Novels* (Bloomington, Ind., 1967), 80.
[136] Canto 1, st. 16.

Byron's mockery shows that within ten years of publication *Coelebs* had become a cultural reference point, a book that was talked about even when not read. This continued well into the Victorian age. In Percy Fitzgerald's *Young Coelebs* (1879) a character says, 'That was a book we all read when I was a lad, written by some tabby of an old maid.'[137] Commenting on his status as a confirmed bachelor, the philosopher Herbert Spencer wrote, 'the chances are that I shall continue a melancholy Coelebs to the end of my days'.[138] Edmund Gosse recalled that, in his cramped Plymouth Brethren childhood, *Coelebs* was one of the few novels to be found in his parents' library. He read it avidly, lingering over its 'pictures of frivolous society and even perilous intrigue', its glimpses of a naughty world.[139] As Charlotte M. Yonge pointed out, 'To the more seriously disposed persons who barely tolerated fiction of any sort, *Coelebs*, with its really able sketches of character, and epigrammatic turns, was genuinely entertaining and delightful.'[140] More had given an Evangelical world deeply suspicious of novels permission to read fiction; the publication of *Coelebs* led the *Christian Observer* to begin reviewing the occasional novel, though the policy was abandoned for a while in the stricter atmosphere of the late 1820s.[141] She had also provided encouragement for other women to use the novel form to propagate the Evangelical message. Evangelical productions such as Mary Martha Sherwood's *The Fairchild Family* (1818) and Charlotte Elizabeth Tonna's social-realist *Helen Fleetwood* (1841) were part of her legacy to the next generation.

---

[137] Colby, *Fiction with a Purpose*, 318 n. 20.

[138] Quoted in G. S. Haight, *George Eliot: A Biography* (Oxford, 1968), 119.

[139] A. Thwaite, *Edmund Gosse: A Literary Landscape* (Oxford, 1984), 48–9.

[140] C. M. Yonge, *Hannah More* (London, 1888), 154.

[141] E. Jay, *The Religion of the Heart: Anglican Evangelicalism and the Nineteenth-Century Novel* (Oxford, 1979), 198.

Chapter 13

━━━⟫●⟪━━━

High Priestess
1809–1816

'BY 1805', writes a generally sympathetic commentator, 'More had said everything of interest which she had to say. Her later writings reveal a decline into old age that it is charitable to ignore.'[1] But Hannah More's significance was not over by the time she reached her sixtieth birthday. Far from being a fading memento of a bygone age, she was, through her writings, her hospitality, her powers of organization, and her sheer longevity, one of the most influential figures in the rapidly growing Evangelical movement: its 'high priestess' in the words of one of its historians.[2] 'What Wilberforce was among men', declared her *Christian Observer* obituarist, 'Hannah More was among women.'[3]

Not everyone saw this as a compliment. To William Cobbett she was 'the Old Bishop in petticoats'.[4] In its obituary notice the High Church *Quarterly Review* was to state rather sourly that 'Mrs Hannah More, in the later years of her life, lent the distinction of her too exclusive favour' to a 'religious sect'—that is to the Evangelical party.[5] The accusation of exclusivity is not quite fair. Though More's commitment to Evangelicalism

[1] R. Hole (ed.), *Selected Writings of Hannah More* (London, 1996), p. xv. Hole's interpretation is based on J. C. D. Clark's influential *English Society, 1688–1832: Ideology, Social Structure and Political Practice during the Ancien Regime* (Cambridge, 1985).

[2] I. Bradley, *The Call to Seriousness: The Evangelical Impact on the Victorians* (London, 1976), 19.

[3] *Christian Observer*, 33 (1833), 632; see also 34 (1834), 168.

[4] *Weekly Political Register*, 20 (Apr. 1822), 188. Earlier the Paineite writer Charles Pigott had described her as 'a *downright* Bishop Horsley in petticoats'. *The Female Jockey Club; or, A Sketch of the Manners of the Age* (London, 1794), 200.

[5] *Quarterly Review*, 104/52 (1834), 416.

was total and unquestioned, her instincts were for tolerance and inclusiveness. In the bruising aftermath of the Blagdon controversy, she wrote in her
diary:

My soul is sick of religious controversy. How I hate the little narrowing names of
Arminian and Calvinist! Christianity is a broad basis. *Bible* Christianity is what I
love; that does not insist on opinions indifferent in themselves;—a Christianity
practical and pure, which teaches holiness, humility, repentance, and faith in
Christ, and which after summing up all the Evangelical graces, declares that the
greatest of these is charity.[6]

She tried to broaden her charity to those outside the Evangelical community,
and she acknowledged the spiritual insights of devout High Church people
with a readiness that makes nonsense of the supposition that the two wings
of the Church of England were permanently locked in internecine warfare.
There were many intricate connections between Evangelicals and the so-
called Orthodox, and it was possible for friendships, cemented by a common
spirit of devotion, to cross the divide of churchmanship.[7] As Alexander
Knox put it, 'Hannah More and I are both substantially of the same school;
that is, we both make it our object to pass through the form of godliness to
the power thereof.'[8] Another friend from outside the Evangelical circle was
Thomas Burgess, bishop of St David's, who founded a college for the Welsh
clergy at Lampeter in 1822. More claimed part of the credit for this much
needed venture, telling Mrs Thornton, 'I hardly know so pressing a cause.
There will, unavoidably, to save [Burgess's] credit, be mixed with it a little
too much High Church, but we must be glad to do something if we cannot
do all that is wanted.'[9]

But friendship could not gloss over all differences, and eventually Knox,
devoted admirer though he remained, detected blind spots.[10] He came to see
her as a somewhat dubious churchwoman, who downplayed the importance
of the sacraments and ecclesiastical structures because of her Evangelical
insistence that the only means of salvation was faith in Christ. She refused to
accept the High Church belief that baptism was a means of regeneration. She
did not believe that bishops were essential to the Church, and that therefore
non-episcopal churches such as the Church of Scotland were in a state of
schism. These doctrinal issues were not angels-on-pinhead matters, but involved fundamental beliefs about the meaning of Christianity. To Hannah

[6] Roberts, iii. 196.
[7] D. Newsome, 'Father and Sons', *Historical Journal*, 6 (1963), 295–310; id., *The Parting of
Friends: A Study of the Wilberforces and Henry Manning* (London, 1966), 5–15.
[8] A. Knox *Remains* (London, 1837), iv. 174–5.
[9] Thornton, Add. MS 7674/1/E/2, More to Mrs H. Thornton, 5 Apr. [1808]. For Burgess, see
J. S. Harford, *The Life of Thomas Burgess, DD, Late Bishop of Salisbury* (London, 1840).
[10] Knox, *Remains*, iv. 227–9.

More, personal faith mattered more than institutional correctness, and here she had more in common with Dissenters like William Jay than with many in her own Church.

One historian of Evangelicalism has detected a common core of doctrine and practice that united all those who claimed the name, whatever their denomination: the necessity of conversion, a commitment to activism in spreading the gospel, a belief in the sole authority of the Bible, and a theology centred round the atoning death of Christ.[11] Within this broad range of agreement, however, there were inevitable conflicts and differences of emphasis. Because there was no single church to impose institutional and doctrinal unity, Evangelicals carried the baggage of their denominations and of their differing theological positions. Baptists rejected infant baptism; Calvinists and Arminians disputed predestination and free will; Anglicans held to an established Church, a formal liturgy, and an episcopal hierarchy, all rejected by Evangelical Dissenters. The deceptively simple belief that the Bible contained all the truths necessary for salvation was fraught with problems. Which Bible? Whose interpretation? What was to be done when good people sincerely disagreed?

For all their differences, however, Evangelicals usually recognized each other, if only because they communicated in a common code. To be converted was to come under 'serious impressions'; an Evangelical clergyman was a 'serious', 'religious' or 'gospel' clergyman; 'good people' were Evangelicals; 'good sort of people' or 'nominal Christians' were those non-Evangelicals whose respectable lives made them unaware of their spiritual dangers; 'prejudiced' people were those who were hostile to the Evangelical gospel. There was an underlying unity on the necessity of conversion or the 'new birth'. 'However the *term* may offend,' More wrote, 'there is nothing ridiculous in the *thing*.'[12] But she used the language of conversion with caution and humility. The new birth was a secret transaction between the believer and God which could not be reduced to an easy formula. It was presumptuous to insist that every individual go through the same experience, and that this experience had to be intense, dramatic, and take place at a specific moment in time. This, after all, had not happened to her. She was therefore inclined to judge people generously in this delicate area, and give the benefit of the doubt to many who could not use the Evangelical formulae—a stance which set her apart from many in the growing Evangelical community.

It is not always recognized that *Coelebs* was a work of religious controversy as well as a fictional conduct book, and that much of the book was polemic against the excesses of some of her fellow believers. Ultra-Calvinist readers

[11] D. W. Bebbington, *Evangelicalism in Modern Britain* (London, 1989), 1–17.
[12] *Practical Piety*, i. 59.

might have been deeply offended by her attack on Evangelical exclusivity in the person of Mrs Ranby, who

seems to consider Christianity as a kind of free-masonry, and therefore she thinks it superfluous to speak on serious subjects to any but the initiated. If they do not *return the sign*, she gives them up as blind and dead... She holds very cheap that gradual growth in piety which is, in reality, no less the effect of divine grace that those instantaneous conversions, which she believes to be so common... Though her Redeemer laid down his life for all people, nations and languages, she will only lay down her money for a very limited number of a very limited class. To be religious is not claim sufficient on her bounty, they must be religious in a particular way.[13]

Later in the novel Mr Stanley, the character who most expresses her own views, makes a pointed contrast between the 'enthusiast' and the 'sober Christian', who does not presume in his own case 'to fix the *chronology of conversion*'.[14] 'Sober' was one of More's key words when she wrote about religion. It was very Anglican, very Augustan, very much a reflection of the anti-Romantic who preferred Pope to Wordsworth and Matthew Prior to Sir Walter Scott. She spoke for a generation poised between the excitable pieties of the Methodist revival and the charismatic fervour which came to be associated with Edward Irving in the 1820s. Her piety and that of the Clapham sect was calm and measured; in the spirit of Lockean empiricism they judged the sincerity of a person's religion by its outcome in a life spent in godly living and deeds of charity. This was the message of the religious works of More's later years, which, unlike most of her earlier publications, went out under her own name. Their revealing titles, *Practical Piety* (1811), *Christian Morals* (1813), *Moral Sketches* (1819), show that they were declarations of war on Calvinist Antinomianism, the belief that because Christians are saved by God's unmerited grace rather than by good works, the moral code was an Old Testament relic not applicable to God's elect. To More this was a dangerous presumption. As she trenchantly declared in *Practical Piety*, 'To suppose that the blood of Christ redeems us from sin, while Sin continues to pollute the Soul, is to suppose... that it acts like an amulet, an incantation, a talisman, which is to produce its effect by operating on the imagination and not on the disease.'[15]

As Calvinism revived in the early years of the nineteenth century, she believed that her fears were being realized, and her distance from London did not protect her from the storms of controversy. From 1815 a group of prominent Evangelicals, including some West Country clergy and their wives, left

---

[13] *Coelebs*, i. 62–3, 67.   [14] *Coelebs*, ii. 220–2.
[15] *Practical Piety; or, The Influence of the Religion of the Heart on the Conduct of the Life* (London, 1811), i. 55.

the Church of England, underwent believers' baptism, and started a small sect of their own, the 'Trinitarian and Particular Baptists'.[16] They talk, More wrote with angry sarcasm, 'of putting forth a Liturgy from which the ten commandments and many other such *excrescences* are to be expunged— for that Christians have nothing to do with the Law'.[17] She heard that High Calvinist fellow travellers in Bristol were strongly hostile to her stress on morality: 'When they happened to speak of poor me, they said "She makes us sick of practice." '[18] These were dangerous times for Evangelicals, and many, anxious to preserve their hard-won respectability, went out of their way to condemn the 'Western Schism' in the strongest language. Even-tually many of the seceders quarrelled with each other and went their separate ways, some even returning to the Church of England; but the prob-lems surrounding the possible misuses of the doctrine of salvation had not gone away.

But though More did not shrink from controversy, she found it more congenial to play an active role in a cause that united all Evangelicals, and also brought in some High Church, Unitarians and even Roman Catholics. This was the Bible Society, one of the first of the great interdenominational societies which were to play such a significant role in fashioning Evangelical culture in the nineteenth century.

Around 1802, so every Evangelical child used to be told, a girl called Mary Jones lived in a small cottage in the Welsh countryside, a remote and beauti-ful region with few English speakers. Like a child in one of Hannah More's Cheap Repository stories, she learned to read at a school opened in the village and acquired an ambition to possess a Bible for herself. Learning that a man in Bala, the Revd Thomas Charles, had a number of Bibles to sell, she walked the twenty-mile journey over rough countryside in order to obtain one. Fortunately Charles had a Bible, the last in his possession. The child stared at it in silent rapture, then took it in both hands and began her walk back home. But Charles had now run out of Welsh Bibles, and the Society for the Propagation of Christian Knowledge had recently declined to publish any further editions. Shortly after his encounter with Mary Jones, he went to London, where he submitted a question to the Religious Tract Society: 'How a large and cheap edition of the Bible could be had in Welsh'. A Baptist minister suggested the formation of a society for this purpose, adding the

[16] G. Carter, *Anglican Evangelicals: Protestant Secession from the Via Media, c.1800–1850* (Oxford, 2001), ch. 4.

[17] Clark, More to Olivia Sparrow, 18 Oct. 1815. The secessionists responded in kind. More heard that one of them, Thomas Cowan, 'the other day made a long quotation in his Sermon from the *Essay on St Paul!!!*', holding it up to criticism for its 'unsound' theology. Huntington, HM 30598, More to Charles Hoare, 8 Jan. [1816].

[18] Huntington, HM 30598, More to Charles Hoare, 8 Jan. [1816].

question 'and if for Wales, why not for the Kingdom? why not for the whole world?'[19] After a bout of strenuous networking the Anglicans of the Clapham sect were won over to the idea; so, with some misgivings, was the more cautious Beilby Porteus, though the archbishop of Canterbury kept his distance. The result was the founding of the British and Foreign Bible Society at a public meeting in London on 7 March 1804.

The society was interdenominational from the start, and even included some non-Evangelicals like Bishop Burgess. Its three secretaries were John Owen, curate, lecturer of Fulham, and Porteus's chaplain, a Welsh Baptist, and a German Lutheran; the committee consisted exclusively of laymen, fifteen Anglicans, fifteen Dissenters, and six foreigners resident in London. Henry Thornton was treasurer and the Claphamite Lord Teignmouth, former governor-general of India, its president. In drawing together Evangelicals of all denominations, the society provided them with the institutional unity they had previously lacked. Its deliberately minimalist agenda was 'the circulation of the Scriptures, and of the Scriptures only, *without note or comment*' (a proviso insisted on by the wary Porteus, worried about possible partisan interpretations of the Bible). Unlike the denominational missionary societies, it did not send out clergy to found churches. Its deceptively simple remit was to disseminate (and where necessary translate) the one text all Christians could (apparently) agree on.

So far so ecumenical. But this coming together of Evangelicals aroused the wrath of some High Churchmen, infuriated at the unspoken criticism of the older Anglican societies, the apparent downgrading of the Prayer Book, and the mingling of churchmen and Dissenters as equal partners in a common enterprise. Archdeacon Daubeny, one of many clerical *enragés*, charged head down into the arena against this 'wild deviation from the established order of things', part of the modern liberal heresy 'that every man has a right to worship God *in his own way*'.[20] To More's dismay, Alexander Knox agreed with her old enemy. The inclusiveness of the Bible Society, he argued, resembled 'real Christianity about as much as that two legged unfeathered animal, a plucked cock, resembled Plato's man'; anticipating the Tractarian doctrine of reserve, he feared 'an epidemic of contempt of the sacred volume thus...rashly vulgarized'.[21] Saddened by Knox's reasoning, More brutally

[19] For the Bible Society, see W. Canton, *A History of the British and Foreign Bible Society*, (London, 1904–10); J. Owen, *The History of the Origin and First Ten Years of the British and Foreign Bible Society* (London, 1816); L. Howsam, *Cheap Bibles: Nineteenth-Century Publishing and the British and Foreign Bible Society* (Cambridge, 1991). See also R. H. Martin, *Evangelicals United: Ecumenical Stirrings in Pre-Victorian Britain, 1795–1830* (Metuchen, NJ, 1983), 82.

[20] C. Daubeny, *Reasons for Supporting the Society for Promoting Christian Knowledge in Preference to the New Bible Society* (London, 1812), 11, 56.

[21] J. Jebb and A. Knox, *Thirty Years' Correspondence between John Jebb and Alexander Knox*, ed. C. Forster (London, 1836), ii. 164, 343.

dismissed another High Church pamphleteer, Edward Maltby, future bishop of Durham, as 'abominable'.[22] Her *ad hominem* language was extreme but also typical. Nothing had so set Anglican against Anglican since the Blagdon controversy. That had been the dress rehearsal; this was the full performance.

Yet none of this impeded the society's success. Its genius lay in its ability to mobilize the energies of its supporters throughout the country, using women and even children, and playing a vital role in the creation of the energetic Evangelical culture which was to be such an important feature of Victorian society. It happened spontaneously, as auxiliary associations began to mushroom throughout the country. The Bristol Auxiliary was founded in February 1810, and all the More sisters except Mary contributed 5 guineas each.[23] In the first year of its existence it distributed over 4,000 Bibles and Testaments. The auxiliaries then spawned their own outgrowths in the form of Ladies' Associations, and the arguments for female philanthropy that More had advocated in *Coelebs* were given practical application. By the 1830s middle-class women had cornered the market in selling cheap Bibles to the poor. Conservatives fretted at this 'amazonian' conduct, a blatant display of the unfeminine qualities of 'zeal and boldness' rather than 'the softened diffidence and female modesty which forms the great charm of the female bosom'.[24] Some feared that the women would neglect their families and undermine male authority by becoming tub-thumping fanatics; or, more insultingly still, that they would be unable to add up the collections. But perhaps the women themselves took heart from the support of that model of female propriety Hannah More, who, as will be shown, conspicuously led by example.

More's activities in her seventh decade can be seen as a triumph of endurance at a time when her life was dominated by increased frailty and the inexorable progress of bereavement. Her toothless gums were one reminder of the passing of time; the death of Porteus in May 1809 was another. 'I seem to be outliving my age,' she told Wilberforce in a sad acknowledgement of the fate of the long-lived elderly.[25] 'Twenty years did we three spend the month of May together!' she mourned to Ann Kennicott; now she would never see Fulham again.[26] He left her £200 in stock, and she set up an urn to his memory in a plantation near Barley Wood: 'in memory of long and faithful friendship'.[27] Though he had never formally identified himself with the Evangelicals, they were now deprived of their chief supporter on the

[22] Clark, More to Zachary Macaulay, 21 Sept. [1812].   [23] *FFBJ*, 3 Feb. 1810.
[24] Quoted in Martin, *Evangelicals United*, 114.
[25] Duke, More to Wilberforce, 12 July 1809.
[26] Clark, More to Ann Kennicott, 21 July 1809.   [27] Roberts, iii. 264.

episcopal bench. More mourned for the loss of her friend, 'but much more do I mourn for the Church—What a Successor!'[28] The unworthy successor was Dr John Randolph, former bishop of Oxford, an uncompromising opponent of the Bible Society. In 1813 he punished John Owen for his Bible Society activities by forcing him to resign his curacy at Fulham so that he could be resident in his Essex parish. To More, apparently unperturbed by the pluralism, this was religious persecution and Owen the society's 'Proto Martyr'; mentally dusting down her old poem, she promptly christened Randolph 'Bp. Bonner the 2nd'.[29] When he died suddenly in July 1813, she found it an 'awful consideration . . . he had in the press a circular letter to his Clergy not to preach on or for the Bible Society . . . It pleased God to move him before this mandate was passed.'[30]

Though old friends (and enemies) were passing away, More was making new, younger ones. Some were local dignitaries such as John Scandrett Harford, a former Quaker, the owner of the imposing Blaise Castle, and Sir Thomas Dyke Acland, Tory MP for Devon from 1812. Others were promising Evangelical clergy such as Acland's brother-in-law Charles Hoare, son of the Fleet Street banker and vicar of Blandford Forum in Dorset from 1807; and Daniel Wilson, later to become an especially zealous bishop of Calcutta. Another important new friend was the widowed Lady Olivia Bernard Sparrow, daughter of the Irish peer the earl of Gosford, an influential landowner in Huntingdonshire and a noted Evangelical philanthropist. A Swiss couple, François and Marie-Aimée Huber, who were distantly related to Madame de Staël, kept her informed about the progress of Evangelical religion in Geneva, and in 1816 M. Huber translated *Coelebs* into French.[31] Through all these contacts she became an important part of the network of communications that was turning the Evangelical movement into one of the most formidable forces of the age.

Some of her friends were of an even younger generation. One of the most attractive features of More's character is her delight in the company of her friends' children, for whom Barley Wood became the summer playground. She quickly recognized Tom Macaulay's extraordinary gifts and did her best to cultivate them. 'He is a jewel of a boy,' she told his proud father. She advised him on his reading, and admired his poetical compositions. Like a kindly aunt, she gave him money to buy a book at Hatchards.[32] Much as she

[28] Duke, More to Wilberforce, 12 July 1809.
[29] Huntington, HM 30593, More to Charles and Jane Hoare, 2 Nov. [1813]; Duke, More to Wilberforce, 7 Sept. [1813].
[30] Huntington, HM 30593, More to Charles Hoare, 2 Nov. 1813.
[31] I am grateful to Dr Clarissa Campbell Orr for information about the Hubers.
[32] Clark, More to Zachary Macaulay, 8 July 1811; 21 Sept. [1812]; Aug. 1813.

loved him, however, she was not blind to his faults, and she presciently warned his parents that 'he is a little inclined to undervalue those who are not considerable or distinguished in some way or other'.[33] Her friendship with this very brilliant young man was ended by political differences, but it made its mark on Macaulay. In 1831 he was to write a famous essay on Johnson ending with a dazzling word picture of 'the gigantic body, the black worsted stockings, the grey wig with the scorched foretop, the dirty hands, the nails bitten and pared to the quick'.[34] His picture obviously owes a great deal to Boswell's *Life*, but also to the fact that he had spent so many weeks of his childhood in the company of a survivor of the age of Johnson.

Another child to be fascinated by More's accounts of those days was Marianne Thornton, who left a vivid and evocative picture of golden summers spent with five benevolent and cultivated old ladies. Marianne's account is based on no particular year; it is an amalgam of nostalgic memories of 'that Paradise of my Childhood, Barley Wood', recollected in middle age and written down for her great-nephew E. M. Forster.

Surely there never was such a house, so full of intellect and piety and active benevolence. They lived in such uninterrupted harmony with each other...that young or old one felt oneself in a brighter and happier world...I can now imagine our arrival at the door covered with roses, and 'the Ladies', as they were always called, rushing out to cover us with kisses, & then take us into the kitchen to exhibit us to Mary and Charles, the housemaid and Coachman, then running themselves to fetch the tea things, Mrs Betty letting no one but herself to fry the eggs for 'the darling', the brown loaf brought out, the colour of a mahogany table, baked only once a week, of enormous size, but excellent taste...the peas we were set to pick, and then shell, perched upon the kitchen dresser, while Mrs Sally made the room resound with some of her merry stories of the Cottagers round, & then we were sent off by ourselves or with some village child to buy chickens at the next farm, and when we returned dragging along our purchases, how we were fed with strawberries and cream, & told to lie down on the hay whilst Charles, the Coachman, Gardener, Bailiff & Carpenter, made us a syllabub under the cow.[35]

Even when Hannah More was ill, Marianne recollected, she loved the company of young people. One night in 1813 she encouraged her to hide behind the curtains so that the maid would not spot her and send her away. 'No girl of sixteen could have enjoyed the trick more.'[36]

[33] BL, Add. MS 63084, More to the Macaulays [1812].
[34] *Lord Macaulay's Essays and Lays of Ancient Rome* (London, 1905), 184–5.
[35] Thornton, Add. MS 7674/1/L10, fos. 35–8. Forster's (not completely accurate) transcription is in his *Marianne Thornton* (London, 1956), 38–41.
[36] Thornton, Add. MS 7674/1/L10, fo. 41.

Occasionally Hannah More was still well enough to travel. In 1811 she and Patty undertook a marathon seven-week journey to the Midlands, principally to visit Yoxall Lodge in Staffordshire, the home of the Revd Thomas Gisborne, author of the much admired *Essay on the Duties of the Female Sex* (1797). She found it 'the abode of peace, piety, literature, friendship and elegant hospitality', and, to make the visit even more pleasant, Ann Kennicott was also there.[37] She would certainly have paid attention to the children, but her reactions to Gisborne's 11-year-old daughter are unrecorded; thirty-two years later Lydia Gisborne was to become the notorious Mrs Robinson, whose affair with her children's tutor, Branwell Brontë, led to his ruin. At Yoxall, too, she met a man who became one of her closest friends, Henry Ryder, incumbent of two Leicestershire parishes. A distinguished though turbulent future lay ahead of him. In 1812 he became her neighbour when he was appointed dean of Wells, and in the following year she reported to Wilberforce that 'He is filling the Cathedral every Sunday tho he preaches near an hour. He hints at his difficulties; I understand him, he has not one congenial spirit in Wells.'[38] Three years later, partly through the influence of his brother Lord Harrowby, he became bishop of Gloucester, the first Evangelical on the episcopal bench.

Three weeks of this tour were spent in general sightseeing. In Shrewsbury she saw 'the Field where Hotspur fell and where Falstaff proved that "Discretion is the better part of valour"'. Like many other visitors, she was appalled at the ironworks at Coalbrookdale, set in the otherwise beautiful Severn Valley.

Wherever I went I was disgusted with what I ought as a good citizen to have rejoyced at, the injury usefulness had done to beauty. Every lovely piece of scenery is so defiled with stinking, dingy, disfiguring manufactures that the charms of nature are more than half defaced. There is especially at Coalbook Dale a wonderful mixture of Elysium and Factories, but the infernal predominates.[39]

Later in the year the strains of rapid industrialization and wartime disruption were to lead to the Luddite disturbances, as stocking frames were smashed throughout the East Midlands.

The tour was rounded off by a visit to see one of the Welsh tourist attractions, the celebrated 'Ladies of Llangollen'. About thirty-five years earlier Lady Eleanor Butler and her friend Miss Sarah Ponsonby had defied the wishes of their families and set up house together in Plas Newydd in the vale of Llangollen. They lived there in the most celebrated sentimental

[37] Clark, More to Sarah Holroyd, 28 Sept. [1811]; Roberts, iii. 350–1.
[38] Duke, More to Wilberforce, 7 Sept. [1813].
[39] Clark, More to Sarah Holroyd, 28 Sept. [1811]. For Sarah Holroyd, see J. H. Adeane (ed.), *The Girlhood of Maria Josepha Holroyd* [*Lady Stanley of Adlerley*] (London, 1896).

friendship of the age, wearing semi-masculine costume, and adding fashionable Gothic features to their house; neither of them ever spent a single night away from the house or each other. More was delighted with them. 'I have hardly since the loss of my dear Mrs Montagu met with so much spirit, sense, and animation, so much knowledge of the world and of books with a vivacity peculiarly her own as in Lady E. Butler. Miss Ponsonby seems equally excellent in another way.'[40] Did she feel a pang at the recollection of an earlier period in her life? She wistfully told Sir William Weller Pepys, one of the few survivors, that his letters conveyed 'certain associations inseparable from the recollection of pleasure never to be repeated, in a society never to be again enjoyed'.[41] Amid all the talk of Bible Societies and missions to the heathen, there was a part of her that still longed for elegant and civilized bluestocking conversation. She did not speculate about the sexuality of the two ladies or see anything odd in a relationship that bore many resemblances to the earlier close friendship of Elizabeth Bouverie and Margaret Middleton.[42]

Private affairs could not be divorced from the huge strains imposed on a nation at war, and with Britain and France imposing economic sanctions on each other, many manufacturing districts plunged into ever deeper crises. In an unwelcome by-product of the sanctions, the United States declared war over the British insistence that the Royal Navy search neutral shipping for embargoed French goods: 'an awful event', Thornton declared to his wife.[43] But George III, who had experienced one war with America, knew nothing of this. In 1811 he was declared incurably insane, and his remaining nine years were spent in a half-life at Windsor, where he prowled the corridors, a ghostly figure in a nightgown. In the following year his son the regent assumed full powers, and, to the disgust of his Whig daughter, he abandoned his former political allies and kept Spencer Perceval's Tory government in office. Wilberforce and Thornton saw themselves as critical friends of the administration, and regarded the devout prime minister as almost one of them. It was therefore a huge blow when, on 11 May 1812, Perceval was assassinated in the lobby of the House of Commons by a Liverpool bankrupt, John Bellingham, thus gaining the unenviable distinction of being the only British prime minister to be assassinated. More was appalled at the crime, but even more so at the sympathetic reception given to Bellingham at the gallows by a crowd that was sick of war and politicians. She wrote to Ann Kennicott,

I have seen with indignation the half penny papers that are cried about London streets...drawn up with so much wicked art that the assassin seems the martyr

[40] Clark, More to Sarah Holroyd, 28 Sept. [1811].
[41] Roberts, iii. 337.   [42] See *Gambier*, i. 139.
[43] Thornton, Add. MS 7674/1/L5, fo. 49, Thornton to Mrs H. Thornton, 25 Jan. 1812.

and hero and Perceval the oppressor. It is quite astonishing what a mischievous effect this has produced on the minds of the vulgar; and even some of the higher class speak of this execrable villain with a sort of respect as they would of Brutus . . . Medals too are struck of Bellingham, and sold in the Booksellers Shops! I never wished to be Bishop of London before, at least not the Eveque regnant [Randolph, the opponent of the Bible Society], but if I were so at present, I certainly should call to account the Clergyman who administered the Sacrament to an assassin who died glorying in his crime . . . had he expressed contrition . . . the case would have been otherwise.[44]

Even in the face of the grim events, Mrs Kennicott had to smile sceptically at her friend's declaration that she had never before wished to be bishop of London.[45]

By this time Barley Wood had a new inmate, a little girl who came to them in 1811 aged 2, and became a sort of adopted granddaughter. Her name was Louisa Tidy, the daughter of Charles, their coachman and general factotum, whose wife had died recently. More told the Hubers, 'The girl who is a pleasant child is here half the time in order to help out his exhausted finances, as he has two to pay for.'[46] She loved watching her play. Louisa's quick ear picked up the sisters' refrains as they fretted about Lady Olivia Sparrow's health, and one day More

overheard the little brat . . . singing in a plaintive note to her doll

> 'Lady Livy
> poor Lady Livy
> dear Lady Livy
> poor dear Lady Livy'.[47]

Three years later she fondly reported to Lady Olivia that 'Little Tidy . . . is the most amusing, sprightly, idle little witch imaginable. The greatest lover of humour and hater of *literature*, a wit and a dunce. Your beautiful books are kept on a high shelf in her sight, nor is she allowed to see the pictures which are her delight till she can read the words.'[48] Lady Olivia persisted, and sent Louisa another book later in the year. 'The little brat was out of her wits with joy, and when any company comes, runs down with her *Livrary* in her frock. But she is a dunce at her book tho' keen in her understanding.'[49]

44 Clark, More to Ann Kennicott, 10 June [1812].
45 Clark, Ann Kennicott to More, Windsor, 13 July [1812].
46 Clark, More to F. Huber, 1812.
47 BL, Egerton MS 1965, fo. 7a, More to Olivia Sparrow [Dec. 1812].
48 BL, Egerton MS 1965, fo. 30b, More to Olivia Sparrow, 17 Feb. 1815.
49 Clark, More to Olivia Sparrow, 18 Oct. 1815.

When the Hubers tried to tell More that she was being exploited, she responded indignantly, 'We took her at two years old, a poor diseased help-less creature who must otherwise have starved . . . Her health is very bad, her mind very acute.' She added that she was now paying 8 guineas a year for her to go to school, where she was learning to read and write (the writing an unmistakable sign that Louisa was being taken out of her class). She would send her to boarding school it she could afford it, she added unrepentantly. 'As I am naturally fond of children I teach her myself of an evening when we are alone.'[50] This of course was the point; she had 'adopted' Louisa because her chatter and her laughter added life and sparkle to the elderly household. Later, in the sad aftermath of Patty's death, she took comfort when Louisa read to her from the Bible in her strong Somerset accent: 'She reads very well and I do not mind her *hidols* and her *himages*, her *eaven* and her *hearth*.'[51]

In 1813 the sisterhood suffered its first rupture with the death of Mary on 18 April (Easter Sunday). John Scandrett Harford remembered her as a stately and rather deaf old lady who dressed in an old-fashioned style, with 'a high cap surmounting a large ruff of powdered hair'.[52] For the past year, however, she had been 'almost as weak as an infant',[53] but, though the loss had been long anticipated, it was hard to bear. The sisters visited 'the cold remains twenty times a day' before she was buried in Wrington churchyard, where they were one by one to join her.[54]

Yet in the midst of this grief Hannah More's energies had returned. The Clapham Saints had begun a new campaign. In 1813 the East India Compa-ny's charter was up for renewal, and the Evangelicals wished to insert a clause in the new charter allowing Christian missionaries to operate in the parts of India controlled by the Company. They faced fierce opposition from the Company, which had always forbidden proselytizing for fear that this would exacerbate religious tensions—an apprehension that the terrible events of 1857 might appear to justify. But to Evangelicals, believing as they did that the only way to God was the Christian way, this denial of the gospel to the Indians was the supreme national sin, comparable to the now abolished slave trade. With tactics learned from the abolitionist movement, Wilberforce planned to bring pressure on his fellow parliamentarians from the country at large. In March he wrote to Hannah More asking her 'to stir up a petition in Bristol, and in any other place'.[55] She acted speedily. On 3 April a letter from 'Philanthropos' appeared in the *Bristol Journal* setting out the case for

[50] Huntington, HM 31109, More to the Hubers, 21 Mar. [1817].
[51] Clark, More to Macaulay [1819?].
[52] J. S. Harford, *Recollections of William Wilberforce Esq.* (London, 1864), 267.
[53] Folger, W.b. 488, fo. 25, More to Eva Garrick, 26 Mar. 1812.
[54] Roberts, iii. 384.   [55] *Life of Wilberforce*, iv. 103.

spreading the Christian message to India 'in a gradual and prudent way'. In the following week the paper informed its readers that 'the Petitions to both Houses of Parliament, relative to the promotion of Christianity in India, will remain for signatures at the Council-House and Commercial-Rooms till three o'clock on Monday next'.[56] Two days later More wrote to Wilberforce,

I hope you will think we have done wonders in Bristol considering the shortness of the time—I next thought of Manchester. I named to my valuable neighbour Mrs Quincey [mother of Thomas the opium addict], your idea about getting petitions for Christianizing India, she sent me the enclosed desiring me to get a Frank and send it, but we are both so afraid we have not correctly met your wishes that I think it safer to trouble you to read it . . . Send me half a line to say whether you approve of the Manchester plan . . .[57]

The petitions were successful in Manchester, Bristol, and throughout the provinces. Armed with this impressive support, Wilberforce stood up in the Commons on 22 June and delivered a diatribe on 'the degraded character of the Hindoo superstition'[58] that reads shockingly two centuries later, though at the time the evils of *sati* and female infanticide seemed to present powerful arguments for Christian proselytizing. His motion was carried by 89 votes to 36. The consequences for India were momentous. The Evangelical success in opening up India to Christianity was paralleled a generation later by the secular Utilitarian programme of Westernization, an agenda that was summed up in the confident persona of Thomas Babington Macaulay, who went to India as the new law member in 1834. In a resolution of the following year he declared 'that the great objects of the British government ought to be the promotion of European literature and science . . . through the medium of the English language'.[59] Such was the success of this programme that later generations of bemused Indian schoolchildren were made to learn Wordsworth's *Daffodils* by heart, without having the least idea what these exotic flowers looked like.

The success of Wilberforce's campaign had profound implications for Britain as well as India. The mass petitioning of Parliament once again proved its usefulness. A wider public—going far beyond the formal electorate—had gained access to the political process: women in particular. Hannah More and Elizabeth De Quincey, networking, persuading, searching for the right words, following the parliamentary debates with enthusiasm, were part of an emerging culture that, in paradoxical fashion, told women to confine themselves to domestic concerns, and at the same time, when the cause was good, encouraged them to take on roles that looked suspiciously masculine and to enter a public sphere that in theory was reserved for men.

---

[56] *FFBJ*, 3 and 10 Apr. 1813.
[57] Bodleian, MS c. 48, fo. 54, More to Wilberforce [12 Apr. 1813].
[58] *Life of Wilberforce*, iv. 119.
[59] P. Spear, *A History of India* (Harmondsworth, 1965), ii. 126–7.

But there were limits to the political influence of a disfranchised woman, as Hannah More realized in the spring and summer of 1813 when Wilberforce—of all people—let her down. In February the Commons voted on a bill to allow Catholics to enter Parliament. This created a dilemma for the Clapham Saints, torn between their hostility to Rome and their fear that, if this measure were defeated, Ireland would erupt once more—a prospect that was painstakingly set out in Knox's immense letters to Wilberforce. In 1812 Henry Thornton had admitted to More that 'I voted for the Catholics, so also did Charles Grant jun^r, & the scale vibrated a little with Babington & Wilberforce.'[60] Now—a year later—Wilberforce argued in committee that Parliament had a golden opportunity to secure peace in Ireland by conceding the Catholic claims. This caused a sensation in an Evangelical world that took it for granted that the Pope was Antichrist and that 'popery' was the implacable enemy of civil liberty, religious freedom, and gospel truth. Wilberforce knew many of his friends were going to give him a hard time—not least the fervently Protestant More sisters.

In the summer he passed a day with them and saw from the start 'that a storm was lowering over him', the main thunderclouds heading from Patty's direction. He decided that attack was the best mode of defence, and, when the subject was raised, he said gravely, 'How shocking it is that you who know so much of the misery which Popery has brought on Ireland, should advocate a system which perpetuates its falling yoke!' For once, Patty was silenced, and the rest of the visit passed off pleasantly.[61] But all was not well. Hannah More was too polite, too reverential even, to pick a quarrel with this greatest of Evangelicals, but this did not stop her brooding on his defection. Six years later, when he transgressed again, she was to write unhappily to Henry Ryder, bishop of Gloucester,

We have been sadly cast down by the miserable majority on the Catholic question. Why would that dear Wilberforce throw his great weight, probably not much short of forty votes, into the wrong side? His enemies too are making a handle against him, of what I must confess appears even to partial *me* an error, his high panegyric on Sir Samuel Romilly [the Whig reformer, who had committed suicide in November 1818]! I grieve to see the noblest minds *can* be a little warped by their partialities. Our dear friends ... Babington, Macaulay &c are too much disposed to defend Romilly and even Brougham on account of their use in the abolition business—all this is natural, but a Socinian and a Suicide (tho' I hope an insane one) should not have been painted in such glowing colours by our incomparable friend. I would not say this but to your Lordship.[62]

[60] Thornton, Add. MS 7674/1/L5, fo. 85, Thornton to More, 25 Apr. 1812.

[61] *Life of Wilberforce*, iv. 99–100.

[62] Harrowby MS Trust, Ryder Papers, MS 262, More to Ryder, 7 May 1819. Quoted by kind permission of the seventh earl of Harrowby.

More's fear that the cause of abolition had created unnatural political alliances between conservatively minded Evangelicals and Rational Dissenters shows that a breach had been opened between the parliamentary Evangelicals and the wider movement in the provinces. For all her love of Wilberforce, she had cast her lot with the 'country Evangelicals', an increasingly conservative body, often suspicious of the relatively liberal and open-minded Clapham sect.[63] (She must have been mortified when Ryder reluctantly voted for emancipation in 1829.)

In the summer of 1813 Hannah and Patty embarked on another tour.[64] For the first time since 1806 they planned to go to the environs of London to meet old friends. First they visited Brampton Park, Olivia Sparrow's home in Huntingdonshire, where predictably Hannah was taken ill. A journey to Kent, intended to revive happy memories of spring days at Teston, was cancelled on the news of the death of Lord Barham; he was 86, and died knowing, like Othello, that he had done the state some service. However, they were able to visit to the Thorntons at Battersea Rise, the Wilberforces at Kensington Gore, and Lady Waldegrave at Strawberry Hill, where More was preoccupied with thoughts of its former master. They then called at Hampton, but Mrs Garrick was out. More 'saw over the Garden, the Temple &c where I had passed so many days of various colours, and concluded with the Preacher that *all is vanity*'.[65] But she wrote later to Mrs Garrick in a lighter vein, telling her how she had been 'much diverted' with the maid.

Fearing she might take us for thieves...I said, 'we are very old friends of Mrs Garrick, my name is More, I don't [know] whether you ever heard my name'—'O yes, Ma'am said she I have heard a great deal about you because you used to have your Cloaths washed by Mrs Jones'—so you see there are many roads to fame. How many thousand things we should have had to talk of had we met?[66]

But they were never to meet again.

Back home the sisters plunged into another round of activity. It began in August 1813, when More told Zachary Macaulay that 'On Friday we are to have a meeting to establish a Bible Society of our own at Wrington. I am busy in writing notes, as all distant members, and all orators, are to have a breakfast prepared for them at Barley Wood before the meeting.'[67] The Wrington

[63] I. Bradley, 'The Politics of Godliness: Evangelicals in Parliament, 1784–1832', D. Phil. thesis (Oxford, 1974), 63–66.

[64] Roberts, iii. 396–401.

[65] Clark, More to Mrs H. Thornton, 4 July 1813.

[66] New York Public Library, Berg Collection of English and American Literature, 221719B, More to Eva Garrick, 7 Aug. [1813].

[67] Clark, More to Zachary Macaulay, Aug. 1813.

Society was not one of the Ladies' Societies but was a branch of the Somerset Auxiliary, open to both sexes. It had been founded on 21 April 1813, after what More described as 'many draw backs and vexatious interruptions' (including the opposition of Bishop Beadon), under the auspices of John Scandrett Harford.[68] After much assiduous letter-writing, eighteen clergy attended the inn at Wrington for the inaugural meeting. The assembly met 'in a waggon house—I was indulged with a room in the house which looked down on it . . . *We* kept open house for the distant pilgrims and had near 20 to breakfast, dinner and tea.'[69] In all, £170 was raised for the Society.

The Wrington anniversaries became a regular summer feature, and Hannah and Patty More battled through ill health and old age to keep them going. In 1818 More told Wilberforce that, far from being what a local clergyman called a 'Hotbed of Heresy and Schism', they had entertained 'near 40 Clergymen of the Establishment, and only one Dissenter'. The weather was good, so most were able to eat out of doors. 'They all enjoy'd themselves exceedingly, and it had all the gaiety of a public garden.' On purely economic grounds, she knew that the work in arranging such events was hard to justify ('Some may think that it would be better to add £20 to our Subscription, and save ourselves so much trouble') but she was shrewd enough to recognize the importance of sociability and celebration to the creation of Evangelical culture. 'The many young persons of fortune present, by assisting at this little festivity, will learn to connect the idea of innocent cheerfulness with that of religious societies, and may go and do likewise.'[70] After another successful anniversary she told young Marianne Thornton that the 'White robed nymphs and black Clericals make a pretty motley mixture on the Hill'.[71] It was a treat for the eye as well as the soul and stomach, a recognition that even Protestant man cannot live by sermons alone. Just as much of post-Napoleonic Europe saw the revival of Catholic ceremonies and associations, the Evangelicals could mount their own rituals and theatre. Again, Hannah More was at the forefront of a changing culture.

The signs of change were all around. In 1811 the Evangelical movement had fought off an attempt by the home secretary, Lord Sidmouth, to limit the freedoms of Dissenters by clamping down on itinerant preaching. In the following years they began to assemble in London every May to attend the meetings of the various Evangelical societies. In 1813 Mrs Thornton wrote excitedly to More of 'such a week of religious dissipation that I have wished

[68] W. Canton, *A History of the British and Foreign Bible Society* (London, 1904–10), 478; Huntington, HM 30592, More to Jane Hoare, 4 Feb. [1813].

[69] Clark, More to Olivia Sparrow, 21 Aug. 1813.

[70] Duke, More to Wilberforce [1818].

[71] Thornton, Add. MS 7674/1/E/6 [1816].

for Mrs Sally here amongst us. Such sermons for Missions & Jews & Heretics! such meetings after each sermon—such collections & above all such a parent bible meeting that I think all the good people look ten years younger than they did.'[72] The Evangelical ritual calendar was now established, and one week in May—what More, appropriating an older terminology, sometimes called its *sainte semaine* and at other times its 'Christian carnival'—was its highlight.[73] In 1831 the Evangelicals acquired their temple, Exeter Hall in the Strand. Though old age kept More away, she loomed over the debates and transactions. On one occasion in the 1820s a fractious Bible Society meeting was brought to a reverential silence by the reading of a passage from 'the venerable and illustrious Hannah More'.[74] Wilberforce apart, few could match her moral authority.

In the spring of 1814 the Allies marched into Paris, Napoleon abdicated, and the Bourbon monarchy was restored. 'This hath God done,' Wilberforce wrote to More, only regretting that Pitt was not alive to witness it.[75] Though Bonaparte was to make his dramatic 'hundred days' comeback in the following year, Britain's endless war with France was virtually over. At about the same time Hannah More received a distinguished and unexpected guest. This was 'Coleridge the poet of the Lakes', who was on an extended visit to Bristol to deliver a course of lectures on Shakespeare. She had previously avoided him because of his radical politics and Unitarian theology, but he had long abandoned these and was now eager to meet her. She told Wilberforce, 'As that fiddling monosyllable *No* is the hardest word I ever learnt to pronounce—I gave him leave.' He arrived one morning in April with his friend Joseph Cottle the bookseller, who had known More for many years. Like almost everyone who met him, she found Coleridge 'very eloquent, entertaining and brimfull of knowledge'. She was also pleasantly surprised at his knowledge of Evangelicalism.[76] He seems to have enjoyed the visit, finding More 'the *first* literary female I ever met with—In part, no doubt, because she is a Christian'.[77]

However, More's bland account did not convey the full flavour of the visit. While he was with her, the watchful Cottle noticed his friend's hands shake 'to an alarming degree, so that he could not take a glass of wine without spilling it, though one hand supported the other'.[78] It was impossible to hide

[72] Thornton, Add. MS 7674/1/L5, fo. 130, Mrs H. Thornton to More, 6 May 1813.

[73] Roberts, iv. 74; Clark, More to Olivia Sparrow [1814].

[74] Thornton, Add. MS 7674/1/F/9, Marianne Thornton to More, n.d. The sentence was from *Practical Piety*.

[75] *Life of Wilberforce*, iv. 171.

[76] Duke, More to Wilberforce, 13 Apr. 1814.

[77] *Collected Letters of Samuel Taylor Coleridge*, ed. E. L. Griggs (Oxford, 1959), iii. 499–500.

[78] J. Cottle *Reminiscences of Samuel Taylor Coleridge and Robert Southey* (London, 1847, repr. Highgate, 1970), 360–1.

the deadly effects of his opium addiction, and, if More took note of the symptoms, this may have reinforced her anxieties over Wilberforce's well-known dependency. Though he was fortunate to escape many of the drug's devastations, the deterioration of his eyesight was probably a symptom of the prolonged effects of morphine.[79] The substance was legal and widely available and she took it herself, under prescription, as did Henry Thornton. She too suffered from 'weak eyes' from at least 1807, though the vagueness of her descriptions of her symptoms makes it hard to determine whether she was suffering from opium poisoning or simply from a degenerative eye disease.[80] (When Thomas De Quincey's *Confessions of an English Opium Eater* was published, her attitude to her friend's son was harsh: 'Mrs Quincey must be terribly mortified at the Opium eater.'[81] Because her consumption was purely medicinal and never approached De Quincey's enormous intake, she made little if any connection between his crippling addiction and her mild one.)

That summer saw the usual round of feasts, with More, who had been confined by illness for eight months, at last able to venture outdoors. Twenty-four people came to dinner and tea on 'Bible day' and Henry Ryder 'spoke excellently'; 700 children attended the school feasts, though More still mourned the missing 500 from Blagdon.[82] By this time much of the euphoria attending the end of the war had died down, and More along with many others was lamenting the 'shocking blot on the fair face of peace'.[83] In June the foreign secretary, Knox's old employer Lord Castlereagh, returned to London, having negotiated the Treaty of Paris, which allowed the French to resume the slave trade for a further five years. Wilberforce immediately denounced this 'Additional Article', and once more the abolitionists appealed to their networks throughout the country. The result was a series of petitions, three quarters of a million signatures in all, which forced the hand of the duke of Wellington, Britain's new ambassador to France. Such was the pressure of public opinion that the Treaty of Paris was renegotiated, and the European powers signed a general declaration opposing the slave trade.[84] Even though the declaration was too vague to have much immediate effect, it represented a further triumph for British pressure group politics.

[79] As early as 1797 More had expressed the hope that the waters at Bath 'will enable him to reduce the quantity of opium he now takes'. *Gambier*, i. 241, More to Elizabeth Bouverie [1797]. For a discussion of Wilberforce and narcotics, see J. Pollock, *Wilberforce* (London, 1977), 79–81. For opium, see V. Berridge and G. Edwards, *Opium and the People: Opiate Use in Nineteenth-Century England* (London, 1981).

[80] Bodleian, MS d. 14, fo. 8, More to Wilberforce, n.d.; Duke, 14 June 1813, *c*.10 Jan. 1815, and 26 June 1819.

[81] Huntington, MY 704, More to Selina Macaulay, 12 Dec. [1822].

[82] Duke, More to Wilberforce, 27 June 1814.   [83] Ibid.

[84] S. Drescher, 'Whose Abolition? Popular Pressure and the Ending of the British Slave Trade', *Past and Present*, 43 (1994), 136–43.

While Wilberforce was mounting his campaign, More was at work on another book, her two-volume *Essay on the Character and Practical Writings of St Paul* (the word 'practical' being highly characteristic). She published under her own name, and such was her prestige in the Evangelical world that the first impression sold out before it was published early in 1815.[85] The success is all the more remarkable considering that in a third-person author's preface she realistically admitted 'her incompetency to the proper execution of such a work...her deficiencies in ancient learning, Biblical criticism, and deep theological knowledge'.[86] Though she made an effort to place him in context, her St Paul turned out to be Burkean in his politics, sober and rational in his piety, with (by implication) strong views on the errors of the ultra-High Churchmen and hyper-Calvinists; she had fashioned the great apostle in her own image.

1814 had been a good year for More, a time of improved health and vigour. She was lucky, however, to see in the new year, having narrowly escaped being burned to death. One November day, she told Eva Garrick,

I was standing about noon in my own room with my back to the fire; all at once I heard a noise which I thought was the roaring of the wind in the Chimney, on looking round I saw myself all in flames...I went to the top of the Stairs and called for help. They all ran and found me a flaming spectacle.[87]

She owed her life to one of the Miss Robertses, a pair of sisters who had taken to staying with her. With great presence of mind she grasped More 'flaming as I was, as if I had been an infant, and laying me on the carpet... burned her hands...terribly'.[88] The incident was reported in the papers (accompanied by recommendations for the use of fireguards) and More received about 100 letters from concerned friends.[89] As her burns healed, she was able to give a piece of grimly satisfying news to Macaulay: Thomas Bere was 'dead after a period of insanity'.[90] She was to find the new curate much more amenable: 'He takes my advice kindly and allows me to say anything to him...He has of course much to learn, being just escaped from Christ Church.'[91] When it came to lecturing the local clergy, old habits died hard.

The year had ended dramatically. The new one—the year of her seventieth birthday—opened dreadfully. At the end of 1814 Thornton had written

[85] Huntington, MY 668, More to Macaulay, 20 Feb. [1815].
[86] *An Essay on the Character and Practical Writings of St Paul* (London, 1815), vol. i, p. iii.
[87] Berg, 221718B, More to Eva Garrick, 3 Dec. [1814].
[88] Roberts, iii. 414–15, 417–19.
[89] Ibid. 419–20; *FFBJ*, 19 Nov. 1814.
[90] Clark, More to Zachary Macaulay, 21 Dec. 1814; *FFBJ*, 5 Nov. 1814.
[91] BL, Egerton MS 1965, fos. 43–4, More to Olivia Sparrow, 13 Sept. [1815].

to tell her that he had been 'very poorly for some weeks past'. Even as he wrote, he was interrupted by his cough and the letter was finished by his wife.[92] He was presenting the classic symptoms of tuberculosis, the 'white plague', which after a period of decline was about to reach a new peak in the nineteenth century: the cough producing thick yellow sputum streaked with blood, the rapid weight loss, and the fever. The sudden removal of such a man, Wilberforce told More, 'would be a most mysterious Providence';[93] he had been his right-hand man in the abolition campaign, the chief financial support of the Mendip schools, the patron of innumerable charities, the half of an unusually devoted couple, the father of nine children, the eldest a girl of 18, her brother still too young to take over the family bank. Surely God would not remove him in the middle of such usefulness? But he died on 16 January aged 54, and was buried in the freezing cold eight days later. Wilberforce was too ill to attend. A week later another friend, the barrister John Bowdler junior, Evangelical member of a High Church family, died. Before this news had properly sunk in, another prominent Clapham connection, the oriental scholar and biblical translator Dr Claudius Buchanan, also died, possibly from a chill caught at Thornton's funeral. 'Who next, Lord?' a distraught Wilberforce wrote to More.[94] She was equally devastated. 'Thornton, Bowdler, Buchanan: the blows come thick upon each other. How wounding to the heart! how awakening to the soul!' She urged Wilberforce to make his own health a priority. 'As Knox once said to me, "let the dead bury their dead".'[95]

She was at her best when her friends were bereaved, ready to give practical advice as well as spiritual consolation. Though Mrs Thornton was bearing up well, she had a sensible warning for her. 'I am afraid you will think me but a worldly Counsellor when I say I wish you not too much to suppress emotions which nature dictates and which grace does not forbid.'[96] In the summer Mrs Thornton and five of her children came to stay at Barley Wood. Yet the change of scene could not accomplish the desired purpose, and by the autumn she was showing the symptoms of her husband's illness. She died peacefully at Brighton in October. More wrote to Marianne immediately: 'Glory & honour & praise be unto Him that sitteth on the Throne & unto the Lamb for ever.'[97] The words were sincere and apposite, for, if the Thorntons were not rejoicing in heaven, who then could be saved? But it was 'a very trying as well as mysterious dispensation', and she could not help fretting about the 'poor dear orphans'.[98] Following the provisions of their

---

[92] Thornton, Add. MS 7674/1/L6, fos. 68–73.   [93] *Life of Wilberforce*, iv. 228–9.

[94] Ibid. 235.   [95] Duke, More to Wilberforce, 13 Feb. 1815.

[96] Thornton, Add. MS 7674/1/L6, fos. 141–2, More to Mrs H. Thornton, 20 Jan. 1815.

[97] Ibid., fo. 134, More to Marianne Thornton, 14 Oct. 1815. See also Add. MS 7674/1/N, fo. 433.

[98] BL, Egerton MS 1965, fo. 40a, More to Olivia Sparrow [Oct. 1815].

father's will, the children were placed under the guardianship of a childless young couple, Robert Inglis and his wife, Mary. Inglis was the heir to a baronetcy and a member of Parliament, with strong Tory views at odds with Henry Thornton's more liberal politics. But the couple proved excellent guardians, and it must be a tribute to their kindness and sensitivity that the Thornton children were so little traumatized by their double bereavement.

Thornton's death marked the first serious rupture in the ranks of the Clapham sect. Wilberforce himself was cutting down on his public activities in order to concentrate more on his six children. From 1812 he had ceased to represent the 'popular' constituency of Yorkshire and had become member for a pocket borough in the gift of his wife's cousin the third Baron Calthorpe. ('Old Corruption' had its uses.) Hannah More herself continued to struggle through bilious attacks, chest infections, and fever. Yet the demands on her time and her energies, not all of them self-induced, continued relentlessly. Too celebrated, too conveniently close to Bath and Clifton, those centres of Georgian sociability, to live in seclusion, she had become, in the words of one of the Thornton children, 'a sort of lioness'.[99] At the beginning of 1816 she admitted wearily to Wilberforce that 'the retirement I sought I have never been able to find ... I never saw more people known and unknown in my gayest days.' No visiting Evangelical would wish to leave the area without a sight of the mother of the movement. In a wry recognition of her iconic status she added, 'They come to me as to the Witch of Endor and I suppose I shall soon be desired to tell fortunes and cast nativities.'[100] She was the nearest a Protestant culture could come to a holy woman, endowed with particular insights and a privileged access to the deity. After her death an American visitor remembered her 'celebrated cottage', her appearance, her conversation with a wealth of reverential detail that would not be out of place in a description of a pilgrimage.[101] Barley Wood was a sacred place, and More the oracle to be found within its walls. She had become public religious property who could only retreat into a private world on her doctor's orders.

Not all who came to Barley Wood were Evangelicals in quest of their high priestess. Her list of visitors reads like a late Georgian *Who's Who*. Some came out of kindness. In 1813 Sarah Siddons, staying with Thomas Sedgwick Whalley, came over and recited parts of *Paradise Lost* to the sisters; they were impressed with her reading and politely kept to themselves their disapproval of her profession.[102] Others came from curiosity. In the summer of 1816 More once more complained of being 'sadly overdone with com-

[99] Thornton, Add. MS 7674/1/N, fo. 617, Sophia Thornton to Laura Thornton, 1827.
[100] Duke, More to Wilberforce, 30 Jan. 1816.   [101] *Christian Observer*, 33 (1833), 629–31.
[102] Duke, More to Wilberforce, 7 Sept. 1813.

pany. Yesterday we had above twenty, more than half of them strangers.' Some were welcome. On one occasion she was taken aback when 'a servant came up in a hurry to tell me that there was a Coach at the door with eight Arabians'. The visitors 'proved to be eight Moravians, no formidable race. These holy Sisters made me a kind visit.'[103] A less congenial visitor was the Revd Thomas Malthus, author of the famously alarmist essay on population, whom More found 'too thorough a Brougham-ite & Edinburgh Reviewer for me to like'.[104] His prescription for starving the poor out of their propensity to breed beyond their means would have struck no chord of sympathy with a woman who had devoted so much of her time to feeding malnourished children. A more Evangelically orthodox visitor was 'my charming friend Mrs Gladstone of Liverpool',[105] whose husband was responsible for shipping copies of her books to the United States. On one occasion she visited accompanied by her young son William, and More presented the future prime minister with an inscribed copy of *Sacred Dramas*.[106]

A letter to Pepys opens up the possibility of another famous visitor. 'I am ashamed of myself for not having read any of Miss Austen's novels,' she wrote in 1816. 'It is merely want of time.' (This was a coded way of saying that, with the exceptions of the works of Madame de Staël and Sir Walter Scott, she now read little fiction.) She added, 'Two of the sisters have been here, and seemed to be amicable, interesting women, and well bred.'[107] As there were only two Austen sisters, the visitors must have been Cassandra and Jane, who could have called on her during their stay at Clifton in the summer of 1806. But would More have remembered this after ten years? Though one would dearly love to believe in the meeting, it is possible that one visitor might have merged into another, and that More might have confused the Austen sisters with two other young women. 'I am worn out with company,' she told Zachary Macaulay. 'I am sometimes tempted to run away.'[108]

Another unwelcome by-product of fame was the problem of pirated editions of her books. Reckoning up her earnings in the spring of 1816, she estimated that *Strictures*, *Coelebs*, and *Practical Piety* had netted her £6,000, and 'the other twelve volumes probably about as much more'.[109] She had come to regret her decision, made in the days when she knew little of publishers, to sell the copyright of her early works to Cadell. Now, however, the pirates were injuring both her and her publishers by printing them 'in small tempting forms, full of vignettes and deceptions and most impudently

---

[103] Ibid., 2 Sept. 1823. [104] Ibid., 4 July 1816. [105] Ibid. [Autumn 1818].
[106] J. Morley, *The Life of William Ewart Gladstone* (London, 1903), i. 12.
[107] Clark, More to Pepys, 16 Mar. 1816.
[108] Huntington, MY 671, More to Zachary Macaulay, 23 Sept. 1815.
[109] Clark, More to Pepys, 16 Mar. 1816.

prefix[ed] to the volumes *"with Memoirs of the Author's Life"*.[110] But though Cadell rushed out his own editions,[111] the pirates continued to sell: proof that Hannah More continued to be hot literary property. At the age of 71 she had not yet reached the end of her active life.

[110] Duke, More to Wilberforce, 30 Jan. 1816.
[111] Clark, More to Pepys, 16 Mar. 1816.

Chapter 14

'Loyal and Anti-Radical Female' 1816–1833

THE final years of Hannah More's life saw her engaged in a wearying struggle against frail health, a steady stream of bereavements, and what she saw as the contagion of radical politics. Her life was a succession of fevers and bronchial illnesses that confined her to her room for months on end. 'I believe my constitution is a Presbyterian', she told Wilberforce wryly at the beginning of 1823, 'for it hates all Festivals, Tides and red letter days. I was seriously ill Christmas Day, got better, but relapsed New Years day...I should be better if I had less to do but I am willing to die in the harness.'[1] Until the onset of senility in her late eighties, the urge to be active kept her involved in the wider world during a particularly disturbed and anxious period. With the problems of peace proving as pressing as the strains of war, she felt obliged to add her support to the repressive policies of the post-war government. Yet, as her politics became ever more reactionary, she continued to open up avenues for the participation of women in public life and to applaud younger woman who were able to go beyond her own innovations. She died bewildered and angry at political change, without recognizing her own contribution to the new order.

The deaths of her friends continued relentlessly. With the passing of the *mater dolorosa* Lady Waldegrave at the beginning of 1816, her connection with Strawberry Hill came to an end. They were all dead now: the three Ladies Waldegrave, the society beauties of the 1780s; the duchess of

---

[1] Bodleian, MS c. 48, fo. 31, More to Wilberforce, 8 Jan. 1823.

Gloucester, the thorn in the side of the royal family; the great Horace Walpole. She told Marianne Thornton, 'I have seen them all go down to the grave—for *one* alas! the brightest of the band, I have not ceased to mourn not on account of his death but his unhappy prejudices against religion.'[2] The great consolation was the behaviour of Lady Waledgrave's half-brother the duke of Gloucester, ridiculed as 'Silly Billy', but a patron of the Bible Society and the only male member of the royal family to support the abolition of the slave trade.

The next to die was Betty, the silent More sister, who suffered a stroke in 1814. In April 1816 she developed gangrene in her leg and lost the power of swallowing and of speech.[3] She died on 16 June, leaving More to reflect that she had never really known her sister. 'She was always reserved, and thought much more than she spoke.'[4] In the verdict of an early biographer, she was the only one of the sisters to conform to gender stereotypes. 'She was formed for woman's ordinary province; to be the active but invisible agent in a well-economized household... She was the WIFE of Barley Wood.'[5] The terrible enforced speechlessness of her last weeks may reflect a deeper reality. A kind-hearted, domesticated woman, who had taught needlework at the Park Street school and fried eggs for the Thornton children, she had spent a lifetime awed into silence by four strong-willed articulate sisters.

The ebullient Sally died in agony in the following year, possibly from cancer. In her last weeks her leg, like Betty's, became gangrenous 'from below the knee to the toes. It seemed enclosed in a black boot,' More wrote in horror to Ann Kennicott.[6] Though often delirious from the immense quantities of laudanum her sisters poured into her, she died secure in her faith. Of all the sisters, she raises the most tantalizing questions of what might have been. She leaves an impression of vitality and energy that never found an appropriate outlet. In Marianne Thornton's opinion, she was the most talented of the five: though she lacked 'the Bas bleu sort of Bon Motism', she had 'more wild unrestrained wit than I almost ever saw'.[7] A light had gone out in Barley Wood, and Hannah and Patty were now all to each other.

Two months later the conservative press was moralizing over the death of Madame de Staël, that 'splendid error',[8] who had fascinated More for years. For a brief, dangerous period she had also fascinated Wilberforce, who dined with her in March 1814 and found 'the whole scene... intoxicating

---

[2] Thornton, Add. MS 7674/1/E5a, More to Marianne Thornton [1816].
[3] Clark, More to Olivia Sparrow [1814], 8 June [1816].
[4] Huntington, MO 30606, More to Charles Hoare [1816].
[5] H. Thompson, *The Life of Hannah More* (London, 1938), 268–9.
[6] Roberts, iv. 26.
[7] Thornton, Add. MS 7674/1/N, fo. 439, Marianne Thornton to Patty Smith, 21 Aug. 1815.
[8] Duke, More to Wilberforce, 21 Mar. 1814.

even to me. The fever arising from it is not yet gone off.' Fearful that his dalliance with such a notorious woman might ruin his reputation, he wrote an anguished confidential letter to More, who soothingly told him that he had nothing to fear from 'the religious gossips or the worldly critics'.[9] By this time she had read another of de Staël's works, *De l'Allemagne* (1810), her famous exposition of German Romanticism, which had so angered Napoleon that he had ordered her expulsion from France. As with *Corinne*, she was both fascinated and repelled. She found within it 'passages of the greatest beauty, flashes of light bursting thro the darkness of those dull German Metaphysics', but thought de Staël's religion 'of a very questionable sort... its sublimities she ranks with those of literature, poetry and the fine arts'.[10] This ran counter to her own conviction that Christianity was open to the poor and uneducated as well as those of great abilities and refined sensibilities, and in her *St Paul* she mounted an attack against the semi-mystical elitism of 'the learned speculatists of the German school, as recently presented to us by their eloquent and accomplished eulogist'.[11] Yet for all her buffeting at More's hands, de Staël continued to think well of her; she had wished to come to Barley Wood in 1814, and just before her death she wrote 'a most flattering *Annonce*' of *Coelebs* in the *Constitutionel*. More thought this 'a proof that whatever she wants, she does not want Candour, for I had little mercy on her and her party'.[12] She was saddened to hear of her death: 'What good she might have done with those super-eminent talents!'[13] But as she later insisted to the Hubers (tactfully because they were her relatives), the genius so prized by the Romantics was a gift of God but had no 'necessary connection with religion... I mean the religion of Christ, not that of Plato.'[14]

Post-victory euphoria quickly gave way to post-war crisis, four years of tumultuous radicalism that threw the propertied classes into panic.[15] Reduced demand for wartime products threw thousands out of work, threatening the collapse of the already creaky system of poor relief. The victors returned to a land of no employment and dear bread, and a government which seemed impervious to the grievances of the poor. Radicals demanded parliamentary reform and manhood suffrage; some turned to

[9] *Life of Wilberforce*, iv. 164–5; Duke, More to Wilberforce, 21 Mar. 1814.
[10] Duke, More to Wilberforce, 21 Mar. 1814.
[11] *An Essay on the Character and Practical Writings of St Paul* (London, 1815), i. 278.
[12] Duke, More to Wilberforce [1817].
[13] Ibid.   [14] Roberts, iv. 139.
[15] E. P. Thompson, *The Making of the English Working Class* (Harmondsworth, 1968), ch. 15; I. McCalman, *Radical Underworld: Revolutionaries and Pornographers in London, 1795–1840* (Cambridge, 1988); K. Gilmartin, *Print Politics: The Press and Radical Opposition in Early Nineteenth-Century England* (Cambridge, 1996). For the conservative response, see P. Ziegler, *Addington: A Life of Henry Addington, First Viscount Sidmouth* (London, 1965), 338–66.

conspiracy and violence. A mass meeting at Spa Fields at the end of 1816 resulted in an abortive attempt to attack the Tower of London. Wilberforce was one of many politicians who supported a clampdown on public meetings and the temporary suspension of Habeas Corpus, both rushed through Parliament in February 1817.

These severe measures failed to quell the anxieties of Viscount Sidmouth, the former Henry Addington, one of the most reactionary home secretaries in British history. He saw the virus of radicalism invading the political bloodstream through cheap periodicals, such as Cobbett's *Political Register* and T. J. Wooler's *Black Dwarf*, and through irreverent songs composed by the plebeian anticlericals of the Spencean societies. In imitation of the tactics used by the Cheap Repository, this material was distributed throughout the country by chapmen and hawkers. Hannah More's future biographer William Roberts brought her a sample of this literature. She read out an extract to Patty, who made her stop after a few lines, while the dying Sally was 'agitated painfully'. Outraged, More wondered if the magistrates had the power to punish the vendors of this 'unparalleled blasphemy'.[16] In the home secretary's view they did indeed have this power, and on 27 March he issued a round robin to the lords-lieutenant of the counties, instructing them to inform the magistrates within their jurisdiction that they had the power and the duty to prevent the circulation of 'blasphemous and seditious pamphlets and writings'.[17] As part of the same strategy, Hannah More was wheeled out, probably by Sidmouth's brother, her neighbour Hiley Addington, in order to repeat her performances of the 1790s and write 'songs, papers &c. by way of antidote to this fatal poison'.[18] They were sold at Hatchard's bookshop in Piccadilly, and reprinted by Rivington in 1819 as *Cheap Repository Tracts Suited to the Present Times*. One ballad, 'The True Rights of Man, or the Contented Spitalfields Weaver', gives an idea of the flavour of the collection.

> Tho' different our stations, some great and some small,
> One labours for each, and each labours for all . . .
> And the true *Rights of Man* and the life of his cause
> Is not equal POSSESSIONS but equal just laws.[19]

'False, whining, and hypocritical' was the radical William Hone's enraged verdict on the collection. 'The general tenor of the *trash* is "work if you can get any thing to do, and if not apply to the overseers: and if they cannot

---

[16] Roberts, iv. 5.

[17] For the implications of the circular, see P. Harling, 'The Law of Libel and the Limits of Repression, 1790–1832', *Historical Journal*, 44 (2001), 107–34; O. Smith, *The Politics of Language, 1791–1819* (Oxford, 1984), 154–201.

[18] Roberts, iv. 10–11.

[19] *Cheap Repository Tracts Suited to the Present Times* (London, 1819), 151.

provide for you, you will do your utmost to starve with as much propriety as the most respectable among your neighbours".'[20]

In recycling her familiar arguments, More failed to take account of the changes that had taken place since the 1790s. Revolutionary France was now Bourbon France, no longer an external threat, while the onward march of industrialization and the spread of elementary education (partly through Sunday schools) had created a new type of working man immune to her Burkean pieties. If, as has been asserted, the loyalists 'won' the political argument in the 1790s, they were unable to repeat their success in the post-war period.[21] Perhaps aware that she had no realistic political answer to radicalism, she tried another strategy in 1821 when she published *Bible Rhymes*, a verse summary of the themes of each book of the Bible to counter-act the irreverence of the radical literature.[22] As usual, she fretted over whether to publish anonymously and feared, with some justification, that the project would not succeed in its purpose.[23] Compared with her previous work, *Bible Rhymes* was a slight and trite product: the type of improving literature Evan-gelical parents might buy their children, but unlikely to have wide appeal.

In one respect, Hone was unfair to More. Though she had little under-standing of the grievances of distant millworkers and handloom weavers, she was acutely sensitive to the sufferings of those close to home, whom she knew as individuals. The Mendip villages of Shipham and Rowberrow, where she had set up schools and a women's benefit club, were suffering terribly. With the coming of peace the demand for brass had dried up and there was no longer a market for the calamine they mined. By the end of 1816 over 1,000 people were near starvation, with both the poor law and private charity proving ineffectual, as there was 'not one person in the two parishes rich enough to give a basin of broth'.[24] 'Be so good as to speak to the King,' More wrote to Sir Thomas Dyke Acland, 'and desire him . . . to use brass Harness, it would become the fashion, and my miners would become Gentlemen.'[25] Seizing on an imaginative remedy, she told Wilberforce triumphantly, 'I am turned *Merchant*'; she and Hiley Addington had bought up some of the dead stock of ore. 'If times mend, we shall hope to see our stock, but we must stand the chance of other trades.'[26] There was political calculation mixed up with

[20] *Hone's Reformists' Register and Weekly Commentary*, 11 (Apr. 1817), i. 325–6.

[21] E. Groth Lyon, *Politicians in the Pulpit: Christian Radicalism in Britain from the Fall of the Bastille to the Disintegration of Chartism* (Aldershot, 1999), 55–60.

[22] *Bible Rhymes on the Names of All the Books of the Old and New Testament with Allusions to Some of the Principal Incidents and Characters* (London, 1821).

[23] Harrowby MS Trust Ryder Papers, MS 249, More to Henry Ryder, 21 Mar. [1821]; Cam-bridgeshire County Record Office, Manchester Collection, M10A/8/14, More to Millicent Sparrow, 31 Mar. [1821].

[24] Clark, More to Ann Kennicott, 24 Dec. 1816.

[25] Thornton, Add. MS 7674/1/E/10, More to Acland [1817].

[26] Duke, More to Wilberforce [1817].

the compassion, as desperate miners had recently rioted in Paulton and Rad-stock, bringing back memories of the riots of the 1790s.[27] Perhaps because of More's actions, the Shipham men remained quiet, but their problems did not go away. As late as 1827 she told Harford that they 'lie heavy on my heart'. Unable to buy bread, they were subsisting on potatoes which she had bought in bulk when they were cheap and then buried in a pit in order to preserve them.[28] 'I asked my School Master what they were to do now?' she reported bleakly to Wilberforce. 'His answer was, "they must eat one another".'[29]

At the end of 1817 a national tragedy jolted the nation into mourning. In the previous year Princess Charlotte had married Prince Leopold of Saxe-Coburg, and the attractive young couple gave an immediate lift to the jaded monarchy, with its pathetic mad king and unsavoury, self-indulgent princes. The news of Charlotte's pregnancy was greeted with delight and bets were taken on the sex of the child. In early November the princess went into an exhausting forty-eight-hour labour, giving birth at last to a dead son on 5 November. She died herself in the early hours of the next day from causes that have never been satisfactorily explained, and with her died for a while Hannah More's hopes for a patriotic queen who would lead a providentially chosen nation into the paths of righteousness.

Throughout the country the news was announced by the mournful tolling of bells. Linen drapers stocked up on black cloth and were quickly sold out. Such public grief had not been seen since the death of Queen Mary in 1694. More later recollected, 'It was a sorrow not the less felt by every one because it was shared by all: it was as much an individual as an universal sorrow. Every Briton seemed to feel it as acutely as if he alone felt it.'[30] The ever-emotional Patty cried for a fortnight; in her calmer way More lamented the 'lovely happy Princess' and her heart went out to her 'desolate husband. With his sound sense and religious principles, what a pilot would he have been to her thro the stormy sea she might have had to weather.'[31] In an astonishing letter to Marianne Thornton she declared,

If ever I could be disposed to wish myself a Papist it would be immediately on the death of one in whom one had taken a warm interest. It seems comfortless that after one has watched over them and offered up petitions for them that in the moment of the greatest interest, that of their dissolution, prayer must cease ... and what was duty one moment is become unlawful in the rest.[32]

---

[27] *FFBJ*, 8 Mar. 1817.   [28] A. Harford, *Annals of the Harford Family* (London, 1909), 105.
[29] Duke, More to Wilberforce [Dec. 1827].
[30] *Works* (London, 1830), vol. vi, p. xiii; S. C. Behrendt, *Royal Mourning and Regency Culture: Elegies and Memorials of Princess Charlotte* (Basingstoke, 1997).
[31] Clark, More to Ann Kennicott, 13 Dec. 1817. More later sent Leopold a copy of *Practical Piety*. Duke, More to Wilberforce, 19 Feb. [1818].
[32] Thornton, Add. MS 7674/1/E/7, More to Marianne Thornton, Nov. 1817.

She was to brood on Charlotte's death for a good while and eventually, at the height of the Queen Caroline agitation, to see it as providential. 'Had her precious life been spared how dreadfully would it have aggravated the public tumults, she loved her unhappy Mother, and was not unfriendly to the Opposition. It must have created a civil war, so much was she the general darling.'[33] By this time the future Queen Victoria had been born, daughter of the duke of Kent and Prince Leopold's sister: a 'fine animated child', Wilberforce told More. He had called on her mother, and, characteristically, ended up on the floor with the little princess and her toys.[34] At the end of More's life, when it was a near certainty that Victoria would succeed to the throne, she sent her mother a copy of the *Hints to a Princess* as an indication that she believed that her hope of a virtuous female sovereign would at last be fulfilled.[35] After strenuous efforts More's biographer Henry Thompson was given permission to dedicate his *Life*, published in 1838, to the young queen.[36]

The need for virtue in high places seemed more urgent than ever. The coming of peace opened up the Continent to the travel-starved British, and, with disconcerting rapidity, the old enemy became a popular destination. 'I do not much admire this unrighteous speed,' More complained ineffectually.[37] To her dismay, one of the most enthusiastic of the tourists was Marianne Thornton, who made three trips over to France between 1816 and 1818. Her feelings were hardly assuaged by the irrepressible Marianne's tongue-in-cheek letter, cunningly sent the day before her departure, begging her 'to write her some *warnings*'—which, of course, would be ignored. 'Poor dear Marianne!' she sighed to Macaulay. 'I would speak with all due tenderness, but I must say that *three* visits to France within two years of the death of her excellent mother is not a good example for Henry Thornton's daughter.'[38] She was especially indignant with the urbane and tolerant Harfords, who had gone to Italy, visited the Pope, and returned 'overflowing with accounts of *His Holiness* and their friends the *Cardinals*'.[39] Her dismay at the travellers' conduct ran deep. 'They have turned their numerous servants upon the world to beg or to steal. They injure Government by escaping the Taxes and starve the poor for want of labour.' Even worse, once abroad the English were contaminated by lax foreign manners. 'The Pope himself expressed his disappointment at the character of the English ladies at

[33] Clark, More to the Hubers, 9 July 1820.
[34] *Life of Wilberforce*, v. 71–2.
[35] Roberts, iv. 335–6.
[36] Thompson's correspondence is in the Yale University, Beinecke Rare Book and Manuscript Library, Osborn Collection.
[37] BL, Egerton MS 1965, fo. 16, More to Olivia Sparrow, 26 Oct. [1814].
[38] Huntington, MY 675, More to Zachary Macaulay, 11 Apr. 1818.
[39] BL, Egerton MS 1965, fo. 69, More to Olivia Sparrow, 2 Oct. 1817.

Florence, Naples, and Rome, the gayest Sunday assemblies are held by our Countrymen.'[40] Brooding on Princess Charlotte's death, she saw it as a mark of divine displeasure that 'not only our Nobles and Gentry but the middle classes' were 'learning to desecrate the Sabbath, and to educate their children in the French city of sin'.[41]

With the 'French mania' showing no sign of dying down, she published the last of her major works, *Moral Sketches*, written in haste in the early months of 1819. 'I expect to give offence to many of my friends', she told Olivia Sparrow, 'but I have delivered my own soul and I must soon stand at a higher bar than the world's judges.'[42] It was the soul of a woman who had never left Britain, whose long life had seen four major wars with France, and the whole book was infused with her Francophobia. 'We are losing our national character,' she lamented. 'In a few years . . . the strong and discriminating features of the English heart and mind will be obliterated.'[43] The book came out at the end of the summer, a bad time for sales, though it had gone into a respectable three editions by October.[44] But, as More had predicted, her exaggerated fear of France did not go down well. Her old enemy the *Anti-Jacobin* could not 'admit any justness of comparison between Caesar's crossing the Rubicon to overturn the laws and liberties of his country, and a gentleman's going upon and returning from his travels of pleasure'.[45] More's fellow Evangelicals gave her little support. To a cosmopolitan like Zachary Macaulay, gently protesting that he would be unable to show her book to his French friends, she had become like a much loved elderly relative whose forthright views are an increasing embarrassment to the more liberally minded younger generation.[46]

'When I lose Patty,' More predicted, 'I shall lose my hands, eyes & ears.'[47] Her sole surviving sister had been ailing for years. In September 1817 they were visited by Knox's friend John Jebb, who was to be made bishop of Limerick in 1822. For all their differences over the Bible Society, the visit was cordial, and he was able to report to Knox that 'neither their talents nor their vivacity are in the least subdued'. But Patty was suffering agonizing spasms, especially at night, and Jebb lay in bed helplessly listening to her cries.[48]

[40] BL, Egerton MS 1965, fo. 56, More to Olivia Sparrow, 30 Aug. 1817.

[41] Duke, More to Wilberforce [*c*.12 Nov. 1817].

[42] BL, Egerton MS 1965, fos. 74b–75a, 23 June 1819.

[43] *Moral Sketches of Prevailing Opinions and Manners* (6th edn. London, 1820), 10.

[44] BL, Egerton MS 1965, fo. 79b, More to Olivia Sparrow, 30 Oct. 1819. One of the purchasers was the Revd. Patrick Brontë. J. Barker, *The Brontës* (London, 1994), 145.

[45] *Anti-Jacobin Review*, 57 (Feb. 1820), 564.

[46] M. Knutsford, *Life and Letters of Zachary Macaulay* (London, 1900), 350.

[47] M. J. Crossley-Evans, 'The Curtain Parted', *Transactions of the Bristol and Gloucestershire Archaeological Society*, 110 (1992), 203.

[48] *Thirty Years' Correspondence between John Jebb and Alexander Knox*, ed. C. Forster (London, 1836), i. 337–8.

A year later she had a period of fever and delirium, which left her 'a poor shattered creature'.[49] But her energy seemed to revive in the following September (1819) when the Wilberforces came to Barley Wood for a week. She insisted on accompanying them on outings to the local beauty spots, and on the evening of the 9th she kept Wilberforce up until nearly midnight, talking animatedly about Hannah's early life. Then a couple of hours after retiring to bed, 'she awoke in the pangs of death' with 'agonies unspeakable' and 'shrieks' that rent her sister's heart. At eight o'clock next morning Wilberforce, who had slept through it all, came out of his bedroom and found a distraught Hannah at the door: 'Have you not heard, Patty is dying?' They sent for the doctor, but nothing could save her. A few hours before her death she 'rambled a good deal, but in a quiet way, full of piety and charity, ordering stockings & shoes for the poor &c'. She died on 14 September and was buried too early for Wilberforce and Henry Ryder to attend the funeral.[50]

'Poor Mrs H. More!' wrote Knox, reflecting the anxieties of all her friends. 'It is impossible to think of her without heartfelt pain.'[51] She found comfort of a sort in her dead sister's peaceful face, in the funeral sermons, and in the scores of letters of condolence. There was comfort too in the touching devotion of the Mendip people, who wore scraps of black cloth round their ragged sleeves, and in the tears of Hedges, the Barley Wood gardener, who remembered the many garments she had made for the poor. Another servant was so distressed that More sent her away for a few days to help her recover her spirits.[52] Though she tried to accept the divine will, there was no getting round the loss. 'My house is left to me desolate!' she wrote to Charles Hoare, '... I have no one with whom to share my joys and my sorrows.'[53] For the first time in her life, she was on her own.

The accession of the unpopular regent George IV in January 1820 plunged the storm-tossed state into yet another crisis. The king had long been estranged from his wife, Caroline of Brunswick, and on his accession he refused to allow her name to be inserted in the prayers for the royal family in the liturgy. Caroline was abroad when her father-in-law died. For the last seven years she had been travelling on the Continent in the company of her Italian courtier Bartolomeo Pergami. Their behaviour affronted the sensibilities of the most hardened British tourists; but then her husband's adulteries had been equally flagrant. Caroline's treatment outraged many women, already infuriated at the double standard that punished erring wives but not profligate

[49] Duke, More to Wilberforce [Autumn 1818].
[50] Clark, More to Selina Macaulay, 25 [Sept.] 1819; *Life of Wilberforce*, v. 32.
[51] Jebb and Knox, *Thirty Years' Correspondence*, i. 387.
[52] Clark, More to the Hubers, 18 Nov. 1819; London Guildhall University, Women's Library, More to the Misses Roberts, 'Thursday' [1819]; Roberts, iv. 102.
[53] Huntington, HM 30607, More to Charles Hoare [1819].

husbands, while radicals saw a useful stick with which to beat the government. The queen had become the improbable symbol of the nation's troubles and discontents.[54]

It was Caroline herself who set events in motion. Determined to claim her rights, she landed at Dover in June, and made a triumphal entry into London, where she lodged at the house of her friend the radical MP Alderman Wood. This forced the hand of the harassed government of Lord Liverpool, who were badgered by the king into drawing up a Bill of Pains and Penalties, which, if passed, would deprive Caroline of her title. The nation settled down to enjoy a dramatic set-piece, the trial of the queen before her peers in the House of Lords; the charge adultery with Pergami.

In retrospect Queen Caroline, slatternly and malodorous, deeply eccentric, yet oddly sympathetic, has greatly added to the gaiety of historical studies. Yet, as Wilberforce recognized, the whole business was a tragedy for the couple involved, forced into a marriage of convenience, and then obliged to act out their disharmony before the readers of the newspapers. He tried to secure a compromise, to ensure that, while she was still legally queen, Caroline's name was reinserted into the liturgy, but his well-meaning efforts merely led to accusations of sanctimony. The whole business, he wrote to More, 'teems with as many nauseous ingredients as Macbeth's witches' cauldron'.[55] Reflecting the opinions of the more conservative 'country' Evangelicals, More showed no compassion for Caroline. 'What do you mean to do with the Queen of the Radicals?' she asked Zachary Macaulay. 'O! expatriate her, at any rate, at any cost!'[56] Her certainty about the queen's guilt led her to abandon her strict propriety. Writing to Olivia Sparrow, woman to woman, she repeated some salacious gossip about Caroline and Pergami sleeping in the same bed in an inn in Italy.[57] Still more indelicately (though she was perhaps unaware of the double meaning) she passed on to Selina Macaulay a joke about Caroline and her champion Alderman Wood: 'I just asked Louisa why the Queen is like the Shrubs in a forest, and she answered because she is Under-Wood.'[58] Even with Wilberforce her guard slipped. 'A friend of mine who spoke of his own knowledge told me that this pernicious woman's chief champion, I had almost said bully, Lord Carnarvon, has repeatedly called the Q a d——d brimstone—*pray burn*.'[59] In a moment of

---

[54] For the Queen Caroline affair, see F. Fraser, *The Unruly Queen: The Life of Queen Caroline* (London, 1996), chs. 14–17; L. Colley, *Britons: Forging the Nation, 1707–1837* (New Haven, 1992), 265–8; J. Fulcher, 'The Loyalist Response to the Queen Caroline Agitations', *Journal of British Studies*, 34 (1995), 481–502.

[55] *Life of Wilberforce*, v. 70.

[56] Clark, More to Zachary Macaulay [1820].

[57] BL, Egerton MS 1965, fo. 85a, Mar. 1820.

[58] Huntington, MY 700, 15 Feb. [1820, catalogued 1821?].

[59] Bodleian, MS c. 48, fo. 29, More to Wilberforce, n.d.

self-criticism, she had to confess that the queen's sins 'occupy my thoughts more than my own'.[60]

The trial ended inconclusively. In November the bill was passed in the Lords, but by such a narrow margin that the government decided to adjourn it, allowing Caroline's friends to claim that she had, in effect, been acquitted. 'Thank God the country is saved!' a jubilant Tom Macaulay wrote to his parents from Cambridge: they prudently did not inform More of his 'Queen-ite' sentiments.[61] In the following summer Caroline turned up at her husband's coronation, but in a moment of great public humiliation she was denied admittance. She was taken ill at the end of July and died suddenly on 7 August. Her funeral was as disorderly as her life, and in the skirmishes two men were killed. She was buried in her native Brunswick and was quickly forgotten. For a brief moment, however, she had been a potent national symbol, encapsulating in her ungraceful person the conflicts of a changing culture.

The Queen Caroline affair came at a pivotal moment. Politically it occurred when memories of the Peterloo massacre and the Cato Street conspiracy, Arthur Thistlewood's mad attempt to assassinate the whole Cabinet, were fresh in the public mind. It coincided too with a new emphasis on domesticity and family values. At the close of the abolition debates in 1807 Wilberforce had been contrasted with Napoleon: the one a man who returned every evening to the bosom of his loving family, the other a destroyer of public order. In her tribute to George III, published as a preface to the sixth edition of *Moral Sketches*, Hannah More had declared that 'his domestic duties were filled with eminent fidelity and uniform tenderness'.[62] Set against these shining examples of domestic probity, George IV seemed a tarnished figure who, as even More admitted, had brought some of his marital disaster on his own head.[63] The all-conquering ideology of domesticity raised some urgent questions of gender. How were men and women to behave? What were their respective duties? Was the domestic sphere a place of rigid confinement for women or could it open up new avenues for public action? The paradox of the 'Tory feminism' of More's final years is that, as her politics grew ever more reactionary, so her views on gender became more fluid. The woman who, in her youth, had seen fit to quote Pericles and urge women to shun public life was in her old age an ardent supporter of female activism, provided it kept within the bounds of modesty—though even here she could be surprisingly flexible.

[60] Duke, More to Wilberforce [1820].
[61] G. O. Trevelyan, *The Life and Letters of Lord Macaulay* (London, 1876), i. 99.
[62] *Moral Sketches*, pp. vi–vii.
[63] 'Poor King! How are the sins of youth brought home to him!' Huntington, MY 690, More to Zachary Macaulay [1820].

'Loyal and Anti-Radical Female'

The death of Princess Charlotte and the trial of Queen Caroline help to account for the growing pessimism of More's politics. In the nation at large she saw 'the overflowings of Ungodliness'.[64] Locally, as she told Wilberforce, radicalism was gaining recruits. 'My loyal neighbour Mr Wylde, a Rector at two parishes and a magistrate, at his Tythe dinner could only get five men of fifty to drink the king's health.' A new radical paper, the *Bristol Mercury*, was 'doing infinite harm in my village. The advertisements are stuck up at every corner, and the vender [*sic*] with his horn affronts every body around him.'[65] This made her sometimes impatient with the more measured attitudes of her Clapham friends. At the height of the Queen Caroline agitation she defended Liverpool's government against criticisms in the *Christian Observer*.

We did indeed, think you rather hard upon Ministers ... we have great obligations to them. They put a glorious end to a war which neither the gigantic intellect of Pitt, not that of Fox, could achieve ... I believe Wellington is the only vicious man in the Administration—yet as an instrument, what do we not owe him? the very roof perhaps which covers us ... I do think that the independent party, as they are called, have a strong leaning to opposition.[66]

Her political arteries were hardening rapidly. In 1821, 'sick of that liberty I used to prize',[67] she joined the Constitutional Association, an ultra-conservative body set up at the end of the previous year to undertake private prosecutions of the writers and disseminators of radical literature. (She is probably the 'Loyal and Anti-Radical Female' listed in the *Bristol Journal* as subscribing 5 guineas.[68]) She sent her donation to the home secretary, together with a letter setting out her political views. 'I honour the kingly office and I love the king. I have no doubt but he will continue to be a truly patriotic monarch, but the worst of kings I shall obey & think better than *king Mob*.'[69] Yet she had earlier warned Princess Charlotte that the people would not stomach a tyrannical monarch. She had always stressed the need for obedience, but now the emphasis had changed, with the language of the balanced constitution and the rule of law sidelined in favour of a more authoritarian discourse. By this stage, as Zachary Macaulay told the Whig lawyer and future lord chancellor Henry Brougham, her 'feelings and prepossessions are all on the side of toryism—and she certainly has been ... and is still a strong antiwhig'.[70] He added, 'I speak of Whigs and Tories as they now are.' This is an important point. More had shifted but so had British

---

[64] Duke, More to Wilberforce [1820].
[65] Bodleian, MS c. 48. fo. 30, More to Wilberforce, 1820.
[66] Clark, More to Zachary Macaulay [Dec. 1820].   [67] Roberts, iv. 156.
[68] *FFBJ*, 2 June, 1821.
[69] Bristol City Council, Bristol Record Office, 39015, More to Sidmouth, 26 May 1821.
[70] University College London Library, Brougham 10531, Macaulay to Brougham, 31 May 1820. By permission of University College London Library Services.

politics, with right-wing politicians increasingly happy to describe themselves as Tories.[71] The great polarizing issue was Catholic emancipation, with fears of 'popery' driving many into the ranks of the extreme Tories, or 'Ultras'. A Roundhead by instinct and ancestry, who thoroughly detested the Stuart monarchs,[72] Hannah More had never been a Tory in the traditional sense. For once William Roberts got it right when he pointed out that her robust defence of the Glorious Revolution, her patriotic Protestantism, and her fear and hatred of Catholicism would have made her a mainstream Whig a century earlier.[73] (Though she named her two cats Non-Resistance and Passive Obedience, this is more likely to have been a playful comment on feline nature than an exact statement of her political principles.)

Her move from conservative Whig to vehement Ultra coincided with changes in the wider Evangelical movement, which in the 1820s became increasingly fractious, turbulent, and intolerant.[74] The Clapham Saints, influenced by Enlightenment ideas of progress, believed that human life could be changed for the better through political action. However, many of the younger generation, touched by the Romanticism of Coleridge and the prophetic books of Daniel and Revelation, were impatient with this gradualist programme and looked increasingly to the second coming of Christ, a cataclysmic event that would be heralded by the conversion of a remnant of the Jewish nation and by the return of the Jews to Palestine. The new era was symbolized by two men in particular: the strange and compelling Scotsman Edward Irving, minister of the Caledonian Chapel in Hatton Garden, and the wealthy and charismatic Lewis Way, president of the London Society for Promoting Christianity among the Jews.[75] More had been one of the first subscribers to

---

[71] J. Sack, *From Jacobite to Conservative: Reaction and Orthodoxy in Britain, c.1760–1832* (Cambridge, 1993), 66–74.

[72] See e.g. her comments to Henry Thornton on Charles James Fox's posthumous *History of England*: 'I abandon to Fox all the Royal Stuarts. I think he has not been at all unjust to them.' Clark, More to Thornton, 18 June 1808.

[73] Roberts, iv. 354.

[74] D. W. Bebbington, *Evangelicalism in Modern Britain: A History from the 1730s to the 1980s* (London, 1989), ch. 3; E. Jay (ed.), *The Evangelical and Oxford Movements* (Cambridge, 1983), 1–19. A particularly bitter dispute in the mid-1820s was the so-called Apocrypha controversy. Some members of the Bible Society argued that in order to placate Continental Roman Catholics, the apocryphal books (which Protestants did not believe to be part of the canonical Scriptures) should be included in the Society's Bibles, but this position was vehemently contested by many Scots Presbyterians and by Ulstermen, such as the Revd. Patrick Brontë. More lamented to Daniel Wilson that 'this unhappy schism in the Bible Society afflicts me by day, and keeps me awake by night. . . . I do heartily wish the Apocrypha was out of every Bible; but if the Papists will not take a Bible without it, is there any comparison between having a Bible with it, and having *no Bible at all*?' Roberts, iv. 281–2.

[75] S. Gilley, 'Edward Irving: Prophet of the Millennium', in J. Garnett and C. Matthew (eds.), *Revival and Religion since 1700: Essays for John Walsh* (London, 1993), 95–110; G. Carter, *Anglican Evangelicals: Protestant Secessions from the Via Media, c.1800–1850* (Oxford, 2001), 172–94.

Irving's church,[76] but by 1823 she had become disillusioned with 'the peer-less Northern Star', finding him destitute of 'taste and correct writing...the grace of classic parts or even intelligible simplicity'.[77] She was objecting, in her thoroughly eighteenth-century fashion, to his breathless and high-flown style, an almost exact replica of that of his friend and fellow country-man Thomas Carlyle. To her the style represented a fundamental instabil-ity—an 'insufferable bombast' and a 'levity' and 'profaneness'.[78] Her fears were confirmed when Irving turned out to be a false prophet, breaking with Evangelicalism to found his own charismatic Catholic Apostolic Church. But she never ceased to be charmed with 'Rabbi Way' and was full of enthusiasm for his schemes to convert the Jews. When he visited her in the sad after-math of Patty's death, she could not help being inspired by 'his sanguine, not hopes but certainties, of the near approach of the last days. While he is talking in his heavenly anticipation...one cannot help adopting his views and hoping as he hopes.'[79] In her will she left £200 to the 'Jew Society'. Increasingly conservative and pessimistic, ever more fearful of 'popery', inclined at times to millenarianism, she half-hoped for a divine cataclysm that would put a troubled world to rights.

Her deepening conservatism, however, had little in common with what she continued to see as the intolerant, exclusive *Anti-Jacobin* agenda with its formal religion and narrow definition of loyalty.[80] In *Village Politics* she had criticized those who would exclude Dissenters from any meaningful role in religion and politics. A generation later she found a loyalist meeting in Wrington

much too loyal for me...a set of Justices of the lowest order, belonging to another district...brought their own address ready cut and dried, very ill written, and so very High Church (the common case of men who have little knowledge and no religion) that *our* Clergy and Magistrates strongly opposed it, on the ground that it positively excluded every Dissenter, however well disposed, from signing.[81]

Other traces of more liberal attitudes remained. When the Greeks began their war of independence, she became 'a most strenuous champion for the land of Homer'; rebellion at a safe distance could still win her approval.[82] Except when fulminating against home-grown radicals, her discourse was

---

[76] Huntington, MY 680, More to Zachary Macaulay [1823].

[77] Duke, More to Wilberforce, 2 Sept. 1823.

[78] Huntington, MY 681, More to Zachary Macaulay, 1823.

[79] BL, Egerton MS 1965, More to Olivia Sparrow, 30 Oct. 1819, fo. 78b.

[80] See her letter to Mrs Thornton on the death of John Bowles, founder of the Society for the Suppression of Vice: 'I do not doat on that formal antijacobin sort of religion.' Clark, 9 May [1809; catalogued 1813].

[81] Clark, More to Zachary Macaulay [1820].

[82] W. W. Pepys, *A Later Pepys: The Correspondence of Sir William Weller Pepys, Bart.* (London, 1904), ii. 367.

libertarian. As she told Daniel Wilson, 'I think that if I could see the abolition of the slavery of the body in the West Indies, and of the slavery of the soul in Ireland and Popish Europe, I could sing my *nunc dimittis* with joy.'[83]

The question of slavery was never far from her mind. In 1818 she received a letter from Sir Alexander Johnstone, chief justice of Ceylon (Sri Lanka), a British crown colony since 1802, who wrote to her from Cheltenham to tell her that he had translated her *St Paul* into Tamil and Sinhalese. Shortly afterwards he sent her some palm leaves on which the story of Moses from her *Sacred Dramas* had been transcribed into Sinhalese.[84] An enthusiastic modernizer, a future founder of the Royal Asiatic Society, and an opponent of slavery, Johnstone had enacted that every child on the island born after 12 August 1816 (the prince regent's birthday) should be free, and he wanted the anniversary of this triumph to be celebrated by a public holiday and a commemorative ballad. The result was More's 'little trumpery poem'[85] *The Twelfth of August or the Feast of Freedom*, which was published anonymously and later translated into Sinhalese by two Buddhist monks. In 1827 the composer Charles Wesley set it to music. The finished product sets out a message of benevolent imperialism. Woodcuts show happy, scantily clad natives dancing round a cocoa tree to celebrate their manumission, while the text asserts

> ENGLAND, fair FREEDOM's choicest friend
> Conveys the SACRED FRUIT.[86]

In the meantime a girls' school named Barley Wood had been founded on the island in her honour, neatly linking three of her pet causes, the advancement of Evangelical Christianity, the education of girls, and the abolition of slavery.

From the campaign of 1788 onwards abolition had been a means by which women—conservative and radical—could enter political debates.[87] In one respect this had nothing to do with feminism, as, far from challenging their formal exclusion from power, campaigning women idealized their subordination and held it up as a model for all women. But for all its limitations,

---

[83] Roberts, iv. 257.

[84] Ibid. 43–4; Pierpont Morgan Library, New York, MA 4500 M, Collection Gordon Ray, More to Cadell and Davies, 6 Oct. 1818.

[85] Huntington, MY 704, More to Selina Macaulay, 12 Dec. [1822].

[86] *The Twelfth of August; or, The Feast of Freedom* (London, 1819), 4.

[87] K. Corfield, 'Eliza Heyrick: Radical Quaker', in G. Malmgreen (ed.), *Religion in the Lives of English Women, 1760–1930* (London, 1986), 41–67; L. Billington and R. Billington, ' "A Burning Zeal for Righteousness": Women in the British Anti-Slavery Movement, 1820–1860', in J. Rendall (ed.), *Equal or Different: Women's Politics, 1800–1914* (Oxford, 1987), 82–111; C. Midgley, *Women Against Slavery: The British Campaigns, 1780–1870* (London, 1992); M. Ferguson, *Subject to Others: British Women Writers and Colonial Slavery, 1670–1834* (London, 1992).

anti-slavery was a means by which women could make domestic ideology work to their advantage. They were the home-makers, the purchasers of consumer goods, and boycotts of sugar and other slave-manufactured products could only be effective if initiated by them. A letter More wrote to Wilberforce shows how decisions on consumption could become a matter of family discussion.

I must tell you a little story of three little boys who were brought to see me yesterday by their mother, an amiable quaker lady—Nothing will induce these children, they have such an abhorrence of Slavery, to touch any thing made with sugar, but they tell me they were under a great temptation, their aunt who was here, was going to be married, of course she would have a fine Wedding Cake, and they were told a Cake could not be made without sugar. What *could* they do? but they would not eat it, They would consider it an atrocity.[88]

Would-be ethical consumers were increasingly easing their consciences by buying East Indian sugar. Like many other women, More made a point of serving it to her guests, as it had 'no blood on it'.[89]

In the mid-1820s some women campaigners began to form their own 'ladies' associations'. This was a controversial development. While Zachary Macaulay was an enthusiast, Wilberforce was alarmed at the licence this gave for women 'to meet, to publish, to go from house to house stirring up petitions', thinking such activities 'unsuited to the female character as delineated in Scripture'.[90] But the Bible Society had set a precedent, as had Wilberforce's campaign to open up British India to Christian missionary activity, and the subsequent agitation against the practice of *sati* (the burning of widows).[91] On this issue More seems to have sided with Macaulay, and at the age of 83, though too old and infirm to be an active campaigner, she joined the committee for the Female Anti-Slavery Society for Clifton, which had been founded by her friends Margaret and Mary Roberts. In doing so, she set herself at odds with conservative advocates of slavery, outraged at what they saw as a blatant 'deviation from female retirement'.[92]

One woman in particular came to exemplify for More all that was best in female activism. This was the Quaker prison reformer Elizabeth Fry, 'that wise and active disciple of her great master', who put her in mind of 'Deborah judging Israel under a palm tree'; this made her a true 'Mother in

[88] Duke, More to Wilberforce, 5 May 1825.

[89] *Christian Observer*, 34 (1834), 578.

[90] *Life of Wilberforce*, v. 264-5.

[91] C. Midgley, 'From Supporting Missions to Petitioning Parliament: Women and the Evangelical Campaign against *Sati* in India, 1813-30', in K. Gleadle and S. Richardson (eds.), *Women in British Politics, 1760-1830: The Power of the Petticoat* (Basingstoke, 2000), 74-92.

[92] Midgley, *Women Against Slavery*, 48; Duke, More to Wilberforce [Dec. 1827]; *An Address to the Females of Great Britain on the Propriety of their Petitioning Parliament for the Abolition of Negro Slavery, by an Englishwoman* (London, 1833), 10.

Israel' in the manner of the long dead Sarah Baber.[93] From the younger woman's experiences she reached a conclusion which she never previously thought through, because it ran counter to all her previous writings: that women's reluctance to challenge the male prerogative of public speaking derived not from innate modesty but from lack of confidence. A registered minister in the Society of Friends from 1811, Elizabeth Fry had permission to travel and to preach. It was one of the very few avenues for public speaking open to a woman, and More was quick to recognize its significance. 'None but a woman, and none but a quaker woman, *could* have ventured, or if venturing, could have succeeded. Their habits of public speaking have taken away that fear of men which would have intimidated one of *us*, even if we had more zeal and piety than are commonly found amongst us.'[94]

In *Moral Sketches* she described Mrs Fry as a feminine version of the prophet Daniel (with a few overtones of the Gothic novel), venturing 'unprotected and alone' into 'the dreary abodes of calamity and crime', her 'mild demeanour' awing them into peace.[95] Her achievements were especially remarkable because, with no devoted sisters to keep house for her, she had constantly to juggle her public and private roles. 'If she stole some hours from her family to visit the prison, she stole some hours from sleep to attend to her family.'[96] As a token of her esteem she sent Elizabeth Fry copies of *Moral Sketches* and of her last work, *The Spirit of Prayer* (1825), a compilation of her earlier writings on the subject of prayer.[97] In 1823 Mrs Fry and her brother Joseph John Gurney called at Barley Wood. Like many other visitors, Gurney found her 'an extraordinary and excellent person. She is now seventy-eight years old but most vivacious and productive. *Very* like Wilberforce.'[98]

The example of Elizabeth Fry showed what a woman could achieve, given the right set of (providentially ordained) circumstances. But it was not given to every woman to be Superwoman, blessed with great energy and a self-effacing, supportive husband, and More's prescriptive ideal remained the more achievable goal of Lucilla Stanley's domestic philanthropy. Within the growing Evangelical culture the scope for philanthropy was expanding all the time, with the Bible Society's 'ladies' associations' in particular opening up new avenues. Yet, although women did most of the work on the ground, they were excluded from the Society's anniversary meetings until 1831. More's resentment at this discrimination comes over in a letter to Marie-Aimée Huber: 'Was Mr Huber able to attend the Bible meeting? *Your* unfortunate sex, I know, excluded *you* from that glorious holiday.'[99] In *Moral*

---

[93] Roberts, iv. 63.   [94] Ibid. 68.   [95] *Moral Sketches*, 213.
[96] Ibid.
[97] Clark, box 28, More to Cadell and Davies [1819]; Boston (Mass.) Public Library, Dept. of Rare Books and Manuscripts, MS Eng. 183 (58), Elizabeth Fry to More, 7 Feb. 1825.
[98] Quoted in M. G. Jones, *Hannah More* (Cambridge, 1952), 215.
[99] Clark, More to M.-A. Huber, 28 May 1818.

Sketches she took up the cudgels for the slighted women, arguing that 'we know not what reasonable objection can be made to their being modest and silent auditors on these occasions'. With a swipe at her travelling friends, she added that the women's 'little absences from home' were negligible, compared with the 'long and frequent desertion' of those who left their own country for months at a time.[100]

From the 1820s women found another outlet for activity in the charity bazaar, a female-dominated institution which became one of the great money-raisers of the nineteenth century.[101] (In *The Mill on the Floss* George Eliot shows how this apparently decorous activity, where young women presided over the stalls and the men bought their goods, could become the focus for explosive sexual tensions.) Bazaars proved an ideal outlet for More's failing energies, giving her something to do at a time when her options were closing. She became ill again at the beginning of 1822, and for most of the rest of the year she was confined to her apartment. Her schools were now in the hands of Miss Mary Frowd, a niece of Lord Exmouth, who had become her companion and secretary (the role she had once performed for Mrs Garrick). Shut off from her former active life, confined to a few rooms, unable to attend church, she turned to 'knitting Gent's Cuffs and babies shoes for the benefit of the Missionary and Jew Societies. I send them to the public bazaars at Bath and Clifton with my name appended to each. They are sold for *ten* some of them for *twenty* times their value.'[102] In 1827 she wrote a little poem, 'The Bazaar', which circulated in manuscript among her friends.

> Time was, each Lady thought no harm,
> By ornaments she *wore* to charm:
> Self-love bade Industry make haste,
> And Vanity was fed by Taste:
> Oh then—the Time's not distant far
> Up sprang the bountiful Bazaar.
>
> Here charity assumes new grace
> By wearing Decoration's face.
> Long may the liberal scheme abide!
> For taste is virtue, *so* applied.[103]

The death of Mrs Garrick in October 1822 at the age of 98, and those of Sir William Weller Pepys and James Jones, faithful minister at Shipham, in 1825, were further reminders to More of her own mortality. In 1827 she told

---

[100] *Moral Sketches*, 203–6.

[101] F. K. Prochaska, *Women and Philanthropy in Nineteenth-Century England* (Oxford, 1980), ch. 2.

[102] Clark, More to the Hubers, 24 Jan. 1823. For bazaars at Clifton, see e.g. *FFBJ*, 10 Mar. 1827.

[103] BL, Add. MS 42511, fo. 16.

Wilberforce that she had 'not one Contemporary left. My youthful set, the Johnsons, the Garricks, the Burkes... the Reynolds &c I do not reckon, as *they* were old; of my second set, the Bp of Durham and Lady Cremorne were the last both 94.—Of your period (alas for H Thornton) there remain yourself... the Gisbornes, the Babingtons... &c &c.'[104] (She had momentarily forgotten Ann Kennicott, who was to die in February 1830.) She was also outliving her doctors, and fretting about their welfare. Her devoted attendant Dr Carrick frequently rode up from Clifton, a two-hour ride, stayed with her for two hours, and then refused to take any fees. Oppressed at her helplessness, worried about his family, she begged Wilberforce to try to persuade him to accept what was owed him.[105]

Another letter shows the same fundamental kindness, this time cutting across the unjust code of sexual morality. It was a plea to Selina Macaulay for a disgraced servant, Jane Crump, lady's maid to a neighbour, a Mrs Miles (probably More's relation Harriet Miles), and sister to two of her own servants, Mary and Susan Crump. The girl 'was found to be intimate with one of her male companions', and 'Mrs M. M not chusing to part from the man, this unhappy girl was of course the victim, as she deserved to be', and was dismissed. More did not question the double standard, but she was worried for Jane Crump, now unable to find work. She was honest and hard-working, and 'great as the fault is, she must not be left to starve, happily there are no *consequences*'. Could Mrs Macaulay or Mrs Inglis find a post for her in London?[106]

The Macaulays had problems of their own. More was now increasingly dependent on Zachary Macaulay, who, with great patience, dealt with her many anxious complaints about her convoluted relations with her publishers, while his own affairs continued to harass him. He was constantly pilloried in the right-wing press. Even more distressingly, a poor commercial climate and his partner's mismanagement of the Sierra Leone Company caused him severe financial losses, forcing the family to move to the then downmarket Great Ormond Street.

Wilberforce, too, was in trouble, his finances drained by the antics of his eldest son. At Cambridge William Wilberforce junior had drunk heavily, run up debts, and refused to work, causing his father to remove him. At the beginning of 1820, while he was meant to be studying law, he married Mary Owen, the penniless daughter of the secretary of the Bible Society. The newly-weds visited Barley Wood, and, when they left, More confided her anxieties (with more emotion than grammar) to Olivia Sparrow.

---

[104] Duke, More to Wilberforce, 25 May [1827].   [105] Ibid. [1822].
[106] Huntington, MY 706, More to Selina Macaulay, 19 July 1823.

He is gentlemanly and agreeable in his manners ... She is handsome, but I thought her vapid and uninteresting. It is all very well now that they are visiting about, and the days are all halcyon; but what is to become of them I cannot guess, nor can their dear father. *Il faut manger* dans ce pauvre monde. And how that father is to provide a separate Establishment for one, who neither *can*, nor probably *will* do nothing I cannot guess. It goes to my heart as I know he has nothing to spare.[107]

She was proved right. William's debts severely cut into his father's income, causing him to sell the large house in Middlesex he had bought after his retirement from politics in 1825. The great emancipator, who could have died a reasonably wealthy man if he had not allowed his son to waste the family fortune, ended his days without a home of his own, spending much of his time at Bath or in the houses of his younger sons. Easy assumptions that the virtues of the Clapham Saints earned them a sleek prosperity in this world as well as a heavenly reward in the next are wide of the mark.

Hannah More herself frequently complained about lack of money, and began to entertain the possibility of selling Barley Wood. Much of her income from her books went on improvements to her estate or her numerous charities (such as her subscription at the end of 1823 to the newly founded Clergy Daughters' School at Cowan Bridge in Yorkshire, which at that time was attended by four of the Brontë sisters, and was later to be made notorious as Lowood School in *Jane Eyre*).[108] She was living above her income, purchasing land she surely did not need, yet her investments were not as profitable as they had been.[109] She added to her expenses by taking in 'two starving orphans' at the end of 1827. 'I am blamed for this,' she told Wilberforce, 'but I cannot see them perish for hunger.'[110] Her household, she knew, was overstaffed and 'most of my servants are clogs to me in the way of expence'.[111] On a visit to Barley Wood in 1827, one of the young Thorntons noted the friendly, almost familiar, relations between More and her servants, though she saw nothing amiss, taking it for granted that the servants' relaxed manners in the presence of their mistress were signs of affection and respect.[112] She failed to grasp the situation. While Mary Frowd or the Roberts sisters were lodging with her, More was safe, but in their absence, a frail old lady confined to the upstairs rooms, she was more vulnerable than she knew.

In March 1828 she received a letter from Zachary Macaulay that was to change her life. He had learned 'from a friend' (John Scandrett Harford?)

---

[107] BL, Egerton MS 1965, fos. 85–6, Mar. 1820.
[108] Barker, *The Brontës*, 119.
[109] Duke, More to Wilberforce, 25 May [1827]; Clark, More to Zachary Macaulay, 4 Feb. 1826.
[110] Duke, More to Wilberforce [Dec. 1827].
[111] Huntington, MY 706, More to Selina Macaulay, 19 July 1823.
[112] Thornton, Add. MS 7674/1/N, fos. 617–19, Sophia Thornton to Laura Thornton, 1827.

that her servants were engaging in practices 'highly objectionable and indecorous', wasting her money and squandering her food. They were even putting her at risk, being 'sometimes engaged in night revelries in the village, in
which they induced even Louisa to take a part; leaving you and your house
to their fate'. They were pillaging her property and 'in particular Charles
took advantage of your stage of health to turn your farming concerns into a
source of gain to himself'.[113] His remedy was brutally practical: she must
leave Barley Wood and move to a ready furnished, easily maintained house
at Clifton, where she would be looked after by kind friends, her physician,
and reliable servants. In effect, she was being offered sheltered housing.

There is a tendency to assume that More must have somehow 'deserved'
her misfortune: how had she treated her servants in order to be repaid with
negligence and deceit? Yet all the evidence points the other way. She had
taken his daughter off Charles Tidy's hands when he was too poor to look
after her properly; she had educated this daughter, given her a home, and
recently spent £120 apprenticing her to a milliner.[114] (She might have done
even more had the young woman been as ambitious and as academically
inclined as she had been at her age.) She had kept on a larger staff of
servants than she needed because she could not bear to turn them out onto
an uncertain labour market. She had done her best to help Mary Crump's
sister find new employment after her disgrace. Knowing all this, the temptation to descend to self-pity must have been immense; yet nothing in Hannah
More's life became her better than her dignified response to her calamity.
The 'Ultra Anti-Procrastinator',[115] she decided immediately to follow Macaulay's advice. The reversion of Barley Wood was sold to Harford's brother
William, and on 18 April she took her last look at the urn to Locke, the
monument to Porteus, the trees and flowerbeds she had planted and lovingly
nurtured. She was bidding farewell to the one youthful enthusiasm that had
never left her, 'a passion for scenery, raising flowers, and landscape
gardening', which she had first learned at William Turner's Belmont.[116] The
Macaulays had come up from London to help her move. As they put her
into the carriage, her thoughts turned to Milton: 'I am driven like Eve out of
Paradise, but not like Eve by angels.'[117]

The house was 4 Windsor Terrace, a new four-storey building, situated
on high ground at the edge of the elegant and rapidly expanding suburb of
Clifton, with a view over to the wooded Avon gorge in one direction and the
city of Bristol in the other. Six months into her new life More could count
her blessings. She was sad to lose her 'pretty horses', but the sale had netted
her £60. With fewer servants (four instead of eight) and no coach, she had

---

[113] Knutsford, *Macaulay*, 448.   [114] Clark, More to Zachary Macaulay [1827].
[115] Duke, More to Wilberforce, 25 May [1827].   [116] Roberts, iv. 303.
[117] Knutsford, *Macaulay*, 449.

more disposable income and could more easily afford the £250 a year which the schools were costing her. Though trimmed down, the work she and Patty had begun was on a firm footing and would survive her death. Under Miss Frowd's direction the house was running smoothly, and her other friends Mary and Margaret Roberts were living fifty yards away. Unable to attend church, she was regularly visited by two clergymen, 'whom I call my Chaplains'; and hard-working Dr Carrick would no longer have to make a twelve-mile journey to visit her.[118] In one respect her life had changed little. To her dismay, she found that the visitors kept on coming, and she resolved that she would only be 'at home' to company from one to three in the afternoon.[119]

Surprisingly, perhaps, she did not lose touch with her former servants. Mary Crump took lodgings in Wrington, and agreed to look after More's pet squirrel and caged birds; however, a fire in the house made Mary homeless and smothered the pets. In May she married Charles Tidy, the banns having been published the day they were dismissed; it transpired that they had been lovers for some time. Louisa could not be abandoned. Mary Frowd and the Misses Roberts visited her in Bath and found her tearfully penitent, and More allowed herself to believe that she would eventually make a successful milliner.[120]

In the outside world the political turbulence intensified. In March 1829 two politicians she had previously admired, the duke of Wellington, the prime minister, and Sir Robert Peel,[121] the home secretary, did the unthinkable and brought in a bill to allow Catholics to enter Parliament. Their dramatic conversion was a response to Daniel O'Connell's victory in the County Clare by-election and the renewed prospect of violence in Ireland if he was not allowed to take his seat. From a later perspective the bill can be seen as a belated victory for tolerance, but the many vehement opponents of Catholic emancipation were perfectly right to argue that it marked the end of the Protestant constitution set up after the Glorious Revolution. This was the case 'Orange Peel' himself had argued in a brilliant speech in 1817, and his defection aroused bitter anger in his constituency of Oxford University, the most Anglican in the country. In February 1829 (before the bill was even introduced) he daringly submitted himself for re-election. The country cler-gyman who formed the bulk of the Oxford MAs rode into town to cast their

---

[118] Huntington, MY 692, More to Selina Macaulay [1828]; Duke, More to Wilberforce [27 Oct. 1828]; BL, Egerton MS 1965, fo. 98, Mary Roberts to Olivia Sparrow, 1 May 1830.

[119] Huntington, MY 692, More to Selina Macaulay [1828].

[120] Ibid.

[121] In 1826 More sent Peel a copy of a ballad she had written, and praised him for his 'wise and well directed zeal for the public good'. Peel's reply was non-committal. Clark, Hannah More MSS box 43, More to Sir Robert Peel, 6 May 1826.

votes for his opponent, the Thornton children's guardian, Sir Robert Inglis, one of the leaders of the parliamentary Ultras. The household at Clifton could not contain their feelings. 'I did not expect to see the king surrounded by a half Protestant ministry,' More wrote feverishly to Marianne Thornton; 'had it been Turkish or Jewish I might have put up with it...the Miss Roberts's and Miss Frowd are running about like mad folks; and I am not over sound.'[122] When Inglis defeated Peel, Marianne, apparently forgetting that her own father had voted for Catholic emancipation along with Wilber-force and most of the Clapham Saints, was ecstatic.[123] So was More. 'Joy, joy, joy to you, to me! Joy to the individual victorious Protestant! Joy to the great Protestant cause!' she wrote to Marianne.[124] Her triumphalist language was echoed by many in Oxford, including John Henry Newman, the future cardinal, then a fellow of Oriel and, of course, an Anglican. But winning a battle is not winning a war; another seat was found for Peel and on 13 April the bill was signed by a tearful king, perhaps imagining his old father spin-ning in his grave.

More's unrestrained language was far removed from the carefully moderate arguments of the *Princess*, with its calm and balanced sentences and its metaphors of rootedness and stability. It is tempting to suggest that she was simply too old to cope with the new world and that her anti-Catholicism was a symbol of her inability to adapt to changed circumstances. Yet public opinion in general was overwhelmingly against Catholic emancipation, and thousands of petitioners, the great majority considerably younger than More, felt exactly as she did. Protests were especially fierce in her own West Country, where both Monmouth and William III had landed and where it was second nature to associate Protestantism with the defence of English liberties. On this issue, as on so many others, her gut reactions represented a substantial body of opinion. If anything, anti-Catholicism intensified over the next twenty years, so, however deplorable, More's prejudices were hardly backward-looking.[125]

The ravages of old age were becoming more apparent. She was rapidly losing her once remarkable memory, and was confused when strangers visited her. Formerly so methodical, she was scattering her letters over the room. There were times when she seemed to believe that Burke (dead thirty years) was still alive.[126] Yet she managed to follow the election of 1830 and

---

[122] Roberts, iv. 334.
[123] E. M. Forster, *Marianne Thornton, 1797–1887* (London, 1956), 88–9.
[124] Roberts, iv. 335.
[125] See E. Norman, *The English Catholic Church in the Nineteenth Century* (Oxford, 1984), 15–22; J. Wolffe, *The Protestant Crusade in Great Britain, 1829–1860* (Oxford, 1991).
[126] BL, Egerton MS 1965, fos. 98–101, Mary Roberts to Olivia Sparrow, 1 May 1830, 14 Apr. [?]; Thornton, Add. MS 7674/1/E/11, More to Sir Thomas Dyke Acland, n.d. [incomplete].

the subsequent turbulent events surrounding the passing of the 1832 Reform Act. After the election she received a visit from one of the new members, Tom Macaulay, elected MP for Calne on a reform platform, who tactlessly brought with him his fellow Whig Edward Protheroe, member for Bristol. Predictably, the visit was ruined by an argument over politics, and More never saw her former protégé again.

When the new Parliament resumed, Wellington's government quickly fell, and was replaced by a Whig administration. On 2 March 1831 Macaulay spoke in favour of the Reform Bill, but when his mother wanted him to send More a copy of his speech, he wrote with some prescience, 'Oh, no, don't send it; if you do, she'll cut me off with a Prayer-book.'[127] (He overestimated his legacy.) In October the bill was thrown out by the Lords, and Bristol erupted into three days of looting and burning. Private houses in affluent Queen Square, the Bridewell, two gaols, and the Bishop's Palace on College Green (near the site of the More sister's first school) were burned down.[128] The glow from the fires lit up the sky from as far away as Newport across the Bristol Channel, and from the high windows of her house in Clifton More would have had a panoramic view of the destruction. All her life she had deplored the actions of the mob and now its depredations were on her own doorstep. Worse still, the riots panicked Parliament into passing the bill, which received the royal assent in the spring of 1832. She was as angry as she had ever been in her life, and, as he had ruefully predicted, she vented her wrath on Tom Macaulay. A codicil of 11 August 1832 revoked the legacy of her books, and transferred the bequest to Charles Popham Miles, son of her relative Harriet Miles and the future principal of the Malta Protestant College.[129] It was a poor return for the long friendship shown her by Macaulay's parents, but she was no longer thinking rationally. Macaulay, who never bore her malice for his disinheritance, wrote later, 'I kept her friendship as long as she kept her wits.'[130]

In the same month Harford's wife and sister-in-law visited her. They found her animated but occasionally confused. Louisa Harford commented that her room was 'a pleasant cage'. More diplomatically, perhaps, her sister added, 'It contains a bird of paradise.' More, who had in former times been burdened by the demands of company, now showed her loneliness by beg-

---

[127] *Letters of Thomas Babington Macaulay*, ed. T. Pinney (Cambridge, 1974–81), i. 277 n. 3.

[128] S. Thomas, *The Bristol Riots* (Bristol, 1995), 1. The bishop, who was forced to flee from his palace, was Dr Robert Gray, who in 1804 had encouraged More to write *Hints to a Princess*.

[129] In the previous decade More had given the family considerable financial support.

[130] Quoted in *Letters of Macaulay*, vol. i, p. xxix. Macaulay was not the only sufferer. Bishop Ryder, who had also voted for the bill, had his legacy reduced from £1,000 to £500, the difference being transferred to Wilberforce. The reasons are unclear, but if this was a punishment, it is difficult to believe that More, with her great admiration for Ryder, could have been in her right mind.

ging them to come again soon.[131] During a visit made at the end of 1831 Harford was disturbed by her 'strange and incoherent' ramblings, in which she imagined herself 'not in her own house, and suffering unkind treatment'.[132] One day, Mary Frowd reported, she put her hand to her head and exclaimed, 'I am all confusion. I seem quite to have lost my understanding.'[133] It is unlikely that she took in the news of Wilberforce's death in July 1833, only days after the abolition of slavery in the British empire. She did not know of his funeral in Westminster Abbey, of the solemn procession to the north transept where his body was laid close to the tombs of his great parliamentary contemporaries Pitt, Fox, and Canning.

On one of his last visits Harford stood at More's bedside and 'took her hand and kissed it. She opened her eyes, and drawing my hand to her lips, kissed it more than once, and then stretched out both her arms to me.' Did she recognize him or did she believe him to be someone else? He did not know.[134] On 6 September he and Sir Robert Inglis visited her for the last time. She was now refusing food and clearly dying. The following evening, Friday 6 September 1833, watched by William Roberts, her face became 'smooth and glowing'. She smiled, tried to raise herself from her pillow, reached out her arms and called out 'Patty!' and then 'Joy!' She then fell into a gentle sleep and died in the following afternoon.[135]

Because women did not attend funerals, Louisa Harford and her sister paid their respects at Windsor Terrace, where they strewed flowers over her body. On 13 September she was taken to Barley Wood; a stream of coaches following the cortège, and, as they passed through the streets, the bells of the churches tolled out in tribute to the city's famous daughter. When they reached Wrington, they found that most of the shops were closed and the schoolchildren had been kitted out in mourning. From Barley Wood the procession, led by the children and accompanied by local dignitaries, set out for the church, where they were met by Henry Thompson, the resident clergyman and a future biographer. The interior of the church was hung in black and the number of mourners was so great than many had to wait outside. After the service, read by her old friend and protégé the Bristol Evangelical clergyman Thomas Tregenna Biddulph, she was laid alongside her four sisters in a corner of the churchyard.[136]

When her will was proved, she was found to possess the very substantial sum of £27,500.[137] Most of the money went to about 200 selected charities. The Bristol Infirmary and the Bible Society received £1,000 each. £200 went

---

[131] J. S. Harford, *Recollections of William Wilberforce, Esq.* (London, 1864), 284.
[132] Bristol Record Office, 28048 C78, journal of J. S. Harford, 1 Jan. 1831–4, Feb. 1842.
[133] Roberts, iv. 344.   [134] *Recollections of Wilberforce*, 285.   [135] Roberts, iv. 349.
[136] See *Bristol Mirror* and *Bristol Mercury*, 21 Sept. 1833.
[137] *Bristol Mercury*, 28 Sept. 1833.

to the Burman Mission, where another of More's enterprising, courageous heroines, the 'wonderful' American Baptist missionary Ann Hasseltine Judson was busy adopting orphan girls and redeeming slaves.[138] The Jew Society received another £200, as did the Clergy Daughters' School at Cowan Bridge (the surviving Brontë girls—Charlotte and Emily—had been removed from the school eight years earlier). £50 went to the Shipham poor, £5 and £50 to the Shipham and Cheddar Female Clubs respectively. Other sums of money and personal effects went to various relations and godchildren. Her executrices were Mary Frowd and Margaret Roberts (Mary Roberts had died in 1832), and it was their well-meaning decision to entrust the writing of her biography to Margaret's brother William that did so much to damage her posthumous reputation.

How was Hannah More to be assessed? Her unconventional life left William Howley, archbishop of Canterbury, grappling with the problem of an appropriate epitaph.

That part of the Epitaph which concerns the entrance on Life is extraordinarily difficult: were the subject a man, the abandonment of wealth, distinction and honors would be quite appropriate and sufficiently important in the eyes, even of the wiser part of the world, to constitute a sacrifice. But a woman however distinguished, has only to give up that which contributes to amusement or gratifies vanity.[139]

The limited vocabulary applied to women could not cope with the rich complexity of More's life. Her career as poet and playwright—and her sisters' success in creating a successful school—could not be fitted into the trivializing constraints of Howley's language. Yet the achievements were plain for those with eyes to see. Five spinsters, born into circumstances of failure and near poverty, forced to earn their livings, and succeeding triumphantly in their vocations, they had shown what it was possible for women to achieve in an environment that was at best ambivalent and at worst hostile to women on their own. Twenty-five years after Hannah's death Marianne Thornton stood by the quiet grave, remembered the golden childhood summers, the anecdotes of Garrick and Johnson, the schools and clubs, the inspiring teaching, the bustling kindness, and reflected, 'God has indeed given them a better name than that of sons and daughters.'[140]

---

[138] For More's support for this campaign, see Huntington, MY 704, More to Selina Macaulay, 12 Dec. [1822].

[139] Bristol Record Office, 28048/C82/1, letter to an unnamed correspondent, 10 Nov. 1834.

[140] Thornton, Add. MS 7674/1/L10, fo. 41. Marianne was quoting Isa. 56: 5; also Add. MS 7674/1/N, fo. 35.

Conclusion

THE Bristolians were surely right to honour Hannah More as she made her final journey through their city. They recognized that few of her contemporaries—male or female—could match her extraordinary career. Far from being a footnote in the history of her age, she was one of its prime movers, leaving her imprint on the theatre, the bluestocking circle, the political debates sparked by the French Revolution, elementary education, the anti-slavery movement, the growth of Evangelical religion, foreign missions, and female philanthropy. The two halves of her life, divided by the watershed of her conversion, neatly spanned the seismic shift which saw the relatively relaxed culture of the eighteenth century give way to the earnest moralism of the nineteenth. The friend of such quintessentially eighteenth-century figures as Horace Walpole, David Garrick, and Samuel Johnson, she witnessed the promising beginnings of the careers of Thomas Babington Macaulay and William Ewart Gladstone.

During her last years at Clifton the new world came into being. Daniel O'Connell became the first Roman Catholic member of Parliament since the Reformation. Charles Darwin was appointed ship's naturalist on the *Beagle*. The railway age claimed its first victim, but, undeterred, the Bristolians were ready to welcome the proposed 'Great Western Rail-Road'. The death of George IV brought the young Princess Victoria a step nearer the throne. Prince Leopold, Princess Charlotte's widower, was chosen king of the newly independent Belgians. Manchester, Birmingham, and Leeds gained parliamentary representation at the expense of the picturesque anachronisms of Dunwich and Old Sarum. John Keble launched the Oxford Movement. Had More lived a few years longer and retained her mental faculties, she would have found much of this new world alien and bewildering. Rather cruelly, the obituary in the Evangelical *Eclectic Review* placed her firmly in the past: 'She had become, as an author, posthumous to the present age, long before she quitted life: and her writings have probably produced very nearly the full amount of good they are adapted to effect.'[1] With the exceptions of the Cheap Repository tracts and their imitators and *Coelebs in Search of a Wife*, most of her writings quickly faded into obscurity. A new age needed new voices.

Yet it is wrong to locate her so firmly in an eighteenth-century *ancien régime* that she seems totally out of place in the new culture. More in her old age, writing anti-slavery poems, knitting for bazaars, entertaining pious aristocratic ladies, and organizing Bible Society auxiliaries, rightly believed that she had lived through momentous changes; and, though she despaired of political developments, she was generally optimistic about the cultural transformation taking place around her. How could she be totally gloomy about the future when she had done so much to shape it?

Not all Victorians found her congenial. 'I like neither her letters, nor her books, nor her character, nor her beliefs,' wrote the future George Eliot.[2] Others could not accept her prescription of active philanthropy as a panacea for women's continuing disadvantages. Elizabeth Barrett Browning's Aurora Leigh is cruelly contemptuous of her pious aunt's insipid good works.

> The poor-club exercised her Christian gifts
> Of knitting stockings, stitching petticoats,
> Because we are of one flesh after all
> And need one flannel (with a proper sense
> Of difference in the quality ...)
>   She had lived
> A sort of cage-bird life, born in a cage,
> Accounting that to leap from perch to perch
> Was act and joy enough for any bird.
> Dear heaven, how silly are the things that live
> In thickets and eat berries.[3]

Emily Davies, the founder of Girton College, Cambridge, deeply resented her inferior education, and rebelled against the expectations that, as a clergyman's daughter, she would do good works in the parish.[4] More's influential argument that philanthropy was a woman's profession had its weaknesses as well as its strengths. While it validated female activism and subtly undermined the ideology that sought to confine women to the purely domestic sphere, it remained a one-size-fits-all model that could never do justice to the diversity of their needs and abilities.

Yet for all the limitations of her approach, she cast a long shadow over the generations that followed. George Eliot's dismissive comments on More were

---

[1] *The Eclectic Review*, 3rd ser. 12 (1834), 446.

[2] *The George Eliot Letters*, ed. G. S. Haight, i. (London and New Haven, 1954), 245.

[3] E. Barrett Browning, *Aurora Leigh* (rev. 1859), ed. M. Reynolds (New York, 1995), bk. 1, lines 297–301, 304–9.

[4] B. Caine, *Victorian Feminists* (Oxford, 1993), 64–5.

part of her painful rejection of Evangelical dogmatism. She later came to view the religion of her adolescence in a more sensitive light, and to acknowledge its potential to make life bearable for suffering men and women. Her agnosticism was always infused with Evangelical seriousness. The earnestness was catching. 'Nobody is gay now,' the languid prime minister Lord Melbourne complained to the young Queen Victoria; 'they are all so religious.'[5] For much of the nineteenth century Evangelicalism was the dominant religious force in British life. The Great Exhibition was closed on Sundays because of Evangelical pressure. Gladstone, son of one of More's friends, became a High-Churchman, but kept many of his earlier Evangelical characteristics.[6] Three successive Victorian lord chancellors taught in Sunday schools for most of their lives.[7] In a more secular form, Evangelicalism was transformed into the 'respectability' which was one of the defining marks of the middle classes.

These middle classes were rapidly discovering their power. More's efforts in the causes of anti-slavery and missionary work were part of a mass mobilization later imitated by Anti-Corn Law League. Pressure group politics were here to stay, and women were an important part of the new assertiveness. The Victorian feminist Barbara Leigh Smith Bodichon learned some of her political activism when she attended the Ladies' Free Trade Bazaar held in May 1845 at the Theatre Royal, Covent Garden, site of Hannah More's theatrical triumph.[8] A Unitarian by upbringing, with reforming political views, she was hardly More's ideological sister, but her early campaigning methods were remarkably similar. The paradox was picked up by one of the first historians of feminism, who gave More an important role in the expansion of women's activities: 'Without in the least intending to do so, she was marking out a new sphere for the young women of the middle classes, and their revolt against their own narrow and futile lives followed as a matter of course.'[9] Though this is perhaps too neat and deterministic, it can hardly be denied that many Victorian women philanthropists were deeply inspired by Hannah More's pioneering work.[10] 'Her truly valuable legacy', wrote Charlotte Mary Yonge, 'was not only the example of what one woman could be, and could do, but a real influence on the tone of education in all classes of English women.'[11]

[5] Quoted in I. Bradley, *The Call to Seriousness: The Evangelical Impact on the Victorians* (London, 1976), 13.

[6] H. C. G. Matthew, *Gladstone, 1809–1898* (Oxford, 1999), 27–8.

[7] R. C. K. Ensor, *England, 1870–1914* (Oxford, 1936), 139 n.

[8] P. Hirsch, *Barbara Leigh Smith Bodichon, 1827–1891: Feminist, Artist, and Rebel* (London, 1999), 27–9.

[9] R. Strachey, *The Cause: A Short History of the Women's Movement in Britain* (London, 1928), 13.

[10] F. K. Prochaska, *Women and Philanthropy in Nineteenth-Century England* (Oxford, 1980), 223.

[11] C. M. Yonge, *Hannah More* (London, 1888), 196.

Conclusion

Although Hannah More never left Britain (and only left England for brief trips over the border into Wales), her influence extended far beyond her own country. This was symbolized by the founding of the Barley Wood school in Ceylon, and by the policy of the Church Missionary Society to name orphaned African girls after her.[12] She rejoiced in Britain's imperial mission, seeing it as, among other things, a liberating force in the lives of women. Already, the movement for women's education in the Indian subcontinent had begun with the Society for Promoting Female Education in the East, and it was to be continued in the work of the *zenana* missions.[13] With the abolition of the slave trade and the expansion of missionary work, the way was open for More and those who thought like her to argue that the British empire was part of a divine plan to spread Christian truth and civilization throughout the world. It is no accident that the quintessential mid-Victorian hero was the charismatic Evangelical soldier Henry Havelock, the general who raised the siege of Lucknow in 1857. More, who had deeply admired his father-in-law, the Baptist missionary Dr Joshua Marshman, would have relished his exemplary death.

The children who visited More at Barley Wood reached their maturity in the Victorian era. Macaulay and Gladstone were only two of the many political, literary, and religious figures who had Evangelical childhoods. Even when, as in so many cases, the belief departed, the inherited sense of mission, the compulsion to do good in an imperfect world, remained. Because of this residual Evangelicalism, many Victorians who could not share her political or religious views were happy to celebrate Hannah More. As the temperance campaigner Clara Lucas Balfour wrote, 'The woman who, for many years, educated at her own expense a thousand children annually, and whose munificent charities were not maintained by any inherited wealth or rank, but by the product of her own talents, is one of whom England may be justly proud.'[14] Active, enterprising, and generous, a meritocrat not the inheritor of privilege, More was an invaluable role model for the women who came later: the 'mother' of Victorianism possibly;[15] certainly one of the midwives of the new age.

[12] E. Stock, *The History of the Church Missionary Society* (London, 1899), i. 126.

[13] J. Murray, 'Gender Attitudes and the Contribution of Women to Evangelism and Ministry in the Nineteenth Century', in J. Wolffe (ed.), *Evangelical Faith and Public Zeal* (London, 1995), 102–3.

[14] C. L. Balfour, *A Sketch of Mrs Hannah More and her Sisters* (London, 1854), 4.

[15] C. H. Ford, *Hannah More* (New York, 1996), 77.

CHRONOLOGY OF HANNAH MORE'S LIFE AND WRITINGS

1745	Born 2 February at Fishponds, Stapleton, Gloucestershire
1758	Mary More opens a boarding school in Trinity Street, Bristol
c.1762	The More sisters build a school in Park Street, Bristol
c.1767	Visits the estate of William Turner at Belmont; later accepts his proposal of marriage
1769	Death of the Bristol actor, William Powell
1773	Engagement to Turner finally broken off; accepts an annuity of £200 p.a.; *The Search after Happiness* published by Bristol printer Sarah Farley
1774	Goes to London; on her second visit meets David Garrick, Samuel Johnson, Edmund Burke, and Elizabeth Montagu; supports Burke's election campaign in Bristol; Thomas Cadell publishes *The Inflexible Captive* and becomes her main publisher
1775	*The Inflexible Captive* performed at the Theatre Royal, Bath
1776	Becomes the Garricks' permanent house guest; meets Beilby Porteus, bishop of Chester (bishop of London from 1787); witnesses Garrick's farewell performances; publishes *Sir Eldred of the Bower and the Bleeding Rock*
1777	Publishes *Essays on Various Subjects*
1777–8	*Percy* performed at the Covent Garden theatre
1778	Richard Samuel depicts her as one of the 'Nine Living Muses of Great Britain'
1779	Death of Garrick; becomes Eva Garrick's companion; failure of *The Fatal Falsehood*
1780	Begins friendship with Horace Walpole; reads John Newton's *Cardiphonia*
1781	Begins to help 'Louisa', the 'Lady of the Haystack'
1782	Publishes *Sacred Dramas* and *Sensibility*
1783	Death of Jacob More; writes *The Bas Bleu*, which circulates in manuscript
1784	Begins to correspond with Horace Walpole; begins visits to the Middletons at Teston in Kent; befriends Ann Yearsley
1785	Buys Cowslip Green; quarrels with Ann Yearsley
1786	Death of Mary More (mother); at Teston becomes involved in the abolitionist movement; publishes *Florio* and *The Bas Bleu*
1787	Meets John Newton and William Wilberforce; meets Thomas Clarkson in Bristol

1788   Publishes *Slavery* and *Thoughts on the Importance of the Manners of the Great to General Society*

1789   Horace Walpole publishes *Bishop Bonner's Ghost* on the Strawberry Hill Press; Hannah and Patty More found the first of the Mendip schools at Cheddar; other schools follow at Shipham, Rowberrow, Nailsea, Blagdon, and Wedmore (also smaller schools)

1790   The More sisters hand over the Park Street school to the Mills sisters, and settle in Bath

1791   Publishes *Estimate of the Religion of the Fashionable World*; Clementina Clerke elopes from the Park Street school

1792   Founds women's benefit clubs at Cheddar and Shipham

1793   Publishes *Village Politics* and *Remarks on the Speech of M. Dupont*

1794   Richard Vining Perry acquitted of the charge of abducting Clementina Clerke; More becomes friendly with the Waldegrave family

1795–8   Edits the Cheap Repository tracts

1795   Founds the Blagdon school

1798   Founds the Wedmore school in the face of opposition from local clergy and farmers

1799   Publishes *Strictures on the Modern System of Female Education*

1799–1802 The Blagdon controversy

1801   Builds Barley Wood

1803   Publishes patriotic ballads

1804   Hannah More's sisters sell their Bath house and move into Barley Wood; 'The White Slave Trade' published in the *Christian Observer*

1805   Publishes *Hints towards Forming the Character of a Young Princess*

1808   Publishes *Coelebs in Search of a Wife*

1811   Visits the West Midlands and Wales; Publishes *Practical Piety*

1813   Final visit to the London area; death of Mary More (sister); supports the sending of missionaries to India; founds auxiliary Bible Society at Wrington; publishes *Christian Morals*

1815   Deaths of Henry and Marianne Thornton; publishes *Essay on the Character and Practical Writings of St Paul*

1816   Death of Betty More

1817   Writes new loyalist tracts; deaths of Sally More and Princess Charlotte

1819   Death of Patty More; loyalist tracts published as *Cheap Repository Tracts Suited to the Present Times*; publishes *Moral Sketches*, and *The Twelfth of August; or, The Feast of Freedom*

1821   Publishes *Bible Rhymes*

1825   Publishes *The Spirit of Prayer*

1828   Leaves Barley Wood; settles at Clifton

1833   Death of Wilberforce; dies at Clifton; buried at Wrington

SELECT BIBLIOGRAPHY

Primary Sources

Works by More

The Search after Happiness: A Pastoral Drama (5th edn. London, 1774).

The Inflexible Captive: A Tragedy (London, 1774).

Sir Eldred of the Bower and The Bleeding Rock: Two Legendary Tales (Dublin, 1776).

Ode to Dragon, Mr Garrick's House Dog at Hampton (London, 1777).

Essays on Various Subjects, Principally Designed for Young Ladies (London, 1777).

Percy: A Tragedy (London, 1778).

The Fatal Falsehood: A Tragedy (London, 1779).

Sacred Dramas: Chiefly Intended for Young Persons: The Subjects Taken from the Bible. To which is added, Sensibility, a Poem (London, 1782).

Florio: A Tale for Fine Gentlemen and Fine Ladies; and, The Bas Bleu; or, Conversation: Two Poems (Dublin, 1786).

Slavery: A Poem (London, 1788).

Thoughts on the Importance of the Manners of the Great to General Society (4th edn. London, 1788).

Bishop Bonner's Ghost (Twickenham, 1789).

An Estimate of the Religion of the Fashionable World by One of the Laity (3rd edn. London, 1791).

Village Politics Addressed to all the Mechanics, Journeymen and Day Labourers in Great Britain, by Will Chip, a Country Carpenter (4th edn. London, 1793).

Remarks on the Speech of M. Dupont, made in the National Convention of France on the Subjects of Religion and Public Education (London, 1793).

Cheap Repository Tracts Published during the Year 1795 (London and Bath, [1797]).

Cheap Repository Tracts Published during the Year 1796 (London and Bath, [1797]).

Cheap Repository Tracts, Entertaining Moral and Religious (London, 1798).

Cheap Repository Shorter Tracts (London, 1798).

Cheap Repository Tracts for Sunday Reading (London, 1798).

Strictures on the Modern System of Female Education, with a View of the Principles and Conduct Prevalent among Women of Rank and Fortune, 2 vols. (5th edn. London, 1799).

The Works of Hannah More in Eight Volumes: including several pieces never before published, 8 vols. (London, 1801).

'The White Slave Trade', *Christian Observer*, 3 (Mar. 1804), 151–4.

Bibliography

Hints towards Forming the Character of a Young Princess, 2 vols. (2nd edn. London, 1805).

Coelebs in Search of a Wife: Comprehending Observations on Domestic Habits… Religion, and Morals, 2 vols. (9th edn. London, 1809).

Practical Piety; or, The Influence of the Religion of the Heart on the Conduct of the Life, 2 vols. (London, 1811).

Christian Morals, 2 vols. (London, 1813).

An Essay on the Character and Practical Writings of St Paul, 2 vols. (London, 1815).

The Works of Hannah More: A New Edition, 18 vols. (London, 1818).

Moral Sketches of Prevailing Opinions and Manners, Foreign and Domestic (6th edn. London, 1820).

The Twelfth of August; or, The Feast of Freedom (London, 1819).

Cheap Repository Tracts Suited to the Present Times (London, 1819).

Bible Rhymes on the Names of All the Books of the Old and New Testament with Allusions to Some of the Principal Incidents and Characters (London, 1821).

The Spirit of Prayer by Hannah More. Selected and Compiled by her from Various Portions exclusively on the subject in her published volumes (London, 1825).

The Works of Hannah More, with Editions and Corrections, 11 vols. (5th edn. London, 1830).

Letters of Hannah More to Zachary Macaulay, Esq., containing Notices of Lord Macaulay's Youth, ed. Arthur Roberts (London, 1860).

Manuscript Sources

Anson MSS, letters and diaries of Mary Hamilton, property of Sir Peter and Dame Elizabeth Anson

Bodleian Library, Oxford, MSS Wilberforce.

Boston (Mass.) Public Library, Dept. of Rare Books and Manuscripts.

Bristol City Council, Bristol Record Office, miscellaneous correspondence.

Bristol City Council, Bristol Reference Library, miscellaneous correspondence and pamphlets.

British Library, Add. MSS 16919–16931, Reeves Papers.

British Library, Add. MS 22907, Cobbett Papers.

British Library, Add. MS 37835, Windham Papers.

British Library, Add. MS 42511, Hannah More Papers.

British Library, Add. MS 46362, fo. 62, letter to Dowager Countess of Haddington.

British Library, Add. MS 63084, fos. 4–11, miscellaneous correspondence.

British Library, Egerton MS 1958, miscellaneous correspondence.

British Library, Egerton MS 1965, letters to Lady Olivia Sparrow.

Cambridgeshire County Record Office, Huntingdon, Manchester Collection, letters to Millicent Sparrow, Viscountess Mandeville.

Cambridge University Library, Thornton Papers.

Cambridge University, St John's College Library, MS k. 34, letter to Richard Beadon, Bishop of Bath and Wells.

Centre for Kentish Studies (Maidstone), Stanhope MS U1590/S5/03/6, letters to George Pretyman-Tomline.

College of William and Mary, Swem Library, Williamsburg, Virginia, Jonathan Boucher Papers.

Duke University, Durham, NC, Rare Book, Manuscript and Special Collections Library, William Wilberforce Papers.

Flintshire County Record Office, Gwynn-Gladstone MSS, 335, 396, letters to Anne and John Gladstone.

Folger Shakespeare Library, Washington, letters to Eva Marie Garrick.

Harrowby Manuscript Trust, Ryder Papers, letters to Henry Ryder.

Henry E. Huntington Library, San Marino, letters to Elizabeth Montagu, Zachary and Selina Macaulay, Marianne Thornton, Charles and Jane Hoare.

Indiana University, Lilly Library, Gwatkin MSS, letters of Sally and Martha More to Ann Lovell Gwatkin.

Lambeth Palace Library, Porteus correspondence and papers.

London Guildhall University, Women's Library.

New York Public Library, Berg Collection of English and American Literature, Astor Lennox and Tilder Foundations, miscellaneous correspondence.

Pierpont Morgan Library, New York, Misc. English, miscellaneous correspondence.

Public Record Office, Kew, wills of William Turner, Martha More, Hannah More.

Somerset County Record Office, parish registers; records of the Cheddar and Shipham Female Societies.

Trustees of the Mary Webb Charities and the Hannah More Building, Fishponds, Bristol, 'Memorandum and Accounts relating to Mrs Webb's Charity'.

University of California at Los Angeles, William Andrews Clark Memorial Library, Hannah More MSS (uncatalogued) and Hannah More MS Box (catalogued).

University College London Library, Brougham MSS.

Victoria and Albert Museum, Garrick Papers.

Yale University, Beinecke Rare Book and Manuscript Library, Osborn Collection, miscellaneous correspondence.

Newspapers and Journals

Analytical Review
The Anti-Cobbett; or, The Weekly Patriotic Register
Anti-Jacobin Review
Bath Chronicle
Bonner and Middleton's Bristol Journal
Bristol Mercury
Bristol Mirror
British Critic
Christian Observer
Cobbett's Weekly Political Register
Eclectic Review
Edinburgh Review

Bibliography

Family Magazine
Felix Farley's Bristol Journal
Gentleman's Magazine
Hone's Reformists' Register and Weekly Commentary
Ladies' Monthly Museum
Monthly Review
Morning Chronicle
Morning Herald
Morning Post
Orthodox Churchman's Magazine
Quarterly Review
St James's Chronicle
Sarah Farley's Bristol Journal
The Times
Weekly Political Register
Woodfall's Register

Printed Primary Sources

An Address to the Females of Great Britain on the Propriety of their Petitioning Parliament for the Abolition of Negro Slavery, by an Englishwoman (London, 1833).

ADEANE, J. H. (ed.), The Girlhood of Maria Josepha Holroyd [Lady Stanley of Alderley] (London, 1896).

The Affecting History of Louisa, the Wandering Maniac; or, 'Lady of the Haystack'... supposed to be a Natural Daughter of Francis I, Emperor of Germany (London, 1803).

ANSON, ELIZABETH and FLORENCE (eds.), Mary Hamilton, afterwards Mrs John Dickenson at Court and at Home. From Letters and Diaries 1756 to 1816 (London: John Murray, 1925).

ASHTON, JOHN (ed.), Chapbooks of the Eighteenth Century (London, 1882; repr. n.d.).

ASTELL, MARY, A Serious Proposal to the Ladies (London, 1696).

AUSTEN, JANE, Lady Susan, The Watsons, Sanditon, ed. Margaret Drabble (Harmondsworth: Penguin, 1974).

—— Catherine and Other Writings, ed. Margaret Anne Doody and Douglas Murray (Oxford: Oxford University Press, 1993).

—— Jane Austen's Letters, ed. Deidre Le Faye (Oxford: Oxford University Press, 1995).

BERE, THOMAS, The Controversy between Mrs Hannah More and the Curate of Blagdon, relative to the Conduct of her Teacher of the Sunday School in that Parish (London, 1801).

—— An Appeal to the Public on the Controversy between Hannah More, the Curate of Blagdon, and the Rev. Sir A. Elton (Bath, 1801).

—— *An Address to Mrs Hannah More on the Conclusion of the Blagdon Controversy* (Bath and London, 1801).

BERRY, MARY, *Extracts from the Journals and Correspondence of Miss Berry from the Year 1783 to 1852*, ed. Lady Theresa Lewis, 3 vols. (London, 1865).

BIRRELL, AUGUSTINE, *Collected Essays*, 2 vols. (London: Elliot Stock, 1899).

—— *In the Name of the Bodleian and Other Essays* (London: Elliot Stock, 1905).

[BOAK, JOHN] *A Statement of Facts relative to Mrs H. More's Schools Occasioned by Some Late Misrepresentations*, (3rd edn. Bath and London, 1801).

BOSWELL, JAMES, *Life of Johnson*, ed. George Birkbeck Hill, 6 vols. (Oxford: Clarendon Press, 1934).

—— *Boswell's London Journal, 1762–1763* (Yale edn.), ed. Frederick A. Pottle (London: Heinemann, 1950).

BOUCHER, JONATHAN, *A Sermon Preached at the Assizes held at the City of Carlisle, August the 12, 1798* (Carlisle, 1798).

BROWNING, ELIZABETH BARRETT, *Aurora Leigh* (rev. edn. 1859), ed. Margaret Reynolds (New York: W. W. Norton, 1995).

—— *Correspondence of Edmund Burke (1774–1797)*, gen. editor Thomas W. Copeland, 10 vols. (Cambridge: Cambridge University Press; Chicago: Chicago University Press, 1958–78).

BURKE, EDMUND, *Reflections on the Revolution in France*, ed. Conor Cruise O'Brien (Harmondsworth: Penguin, 1982; repr. 1986).

BURNEY, FANNY, *Memoirs of Dr Burney*, ed. Madame d'Arblay, 3 vols. (London, 1832).

—— *Diary and Letters of Madame d'Arblay*, 7 vols. (London, 1842).

—— *The Journals and Letters of Fanny Burney (Madame d'Arblay)*, i: *1791–2*, ii: *Courtship and Marriage, 1793*, ed. Joyce Hemlow (Oxford: Clarendon Press, 1972).

—— *The Early Journals and Letters of Fanny Burney*, i: *1768–1773*, ed. Lars E. Troide (Oxford: Clarendon Press, 1988).

—— The *Early Journals and Letters of Fanny Burney*, iii: *The Streatham Years*, pt. 1: *1778–1779*, ed. Lars E. Troide and Stewart J. Cooke (Oxford: Clarendon Press, 1994).

CARTER, ELIZABETH, *Letters from Mrs Elizabeth Carter to Mrs Montagu*, ed. Montagu Pennington, 3 vols. (London, 1817).

A Charitable Morsel of Unleavened Bread for the Author of a Letter to the Rev William Romaine, entitled Gideon's Cake of Barley Meal, being a reply to that pamphlet (London, 1793).

CHATTERTON, GEORGIANA, LADY (ed.), *Memorials, Personal and Historical of Admiral Lord Gambier*, 2 vols. (London, 1861).

CLARK, J. C. D. (ed.), *Memoirs of James, Second Earl Waldegrave* (Cambridge: Cambridge University Press, 1988).

CLARKSON, THOMAS, *History of the Rise, Progress, and Accomplishment of the Abolition of the African Slave Trade by the British Parliament* (London, 1839).

COLERIDGE, SAMUEL TAYLOR, *The Collected Letters of Samuel Taylor Coleridge*, ed. Earl Leslie Griggs, 4 vols. (Oxford: Clarendon Press, 1959).

Bibliography

COLLINSON, JOHN, *The History and Antiquities of the County of Somerset*, 3 vols. (Bath, 1791).

COLQUHOUN, PATRICK, *A Treatise on the Police of the Metropolis* (London, 1796).

COTTLE, JOSEPH, *Reminiscences of Samuel Taylor Coleridge and Robert Southey* (London, 1847; repr. Highgate: Lime Tree Bower Press, 1970).

A Country Carpenter's Confession of Faith (London, 1794).

COWPER, WILLIAM, *The Task and Selected Other Poems*, ed. James Sambrook (London: Longman, 1994).

DAUBENY, CHARLES, *A Guide to the Church in Several Discourses... Addressed to William Wilberforce, Esq., MP* (London, 1798).

—— *A Letter to Mrs Hannah More on Some Part of her Late Publication Entitled 'Strictures on Female Education'* (Bath and London, 1799).

—— *Vindiciae Ecclesiae Anglicanae in which some of the false reasonings and palpable misrepresentations in a publication entitled 'The True Churchman Ascertained'... are pointed out* (London and Bath, 1803).

—— *Reasons for Supporting the Society for Promoting Christian Knowledge in Preference to the New Bible Society* (London, 1812).

DAVIES, THOMAS, *Memoirs of the Life of David Garrick, Esq.*, 2 vols. (London, 1780).

DE QUINCEY, THOMAS, *Collected Writings*, ed. David Masson, 14 vols. (Edinburgh: Adam & Charles Black, 1890).

DEVERELL, MARY, *Sermons on the Following Subjects* (Bristol [1774]).

EASTERBROOK, JOSEPH, *An Appeal to the Public Respecting George Lukins, Called the Yatton Demoniac* (Bristol, 1788).

ELIOT, GEORGE, *The George Eliot Letters*, ed. Gordon S. Haight, 6 vols. (London: Oxford University Press; New Haven: Yale University Press, 1954).

—— *Scenes of Clerical Life*, ed. Thomas A. Noble (Oxford: Oxford University Press, 1988).

ELTON, SIR ABRAHAM, *A Letter to the Rev. Thomas Bere... Occasioned by his Late Unwarrantable Attack on Mrs HANNAH MORE* (London and Bath, 1801).

The First Report of the Society for Bettering the Conditions and Increasing the Comforts of the Poor (London, 1797).

FOSTER, JOHN, *An Essay on the Evils of Popular Ignorance* (London, 1820).

GARRICK, DAVID, *The Private Correspondence of David Garrick with the Most Celebrated Persons of his Time*, ed. James Boaden, 2 vols. (London, 1821).

—— *The Letters of David Garrick*, ed. David M. Little and George M. Kahrl, 3 vols. (Cambridge: Cambridge University Press, 1963).

[George Prince of Wales] *The Correspondence of George Prince of Wales, 1770–1812*, ed. A. Aspinall, 8 vols. (London: Cassell, 1968).

Gideon's Cake of Barley-Meal: A Letter to the Rev. William Romaine on his preaching for the emigrant popish clergy, with some Strictures on Mrs Hannah More's Remarks published for their benefit (London, 1793).

GILPIN, WILLIAM, *Observations on the River Wye and Several Parts of South Wales,* (2nd edn. London, 1789).

GISBORNE, THOMAS, *An Enquiry into the Duties of the Female Sex* (London, 1797).

344

[GLASSE, GEORGE HENRY] *Inconnue: Louisa. A Narrative of Facts supposed to throw light on the Mysterious History of 'The Lady of the Haystack'*, (3rd edn. London, 1801).

HARFORD, JOHN SCANDRETT, *The Life of Thomas Burgess, DD, Late Bishop of Salisbury* (London, 1840).

—— *Recollections of William Wilberforce, Esq.* (London, 1864).

HODGSON, ROBERT, *The Life of the Right Reverend Beilby Porteus, DD, Late Bishop of London* (2nd edn. London, 1811).

HORSLEY, SAMUEL, *The Charge of Samuel, Lord Bishop of Rochester, to the Clergy of his Diocese* (London, 1800).

House of Commons Sessional Papers: Select Committee on Education, 1835, vol. 7.

JAY, WILLIAM, *The Autobiography and Reminiscences of the Rev. William Jay*, ed. George Redford and John Angell James (London, 1855).

JEBB, JOHN, and KNOX, ALEXANDER, *Thirty Years' Correspondence between John Jebb and Alexander Knox*, ed. Charles Forster, 2 vols. (London, 1836).

JOHNSON, SAMUEL, *The Letters of Samuel Johnson*, ed. Bruce Redford, iv: *1782–1784* (Princeton: Princeton University Press, 1994).

[JONES, WILLIAM] *Liberty and Property Preserved against Republicans and Levellers: A Collection of Tracts*, i: *Nos. 1 and 11* (London [1792]).

—— *The Jubilee Memorial of the Religious Tract Society* (London, 1850).

KELLY, GARY (ed.), *Bluestocking Feminism: Writings of the Bluestocking Circle, 1738–1785*, 6 vols. (London: Pickering & Chatto, 1999).

KNOX, ALEXANDER, *Remains*, 2nd edn., 4 vols. (London, 1836–7).

LEADBETTER, CHARLES, *The Royal Gauger; or, Gauging Made Easy* (London, 1739).

A Letter to the Rev. Charles Daubeny on Some Passages Contained in his Guide to the Church and his Letter to Mrs Hannah More, by a Minister of the Church of England (Bath and London, 1799).

The Life of James Aitken, Commonly Called John the Painter, 2nd edn. (London, 1777).

MACAULAY [GRAHAM], CATHARINE, *Letters on Education with Observations on Religious and Metaphysical Subjects* (London, 1790).

MACAULAY, THOMAS BABINGTON, *Lord Macaulay's Essays and Lays of Ancient Rome* (London: Longmans, Green, 1905).

—— *Letters of Thomas Babington Macaulay*, 6 vols., ed. Thomas Pinney (Cambridge: Cambridge University Press, 1974–81).

MATHEWS, J., *The Bristol Guide*, 5th edn. (Bristol, n.d.).

MAYETT, JOSEPH, *The Autobiography of Joseph Mayett of Quainton (1783–1839)*, ed. Ann Kussmaul, Buckinghamshire Record Society, no. 23 (1986).

METASTASIO, PIERO, *Biblioteca Teatrale Italiana*, iii (Lucca, 1762).

MITFORD, MARY RUSSELL, *Our Village: Sketches of Rural Character and Scenery*, 5 vols. (London, 1824).

MONTAGU, ELIZABETH, *Mrs Montagu, 'Queen of the Blues': Her Letters and Friendships from 1762 to 1800*, ed. Reginald Blunt, 2 vols. (London: Constable, 1904).

Bibliography

MORE, MARTHA, *Mendip Annals; or, The Narrative of the Charitable Labours of Hannah and Martha More*, ed. Arthur Roberts (London, 1859).

A Narrative of the Extraordinary Case of George Lukins of Yatton (Bristol, 1788).

NEWMAN, JOHN HENRY, *Apologia pro Vita Sua*, ed. Ian Ker (Harmondsworth: Penguin, 1994).

NEWTON, JOHN, *Cardiphonia; or, The Utterance of the Heart; in the Course of a Real Correspondence. By the Author of Omicron's Letters*, 2 vols. (London, 1781).

[——] An *Authentic Narrative of Some Remarkable and Interesting Particulars*, 6th edn. (London, 1786).

—— *Thoughts upon the African Slave Trade* (London, 1788).

[—— and COWPER, WILLIAM] *Olney Hymns in Three Books* (5th edn. London, 1788).

NORMAN, SAMUEL, *Authentic Anecdotes of George Lukins, the Yatton Demoniac* (Bristol, n.d.).

Of the Education of the Poor; being the first part of a Digest of the Reports Society for Bettering the Condition of the Poor (London, 1809).

OWEN, JOHN, *The History of the Origin and First Ten Years of the British and Foreign Bible Society*, 2 vols. (London, 1816).

PAINE, THOMAS, *Rights of Man*, ed. Eric Foner (Harmondsworth: Penguin, 1969; repr. 1987).

PEPYS, WILLIAM WELLER, *A Later Pepys: The Correspondence of Sir William Weller Pepys, Bart., Master in Chancery 1758–1825*, ed. Alice C. C. Gaussen, 2 vols. (London: Bodley Head, 1904).

[PIGOTT, CHARLES] *The Female Jockey Club; or, A Sketch of the Manners of the Age* (London, 1794).

PIOZZI, HESTER LYNCH, *Anecdotes of the Late Samuel Johnson, LLD, during the Last Twenty Years of his Life* (Dublin, 1786).

—— *The Piozzi Letters: Correspondence of Hester Lynch Piozzi (formerly Mrs Thrale)*, ed. Edward A. Bloom and Lilian D. Bloom (Newark: University of Delaware Press; London: Associated University Presses), i: *1784–1791* (1989); ii: *1792–1798* (1991); iii: 1799–1804 (1993).

—— *Thraliana: The Diary of Mrs Hester Lynch Thrale (Later Mrs Piozzi) 1776–1809*, ed. Katherine C. Balderston, 2 vols. (Oxford: Clarendon Press, 1942).

PLACE, FRANCIS, *Improvement of the Working People* (London, 1834).

—— *Autobiography of Francis Place (1771–1854)*, ed. Mary Thale (Cambridge: Cambridge University Press, 1972).

PORTEUS, BEILBY, *A Sermon Preached before the Incorporated Society for the Propagation of the Gospel in Foreign Parts* (London, 1783).

—— *A Letter to the Clergy of the Diocese of Chester concerning Sunday Schools* (London, 1786).

—— *A Charge Delivered to the Clergy of the Diocese of London in the Years 1798 and 1799* (London, 1799).

PRATT, J. H. (ed.), *Eclectic Notes; or, Notes of Discussions on Religious Topics at the Meetings of the Eclectic Society, London, during the Years 1798–1814* (2nd edn. London, 1856).

[Princess Charlotte] *Letters of Princess Charlotte, 1811–1817*, ed. A. Aspinall (London: Home & Van Thal, 1949).

RAMSAY, JAMES, *An Essay on the Treatment and Conversion of African Slaves in the British Sugar Colonies* (London, 1784).

—— *An Enquiry into the Effects of Putting a Stop to the African Slave Trade* (London, 1784).

[ROBINSON, MARY] *A Letter to the Women of England on the Injustice of Mental Subordination* (London, 1799).

—— *Perdita: The Memoirs of Mary Robinson (1758–1800)*, ed. M. J. Levy (London: Peter Owen, 1994).

SABOR, PETER (ed.), *Horace Walpole: The Critical Heritage* (London: Routledge & Kegan Paul, 1987).

[SHAW, WILLIAM] *The Life of Hannah More, with a Critical Review of her Writings, by the Rev. Sir Archibald MacSarcasm, Bart* (London, 1802).

SPENCER, EDWARD, *Truths respecting Mrs Hannah More's Meeting-Houses and the Conduct of her Followers* (Bath, 1802).

[THORNTON, HENRY] *A Plan for Establishing by Subscription a Repository of Cheap Publications, on Religious & Moral Subjects* ([1795]).

The Trial of Richard Vining Perry (Bristol, 1794).

TRIMMER, SARAH, *The Oeconomy of Charity; or, An Address to Ladies concerning Sunday Schools* (London, 1787).

—— *The Servants' Friend: An Exemplary Tale Designed to Enforce the Religious Instructions Given at Sunday and Other Charity Schools* (2nd edn. London, 1787).

WALPOLE, HORACE, *A Description of the Villa of Mr Horace Walpole* (Twickenham, 1784).

—— *Horace Walpole's Correspondence with Mary and Agnes Berry*, ed. W. S. Lewis and A. Dayle Wallace, xi (New Haven: Yale University Press; London: Oxford University Press, 1944).

—— *Horace Walpole's Correspondence with Sir Horace Mann*, ed. W. S. Lewis, Warren Hunting Smith, and George G. Lam, xxiv (London: Oxford University Press; New Haven: Yale University Press, 1967).

—— *Horace Walpole's Correspondence with William Mason*, ed. W. S. Lewis, Grover Cronin Jr., and Charles H. Bennett, xxix (London: Oxford University Press; New Haven: Yale University Press, 1955).

—— *Horace Walpole's Correspondence with Hannah More et al.*, ed. W. S. Lewis, Robert A. Smith, and Charles H. Bennett, xxxi (London: Oxford University Press; New Haven: Yale University Press, 1961).

—— *Horace Walpole's Correspondence with the Countess of Upper Ossory*, ed. W. S. Lewis and A. Dayle Wallace, xxxiii (London: Oxford University Press; New Haven: Yale University Press, 1965).

—— *Horace Walpole's Correspondence with the Walpole Family*, ed. W. S. Lewis and Joseph W. Reed Jr., xxxvi (London: Oxford University Press; New Haven: Yale University Press, 1973).

347

Bibliography

Wesley, Charles, *The Journal of Charles Wesley*, ed. Thomas Jackson, 2 vols. (London, 1849).

Wesley, John, *The Journal of John Wesley*, vi, ed. Nehemiah Curnock (London: Charles H. Kelly, 1915).

Whalley, Thomas Sedgwick, *Animadversions on the Curate of Blagdon's Three Publications... with Some Allusions to his Cambrian Descent* (London, 1802).

—— *Journals and Correspondence of Thomas Sedgwick Whalley, D.D.*, ed. Hill Wickham, 2 vols. (London, 1863).

Wilberforce, William, *A Practical View of the Prevailing Religious System of Professed Christians in the Higher and Middle Classes... contrasted with Real Christianity* (London, 1797).

—— *The Correspondence of William Wilberforce*, ed. Robert Isaac and Samuel Wilberforce, 2 vols. (London, 1840).

[Wolcot, John] *Nil Admirari; or, A Smile at a Bishop... by Peter Pindar Esq.* (London, 1799).

Wollstonecraft, Mary, *Political Writings*, ed. Janet Todd (Oxford: Oxford University Press, 1994).

Wordsworth, William and Dorothy, *The Letters of William and Dorothy Wordsworth*, i: *The Early Years, 1785-1805*, ed. Ernest de Selincourt, 2nd edn., rev. Chester L. Shaver (Oxford: Clarendon Press, 1967).

—— *The Letters of William and Dorothy Wordsworth*, iii: *The Middle Years*, p. 11: *1812-1820*, ed. Ernest de Selincourt, rev. Mary Moorman and Alan G. Hill (Oxford: Clarendon Press, 1970).

Yearsley, Ann, *Poems on Several Occasions, by Ann Yearsley, a Milkwoman of Bristol* (London, 1785).

—— *Poems on Various Subjects, by Ann Yearsley, a Milkwoman of Clifton, near Bristol* (London, 1787).

Yonge, Charlotte M., *The Cunning Woman's Grandson: A Tale of Cheddar a Hundred Years Ago* (London, n.d.).

Secondary Sources

Allen, W. O. B., and MacClure, Edmund, *Two Hundred Years: The History of the Society for Promoting Christian Knowledge, 1698-1898* (London, 1898).

Altick, Richard D., *The English Common Reader: A Social History of the Mass Reading Public, 1800-1900* (Chicago: University of Chicago Press, 1957).

Anderson, Patricia, *The Printed Image and the Transformation of Popular Culture, 1790-1860* (Oxford: Clarendon Press, 1991).

Andrew, Donna T., 'The Code of Honour and its Critics: The Opposition to Duelling in England, 1780-1850', *Social History*, 5 (1980), 409-34.

—— *Philanthropy and Police: London Charity in the Eighteenth Century* (Princeton: Princeton University Press, 1989).

—— 'Popular Culture and Public Debate: London 1780', *Historical Journal*, 39 (1996), 405-23.

—— ' "Adultery à-la-Mode": Privilege, the Law and Attitudes to Adultery, 1770–1809', *History*, 82 (1997), 5–23.

ANDREWS, S., 'Pitt and Anti-Jacobin Hysteria', *History Today*, 48 (Sept. 1998), 49–54.

ANNAN, N. G., 'The Intellectual Aristocracy', in J. H. Plumb (ed.), *Studies in Social History* (London, Longmans, Green, 1955), 243–87.

ANSTEY, ROGER, *The Atlantic Slave Trade and British Abolition* (London: Macmillan, 1975).

ASPINALL-OGLANDER, CECIL, *Admiral's Wife: Being the Life and Letters of the Hon. Mrs Edward Boscawen from 1719 to 1761* (London: Longmans, Green, 1940).

—— *Admiral's Widow: Being the Life and Letters of the Hon. Mrs Edward Boscawen from 1761 to 1805* (London: Hogarth Press, 1942).

ASTON, NIGEL, 'Horne and Heterodoxy: The Defence of Anglican Beliefs in the Late Enlightenment', *English Historical Review*, 108 (1993), 895–919.

—— 'A "lay divine": Burke, Christianity, and the Preservation of the British State, 1790–1797', in id. (ed.), *Religious Change in Europe, 1650–1914: Essays for John McManners* (Oxford: Clarendon Press, 1997), 185–211.

BAINES, PAUL, *The House of Forgery in Eighteenth-Century Britain* (Aldershot: Ashgate, 1999).

BALFOUR, CLARA LUCAS, *A Sketch of Mrs Hannah More and her Sisters* (London, 1854).

BARKER, HANNAH, and CHALUS, ELAINE (eds.), *Gender in Eighteenth-Century England: Roles, Representations, and Responsibilities* (London: Longman, 1997).

BARKER, JULIET, *The Brontës* (London: Weidenfeld & Nicolson, 1994).

BARKER, KATHLEEN, 'The Theatre Royal, Bristol: The First Seventy Years', in Patrick McGrath (ed.), *Bristol in the Eighteenth Century* (Newton Abbott: David & Charles, 1972), 63–87.

—— 'William Powell: A Forgotten Star', in Kenneth Richards and Peter Thompson (eds.), *The Eighteenth-Century English Stage* (London: Methuen, 1972), 73–83.

—— *The Theatre Royal, Bristol, 1766–1966: Two Centuries of Stage History* (London: Society for Theatre Research, 1974).

BARKER-BENWELD, G. J., *The Culture of Sensibility: Sex and Society in Eighteenth-Century Britain* (Chicago: University of Chicago Press, 1992).

BARRY, JONATHAN, 'The Cultural Life of Bristol, 1640–1775', D.Phil. thesis (Oxford, 1985).

—— 'The Press and the Politics of Culture in Bristol, 1600–1775', in Jeremy Black and Jeremy Gregory (eds.), *Culture, Politics and Society in Britain, 1660–1800* (Manchester: Manchester University Press, 1991), 49–81.

BEBBINGTON, D. W., *Evangelicalism in Modern Britain: A History from the 1730s to the 1980s* (London: Unwin Hyman, 1989).

BEHRENDT, STEPHEN C., *Royal Mourning and Regency Culture: Elegies and Memorials of Princess Charlotte* (Basingstoke: Macmillan, 1997).

Bibliography

BELHAM, P., 'The Origins of Elementary Education in Somerset, with Particular Reference to the Work of Hannah More in the Mendips', MA thesis (Bristol, 1953).

BELLINGER, D., 'The Émigré Clergy and the English Church, 1789–1815', *Journal of Ecclesiastical History*, 34 (1983), 392–410.

BENEDETTI, JEAN, *David Garrick and the Birth of the Modern Theatre* (London: Methuen, 2001).

BENNETT, C. H., 'The Text of Horace Walpole's Correspondence with Hannah More', repr. rev. in *The Yale Edition of Horace Walpole's Correspondence*, xxxi, ed. W. S. Lewis (New Haven: Yale University Press, 1961), pp. xix–xxiv.

BERRIDGE, VIRGINIA, and EDWARDS, GRIFFITH, *Opium and the People: Opiate Use in Nineteenth-Century England* (London: Allen Lane/St Martin's Press, 1981).

BIDDULPH, VIOLET, *The Three Ladies Waldegrave* (London: Peter Davies, 1938).

BILLINGTON, LOUISE, and BILLINGTON, ROSAMUND, ' "A Burning Zeal for Righteousness": Women in the British Anti-Slavery Movement, 1820–1860', in Jane Rendall (ed.), *Equal or Different: Women's Politics, 1800–1914* (Oxford: Basil Blackwell, 1987), 82–111.

BINDMAN, DAVID, *The Shadow of the Guillotine: Britain and the French Revolution* (London: British Museum Publications, 1989).

BLAKEY, DOROTHY, *The Minerva Press, 1790–1820* (London: Oxford University Press, 1939).

BOLT, CHRISTINE, and DRESCHER, SEYMOUR (eds.), *Anti-Slavery, Religion and Reform: Essays in Memory of Roger Anstey* (Folkestone: Dawson & Archon, 1980).

BORSAY, PETER, *The English Urban Renaissance: Culture and Society in the Provincial Town, 1660–1770* (Oxford: Clarendon Press, 1989).

BRADLEY, IAN, 'The Politics of Godliness: Evangelicals in Parliament, 1784–1832', D.Phil. thesis (Oxford, 1974).

—— *The Call to Seriousness: The Evangelical Impact on the Victorians* (London: Jonathan Cape, 1976).

BRADLEY, JAMES E., *Religion, Revolution, and English Radicalism: Nonconformity in Eighteenth-Century Politics and Society* (Cambridge: Cambridge University Press, 1990).

BREWER, JOHN, *The Sinews of Power: War, Money, and the English State, 1688–1783* (London: Unwin Hyman, 1989).

—— *The Pleasures of the Imagination: English Culture in the Eighteenth Century* (London: HarperCollins, 1997).

BROWN, FORD K., *Fathers of the Victorians: The Age of Wilberforce* (Cambridge: Cambridge University Press, 1961).

BROWNELL, MORRIS R., *The Prime Minister of Taste: A Portrait of Horace Walpole* (New Haven: Yale University Press, 2001).

BURNIM, KALMAN, A., *David Garrick, Director* (Pittsburgh: University of Pittsburgh Press, 1961).

BURNS, ARTHUR, *The Diocesan Revival in the Church of England, c.1800–1870* (Oxford: Clarendon Press, 1999).

BUTLER, MARILYN, *Jane Austen and the War of Ideas* (2nd edn. Oxford: Clarendon Press, 1987).

CAINE, BARBARA, *Victorian Feminists* (Oxford: Oxford University Press, 1993).

—— *English Feminism, 1780–1980* (Oxford: Oxford University Press, 1997).

CANTON, WILLIAM, *A History of the British and Foreign Bible Society*, 5 vols. (London: John Murray, 1904–10).

CARPENTER, KIRSTY, *Refugees of the French Revolution: Émigrés in London, 1789–1802* (Basingstoke: Macmillan; New York: St Martin's Press, 1999).

—— and MANSELL, PHILIP (eds.), *The French Émigrés in Europe and the Struggle against Revolution, 1789–1814* (Basingstoke: Macmillan; New York: St Martin's Press, 1999).

CARTER, GRAYLING, *Anglican Evangelicals: Protestant Secessions from the Via Media, c.1800–1850* (Oxford: Oxford University Press, 2001).

CHARTIER, ROBERT, 'Culture as Appropriation: Popular Cultural Uses in Early Modern France', in Steven L. Kaplan (ed.), *Understanding Popular Culture: Europe from the Middle Ages to the Nineteenth Century* (Berlin: Mouton, 1984), 229–53.

CHISHOLM, KATE, *Fanny Burney: Her Life, 1752–1840* (London: Chatto & Windus, 1998).

CLAEYS, GREGORY, *Thomas Paine: Social and Political Thought* (Boston: Unwin Hyman, 1989).

—— 'The French Revolution Debate and British Political Thought', *History of Political Thought*, 11 (1990), 59–80.

CLARK, J. C. D., *English Society, 1688–1832: Ideology, Social Structure and Political Practice during the Ancien Regime* (Cambridge: Cambridge University Press, 1985).

CLARK, PETER, *British Clubs and Societies, 1580–1800: The Origins of an Associational World* (Oxford: Clarendon Press, 2000).

CLARKE, NORMA, *Dr Johnson's Women* (London: Hambledon Press, 2000).

CLIFFORD, JAMES L., *Hester Lynch Piozzi (Mrs Thrale)* (Oxford: Clarendon Press, 1941).

CLOYD, E. L., *James Burnett, Lord Monboddo* (Oxford: Clarendon Press, 1972).

COBBAN, ALFRED, *The Debate on the French Revolution, 1789–1800* (2nd edn. London: A. & C. Black, 1950).

COLBY, ROBERT A., *Fiction with a Purpose: Major and Minor Nineteenth-Century Novels* (Bloomington: Indiana University Press, 1967).

COLLEY, LINDA, 'The Apotheosis of George III: Loyalty, Royalty and the British Nation', *Past and Present*, 102 (1984), 94–129.

—— *Britons: Forging the Nation, 1707–1837* (New Haven: Yale University Press, 1992).

CORFIELD, KENNETH, 'Eliza Heyrick: Radical Quaker', in Gail Malmgreen (ed.), *Religion in the Lives of English Women, 1760–1930* (London: Croom Helm, 1986), 41–67.

Bibliography

CORFIELD, P. J., *The Impact of English Towns, 1700–1800* (Oxford: Oxford University Press, 1982).

CROSSLEY-EVANS, M. J. (ed.), 'The Curtain Parted; or, Four Conversations with Hannah More, 1817–1818', *Transactions of the Bristol and Gloucestershire Archaeological Society*, 110 (1992), 181–211.

DARNTON, ROBERT, 'Readers Respond to Rousseau: The Fabrication of Romantic Sensibility', in id., *The Great Cat Massacre and Other Episodes in French Cultural History* (New York: Basic Books, 1984), 215–56.

DAVIDOFF, LEONORE, and HALL, CATHERINE, *Family Fortunes: Men and Women of the English Middle Class, 1780–1850* (London: Routledge, 1987).

DEMERS, PATRICIA, ' "For mine's a stubborn and a savage will": "Lactilla" (Ann Yearsley) and "Stella" (Hannah More) Reconsidered', *Huntington Library Quarterly*, 56 (1993), 135–50.

—— *The World of Hannah More* (Lexington: University Press of Kentucky, 1996).

DEUTSCH, PHYLLIS, 'Moral Trespass in Georgian London: Gambling, Gender, and Electoral Politics in the Reign of George III', *Historical Journal*, 39 (1996), 637–56.

DICKINSON, H. T., *Liberty and Property: Political Ideology in Eighteenth-Century Britain* (London: Methuen, 1977).

—— 'Popular Loyalism in Britain in the 1790s', in Eckhart Hellmuth (ed.), *The Transformation of Political Culture: England and Germany in the Late Eighteenth Century* (Oxford: Oxford University Press, 1990), 503–33.

—— *The Politics of the People in Eighteenth-Century Britain* (Basingstoke: Macmillan, 1995).

—— (ed.), *Britain and the French Revolution, 1789–1815* (London: Macmillan, 1989).

DINWIDDY, JOHN, 'Conceptions of Revolution in the English Radicalism of the 1790s', in Eckhart Hellmuth (ed.), *The Transformation of Political Culture: England and Germany in the Late Eighteenth Century* (Oxford: Oxford University Press, 1990), 535–60.

DONKIN, EILEEN, *Getting into the Act: Women Playwrights in London, 1776–1829* (London: Routledge, 1995).

DOODY, MARGARET, *Frances Burney: The Life in the Works* (New Brunswick, NJ: Rutgers University Press, 1988).

DOYLE, WILLIAM, *The Oxford History of the French Revolution* (Oxford: Oxford University Press, 1989).

DOZIER, ROBERT, *For King, Constitution and Country: The English Loyalists and the French Revolution* (Lexington: University Press of Kentucky, 1983).

DRESCHER, SEYMOUR, *Econocide: British Slavery in the Era of Abolition* (Pittsburgh: University of Pittsburgh Press, 1977).

—— *Capitalism and Antislavery: British Mobilization in Comparative Perspective* (New York: Oxford University Press, 1987).

—— 'Whose Abolition? Popular Pressure and the Ending of the British Slave Trade', *Past and Present*, 43 (1994), 136–43.

DYCK, I., *William Cobbett and Rural Popular Culture* (Cambridge: Cambridge University Press, 1992).

EASTWOOD, DAVID, 'Patriotism and the English State in the 1790s', in Mark Philp (ed.), *The French Revolution and British Popular Politics* (Cambridge: Cambridge University Press, 1991), 146–68.

—— 'Robert Southey and the Meanings of Patriotism', *Journal of British Studies*, 31 (1992), 265–87.

ELBOURNE, ELIZABETH, 'The Foundation of the Church Missionary Society: The Anglican Missionary Impulse', in J. Walsh, C. Haydon, and S. Taylor (eds.), *The Church of England, c.1689–c.1833: From Toleration to Tractarianism* (Cambridge: Cambridge University Press, 1993), 247–64.

ELLERY, ELOISE, *Brissot de Warville: A Study in the History of the French Revolution* (Boston: Houghton Mifflin, 1915).

ELTON, MARGARET, *Annals of the Elton Family, Bristol Merchants and Somerset Landowners* (Far Thrupp, Stroud: Alan Sutton, 1994).

EMSLEY, CLIVE, *British Society and the French Wars, 1793–1815* (London: Macmillan, 1979).

ENSOR, R. C. K., *England, 1870–1914* (Oxford: Oxford University Press, 1936).

ESTABROOK, CARL B., *Urbane and Rustic England: Cultural Ties and Social Spheres in the Provinces, 1660–1780* (Manchester: Manchester University Press, 1998).

FEATHER, JOHN, *The Provincial Book Trade in Eighteenth-Century England* (Cambridge: Cambridge University Press, 1986).

FERGUSON, MOIRA, *Subject to Others: British Women Writers and Colonial Slavery, 1670–1834* (London: Routledge, 1992).

FISSELL, MARY E., *Patients, Power, and the Poor in Eighteenth-Century Bristol* (Cambridge: Cambridge University Press, 1991).

FORD, CHARLES HOWARD, *Hannah More: A Critical Biography* (New York: Peter Lang, 1996).

FOREMAN, AMANDA, *Georgiana, Duchess of Devonshire* (London: HarperCollins, 1999).

FORSTER, E. M., *Marianne Thornton, 1797–1887: A Domestic Biography* (London: Edward Arnold, 1956).

—— *Abinger Harvest* (Harmondsworth: Penguin, 1967).

FOUCAULT, MICHEL, *Madness and Civilisation*, trans. Alan Sheridan-Smith (London: Tavistock, 1967).

FRASER, FLORA, *The Unruly Queen: The Life of Queen Caroline* (London: Macmillan, 1996).

FULCHER, JONATHAN, 'The Loyalist Response to the Queen Caroline Agitations', *Journal of British Studies*, 34 (1995), 481–502.

GASKELL, ELIZABETH, *The Life of Charlotte Brontë* (Harmondsworth: Penguin, 1975).

GILLEY, SHERIDAN, 'Edward Irving: Prophet of the Millennium', in Jane Garnett and Colin Matthew (eds.), *Revival and Religion since 1700: Essays for John Walsh* (London: Hambledon Press, 1993), 95–110.

—— and SHEILS, W. J. (eds.), *A History of Religion in Britain: Practice and Belief from Pre-Roman Times to the Present* (Oxford: Basil Blackwell, 1994).

Bibliography

GILMARTIN, KEVIN, *Print Politics: The Press and Radical Opposition in Early Nineteenth-Century England*, Cambridge Studies in Romanticism, 21 (Cambridge: Cambridge University Press, 1996).

GOLDSMITH, NETTA MURRAY, *The Worst of Crimes: Homosexuality and the Law in Eighteenth-Century London* (Aldershot: Ashgate, 1998).

GREEN, EMANUEL, *Bibliotheca Somersetensis: A Catalogue of Books, Pamphlets, Single Sheets and Broadsides in some way connected with the County of Somerset*, 3 vols. (Taunton: Barnicott & Pearce, 1902).

GREEN, SAMUEL G., *The Story of the Religious Tract Society for One Hundred Years* (London, 1899).

GREGORY, JEREMY, 'The Eighteenth-Century Reformation: The Pastoral Task of the Anglican Clergy after 1689', in J. Walsh, C. Haydon, and S. Taylor (eds.), *The Church of England: From Toleration to Tractarianism c.1689–c.1833* (Cambridge: Cambridge University Press, 1993), 67–85.

GRUNDY, ISOBEL, 'Samuel Johnson as Patron of Women', in P. J. Korshin (ed.), *The Age of Johnson: A Scholarly Annual*, (New York: AMS Press), (1987), 59–77.

GUEST, HARRIET, *Small Change: Women, Learning, Patriotism, 1750–1810* (Chicago: University of Chicago Press, 2000).

GUNSTONE, J. T. A., 'Alexander Knox, 1757–1831', *Church Quarterly Review*, 157 (1956), 463–75.

HABERMAS, JÜRGEN, *The Structural Transformation of the Public Sphere: An Inquiry into a Category of Bourgeois Society*, trans. Thomas Burgess (Oxford: Polity Press, 1989).

HAIGHT, GORDON S., *George Eliot: A Biography* (Oxford: Clarendon Press, 1968).

HALL, CATHERINE, 'The Early Formation of Victorian Domestic Ideology', in Sandra Burman (ed.), *Fit Work for Women* (London: Croom Helm, 1979), 15–32.

HARFORD, ALICE, *Annals of the Harford Family* (London: Westminster Press, 1909).

HARLING, PHILIP, 'The Law of Libel and the Limits of Repression, 1790–1832', *Historical Journal*, 44 (2001), 107–34.

HARMAN, CLAIRE, *Fanny Burney: A Biography* (London: HarperCollins, 2000).

HARRIS, TIM, 'Problematising Popular Culture', in id. (ed.), *Popular Culture in England, c.1500–1850* (London: Macmillan, 1995), 1–27.

HASTINGS, ADRIAN, *The Construction of Nationhood: Ethnicity, Religion, and Nationalism* (Cambridge: Cambridge University Press, 1997).

HEMLOW, JOYCE, *The History of Fanny Burney* (Oxford: Clarendon Press, 1958).

HEMPTON, DAVID, *Methodism and Politics in British Society, 1750–1850* (London: Hutchinson, 1984).

—— *Religion and Popular Culture in Britain and Ireland from the Glorious Revolution to the Decline of Empire* (Cambridge: Cambridge University Press, 1996).

HENNELL, MICHAEL, *John Venn and the Clapham Sect* (London: Lutterworth Press, 1958).

HERZOG, DON, *Poisoning the Minds of the Lower Orders* (Princeton: Princeton University Press, 1998).

HIBBERT, CHRISTOPHER, *George IV* (Harmondsworth: Penguin, 1976).

HILL, BRIDGET, *The Republican Virago: The Life and Times of Catharine Macaulay, Historian* (Oxford: Clarendon Press, 1992).

HILTON, BOYD, *The Age of Atonement: The Influence of Evangelicalism on Social and Economic Thought, 1785–1865* (Oxford: Clarendon Press, 1991).

HINDMARSH, D. BRUCE, *John Newton and the English Evangelical Tradition between the Conversions of Wesley and Wilberforce* (Oxford: Clarendon Press, 1996).

—— 'The Olney Autobiographers: English Conversion Narrative in the Mid-Eighteenth Century', *Journal of Ecclesiastical History*, 49 (1998), 61–84.

HIRSCH, PAM, *Barbara Leigh Smith Bodichon, 1827–1891: Feminist, Artist, and Rebel* (London: Pimlico, 1999).

HOLE, ROBERT, *Pulpits, Politics, and Public Order in England, 1760–1832* (Cambridge: Cambridge University Press, 1989).

—— *Selected Writings of Hannah More* (London: William Pickering, 1996).

—— 'Hannah More on Literature and Propaganda', *History*, 85 (2000), 623–33.

HOLME, T., *Prinny's Daughter: A Biography of Princess Charlotte of Wales* (London: Hamish Hamilton, 1976).

HOPKINS, MARY ALDEN, *Hannah More and her Circle* (New York: Longmans, Green, 1947).

HOWSAM, LESLIE, *Cheap Bibles: Nineteenth-Century Publishing and the British and Foreign Bible Society* (Cambridge: Cambridge University Press, 1991).

HOWSE, E. M., *Saints in Politics: The 'Clapham Sect' and the Growth of Freedom* (London: George Allen & Unwin, 1952).

HUFTON, OLWEN, *The Prospect before Her: A History of Women in Western Europe*, i: *1500–1800* (London: HarperCollins, 1997).

INNES, JOANNA, 'Politics and Morals: The Reformation of Manners Movement in Later Eighteenth-Century England', in Eckhart Hellmuth (ed.), *The Transformation of Political Culture: England and Germany in the Late Eighteenth Century* (Oxford: German Historical Institute; London: Oxford University Press, 1990), 57–118.

—— 'The "Mixed Economy of Welfare" in Early Modern England: Assessments of the Options from Hale to Malthus (*c.*1683–1803)', in Martin Daunton (ed.), *Charity, Self-Interest, and Welfare in the English Past* (London: UCL Press, 1996), 139–80.

JACOB, W. M., *Lay People and Religion in the Early Eighteenth Century* (Cambridge: Cambridge University Press, 1996).

JAY, ELISABETH, *The Religion of the Heart: Anglican Evangelicalism and the Nineteenth-Century Novel* (Oxford: Clarendon Press, 1979).

—— (ed.), *The Evangelical and Oxford Movements* (Cambridge: Cambridge University Press, 1983).

JENKINS, RICHARD, *Memoirs of the Bristol Stage* (Bristol and London, 1826).

JOHNSON, CLAUDIA L., *Jane Austen: Women, Politics and the Novel* (Chicago: University of Chicago Press, 1988).

JONES, ANN H., *Ideas and Innovations: Best Sellers of Jane Austen's Age* (New York: AMS Press, 1986).

Bibliography

JONES, CHRIS, *Radical Sensibility: Literature and Ideas in the 1790s* (London: Routledge, 1993).

JONES, COLIN, *Britain and Revolutionary France: Conflict, Subversion, and Propaganda* (Exeter: University of Exeter Press, 1983).

JONES, M. G., *Hannah More* (Cambridge: Cambridge University Press, 1952).

—— *The Charity School Movement: A Study of Eighteenth-Century Puritanism in Action* (Cambridge: Cambridge University Press, 1983).

JONES, VIVIEN (ed.), *Women in the Eighteenth Century: Constructions of Femininity* (London: Routledge, 1990).

KAHN, MADELEINE, 'Hannah More and Ann Yearsley: A Collaboration across the Class Divide', *Studies in Eighteenth-Century Culture*, 25 (Baltimore: Johns Hopkins University Press, 1996), 203-23.

KEANE, JOHN, *Tom Paine: A Political Life* (London: Bloomsbury, 1996).

KETTON-CREMER, R. WYNDHAM, *Horace Walpole* (London: Duckworth, 1940).

KINNAIRD, J. K., 'Mary Astell and the Conservative Contribution to English Feminism', *Journal of British Studies*, 19 (Fall 1979), 53-75.

KNUTSFORD, MARGARET, VISCOUNTESS, *Life and Letters of Zachary Macaulay* (London: Edward Arnold, 1900).

KOWALESKI-WALLACE, ELIZABETH, *Their Fathers' Daughters: Hannah More, Maria Edgeworth and Patriarchal Complicity* (New York: Oxford University Press, 1991).

KRUEGER, CHRISTINE L., *The Reader's Repentance: Women Preachers, Women Writers and Nineteenth-Century Social Discourse* (Chicago: University of Chicago Press, 1992).

LANDRY, DONNA, *The Muses of Resistance: Laboring-Class Women's Poetry in Britain, 1739-1796* (Cambridge: Cambridge University Press, 1990).

LANGFORD, PAUL, *Public Life and the Propertied Englishman, 1698-1798* (Oxford: Clarendon Press, 1994).

LAQUEUR, T. W., *Religion and Respectability: Sunday Schools and Working-Class Culture, 1780-1850* (New Haven: Yale University Press, 1976).

LATIMER, JOHN, *The Annals of Bristol in the Eighteenth Century* ([Bristol], 1893).

LOVEGROVE, DEREYCK W., *Established Church, Sectarian People: Itinerancy and the Transformation of English Dissent, 1780-1830* (Cambridge: Cambridge University Press, 1988).

LOVELL, TERRY, 'Subjective Powers? Consumption, the Reading Public and Domestic Woman in Early Eighteenth-Century England', in Ann Bermingham and John Brewer (eds.), *The Consumption of Culture, 1600-1800: Image, Object, Text* (London: Routledge, 1995), 23-41.

LYON, EILEEN GROTH, *Politicians in the Pulpit: Christian Radicalism in Britain from the Fall of the Bastille to the Disintegration of Chartism* (Aldershot: Ashgate, 1999).

MCCALMAN, IAIN, *Radical Underworld: Revolutionaries and Pornographers in London, 1795-1840* (Cambridge: Cambridge University Press, 1988).

MCGRATH, PATRICK (ed.), *Bristol in the Eighteenth Century* (Newton Abbot: David & Charles, 1972).

MCINTYRE, I., *Garrick* (London: Allen Lane/Penguin Press, 1999).

MACLEOD, EMMA VINCENT, *A War of Ideas: British Attitudes to the Wars against Revolutionary France, 1792–1802* (Aldershot: Ashgate, 1998).

MCMANNERS, JOHN, *Church and Society in Eighteenth-Century France*, i: *The Clerical Establishment and its Social Ramifications* (Oxford: Clarendon Press, 1998).

MALCOLMSON, ROBERT W., *Popular Recreations in English Society, 1700–1850* (Cambridge: Cambridge University Press, 1973).

——‘"A Set of Ungovernable People": The Kingswood Colliers in the Eighteenth Century', in J. Brewer and J. Styles (eds.), *An Ungovernable People: The English and their Law in the Seventeenth and Eighteenth Centuries* (London: Hutchinson, 1980), 85–127.

MARSHALL, PETER, *The Anti-Slave Trade Movement in Bristol* (Bristol: Historical Association, 1996).

MARSHALL, P. J., and WILLIAMS, GLYNDWR, *The Great Map of Mankind: British Perceptions of the World in the Age of Enlightenment* (London: Dent, 1982).

MARTIN, R. H., *Evangelicals United: Ecumenical Stirrings in Pre-Victorian Britain, 1795–1830* (Metuchen, NJ: Scarecrow Press, 1983).

MASON, MICHAEL, *The Making of Victorian Sexual Attitudes* (Oxford: Oxford University Press, 1994).

MATHER, F. C., *High Church Prophet: Bishop Samuel Horsley (1733–1806) and the Caroline Tradition in the Later Georgian Church* (Oxford: Clarendon Press, 1992).

MATTHEW, H. C. G., *Gladstone, 1809–1898* (Oxford: Oxford University Press, 1999).

MEACHAM, STANDISH, *Henry Thornton of Clapham, 1760–1815* (Cambridge, Mass.: Harvard University Press, 1964).

MEYERSTEIN, E. H. W., *A Life of Thomas Chatterton* (London: Ingpen & Grant, [1930]).

MIDGLEY, CLARE, *Women Against Slavery: The British Campaigns, 1780–1870* (London: Routledge, 1992).

——‘From Supporting Missions to Petitioning Parliament: British Women and the Evangelical Campaign against *Sati* in India, 1813–30', in Kathryn Gleadle and Sarah Richardson (eds.), *Women in British Politics, 1760–1830: The Power of the Petticoat* (Basingstoke: Macmillan, 2000), 74–92.

MITCHELL, L. J., *Charles James Fox* (Harmondsworth: Penguin, 1997).

MONTLUZIN, EMILY LORRAINE DE, *The Antijacobins, 1798–1800: The Early Contributors to the 'Anti-Jacobin Review'* (Basingstoke: Macmillan, 1989).

MORGAN, KENNETH, *Bristol and the Atlantic Trade in the Eighteenth Century* (Cambridge: Cambridge University Press, 1993).

MORI, JENNIFER, *William Pitt and the French Revolution, 1785–1795* (Edinburgh: Keele University Press, 1997).

MORLEY, JOHN, *The Life of William Ewart Gladstone*, 3 vols. (London: Macmillan, 1903).

357

Bibliography

MOWL, TIMOTHY, *Horace Walpole: The Great Outsider* (London: John Murray, 1996).

MULLAN, JOHN, and REID, CHRISTOPHER, *Eighteenth-Century Popular Culture: A Selection* (Oxford: Oxford University Press, 2000).

MURRAY, JOCELYN, 'Gender Attitudes and the Contribution of Women to Evangelicalism and Ministry in the Nineteenth Century', in John Wolffe (ed.), *Evangelical Faith and Public Zeal: Evangelicals and Society in Britain, 1780–1980* (London: SPCK, 1995).

MYERS, MITZI, 'Reform or Ruin: "A Revolution in Female Manners" ', *Studies in Eighteenth-Century Culture*, 11 (1982), 199–216.

—— 'Hannah More's Tracts for the Times: Social Fiction and Female Ideology', in Mary Anne Schofield and Cecilia Macheski (eds.), *Fett'rd or Free? British Women Novelists 1670–1815* (Athens: Ohio University Press, 1986), 264–84.

—— ' "A Peculiar Protection": Hannah More and the Cultural Politics of the Blagdon Controversy', in Beth Fowkes Tobin (ed.), *History, Gender, and Eighteenth-Century Literature* (Athens: University of Georgia Press, 1994), 227–57.

MYERS, SYLVIA HARCSTACK, *The Bluestocking Circle: Women, Friendship, and the Life of the Mind in Eighteenth-Century England* (Oxford: Clarendon Press, 1990).

NARDIN, JANE, 'Hannah More and the Rhetoric of Educational Reform', *Women's History Review*, 10 (2001), 211–27.

NEUBURG, VICTOR E., *Popular Education in Eighteenth-Century England* (London: Woburn Press, 1971).

NEWMAN, GERALD, *The Rise of English Nationalism: A Cultural History, 1740–1830* (London: Weidenfeld & Nicolson, 1987).

NEWSOME, DAVID, 'Father and Sons', *Historical Journal*, 6 (1963), 295–310.

—— *The Parting of Friends: A Study of the Wilberforces and Henry Manning* (London: John Murray, 1966).

NICHOLLS, J. F., and TAYLOR, JOHN, *Bristol Past and Present*, 3 vols. (Bristol, 1881–2).

NOCKLES, PETER, 'Church Parties in the Pre-Tractarian Church of England 1750–1833: The "Orthodox"—Some Problems of Definition and Identity', in John Walsh, Colin Haydon, and Stephen Taylor (eds.), *The Church of England: From Toleration to Tractarianism c.1689–c.1833* (Cambridge: Cambridge University Press, 1933), 334–59.

—— *The Oxford Movement in Context: Anglican High Churchmanship, 1760–1857* (Cambridge: Cambridge University Press, 1994).

NOLL, M. A., BEBBINGTON, D. W., and RAWLYK, G. A. (eds.), *Evangelicalism: Comparative Studies of Popular Protestantism in North America, the British Isles, and Beyond, 1700–1900* (Oxford: Oxford University Press, 1994).

NORMAN, EDWARD, *The English Catholic Church in the Nineteenth Century* (Oxford: Clarendon Press, 1984).

O'DONNELL, SHERYL, 'Mr Locke and the Ladies: The Indelible Words on the *Tabula Rasa*', *Studies in Eighteenth-Century Culture*, 8 (1979), 151–64.

OLDFIELD, J. R., *Popular Politics and British Anti-Slavery: The Mobilisation of Public Opinion against the Slave Trade, 1787–1807* (Manchester: Manchester University Press, 1995).

OMAN, CAROLA, *David Garrick* (London: Hodder & Stoughton, 1958).

PALMER, RAY (ed.), *A Ballad History of England from 1588 to the Present Day* (London: Batsford, 1979).

PEARSON, JACQUELINE, *Women's Reading in Britain, 1750–1835: A Dangerous Recreation* (Cambridge: Cambridge University Press, 1999).

PEDERSEN, SUSAN, 'Hannah More Meets Simple Simon: Tracts, Chapbooks, and Popular Culture in Late Eighteenth-Century England', *Journal of British Studies*, 25 (1986), 84–113.

PERRY, RUTH, *The Celebrated Mary Astell: An Early English Feminist* (Chicago: University of Chicago Press, 1986).

PHILP, MARK, 'Vulgar Conservatism, 1792–3', *English Historical Review*, 110 (1995), 42–69.

—— (ed.), *The French Revolution and British Popular Politics* (Cambridge: Cambridge University Press, 1991).

POCOCK, J. G. A., 'Catharine Macaulay: Patriot Historian', in Hilda L. Smith (ed.), *Women Writers and the Early Modern British Political Tradition* (Cambridge: Cambridge University Press, 1998), 243–58.

PODMORE, C., *The Moravian Church in England, 1728–1760* (Oxford: Clarendon Press, 1998)

POLLOCK, JOHN, *Wilberforce* (London: Constable, 1977).

PORTER, ROY, *Mind-Forg'd Manacles: A History of Madness in England from the Restoration to the Regency* (London: Athlone Press, 1987).

—— *Enlightenment: Britain and the Creation of the Modern World* (London, Penguin: 2001).

PORTUS, G. V., *Caritas Anglicana; or, An Historical Inquiry into those Religious and Philanthropical Societies that Flourished in England between the Years 1678 and 1740* (London: A. R. Mowbray, 1912).

POYNTER, J. R., *Society and Pauperism: English Ideas on Poor Relief, 1795–1834* (London: Routledge & Kegan Paul; Toronto: University of Toronto Press, 1969).

PRICE, C., 'Thomas Harris and the Covent Garden Theatre', in Kenneth Richards and Peter Thompson (eds.), *Essays on the Eighteenth-Century English Stage* (London, 1972), 105–22.

PRIOR, KAREN IRENE SWALLOW, 'Hannah More and the Evangelical Contribution to the English Novel', Ph.D. thesis (Buffalo, NY, 1999).

PROCHASKA, F. K., *Women and Philanthropy in Nineteenth-Century England* (Oxford: Oxford University Press, 1980).

PYM, DOROTHY, *Battersea Rise* (London: Jonathan Cape, 1934).

QUINLAN, MAURICE, *Victorian Prelude: A History of English Manners, 1770–1830* (New York: Columbia University Press, 1941).

RANDALL, ADRIAN, and CHARLESWORTH, ANDREW (eds.), *Moral Economy and Popular Protest: Crowds, Conflict and Authority* (Basingstoke: Macmillan, 2000).

Bibliography

RAVEN, JAMES, *Judging New Wealth: Popular Publishing and Responses to Commerce in England, 1750–1800* (Oxford: Clarendon Press, 1992).

RENDALL, JANE, *The Origins of Modern Feminism: Women in Britain, France and the United States, 1780–1860* (Basingstoke: Macmillan, 1985).

RICHARDSON, DAVID, *The Bristol Slave Traders: A Collective Portrait* (Bristol: Historical Association, 1996).

RIVERS, ISABEL (ed.), *Books and their Readers in Eighteenth-Century England* (Leicester: Leicester University Press, 1982).

RIZZO, BETTY, *Companions without Vows: Relationships among Eighteenth-Century British Women* (Athens: University of Georgia Press, 1994).

ROBERT, CHARLES, *Urbain de Hercé, Dernier Évêque et Comte de Dol* (Paris: Victor Retaux, 1900).

ROBERTS, J. M., *The Mythology of the Secret Societies* (London: Secker & Warburg, 1972).

ROBERTS, M. J. D., 'The Society for the Suppression of Vice and its Early Critics, 1802–1812', *Historical Journal*, 26 (1983), 159–76.

ROBERTS, WILLIAM, *Memoirs of the Life and Correspondence of Hannah More*, 4 vols. (2nd edn. London, 1834).

ROGERS, NICHOLAS, *Crowds, Culture, and Politics in Georgian Britain* (Oxford: Clarendon Press, 1998).

ROWELL, G., STEVENSON, K., and WILLIAMS, R. (eds.), *Love's Redeeming Work: The Anglican Quest for Holiness* (Oxford: Oxford University Press, 2001).

ROYLE, EDWARD, *Revolutionary Britannia? Reflections on the Threat of Revolution in Britain, 1789–1848* (Manchester: Manchester University Press, 2000).

RULE, JOHN, 'Explaining Revivalism: The Case of Cornish Methodism', *Southern History*, 20–21 (1998–9), 168–88.

SACK, JONATHAN, *From Jacobite to Conservative: Reaction and Orthodoxy in Britain, c.1760–1832* (Cambridge: Cambridge University Press, 1993).

SAPIRO, VIRGINIA, *A Vindication of Political Virtue: The Political Theory of Mary Wollstonecraft* (Chicago: University of Chicago Press, 1992).

SCHAMA, SIMON, *Citizens: A Chronicle of the French Revolution* (London: Viking, 1989).

SCHLENTHER, BOYD STANLEY, *Queen of the Methodists: The Countess of Huntingdon and the Eighteenth-Century Crisis of Faith and Society* (Durham: Durham Academic Press, 1997).

SCHWOERER, LOIS, 'Images of Queen Mary II, 1689–95', *Renaissance Quarterly*, 42 (1989), 82–101.

SHOEMAKER, ROBERT B., *Gender in English Society, 1650–1850: The Emergence of Separate Spheres?* (London: Longman, 1998).

SHYLLON, FOLARIN, *James Ramsay: The Unknown Abolitionist* (Edinburgh: Canongate, 1977).

SIMMONS, CLARE A., *Reversing the Conquest: History and Myth in Nineteenth-Century British Literature* (New Brunswick, NJ: Rutgers University Press, 1990).

SKEDD, SUSAN, 'Women Teachers and the Expansion of Girls' Schooling in England, *c.*1760–1820', in Hannah Barker and Elaine Chalus (eds.), *Gender in Eighteenth-Century England: Roles, Representations, and Responsibilities* (London: Longman, 1997), 101–25.

SKRINE, PETER, 'Die Brautschauerzählung bei Jeremias Gotthelf und Hannah More', *Erzählkunst und Volkserziehung. Das literarische Werk des Jeremias Gotthelf* (Tübingen, 1999), 289–303.

SMITH, E. A., 'The Yorkshire Elections of 1806 and 1807: A Study in Electoral Management', *Northern History*, 2 (1967), 62–80.

SMITH, OLIVIA, *The Politics of Language, 1791–1819* (Oxford: Clarendon Press, 1984).

SNELL, K. D. M., 'The Sunday-School Movement in England and Wales: Child Labour, Denominational Control, and Working-Class Culture', *Past and Present*, 164 (Aug. 1999), 122–68.

SOLOWAY, R. A., *Prelates and People: Ecclesiastical Social Thought in England, 1783–1852* (London: Routledge & Kegan Paul; Toronto: University of Toronto Press, 1969).

SPATER, GEORGE, *William Cobbett: The Poor Man's Friend*, 2 vols. (Cambridge: Cambridge University Press, 1982).

SPEAR, PERCEVAL, *A History of India*, 2 vols. (Harmondsworth: Penguin, 1965).

SPINNEY, G. H., 'Cheap Repository Tracts: Hazard and Marshall Edition', *The Library*, 4th ser., 20, 3 (Dec. 1939), 295–340.

SPUFFORD, MARGARET, *Small Books and Pleasant Histories: Popular Fiction and its Readership in Seventeenth-Century England* (London: Methuen, 1981).

STEPHEN, JAMES 'The Clapham Sect', *Edinburgh Review*, 80 (1844), 251–307.

—— *Essays in Ecclesiastical Biography* (London, 1875).

STEVENSON, JOHN, 'Popular Radicalism and Popular Protest', in H. T. Dickinson (ed.), *Britain and the French Revolution, 1789–1815* (London: Macmillan, 1989), 61–81.

—— *Popular Disturbances in England 1700–1832* (2nd edn. London: Longman, 1992).

STOCK, EUGENE, *The History of the Church Missionary Society*, 4 vols. (London, 1899).

STOKES, G. T., Alexander Knox and the Oxford Movement', *Contemporary Review*, 3 (1887), 184–205.

STONE, GEORGE WINCHESTER, and KAHRL, GEORGE M., *David Garrick: A Critical Biography* (Carbondale: Illinois University Press, 1979).

STOTT, ANNE, ' "Female Patriotism": Georgiana, Duchess of Devonshire and the Westminster Election of 1784', *Eighteenth-Century Life*, 17 NS (Nov. 1993), 60–84.

—— 'Hannah More: Evangelicalism, Cultural Reformation, and Loyalism', Ph.D. thesis (London, 1998).

—— 'Patriotism and Providence: The Politics of Hannah More', in Kathryn Gleadle and Sarah Richardson (eds.), *Women in British Politics, 1760–1860: The Power of the Petticoat* (Basingstoke: Macmillan, 2000), 39–55.

Bibliography

—— 'Hannah More and the Blagdon Controversy, 1799–1802', *Journal of Ecclesiastical History*, 51 (2000), 319–46.

—— '"A singular injustice towards women": Hannah More, Evangelicalism and Female Education' in Sue Morgan (ed.), *Women, Religion and Feminism in Britain 1750–1900* (Basingstoke: Palgrave, 2002), 23–38.

STRACHEY, RAY, *The Cause: A Short History of the Women's Movement in Britain* (London: G. Bell & Sons, 1928).

SUTHERLAND, KATHRYN, 'Hannah More's Counter-Revolutionary Feminism', in Kelvin Everest (ed.), *Revolution in Writing: British Literary Responses to the French Revolution* (Milton Keynes: Open University Press, 1991), 27–63.

TAYLOR, STEPHEN, 'Queen Caroline and the Church of England', in Stephen Taylor, Richard Connors, and Clyve Jones (eds.), *Hanoverian Britain and Empire: Essays in Memory of Philip Lawson* (Woodbridge: Boydell Press, 1998), 82–101.

THOMAS, HUGH, *The Slave Trade: The History of the Atlantic Slave Trade, 1440–1870* (Basingstoke: Macmillan, 1998).

THOMAS, SUSAN, *The Bristol Riots* (Bristol: Bristol Historical Association, 1995).

THOMPSON, E. P., *The Making of the English Working Class* (Harmondsworth: Penguin, 1968).

—— *Customs in Common* (Harmondsworth: Penguin, 1991).

THOMPSON, HENRY, *The Life of Hannah More with Notices of her Sisters* (London, 1938).

THOMPSON, KENNETH, 'Religion, Class, and Control', in Robert Bocock and Kenneth Thompson (eds.), *Religion and Ideology* (Manchester: Manchester University Press, 1985), 126–53.

THWAITE, ANN, *Edmund Gosse: A Literary Landscape* (Oxford: Oxford University Press, 1984).

TOBIN, BETH FOWKES, *Superintending the Poor: Charitable Ladies and Paternal Landlords in British Fiction, 1770–1860* (New Haven: Yale University Press, 1993).

TODD, JANET, *Sensibility: An Introduction* (London: Methuen, 1986).

—— *Mary Wollstonecraft: A Revolutionary Life* (London: Weidenfeld & Nicolson, 2000).

TOLLEY, CHRISTOPHER, *Domestic Biography: The Legacy of Evangelicalism in Four Nineteenth-Century Families* (Oxford: Clarendon Press, 1997).

TOMALIN, CLAIRE, *Jane Austen: A Life* (Harmondsworth: Penguin, 1998).

TOMASELLI, SYLVANA, 'The Enlightenment Debate on Women', *History Workshop Journal*, 20 (1985), 101–24.

TOMKINS, J. M. S., *The Polite Marriage, also the Didactic Lyre, the Bristol Milkwoman, the Scotch Parents, Clio in Motley and Mary Hays, Philosophess* (Cambridge: Cambridge University Press, 1938).

TREVELYAN, GEORGE OTTO, *The Life and Letters of Lord Macaulay*, 2 vols. (London, 1876).

VALENZE, DEBORAH, *Prophetic Sons and Daughters: Female Preaching and Popular Religion in Industrial England* (Princeton: Princeton University Press, 1985).

VICKERY, AMANDA, 'Golden Age to Separate Spheres? A Review of the Categories and Chronology of English Women's History', *Historical Journal*, 36 (1993), 383–414.

—— *The Gentleman's Daughter: Women's Lives in Georgian England* (New Haven: Yale University Press, 1998).

WALDRON, MARY, 'Ann Yearsley and the Clifton Records', *The Age of Johnson: A Scholarly Annual*, 3, ed. P. J. Korshin (New York, 1990), 301–25.

—— 'The Frailties of Fanny: *Mansfield Park* and the Evangelical Movement', *Eighteenth-Century Fiction*, 6 (1994), 259–81.

—— *Lactilla, Milkwoman of Clifton: The Life and Writings of Ann Yearsley, 1753–1806* (Athens: University of Georgia Press, 1996).

—— *Jane Austen and the Fiction of her Time* (Cambridge: Cambridge University Press, 1999).

WALSH, JOHN, 'Origins of the Evangelical Revival', in J. D. Walsh and G. V. Bennett (eds.), *Essays in Modern English Church History* (London: A. & C. Black, 1966), 132–62.

—— 'The Anglican Evangelicals in the Eighteenth Century', *Aspects de l'Anglicanisme: Colloque de Strasbourg, 14–16 juin, 1972* (Paris: Presses Universitaires de France, 1974), 87–102.

WALSH, JOHN, 'The Church and Anglicanism in the "Long" Eighteenth Century', in John Walsh, Colin Haydon, and Stephen Taylor (eds.), *The Church of England, c.1689–c.1833: From Toleration to Tractarianism* (Cambridge: Cambridge University Press, 1993), 1–64.

WARD, W. R., *The Protestant Evangelical Awakening* (Cambridge: Cambridge University Press, 1994).

—— 'The Evangelical Revival in Eighteenth-Century Britain', in Sheridan Gilley and W. J. Sheils (eds.), *A History of Religion in Britain: Practice and Belief from Pre-Roman Times to the Present* (Oxford: Blackwell, 1994), 252–72.

WATT, TESSA, *Cheap Print and Popular Piety, 1550–1640* (Cambridge: Cambridge University Press, 1994).

WATTS, G. TRACEY, *Theatrical Bristol* (Bristol: Holloway & Son, 1915).

WEISS, HARRY B., *Hannah More's Cheap Repository Tracts in America* (New York: New York Public Library, 1946).

WELLS, ROGER, *Wretched Faces: Famine in Wartime England, 1763–1803* (Gloucester: Alan Sutton, 1988).

WHITAKER, W. B., *The Eighteenth-Century English Sunday: A Study of Sunday Observance from 1677 to 1837* (London: Epworth Press, 1940).

WILBERFORCE, ROBERT ISAAC and SAMUEL, *The Life of William Wilberforce*, 5 vols. (London, 1838).

WILLIAMS, CAROLYN D., 'Poetry, Pudding, and Epictetus: The Consistency of Elizabeth Carter', in Alvaro Ribeiro and James G. Basker (eds.), *Tradition and Transition: Women Writers, Marginal Texts, and the Eighteenth-Century Canon* (Oxford: Clarendon Press, 1996), 3–24.

WILSON, ELLEN GIBSON, *Thomas Clarkson: A Biography* (Basingstoke: Macmillan, 1989).

Bibliography

WITTMANN, REINHARD, 'Was there a Reading Revolution at the End of the Eighteenth Century?', in Guglielmo Cavallo and Robert Chartier (eds.), *A History of Reading in the West*, trans. Lydia G. Cochrane (Cambridge: Polity Press, 1999), 284–312.

WOLFFE, JOHN, *The Protestant Crusade in Great Britain, 1829–1860* (Oxford: Clarendon Press, 1991).

—— *Evangelicals, Women and Community in Nineteenth-Century Britain* (Milton Keynes: Open University, 1994).

—— (ed.), *Evangelical Faith and Public Zeal: Evangelicals and Society in Britain 1780–1980* (London: SPCK, 1995).

WOOD, MARCUS, *Radical Satire and Print Culture 1790–1832* (Oxford: Clarendon Press, 1994).

WOODS, LEIGH, *Garrick Claims the Stage: Acting as Social Emblem in Eighteenth-Century England* (Westport, Conn.: Greenwood Press, 1984).

WOODWARD, LIONEL-D., *Une Anglaise Amie de la Révolution française: Hélène-Maria Williams et ses amis* (Paris: Champion, 1930).

YEO, EILEEN JANES, *The Contest for Social Science: Relations and Representations of Gender and Class* (London: Rivers Oram Press, 1996).

—— (ed.), *Radical Femininity: Women's Self-Representation in the Public Sphere* (Manchester: Manchester University Press, 1998).

YONGE, CHARLOTTE M., *Hannah More* (London, 1888).

ZIEGLER, PHILIP, *Addington: A Life of Henry Addington, First Viscount Sidmouth* (London: Collins, 1965).

ZIONKOWSKI, L., 'Strategies of Containment: Stephen Duck, Ann Yearsley, and the Problem of Polite Culture', *Eighteenth-Century Life*, NS 13/3 (1989), 91–108.

Works of Reference

The Biographical Dictionary of Actors, Actresses, &c, ed. A. Philip H. Highfill Jr, Kalman A. Burnim, and Edward A. Langhans, 16 vols. (Carbondale: Southern Illinois University Press, 1975).

The Blackwell Dictionary of Evangelical Biography, 1730–1860, 2 vols. (Oxford: Blackwell, 1995).

The Bristol Directory.

British Museum Catalogue of Political and Personal Satires, vi, ed. Mary Dorothy George (London: HMSO, 1978).

Clerical Guide, 2nd edn. (London, 1822).

Dictionary of Christian Biography, ed. Michael Walsh (London: Continuum, 2001).

Dictionary of English Church History, ed. S. Ollard and J. Crosse, 2nd edn. (London: A. R. Mowbray, 1919).

Dictionary of National Biography, ed. Leslie Stephen and Sidney Lee, 22 vols. (1908–9).

History of Parliament: The House of Commons 1790–1820, ed. R. G. Thorne (London: Secker & Warburg, 1986).

The London Encyclopaedia, ed. Ben Weinreb and Christopher Hibbert (rev. edn. London: Macmillan, 1992).

The London Stage, 1600–1800, pt. 5, i: *1776–1800*, ed. Charles Beecher Hogan, 3 vols. (Carbondale: Southern Illinois University Press, 1988).

The Longman Companion to the French Revolution, ed. Colin Jones (Harlow: Longman, 1990).

The Revels History of English Drama, vi: *1750–1880*, ed. John Lofts, Richard Southern, Marion Jones, A. H. Scouted (London: Methuen, 1976).

The Victoria History of the Counties of England: A History of Somerset, ed. William Page, 5 vols. (repr. From 1st edn. London, 1911; London: Damsons of Pall Mall for University of London, Institute of Historical Research, 1986).

INDEX

Index

Index

Index

Index

Index

Index

Index

Index

Index